"Your pa[th]
 it may [...]
But it is one of the brightest
 paths out there." —Satty.

DIVIDED PROVINCE

"When ever you think you
Lack marks, Remember
one thing they do Not
Define you in anyway"
"SO THANKFUL FOR EVERYTHING"

"Satty you will Get in
 to Law school,
   you will become
    a Lawyer that they"
"ALL WILL REMEMBER"
      11:11 ☺

one day it will all pay off,
All these nightshifts, school work,
Lack of support, everything will
come together! You are meant
to be the best version of your
self!.

year 2025 will be in Law school 2nd year, with Kimberly's side and a king on my toe —Satty 12/30/2019.

DIVIDED PROVINCE

Ontario Politics in the Age of Neoliberalism

EDITED BY GREG ALBO AND BRYAN M. EVANS

McGill-Queen's University Press
Montreal & Kingston | London | Chicago

© McGill-Queen's University Press 2018

ISBN 978-0-7735-5473-3 (cloth)
ISBN 978-0-7735-5474-0 (paper)
ISBN 978-0-7735-5567-9 (ePDF)
ISBN 978-0-7735-5568-6 (ePUB)

Legal deposit first quarter 2019
Bibliothèque nationale du Québec

Printed in Canada on acid-free paper that is 100% ancient forest free (100% post-consumer recycled), processed chlorine free

This book has been published with the help of a grant from the Canadian Federation for the Humanities and Social Sciences, through the Awards to Scholarly Publications Program, using funds provided by the Social Sciences and Humanities Research Council of Canada.

We acknowledge the support of the Canada Council for the Arts, which last year invested $153 million to bring the arts to Canadians throughout the country.

Nous remercions le Conseil des arts du Canada de son soutien. L'an dernier, le Conseil a investi 153 millions de dollars pour mettre de l'art dans la vie des Canadiennes et des Canadiens de tout le pays.

Library and Archives Canada Cataloguing in Publication

Divided province : Ontario politics in the age of neoliberalism / edited by Greg Albo and Bryan M. Evans.

Includes bibliographical references and index.
Issued in print and electronic formats.
ISBN 978-0-7735-5473-3 (cloth). – ISBN 978-0-7735-5474-0 (paper). –
ISBN 978-0-7735-5567-9 (ePDF). – ISBN 978-0-7735-5568-6 (ePUB)

1. Neoliberalism – Ontario – History – 20th century. 2. Neoliberalism – Ontario – History – 21st century. 3. Ontario – Politics and government – 1995–2003. 4. Ontario – Politics and government – 2003–. 5. Ontario – Economic policy. 6. Ontario – Social policy. I. Albo, Gregory, editor II. Evans, Bryan, 1960–, editor

FC3077.2.D58 2018   971.3'04   C2018-905404-2
                                 C2018-905405-0

Set in 11/14 Minion Pro with Ordax and Univers
Book design & typesetting by Garet Markvoort, zijn digital

Contents

Tables, Figures, and Maps | ix

Preface | xiii
Greg Albo and Bryan Evans

1 Divided Province: Democracy and the Politics of State Restructuring in Ontario | 3
Greg Albo

| PART ONE |
THE POLITICAL ECONOMY OF NEOLIBERALISM IN ONTARIO

2 The Ontario Growth Model: The "End of the Road" or a "New Economy"? | 43
John Peters

3 The Geography of the Ontario Service Economy | 77
Steven Tufts

4 A Neoliberal Pause? The Auto and Manufacturing Sectors in Ontario since Free Trade | 103
Dimitry Anastakis

5 Northern Ontario and the Crisis of Development and Democracy | 130
David Leadbeater

| PART TWO |
TRANSFORMING THE ONTARIO STATE

6 New Bargains? Ontario and Federalism in the Neoliberal Period | 187
 Robert Drummond

7 Gendering State: Women and Public Policy in Ontario | 212
 Tammy Findlay

8 Municipal Neoliberalism and the Ontario State | 247
 Carlo Fanelli

9 Class, Power, and Neoliberal Employment Policy in Ontario | 275
 Charles W. Smith

| PART THREE |
CONSOLIDATING THE NEOLIBERAL POLICY REGIME IN ONTARIO

10 Poverty and Policy in Ontario: You Can't Eat Good Intentions | 309
 Peter Graefe and Carol-Anne Hudson

11 Reforming Health Services in Ontario: Contradictions | 334
 Pat Armstrong and Hugh Armstrong

12 Competing Policy Paradigms and the Search for Sustainability in Ontario Electricity Policy | 359
 Mark Winfield and Becky MacWhirter

13 Schooling Goes to Market: The Consolidation of Lean Education in Ontario | 394
 Alan Sears and James Cairns

| PART FOUR |
DEMOCRATIC POLITICS AND SOCIAL MOVEMENTS

14 Colonialism, Indigenous Struggles, and the Ontario State | 423
    James Lawson

15 Unequal Futures: Race and Class under Neoliberalism
    in Ontario | 461
    Grace-Edward Galabuzi

16 The Democratic Imagination in Ontario and
    Participatory Budgeting | 493
    Terry Maley

17 The Challenges of Union Political Action in
    the Era of Neoliberalism | 522
    Stephanie Ross

Contributors | 549

Index | 553

Tables, Figures, and Maps

TABLES

3.1 Employment composition of Ontario CMAs, selected service industries, 2016 | 86

3.2 Demographic characteristics of service industry employment, Ontario, 2016 | 88

4.1 Decade of decline: Ontario automotive plant closures, 2001–13 | 114

4.2 Automotive investment in the US, 1993–2002 (US$ millions) | 119

5.1 Class structure compared for Northern Ontario and Southern Ontario, 2017 (employed persons, in thousands) | 140

5.2 Industry structure of employment compared for Northern and Southern Ontario, 2017 | 142

5.3 Northern Ontario employment by industry, selected years, 1987–2017 (employed persons, in thousands) | 144–5

8.1 Municipal structure in Ontario as of 2013 | 251

8.2 City of Toronto operating revenue, 2017 | 252

8.3 City of Toronto operating expenditures, 2017 | 252

9.1 Ontario permanent and temporary employment, 1997–2012 | 291

10.1 Ontario labour market and poverty trends, 1985–2018 | 310

12.1 Policy paradigms in Ontario electricity policy, 1906–2017 | 386

14.1 Specific claims cases, Ontario and Canada, 2013 and 2018 | 435

14.2 Current claims and land-related negotiations involving Ontario | 435

15.1 Racialized population in Ontario, 2011 | 464

15.2 Aboriginal Peoples in Canada and Ontario | 464

15.3 Racialized groups in low-income areas in Ontario urban centres, 2001–06 | 467

15.4 Labour market profile, Aboriginal Peoples in Ontario, 2011 (%) | 473

15.5 Average employment income for Aboriginal groups in Ontario, 2011 ($) | 473

15.6 Labour market profile of racialized groups in Ontario, 2011 (%) | 474

15.7 Labour market profile by racialized groups in Ontario, 2011 (%) | 475

15.8 Gender, race, and employment income in Ontario, 2011 ($) | 475

15.9 Average employment income by racialized group in Ontario, 2010 ($) | 476

15.10 Racialized labour market distribution by occupation in Ontario, 2011 (%) | 477

15.11 Low income by racialized group after tax in Ontario, 2010 (%) | 478

FIGURES

2.1 The decline of Ontario private sector unionized manufacturing employment, 1997–2015 | 52

2.2 Canada's new "financial" economy | 59

2.3 Ontario's new economy and employment, 1990–2010 | 60

2.4 Precarious and atypical employment in Ontario, 1995–2015 | 65

2.5 Ontario non-standard employment and wage penalties, 1999–2011 (median hourly wages) | 66

3.1 Service employment as percentage of all Ontario employment, fifteen years and over by sex, 1976–2016 | 85

3.2 Occupational distribution of service sector employment, 1976 and 2016 (% of all service employment) | 85

3.3 Average hourly wage rate and union coverage by industry, 2016 | 89

4.1 Car and commercial vehicle production in ten nations, 1999, 2012, and 2017 | 111

4.2 Canadian car and commercial vehicle production, 1999–2017 | 111

4.3 Employment in the Canadian auto industry, 1991–2016 | 115

7.1 Ontario Women's Directorate budget 1987–2016 (inflation adjusted in 2010 dollars) | 217

9.1 Ontario unemployed and discouraged workers, annual average (%), 1947–2016 | 279

9.2 Employment in Ontario's manufacturing industry, 1991–2016 | 289

9.3 Union density in Ontario (% of workforce unionized), 1976–2017 | 293

9.4 Union density, public and private sector in Ontario (%), 1997–2017 | 294

12.1 Ontario electricity consumption in terawatt hours/year (tWh/yr) | 375

MAPS

5.1 Northern Ontario as defined by the Growth Plan for Northern Ontario | 131

5.2 Northern Ontario transportation | 133

5.3 Historical and new treaties in Canada | 137

Preface

Ontario's official motto, "Loyal she began, loyal she remains," recalls the province's fidelity to the British monarchy, and its anti-democratic, elitist, and counter-revolutionary ideological origins in the eighteenth century. From these sources onward, the Upper Canadian colonial state established a conservative political and administrative template as it fostered settlement and capitalist development in the province. This political project and consensus endured even through the postwar period of welfare state construction. Patronage, clientelism, brokerage politics, and modest state capacity were – and remain – the hallmark features of the Ontario state. Unlike other jurisdictions, where the resources and capacities of subnational states were often actively put toward development and projects of social reform, the Ontario case is one of, at best, limited ambitions, apart from building capitalism and protecting the rights of private property in the province.

The passage from this conservative state form (with its close alliances between state elites and capitalist classes) to a neoliberal one is still consequential in many respects. First, the centralizing and increasingly authoritarian tendencies within neoliberalism are strengthened, and, secondly, the fragility and weakness of the existing administrative state structures easily lend themselves to neoliberal restructuring efforts that meet with little or no resistance within or outside of the state. Ontario's turn to neoliberalism started in the 1980s, but had not been clearly set until the arrival of the Mike Harris-led "Common Sense Revolution" in 1995, which firmly embedded the neoliberal project within the Ontario state and political economy. The Harris Conservatives jettisoned the party's previous "One Ontario" ideology and practice, in the wake of its historic 1985 defeat, and became a party of the "hard right." A decade of the Dalton McGuinty Liberal government amply demonstrated that while the rather crude and aggressive variant of neoliberalism expressed by the Common Sense Revolutionaries may have been defeated in 2003, neoliberalism itself endured. Indeed, this project was deepened and advanced by the Liberals as a more politically sustainable endeavour under their leadership, including over the premiership of Kathleen Wynne after 2013. The defeat of the Liberals and the election of a Progressive Conservative government led by Doug Ford in June 2018 disrupted the political hegemony of the Liberals. But the hard right populist platform of the Conservatives is even more firmly committed to the market-expanding policies of neoliberalism.

At this juncture, Ontario's state and economy share several characteristics synonymous with neoliberal markets and administration. These include: the dominance of the service and financial sectors; an increasingly internationalized economy; decentralized and marketized public service delivery; a highly centralized decision-making process at the apex of the state relatively insulated from legislative accountability; and a politicized senior bureaucratic elite circulating between the corporate and state sectors. This trajectory in institutional form and policy practices has serious implications for further eroding already "thin" and formal liberal democratic structures and processes, as well as circumventing any serious consideration of a more radical democracy and redistributive policy agenda.

In addition to these general institutional characteristics, neoliberalism as a policy regime can be defined as a market-enhancing approach to governance and, as such, represents an ideological shift toward a different – and in many ways more active – role of the state in expanding capitalist-led economic and social development. In attempting to enhance the scope of market allocation and private power, neoliberal policies build upon principles of competition, laissez-faire, efficiency, productivity, profitability, and individual autonomy. These are manifested in policy forms such as liberalization, deregulation, privatization, and an erosion of worker protections as well as redistributive programs. In other words, neoliberal policy regimes attempt to ensure the social reproduction of the class and extra-market institutional conditions for capital accumulation through various market and pricing mechanisms. Neoliberal policy practices have major effects institutionally: the hollowing out of certain regulatory capacities of the state; the monetizing and marketizing of public assets; the concentration of political power in the central executive, particularly in the leader's office; and the re-ordering of state apparatuses to increase the control and management functions of the central economic agencies, strengthen the mandates and capacities of the policing, carceral, and security apparatuses, and limit the resources and role of other departments and agencies of the state. Neoliberalism is fundamentally misconceived, then, if interpreted as a policy regime setting markets against states. Quite the opposite, the neoliberal state form plays a crucial role in building, extending, and internationalizing markets.

The election of McGuinty's Liberals in 2003 was a rejection of the hard edges of the Common Sense Revolution but not a defeat of neoliberalism. Indeed, the Liberals successfully rebuilt a "One Ontario" political coalition. This "popular front" included a diverse spectrum of forces, incorporating finance capital, green entrepreneurs, and certain public sector professionals, notably teachers. The policy expression of this coalition incorporated a sharp turn to public-private partnerships (P3s), industrial subsidies (especially in the auto sector), competitive contracting-out of service delivery in conjunction with an expansion of post-secondary education and health care services, and the deployment of an inclusionary discourse of citizen diversity. This is what most differentiates the neoliberalism of the McGuinty-Wynne Liberals from the Common Sense Revolutionaries. In the process, social democracy under the NDP adopted much of the same in their "third way" approach to state policies and capitalist markets. As such, the NDP became less of a clear policy alternative, and even, as witnessed in the 2014 general election, adopted much of the anti-tax populism of the hard right Conservatives led by Tim Hudak or now by Doug Ford (both acolytes of the Harris years in power).

The June 2018 election marked the end of fifteen years of Liberal government, and underscored the social divisions in Ontario after some three decades of the market-centred policies of neoliberalism. As premier, Wynne maintained the commitment to fiscal constraint and a return to balance budgets, embraced the new public management agenda for the public sector, and stumbled into the partial privatization of Ontario Hydro. In contrast (and without ever resolving the contradiction), she wanted to shift away from the imagery of an austere government lacking social ambition that the Liberals projected under McGuinty. In particular, she sought to repair relations with the province's large and politically savvy teachers' unions – part of a wider policy agenda that also promoted social inclusion for First Nations and marginalized groups and re-investment in public services and transportation infrastructure. In her last year of governing, Wynne added labour law reforms, a commitment to increasing the minimum wage to $15/hour, and election proposals of publicly subsidized child care as well as dental and drug coverage. The Liberals' intent was to present voters with a clear and progressive alternative to the Conservatives, and to avoid being outflanked on the left (as in the Liberals' 2014 campaign, the NDP forwarded similar proposals, although with more comprehensive coverage and modest tax increases).

The Conservative platform, in contrast, followed the populist playbook of the right: various tax cuts on gas, income, and corporate earnings; withdrawal of commitments to address climate change by scrapping the market-based "cap and trade" system; freezing any further increases in the minimum wage; rolling back changes to the sex education curriculum with its efforts to address sexual differences; and a host of other largely symbolic commitments. Over fifteen years in government, the Liberals accumulated more than their fair share of policy and political blunders. In his persona and utterances, Ford appealed to the stresses, fears, and insecurities that so much of the Ontario population feels, and fused "social conservatism" with "market populism" to win a legislative majority. In this, the Ford government joins a host of other right-wing populist movements gaining political support and occasionally achieving government around the world. The claims of a historical democratic civility in Ontario politics sustained by a "fairer" regional capitalism no longer bears even casual scrutiny.

If neoliberalism is to be contested and rolled back in Ontario, a profound rethinking of the role and structure of the provincial state would necessarily compose part of that alternative political program. This would include a strategy to construct a more democratic administrative state, entailing new mechanisms both to support planning at the centre of the state and to extend democratic controls into workplaces and over productive assets. The agenda for such an alternative policy regime and institutional base would be to enable genuine and broadly based participation in the policy process by building sectoral and community-level input. The logic of such a regime would be to radically extend the scale and scope of capacities and control over productive assets while reducing the scale and scope of hierarchical and command organizations, and of private control over the social surplus and accumulation of productive assets. Of course, even getting to this stage requires something that does not exist – a structured political movement and organization that is explicitly anti-neoliberal, and anti-capitalist, in programme and action. Neither the NDP nor any of the social movement coalitions represents such a vehicle at this moment in Ontario. Until such time as there exists a critical mass and organizational capacity to mobilize toward the defeat of neoliberalism, there will be no exit from the deepening social polarization in Ontario, in all of its manifestations, and no preventing the further deterioration of the already fragile state of democracy. Resisting neoliberalism today is about building an alternative future based on equality and popular participation in our workplaces and communities. Such new forms of democracy will also depend upon contesting current democratic institutions in both legislatures and state administration. This collection of essays is both an examination of the history and practice of neoliberalism in Ontario and an exploration of its alternatives.

As Canada's most populous province, and the core axis of power shaping the country's political economy and its place in global capitalism, Ontario is the subject of a great deal of noteworthy research and political writing. There are a number of volumes that have gained an audience of students and informed them – and their professors as well – about Ontario politics. These texts have largely been guided by an agenda of describing the institutional matrix of Ontario government, analyzing the way that Queen's Park fits into the inter-governmental relations of Canadian federalism, coordinating research agendas of academics and policy networks, and serving as an educational platform for the political integration of Ontario.

The mandate we set for this volume is quite different (though we hope it also provides a valuable resource for students and researchers alike). It is our view that Ontario is an increasingly divided political space wracked by the social cleavages of class, race, colonial legacies, and its own regionalisms. These divisions are the source of a deep-seated and widespread political alienation from the liberal democratic institutions of the Ontario state and the "one province" consensus discourse that has typically guided the three main political parties and blocked the emergence of alternatives to neoliberalism. In the context of managing public austerity and neoliberal capitalism today, these contradictions are ceding political space to a growing populist hard right (found in Ontario in the Conservative Party and Toronto's "Ford Nation"). In some circles, these developments are described as a condition of post-democracy. But this concedes too much to the democratic qualities of liberal democratic capitalism – certainly in Ontario. They are better, and more simply, identified as the authoritarian and non-democratic tendencies of neoliberalism, from placing limits on parliamentary processes, to concentrating executive power, to allocating ever-more resources to policing and surveillance.

To this end, we sought to draw together leading social scientists of Ontario politics, from both Marxist and critical institutionalist political economy traditions, to dissect the contours, contradictions, and pitfalls of capitalism and politics in Ontario over the now painfully long period that neoliberalism has set the policy agenda. As such, these essays do not share a common theoretical approach or political stance, representing a variety of critical perspectives and deploying a range of concepts. But they do share a deep dissatisfaction – even anger – with the way that the class divisions and social inequalities in Ontario continue to grow; and a common despair at an elite political culture far removed from – and oppositional toward – a participatory and egalitarian democracy. Ontario is, of course, not isolated in confronting this difficult political moment. It is a regional zone of a world market beset by the mounting contradictions and polarizations of a global capitalism at odds with the world's people and the earth's ecology. These are the themes concerning the political economy of contemporary capitalism, as pressing in Ontario as they are in the rest of Canada and the world.

We need, of course, to thank all the contributors to this volume. They worked with great patience and enthusiasm to produce essays that are innovative in research and unique in their argument, and which contribute to an alternative political agenda for Ontario. As well, we want to underline the assistance of Bob MacDermid, Aidan Conway, Chris

Bailey, Robin Chang, Jordan House, and Gideon Kalman-Lamb with bringing the manuscript together. The support of the Centre for Social Justice (Toronto), the Scholarly Publications Program of the Federation for the Humanities and Social Sciences, York and Ryerson Universities, and the editorial staff at MQUP was indispensable in seeing this project to completion. We would like in particular to single out the superb editorial assistance of Scott Howard in the preparation of the final manuscript.

Finally, it is important to recognize, indeed insist upon the fact, that present-day Ontario emerges out of a settler-colonial process, set in motion by the development of European capitalism, whose dislocations continue to beset the province. The Truth and Reconciliation Commission established by the government of Canada sought to re-examine this history as part of remaking our present. In this spirit and intent, we wish to acknowledge that our research and work takes place in the traditional territories of the many First Nations and Métis Peoples of Ontario. These territories are covered by several treaties and agreements between First Nations and Métis and the Ontario and Canadian states. As we write in Toronto, we wish in particular to acknowledge the ancestral traditional territories of the Ojibway, the Anishinaabe, Wendat, Haudenosaunee, and the Mississaugas of the New Credit. Many areas of Ontario are still in dispute and subject to ongoing claims. These struggles of the First Nations and Métis are a central component of the many demands for justice and democracy that remain to be accounted for in Ontario.

Greg Albo
Bryan Evans

DIVIDED PROVINCE

| 1 |

Divided Province: Democracy and the Politics of State Restructuring in Ontario

GREG ALBO

Analysts of the Canadian political system are infamous for trumpeting its stability and elite consensus in comparison with the conflict and turbulence of the European – and even American – political scenes. The solidity of Canada's national party system has been built, it is argued, on the overwhelming electoral dominance of the Conservative and Liberal parties, with their overlapping systems of support from Canada's business elites. The social democratic New Democratic Party (NDP), with its historical links to the labour movement, occupies a subordinate place within the system. But the NDP is equally committed to building a market economy (if balanced by a measure of social supports), and offers an alternate channel for political integration.

None of the sub-national political systems in Canada have replicated this pattern more closely than Ontario, the second largest province by geography and largest by population. One political commentator after another, from journalists to academics, has drawn a linkage between the federal state and Ontario as the governance compact underlying Canada's venerated social stability. The "policy intellectual" who did much to inspire the neoliberal redesign of Ontario's regional political economy, for example, pinned his analysis on the unifying role of the provincial political culture in the federation, even as Ontario transitioned from Canada's historic "economic heartland" to a "North American economic region state" in an era of globalization (Courchene 1998).[1]

The history of Ontario's electoral politics does indeed provide ample support for the integrative role of the provincial political system. In Ontario's slow march to responsible government in the post-Confederation period, the Liberals and Conservatives alternated in long stretches of command over political loyalties, but for a spell in government by the United Farmers of Ontario after the Great War. As for the postwar period, it neatly divides into two phases of partisanship. The postwar boom was facilitated by Keynesian economic policy and was politically dominated by the Progressive Conservative Party in its entirety. A transitional interlude begins in 1985 with the Liberal governments of David Peterson, followed by Bob Rae's unexpected NDP majority in 1990, which was in turn quickly succeeded in 1995 by Mike Harris's Conservative governments. The Liberal Party governed from 2003 to 2018, initially under the leadership of Dalton McGuinty and from 2013 under the leadership of Kathleen Wynne, which recalled earlier phases of electoral hegemony in Ontario. The Liberals consolidated their hold on power not by rejecting the neoliberal policies that came to the fore in Ontario under Harris in the 1990s, but by adapting their governance modes to the new policy regime, while successfully propagating their self-styled "progressive," inclusionary amendments. In overturning the Liberal reign in the June 2018 election, the Doug Ford-led Conservatives took aim at those "progressive" amendments while proposing to deepen the neoliberal policy regime. Such has been the course of electoral democracy in Ontario.

The thematic of Ontario as a regional zone of political stability and social integration dangerously veers – particularly in mainstream political accounts – toward a gross simplification of the provincial political economy. As the central Canadian offshoot of European colonialism, Ontario could only emerge as a specific "political space" in the late eighteenth century out of the conquest and marginalization of the First Nations (Rogers and Smith 1994). These territorial dispossessions – still heatedly contested across the province for their legitimacy in numerous land claims disputes and Indigenous struggles for self-government – provided an essential precondition for the formation of the agro-industrial capitalism that would situate Ontario as one of the central zones of the developing capitalist world market in the late nineteenth century. The class and racial stratifications that came with the coerced migration of African slaves and of displaced peasantry from land enclosures in Europe, and that would form the Ontario producing classes, were another pre-condition. As North American capitalism consolidated, and Ontario evolved into one of its industrial heartlands across the twentieth century, the province gave birth to an industrial working class and labour revolts that laid, in turn, key foundations for the growth of the Canadian labour and socialist movements (Heron 2012).

These historical cleavages continue to define central lines of social conflict in Ontario; today these divisions need to be placed in the second phase of postwar political stability and neoliberalism. In the 1980s, the political parties in Ontario divided over the building of a "competition state" through activist economic policies that would foster elaborate training systems for high-skilled workers in high value-added sectors, supported by an industrial policy fostering firm-centred innovation. By the 1990s, however, all three mainstream political parties converged – by policy reversal in the cases of the NDP and the Liberals, and by political conviction for the Conservatives – around a neoliberal policy regime of reinforcing a market-led social order. For Ontario, like the other provincial states, the implementation of NAFTA and the retrenchment of the Canadian welfare state by the federal Liberal government in the mid-1990s played a decisive role in forging a new political consensus in neoliberalism, and in setting the parameters for provincial policy since. No political jurisdiction in Canada has withstood the neoliberal transformation of its policy regime. Or the common pattern of social polarization associated with the decline of manufacturing and its associated unionized workforce, the explosion of precarious and racialized work, stagnant wages and incomes, the massive concentration of productive assets and financial wealth, and so forth (Evans and Smith 2015). But the radical shift of the guiding public policy framework, from being the industrial heartland of Keynesianism to the centre of neoliberal experimentation, may well be the defining feature of Ontario's place among the Canadian provinces and territories.

There are many potential ways to distinguish a neoliberal state and policy regime. The simplest – and most common – is to counterpose an economic policy regime of Keynesian state-led economic and welfare policies against a Hayekian focus on extending the realm of exchange, contracts, and "free markets." Such a categorical opposition, however, leaves a misleading impression of a once-"liberal" market governed by a limited state breached by the Keynesian interventionist state, and now returning to a more "natural" order of a liberalized economy and state. If neoliberalism as a historical phase of capitalism cannot be understood in terms of idealized policy norms, it still needs to be specified initially in terms of its abstract conception of capitalism as a liberal market order organized through individualized market agents freely entering into exchanges and contracts to maximize their self-interest, subject to the disciplines provided by competitive markets. As such, neoliberal ideology carries an explicit orientation toward a particular political-economic policy regime: self-regulation by markets and prices; accumulation driven by private savings, entrepreneurship, and contracts; free mobility of the factors of production between labour processes, markets, and geographical spaces; individualized formation of needs met by either capitalist firms or voluntary agencies; a stable monetary unit facilitating market exchanges; monetization of public assets; and a constitutionally confined state providing law, order, and contract enforcement.

There are, however, no invariant features of neoliberalism to be uncovered in each and every capitalist state. The neoliberal state emerges at a specific historical juncture, in a wide range of political circumstances, deployed across multiple scales of governance. Subnational states, for example, will each establish spatially specific neoliberal policy regimes even within a common federation; there is no singular social logic unmediated by political struggle leading to a convergence in the administrative modes in which neoliberal norms are implemented. A neoliberal state can be summarized, then, as a particular form of social rule whose modes of administration and policy practices are "market-expanding"; that is, the state is reorganized to advance the social conditions that allow the propertied classes to extract value from the working classes.

The central paradox of the neoliberal phase of capitalism may be that sharpening social divisions of region, race, and class rest alongside party and policy convergence within the political system. The political parties still offer different policy platforms, of course, but there is a "de-contestation" of substantive politics. As Peter Mair (2013, 59) comments with respect to the evolution of political systems over the last few decades, "the parties now share government with one another more easily and readily, with any lingering differences in policy-seeking goals appearing to matter less than the shared cross-party ambition for office ... The parties have become markedly less distinct from one another, while partisan purpose is itself seen as less meaningful or even desirable."[2] Even in the new "age of austerity" since the financial crisis erupted in 2008, the core economic practices of neoliberalism remain, it is contended here, de-politicized within the Ontario political system.

From this reading of the Ontario political system and neoliberalism, two claims are put forward. First, with the impasse of the postwar "one province, one society" development model, Ontario's economic policy entered a transition period of uncertainty, conflict, and failed projects of reform. Second, the neoliberal economic policy regime initially emerged through the Conservative Party as a polarizing "two provinces, two societies" strategy of "class struggle from above" to sustain Ontario's competitiveness in the continental economic bloc formed by NAFTA. But despite oppositional bluster and a wave of political protest, neoliberalism formed the basis for a "one-province" governing consensus under the administration of the Liberal Party. A further contention is, therefore, returned to in the conclusion. It is urgent that the growing dissent from neoliberal austerity across an increasingly divided province begins to cohere into an anti-neoliberal coalition with an assertion of political ambitions not confined by the "actually existing" Ontario political system. But before developing these claims further, it will be helpful to raise a few critical themes for situating subnational regions within the state system.

REGIONAL SPACE AND STATE POLICY

Regional states such as Ontario form pivotal nodes in the multiple scales of governance implicated in the accumulation of capital. In a continual process of emulation and differentiation of social relations and technological innovation, competitive imperatives oblige weaker firms and regions to try to equalize productive capacities, while leading firms and regions are compelled to continually invest in new commodities, techniques, and skills. For Ernest Mandel (1975, 102), this constituent feature of capitalism also forms the basis for the so-called regional question as "the uneven development of states, regions, branches of industry and firms [is] unleashed by the quest for superprofits."

If it is quite misleading to theorize states and markets as enclosed institutional spaces, it would be just as misguided to posit two different social logics, one determining the spatial organization of states and the other the accumulation and circulation of capital. The processes of capitalist development – including both the regionalization and internationalization of capital – cannot be conceptualized apart from the historical forms and modes of state intervention into the economy. Henri Lefebvre (1991, 378) notes that "the state and its bureaucratic political apparatuses intervene continually in space ... in order to intervene at all levels and through every agency of the economic realm." National states and political systems provide the extra-market institutional infrastructure that necessarily underpin market processes – through law, contract enforcement, product standardization, the provision and backing of monetary and credit relations, expenditures for social control, and industrial subsidies, to name but a few. For these reasons alone, states are indispensable to the mediation of the internationalization of capital. But national states also have to develop institutional capacities and policy strategies to manage capital flows and the international value of the currency, guide adherence to the international trading regime, arbitrate international regulatory standards and legalities, and plot the governance of geo-economic and security relations. Hence national state policies form the regulatory institutions that are integral to the real forms of competition in the inter-state system.

Regional states have a special prominence in the complex territorialization that accompanies capitalist development. As capital accumulates, the social division of labour is intensified alongside the increase in the mass and sophistication of the fixed capital investments, in machines and buildings underpinning the production and circulation of commodities. Once the mistaken thesis of markets forming independent of states is discarded, it is easy – even obvious – to suggest that the functions and administrative capacities of the regional state have to develop in combination (this does not imply uniformity) with the expansion of the capital stock, and its circulation as money and commodity capital in a proliferation of "institutionalized scales of political decision-making" (Jessop 2004, 64). For the regional state and the subnational political system (and the local state as well), the implication is an expanded mandate and responsibility for managing an increasingly socialized and territorially specific matrix of social relations, capital investments, and exchange flows.

If liberal democratic states are defined, at least in part, by their constitutionalism, their particular allocation of powers to subnational governments in federal systems can always be "formally" identified, including any asymmetrical allocation of powers where boundaries coincide with linguistic and national "minorities." Economic policy regimes at the subnational level thus are interdependent with the national state for the "coordination" of policies governing the production and internationalization of capital, extra-market institutional supports, and fiscal capacity, but subnational governments are also assigned responsibility and a specific institutional autonomy for the determination of their own policy regimes within these constraints.

Apart from their own fiscal and administrative capacities, regional states typically have a major responsibility for the regional organization of the welfare state, as health, education, welfare, and so forth always need to be delivered in spatially diverse and localized settings. And, to one degree or another, all functions of the national state have a territorial counterpart in the subnational state (although the precise administrative responsibility will always vary by the division of powers and branch of the state). This is why there is always an institutional actuality of "blurred jurisdictions" in federal systems, rather than the "watertight compartments" of powers abstractly conjured by constitutional literalists. For assessing regional policy regimes, these are important points to bear in mind as "the making of a regional economy involves not just the development of a productive apparatus on the basis of the atomised decisions of firms ... but also ... the social construction of those institutional-regulatory structures that must be present to secure economic order" (Scott and Storper 1992, 19). The "socialization of capital," in the sense of the organizational complexity and internationalization tendencies of individual units of capital through time, has been particularly hostile to maintaining the jurisdictional integrity – and thus the policy practices – of any scale of governance. It is the facilitation of the agglomeration of capital, however, with its parallel deepening of the spatial division of labour, that preoccupies all subnational states (especially one the size of the Ontario state). Indeed, to the extent that some of these functions are jurisdictionally shared between national and subnational levels, they will also form the basis for intra-state competition over taxes, subsidies, labour laws, regulatory enforcement, and even social policies to influence the locational decisions of capital.

Historically, regional economic policy regimes have focused on equalizing (or sustaining) uneven economic development through direct subsidies, nationalizations, infrastructure investments, education and training regimes, and so forth, to generate production and export capacities. In other words, regional state-building has meant targeted industrial policies of "market control" (often summarized as "regional production systems" to incorporate the extra-market institutions of market coordination) and modernization of regional (and local) state administrative capacities "to mobilize a variety of compensatory regional and social policies ... to alleviate inherited patterns of spatial uneven development" (Brenner 2004, 101).

Since the 1980s, however, the ideology of neoliberalism has been central to the remaking of the political form as well as policy content of regional states. The fiscal and administrative devolution of many areas of regulation and social policy, to raise the most noted examples, has typically occurred without the transfer of adequate fiscal resources in the federal transfer regime, with the express intent of stepping up market disciplines and social austerity. This has generated, in turn, further policy devolution to local governments where the administrative and fiscal capacities are even more fragile. Thus fiscal crises and austerity have been endemic to subnational and local states across the entire period of neoliberalism.

The metaphor of a neoliberal "hollowing-out" of the state has often been invoked to describe this rescaling process. This thesis can lead, however, to analytical errors and political misconceptions, and too often mimics neoliberalism's ideological self-image. Both national and regional states have become more active – not less – in orienting their administrative capacities and policies toward regional competitiveness and facilitating the internationalization of capital. Subnational states have become intensely engaged in a kind of inter-jurisdictional "economic warfare," to invoke another metaphor, cutting across regional state apparatuses to provide the most fertile conditions for the territorial accumulation of capital. The territorial logic of regionalization cannot be disentangled from the accumulation of capital.

Indeed, regional policies play a powerful role in "market-expanding" policies that directly attempt to support the regional accumulation of capital through P3s, tax incentives, loan support, leasing arrangements, infrastructure support, and innumerable other policy tools. These are often discussed in terms of "incubating" regional centres of innovation formed around particular technological paradigms and industrial applications, linking education, research, and even sectoral coordination across competing firms. The education and training branches of subnational states, for example, have been "instrumentalized" in their curriculum and research mandates – what some have called a corporatization of universities – to facilitate the competitiveness of regional production systems. Similar reorientations of other branches and departments of the regional state, such as taxation, energy policies, transportation, and housing can also be identified. This is what Philip Cerny (1995, 620) refers to as the regional competition state – "an agent for the commodification of the collective, situated in a wider, market-dominated playing field." These various modes of public administration are, of course, not invented anew. Some are scrapped, others are reworked and adapted, and new procedures and practices are implemented as the various state apparatuses are aligned with the neoliberal policy regime.

The regional economic policy regime adjusts to the world market not as an external constraint acting on the regional economic space, but as a market logic internalized inside the state. Market imperatives are inscribed in the institutional apparatuses of the regional state, that is, in budgetary mandates, in departmental operational plans and organization, in forms of governance of boards and agencies, and so on. Regional space is, as Edward Soja (1989, 171) suggested, always a terrain of conflict and contradiction "for control over the restructuring of space." The Ontario region-state, across and within its long periods of "one-province," "one-party-dominant" political rule, is no exception to these divisions.

THE TORIES AND THE ONTARIO REGION-STATE: FROM BOOM TO NEOLIBERALISM

It is helpful to frame the current neoliberal policy regime in Ontario in relation to its historical antecedents. This is not a claim that these policies are, in fact, long-standing, although Ontario has never strayed very far from an instrumentalist state committed to market expansion. The intent is, rather, to locate the political path that led to today's neoliberal governance modes and state.

Ontario, and indeed the world market, had never seen anything like the "long boom" that followed the Second World War. Over a period of some thirty-odd years, from the 1940s to the 1970s, Ontario was transformed from an agrarian and extractive economy into one of the world's leading zones of advanced manufacturing and high finance. Over this period, real annual average growth hovered around 5 per cent, built on a rapidly expanding population but with per capita incomes still trebling. The impact on the regional production system was spectacular. In the early 1940s, the primary extractive sector provided just over a quarter of output and employment, but by the mid-1970s it had fallen to just over 6 per cent of output and under 5 per cent of employment; in the 1940s, the manufacturing share of total employment was at a similar level at almost half of output, but fell to under a third of employment and under 40 per cent of output by the 1970s. Astonishingly, services (with all their public and private sector diversity) were approaching 60 per cent of output and two-thirds of employment by the end of the 1970s (Rea 1985, chaps. 1 and 5; Richmond 1974). As a consequence, the small capital and independent agrarian producers that had such a profound impact on the pre-Depression Ontario economy were increasingly displaced by a professional middle class spread across all sectors and a massive expansion of public and private sector working classes.

The postwar boom in the advanced capitalist countries is commonly summarized as "Fordism." A lead role in accumulation was played by the mass production industries of autos, consumer durables, and personal consumption; and these industries tended to employ a unionized workforce able to push for wage and benefits increases in line with the gains in productivity and social spending in tandem with growth. By any measure, Ontario emerged as one of the world centres of Fordist production benefitting from foreign direct investment in Canadian branch-plants, powerful linkages from the extractive sector to manufacturing, and, as the national hub for retail, financial and government services in Canada. The regional production system was, moreover, reinforced by national Keynesian economic policies. An implicit import substitution industrialization strategy encouraged extractive sector exports from the rest of Canada (oil and gas, grains, fish, hydro, minerals) to finance the development of Ontario-centred manufacturing producing for the national market. The federal government policies included a competitive Canadian dollar, the smoothing of inward flows of foreign capital, tariffs, skilled immigrant labour flows, and sectoral trade pacts with the US in defence products and autos, among others. The building of the national welfare state, even one as modest as Canada's, further provided the government employment, educational skills, and accommodative effective demand that benefitted the Ontario economy.

With national policies so integral to building the regional production system, the Ontario state needed much less of its own planning capacities. It simply had to not be a political obstacle (as it often was in the post-Confederation period or in its hesitations to support the CPP and medicare). Still, the regional policies of the Ontario state played their own part through the one-party domination of the Conservatives from 1940 to 1985. This was old-style Toryism that sought, across the premierships of Drew, Frost, Robarts, and Davis, a "one-province" consensus. Ontario's economic policies were, then, hardly ambitious or innovative, and always foremost concerned, as Premier Frost put it, to "clear the way for the private sector" (quoted in Brownsey and Howlett 1992, 156). Initially, "activist" regional industrial policies simply consisted of extensive use of subsidies, special tax and investment legislation, export promotion, development grants, and the like. They also included building the infrastructure to supply cheap energy via Ontario Hydro and cheap transport through inter-governmental cooperation, constructing the St Lawrence Seaway and the Trans-Canada Highway to link the continental market.

This modest economic policy activism still required a significant expansion of an initially tiny provincial bureaucracy. Every major sector had its particular government department, agency, or program, with the ties that then developed between local business elites and the Conservative government forming a powerful network of power. A massive expansion of the college and university system over the period was another measure to ensure a continual supply of skills as the technical division of labour increased and services became more important. But the lack of administrative capacities meant that postwar activist regional economic policy in Ontario mounted to a lot less than the sum of ad hoc policies occurring in each sector and each sub-region of the province.

Other areas of social policy also expanded as the Ontario state was prodded into policy activism by the expansion of federal shared-cost programs building out the Canadian welfare state. But cost containment and keeping per capita social expenditures modest relative to other provinces meant that Ontario was always a laggard and never a leader, apart from a labour relations regime that was at least permissive of unionization. It is hard not to concur with one thorough assessment of Ontario provincial politics that, for the Conservative regime, "the role of the state was to maintain and enhance conditions for the private accumulation of capital" (Brownsey and Howlett 1992, 157).

Despite the evident prosperity and the pull of Ontario and Toronto for immigration, the relative economic underperformance compared to other core capitalist countries began to raise concerns. Ontario's long boom was propelled by intensive and extensive accumulation as productivity increases from adopting branch-plant technology provided about half the increase in output, with the rest coming from the rapid increase in the size of the labour force. But the Ontario strategy for the regional production system was little more than facilitating resource development and laying infrastructure, with the Ontario Development Councils attempting to spur technology but never building industrial planning capacity inside the state. Already in 1969, the Committee on Government Productivity established by the Conservative government revealed the institutional primacy of market-expanding strategies in its calls for cuts in spending, competitive tendering, and contracting-out of public services – what it termed "re-privatization." In 1975, the Special Program Review Committee took up the same themes of fiscal policy constraint to shrink the size of government in the economy for competitiveness (Rae 1985, 232–7; White 1998, 122–6).

By the end of the 1970s, with the general slowdown in the world market cutting growth in half and doubling unemployment rates, Ontario was performing in the bottom half of the Canadian provinces. Industrial rationalization hit Ontario hard, with layoffs spread across almost all manufacturing sectors and hundreds of firms. The "Volcker shock," resulting from the US Federal Reserve driving up interest rates, provoked a deep recession that further decimated Ontario industry and opened a path for neoliberal policies. With economic output sliding and job losses mounting, alongside increasing demands for the expansion of the welfare state from a growing middle class, unions, and new equity-seeking social movements, the Ontario state fell into a series of fiscal deficits into the 1980s.

The Conservative governments of Bill Davis from 1971 to 1985 were committed to the same politics of state "intervention" to support private sector-led growth. But the political scene was radically shifting to neoliberal politics in the US and Britain, with the federal Liberal government taking hesitant steps in the same direction. Already in the mid-1970s, Ontario had begun to introduce budgets of restraint, if not yet the austerity to come, focused on slowing the pace of public sector growth, in terms of expenditures and employment, relative to the private sector (Drummond 1983). By the 1980s, this had formed into an even tighter pattern of restraining expenditure growth below the growth rate of output and population growth. The 1982 Inflation Restraint Act unilaterally placed a ceiling on public sector wage increases and restricted public sector collective bargaining. As budgetary restraint became systemic, the Tories moved to create fiscal space for industry by further restricting social spending in what already was one of the most modest welfare states in Canada. The support for industry was meant to assist the restructuring of the regional production system. But with such weak central planning capacities, the actual policies had little coherence – business tax cuts here and there, the Board for Industrial Leadership and Development (BILD) repackaging standard infrastructure programs, the Innovation Development for Employment Advancement (IDEA) for technological innovation, an Employment Development Fund for industry assistance, a 25 per cent stake in Suncor in the oil sands, and others (Speirs 1986, 9–10). This was still a "one-province" strategy of restraint in an attempt to hold the Tory electoral bloc together. The Conservatives were now, however, unable to deliver the same semblance of shared prosperity for all.

The successive Liberal and NDP governments of Peterson and Rae, spanning the decade from 1985 to 1995, were quite another story. Both parties attempted to come to terms with the backwardness of the administrative capacities of Queen's Park after the long period of Conservative rule. There was, moreover, the pressing need to address the faltering competitiveness of the branch-plant production system. Their common agenda could also be cast as an alternative to the neoliberal policies gaining prominence across the world under the guise of the "Washington consensus," and in Canada via the radical restructuring of Canadian trade and economic policy proposed by the 1984 Royal Commission on the Economic Union. These policies were considered a "low road" to competitiveness based on "flexibilization" and cuts to wages and social policy. The Liberal-NDP compact proposed, in contrast, a "high road" of "progressive competitiveness" by developing high value-added sectors employing high-skilled workers within networks of continual innovation. This was an agenda formulated in Ontario by the Premier's Council, an advisory body established to rethink the regional economy. The premise was that a "competition state" at the regional level was needed to deal with the globalization of trade, finance, and social relations – as expressed in the title of their major report, *Competing in the New Global Economy* (1988).

In a first step, the Liberals signed an accord with the NDP to force the Tories out of office and form a minority government. For both parties, the accord was guided by a modernization project of administrative competencies for service delivery, a measure of centralized coordination across the branches of the state, and the capacity for strategic intervention in the "new economy" beyond the old regional industrial policies of tax incentives and subsidies. Within "a framework for fiscal responsibility," the accord also proposed an overhaul of the welfare state that was suffering from decades of Tory neglect – creating employment and pay equity legislation, upgrading environmental regulations, addressing youth unemployment via targeted training programs, increasing ministry budgets, overhauling employment and welfare programs, building co-op and non-profit housing, introducing plant shutdown legislation, and much else (Ehring and Roberts 1993, 376–9). This was as progressive a modernization of state capacities as Ontario has ever seen. Particularly in the Liberals' second term, it included modest increases in taxes, including to income taxes, and also to sales, payroll, and excise taxes, in order to upgrade the welfare state and infrastructure in Ontario.

The second step in forging a new regional economic policy, however, proved far more difficult. Although given a strong assist by a powerful (if short-lived) boom pushing average annual growth rates for 1983–89 to well above 4 per cent, productivity growth remained flat (Ontario Ministry of Finance 1994; Courchene 1998, 34–6). Despite the elaborate agenda of the Premier's Council, economic caution prevailed. The Peterson industrial policy for the new economy largely consisted of a Ministry of Skills Development consolidating an array of training and adjustment programs, and a Ministry of Industry, Trade and Technology clustering together industry support policies. These hardly moved beyond the community development agreements of the Ontario Development Corporation of the Davis era and the typical ad hoc Ontario state response to industrial restructuring. The most significant economic policy innovation was, perhaps, the establishment of a Ministry of Financial Institutions, which undertook a policy of deregulating the securities industry. It foretold where the Ontario economy was steadily being repositioned – a low-cost production zone within the North American economy anchored by an elaborate financial and producer service sector.

As the Liberals fell into a morass of policy confusions and spending scandals, the newly elected NDP government of 1990 attempted, in a third step, to push even harder for the modernization of a competition state. The NDP's *An Agenda for the People* set itself against the federal government's aggressive adoption of neoliberalism with the turn to continental trade integration, privatization, marketization, and social policy cuts. One part of the *Agenda* was social justice, with a goal of increasing social spending and including "equity" issues in terms of employment, pay, human rights, and poverty reduction. In the midst of the recession of 1990–92, with growth rates turning negative (and real GPD growth per capita at a dismal -1% for 1990–94), the new NDP government accepted a budgetary deficit for 1991–92 of $10 billion (and final estimate deficits remained in the $10–12 billion for each year of the NDP in power); the goal was to provide economic stimulus targeted at social spending and job creation (Ontario Ministry of Finance 2005, 18; Courchene 1998, 130). A range of other initiatives also departed from the emerging neoliberal consensus: labour law changes against scabs and to ease organizing, rent controls and an increased minimum wage, an increase in the personal income tax surtax, modest increases in corporate and capital taxes, support for non-profit housing, a wage protection fund, and many others.

The other key part of the *Agenda* picked up the mantle of a "progressive" industrial policy to meet the global competition Ontario now faced, and was laid out in the 1992 policy paper, *An Industrial Policy Framework for Ontario*. This was pitched as a new "partnership" between capital, labour, and community groups in the province – skills training for flexibility through the colleges and vocational schools, innovation clusters for new high value-added products, universities oriented to new research and development, and support for regional networks of firms. Two institutions, the Ontario Training and Adjustment Board (OTAB) and the Sectoral Partnership Fund (SPF), were at the centre of the strategy. OTAB had its origins in the second Peterson government, but it was the NDP burden to try to establish it in industry, overhaul labour force development and adjustment programs, and support its equity objectives. The SPF was a modestly funded attempt to forge networks between business, unions, and government to build "trust" and encourage cooperative strategies to increase the productivity of Ontario industry (Bradford 1998).

These policy departures had little to do with bringing socialism to Ontario, and were quite measured social democratic efforts to build a more productive, inclusive capitalism – the Ontario NDP's version of a "one-province" strategy. Yet it still ran into hostile – even venomous – opposition. The various Ontario business associations and the mass media ran a vicious campaign against the deficit, insanely warning that Ontario was heading off a "fiscal cliff." The same kinds of doomsday campaigns were waged against public auto insurance, benefits for same-sex couples, and tax reform. Every oppositional campaign was met with full retreat by the Rae regime. With no strategic partnerships to be had, the federal government capping transfer programs in the midst of a recession, the Canadian dollar rising from 70 cents in 1986 to 89 cents in 1991 (eroding any unit labour cost advantage), and the introduction of the GST in 1991, political circumstances turned completely against the NDP and its modest reform ambitions, and in favour of a brutal industrial restructuring.

The government turned to its allies in the labour movement for sacrifices to restore "fiscal integrity" as they saw it. Even before their competition state strategy could gain any administrative capacity, the NDP began to resort to austerity in 1992 with a mix of tax increases and expenditures cuts. This was, however, only the beginning. In 1993–94, the NDP adopted an expenditure control plan, comprising $4 billion in program cuts, tax increases of $1.8 billion, and public sector wage restraint (to save another $2 billion). The absolute cut in government expenditures was the first since the early 1940s. The social contract proposed for public sector workers initially attempted to negotiate wage restraint, and then imposed it, against existing collective agreements, and also cut 11,000 jobs to boot (Walkom 1994, chap. 8).

The "Rae reversal" was not a policy shift isolated to Ontario. European social democracy was also tacking away from interventionist policies for competitiveness under the misleading banner of a "third way." Like the NDP government, this was a retreat from policies attempting to control the market and redistribute unequal market incomes to accommodate the neoliberal policy regime in the 1990s. The strategy of progressive competitiveness through social partnerships mutated, across social democratic parties and in Ontario under the NDP, into the "austerity in one class" of neoliberalism. At the end of the NDP period, the fiscal deficit was contained and per capita spending barely moved from the Liberal years (White 1998, 142).

The Liberal-NDP decade in power in Ontario prepared the grounds for the Conservative Party's "counter-revolution" under the leadership of Mike Harris. Both governments had accepted a "one-province" "partnership for productivity" between capital and labour. In turn, both drifted into policies of austerity for the public sector, restraint from workers in collective bargaining, and flexibility in labour markets and the welfare state, all to contain costs for capital. These were, it hardly needs saying, all central precepts of the neoliberal policy regime, and common to the new right and "third way" social democracy alike.[3]

The political calculation of the Harris Conservatives took the form of the *Common Sense Revolution* (CSR) manifesto trumpeted across the province in the 1995 election. It was, in word and proposed deeds, a militant pledge of neoliberal policies of market discipline to bolster Ontario business – a "two provinces, divided society" strategy to wage class struggle from above. The manifesto provided the policy guideposts for the Conservatives in power from 1995–2003. The Common Sense Revolutionaries who gathered around Harris came from corporate law offices, Bay Street, and a growing group of hard-right MPPs from rural Ontario and the outer suburbs of the major cities. Their gamble was on a decisive mandate to overthrow existing policies. It required a political polarization between the morally upright, entrepreneurial, individual citizens of Ontario and the welfare-scroungers, unions, and collectivist state that had cost Ontario its competitive edge. The programmatic content was clear: cut taxes, spending, regulation, the partnership model, and the size of the Ontario public service; balance budgets; and reform administration in line with the new public management of marketization of the state. In other words, remake the form and policy regime of the Ontario state to restore its competitive position as a low-tax, low-cost regional economy within the NAFTA trade zone.

The Conservative legislative onslaught came with unprecedented rapidity and volume within the first year of power, with massive omnibus bills bullied through the legislature as a standard practice. Without public consultation and with only the slightest legislative debate, an authoritarian concentration of power in the Premier's Office took hold and the size of the provincial assembly was cut. A complete tally of the administrative transformations, policy shifts, layoffs, and budgetary measures of the first Harris government could go on for hundreds of pages.

A first set of measures rolled back the NDP's "social inclusion" agenda to weaken labour protections and increase downward wage flexibility: repealing employment equity legislation; reversing labour law changes; freezing the minimum wage; gutting employee wage protection; radically cutting social assistance in terms of eligibility and income support levels; introducing mandatory workfare; and laying off 10,600 public service jobs. Another focus was a dramatic reorientation of fiscal politics by an income tax cut of some 30 per cent and lowering the initial threshold for when the the Employer Health Tax kicked in, while proposing to systematically cut government spending as a portion of provincial output. Much of this was put forward in the massive enabling legislation called the Savings and Restructuring Act, passed in 1996. This act entailed expenditure cuts in the first year of some $5 billion, or 20 percent of what was called non-priority spending (White 1998, 267–8; Courchene 1998, 174–212).

To make it perfectly clear that the attempt to modernize and build the capacities of the Ontario state were over, the sectoral training and industrial policy strategies were scrapped, with the remnants returned to appropriate ministries. The Conservative strategy, outlined in the 1997 budget, *Investing in Our Future*, returned to the traditional ad hoc policy of tax incentives and subsidies for research and development, with a set of additional incentives for innovation in new technology. The most transformative Conservative measures were the neoliberal remaking of the broad public sector to reduce permanently the capacities of the Ontario state: the breakup and commercialization of Ontario Hydro; the privatization of Highway 407; a mass reduction of the size of the Ontario Public Service (OPS); a radical extension of the contracting-out of employment and service provision in waste management, water, highway maintenance, and much else; a move toward light or self-regulation; extensive downloading of programs and service provision to municipalities (without a parallel shift in revenues and policy capacities); the pushing of commercialization models on school boards, hospitals, parks, and other sectors; a massive amalgamation of hospitals, school boards, and municipalities; a dramatic curtailing of public oversight and consultative processes; the charging of each ministry with forming its own "business plan" to identify core services and restructure service delivery mechanisms; the institutional embrace of NAFTA; and many others. The various Ontario police forces grew in strength and visibility in parallel to the cuts (White 1998, 250–80; Courchene 1998, chap. 7).

The Harris regime cast a harsh anti-democratic shadow over the Ontario state, openly attacking the labour movement, even as it weathered a storm of protests in the "Days of Action": one-day, city-based general strikes across the province from 1995–98. But economic fortune initially favoured the Common Sense Revolutionaries. A lower dollar and lower interest rates after the industrial restructuring from free trade combined with the "Clinton boom" in the US to strengthen export competitiveness and push real growth rates well above 5 per cent for 1997–2000. However, with the bursting of the dot-com bubble and the economic impact of 9/11 and the turn to "permanent war," growth in the regional economy fell to under 2 per cent in 2001, and remained low from then on. As a consequence, with the tax cuts already eroding fiscal capacity, the Ontario budgetary position again deteriorated, despite the radical undermining of public spaces, programs, and infrastructure by Harris, with a deficit of over $5.4 billion for 2003–04 (Ontario Ministry of Finance 2014).

The Harris election mandate of 1999, the so-called *Blueprint Manifesto*, thus lost the original bluster and swagger, if remaining just as determined in its neoliberalism. The second term remained fixed on an agenda of corporate tax cuts, trimming the size of public employment, and bringing provincial government expenditures from about 19 per cent of provincial output when entering office to just under 15 per cent. Other "new public management" measures were also pushed ahead in the remaking of internal management processes, such as detailed commercial-like business plans and performance standards (Ontario Ministry of Finance 2003, 69). Together, the fiscal adjustment and the transformation of the administrative form of the Ontario state consolidated a new logic of competitive austerity centred on regionally flexible labour markets, a tamed union movement, low taxes, minimal program spending, and marketized modes of public administration open to almost any kind of private development.

THE LIBERALS RETURN: NEOLIBERALISM 3.0

By 2003, the political lustre of the CSR was gone, and with it the "two-provinces" strategy of calculated political polarization to tear up the project of a progressive state-led modernization of Ontario. But the coming into power of the Liberals, under the leadership of the tepid Dalton McGuinty, did not signify a departure from neoliberal modes of governance. Indeed, the Liberals sought to rule by restoring the Ontario ideology of "one province," in a new rhetoric of symbolic inclusiveness, but without reversing the regressive modernization of the economic and social policies of the CSR. In the post 9/11 economy, Ontario slipped into economic stagnation, growing at just over 2 per cent for 2003–07 (Ontario Ministry of Finance 2014). It would have taken an administration with considerable political ambition and clear strategic direction to alter the neoliberal course; the McGuinty Liberals had neither.

The initial undertaking was to demonstrate their own commitments to fiscal consolidation and the "low tax" strategy. The Liberal "one Ontario" logic was brutally simple: the Harris tax regime would remain in place, budgetary balances would be sought, but there would be a stop – for progressive gloss – to "irresponsible tax cuts for some, so we can … provide public services for all" (Ontario Ministry of Finance 2004, 1). The first McGuinty budget affirmed that program and capital spending could be expected to continue to decline as a portion of provincial output. This would steadily bring down the $5.6 billion deficit inherited from the Tories, but also lock in the radical Harris cuts to the Ontario public sector.[4] As the Liberals settled into office, their "inclusionary neoliberalism" was illustrated with particular clarity in the 2005 budget. The budgets of most ministries would be steadily cut in real terms in increments to leave space for increased expenditures on health and education, all as a matter of "fiscal discipline." Further, a five-year $30 billion in new infrastructure plans would now occur via "alternate fiscal procurement," as the Liberals termed their particular renewal of privatization via public-private partnerships (P3s). The newly formed Ministry of Public Infrastructure Renewal was charged with building an inventory of public assets – such as major crown corporations like the LCBO, Ontario Lottery and Gaming Corporation, and Hydro One, but also real estate and general government services – that might be suitable for privatization, commercialization, and P3s. As well, the Infrastructure Ontario agency would seek "opportunities … for private sector innovation in design, construction, service delivery, and /or asset use" in specific projects (Ontario Ministry of Public

Infrastructure Renewal 2004, 22; Nugent 2015). The revenues raised would, the Liberals contended, fund infrastructure renewal without the government having to raise taxes or sell bonds.

Within these fiscal constraints, the Liberals struggled to give state policies a progressive veneer. It was quite impossible to rebuild public services and state capacities at existing tax levels; at most, a "selective activism" might be offered, by manipulating various administrative mechanisms for symbolic equity, commercializing public assets to generate funds for specific projects, and targeting special tax measures. A health tax levy, for example, was implemented in 2004 on employer payrolls, given the constraints imposed on general revenue sources. The Green Energy and Green Economy Act of 2009 symbolized concerns over climate change with its phase-out of coal and an attempt to build up renewable energy. But it was characterized by seemingly endless missteps and cost overruns linked to the prior breakup of Ontario Hydro, as well as to the Liberals' fixation on building up private ownership in the renewable energy sector and sacrificing the historical role of public energy in the province. In labour relations, the Liberals cast aside the decade-long aggressive assault on unions, particularly in the education sector, but barely revised labour laws and continued to introduce back-to-work legislation against public sector workers, notably Toronto transit workers in 2008 and CUPE university workers in 2009 (Evans and Smith 2015, 176–80).

The notion of a progressive competitiveness within the "new economy" was central to the Liberal approach to the regional production system of the 1980s.[5] There was only a trace of that regional strategy left in the Ministry of Economic Development and Trade with its inventory of incentives and subsidies, and low-tax, light regulation. Indeed, the McGuinty government now offered up the Ministry of Research, Innovation and Science, formed in 2005, without any of the earlier "sectoral" or "partnership" mandates. The entire Ontario state apparatus was now being instrumentalized to enhance competitiveness via leveraging public funds, across universities and research agencies, into research that would back capitalist-sector product development. Similar efforts formed to enhance incentives for "small business and entrepreneurship." As a result, a focus on the "commercialization" and "human capital formation" of science and technology entered into the mandate of the Ministry of Training, Colleges and Universities.[6] The

2006 $3.2 billion Innovation Ontario Agenda provided a framework for all these efforts with its focus on "industrial clusters [and] convergence networks ... to connect academic research with market opportunities and help early-stage companies to become investor-ready" (Government of Ontario 2015, n.p.). The core of the strategy was presented in the 2008 budget and focused on tax exemptions for corporations, commercializing intellectual property developed by Canadian universities, an innovation tax credit, and a suite of other corporate tax breaks to stimulate capital investments. Under the same initiative, the government proposed the Next Generation Jobs Fund "to support market-driven opportunities in strategic areas," notably the ICT sector, renewable energies, and bio-pharmaceuticals (ibid.). The "networks of coordination" now guiding the Ontario regional production system reworked the Harris CSR, but within the same "low-tax, low-cost" economic strategy.

By their second term election in 2007, the attempt to cast the McGuinty Liberal as "progressive" began to border on parody. In 2008, the government finally put forward minor increases to the core social assistance rates, not even coming close to reversing the punitive cuts of the Tories from a decade earlier. The Liberals' much-hyped anti-poverty strategy, *Breaking the Cycle: Ontario's Poverty Reduction Strategy* (2008), amounted to nothing more than the first in a series of consultations with "community partners" that continued endlessly on. It was only in 2009 that the real minimum wage moved ahead of the rate frozen by Harris in 1995; but the Liberals then turned around and froze the rate for 2011–15, before bumping it up in 2016 (Caledon Institute 2012, 25–7; Battle 2015, 7, 17).[7]

The global financial crisis of 2008–10 further tested the tension between the progressive claims and neoliberal commitments of Ontario Liberalism. The most severe economic crisis since the Great Depression led to trillions in financial assets being wiped out, a decline in the volume of world trade, and a panic over an economic collapse that could not be contained. For Ontario, economic growth completely stalled in 2008 and then declined by 3.1 per cent in 2009 in the depth of the financial crisis, thereafter remaining stagnant at below historical trend rates of growth (Ontario Ministry of Finance 2014). As with other governments, Ontario turned to an "emergency Keynesian" fiscal policy, with monetary and banking policy centred in Ottawa, in the

2009 budget. For the Liberals, this meant a "bold" departure – that is, letting a modest budgetary surplus slide into a significant deficit (eventually hitting $19.3 billion, after a forecast of $14.1 billion). There was, as well, deliberate stimulus. The most significant was the phasing-in of a permanent reduction of the corporate income tax from 14 per cent to 10 per cent by 2013. The bottom income tax bracket was cut by 1 per cent as well, and a range of low income tax credits expanded, as a show of "equity," against the corporate tax cuts (although such a cut had little claim to be redistributional, as changes to the sales tax offset the income tax cuts). The corporate tax cuts of some $4.5 billion over 3 years were stimulative but not inconsistent with neoliberal policy goals (which the budget referred to as "competitive government"). The additional spending was significant in increasing annual program spending by $11.1 billion for the coming year (to an extent levered by the federal government's *Economic Action Plan*), and for proposing stimulus for an additional year before returning to restraint. The measures included expediting an increase in the Ontario Child Benefit, a modest bump in spending on affordable housing, and an increase and acceleration of planned infrastructure spending, notably the Move Ontario public transit plans (Ontario Ministry of Finance 2009, chap. 1).

The respite from austerity was short-lived, however. By the 2010 budget, with the crisis compounding class and regional polarizations across the province, the McGuinty government's "Open Ontario Plan" upped its neoliberal commitments and made it clear that public sector restraint would be the means to "pay for the crisis." The tax cuts of the prior year would be supplemented by further cuts to the minimum corporate tax by a third and the elimination of the capital tax levied on corporate assets. With fiscal capacity now even further constrained, the Liberals' stated objective of bringing the budget back into balance by 2017–18 would require strict austerity, alongside a return to modest growth and low interest rates. The Liberals judiciously avoided dramatic cuts of the sort being pushed by the neo-Harrisites on the Conservative front benches, and even shifted some spending into their "priority areas", such as education, health, and even daycare, to yield the appearance of new programs. Reminiscent of the initial turn to austerity in the 1990s, public sector employees would be singled out: a freeze on compensation was immediately imposed on non-union workers until March 2012, with unionized employees being pushed into accepting a two-year wage freeze. The overall budget trajectory was to be put on a steady reduction of the deficit, the debt, and the overall size of government by locking in an increase in annual real government spending at less than the pace of nominal economic growth. The Open for Business Act shortly followed, and put forward more than a hundred proposals for commercialization and deregulation to foster "competitiveness." These proposals cut across a swath of legislation and departments, laying out easier terms for foreign investment; opening up the so-called Ring of Fire mining zone; further commercializing health care provisions; downgrading environmental reviews; pushing a "self-help" model of enforcing employment standards; and dozens of others (Ontario Ministry of Finance 2010, 50–2, 157–8; Fanelli and Thomas 2011, 152–8).

Although reduced to minority government status in the fall 2011 election, the McGuinty government did nothing to reverse its turn away from fiscal stimulus, even while campaigning under the "one province" theme of "moving forward together." Neither of the inept campaigns by the NDP or Conservatives compelled political reconsideration of "one-province" neoliberalism. By 2012, the transition to permanent austerity began in earnest. The budget set out the strategy for the 2017–18 target of eliminating the deficit, and indeed proposed austerity for the rest of the decade. Although the budget postponed the last step of the corporate tax cuts, new revenue measures focused on increasing user fees across ministries, squeezing more money out of the LCBO and "gaming," and using "alternate financing and procurement" from the commercialization of government assets. These measures were to raise $4.4 billion in new revenues over three years. But the catalogue of proposed cuts over the same period was $17.7 billion: the amalgamation of school boards, the merger of ministries alongside employment cuts, a decline in environmental regulatory and enforcement, delays to increases in the Child Benefit, a hospital budget freeze. Little else was spared. In the fall, the Putting Students First Act (2012) imposed a two-year wage freeze and other compensation cuts on the education sector, in the process suspending collective bargaining and insulating the act from provincial human rights legislation (Ontario Ministry of Finance 2012, 40; OPSEU 2012).[8]

Such a fiscal matrix could only be managed by a further neoliberal radicalization of the public management of the Ontario state, well beyond anything that even the CSR envisioned. The Commission on the Reform of Ontario's Public Service (2012), chaired by the former Bay Street banker Don Drummond, provided the legitimacy and the strategy for the effort. Across its over 500 pages, the commission's report provided the most comprehensive plan for the neoliberalization of fiscal policy and administrative modes that any government in Canada has yet delivered. The commission had no mandate to review taxes: its purpose was to suggest cuts and the rationalization of public assets to meet the deficit targets. Its framing recommendation called for a "fall by 2.5 percent" in real per capita spending per year – a slightly more aggressive target than the pace the Liberals had already set (10). From this constraint, there was hardly a policy field that the Drummond Report left out. It proposed a lengthy list of possibilities for privatization across ministries; an overhaul of government service provision to massively expand contracting-out; sectoral self-regulation; reducing real per capita expenditures by capping health care spending at 2.5 per cent year and postsecondary education at 1.5 per cent to 2017–18; extending local health networks to allow more market provisioning; having seniors pay more for drugs; charging higher user fees for water, parking, and much else; expanding access to slot machines; and hundreds of other proposals.[9]

Increasingly discredited, McGuinty could not survive the growing public antipathy to the austerity turn that he had crafted. The election of Kathleen Wynne to leader in late 2013, and to a majority government in the election of 2015, was to be a "progressive reset" of Liberal governance. The reset proved elusive. The policy restraint was already locked in by the parameters set by the last budgets, and by the authority the Liberals had granted to the Drummond Report. Indeed, the "social justice" government trumpeted that "Ontario was the leanest government in Canada, with the lowest per capita program spending of any province ... and is projected to remain so" (Ontario Ministry of Finance 2016, 174).

Although Wynne scrapped the legislated pay freeze in the education sector in 2013 (as the teachers' unions allied with the government), the Social Assistance Review to address poverty failed to get off the ground. Like the entire Liberal anti-poverty agenda, it mutated into yet further study, alongside proposed pilot projects testing guaranteed annual income. Wynne re-tuned the "one province" discourse, but it was austerity that prevailed. The "low tax, low cost" agenda was the pivot for what remained of regional economic policy. The high-profile Premier's Advisory Council on Government Assets (2014), established under the leadership of (another) former bank executive Ed Clark, was charged with "asset optimization" – the latest term for privatization – to provide some tens of billions in funds for infrastructure and debt reduction. The foremost example of this was the controversial sale of 60 per cent of Hydro One over 2015–16. Similarly, the new "cap and trade" market for carbon emissions relied on excise taxes and market trades in carbon to fund green industry expansion. Innovation policy, too, depended on using public assets to leverage investment through "industry-academic collaborations," such as the Advance Manufacturing Consortium, the Automotive Industry Manufacturing Strategy, the Investment Acceleration Fund, and others (Ontario Ministry of Finance 2016; Block 2016).

After a decade of austerity and an uptick in economic growth to well above 2 per cent for 2017–18, the Liberals announced the achievement of a balanced budget. But in the run-up to the June 2018 provincial election, an increasingly unpopular Wynne proposed to relax spending and allow the budget to slide slightly into deficit at 1 per cent of GPP. Indeed, a series of initiatives presented a progressive turn to the policy regime: the Fair Workplaces, Better Jobs Act (2017), an anti-racism directorate, a basic income pilot project, pharmacare, and increased funding (often spread over many years) for child care, health care, transit, housing, and other initiatives (both symbolic and involving modest expenditures) across the range of ministries. With no planned shift in taxes and pressures for further tax cuts, budgetary policy was to return in the near future to the Ontario fiscal austerity norm of declining per capita expenditures (Block and Hennessy 2017; Giovannetti 2018). As when they won an unexpected surge of support in the 2015 election, the Wynne Liberals planned to outflank a directionless NDP on the left and polarize voters against a Conservative Party led by the hard right figure of Doug Ford. Yet, under the "one province" political dominance of the Liberal Party, the Ontario state was transformed into one of the leading zones of neoliberal policy in the core capitalist countries.

If it is not yet clear the extent to which Ford will return to the deliberately polarizing strategy of Harris, there is no doubt that Ontario's neoliberal commitments are not under threat. In campaigning "for the people" against "liberal elites," Ford promised in his government's initial Throne Speech that Ontario is now "open for business," echoing Harris and McGuinty before him (Ontario Progressive Conservatives 2018; Ontario Office of the Premier 2018). The policies proposed are also utterly conventional in their neoliberal roots (if extreme in their social implications): cut gas and income taxes and hydro rates; scrap the carbon trading system; reduce regulation hindering small business; audit the government books to find "efficiencies" (which will pay for the tax cuts without cuts to services or jobs); expand social programs through targeted tax credits (not bureaucracy); and many others. But with the Conservative cuts to government revenues forecast to drive the budgetary deficit up, the cuts can only be financed by fiscal austerity, privatizations, contracting-out, and public sector compensation cuts. These are all part of the standard neoliberal policy arsenal that the Conservatives left unmentioned. With the Ontario public sector already the most austere in Canada, the contradictions of the Conservative program will, no doubt, confront unexpected political challenges.

OUT OF THE NEOLIBERAL IMPASSE?

As the postwar ideology and political consensus of "one-province" Toryism began to unravel from the economic turbulence of the 1970s, Ontario entered a phase of instability in its political system across the 1980s, reflected in the splintering of historical patterns of partisanship and a series of minority governments. The "two provinces" strategy of "class struggle from above" pursued by the Harris government in the 1990s imposed neoliberalism across the province, eclipsing the old brokerage politics. But it was the Liberals under McGuinty and Wynne who pushed an increasingly hard right Conservative Party to the electoral margins and gained electoral hegemony. They did so, however, by governing from within the new market-centred policy framework the

Conservatives had forged. More than twenty years of austerity, beginning with the Rae reversal through the Common Sense Revolution to Liberal domination, returned Ontario to "one-province" politics. The formal political system again cohered in political consensus, more or less, but now within the policy regime of neoliberalism.

The economic crisis since 2008 has, if anything, reinforced the adherence of political elites and the business classes to neoliberal policies in Ontario and Canada. The main economic policy response has been to increase the autonomy and capacity of the Bank of Canada to restore bank liquidity, via a "quantitative easing" of the money supply to enforce low interest rates and relaxed credit conditions. With federal fiscal policy quickly reverting back to austerity and "market-expanding" federalism under the Harper Conservatives, the Ontario state opted for a policy regime consistent with this budgetary constraint. The Liberal government did so with its own variety of neoliberalism: a selective expansion of state spending in a few areas coupled with non-expenditure symbolic policies in others, all tightly controlled within an overall fiscal program of public sector wage restraint, spending cuts, and the monetization of public assets.

Without systematic opposition from any of the political parties, neoliberal policy governance has, in effect, become "de-politicized" within the Ontario political system and the state. The formal institutions of liberal democracy continue on; indeed, they have become even more vigorously defended by Ontario's political and media elites. But mass citizen disengagement from – and cynicism toward – conventional politics prevails as the commonsensical stance toward politics. According to Antonio Gramsci (1971, 267), the political party system and the state apparatuses form the matrix from within which a ruling class exercises its hegemony – "it will develop integrally into a State (an integral State, and not into a government technically understood)." In the Ontario region-state, the neoliberal matrix provides a secure fortress insulating the province's ruling classes from popular pressures, with Queen's Park itself little more than another state apparatus for forging regional stability.

The neutralization of political divisions in the parliamentary field in Ontario is also a register of the disarray of social alternatives in the extra-parliamentary sphere. Truncated social ambitions, in both popular mobilizations and political imaginaries, has made for an "anti-politics" sensibility in social movements in Ontario over the last decade or so (running parallel to the de-contestation within the political system). This detachment from the parties and the political system of liberal democracy – a sense of alienation cutting across the entire federal system in Canada – does not mean that political opposition is eliminated. But this dissent (at least among the political left) is now expressed in an ever-more pragmatic and fragmented politics that disavows the party form as the means to formulate and build political alternatives: a turn to strategic voting to keep the "worst of the neoliberal lot" out; sectoral lobbying for delimited campaign goals to get "whatever is possible" out of a corrupted political system; pursuit of "localist" community-based alternatives under the (quite naïve) assumption that these initiatives are independent of the political system; and sporadic outbursts of political discontent – such as in the recent and inspiring Occupy and Idle No More uprisings – that just as quickly recede into the background, all too often recorded as another disappointing attempt to "change things" that falls short.

The retreat into a posture of anti-politics by so many sections of the progressive movement in Ontario (to cast the net on this point widely) reflects, in good part, the steady erosion of the coalition of unions, social agencies, activists, and social movements that came together in the mid-1990s to oppose the Harris Conservative government, to some extent as a regional outgrowth of the struggles against free trade agreements and globalization. The Ontario coalition of resistance to neoliberalism unfolded under the banner of "Days of Action" from 1995–98 with a series of militant city-wide demonstrations in eleven Ontario cities (Kellogg 2011). The "mass strikes" were led by the Ontario Federation of Labour (OFL), but hinged on an alliance between the Canadian Auto Workers (CAW), public sector unions like CUPE, and the local social justice networks that had formed across Ontario. The inability of the "Days" coalition to block the Common Sense Revolution led, however, to a strategic impasse and eventual organizational disarray. The OFL retreated into a managerialist mode and empty political shell, and relations among the affiliate unions became increasingly fractious, with political energies too often focused on arcane jurisdictional issues and personality conflicts. The army of social agencies and community groups, too, moved to a defensive posture of self-preservation, and accommodation to the new policy terrain. And activist groups and social movements typically avoided, for all their radicalism in discourse, any rethinking of political organization and strategy, as if things could just continue on as usual.

For a brief moment, the anti-globalization movement raised the banner of "another possible world" – an anti-capitalist politics that would cut across the world market and breach compartmentalized scales of governance. This astonishing global rebellion included major demonstrations and activist groups in almost every Ontario community. In retrospect, however, the movement only succeeded in the mobilization of political outrage at the expansion of corporate property rights at the expense of "citizen rights" to secure jobs and incomes. The consolidation of the market disciplines of neoliberalism was barely impeded. The alternatives that the anti-globalization movement insisted to be possible, across a flood of manifestos and policy planks, receded into the background in the face of the "global war on terror" after September 2001.

Since 2003, it was the Liberal governments of both McGuinty and Wynne that electorally benefitted from this coalition of opposition as it fragmented and turned away from social – even anti-capitalist – militancy in political tactics. The Liberals' retrieval of the "one-province" discourse, even if neoliberal in policy and adding to social inequalities in practice, looked enlightened in contrast to the socially divisive and market-worshipping policies and discourse of the Conservatives. Many of Ontario's leading oppositional forces – notably, the CAW (now Unifor), the teachers' unions, the vast majority of the ecology movement, and a range of anti-poverty and equity-seeking groups – adopted an approach of "social dialogue" with the Liberal governments (and they may yet do so with the Ford Conservatives). In exchange for reining in political resistance to neoliberalism and supporting strategies for regional competitiveness, there was an effort to broker from the Liberal government social concessions such as raising minimum wages and low income assistance, improvements in school funding, adoption of a minimal strategy for energy conversion, and the like. But since the economic crisis and the more vigorous policy of austerity by the Liberal governments of McGuinty and Wynne, the fiscal space for even these modest social compromises had all but disappeared.

Sustained opposition to austerity from the labour movement remained, in this context, limited by "multiple crises of solidarity" – sectional divisions, defensive efforts to preserve jobs, and the truncation of the social ambitions of union leadership (Swartz and Warskett 2012, 28–31). The Ontario Common Front (OCF), an alliance led by the OFL with community organization allies since 2012, was initially effective in electoral mobilization against the Conservatives under banners such as "We are Ontario" and "#StopHudak." However, the alliance has been wracked by divisions over tactical electoral support for the Liberals or the NDP and by non-electoral organizing. The OCF also assisted in organizing occasional anti-austerity demonstrations in a number of cities, and providing support for other campaigns led by individual unions, such as the fight against income inequalities and the defense of public services, pensions, and steel plants. But the *Action Plan* of the OFL (2015; 2017), released biennially and by default serving as the main alternate tactical document for oppositional forces in the province, still lacks a wider programmatic agenda, a strategy for the mobilization of workplaces for the coming period, and even commitment (least of all over electoral strategies) from its member unions. By the 2018 election, the OCF was notable only for its absence, with ad hoc arrangements between particular unions and specific campaigns widespread – even to the point of the labour movement running three separate anti-privatization campaigns. As Larry Savage (2017, 307) has commented, "Ontario has become home to the most divided labour movement in Canada."

Still, a new landscape of resistance appears to be slowly but steadily emerging out of the growing social divisions in Ontario (Gray 2015). The long-standing campaign against health care privatization led by the Ontario Health Coalition and CUPE, for example, has been given new urgency by further cuts and the marketizaton of health care, with protests and campaigns strung out across the province over the last several years. The "Fight for $15" campaign for a living minimum wage and decent work has spread rapidly across the province, gaining active chapters on university campuses and many cities. During the 2018 election, the campaign opted for conventional "candidate pledges" of support for the Bill 148 reforms and studiously avoided partisan support between the Liberals and the NDP. The Ford government will, no doubt, challenge the labour reforms, and this will quickly become a test for linking movements together in this struggle (Fodor 2018).

A range of other campaigns are also gaining traction: against the privatization of Ontario Hydro and local electricity utilities; for the expansion of affordable – even free – public transit; in opposition to systematic racialized biases in policing and the judicial system through Black Lives Matter; for improved funding for education across all levels; for stronger climate change policies; through the spirited Women's March in 2017, and the more recent #MeToo movement of 2018; and others. First Nations resistance has followed its own pattern, alternating between popular demonstrations (as with the Idle No More demonstrations) and blockades of roads, pipelines, and rail lines, in struggles to assert greater community control over resource development and self-government in Aboriginal territories (Camfield 2011; Harden 2013, 70–82; Karim and Bush 2018). These campaigns do not yet amount to an Ontario-wide, united front able to overturn the hegemony of the "one-province" political consensus in the neoliberal policy regime. But they are suggestive of the potential to forge a wide range of sectoral campaigns against austerity and cuts to public services, and embed them in place-based community struggles concretely linking workers and users.

If new radical formations and political agendas are to emerge in Ontario, this will require an explicit break from the "anti-politics" discourse and political "common sense" of the last two decades. The de-politicization of neoliberal policies within Ontario – and across the Canadian state – underpins the austerity consensus of the "one-province" political system. The political elites, across all three main political parties, only offer rival sets of policies that operate within the neoliberal regime, with Ford proposing not to break the system but take a few further radical steps to entrench it. In an increasingly divided province, direct action, demonstrations, and community organizing remain an indispensable part of the tactical arsenal of the union and social movements. But there is also a critical need for an explicit confrontation with neoliberalism as it resides in the institutions of the integral state of Ontario. An alternate politics in this age of austerity will necessarily require a bold reimagining of democratic possibilities, anti-capitalist politics, and the remaking of regional spaces. Such a radical democratic movement is not just a project for Ontario, but a call for audacious initiatives across Canada and, indeed, North America.

NOTES

1. In the long-standing textbook on Ontario politics, Desmond Morton (1990, 7, 17) refers to the "durability of Ontario governments ... [as] Ontario has been easy to govern" and has "an earned reputation for political stability."
2. Mair (2013, 12) observes that the "new public management" associated with the administration of neoliberal economic policy deliberately eschews democratic channels for an emphasis on values of cost efficiency and others.
3. From a different vantage point, Ibbitson (1997, 93–5) notes how all parties had moved in the direction of austerity and neoliberalism.
4. As the Canadian Centre for Policy Alternatives (CCPA) (2004, 3–7) noted, the Liberals' response to the Harris cuts to public services was a fiscal plan that would push government spending to "historical lows."
5. The concerns with long-term economic growth and relative productivity performance remained, however, as the Harris neoliberal push did little to alter the trajectory, generating a huge number of studies (see Ontario Ministry of Finance 2005).
6. Universities were given a big boost in funding in McGuinty's initial terms as part of this focus. This did not, however, fully reverse the decline in per capita post-secondary education funding in Ontario since the Harris cuts, or Ontario's place in the bottom group among provinces, or the increased portion of funding coming from tuition.
7. One of the many post-crisis neoliberal measures to increase wage flexibility to aid employers and have workers pay for the crisis in Ontario (Fanelli and Thomas 2011).
8. In 2016, the Ontario Superior Court found the act unconstitutional under the Charter of Rights and Freedoms.
9. The report infamously overstated deficit projections through its forecasting assumptions. The return to economic growth would have addressed the deficit, even leaving to the side restoring tax capacity (Mackenzie 2014).

REFERENCES

Block, Sheila. 2016. *No Crisis on the Horizon: Ontario Debt, 1990–2015*. Ottawa: CCPA.

Block, Sheila, and Trish Hennessy. 2017. "Ontario Budget is Balanced, But Province Still in Fiscal Straightjacket." *Behind the Numbers*, CCPA-ON, 27 April.

Bradford, Neil. 1998. "Ontario's Experiments with Sectoral Initiatives." In *Forging Business-Labour Partnerships: The Emergence of Sectoral Councils in Canada*, edited by Morley Gunderson and Andrew Sharpe. Toronto: University of Toronto Press.

Brenner, Neil. 2004. *New State Spaces: Urban Governance and the Rescaling of Statehood*. Oxford: Oxford University Press.

Brownsey, Keith, and Michael Howlett. 1992. "Ontario: Class Structure and Political Alliances in Industrialized Society." In *The Provincial State: Canada's Provinces and Territories*, edited by Keith Brownsey and Michael Howlett. Mississauga: Copp Clark.

Caledon Institute. 2013. *Canada Social Report: Welfare in Canada 2012*. Ottawa: Caledon Institute.

Camfield, David. 2011. *Canadian Labour in Crisis: Reinventing the Workers' Movement*. Halifax: Fernwood.

Canadian Centre for Policy Alternatives. 2004. *The Ontario Alternative Budget*. Ottawa: CCPA.

Cerny, Philip. 1995. "Globalization and the Changing Logic of Collective Action." *International Organization* 49 (4).

Commission on the Reform of Ontario's Public Services. 2012. *Public Services for Ontarians: A Path to Sustainability and Excellence*. Toronto: Queen's Printer.

Courchene, Thomas. 1998. *From Heartland to North American Region State: The Social, Fiscal and Federal Evolution of Ontario*. Toronto: University of Toronto Press.

Drummond, Robert. 1983. "Ontario Revenue Budgets, 1960–1980." *Journal of Canadian Studies* 18 (1).

Ehring, George, and Wayne Roberts. 1993. *Giving Away a Miracle: Lost Dreams, Broken Promises and the Ontario NDP*. Oakville: Mosaic Press.

Evans, Bryan, and Charles Smith. 2015. "The Transformation of Ontario Politics: The Long Ascent of Neoliberalism." In *Transforming Provincial Politics: The Political Economy of Canada's Provinces and Territories in the Neoliberal Era*, edited by Bryan Evans and Charles Smith. Toronto: University of Toronto Press.

Fanelli, Carlo, and Mark Thomas. 2011. "Austerity, Competitiveness and Neoliberalism Redux: Ontario Responds to the Great Recession." *Socialist Studies* 7 (1/2): 141–70.

Fodor, Matt. 2018. "Ontario Election 2018: Right-Wing Populism Prevails Over Moderate Social Democracy." *The Bullet*, 9 July. www.socialistproject.ca.

Giovannetti, Justin. 2018. "Ontario Heading into Deficit in Pre-Election Budget." *Globe and Mail*, 8 March.
Government of Ontario. 2015. *Seizing Global Opportunities: Ontario's Innovation Agenda*. https://www.ontario.ca/page/seizing-global-opportunities-ontarios-innovation-agenda.
Gramsci, Antonio. 1971. *Selections from the Prison Notebooks*. New York: International Publishers.
Gray, Paul. 2015. "The Wynne-ter of Our Discontent." *Canadian Dimension* 49 (3): 15.
Harden, Joel. 2013. *Quiet No More: New Political Activism in Canada and around the Globe*. Toronto: Lorimer.
Heron, Craig. 2012. *The Canadian Labour Movement*. 3rd ed. Toronto: Lorimer.
Ibbitson, John. 1997. *Promised Land: Inside the Mike Harris Revolution*. Scarborough: Prentice-Hall.
Jessop, Bob. 2004. "Multi-Level Governance and Multi-Level Meta-Governance." In *Multi-Level Governance*, edited by I. Bache and M. Flinders. Oxford: Oxford University Press.
Karim, Alia, and Dave Bush. 2018. "The Road to Bill 148: The Fight for $15 and Fairness in Ontario." *Working Paper N. 3*. York University: Global Labour Research Centre.
Kellogg, Paul. 2011. "Workers Versus Austerity: The Origins of Ontario's 1995–1998 'Days of Action.'" *Socialist Studies* 7 (1/2): 116–40.
Lefebvre, Henri. 1991. *The Production of Space*. Cambridge: Blackwell.
Mackenzie, Hugh. 2014. "Tackling Ontario's Public Services Deficit." *Behind the Numbers*, CCPA-ON, February.
Mair, Peter. 2013. *Ruling the Void: The Hollowing of Western Democracy*. London: Verso.
Mandel, Ernest. 1975. *Late Capitalism*. London: Verso.
Morton, Desmond. 1990. "*Sic Permanet*: Ontario People and Their Politics." In *The Government and Politics of Ontario*, 4th ed., edited by Graham White. Toronto: Nelson.
Nugent, James. 2015. "Ontario's Infrastructure Boom: A Socioecological Fix for Air Pollution, Congestion, Jobs, and Profits." *Environment and Planning A* 47 (12): 2465–84.
Ontario Federation of Labour. 2015. *The Ontario We Want: 2015–2017 OFL Action Plan*. Toronto: OFL.
– 2017. *Power On: The Ontario We Want: 2018–2019 OFL Action Plan*. Toronto: OFL.
Ontario Ministry of Finance. (various years). *Ontario Budget*. Toronto: Queen's Printer.
– 1994. *Ontario Economic Outlook, 1994–1998*. Toronto: Queen's Printer.
– 2004. *Ontario Budget Speech: The Plan for Change*. Toronto: Queen's Printer.

– 2005. *Towards 2025: Assessing Ontario's Long-Term Outlook*. Toronto: Queen's Printer.
– 2014. *Ontario Economic Outlook and Fiscal Review. Economic Data Tables*. Toronto: Queen's Printer. http://www.fin.gov.on.ca/en/budget/fallstatement/2014/ecotables.html.
Ontario Ministry of Public Infrastructure Renewal. 2004. *Building a Better Tomorrow*. Toronto: Queen's Printer.
Ontario Office of the Premier. 2018. "Speech from the Throne: A Government for the People." 12 July. https://news.ontario.ca/opo/en/2018/07/a-government-for-the-people.html.
Ontario Progressive Conservatives. 2018. *For the People: A Plan for Ontario*. www.ontariopc.ca.
OPSEU. 2012. *The "Shock Doctrine" Comes to Ontario*. Toronto: OPSEU.
Premier's Advisory Council on Government Assets. 2014. *Initial Report*. www.ontario.ca.
Rea, K.J. 1985. *The Prosperous Years: The Economic History of Ontario, 1939–75*. Toronto: University of Toronto Press.
Richmond, D.R. 1974. *The Economic Transformation of Ontario, 1945–1973*. Toronto: Ontario Economic Council.
Rogers, Edward, and Donald Smith, eds. 1994. *Aboriginal Ontario: Historical Perspectives on the First Nations*. Toronto: Dundurn.
Savage, Larry. 2017. "The Politics of Labour and Labour Relations in Ontario." In *The Politics of Ontario*, edited by Cheryl Collier and Jonathan Malloy. Toronto: University of Toronto Press.
Scott, Allen, and Michael Storper. 1992. "Industrialization and Regional Development." In *Pathways to Industrialization and Regional Development*, edited by Allen Scott and Michael Storper. London: Routledge.
Soja, Edward. 1989. *Postmodern Geographies*. London: Verso.
Speirs, Rosemary. 1986. *Out of the Blue: The Fall of the Tory Dynasty of Ontario*. Toronto: Macmillan.
Swartz, Donald, and Rosemary Warskett. 2012. "Canadian Labour and the Crisis of Solidarity." In *Rethinking the Politics of Labour in Canada*, edited by Stephanie Ross and Larry Savage. Halifax: Fernwood.
Walkom, Tom. 1994. *Rae Days: The Rise and Follies of the NDP*. Toronto: Key Porter.
White, Randall. 1998. *Ontario Since 1985*. Toronto: Eastend Books.

PART ONE

The Political Economy of Neoliberalism in Ontario

| 2 |

The Ontario Growth Model: The "End of the Road" or a "New Economy"?

JOHN PETERS

In the 1960s and 1970s, Ontario was Canada's "manufacturing heartland." The province had large export-oriented auto, steel, and aerospace industries. It was also Canada's largest and most diversified provincial economy, home to Canada's major national banks, leading construction industries, and expanding service sectors. In addition, Ontario businesses were major exporters of ores, agricultural produce, and forest products. The majority of jobs in Ontario were full time, many of which were unionized in both the private and public sectors. Strikes were widespread across industries, and business and worker relations were often highly conflictual.

Nevertheless, governments often listened to organized labour, sought labour peace, and worked to put in place legislation that improved work conditions for unionized and non-unionized workers alike. The balance of power between firms and workers (uneven though it was) ensured that the productivity gains of companies were shared with the workforce through better collective agreements and wage increases that non-union employers had to pay to attract and retain workers. Better wages also that meant that more of the province's income was tied to the well-being of the province's workers, and that long-term growth depended on good jobs and labour relations that secured wage increases.

Much of this has changed. Over the past decade, Ontario has lost more than 300,000 manufacturing jobs, the vast majority in the unionized auto, steel, and forest industries. Global finance, information technology, and biotechnology industries have flourished, financed by new venture capital, pension funds, and booming stock markets. But this has brought only wealth and good jobs for a few. Far more notable has been the growth of low-wage and precarious employment found everywhere from construction and low-end manufacturing to hotels and the farms of Southern Ontario. Across the province, since the mid-1990s, full-time/full-year jobs have been replaced by the growth of temporary, part-time jobs and self-employment, which now make up 52 per cent of all available jobs (see figure 2.4). Unemployment has nearly doubled from 354,000 to 626,000. In 2010, 50 per cent of Ontarian workers annually earned less than $22,900, well below a low-wage cut-off of two-thirds of annual median income of a full-time, full-year worker.

What this has meant is a fundamental change in Ontario's growth model – in how its economy grows, who benefits, and in the kinds of jobs that people work. For rather than based on a more "intensive" manufacturing and resource model, with full-time jobs, strong unions, and improving employment standards, Ontario's economy today is based on an "extensive" open market strategy. In this model, public officials seek to further economic growth by increasing the quantity of foreign direct investment, expanding the number of takeovers, boosting new capital ventures, and increasing the profitability of American and Canadian businesses through lower taxes and expanded tax credits at the expense of labour income and better wages. On top of this, for Ontario's workers, these economic policies of "extensive" development have created a labour market that is increasingly "dualized" – a labour market that is split between rich and poor, and divided between "insiders" with "good" jobs and "outsiders" with "bad" jobs characterized by poor wages, little job security, and few prospects. Unfortunately, more often than not, it is women, immigrants, and young people who work in these low-wage and often precarious jobs, with little access to benefits and training. The result of these shifts is rising job insecurity and unemployment for more and more Ontario workers, while at the same time, the benefits of globalization – such as rising incomes, better jobs, or greater capital returns – go largely to the wealthiest and most powerful of top income earners.

This chapter is concerned with how these changes to Ontario's economy, labour markets, and jobs have come about. It focuses on the interrelationship between labour policy developments, politics, and economic globalization. It examines how federal and provincial governments have influenced the structure and operation of private and financial markets, and how government policy has grown more generous towards those at the top, while passing laws that disadvantage unions and low-wage workers. It assesses how those in positions of power – most notably American, global, and Canadian multinational firms as well as small and medium businesses – have had an enormous influence over the economy, the distribution of income, and the life chances of Ontario's workers and families. Finally, it looks at the waning power of organized labour to influence business or government policy.

THE COMPARATIVE POLITICAL ECONOMY OF ONTARIO

Many analyses of current economic trends claim that inequality is primarily the result of technological development, globalization, or vulnerable family arrangements (Esping-Anderson 1999; Crompton 2006; OECD 2008). But a good deal of recent literature emphasizes the role of *politics* and *policies* resulting in rising inequality (Glyn 2006; Emmenger et al. 2011a; Hacker and Pierson 2010). This work highlights how jobs and inequality have grown side by side as a result of politics – and particularly how the organizational landscape has shifted to advance the interests of business and employer interests at the expense of wider public concerns about jobs and equality. Throughout much of the postwar period, economic policy models typically revolved around a mixed economy based on markets regulated and supported by governments, and government provision of public goods coupled with a careful balancing of labour and business interests through a range of labour laws and employment regulations (Western 1997). But starting in the 1970s and continuing well into the 2000s, governments fundamentally recast policy priorities to emphasize the profitability of business – most typically at the expense of workers' bargaining power and political clout (Harvey 2006).

This transformation – typically characterized as "neoliberalism" or a "liberal" market model – did not happen by accident. Rather, as Crouch (2006, 2011, 2014) and Hacker and Pierson (2010, 2016) have shown, it was a product of policy reforms to the legal and institutional organization of markets – all pushed by powerful corporations and financial interests. The influence of organized business interests on the visible hand of government can be seen in policy reforms that promoted economic globalization and booming financial markets (Duménil and Lévy 2011; Panitch and Gindin 2013). But it can also be seen in how states around the world adopted new labour and employment policies – or failed to update or improve policies – while weakening union strength and fostering the growth of lower-paid flexible employment (Baccaro and Howell 2017; Luce 2014).

One area that recent research has explored is the role of business interests and employer associations in the policy and legislative processes aimed at fostering new market models and unleashing finance to spur economic growth (Durand 2017; Panitch and Gindin 2013). Piketty (2014) and Lapatavisas (2014) provide economic accounts of the rise of finance and its new economic importance, identifying financialization as a consequence of wealthy rentiers and investors turning to financial activities to improve the existing rate of wealth accumulation. These theories have stressed that because of falling profitability across industrial countries in the 1970s and 1980s, firms and finance pressed governments for reforms that would improve cost considerations and allow major economic sectors to find new profitable investment opportunities and new markets for consumption at home and abroad. Arguing in a similar vein, Panitch and Gindin (2013) have tracked how rapidly officials around the world under American auspices institutionalized financial reforms, removed capital controls, signed trade and investment treaties, and instituted independent central banks under US-led pressures, in order to boost global economic growth. These reforms, they demonstrate, were central in the growth of global multinationals and stock and financial markets, as well as in the rise of financial markets as key drivers of economic growth and profitability, all of which have ultimately redirected contemporary capitalism into new areas of technology and innovation.

It is these changes that help account for the "new economy" found in so many advanced capitalist countries – one dominated by finance, new information technologies, mortgage and housing markets, but also an economy that has undergone wrenching transformation, as older manufacturing and resource industries have been downsized, outsourced, and restructured across countries (Durand 2017; Lapavitsas 2014). New research has demonstrated how a series of regulatory changes freed up large pools of capital for investment in the stock market and the new knowledge economy, fuelling the rise of new financial intermediaries that became entwined with corporate ownership (Lapavitsas 2014; Reich 2015). This included pension legislation that allowed pension funds and insurance companies, for the first time, to hold shares of stock and high-risk bonds in their portfolios (Blackburn 2011; Davis 2016). Also critical to the new finance-led growth models were officials introducing a wave of banking and financial service reforms that opened the way for the massive growth of new financial products and the equally rapid growth of investment banks, institutional investors, and private equity firms with shorter time horizons and higher expectations of return (Batt and Appelbaum 2014). Finally, to foster economic demand, public officials deregulated financial markets and lowered interest rates in order that banks would provide more mortgage credit, and in turn provide a key boost to housing markets, giving individual homeowners the opportunity to purchase and speculate on homes (Crouch 2009). As the late Andrew Glyn (2006) emphasized, what is most notable about this range of economic policy reforms is how they systematically "unleashed" capitalism on a global scale. For with political and policy reforms at national and international levels, new structures were created that were especially favorable to global business, finance, and trade.

A second area of research has detailed how governments have reshaped the competitive contexts for business by revising and weakening regulations that protect workers; making it more difficult for workers to form unions and recruit union members; and by reducing welfare transfers to the poor and the vulnerable (Baccaro and Howell 2017; Brady 2009). Unlike the postwar period of growth, where governments – however reluctantly – introduced legislation to balance labour and capital interests and to ensure that wages increased to bolster growth, over the past twenty years under neoliberal policy models, governments made such changes to labour markets in order to lower labour costs and create more flexible labour markets in order to boost revenues for firms and create more competitive national economies. Consequently, where the postwar growth model was wage-led, this new emphasis on lower labour costs and labour market flexibility has shifted neoliberal growth models to emphasize firms, profits, and capital returns (Dumenil and Levy 2011; Lapavitsas 2014). Such reforms have included changing wage-setting institutions in the effort to restrict and segment wages. Other reforms have looked to reform employment security provisions in order to make it easier to hire and fire workers. Others still have restricted unemployment and other related benefit systems – along with their tax systems – in the attempt create more "active" workers willing to be employed at lower wages in poorer jobs.

The results, as much critical literature has demonstrated, have been rapidly increasing income inequality and the worsening of jobs and wages for the majority. Contrary to neoclassical models that assume that increasing levels of trade and foreign investment, new technology, and higher levels of education will always lead to economies and workers receiving the benefits of policy reforms that promote globalization, critical scholarship has demonstrated that largely the contrary has been true. Over the past twenty-five years, with the rise of the banking sector and new patterns of economic growth based on financial channels becoming commonplace, wealth and income have concentrated at the top (Lapavitsas 2014). Whether in the United States, France, the United Kingdom, or other advanced countries, the common distributional outcome of this financial expansion has not been an improvement to equality or wages, but rather the top 1 per cent receiving a surge of income from new financial investments, racing stock markets, and real estate bubbles (Flaherty 2015; Stiglitz 2010). At the same time, the more governments have adopted macroeconomic policies that internationalized their economies, the more public officials have typically weakened other domestic laws and labour market regulations in order to improve the business climate and entice foreign investors (Baccaro and Howell 2017; Reich 2015). Thus, a global economy driven by global finance and multinational corporations has not only meant labour laws and policies that emphasize flexibility and low costs for employers, but low-wage and non-standard jobs for more and more workers (Standing 2011).

Similar developments can be seen in Ontario over the past twenty-five years. Canadian and international firms operating in Ontario have been primarily interested in increasing profits through lowering taxation, reducing tariff and regulatory barriers, and minimizing social and employment protections for workers. Business has also sought supportive government intervention to facilitate new opportunities in finance and investment in a range of areas. Then, through a series of free trade agreements, tax reductions, pension reforms, and new financial policies, business interests successfully pushed policymakers to deregulate and implement a series of economic reforms designed to restructure Canada's economy through continental market integration. The results, as we shall see, were not only massive new inflows of foreign direct investment for corporate mergers and acquisitions, or new investments in finance and information technologies, but also increased competitive pressures that led major enterprises in auto, steel, forestry, and mining to restructure their operations on North American and global lines, and which led many firms to reduce labour costs through wage concessions, outsourcing, and permanent layoffs.

In terms of labour relation and employment policy, the Harris government also quickly deregulated labour protections across the board, and despite major protests by organized labour and communities across the province, it passed legislation allowing replacement workers during strikes; reduced wage protection for workers in bankrupt firms; eliminated union successor rights in privatized firms; and denied agricultural and domestic service workers the right to unionize (Klassen and Haddow 2006). The Liberal government of Dalton McGuinty elected in 2003 only differed slightly from this pro-economic policy agenda by promising to reinvest more in public services and taking a less confrontational approach to labour relations (Evans 2011). But the Liberal party remained firmly committed to lowering labour costs and creating a flexible labour force for Ontarian and international businesses, and the government made no significant alterations to industrial relations frameworks or employment standards. Rather, ongoing

Liberal policymaking efforts to enhance labour market flexibility and reform were directed at changing incentive structures: liberalizing employment protection legislation to remove obstacles for firms to hire low-wage workers, and enacting stricter conditions to receive social protection and income transfers to spur the job search efforts of the unemployed.

This recasting of economic policy and labour strategies has opened the door to a profound change in Ontario's economy and increasingly inequitable distributional outcomes. As detailed below, financial innovations have given the banking industry and new information technology industries enormous new opportunities to profit, but also provided firms with the opportunity to build global production networks across companies and countries. But building a "new economy" on such lines has also strongly contributed to corporate restructuring, deindustrialization, and the loss of thousands of good jobs. At the same time, the decline in union power has opened the way for Ontario's provincial governments to remove a number of institutional, legal, and legislative supports for unions, and created an economic, social, and political climate for unions that is much more opposed to basic labour law and employment standards. Taking advantage of this shift to a more "flexible" set of labour standards, firms have increasingly chosen to focus on the bottom line rather than social responsibility, and many now operate on the basis of low-wage workers in low-skilled jobs, and fixed-term contracts and bonus incentives for better-paid and higher-skilled employees. Consequently, while a very fortunate few have benefitted from high-paying jobs, the major labour market development in Ontario has been the downward spiral of wages and working conditions for many workers – a development that is often characterized as "dualization."

DEINDUSTRIALIZATION AND THE DECLINE OF UNIONIZED AND FULL-TIME EMPLOYMENT

Since the global recessions of the late 1970s and early 1990s, Canada and other affluent democracies witnessed the transformation of their economies. Across the core Western countries, with the rise of global production and finance, firms expanded their size through takeovers and mergers, and undertook wide-scale restructuring to reduce production and labour costs (Dicken 2015; Moody 2007). The results were deindustrialization and the decline of core manufacturing industries, with the subsequent loss of stable, well-paid full-time jobs and the rise of long-term unemployment (Emmenger et al. 2011a; Peters 2011; Western 1997). Global competition and rising world demand for resources led to the rapid mechanization of resource industries and the precipitous decline of employment with greater productivity gains realized through capital investment. In manufacturing, trade and foreign investment have globalized the production strategies of multinational firms and subsequently led to the displacement of workers and unionized manufacturing in affluent countries with the growth of manufacturing in developing countries (Brady and Denniston 2006; Kollmeyer 2009). Equally important, many global enterprises closed unionized workplaces and transferred their activities to nearby non-union subsidiaries. Other manufacturers in auto, auto parts, and consumer goods established production chains that contracted parts and component production to low-wage companies as well as to non-union contractors in nearby provinces within advanced countries or to neighbouring countries (Moody 2007; Milberg and Winkler 2013).

In Ontario, as figure 2.1 shows, similar trends can be observed over the past thirteen years. Total formal private sector employment grew by over 1,000,000 in the province. But manufacturing employment declined from its peak by more than 320,000 to 144,000, as firms outsourced, closed, laid off, and retired thousands of unionized workers. In Ontario's Big Three auto plants, the Canadian Auto Workers (CAW, now Unifor) experienced the loss of roughly 38 per cent of their members in the assembly and parts sectors over the past ten years (Holmes and Hracs 2010). In steelmaking, centred around Hamilton and Sault Ste Marie, and formerly home to over 60 per cent of Canada's steel manufacturing, job losses of 63,000 totalled more than 40 per cent of employment 1990–2006 (Livingstone, Smith, and Smith 2011). This included the shutdown of US Steel-Stelco facilities in Hamilton and Lake Erie, one of Canada's oldest manufacturing plants, which over the past thirty years has fallen from a peak of 26,000 workers to only 800 today. Northern Ontario's forestry, paper, and wood industries were similarly affected by corporate restructuring and shutdowns, with the loss of

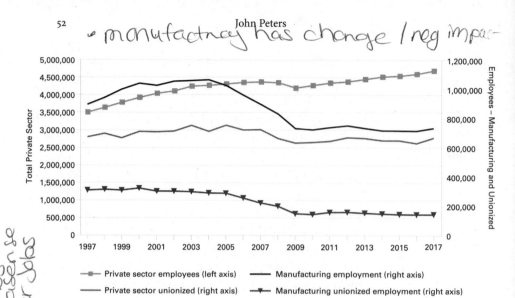

Figure 2.1 | The decline of Ontario private sector unionized manufacturing employment, 1997–2015 (*Source*: Statistics Canada, CANSIM 2820078)

thousands of jobs that accounted for the decline of more than 46 per cent of total employment in the industries.

Centre-right federal and provincial governments, in their attempts to improve business performance, did much to allow companies to restructure and gain greater profits, but did very little for workers or communities undergoing wrenching job loss. Federally, in the 1990s, the passage of the Canada-US Free Trade Agreement (1987) and NAFTA (1994) resulted in the production and marketing of automobiles becoming fully integrated between Canada, the United States and, more recently, Mexico (Stanford 2010). Because of the liberalization of specific sectors and the security that NAFTA provided for increasing cross-border investments, firms launched hundreds of mergers and acquisitions in everything from steel and mining to forestry and chemicals. Such liberalization and cross-border integration led to firms (predominantly but not exclusively American ones) increasing their productivity and lowering their costs by downsizing operations. But it also led to manufacturing operations hiring more part-time and temporary workers, and shifting work to their non-union subsidiaries and low-wage jurisdictions in the United States or Mexico (Murphy and McDonough 2012; Livingstone, Smith, and Smith 2011).

Provincially, corporate tax cuts and lucrative incentive packages for new investment did little to reverse these trends (Stanford 2011, 2012). For with the rise in the Canadian dollar, from $0.62 American in the early 1990s to over $1.03 in 2008, firms continued to restructure their operations throughout North America, seeking the lowest cost jurisdictions and shifting their production to the southern United States and Mexico, and in turn exporting more back into the Canadian market (Holmes 2010; Holmes and Hracs 2010; Peters 2013). Consequently, in a number of industries highly exposed to international trade (including textile mills, machinery, computer and electronics, plastics and rubber, furniture, paper, printing, and transportation equipment), despite tax cuts and investment incentives by the provincial government that were meant to meet the low tax of neighbouring US jurisdictions, the rise of Canada's "petro-dollar" led to widespread shutdowns and layoffs (Beine, Bos, and Coulombe 2009; Stanford 2012).

The financial crisis and the recession that followed (2008–11) has had equally serious consequences for businesses and many high quality jobs (Albo, Gindin, and Panitch 2010). With the collapse of financial markets in North America and Western Europe, there was a significant decline in American demand for Canadian exports. Across Canada, from late 2008 to November 2009 firms laid off more than 450,000 full-time workers, the majority in manufacturing and natural resources, as the number of unemployed workers (seasonally adjusted) jumped to over 1.5 million (Canadian Labour Congress 2009). Highly sensitive to product-market competition, adverse demand or supply shocks, and downturns in financial markets, North American firms reacted quickly to changing economic conditions. Notably, firms began making "quantity" adjustments in the size of their workforces, as well as in work schedules and part-time temporary hiring.

In Ontario's forest and paper industries, the collapse of US housing starts and the drying up demand for paper used in advertising led to the rapid decline of lumber, newsprint, and wood product exports (PWC 2010). In the 1990s and early 2000s, the wood and forest industries had stabilized employment, as Canadian and American multinationals integrated operations across North America, and exported Canadian wood and paper products into the booming American housing and newsprint markets (PWC 2005). But in sharp contrast to the automotive industry, in the wake of the financial crisis, the American firms in Ontario's forestry sector received little financial assistance from the federal and provincial governments to facilitate restructuring and respond to the crisis. Across Northern Ontario, firms closed to focus on core operations in other countries (many in Latin America and China), and workers were forced to leave in search of new employment.

In auto, car sales plummeted in 2008–09 to their lowest level in decades, and the Big Three auto makers responded by shutting down four plants. Auto parts manufacturers folded many more plants, and with the bankruptcy of General Motors and Chrysler in 2009, over 30,000 auto jobs were lost in the assembly and auto parts industry during 2008–10 (Holmes and Hracs 2010). In mining, global giants Vale and Xstrata laid off hundreds of workers as the downturn worsened. Vale then fought a twelve-month strike with the United Steelworkers Local 6500 that resulted in major wage concessions by the local, the retirement of another 10 per cent of their unionized labour force, and the continuing widespread use of part-time contractors (Peters 2010).

Organized labour in Ontario was unable to influence these trends of aggressive corporate restructuring and declining unionized jobs, declining full-time jobs, and declining good jobs with benefits. In auto, the CAW did respond to some bankruptcies and closures with a number of dramatic actions – including plant occupations – to fight for severance benefits for the affected workers (Murnighan and Stanford 2013). But because they were losing members, the far more typical response of unions in the auto, steel, and forestry industries was to focus on improving the competitive position of the company in return for job commitments to ever fewer members. Typically, this involved unions accepting wage and job concessions while accepting speed-up, job-loading, and longer hours in return for the protection of a dwindling core number of jobs. Concessions became central to union plans for labour-management cooperation, and workers were often forced to go along because of threats of plant closures, downsizing, or the failure of the company to secure new products.

The consequences of these setbacks for organized labour in the labour market have been damaging to long-term job prospects (Rubin 2017). In 1999, there were eleven major auto assembly plants in Canada; in 2017, only five remain. Since 2010, with government support, the major auto companies have undertaken major "rationalization" initiatives that have led to layoffs and retirements, and, in the parts industries, concessions that match those of non-unionized workers in the southern US. As notable is the decline of union representation of workers in the auto sector. In the early 1990s, the industry was highly unionized, with over 90 per cent of hourly production workers in assembly, parts, and accessories protected by collective agreements. As of 2014 only 28 per cent of Canada's auto industry was unionized (Rutherford and Holmes 2014).

In other manufacturing and primary industries, the employment future for many workers is just as poor. In Hamilton, US Steel declared bankruptcy and then locked out its workers. Even though it is now legally obligated to pay the federal government more than $40 million in fines, the vast majority of the few hundred workers at its facilities in Hamilton are still unemployed. Across Northern Ontario, the loss of wood and paper jobs has led to a similar exodus of families, with the subsequent bankruptcy of thousands of small businesses; many communities are facing dramatic shortfalls in tax revenues and services.

The auto, steel, and forest industries generated a large number of spin-off jobs and were the biggest consumers of engineered goods, steel, rubber, and processed aluminum, as well as other commodities. Ontario was also the largest automotive producer in North America, home to major vehicle assemblers and the majority of the country's parts producers. But since the financial crisis and the subsequent recession, exports and business spending have declined by record amounts (Rubin 2017). The "Detroit Three" automakers have lost market share and been forced to close many of their manufacturing facilities in Ontario and around the lower Great Lakes (Industry Canada 2012). The 2011 nuclear disaster in Japan and floods in Thailand also affected Japanese manufacturer supply chains, and led Ontario-based operations to lay off workers. Over the period 2012–16, auto sales and profitability improved, due to business fleet and household demand, and firms made plans for new investment and hiring (Sweeney 2017). But with the ongoing difficulties in many parts of the American economy (outside of finance and the global information technology industry), and declines in business investment in manufacturing and forestry, many of Ontario's traditional export industries appear to face further declines and restructuring in the near future. And even in the now-profitable auto assembly sector, new production is based on reduced workforces, typically working at lower wages and benefits.

ONTARIO'S "NEW" ECONOMY

In contrast to the decline of manufacturing and forestry and the waning of exports, Ontario's financial industries and information and communication technologies (ICT), biotechnology, and pharmaceutical industries took on an entirely new level of economic importance, both provincially and in the overall Canadian economy. Following trends like those in the United States and the United Kingdom, one of the key reasons why finance and ICT so rapidly emerged was because of how government constraints were removed from financial markets and those with economic clout. In countries like Canada and the United States, firms rely on high levels of external capital, there are large and active stock markets, and the financial assets of institutional investors play critical roles in financial and stock markets (Amable 2003). But over the past twenty years, finance has taken on an entirely new role – as much in Ontario, Canada, and the United States as around the world (Baker 2009; Stiglitz 2010; Duménil and Lévy 2011).

The deregulation of finance, and the unregulated development of complex new financial products, provides part of the answer for this explosion in finance. As in other advanced industrial countries in the late 1990s, Canadian governments sought to deal with declining profitability in manufacturing and primary industries by demand stimulus through financial deregulation, low interest rates, and support for housing markets (Brenner 2002; Duménil and Lévy 2011). Despite efforts to reduce wages and lower labour and social costs in the 1980s and 1990s, the Chrétien and Harris governments realized further efforts were required to boost corporate growth and spur demand (Stanford 1997). Deregulation and low interest rates increased private debt for businesses and consumers alike, and led to increasing flows of money directed toward stock and housing markets. Government and business expectations were that rising equity prices would provide the means for companies to leverage higher amounts of borrowing, corporate acquisitions, and restructuring. At the same time, rising house prices and the sale of new mortgage-backed securities were to allow individuals to increase equity purchases and housing construction. Together, public officials believed that this would incite ever-higher levels of consumption and investment growth.

To move this "new economy" model forward, the federal and provincial governments enacted financial liberalization and loosened restrictions on the international buying and selling of domestic equity, with the hope that these reforms would boost foreign investment and spur domestic enterprises to restructure and expand, thereby increasing profits and employment growth. The federal government also eased restrictions on the types of assets and equities in which public and private pension fund managers could invest, so as to stimulate changes in corporate finance and corporate operation (CPP Investment Board 2005). The Ontario Securities Commission, following federal approval, passed new laws allowing the "securitization" of loans – that is, giving businesses the opportunity to package loans into bonds that were sold on capital markets to pension and mutual funds, thus turning debts into assets (Bank of Canada 2009b, 2004). Other reforms that induced financial and corporate change included the lowering of bank liquidity ratios, the merger of commercial and investment banking, the repeal of legislation on share buybacks, lower taxation on capital gains from equity sales, and the formal approval of hedge funds.

With these legislative measures in place and the expanding freedom to use them, financial enterprises and non-financial firms rapidly developed new financial instruments and created just as astonishing opportunities to profit. Securitization – the buying and selling of corporate and mortgage market debt – was rapidly developed. Beginning in the late 1990s, companies both large and small also issued thousands of new initial public share offerings (IPOs) on the Toronto Stock Exchange (TSX) to raise capital, fend off takeovers, and allow executives to "cash in their chips" with compensation totalling hundreds of millions of dollars. The expansion of foreign MNCs – as in Ontario and Canada – also led to massive inflows of investment into domestic stock markets, especially into the largest 100 companies on the TSX that account for more than 80 per cent of total market capitalization on the exchange (Peters 2011; Nicholls 2006).

Adding to this financial transformation were companies using collateralized debt obligations and derivatives to drive up their leverage and profits. Canada's burgeoning investment banks, such as CIBC World Markets and RBC Capital Markets, allowed financial and manufacturing firms to increase their debt-to-equity leverage ratios to record levels (Milway et al. 2007). Institutional investors, such as the public sector pension funds of Ontario Teachers and Ontario's municipal employees, along with insurance companies, became major players on Canada's stock and financial markets and contributed to their growth (Archer 2011). Over the period 1990–2000, pension funds across Canada exploded, increasing in size from approximately 5 per cent of Canadian GDP to over 80 per cent between 1990 and 2007. Private equity and venture capital groups invested more than $2 billion in computer, software, and biotechnology industries – the vast majority in Canada's research "triangle" of Kitchener-Waterloo, Toronto, and Ottawa (Durufle 2009). By 2009, Toronto was North America's third largest financial services centre (after New York City and Chicago), with all of Canada's national banks, fifty foreign banks subsidiaries and branches, over 150 credit unions, and 115 securities firms (Milway et al. 2007).

The result of these changes was the explosion of financial and insurance wealth. As figure 2.2 shows, stock trading in Toronto rose to over a trillion dollars annually, exceeding the entire value of the Canadian economy by 20 per cent in 2008, before levelling off in the wake of the crisis to 75 per cent of GDP by 2015. Foreign direct investment in oil and natural resources climbed in Toronto and the other "junior" stock exchanges to record levels, making the Toronto stock and venture exchanges among the most natural resource heavy in the world (Cross 2008; Nicholls 2006). With rising stock trading and equity prices, wages and fees in the banking and brokerage industry took off in the late 1990s, skyrocketing throughout the last decade. The size of Canadian listed companies grew by more than $2 trillion dollars, and chief executive officers paid in salary, bonuses, and stock options regularly made more than $5 million in direct compensation. In 2011, only two years after the financial collapse, top bank executives were again earning more than $10 million in compensation with the return of rising stock and equity prices (Robertson 2011a, 2011b).

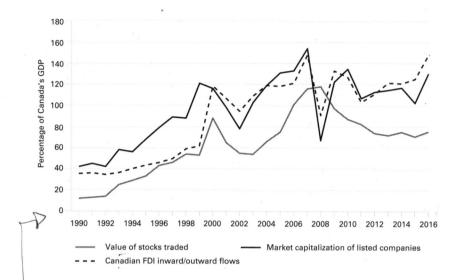

Figure 2.2 | Canada's new "financial" economy (*Sources*: World Bank Development Indicators; UNCTADstat)

New financial investment was also poured into ICT, life sciences, engineering, and biotechology (Industry Canada 2009, 2010). With its open financial markets and firms run by CEOs on the basis of incentive compensation and stock options, international and domestic businesses quickly shifted to new areas of high profitability. In less than fifteen years, more than 16,000 ICT firms were established in Ontario, representing more than 50 per cent of Canada's total ICT industry. Ontario's life sciences industry also grew rapidly in the 1990s, and by the mid-2000s was the ninth largest pharmaceutical industry in the world (Industry Canada 2009).

As figure 2.3 demonstrates, one of the results of this rise in finance, insurance, and "new" economy industries was the steady rise in employment. After declining in the wake of the early 1990s recession, finance, insurance, and real estate (FIRE) saw employment in their sectors rapidly increase, climbing by more than 150,000 from 1995–2015. The business, law, and scientific industries also rose rapidly, doubling in employment size from 1990–2015 to more than 544,000. Together, these two broad sectors accounted for 34 per cent of all new employment growth in Ontario from 1990 to 2015. Officially, median wages in

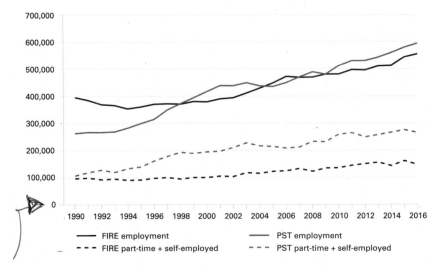

Figure 2.3 | Ontario's new economy and employment, 1990–2010 (*Sources*: Statistics Canada CANSIM tables 2820022, 2820007)

both of these sectors are better than average. But the reality of jobs and employment is highly segmented between a small number of "good" jobs with high income, employment, and benefits, and a vast majority of "bad" jobs with low income, little security, and few or no benefits.

At the top, executives across all the financial and new ICT industries pocketed cash from stock options. Brokerage houses made millions from commissions; investment banks profited from loans and rising stock prices. Eric Sprott, for example, the chair and CEO of the mutual and hedge fund company Sprott Asset Management, earned $27 million in 2010, roughly 11 per cent of the $200 million that the firm earned in performance fees alone (Toronto Life 2011). Lawyers and accounting firms also benefitted, with huge fees for managing money and taxes. The growth of finance and stock market trading favoured the very wealthy, as the top 10 per cent of income earners were estimated to claim 85 per cent of all capital gains from the TSX (which traded over a trillion dollars annually), the 3 trillion dollar pension industry, and the trillion dollar bond and money markets (Stanford 1997).

Yet for the vast majority of administrative assistants, clerks, data entry workers, researchers, paralegals, and other "service" providers, the reality was quite different. With the exponential growth of temporary staffing and employment agencies in Toronto and Ontario to more than 2,500, and with a strong employer preference for part-time and temporary workers (Workers' Action Centre 2007), part-time, temporary, and self-employment more than doubled in the business, professional, and scientific industries (figure 2.3). The rise of precarious employment was as noticeable in finance and insurance, as over 600,000 of the 1 million jobs in finance, insurance, business, and the new economy industries are clerical (Statistics Canada 2011a); the average annual salary among the hundreds of thousands of non-standard employees was less than $23,000 in 2011.

The economic volatility of finance and the new industries has been equally problematic, with even wider consequences for jobs and communities. In telecommunications, as of 2000 Nortel Networks was one of the world's largest suppliers of telecom equipment, with a market capitalization of over $389 billion, and more than 94,500 people employed worldwide – 25,900 of them in Canada (Wahl 2009). By 2009, it was bankrupt, and many of its employees had not only lost their jobs, but their workplace pensions as well. Research in Motion, once seen as Canada's leading tech giant, witnessed the loss of 83 per cent of its value – more than $64 billion in value – and laid off thousands (Olive 2011).

The development of finance also carried other costs for the health of the economy. The collapse of global credit markets in the summer of 2008 caused major losses in mortgage and money markets, as well as layoffs and unemployment for hundreds of thousands of workers in Ontario as across Canada. With declines in real GDP of 3.6 per cent and 2.9 per cent in 2008 and 2009 respectively, the loss of economic growth and employment was the second largest since the Great Depression (Cross 2010). Canada and Ontario did not suffer as severely from the financial crisis as other countries, with the Bank of Canada having to buy up only $110 billion in mortgages, mortgage securities, corporate debt, and commercial paper (Bank of Canada 2009a; CMHC 2009). But from late 2008 to November 2009, more than 220,000 jobs were lost in Ontario, government debt rose rapidly, and more people fell into poverty (Canadian Labour Congress 2009, 2011). Such failings put in question the long-term trajectory of Canada and Ontario's "new" economy.

LOW-WAGE WORK IN ONTARIO

Over the past two decades, inequality and low-wage work in Ontario, in Canada, and in other affluent democracies have increased significantly (Gautie and Schmitt 2010; OECD 2015). Across North America and Western Europe, over 40 per cent of workers are employed in occupations that are strongly affected by unemployment and/or atypical employment (Emmenger et al. 2011b). Workers in atypical employment (those in temporary, part-time, and low-wage self-employment) now annually earn less than half of what workers with high skills and full-time employment do. Workers with discontinuous employment records – including most women and immigrants – have pension incomes that are only half that of workers with full-time unionized careers (Baldwin 2009; LaRochelle-Côté, Myles, and Picot 2009).

"Polarization" and "dualization" are generally used to describe patterns of employment growth that are characterized by the simultaneous creation of high-paid professional and managerial jobs at the top end of the labour market and low-paid personal service jobs at the bottom end, with little or no creation of mid-skilled manual and clerical jobs (Emmenger et al. 2011a). The primary labour market is characterized by good working conditions, high wages, secure jobs, and promotion prospects, while jobs in the secondary labour market are poorly paid and unstable. "Insiders" typically benefit from unionization and standard employment relations; "outsiders" (many of whom are immigrants or visible minorities) are often either unemployed or in employment relationships characterized by low levels of pay and social benefits, and lacking employment or collective bargaining protection.

Canada currently ranks along with the United States as the affluent countries with the *most* "dualized" and segmented labour markets (LaRochelle-Côté and Dionne 2009). Both countries have the highest proportions of workers in low-paid employment (more than 21 per cent of full-time workers), and both have labour markets that are characterized by high levels of atypical employment (more than 31 per cent of total employment) and by limited employment and social protection (King and Rueda 2008). In Ontario as across Canada, provinces have lowered employment standards to allow greater employer flexibility in hiring and firing, and to allow employers to use part-time, contract, and self-employed workers as needed. Provincial governments have also let the minimum wage languish far below the basic median wage, freezing minimum wages and letting them sink with inflation (Murray and Mackenzie 2007). In 2011, the minimum wage ranged from a high of 50 per cent of the median wage in Quebec to a low of 40 per cent in Ontario and British Columbia – figures even lower than those in the United States, the country most commonly believed to have the lowest minimum wage in North America and Western Europe (Lucifora and Salverda 2009; Minimum Wage Advisory Panel 2014).

The Ontario and Canadian governments – like other governments in rich world democracies – have also sought to reduce unemployment by focusing on the control of labour costs and minimizing the state in order to achieve economic competitiveness (McBride 2005; OECD 2006). In the 1980s and 1990s, there was a dramatic increase in labour market exclusion, with unemployment peaking above 12 per cent in 1983, and remaining in double digits for over fifteen years. In response, Conservative and Liberal federal parties, and then provincial governments like that of the Harris Conservatives in Ontario, placed emphasis on reducing income security, shoring up competitiveness, and minimizing employer contributions to social security (Klassen and Haddow 2006). Keys to reform efforts included cost control, expenditure restraint, and the end of passive income security, all measures that were theorized to reduce individual "incentives" to work.

The supply of public goods like social assistance and unemployment insurance were restricted through the tightening of means and jobs tests, the reduction of benefit levels, and cuts to the duration of benefits (Battle, Torjman, and Mendelson 2006). In the early 1990s, Canada's unemployment insurance system provided income benefits for roughly 80 per cent of the unemployed (Mendelson, Battle, and Torjman 2009). By 2005, after a series of "flexibility" improvements, tightening of qualifying conditions, and decentralizing of economic "regions," the Employment Insurance (EI) program was only accessible to 40 per cent of the unemployed. In 2009, following the financial crisis and Conservative reforms to improve EI benefits, in cities like Toronto, with its high immigrant workforce and extensive non-standard employment, only 20 per cent of the unemployed qualified for benefits (Canadian Labour Congress 2011; Mendelson, Battle, Torjman 2009).

The ongoing promotion of immigration likewise contributed to a larger pool of low-wage workers. As in the United States, in Canada the growing numbers of both skilled and less-skilled immigrants (as well as temporary migrant workers) put downward pressure on wages. Prompted by the introduction of new programs such as the Provincial Nominee Programs (PNP) and the Canadian Experience Class (CEC) programs, as well as the Temporary Foreign Worker (TFW) and Seasonal Agricultural Worker programs, employers have picked up ever-larger amounts of labour at below cost. Over the past decade, the total number of TFWs annually working in Canada increased from 150,000 in 1994 to more than 500,000 by 2012 (Citizenship and Immigration Canada 2012), and they typically outnumber newly entering "economic" immigrants by 33 per cent (Gates-Gasse 2010). In Ontario, the vast majority of temporary foreign workers are employed in agriculture and domestic work.

Driving the rise of poor jobs forward were employers – large and small – seeking to compete on the basis of low labour costs. As figure 2.4 illustrates, Ontario businesses, across all sectors, but especially in hotels, restaurants, food, agriculture, janitorial, and warehousing and trucking, use low-wage workers and non-standard employees as part of their competitive strategies. Firms have also been expanding their hiring of workers on a temporary basis, either through temporary agencies and subcontractors, or as individual contractors or "franchisees" (Workers' Action Centre 2007). The lack of adequate staff to enforce employment standards regulations, and the onus on workers to report violations, has left the door open for many employers to take advantage of the system and refuse to pay overtime, cover sick days, or ensure basic health and safety standards.

Taking into account part-time, own-account self-employed, unemployed, and temporary workers on an annual basis, the number of Ontario workers in precarious employment is now 50 per cent. Figure 2.4, while lacking complete data for temporary workers, clearly shows the changing nature of the labour market in Ontario. Over the course of

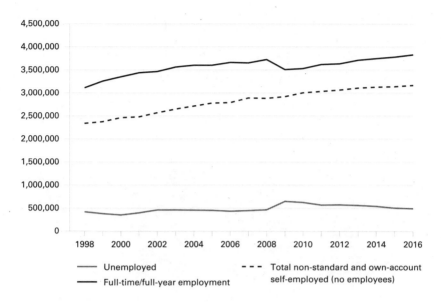

Figure 2.4 | Precarious and atypical employment in Ontario, 1995–2015 (*Sources*: Statistics Canada, CANSIM table 2820020)

1990–2015, full-time/full-year jobs grew very little by only 100,000 to approximately 3.7 million by 2015. This was despite the addition of over 1.4 million workers into Ontario's labour force. By contrast, even though part-time employment grew slowly, temporary and self-employment grew by more than thirty per cent from 1998 on (the period for which we have complete data). In the course of fourteen years, atypical employment rose from 2.3 million in 1998 to more than 3 million in 2015.

The problems with this kind of "flexible" job market are numerous. The vast majority of part-time and temporary workers are regularly paid wages below those with full-time/permanent employment. Few have benefits. Many are forced to work multiple jobs with no job security (Law Commission of Ontario 2012). Those in precarious employment are also more likely to work in unsafe and highly stressful jobs, hurting their health (Lewchuk, Clarke, and de Wolff 2011). Even more notable is that in Ontario, one out of four workers earns less than $10 an hour, effectively making them "working poor" (Murray and Mackenzie 2007).

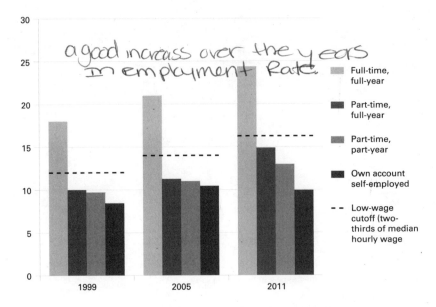

Figure 2.5 | Ontario non-standard employment and wage penalties, 1999–2011 (median hourly wages) (*Source*: Author's figures from custom request, Statistics Canada, Survey of Labour and Income Dynamics [SLID]; and Survey of Consumer Finances [SCF], "Percentage of workers with low-annual earnings and low-hourly wages, Canada and provinces," table C685593)

Overall, as figure 2.5 demonstrates, the results across the 2000s were employers routinely paying part-time and temporary employees, as well as hiring own-account self-employed workers, at little more than half the rate of a full-time, full-year worker. Those working in own-account self-employed jobs fared the worst, with hourly median wages falling to only 40 percent of those in full-time, full-year employment by 2011, approximately 25 cents less than the official minimum of the time. Even those workers in part-time and part-year jobs – which are more typically covered by minimum wage legislation – were paid far less by employers, generally only receiving hourly wages that were 52–55 percent of what a full-time, full-year worker was paid.

Unions and stronger industrial relations frameworks used to put restraints on employers' ability to resort to low-wage and atypical employment. In the postwar period, unions fought to standardize hours and jobs, and influenced working conditions and severance rules across plants and industries (Boeri, Brugiavini, and Calmfors 2001). With greater numbers of full-time unionized jobs, non-union employers often found it necessary to match wages and working conditions in order to draw employees and avoid union organizing drives. Unions could exert influence on employers and wage and income inequality by using strikes. Unions also shaped work and income by pushing for fairer industrial relations law and better employment standards, as well as by influencing policies and partisan politics.

The opposite is now occurring: with the decline of union density and the shift in government policies, unions have much less impact on jobs and wages in the private sector. Consequently, non-union employers are competing more and more on the basis of low labour costs, hiring more temporary, part-time, and contract workers, with little fear of new union organizing. Over the past two decades, unions have engaged in far fewer strikes and those they have taken have been much less effective (Briskin 2007; Peters 2010). Unions have been forced to take wage concessions, with many collective agreements becoming "two-tiered," creating a division between older members and new hires who receive poorer wages, benefits, and protections. Consequently, the appeal and legitimacy of unions among non-unionized workers is in decline.

With Ontario's current economic model being led by finance, ICT, and low-wage service work, the shortcomings in union power and political leverage make it far more likely that government will do substantially less than it did a generation ago to reduce inequality and poverty. The declining influence of organized labour on governments and employers also means that government labour market policies and provincial labour markets will be significantly less egalitarian for the vast majority of Ontarians.

ECONOMIC CRISIS AND SHARPENING SOCIAL DIVISION

Ontario's economic "model" has been transformed over the last two decades. This transformation has fundamentally changed what government does, what its leading economic sectors are, and who benefits. Over the last twenty-five years, government policy has grown more generous towards the wealthy and affluent at the top of corporate operations, especially to those working in the finance, banking, insurance, ICT, and biotechnology sectors. At the same time, government policy on jobs, job quality, and income equality has been remade to emphasize employment growth and "flexible" employment regardless of its consequences for secure jobs and equality. American, international, and domestic firms regularly compete on the basis of lower labour costs and by forcing through layoffs and retirements. And just as frequently, businesses seek to lower costs by pushing for wage concessions, outsourcing, and increasing temporary and self-employment.

For a minority of Ontarians, this new economy is proving very rewarding. But for a growing majority, the risks of finance and the new economy have only been pushed downward, saddling Canadians with greater debt, new holes in the safety net, and broader financial risks as workers, investors, and citizens. Most of the gains of economic growth have gone to the top 10 per cent, and especially to the top 1 per cent. And the shift of income towards the top has been sustained, increasing steadily since 1990. Across Canada, and especially in Ontario, where the majority of high income earners work, the wealthiest 10 per cent of Canadian income earners took more than two-thirds of all income gains from 1992 through to the mid-2000s (Mackenzie 2008; Yalnizyan 2010). By contrast, most Canadians and Ontarians experienced the exact opposite: a decline in income and economic security. For the bottom 20 per cent of full-time income earners, earnings actually fell by 20 per cent between 1980 and 2005 (Conference Board of Canada 2009).

In the wake of the financial crisis, Ontario and Canada experienced the worst economic downturn in more than seventy years, with record numbers of layoffs and job losses, a provincial unemployment rate around 9 per cent, and the share of Ontarians unemployed for more than six months at a near all-time high. In the wake of the crisis, political discussions often centred on the need for better forms of financial regulation and long-term policy planning. Like governments across the world, the Canadian federal and provincial governments reacted to the economic problems with a range of new fiscal policies intended to support the financial sector while stabilizing the economy for business and underpinning income for workers.

Now, only a few years later, the reform window appears closed – with only one significant exception. In the provincial elections of 2011 and 2014, politicians were little interested in the shattering events of 2007 and 2008, or the economic devastation that lingered in the auto and forestry communities throughout Ontario. Instead, attention was focused on when to implement more cuts in domestic spending, the preservation of high-end and corporate tax cuts, and energetic efforts to consider how to restructure Ontario's public services – policies that reflect the organizational and structural transformation of Ontario's political economy.

Before the crisis, the financial, insurance, and ICT sectors were the most powerful economic, political, and social forces in Ontario. After the crisis, the financial, insurance, and ICT sectors are still the most powerful (with the exception of the now much reduced Research in Motion). Before the crisis, the manufacturing sector was in relative decline; there was a growing polarization between rich and poor that left the middle ranks dependent on debt to sustain living standards; public spending on physical infrastructure, education, and social well-being was being slowly constricted; and a growing number of "fees" such as tuition were being raised or newly levied on citizens. Since the crisis, all these same trends continue.

The sole exception recently has been in the introduction of Bill 148, the Fair Workplaces, Better Jobs Act (2017), one of the final and perhaps most significant measures of the Wynne government. Introduced in late 2017, the bill increased the minimum wage to $15 dollars an hour, while also introducing emergency sick days for all workers, boosting protections for workers tied to temporary employment agencies, and improving notice of scheduling changes to workers. The Ontario Ministry of Labour also promised to improve enforcement of employment standards. The legislation marked a major reversal from governments creating few improvements to basic labour standards and regulations, if not actively impeding them.

However, if these reforms are to have meaningful impact, they will have to be followed by further updates to the minimum wage as well as greater efforts to improve the enforcement of employment regulations that have long been left to languish. For even with improvements in

2018, many workers will remain in low-wage work, and many others will likely continue to face aggressive employers given the lack of resources devoted to enforcement and the continuation of an employee-initiated employment standards complaint system that poses real disadvantages for workers in insecure employment. But with the recent election of the Progressive Conservatives under the leadership of Doug Ford, there is little cause for optimism. Alongside the major campaign promises of tax cuts, major reductions in public expenditures, and an end to environmental initiatives to reduce carbon in the economy, there was also a commitment to freeze the minimum wage and other labour market reforms that will only serve to enhance Ontario's low-wage economic model.

Certainly the business community has strongly supported all of these measures, and others that will continue to shape economic outcomes in the favour of a wealthy few. But if Ontarians are to achieve more progressive alternatives and a more egalitarian distribution of incomes and opportunities, then citizens will have to carefully assess the costs of such policies. Equally essential will be citizens rebuilding participatory democracy in the province. For if the new economic model is to be challenged – and its many problems tackled – then new electoral and popular demands are required to counterbalance the operation of ever-more powerful markets and firms.

REFERENCES

Albo, Greg, Sam Gindin, and Leo Panitch. 2010. *In and Out of Crisis: The Global Financial Meltdown and Left Alternatives*. Oakland: PM Press.

Amable, Bruno. 2003. *The Diversity of Modern Capitalism*. New York: Oxford University Press.

Anderson, Christopher J., and Pablo Beramendi. 2008. "Income, Inequality, and Electoral Participation." In *Democracy, Inequality, and Participation: A Comparative Perspective*, edited by P. Beramendi and C.J. Anderson. New York: Russell Sage Foundation.

Archer, Simon. 2011. "Pension Funds as Owners and as Financial Intermediaries: A Review of Recent Canadian Experience." In *The Embedded Firm: Corporate Governance, Labor, and Finance Capitalism*, edited by C. Williams and P. Zumbansen. New York: Cambridge University Press.

Baccaro, Lucio, and Chris Howell. 2017. *European Industrial Relations: Trajectories of Neoliberal Transformation*. New York: Cambridge University Press.

Baker, Dean. 2009. *Plunder and Blunder: The Rise and Fall of the Bubble Economy*. Sausilito: PoliPointPress.

Baldwin, Bob. 2009. *Research Study on the Canadian Retirement Income System*. Toronto: Ministry of Finance, Government of Ontario.

Bank of Canada. 2004. *Financial System Review June 2004*. Ottawa: Bank of Canada.

– 2009a. *Annual Report 2009*. Ottawa: Bank of Canada.

– 2009b. *Financial System Review December 2009*. Ottawa: Bank of Canada.

Batt, Rosemary, and Eileen Appelbaum. 2014. *Private Equity at Work: When Wall Street Manages Main Street*. New York: Russell Sage Publications.

Battle, Ken, Sherry Torjman, and Micheal Mendelson. 2006. *Towards a New Architecture for Canada's Adult Benefits*. Ottawa: Caledon Institute for Social Policy.

Beine, Michel A.R., Charles S. Bos, and Serge Coulombe. 2009. "Does the Canadian Economy Suffer from Dutch Disease?" *Tinbergen Institute Discussion Paper*, N. 09-096/4:36.

Blackburn, Robin. 2011. *Age Shock: How Finance Is Failing Us*. New York: Verso.

Boeri, Tito, Agar Brugiavini, and Lars Calmfors. 2001. *The Role of Unions in the Twenty-First Century*. New York: Oxford University Press.

Bonoli, Giuliano, and David Natali. 2011. *The Politics of the New Welfare State*. New York: Oxford University Press.

Brady, David. 2009. *Rich Democracies, Poor People: How Politics Explain Poverty*. New York: Oxford University Press.

Brady, David, and Ryan Denniston. 2006. "Economic Globalization, Industrialization, and Deindustrialization in Affluent Democracies." *Social Forces* 85 (1).

Brenner, Robert. 2002. *The Boom and the Bubble: The US in the World Economy*. New York: Verso.

Briskin, Linda. 2007. "From Person-Days Lost to Labour Militancy: A New Look at the Canadian Work Stoppage Data." *Relations Industrielles/Industrial Relations* 62 (1).

Canadian Labour Congress. 2009. *Recession Watch Issue 3*. Ottawa: Social and Economic Policy Department.

– 2011. *Recession Watch Issue 5*. Ottawa: Social and Economic Policy Department.

Citizenship and Immigration Canada. 2012. *Facts and Figures: Immigration Overview*. Ottawa: Citizenship and Immigration Canada.

Clarkson, Stephen. 2008. *Does North America Exist? Governing the Continent after NAFTA and 9/11*. Toronto: University of Toronto Press.

CMHC. 2009. *Canadian Housing Observer*. Ottawa: Canada Mortgage and Housing Corporation.

Conference Board of Canada. 2009. *Income Inequality*. Toronto: Conference Board of Canada.

CPP Investment Board. 2005. *Annual Report*. Toronto: Canada Pension Plan Investment Board.

Crompton, Rosemary. 2006. *Employment and the Family*. New York: Cambridge University Press.

Cross, Phillip. 2008. "The Role of Natural Resources in Canada's Economy." *Canadian Economic Observer*, November, Catalog no. 11-010-X.

– 2010. *Year-End Review of 2009*. Ottawa: Statistics Canada.

– 2011. "2010 in Review." *Canadian Economic Observer*. Ottawa: Statistics Canada.

Crouch, Colin. 2006. *Post-Democracy*. Malden, MA: Polity Press.

– 2009. "Privatized Keynesianism: An Unacknowledged Policy Regime." *The British Journal of Politics and International Relation* 11: 382–99.

– 2011. *The Strange Non-Death of Neo-Liberalism*. Malden, MA: Polity Press.

– 2014. "The Neo-Liberal Turn and the Implications for Labour." *The Oxford Handbook of Employment Relations: Comparative Employment Relations*, edited by A. Wilkinson, G. Wood, and R. Deeg. New York: Oxford University Press.

Davis, Gerald F. 2016. *The Vanishing American Corporation*. Oakland: Berrett-Koehler.

Dicken, Peter. 2015. *Global Shift: Mapping the Changing Contours of the World Economy*. New York: Sage Publications.

Duménil, Gérard, and Dominique Lévy. 2011. *The Crisis of Neoliberalism*. Cambridge: Harvard University Press.

Durand, Cedric. 2017. *Fictitious Capital: How Finance Is Appropriating Our Future*. New York: Verso.

Durufle, Gilles. 2009. *Why Venture Capital Is Essential to the Canadian Economy: The Impact of Venture Capital on the Canadian Economy*. Toronto: Canada's Venture Capital and Private Equity Association.

Emmenger, Patrick, Silja Hausermann, Bruno Palier, and Martin Seeleib-Kaiser. 2011a. *The Age of Dualization: The Changing Face of Inequality in De-industrializing Societies*. New York: Oxford University Press.

– 2011b. "Why We Grow More Unequal." In *The Age of Dualization: The Changing Face of Inequality in De-industrializing Societes*, edited by P. Emmenger, S. Hausermann, B. Palier and M. Seeleib-Kaiser. New York: Oxford University Press.

Esping-Anderson, Gosta. 1999. *Social Foundations of Post-Industrial Economies*. New York: Oxford University Press.

Evans, Bryan. 2011. "The Politics of Public Sector Wages: Ontario's Social Dialogue for Austerity." *Socialist Studies/Etudes Socialistes* 7 (1/2): 1.

Flaherty, Eoin. 2015. "Top Incomes under Finance-Driven Capitalism, 1990-2010: Power Resources and Regulatory Orders." *Socio-Economic Review* 13 (3).

Gates-Gasse, Erika. 2010. "'Two Step' Immigration: Canada's New Immigration System Raises Troubling Issues." *The CCPA Monitor*, 1 October.

Gautie, Jerome, and John Schmitt. 2010. *Low-Wage Work in the Wealthy World*. New York: Russell Sage Foundation.

Glyn, Andrew. 2006. *Capitalism Unleashed: Finance, Globalization and Welfare.* New York: Oxford University Press.

Hacker, Jacob, and Paul Pierson. 2010. *Winner-Take-All Politics: How Washington Made the Rich Richer – And Turned Its Back on the Middle Class.* New York: Simon and Schuster.

– 2016. *American Amnesia: How the War on Government Led Us to Forget What Made America Prosper.* New York: Simon and Schuster.

Harvey, David. 2006. *A Brief History of Neoliberalism.* New York: Oxford University Press.

Holmes, John. 2010. "The Forestry Industry." In *What Do We Know? What Do We Need to Know? The State of Canadian Research on Work, Employment, and Climate Change*, edited by C. Lipsig-Mumme. Toronto: York University.

Holmes, John, and Austin Hracs. 2010. "The Transportation Equipment Industry." In *What Do We Know? What Do We Need to Know? The State of Canadian Research on Work, Employment, and Climate Change*, edited by C. Lipsig-Mumme. Toronto: York University.

Industry Canada. 2009. *Ontario Economic Overview February 2009 Update.* Ottawa: Industry Canada.

– 2010. *Ontario Economic Overview February 2010 Update.* Ottawa: Industry Canada.

– 2012. *Ontario Economic Overview January 2012 Update.* Ottawa: Industry Canada.

King, Desmond, and David Rueda. 2008. "Cheap Labor: The New Politics of 'Bread and Roses' in Industrial Democracies." *Perspectives on Politics* 6 (2).

Klassen, Thomas, and Rodney Haddow. 2006. *Partisanship, Globalization, and Canadian Labour Market Policy.* Toronto: University of Toronto Press.

Kollmeyer, Christopher. 2009. "Explaining Deindustrialization: How Affluence, Productivity Growth, and Globalization Diminish Manufacturing Employment." *American Journal of Sociology* 114 (6).

Lapavitsas, Costas. 2014. *Profiting without Producing: How Finance Exploits Us All.* New York: Verso.

LaRochelle-Côté, Sébastien, and Claude Dionne. 2009. "International Differences in Low-Paid Work." *Perspectives on Labour and Income.* Ottawa: Statistics Canada.

LaRochelle-Côté, Sébastien, John Myles, and Garnett Picot. 2009. *Income Security and Stability During Retirement in Canada.* Statistics Canada, Analytical Studies Branch Research Paper Series.

Law Commission of Ontario. 2012. *Vulnerable Workers and Precarious Work.* Toronto: Law Commission of Ontario.

Lewchuk, Wayne, Marlea Clarke, and Alice de Wolff. 2011. *Working without Commitments: The Health Effects of Precarious Employment.* Montreal: McGill-Queen's University Press.

Livingstone, D.W., W. Smith, and D.E. Smith. 2011. *Manufacturing Meltdown: Reshaping Steel Work*. Black Point, NS: Fernwood Publishing.

Luce, Stephanie. 2014. *Labor Movements: Global Perspectives*. Malden, MA: Polity Press.

Lucifora, Claudio, and Weimar Salverda. 2009. "Low-Pay." In *The Oxford Handbook of Economic Inequality*, edited by W. Salverda, B. Nolan, and T.M. Smeeding. New York: Oxford University Press.

Mackenzie, Hugh. 2008. *The Great CEO Pay Race – Over before It Begins*. Ottawa: Canadian Centre for Policy Alternatives.

McBride, Stephen. 2005. *Paradigm Shift: Globalization and the Canadian State*. Halifax: Fernwood Publishing.

Mendelson, Micheal, Ken Battle, and Sherri Torjman. 2009. *Canada's Shrunken Safety Net: Employment Insurance in the Great Recession*. Ottawa: Caledon Institute of Social Policy.

– 2011. *Fixing the Hole in EI: Temporary Financial Assistance for the Unemployed*. Toronto: Mowat Centre School of Public Policy and Governance.

Milberg, William, and Deborah Winkler. 2013. *Outsourcing Economics: Global Value Chains in Capitalist Development*. New York: Cambridge University Press.

Milway, James, Sana Nisar, Claurelle Poole, and Ying Yang. 2007. *Assessing Toronto's Financial Services Cluster*. Toronto: Institute for Competitiveness and Prosperity.

Minimum Wage Advisory Panel. 2014. *Report and Recommendations to the Minister of Labour*. Toronto: Queen's Printer for Ontario.

Moody, Kim. 2007. *US Labor in Trouble and Transition: The Failure of Reform from Above, the Promise of Revival from Below*. New York: Verso.

Murnighan, Bill, and Jim Stanford. 2013. "'We Will Fight This Crisis': Auto Workers Resist an Industrial Meltdown." In *The State, Capitalism, and Labour*, edited by T. Fowler. Ottawa: Red Quill.

Murphy, Fidelma, and Terrence McDonough. 2012. "US Auto Companies' Ownership and Control of Production in Mexico's 'Maquiladoras.'" *Cambridge Journal of Regions, Economy and Society* 5 (3).

Murray, Stuart, and Hugh Mackenzie. 2007. *Bringing Minimum Wages above the Poverty Line*. Ottawa: Canadian Centre for Policy Alternatives.

Nicholls, Christopher. 2006. "The Characteristics of Canada's Capital Markets and the Illustrative Case of Canada's Legislative Response to Sarbanes-Oxley." In *Maintaining a Competitive Capital Market in Canada*, vol. 4. Toronto: Task Force to Modernize Securities Legislation in Canada.

OECD. 2006. *Employment Outlook: Boosting Jobs and Incomes*. Paris: OECD.

– 2008. *Growing Unequal? Income Distribution and Poverty in OECD Countries*. Paris: OECD.

– 2010. *OECD Employment Outlook 2010: Moving Beyond the Jobs Crisis, Employment Outlook*. Paris: OECD.

– 2011. *OECD Employment Outlook 2011*. Paris: OECD.

– 2015. *In It All Together: Why Less Inequality Benefits All*. Paris: OECD.
Olive, David. 2011. "RIM Revival Must Start at Top." *Toronto Star*, 29 July.
Panitch, Leo, and Sam Gindin. 2013. *The Making of Global Capitalism*. New York: Verso.
Peters, John. 2010. "Down in the Vale: Corporate Globalization, Unions on the Defensive, and the USW Local 6500 Strike in Sudbury, 2009-2010." *Labour/Le Travail* 66.
– 2011. "The Rise of Finance and the Decline of Organised Labour in the Advanced Capitalist Countries." *New Political Economy* 16 (1).
– 2013. "Boom, Bust, and Crisis: Canada, Free Markets, and the Decline of Unions and Good Jobs." In *Boom, Bust, and Crisis: Labour, Corporate Power, and Politics in 21st Century Canada*, edited by J. Peters. Halifax: Fernwood.
Piketty, Thomas. 2014. *Capital in the Twenty-First Century*. Cambridge: Harvard University Press.
PWC. 2005. *Global Forest, Paper, and Packaging Industry Survey*. Vancouver: PricewaterhouseCoopers.
– 2010. *Global Forest, Paper and Packaging Industry Survey*. Vancouver: PricewaterhouseCoopers.
Reich, Robert. 2015. *Saving Capitalism: For the Many, Not the Few*. New York: Knopf.
Robertson, Grant. 2011a. "CIBC's McGaughey gets 50% Raise." *Globe and Mail*, 17 March.
– 2011b. "Scotiabank's Rick Waugh Earns $10.7 Million." *Globe and Mail*, 4 March.
Rubin, Jeff. 2017. *How Has Canadian Manufacturing Fared under NAFTA? A Look at Auto Assembly and Parts Industry*. Waterloo: Centre for International Governance Innovation.
Rutherford, Tod, and John Holmes. 2014. "Manufacturing Resiliency: Economic Restructuring and Automotive Manufacturing in the Great Lakes Region." *Cambridge Journal of Regions, Economy and Society* 7 (3).
Standing, Guy. 2011. *The Precariat: The New Dangerous Class*. New York: Bloomsbury Academic.
Stanford, Jim. 1997. *Paper Boom: Why Real Prosperity Requires a New Approach to Canada's Economy*. Ottawa: Canadian Centre for Policy Alternatives.
– 2010. "The Geography of Auto Globalization and the Politics of Auto Bailouts." *Cambridge Journal of Regions, Economy and Society* 3 (3).
– 2011. *Having Their Cake and Eating It Too: Business Profits, Taxes, and Investment in Canada; 1961–2010*. Ottawa: Canadian Centre for Policy Alternatives.
– 2012. "A Cure for Dutch Disease: Active Sector Strategies for Canada's Economy." In *Alternative Federal Budget 2012*. Ottawa: Canadian Centre for Policy Alternatives.
Statistics Canada. 2011a. *LFS National Occupation Classification for Statistics*. CANSIM table 2820010.
– 2011b. *LFS Wages of Employees by Type of Work*. CANSIM table 2820070.

Stiglitz, Joseph E. 2010. *Freefall: America, Free Markets, and the Sinking of the World Economy*. New York: W.W. Norton.

Sweeney, Brendan. 2017. *A Profile of the Automotive Manufacturing Industry in Canada, 2012–2016*. Hamilton, ON: Automotive Policy Research Centre.

Toronto Life. 2011. "The Loaded List: We Catalogue the Astronomical Salaries of Toronto's Ruling Class." *Toronto Life*, 9 November.

Wahl, Andrew. 2009. "The Good, the Bad and the Ugly: Nortel Networks." *Canadian Business*, 30 March.

Western, Bruce. 1997. *Between Class and Market: Postwar Unionization in the Capitalist Democracies*. Princeton: Princeton University Press.

Workers' Action Centre. 2007. *Working on the Edge*. Toronto: Workers' Action Centre.

Yalnizyan, Armine. 2010. *The Rise of Canada's Richest 1%*. Ottawa: Canadian Centre for Policy Alternatives.

| 3 |

The Geography of the Ontario Service Economy

STEVEN TUFTS

Since the 1970s, service economy growth has been commonly considered the natural evolution of late capitalism, central to economic development in so-called knowledge-based, "post-industrial" societies (Bell 1973). Ontario's annual gross domestic product (GDP) from goods-producing industries contracted in the aftermath of the 2007–08 financial crisis and has yet to recover to 2007 levels. At the same time, GDP from service industries increased from $412 billion in 2007 to $490 billion in 2016 (2007 dollars, Statistics Canada 2017a). Services are viewed as an important part of any future employment growth in Ontario's post-industrial, knowledge-based economy, as the sector now employs 3 out of 4 workers.

Ontario's growing service sector is a central component of the province's uneven economic development. Services are integral to broader neoliberal processes including privatization, the reduced presence of labour unions, increased labour market flexibility, intensified competition among regions and cities for investment, and the restructuring of services with the rise of the so-called sharing economy. Employment opportunities in the service sector are geographically uneven and highly segmented: women, young people, racialized workers, and immigrants are overrepresented in some service industries and underrepresented in others. This chapter begins with a brief discussion of the definitional debates about what the "service economy" actually is and its role in the changing economy. The historical growth of service employment, resilient labour market segmentation, and geographically uneven development in Ontario are then detailed. The final section explores the role of services in recent economic development practices and political resistance to such strategies.

DEFINING THE SERVICE ECONOMY

Simple technical definitions of the service sector often use the "tangibility" of the final output as the primary criteria. If a material product results from the production process, then it is a goods-producing industry. For example, the North American Industry Classification System (NAICS) used by Statistics Canada categorizes goods-producing activity into five sectors: agriculture; natural resource extraction; utilities; construction; and manufacturing. Service-producing industries include a range of non-tangible distributive services (e.g., wholesale, retail, transportation) and other types of private and public services (e.g., accommodation and food services, education, health). There are, however, limits to criteria based solely on "tangibility," and many different ways of categorizing economic activity have been developed.

It is important to first ask why social scientists and policymakers have been so obsessed with the typology of economic activity. For many, the shift to services is an indicator of economic progress and the development of advanced consumer societies. For others, service sector expansion relative to goods-producing industries presents a challenge, as perceived lower productivity and the inability to regulate low-wage service work limits real wage growth and contributes to economic inequality.

How best to conceptualize service sector employment growth in advanced capitalist economies has been debated for well over a half century (Schettkat and Yocarini 2003; Wolfe 1955). Early conceptualizations of the economy as comprising different "sectors" date back to the 1930s. The "three-sector hypothesis" developed by Colin Clark (1940) argues that mass consumer demand shifts to services (tertiary sector activity) when markets for manufactured goods (secondary sector) and resources (primary sector) become saturated. Jean Fourastié (1949) added that lower productivity growth in expanding services absorbs workers, stabilizing employment as this shift occurs. These demand-side approaches, emphasizing consumption patterns, were challenged by "supply-side" explanations that argued that lower productivity in services was responsible for employment shifts rather than any real change in demand (Schettkat and Yocarini 2003; Baumol 2001; Fuchs 1968). The legacy of William Baumol's "cost disease thesis," which argued that relative wages in the service sector grow much faster than its lagging productivity, remains influential with policymakers today. Highly "productive" manufacturing jobs remain a goal of much economic development rhetoric in Ontario. At the same time, the state's aggressive attack on the wages of public sector workers in "low productivity" services is a hallmark of austerity programs.

The general claims that services are by their immaterial nature unproductive and incapable of boosting exports or providing high-wage jobs can be challenged. First of all, the "intangibility" of all services is questionable. For example, Andrew Sayer and Richard Walker question the wisdom of conceptually differentiating service and goods production. Consider their characterization of hotels: "hotels principally offer shelter, a useful aspect of a type of *good*, i.e. buildings. Only fine hotels also offer personal labour-services. Having someone take your money and clean-up after you does not count as *service*; it is sales and maintenance work. Restaurants and hotels should therefore be counted partly under manufacturing and partly under retailing, with a residual of labour-services" (1992, 61, emphasis added). While reducing much service-related work to merely "residual labour services" may be an extreme critique, it is important to note that many services do produce tangible goods (e.g., meals) as final output where traditional productivity measures can be used.

Second, information and communication technologies (ICT) have revolutionized many private and public sector services, increasing productivity if measured in terms of the labour input per unit of output. For example, automated tellers and online personal banking services have changed the financial sector. It is, however, difficult to measure traditional "productivity" in services, especially those that provide emotional and caring labour (e.g., childcare) or may have social and economic payoffs over long time horizons such as education and preventative health care.

Third, wages in the sector are not constrained by productivity differentials as much as they are by workers' inability to secure compensation from employers. The low unionization rate in private sector services relative to the public sector is a major factor (Doellgast 2012). There are, however, exceptions where private services have been highly unionized and wages are increased. For example, hotel unions in Las Vegas and other large North American cities have been able to increase standards for hospitality workers (Gray 2004; Tufts 2007).

Fourth, services can contribute to export-led development and strengthen the economic base. Some categorizations differentiate services according to this role. Basic services are those services which are exported (business consulting, tourism-related services) and bring money into the regional economy, while non-basic services are those activities which cater to local needs (e.g., barbershops, convenience stores) (Coffey 1996, 341; Coffey 2001). Distinguishing between basic and non-basic services can be difficult as many firms export and serve domestic markets, but basic services have been the historical preference in terms of economic development priorities, given the higher-added value and wages associated with those sectors.

Fifth, many firms and occupations classed as services (e.g., research and design, mining engineering, building cleaning and maintenance) are, in fact, directly linked to highly productive (yet often environmentally unsustainable) goods production organized at a global scale. Ian Wallace (2002) notes that service economy growth is very much linked to the expansion of flexible commodity chains that integrate a complex global division of labour. He therefore distinguishes producer services (such as advertising) from traditional personal services (e.g., retail, food services) and non-market public services (e.g., education) (see Wallace 2002, 98–9). Some make further distinctions, limiting the "tertiary" sector to distributive services (e.g., retail, transportation) with "quaternary" and "quinary" used to define information-based services utilized by firms and higher decision-making services (e.g., financial consultants) (see Hayter and Patchell 2011, 272–3). These latter categories, which employ highly educated "knowledge workers" or what Robert Reich (1992) calls "symbolic analysts," have been the focus of much contemporary regional economic development policy and practice. The rise of the so-called creative class and the importance of attracting these information workers to regions has been an obsession for policymakers in Ontario.

More recently, traditional service sector activity has been disrupted by gig-economy platforms such as Uber and AirBnB. Here, personal assets of individuals (cars and homes) are appropriated by the revenue-generating sphere of the economy. In some cases, the financialization of these assets (such as car loans and mortgages) are directly related to the owner's capacity to put the assets into circulation with their own service labour. As a result, traditional service industries such as taxi driving and accommodation services have been disrupted by these new technologies. There is some debate over the rise of "crowd workers" associated with these platforms and its impact on labour markets, but in most cases people driving for Uber or Lyft, or renting out space in their homes, are supplementing incomes derived from other forms of contingent work (Huws et al. 2017; Brooks and Moody 2016).

It is here where older conceptualizations of service sector growth also depart from classic demand- and supply-side approaches and focus on the increasingly complex global division of labour. The global economy is not producing fewer goods, but it is producing them in different places with less workers. Export-oriented economies such as China are largely dependent on increased international trade and the nation-state's removal of barriers to the flows of goods, services, and finance. Manufacturing capital can now flee regions with higher wages and strong industrial unions, and financial markets are free to pursue the highest returns on a global scale. At the same time, government attacks against labour since the 1970s in Ontario and other jurisdictions have made it difficult for unions to organize growing numbers of workers in private services and have limited the power of unions in the highly unionized public sector (see Panitch and Swartz 2003; Camfield 2011). The state may not have created the post-industrial economy, but it has enabled its growth. Albo (2010), for example, has argued that the growth of services is part of a much larger neoliberal project and is compatible with the logic of capital to control production through the separation of "mental and manual work," escape unions in the industrial sector, administer global financial and manufacturing systems, and create a large reserve army of contingent workers. (For a state-centred account of post-industrial economic development, see Peters in this volume.)

How to best categorize services and other economic activities will continue to be a challenge, but more recent trends in economic development policy seem less concerned with the numerous ways of classifying services and more concerned with how different services are increasingly interdependent. Over the last decade a great deal of energy has been focused on what types of public and private services make a city "liveable" enough to attract highly skilled "creative" workers to cities (see Florida 2002, 2008). What continues to be neglected in all of these classification schemes, despite the contributions of feminist political economy, is the increasing importance of paid and unpaid services fundamental to social reproduction, such as housework and childcare. Volunteer services are also neglected even as they are increasingly integrated into paid service work (e.g., unpaid internships, community volunteers at cultural events which attract tourists). All types of service work and their interrelationships will continue to define the service economy.

The emergence of services has been central to both Marxist and post-Marxist discussions of a new economy based on knowledge-intensive work. French sociologist Alain Touraine argued thirty years prior to Richard Florida (2002) that economic growth is increasingly based on creative knowledge work: "Growth results from a whole complex of social factors, not just from the accumulation of capital. Nowadays, it depends much more directly than ever before on knowledge, and hence on the capacity of society to call forth creativity" ([1969] 1971, 5).

Touraine further argued that post-industrial society is in fact a "programmed society," where organizations and technocracies are the source of political decision-making power. Class struggle shifts away from traditional labour-management in factories to conflict between technocrats and broader social movements. Touraine's legacy can be seen in more contemporary discussions of an emergent "new economy" based on networked bureaucracies and knowledge workers. Manuel Castells (2000) argues that a new informational economy built of powerful networks linked by communication technologies has radically changed production and social relations. Power is no longer directly linked to the production of tangible goods or services, but rather to the ability to gain control over the global ICT networks that administer their production and distribution. The highly skilled service workers who control the "spaces of flows" (to use Castells's term) are increasingly pivotal.

Similarly, Michael Hardt and Antonio Negri (2004, 2009) have emphasized the "immateriality" of labour as a central component of political and economic change. Flexible, racialized, immaterial labour is crucial to meeting the demands of contemporary advanced capitalist economies. The contradiction for capital is how to exercise control over the knowledge worker when creativity and innovation depends on some degree of individual autonomy. Echoing Touraine, Hardt and Negri (2009, 135) see the growing importance of immaterial production in the new economy as shifting conflict away from issues of material production and toward broader issues of social reproduction. In other words, workplace-based conflict in factories is no longer the most important vehicle for social change. Instead, issues around sustaining communities and social life are argued to be the basis for resistance.

There are, however, important Marxist interventions in such conceptualizations of the "new economy." Doug Henwood (2003), among the harshest of these critics, has argued that productivity increases due to new technology in the service sector, even in finance and banking, are often exaggerated. For Henwood, commentators such as Castells, who fetishize information technologies and knowledge workers, miss the most basic point: service sector expansion is largely due to the increasing commodification of our daily lives and the entry of capital exchange into realms of unpaid labour. Meal preparation in restaurants, commercial laundries, and domestic childcare are all increasingly commodified and compose much low-wage work as capital commodifies everyday life in search of profit (Henwood 2003, 29). Indeed, Uber drivers and AirBnB "hosts" are not "sharing" anything but are part of a larger process of integrating labour (e.g., driving, making beds, cooking and cleaning) into the formal exchange economy.

Debates over how to best conceptualize service industries in the "new economy" have important implications for organizing for social change. Do social movements need to appeal to the shifting identities of "knowledge" and other service workers, or should exploitation in the workplace continue to be the focus? What is clear is that service work is polarized, encompassing some high-wage jobs and many low-wage occupations. It is the uneven development of the service sector and the interdependence of high- and low-wage service employment that typifies Ontario's service economy.

ONTARIO'S UNEVEN SERVICE ECONOMY

In the 1990s, a report produced by the Economic Council of Canada (1991), *Good Jobs, Bad Jobs: Employment in the Service Economy*, touched off a debate over the extent to which service employment growth (and manufacturing employment stagnation) was contributing to economic polarization and more precarious jobs. Those services which serve businesses, such as consulting and commercial finance, are considered to have higher added value than a range of low-wage consumer services. At the same time, higher wages and employment stability are associated with public services such as health care and education. The quantity of these jobs, who has access to them, and where they are located are central contributors to Ontario's uneven political economic development.

Any discussion of the political economy of services in Ontario must consider not only the growth of the sector, but the relative importance of different types of services and their geographical location within the province. There is also labour market segmentation within the service economy that creates resilient inequalities. In terms of overall growth, services now account for over 75 per cent of jobs in Ontario compared to less than 65 per cent in the mid-1970s (see figure 3.1). Further, women participate the most in service sector expansion.

It is important to recognize, however, that while service employment has grown in both absolute and relative terms in Ontario, there have been some significant shifts in the sectoral composition of services over the last thirty years (see figure 3.2). Specifically, as a percentage of overall service employment, trade has declined in Ontario while there has been an increase in the share of professional, scientific, and technical service employment. The increase in professional and technical services employment can be linked to the overall expansion of the knowledge-based economy and the growth of specialized services within complex commodity chains. Despite the rhetoric of expanding public health and social services, their overall share of service employment has increased only slightly. Any relative increase

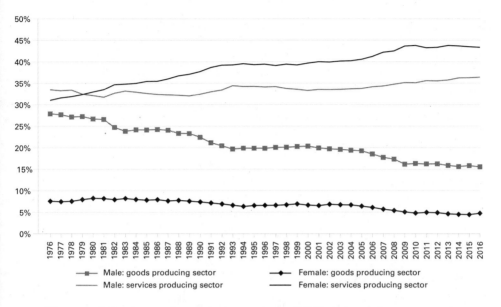

Figure 3.1 | Service employment as percentage of all Ontario employment, fifteen years and over by sex, 1976–2016 (*Source*: Statistics Canada [2017], CANSIM table 282-0008)

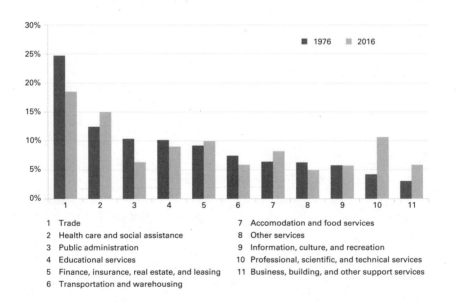

1 Trade
2 Health care and social assistance
3 Public administration
4 Educational services
5 Finance, insurance, real estate, and leasing
6 Transportation and warehousing
7 Accomodation and food services
8 Other services
9 Information, culture, and recreation
10 Professional, scientific, and technical services
11 Business, building, and other support services

Figure 3.2 | Occupational distribution of service sector employment, 1976 and 2016 (% of all service employment) (*Source*: Statistics Canada [2017], CANSIM table 282-0008)

Table 3.1 | Employment composition of Ontario CMAs, selected service industries, 2016

Census Metropolitan Area	Total labour force 15 years and over by industry	Finance and insurance (%)	Professional, scientific, and technical services (%)	Health care and social assistance (%)	Public administration (%)
Ontario	7,141,675	5.3%	8.0%	10.6%	5.8%
Toronto	3,234,350	7.7%	10.5%	8.9%	3.7%
Ottawa-Gatineau	727,045	3.0%	8.6%	10.8%	21.0%
Hamilton	395,005	4.6%	6.6%	12.3%	4.6%
Kitchener-Cambridge-Waterloo	290,425	6.1%	7.5%	9.6%	3.4%
London	258,800	5.2%	6.0%	13.9%	3.8%
St Catharines-Niagara	203,825	2.8%	4.5%	11.5%	4.7%
Oshawa	203,165	4.9%	6.2%	10.8%	5.9%
Windsor	161,790	3.2%	5.0%	12.4%	3.7%
Barrie	110,560	3.0%	5.3%	10.8%	6.1%
Guelph	87,520	3.7%	7.1%	9.1%	4.7%
Greater Sudbury	85,235	2.6%	4.6%	14.4%	7.6%
Kingston	83,430	2.8%	4.7%	15.6%	11.7%
Brantford	70,065	2.4%	4.3%	11.2%	3.7%
Thunder Bay	61,690	2.2%	5.2%	17.5%	7.9%
Peterborough	60,645	2.5%	4.8%	14.3%	5.6%
Belleville	51,140	2.0%	3.4%	12.3%	11.1%

Source: Statistics Canada (2016), Census of Population.

in healthcare employment has been offset by a decline in the share of service workers delivering education. Healthcare employment has expanded faster than employment in educational services in response to the demands of an aging population with fewer children to educate, especially in many Northern Ontario communities. There has also been a relative decline in public administration which can be linked to a significant contraction of public service employment (especially at the federal level) in the 1990s.

There are significant geographical variations if we look at the scale of Ontario's urban system. The structure of service employment varies considerably even among the province's largest cities (table 3.1). In terms of finance and insurance, Toronto is the economic centre of the country, with the most people employed in the sector. Similarly, there are significant numbers of workers in professional, scientific, and technical services in the Greater Toronto and Hamilton Area (GTHA). Canada's capital city region, Ottawa-Gatineau, also employs a high number of people in these services, but is most notably an administrative centre employing one in five workers in public administration. Smaller cities in central, eastern, and northern Ontario depend more on public service employment, especially in health care and social services. Cities such as Thunder Bay and Peterborough are regional service centres with small financial services sectors. Public services are even more important for smaller urban centres, especially in the North.

The diversity of service sector employment among Ontario's cities reflects the hierarchy of the urban system. Large metropolitan cities are hubs for the flows of capital and centres of innovation. Smaller cities outside of southern Ontario are more dependent upon the state for employment. Governments continue be challenged with developing policies that can reverse the trend toward greater concentrations of human and physical capital in large centres and the flight of young people from these centres.

At the urban scale, it is also noted that some producer services have migrated to areas outside of Toronto's central business district (CBD) to a number of nodes in growing suburban centres, such as Mississauga (see Shearmur and Coffey 2002). There is some debate over the extent and nature of this decentralization of employment outside of Toronto's CBD, as it is argued that large institutions (banks, insurance companies, pension funds) are quite robust and actively promote policies to protect significant real estate investments in the downtown core (Charney 2005a, 2005b). Inner-city condominium booms and increased housing costs have seen immigrant groups, traditionally located downtown, move to inner and outer suburbs. Indeed, it is now argued that the most dynamic forms of urban transformation are happening at margins of cities and service growth is part of this process (Keil 2017).

Service sector employment in Ontario is also highly segmented by gender, race, and age (table 3.2). Women constitute almost half of the labour force, but account for two-thirds of the educational service industry and four-fifths of health and social employment. Women

Table 3.2 | Demographic characteristics of service industry employment, Ontario, 2016

	Female	Immigrant and permanent resident	Visible minority (2006)	Age 15–24
Total employees, all industries	48.3%	28.2%	21.5%	14.3%
Retail trade	53.1%	21.3%	22.0%	27.9%
Information and cultural industries	42.8%	26.5%	23.9%	11.8%
Transportation and warehousing	26.5%	36.3%	22.9%	5.9%
Finance and insurance	55.5%	38.1%	30.6%	6.5%
Real estate and leasing	46.4%	33.1%	20.9%	6.9%
Professional, scientific, and technical services	44.2%	34.1%	23.7%	7.4%
Educational services	69.0%	18.7%	14.3%	9.4%
Health care and social assistance	82.2%	27.7%	21.1%	7.1%
Accommodation and food services	57.9%	23.9%	26.5%	41.2%
Public administration	48.0%	12.8%	13.1%	8.9%

Sources: Statistics Canada (2016, 2006), Census of Population.

are also the majority of workers in finance and accommodation and food services, yet are underrepresented in transportation services. "Visible minority" workers are similarly employed in relatively higher numbers in finance and accommodation and food services, but are underrepresented in public services such as education and public administration. A similar pattern exists for immigrant workers in Ontario. Young workers aged fifteen to twenty-four are concentrated in retail trade and accommodation and food services industries that have many entry level positions, require little training, and allow for flexible work arrangements to accommodate secondary and post-secondary education. Overall, the pattern of labour market segmentation raises questions of social exclusion and who has access to more secure, higher-paid employment – particularly in the unionized public sector.

The growth of service industries also has implications for the regulation of work and employment. Industrial unions with a historical

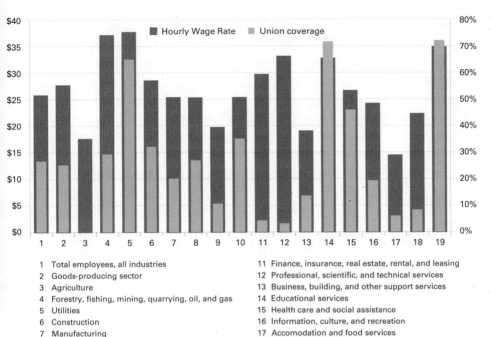

Figure 3.3 | Average hourly wage rate and union coverage by industry, 2016 (*Source*: Statistics Canada [2017], CANSIM tables 282-0078 and 282-0072)

presence in goods-producing industries and public sector unions have failed to organize large numbers of workers in private services (figure 3.3). Wage rates are high in many financial industries despite having a low union presence. In low-wage services such as accommodation and food services, union coverage is less than 10 per cent in Ontario. The fact that these are both growth sectors poses significant challenges for the future of the labour movement, which is strongest in the public sector. Of further concern is that unionized jobs in educational services and public administration are occupied by larger numbers of older, Canadian-born and non-visible minority workers. Immigrants, young workers, and visible minorities continue to work in sectors that the labour movement has failed to organize. As a result, some groups of workers in Ontario have access to labour market institutions that can buffer the impacts of the most brutal neoliberal attacks – deepening inequalities in the labour market. Persistent income inequality has, in part, forced the Ontario government to increase the minimum wage in the province and reform labour law. The significant increase of the provincial minimum wage to $14 an hour in 2018, and another proposed increase to $15 in 2019 (now eliminated), is the result of community organizing such as the $15andFairness movement to improve working conditions for low-wage workers, especially in service industries (see Stephanie Ross, this volume).

THE SERVICE ECONOMY AND NEOLIBERAL ECONOMIC DEVELOPMENT

Services have been increasingly central to both neoliberal economic development processes and policy in Ontario for over two decades. There are developments in which both the non-basic and basic service economy are implicated. In the non-basic service economy the privatization of public services and the "Walmartization" of private services put downward pressure on wages and working conditions. In basic services, intensified place promotion and economic development policy, which focuses on the attraction of "creative talent," aims to capture flows of both tourists and highly skilled workers.

The privatization of public service provision has unfolded over a number of decades preceding the election of Premier Mike Harris and his Common Sense Revolution in 1995. In health care, privatization is not simply increasing provision of services by private for-profit companies, but also the implementation of for-profit management strategies in a range of healthcare services (Armstrong and Armstrong 2001). The driving force of privatization is quite simply the need for capital to expand into sectors where profits are possible. As many government services are unionized, the private sector sees opportunities to provide services (under pseudo-monopolistic conditions) using cheaper labour. As private companies will expect a return on their investment, the savings to taxpayers may be negligible (or non-existent), even as wage rates for workers decline.

The privatization agenda of the Ontario government did not, however, end with the election of Premier Dalton McGuinty in 2003. As a means of financing new infrastructure (such as hospitals), the government continued the practice of public-private partnerships (P3s) as a means of supposedly sharing risk with the private sector that assists with financing. The fear is that P3s will pressure governments to privatize services, as co-investors expect a return. The Ontario government also implements privatization through more incremental policies. For example, the government-owned Liquor Control Board of Ontario (LCBO) has allowed an increasing number of "agency" stores in smaller communities. These franchises operate in for-profit convenience and grocery stores, almost always non-union environments. The LCBO, a Crown corporation that generates billions in revenue each year, has already casualized its unionized workers with large numbers of part-time, temporary workers (see OPSEU 2009).

The Ontario government, facing significant deficits following the global financial crisis of 2007–08, has recently delivered a series of austerity measures. In the spring of 2011, the government appointed Don Drummond, a former economist of Toronto Dominion Bank, to review all government spending and possibilities for the privatization of services (Howlett 2011). The attack on unionized public sector labour providing services also continues at the municipal scale, as Toronto privatized much of the city's waste removal following an unpopular city workers' strike in 2009 (Fanelli 2016).

In private sector services, which remain largely non-union, the restructuring of distributive services pressures both workers and small firms. The "Walmartization" of services most often refers to the competitive effects of big box retail on suppliers, smaller retailers, and labour markets (Greenhouse 2009). In Ontario, the growth of "power retailers" such as Home Depot has significantly changed the retail landscape since the 1990s (Hernandez and Simmons 2006). Ontario local and provincial governments are implicated in the growth of power retail clusters, as land-use planning and regulation shifted to a more "laissez-faire" approach which permitted large auto-dependent retailers to expand rapidly (Jones and Doucet 2001). While some smaller retailers have adapted to power retailers in their communities, downtown businesses are largely unable to compete with value for customers in terms of price and selection (Cotton and Cochon 2007).

Power retailers such as Walmart have a business model that emphasizes low prices achieved through the pressure exerted on suppliers to lower profit margins on high volumes and a low-cost human resource strategy. To maintain low labour costs, Walmart and other power retailers have vehemently resisted unionization in Ontario and abroad (Stout and Pickle 2007). Unions have largely failed to organize in the sector, and as a result unionized workers in competing services such as grocery stores have had downward pressure on their wages and working conditions as part of the greater "Walmart effect." Despite these negative impacts, power retail development companies continue to grow throughout the province.

Ontario governments (provincial and municipal) continue to pursue mega-event and tourism-related economic development strategies. Toronto did host the 2015 Pan-American games. The strategy of sports mega-event-led development in Toronto, however, dates back to the city's failed bids for the 1996 and 2008 Olympic Games. The Olympic bids were integrated into Toronto's waterfront renewal strategies aimed at developing the older industrial lands for higher value-added services and spaces for consumption. Emphasis on mega-events in large cities (and a range of smaller festivals in towns across Ontario) is a significant departure from postwar industrial development strategies based on manufacturing industries. Consumer services that are "exported" to tourists have become pivotal in state economic development strategies. Kipfer and Keil (2002) refer to Toronto as a new model of "competitive city" which stresses not only the entrepreneurial pro-business aspect of the city, but also the way in which "cultural diversity" is increasingly used to market Toronto to tourists, and how the state suppresses dissent and polices poor people to protect consumer and tourist experiences. In this case of mega-event and tourism promotion, the neoliberal state remains very active in an economy which encourages inter and intra-regional competition.

Another important shift in economic policy discourse in Ontario, beginning in the early 2000s, has been the emphasis on policies that attract highly skilled workers to specific places rather than focusing primarily on capital investment. It is argued that in advanced capitalist knowledge-based economies, highly skilled workers are increasingly mobile and capital will follow them to the cities they choose to live in. The importance and increasing power of highly skilled workers in North America's economy has been noted for some time (see Reich 1992). In Ontario, influential policy analyst Tom Courchene (2001) argues that human capital is central to the provincial economy, as the region competes in a global knowledge economy with economic flows that run north and south rather than primarily east and west among provinces. An important caveat to Courchene's argument, however, is that while the flow of goods is largely north-south in Ontario, the province is still greatly dependent upon an east-west flow of interprovincial service trade. For example, the Greater Toronto Area remains a cultural and financial centre for Canada.

There has perhaps been no larger influence on economic development policy in the first decade of the millennium than Richard Florida (2002) and his theories of the rise of the "creative class." At the peak of his popularity, Florida redefined how planners and policymakers think about occupations and sectors. Rather than thinking about services versus goods-producing sectors, work and industries are categorized according to their "creativity" or how much of their value is derived from innovation. Creative class theory proposes that innovation and talent are central to economic development and that innovative or "creative workers" demand specific amenities in the places where they work and live. Florida argues that there are strong correlations between regional economic success, widespread integration of "technology," large numbers of high-skilled "talent," "tolerance" for gays and lesbians, and a range of cultural and consumer related amenities (e.g., museums, galleries, cafés, and restaurants). For many of Florida's followers, the policy implications for cities are readily apparent. A city must be "hip" enough to attract workers who value a "bohemian" lifestyle. It is here where a strong link is made between basic services (e.g., high-tech export services) and non-basic services (e.g., the restaurants and bars that attract high-tech talent). Creative class theory also owes a huge debt to Jane Jacobs (1961), who argued in the early 1960s that diversity and entrepreneurialism are central to the revitalization of urban spaces and economic growth.

Florida is not, however, without critics. Social conservatives (mostly in the US) have accused him of promoting a "gay agenda" because he linked prosperity to thriving gay communities. From a progressive perspective, Jamie Peck (2005) provides a comprehensive critique of creative class theory, largely in terms of how a new round of neoliberal interregional competition for highly skilled workers leads to investment in local amenities at the expense of social services or expenditures which reproduce working-class jobs. Despite these criticisms, Florida (who relocated to the University of Toronto to direct the Martin Prosperity Institute in 2007) continued to capture the imaginations of policymakers. In 2008, the Ontario government commissioned a $2.2 million report, *Ontario in the Creative Age*, authored by Florida and Ron Martin. The authors conclude with a number of broad recommendations for the province, mostly involving investments in human capital formation. The report also emphasizes developing Toronto as the core "mega-region" capable of competing in the global economy. The best that smaller Ontario communities can hope for is greater connectivity to the core. The report was not universally well-received. In his Maclean's magazine review, Andrew Potter (2009) commented that "the Martin/Florida report is weirdly disconnected from both the actual world of work as well as elementary economic realities." Recently, even Florida himself has recognized some of the limits of his previous policy descriptions and the persistent rise of inequality in cities, although he is still very much embedded in a progressive competitive elitism (Florida 2017).The Ontario service economy has become more prominent in economic development practice and policy, but the provincial government has often left the regulation of some of the most significant developments to cities. For example, the entrance of Uber and AirBnB required cities to develop new regulations for the growing "sharing economy" that not only disrupted the taxi and hotel industries but had larger implications for community safety and affordable housing. The regulation of new forms of private service provision continues to prove contentious, but has significant implications for urban development (Wieditz 2017a). As workers and communities resist such changes, complex and contradictory political struggles emerge.

Service industries and employment remain part of persistent patterns of uneven economic development in Ontario and contemporary urban development policy. The 2018 provincial election, won by the Progressive Conservatives led by the right-wing populist Doug Ford, had clear geographical divisions between downtown metropolitan areas supporting the New Democratic Party and Conservative strongholds in car-dependent rural and suburban communities. In part, Ford resonated with voters who, if voting surveys are accurate, often lack access to secure, high-wage service jobs (public and private) in the metropolitan core (in addition to the traditional Conservative base in the business community). Ford campaigned with vows to find "efficiencies" in public spending, and challenged the policies of "Toronto elites" such as a higher minimum wage. New rounds of fiscal austerity and cuts to public sector employment will likely spark new protests and outbreaks of militant political resistance focused on the continuing erosion of the quantity and quality of government services in Ontario.

RESISTANCE AND THE GEOGRAPHY OF SERVICES IN ONTARIO

The reshaping of the geography of Ontario's service economy is not uncontested. Communities continue to lobby the provincial government for the opportunity to provide state services, opposing their concentration in Southern Ontario. In the 1990s, as local economic development strategies, the provincial government decentralized services such as the Ministry of Natural Resources to Peterborough and the offices of the Ontario Lottery and Gaming Corporation to Sault Ste Marie. But there is also grassroots resistance to privatization, Walmartization, tourism-led development, and the "creative-class" project.

In terms of resistance to the privatization and Walmartization of non-basic services, trade unions are attempting to remain relevant forces in the face of attacks by businesses and governments. The Canadian Union of Public Employees (CUPE) has been involved in a battle against the privatization of municipal, provincial, and federal public services for decades (Fanelli 2016). In the 1990s, the union (along with others) helped re-establish the Ontario Health Coalition, an organization of unions and community groups, to fight against cutbacks imposed by the Conservative government. Today, the coalition actively resists privatization and public-private partnerships in health care, and works to remedy the lack of services in smaller communities (see Tattersall 2010, chap. 4). The labour movement is increasingly engaging community groups in coalitions to fight against privatization, such as the Ontario Public Sector Employees Union's "We Own It!" campaign.

Similarly, community groups have fought Walmartization in both small and large cities. Recently, the East Toronto Community Coalition coalition joined the City of Toronto in a fight against the development of "power retail" by Smart Centres in the so-called "studio district" near Leslieville (in the southeastern part of the city). At stake was the encroachment of "big box" retail into designated "employment lands" – areas zoned for non-residential, non-retail commercial activity. As industrial land is scarce in Toronto, the local labour council supported the coalition fighting Walmart-type development (Lehrer and Wieditz 2009). In the end, the development was stopped, one of the few successes in rolling back low-wage big box retail developments that is resistant to unionization. In the end, one of the studios slated for redevelopment announced that it would continue to be used for films in 2012 (Wieditz 2017b).

Community groups have also been active in fighting unbridled growth in basic services. While private sector unions (hotel and building trades workers) supported Toronto's bids for the 1996 and 2008 Olympics, there. was significant community organization against the games (Tufts 2004; Lenskyj 2000). Bread Not Circuses, a group formed to stop the bids, was successful in detailing the limited benefits of mega-event development during the period. However, labour and community organizing failed to emerge in opposition to the Pan Am Games held in Toronto in 2015. Community groups and unions representing hotel workers, a largely female and immigrant workforce, have attempted to forward more sustainable visions of tourism development in the city, which includes greater unionization in hospitality services (Tufts 2006, 2007).

There has been significant resistance against various attempts by the Ontario Lottery and Gaming Corporation to "modernize" the province's publicly owned gaming industry (OLG 2012). The OLG has launched an aggressive program to privatize casino operations and establish a "mega-casino" with an integrated resort in downtown Toronto. The goal is to boost the city's tourism and convention capacity with the promise of thousands of new service jobs. The OLG's strategy is explicitly geographical as it shifts casino development away from racetracks, small border towns, and rural areas to large urban centres. Despite significant state support driven by large casino capital and union endorsements, grassroots groups such as No Casino Toronto have emerged to rally public support against an unpopular form of economic development (Tufts 2017a).

The Geography of the Ontario Service Economy

Community mobilization responded to the low-wage service-led development in Ontario. Unions have supported coalitions and struggles, such as the $15andFairness campaign. Fairbnb, a recent coalition of condo owners, tenant rights activists, and hotel workers in Canada, has led the fight for regulating the short-term rental sector, which has removed housing from the long-term rental markets in large cities with low vacancy rates. Despite the many contradictions of such cross-class coalitions, there has been success in regulating companies such as AirBnB and addressing affordable housing issues (Tufts 2017b). New coalitions emerging in response to addressing disruptive gig-economy services and their impacts on communities are perhaps protecting the creative class from itself.

Organized labour has, however, largely failed to mobilize unorganized private sector service workers in large numbers. There are countless explanations for this failure of unions to organize services, including a crisis of leadership, the bureaucratic structure of unions and industrial relations, the fragmented nature of small service sector employers (e.g., restaurants and retail stores), employer-friendly labour laws, the lack of union appeal to marginalized communities, and changing worker identities not as strongly linked to workplaces. Unions have simply been unable to overcome these barriers. The labour movement in the 1930s experimented with new strategies and models in order to mobilize millions of new industrial workers. The contemporary labour movement has not pursued low-wage service workers in the same aggressive manner. Without a strong labour and social movement presence, the uneven development of the service economy will continue to be an integral part of neoliberalism in Ontario – and everything in the new Ford government agenda reinforces this assessment.

This of course leaves us to consider what role the state can play in the political economy of the services. Despite the fall 2017 changes to labour law in Ontario under Bill 148, there are questions remaining about the state's willingness and ability to enforce labour laws restricting harassment and wage theft. Historically, the Ontario government has limited such enforcement mechanisms (Thomas 2009; Vosko and Thomas 2014). Radical social reform – let alone change – appears only in the distant horizon, but the state could provide a range of transferrable benefits that follow low-wage service workers throughout their careers, attaching benefits to workers rather than employers. Similarly, there have been calls for guaranteed incomes for low-wage service workers as opposed to wage increases. The state will also continue to be challenged as it downloads investments in "knowledge workers" to individuals (in the form of higher tuition fees and student loans). If the service economy is truly dependent on knowledge workers, governments will be pressured by capital to maintain a supply of educated service workers. At the same time, issues of access to high-skilled jobs in the public sector and recognition of foreign training and discrimination will have to be addressed.

What is clearly needed is a comprehensive and coherent service sector development strategy for Ontario that addresses a range of training and sector support needs. A vision for the sector, beyond low-wage consumer services attached to mega-events and mega-casinos and wishful thinking for "creative" investments, will be necessary. Unfortunately, there is little in terms of industrial strategy for even Ontario's manufacturing economy, the presumed economic base of the province.

Absent effective regulation and policy, the geography of Ontario's service economy will continue to develop unevenly, and marginalize women, young people, and racialized workers. Large cities in the GTHA will continue to expand their service economies, and the metropolitan concentration of wealth and employment will challenge smaller cities in other parts of the province. Yet there will also be uneven growth within large centres as service employment shifts between the gentrified downtown core and emerging suburbs, with some groups remaining excluded from more secure service jobs, especially in public services. Labour unions, community groups, and more interventionist governments (at all levels) will be required – and the new Ford government only makes this more challenging – to reshape Ontario's service economy into a more sustainable and just economic landscape.

The changes to Labour Law are extremely hard due to the processing by gov't / because off recent gov't this was not possible. Ford has made it Restrictive. To progress in this sector of law.

REFERENCES

Albo, Greg. 2010. "The 'New' Economy and Capitalism Today." In *Interrogating Work in the New Economy: Restructuring Work in the 21st Century*, edited by Norene Pupo and Mark Thomas. Toronto: University of Toronto Press.

Armstrong, Pat, and Hugh Armstrong. 2001. "Women, Privatization and Health Care Reform: The Ontario Case." In *Exposing Privatization: Women and Health Care Reform in Canada*, edited by Pat Armstrong, Carol Amaratunga, Jocelyne Bernier, Karen R. Grant, Ann Pederson, and Kay Willson. Toronto: Garamond.

Baumol, William. 2001. "Paradox of the Services: Exploding Costs, Persistent Demand." In *The Growth of Service Industries: The Paradox of Exploding Costs and Persistent Demand*, edited by Thijs ten Raa and Ronald Schettkat. Cheltenham: Edward Elgar.

Bell, Daniel. 1973. *The Coming of Post-Industrial Society: A Venture in Social Forecasting*. New York: Basic Books.

Blackwell, Richard. 2011. "Ontario Opens to the Door to Private Partnerships." *Globe and Mail*, 29 March.

Brooks, Chris, and Kim Moody. 2016. "Interview with Kim Moody: Busting the Myths of a Workerless Future." *Labour Notes*, 26 July.

Camfield, David. 2011. *Canadian Labour in Crisis: Reinventing the Workers' Movement*. Halifax: Fernwood.

Castells, Manuel. 2000. *The Rise of the Network Society*. 2nd ed. Malden, MA: Blackwell.

Charney, Igal. 2005a. "Property Developers and the Robust Downtown: The Case of Four Major Canadian Downtown." *Canadian Geographer* 49 (3).

– 2005b. "Re-examining Suburban Dispersal: Evidence from Suburban Toronto." *Journal of Urban Affairs* 27 (5).

Clark, Colin. 1940. *The Conditions of Economic Progress*. London: MacMillan.

Coffey, William. 1996. "The Role and Location of Services in the Canadian Space Economy." In *Canada and the Global Economy: The Geography of Structural and Technological Change*, edited by John Britton. Montreal: McGill-Queen's University Press.

– 2001. "The Geography of Producer Services." *Urban Geography* 21 (2).

Cotton, Barry, and Jean-Charles Cachon. 2007. "Resisting the Giants: Small Retail Entrepreneurs vs. Mega-Retailers; An Empirical Study." *Journal of Small Business and Entrepreneurship* 20 (2).

Courchene, Tom. 2001. *State of Minds: Toward a Human Capital Future for Canadians*. Montreal: IRRP.

Doellgast, Virginia. 2012. *Disintegrating Democracy at Work: Labor Unions and the Future of Good Jobs in the Service Economy*. Ithaca, NY: Cornell University Press.

Economic Council of Canada. 1990. *Good Jobs, Bad Jobs: Employment in the Service Economy*. Ottawa: Ministry of Supply and Services.

Fanelli, Carlo. 2016. *Megacity Malaise: Neoliberalism, Public Services and Labour in Toronto*. Halifax: Fernwood.

Florida, Richard. 2002. *The Rise of the Creative Class: And How It's Transforming Work, Leisure, Community, and Everyday Life*. New York: Basic Books.

– 2017. *The New Urban Crisis: How Our Cities Are Increasing Inequality, Deepening Segregation, and Failing the Middle Class and What We Can Do About It*. New York: Basic Books.

Fourastié, Jean. 1949. *Le Grand Espoir du XXe Siècle*. Paris: Presses Universitaires de France.

Fuchs, Victor. 1968. *The Service Economy*. New York: Colombia University Press.

Gray, Mia. 2004. "The Social Construction of the Service Sector: Institutional Structures and Labour Market Outcomes." *Geoforum* 35 (1).

Greenhouse, Steven. 2009. *The Big Squeeze: Tough Times for the American Worker*. New York: Anchor Books.

Hardt, Michael, and Antonio Negri. 2009. *Commonwealth*. Cambridge: Harvard University Press.

Hayter, Roger, and Jerry Patchell. 2010. *Economic Geography: An Institutional Approach*. Toronto: Oxford University Press.

Henwood, Doug. 2003. *After the New Economy*. New York: New Press.

Hernandez, Tony, and Jim Simmons. 2006. "Evolving Retail Landscapes: Power Retail in Canada." *Canadian Geographer* 50 (4).

Howlett, Karen. 2011. "All Spending Up for Review as Ontario Grapples with Deficit." *Globe and Mail*. 30 March.

Huws, Ursula, Neil Spencer, Dag Syrdal, and Kaire Holts. 2017. *Work in the European Gig Economy: Employment in the Era of Online Platforms; Research Results from the UK, Sweden, Germany, Austria, the Netherlands, Switerland and Italy*. Brussels: FEPS.

Jacobs, Jane. 1961. *The Death and Life of Great American Cities*. New York: Random House.

Jones, Kenneth, and Michael Doucet. 2001. "The Big Box, the Flagship, and Beyond: Impacts and Trends in the Greater Toronto Area." *Canadian Geographer* 45 (4).

Keil, Roger. 2017. *Suburban Planet: Making the World Urban from the Outside In*. London: Wiley.

Kipfer, Stefan, and Roger Keil. 2002. "Toronto Inc? Planning the Competitive City in the New Toronto." *Antipode* 34 (2).

Lehrer, Ute, and Thorben Wieditz. 2009. "Gentrification and the Loss of Employment Lands: Toronto's Studio District." *Critical Planning* 16.

Lenskyj, Helen. 2000. *Inside the Olympic Industry: Power, Politics, and Activism*. New York: State University of New York Press.

Martin, Ron, and Richard Florida. 2009. *Ontario in the Creative Age*. Toronto: Martin Prosperity Institute.

OLG. 2012. *Modernizing Lottery and Gaming in Ontario: Strategic Business Review.* Toronto: OLG.

OPSEU. 2009. *Mt. Albert Wants a Real LCBO Briefing Book.* Toronto: OPSEU.

Panitch, Leo, and Donald Swartz. 2003. *From Consent to Coercion: The Assault on Trade Union Freedoms.* 3rd ed. Toronto: Garamond.

Peck, Jamie. 2005. "Struggling with the Creative Class." *International Journal of Urban and Regional Research* 29.

Potter, Andrew. 2009. "What Would You Pay for a Map with No Roads? For $2.2 Million, Richard Florida and Roger Martin Tell Us Creativity is a Limitless Resource." *Maclean's.* 19 February.

Pupo, Norene, and Mark Thomas. 2010. "Work in the New Economy: Critical Reflections." In *Interrogating Work in the New Economy: Restructuring Work in the 21st Century*, edited by Norene Pupo and Mark Thomas. Toronto: University of Toronto Press.

Reich, Robert. 1992. *The Work of Nations: Preparing Ourselves for 21st Century Capitalism.* New York: Knopf.

Sayer, Andrew, and Richard Walker. 1992. *The New Social Economy: Reworking the Division of Labour.* Oxford: Basil Blackwell.

Schettkat, Ronald, and Lara Yocarini. 2003. *The Shift to Services: A Review of the Literature.* IZA Discussion Paper N. 964. Bonn: IZA.

Shearmur, Richard, and William Coffey. 2002. "A Tale of Four Cities: Intrametropolitan Employment Distribution in Toronto, Montreal, Vancouver, and Ottawa-Hull, 1981–1996." *Environment and Planning A* 34 (4).

Statistics Canada. 2006. *Census of Population.* Catalogue no. 97-564-XCB2006006.

– 2016a. *Census of Population.* Catalogue no. 98-400-X2016092.

– 2016b. *Census of Population.* Catalogue no. 98-400-X2016290.

– 2017a. *Gross Domestic Product (GDP) at Basic Prices, by North American Industry Classification System (NAICS), Provinces and Territories, Annual (Dollars).* CANSIM table 379-0030.

– 2017b. *Labour Force Survey Estimates (LFS), by North American Industry Classification System (NAICS).* CANSIM table 282-0008.

– 2017c. *Census Profiles. 2016 Census of Population.* Catalogue no. 98-316-X2016001. Ottawa. Released 29 November 2017.

– 2017d. *Labour Force Survey Estimates (LFS), Employees by Union Coverage, North American Industry Classification System (NAICS), Sex and Age Group, Annual (Persons).* CANSIM tables 282-0078 and 282-0072.

Stout, John, and Jo-Anne Pickel. 2007. "Wal-Mart Waltz in Canada: Two Steps Forward, One Step Back." *The Connecticut Law Review* 39 (4).

Tattersall, Amanda. 2010. *Power in a Coalition: Strategies for Strong Unions and Social Change.* Ithaca, NY: ILR Press.

Thomas, Mark. 2009. *Regulating Flexibility: The Political Economy of Employment Standards*. Montreal: McGill-Queen's University Press.

Touraine, Alain. (1969) 1971. *The Post-Industrial Society*. New York: Random House.

Tufts, Steven. 2004. "Building the 'Competitive City': Labour and Toronto's Bid to Host the Olympic Game." *Geoforum* 35 (1).

– 2006. "'We Make it Work': The Cultural Transformation of Hotel Workers in the City." *Antipode* 38 (2).

– 2007. "Emerging Labour Strategies in Toronto's Hotel Sector: Toward a Spatial Circuit of Union Renewal." *Environment and Planning A* 39 (10).

– 2017a. "Organized Labor and Casino Politics in Toronto." In *Unions and the City: Negotiating Urban Change*, edited by Ian MacDonald, 53–73. Ithaca, NY: ILR Press.

– 2017b. "Unions and the Gig-Economy: The Case of AirBnB." *The Bullet*, 7 November. https://socialistproject.ca.

Wallace, Ian. 2002. *A Geography of the Canadian Economy*. Toronto: Oxford University Press.

Wieditz, Thorben. 2017a. *Squeezed Out: Airbnb's Commercialization of Home-Sharing in Toronto*. Toronto: Fairbnb.

– 2017b. "Film Unions' Struggle to Defend Studio Space in Toronto." In *Unions and the City: Negotiating Urban Change*, edited by Ian MacDonald. Ithaca, NY: ILR Press.

Wolfe, Martin. 1955. "The Concept of Economic Sectors." *The Quarterly Journal of Economics* 69 (3).

Vosko, Leah, and Mark Thomas. 2014. "Confronting the Employment Standards Enforcement Gap: Exploring the Potential for Union Engagement with Employment Law in Ontario." *Journal of Industrial Relations* 56 (5).

| 4 |

A Neoliberal Pause?
The Auto and Manufacturing Sectors in Ontario since Free Trade

DIMITRY ANASTAKIS

How times have changed. Once the undisputed economic engine of Canada, Ontario's manufacturing sector – especially its auto industry – has faced a dramatic decline since the turn of the century, and especially since 2010. An aptly titled 1985 overview of the postwar economy, *The Prosperous Years,* centred on Ontario's "pre-eminence as the major manufacturing province," and its role in making Ontario the wealthiest region in the country (Rea 1985, 197). The text encapsulated what could be seen as the swaggering arrogance and privileged position of Ontario, an assessment that was echoed by other works on the province and its place in Confederation (Baskerville 2005; Piva 1988; Bothwell 1999). After all, the status of "Empire Ontario" spawned generations of seething regional resentment. For decades, the tariff, the banks, Massey-Ferguson, Eaton's, the National Energy Policy, the media, and a host of other symbols were fodder for grievances real and imagined from the Atlantic to the Pacific, many of them tied to Ottawa's preferential treatment of the province's pampered manufacturing sector.[1]

The swagger, it seems, is no more. By the close of the first decade of the twenty-first century, Ontario had fallen from its pedestal, and in manufacturing, the news was particularly devastating. In the key auto sector, the Big Three of Ford, General Motors (GM), and Chrysler all closed plants in the province even before the great recession and auto sector meltdown of 2009, which saw the bankruptcy of the latter two firms, and their subsequent re-emergence as entities owned by the United States, Canadian, and Ontario governments. In the assembly and parts sector, the workforce was cut from more than 150,000 employees in 2006 to less than 100,000 by 2010. Other sectors were hit just as hard, with a number of high-profile departures that indicated a deeper malaise. Steel giants Stelco and Dofasco were sold or shuttered. Farm implements maker John Deere shut its factory and left the province. After a nasty labour dispute, Caterpillar shuttered its London factory. Firestone closed its Woodstock plant, while General Electric in Peterborough, the city's main employer for nearly a century, announced that by 2018, it would close; at its peak, the plant had employed 6,000 workers. All told, nearly 300,000 manufacturing jobs disappeared in Canada between 2005 and 2009 alone, the vast majority in Ontario (Viera 2009; Statistics Canada 2010). What happened? And what role did public policies towards manufacturing play in this decline?

DEINDUSTRIALIZATION AND ONTARIO MANUFACTURING

Deindustrialization is, of course, neither a new nor solely an Ontario phenomenon, and a lively academic debate has emerged over the causes of the emergence of North America's "rust belt" since the 1970s and 1980s. Unsurprisingly, given the greater impact of deindustrialization upon the United States in the postwar period, American scholars have led the way in this examination, and the first wave of deindustrialization literature largely focused on responses to plant shut-downs and the impact of factory closings upon communities (Bluestone and Harrison 1982; Dudley 1994; Mellon 2002) – and later upon industrial policy or its failure (Reich and Donahue 1986; Podgursky 1984). Initially, traditional Canadian political economy views of deindustrialization, such as those of Robert Laxer (1973) and Daniel Drache (1989), pointed to what they saw as Canada's dependent economic status to explain the decline of Canadian manufacturing. Since Canadian branch-plant firms were dependent upon their American parent companies, when the economy took a downturn in the home market, Canadian firms bore the brunt of downsizing and plant closures to help the multinational (US) firms' bottom line.

More recent assessments have challenged these classic Canadian interpretations of deindustrialization, and questioned even whether

Canada, especially Ontario's "Golden Horseshoe" region, experienced the type of widespread factory closings and decline of manufacturing that was prevalent in the US manufacturing heartland in the Midwest. In tackling the traditional dependency approach, sociologist Michael Del Balso (1997) argued that Canada did not, in fact, deindustrialize in the postwar period, and if anything, "Canada's manufacturing base ha[d] generally grown" before 1995. Historian Steven High (2003) has also argued that in the first great wave of deindustrialization that spread across North America, Canada was largely spared because nationalist workers and their unions effectively challenged governments to force companies to provide notification, and fought closures through collective action. Though these assessments challenged the very debatable notion of widespread deindustrialization in the period before the 1989 Free Trade Agreement, there is no question that since 2000, the manufacturing sector in Canada, and especially Ontario, has declined.

To a large degree, since the 1970s the overall decline in the North American manufacturing sector, and especially in employment within that sector, has been driven by productivity increases, the embrace of automation in manufacturing, and offshore competition from newly industrialized nations such as Japan, South Korea, and later China. Increased efficiency through innovative production systems, computerization, and robotics have made production processes increasingly lean (Womack, Jones, and Roos, 1991). But deindustrialization can also be seen as a consequence of neoliberal policies practised in North America since the 1970s, especially in Ontario, where manufacturing was underpinned by public policies such as the protectionist 1879 National Policy, and then the integrationist managed trade regime of the 1965 Canada-US Automotive Products Trade Agreement (auto pact). The auto pact required the auto makers to maintain production floors in Canada (to build as many vehicles as they sold, and include a certain amount of Canadian content in those vehicles), in exchange for intrafirm duty-free trade across the Canada-US border. As a result, after 1965 the Big Three auto manufacturers integrated their Canadian plants into their North American production, so that Canadian plants that once produced cars only for the Canadian market now produced for all of North America. The emergence after 1973 of neoliberal tenets, such as an embrace of free trade, deregulation, anti-union measures, and a willingness to turn away from these interventionist industrial policies, hastened the deindustrialization of both the United States and Canada, and in the latter case, especially the deindustrialization of Ontario, the manufacturing heartland of the country since Confederation.

This chapter charts the evolution of the political economy of manufacturing in Ontario, focusing on the auto sector, and examines the impact and discourse surrounding provincial and federal government policies from the 1990s to the present day. Since the 1989 Canada-US Free Trade Agreement, manufacturing has been a story of economic integration, the continued threat of deindustrialization, and a sharp debate over the merits of state intervention, at least from the provincial perspective. Overall, federal and provincial trade and fiscal policies towards manufacturing in this period have maintained a laissez-faire, neoliberal approach, one committed to lower corporate taxes, an emphasis upon free trade and tariff removal, and a relatively unfriendly stance towards trade unions.[2]

Yet, surprisingly, when it comes to the province's flagship auto industry, aside from the Mike Harris government, Queen's Park and Ottawa – both Liberal and Conservative governments in the latter case – have, in fact, been largely consistent in maintaining an interventionist approach, one that reflects a pause in an otherwise neoliberal agenda. Indeed, when it comes to auto manufacturing, notwithstanding the Harris interregnum, governments have shown a willingness to provide extensive fiscal support for the sector, exemplified by the 2009 Ontario-Canada bailout of the auto industry led by the avowedly small-government Conservative administration of Stephen Harper. This willingness to utilize interventionist public policy and particularly investment incentives to maintain production reflects a long-standing approach to manufacturing, and especially to the auto industry. In Ontario, public policy has shaped the fate of this keystone industrial sector, more so than automation or production processes, or other market factors such as exchange rates or market presence. However, the price for such direct financial support was steep concessions from the unionized workforce in the auto sector, and a continued adherence to liberalized trade regimes.

This chapter first provides a brief background to manufacturing in Ontario, from the 1980s to today. As the largest industrial sector in the country, manufacturing in Ontario was economically integrated with that of the United States since long before the FTA, owing to the 1965 auto pact (formally the Automotive Products and Trade Agreement). Motor vehicle parts and production (assembly), along with numerous supporting industries such as steel, plastics, and tool and die, have been the predominant element of the Ontario manufacturing sector for decades. The automotive sector and its supporting industries have been the largest single category of employment during this period. Concentrated in southern and southwestern parts of Ontario, this largely unionized workforce has been a key political actor, both federally and provincially (Anastakis 2005; Gindin 1995; Holmes 1990; Yates 1993).

Second, the chapter traces state policies towards the sector in this period, focusing first on provincial approaches, then federal, both within the context of a continentally integrated manufacturing sector. Within the North American industry, state intervention in the form of incentives to lure investment has been the norm since the 1970s. The Progressive Conservative government of Mike Harris was deeply averse to such practices, however, and during its time in office shunned any subsidization policy. As a result, no new plant investment occurred in Ontario in this period, while significant investment was established elsewhere in North America. Nonetheless, Ontario's sector benefitted from a boom in US auto sales from the mid-1990s until the early 2000s. A downturn in the sector's fortunes coincided with the election of Liberal Dalton McGuinty, who had been strongly supportive of spending provincial funds to draw investment and support manufacturing (especially in the auto sector), as was his Liberal successor, Kathleen Wynne.

Federally, both Liberal and Conservative governments have been supportive of auto manufacturing, which is a reflection of the changing political fortunes of these parties within the province, but which has also been influenced by the ongoing support for interventionist policies by labour's traditional ally, the New Democratic Party (NDP). Key electoral battlegrounds in traditional manufacturing locales – Windsor, London, Waterloo, Cambridge, St Catharines, in and around Hamilton, and in the pivotal "905" belt ringing the Greater Toronto Area (especially in auto-producing towns such as Oakville and Oshawa) – have resulted in a largely non-partisan approach to supporting these industries. The willingness of the Canadian Auto Workers union to officially untie itself from the NDP and support the Paul Martin-led federal Liberal Party after 2003 is a further reflection of the political volatility of the sector.

Federal Liberal governments under Jean Chrétien and Martin provided significant support to the auto sector after 2000. In 2002 the Chrétien government was instrumental in the creation of the Canadian Automotive Partnership Council (CAPC), and starting in 2003 the new Paul Martin government provided support in a number of automotive assembly investments in Ontario and promised $500 million in support of the industry (Whittington 2004). Since 2005, and especially during the continental crisis in the auto sector starting in 2008, the Conservative government of Stephen Harper had also been supportive of the sector, providing direct and indirect support, and working with the provincial Liberals to do so. This support reflected a policy evolution for Conservatives in Ottawa, given the strong contingent of former provincial Progressive Conservative members from the Harris era in key positions in the Harper government, and Harper's own personal and political attitudes towards state intervention in specific sectors.

Finally, the chapter will examine the implications of this evolving manufacturing dynamic. Ontario's emergence as a largely service sector-oriented economy has resulted in some conflict over the policies and expenditures of massive amounts of public monies towards what many have concluded are dying manufacturing industries. Much of this discourse has taken on a class-based tinge, one which pits white-collar or service workers against blue-collar and unionized labourers. The relative decline of manufacturing (and especially automotive) has challenged the traditional elements of left-wing power in Ontario: unions, the NDP, and blue-collar workers. One need look no further than Oshawa, a traditional NDP stronghold from the 1960s to the 1980s which was then captured by Conservatives in the 1990s and 2000s, including by former Conservative federal finance minister Jim Flaherty, and provincial Progressive Conservative (and Flaherty's spouse) Christine Elliot.

This cleavage over auto/manufacturing support has also taken on geographical dimensions: support for manufacturing in the Golden Horseshoe remains strong, but less so in Northern Ontario, where there is an emphasis upon resource extraction and newer environmentally friendly industries. The chapter will conclude by examining one more divide: that between Ontario and the rest of the country over federal support for its manufacturing and auto industries. The 2009 auto bailout sparked a rhetorical backlash against Ontario's auto sector, one which reflected a legacy of regional grievances towards the province and its industrial status within Confederation. These grievances have lingered into the Wynne period, despite efforts by the federal government under Justin Trudeau to support the oil sector and spread an industrial policy of high-tech "super-clusters" across the country.

RIDING THE ROLLER COASTER: ONTARIO MANUFACTURING SINCE 1985

Protected for more than a century by both a long-standing federal "national policy" tariff regime and an Ontario policy referred to as the "manufacturing condition," the province's industrial sector flourished for decades. In particular, the Golden Horseshoe area around western Lake Ontario boasted diverse and prosperous manufacturing sectors. Along with auto, industries such as steel, plastics and textiles, pulp and paper, telecommunications equipment, consumer items, machinery, and tobacco processing made Ontario's industrial economy dominant in Canada. Until the 1970s, much of this production flowed east and west to other Canadian provinces, yet in some important sectors such as auto, where a continentalized industry was governed by the managed-trade auto pact regime, the flow was north-south. By the late 1970s and early 1980s, American protectionist impulses, economic malaise, and productivity worries prompted federal policymakers – both Liberal and Progressive Conservative – to push for new economic policies (Hart 2003; Inwood 2005).

The enactment of the Canada-US Free Trade Agreement in 1989 by the federal government of Brian Mulroney marked a sea change for Ontario's manufacturing sector. The provincial government under Liberal David Peterson, the labour movement under Canadian Auto Workers (CAW) leader Bob White, and a number of other economic groups challenged this policy change, but ultimately lost. While the agreement did not fundamentally alter the tariff-free status of Ontario's largest export (and import) sectors, namely automobiles and automotive parts, it did sow the seeds for the auto pact's eventual demise (Anastakis 2013). Meanwhile, free trade unquestionably liberalized many aspects of the Canadian economy, accelerated its integration with the US economy, and coincided with an economic downturn that particularly affected Ontario. In the early 1990s, as the province struggled with the readjustment of free trade, currency fluctuations, and renewed competition, Ontario faced sustained economic difficulties. Goods production shrank from the 1980s to the 1990s as an overall component of Ontario's economy (Ontario 2010, 33). High-profile factory closures, such as the Inglis plant in downtown Toronto, indicated that the worst fears about free trade were coming true and that deindustrialization loomed (Sobel and Meurer 2004).

Yet, by the latter part of the decade, Ontario's industrial sector seemed to have righted itself, largely on the back of a revitalized auto sector. The declining value of the Canadian dollar had a tremendous impact by boosting exports, which were fuelled by massive spending in the US consumables and automotive sectors that were in turn powered by increased lending (including to subprime borrowers) due to historically low interest rates. By 2000, the American ownership ratio for the driving population was 92 per cent (the comparable figure for Canada was 65 per cent), and during the period between 2000 and 2007 North American annual auto sales averaged over 16 million vehicles per year, consistently exceeding previous decades' highest sales.[3]

By the early 2000s, Ontario's auto sector was gigantic, benefitting from the boom in American sales: approximately four-fifths of the province's production flowed southward because of the integration of the industry since the auto pact. In 1999, Canadian plants accounted for one-fifth of the 15 million vehicles produced in North America, or over 3 million vehicles (see figure 4.1). By 2005, Canada was still in the top ten of global producers, with Ontario surpassing Michigan as the largest single auto manufacturing jurisdiction in North America. The province consistently built over 2 million vehicles per year in the period between 2000 and 2008. Moreover, federal and provincial policies in the 1970s and 1980s, which had encouraged offshore foreign direct investment, had led to a diversification of the province's assembly sector, with Toyota and Honda setting up plants in Ontario (Mordue 2007).

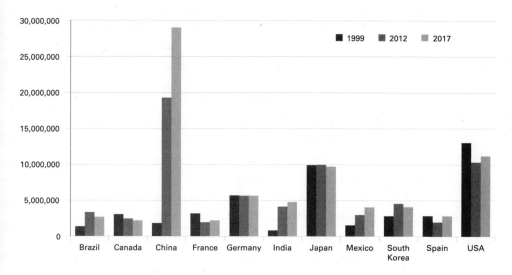

Figure 4.1 | Car and commercial vehicle production in ten nations, 1999, 2012, and 2017 (*Source*: Organisation Internationale des Constructeurs d'Automobiles [2016])

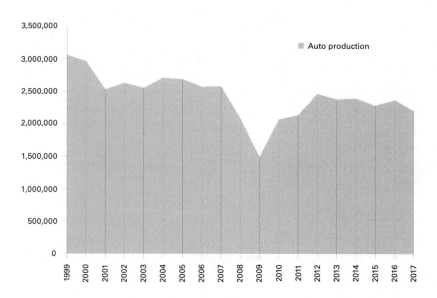

Figure 4.2 | Canadian car and commercial vehicle production, 1999–2017 (*Source*: Organisation Internationale des Constructeurs d'Automobiles [2016])

The bulk of the industry, however, remained tied to the fortunes of the Big Three of GM, Ford, and Chrysler, which dominated the sector.

The direct impact of this automotive boom on other sectors such as steel, plastics, and the parts industry was significant. Magna, headquartered in Aurora, Ontario and Canada's leading auto parts manufacturer, became one of the largest suppliers in the world. Other Ontario parts makers, such as Wescast and Linamar, flourished. The concentration of auto assemblers and parts makers along Highway 401 made southern Ontario one of the most important global auto production clusters (Holmes et al. 2003). Employment boomed as well, as the province's auto sector employment peaked at over 150,000. According to General Motors (2009), by the mid-2000s nearly one in seven jobs in the Canadian economy was tied to the auto industry, versus one in ten in the United States.

What goes up must come down. The successes of the auto sector obscured the ongoing decline of manufacturing overall since 2001, and made the seemingly sudden decline in the auto industry itself, which accelerated after 2008, even more painful. The auto sector's apparent success from the late 1990s to the early 2000s masked a steady erosion of manufacturing in Ontario. Between 2002 and 2008 – even before the sharp cyclical downturn in the auto sector and the recession of 2008 began – manufacturing employment in Ontario had already declined from 18.1 per cent of the province's workers to 13.5 per cent (Ontario 2009, 8). Put another way, in the six years between 2004 and 2011, the number of manufacturing jobs in the province declined from 1.1 million to 781,000. The increase in the value of the Canadian dollar, a slowing US economy, offshore and Mexican competition from lower-waged producers (itself a product of the 1993 North American Free Trade Agreement), and a lack of investment by Canadian manufacturers in new plant and equipment, were all part of this decline. By 2011, industrial sectors such as wood, paper and textiles, food processing, clothing, and rubber and plastics all lost jobs, as Canadian factories closed at twice the rate of those in the United States (Tencer 2013).

In the case of the auto sector itself, a number of factors played a role. As Ontario's auto factories were largely dependent upon the US market (nearly 80 per cent of Canadian vehicles were shipped south), the cyclical downturn in the US car market affected the Canadian assemblers and parts makers significantly. Moreover, GM's decision to introduce "0 per cent" financing in the wake of the terrorist attacks of September 11, 2001, created an unusual car-buying boom that exacerbated the cyclical decline in US consumer demand for autos after 2005 – itself a symptom of economic recession and a well-documented credit crunch. Ongoing issues for US car makers – the quality of their vehicles, their dependency upon large vehicles for profit in the face of rising oil prices, and increased competition of offshore producers – further challenged their ability to remain profitable when consumer demand took a downturn. Another factor in demand was the increased quality and longevity of automobiles themselves, allowing consumers to delay auto purchases longer than usual after the downturn came. Thus, despite technological advances and greater automation which increased productivity and lowered employment, and an outsourcing of assembly jobs to parts makers who specialized in "modularization" (building whole components for the automakers that were shipped to the assembly plants), the Big Three automakers faced increasing challenges.

Policy issues and external factors also clearly played a role. The auto pact's 2001 demise at the World Trade Organization, prompted by Japanese and European complaints over the agreement's protectionist measures, meant that assemblers in Canada were no longer mandated to build as many cars as Canadian consumers purchased, removing a long-standing floor for Canadian production (Anastakis, 2001). As gas prices increased in the mid-2000s, there was a decline in consumer demand for some of the larger vehicle types produced by Canadian factories. Perhaps most significantly, as foreign investors drove up the value of the Canadian dollar by spending billions on Canadian oil and gas ventures in western Canada, the higher value of the dollar made building cars in Canada more costly and thus less desirable. In response to the rising value of the dollar, auto assemblers and parts makers shifted their production to less costly locales, causing plant closures in Ontario. This "Dutch disease" – the phenomenon of an overvalued currency from exports and an influx in foreign investment in one sector causing a decline in another – made Canadian production costs far less competitive than they had been in the 1970s, 1980s, and later 1990s, directly affecting manufacturing employment.

Table 4.1 | Decade of decline: Ontario automotive plant closures, 2001–13

Year	Company/site	Jobs
2001	Chrysler/Bramalea (cut third shift), and Windsor (reduced shift speed at Windsor, cut Pillette second shift)	3,000
2001	Chrysler/Woodstock (Thomas Built Truck), and Kelowna, BC (cut Western Star)	1,000
2002	Ford/Oakville (closed Ontario Truck Plant)	1,500
2002	GM/St Catharines (cut parts production)	900
2003	Chrysler/Windsor (closed Pillette Road plant)	1,200
2003	Navistar/Chatham (closed truck plant)	1,000
2004	Western Star/St Thomas (closed truck plant)	1,000
2008	GM/Oshawa (closed Plant no. 1)	2,600
2008	GM/Oshawa (cut shift at Plant no. 2)	1,000
2009	GM/Oshawa (closed truck plant)	2,700
2010	GM/Windsor (closed transmission facility)	1,400
2011	Ford/St Thomas (closed assembly plant)	1,000
2013	GM/Oshawa (closed assembly line)	2,000
TOTAL		20,300

Sources: Data gathered by author from government reports, *Globe and Mail*, and CAW (2002).

One study found that "63 percent of the manufacturing employment loss due to exchange rate development between 2002 and 2007 are related to a Dutch disease phenomenon" (Beine, Bos, and Coulombe 2009, 1). As a result, in the decade between 2001 and 2011, Ontario auto production faced a severe shake-out, one largely centred on the once-dominant Big Three producers who traditionally underpinned the Ontario sector. More than a dozen plants were shuttered entirely or faced reduced capacity utilization in this period (table 4.1). Total assembly jobs, which had peaked at over 57,000 positions in 1999, dropped to 36,000 by 2010. Many of these high-paying assembly jobs represented a number of additional jobs in the value-added automotive production chain, such as parts makers, tool and die, and moulding positions. For example, GM Canada noted that it purchased $14 billion in parts from Canadian suppliers in 2007, providing a significant source of Canadian employment in the secondary manufacturing sector, one that was to a significant degree Canadian-owned (2009, 25). Indeed, in the parts

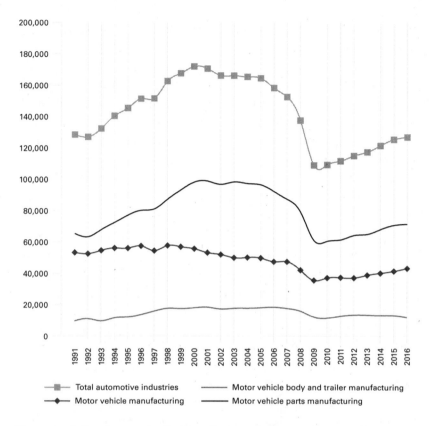

Figure 4.3 | Employment in the Canadian auto industry, 1991–2016 (*Source*: Statistics Canada (2018), CANSIM table 281-0024 for 1991–2012, CANSIM table 301-0008 for 2013–16)

sector, employment peaked in 2001 at just over 100,000 jobs, dropping to 58,000 in 2010 (DesRosiers, 2010). Overall, manufacturing employment declined from more than 1.1 million jobs in 2004 to less than 900,000 in 2008. Amazingly, Ontario's manufacturing job losses accounted for nearly two-thirds of all Canadian job losses between 2004 and 2009 (Ontario 2009, table 4; Sweeney and Mordue, 2017). The sector boasted fourteen auto assembly plants in 2001: three GM, three Ford, three Chrysler, two Toyota, two Honda, and one GM-Suzuki (known as CAMI). By 2017, that figure was reduced to eleven: three GM, one Ford, two Chrysler, three Toyota, and two Honda, even with the 2008 addition of the Toyota Woodstock plant. Further assembly line consolidations at GM's Oshawa facility after 2013 reduced the sector's assembly output even more.

The Big Three restructuring also had a severe impact on parts makers. As assemblers squeezed their suppliers in order to reduce their own costs, margins became even thinner at the parts manufacturers. Canadian parts companies and US subsidiaries such as A.G. Simpson, Alloy Wheels, Johnson Controls, and Oxford Automotive, to name only a few, either laid off workers or faced bankruptcy. The decline in the parts sector even hurt giants such as Magna, Wescast, and Linamar, though these companies have managed to maintain their operations largely by downsizing and shifting some of their production to lower-cost jurisdictions like Mexico. Some, like Linamar, have tried to diversify away from reliance on the auto sector. Between 2005 and 2013, nearly 200 parts plants closed in Canada (Sweeney and Mordue 2017, S7).

St Thomas, Ontario, is a good example of the impact of this overall automotive decline. Once a railway centre, over the course of the twentieth century the town became a manufacturing powerhouse, in large part due to the auto pact. Lower costs (owing to a cheaper dollar and government-covered health care), location, and an excellent workforce also drew Ford and other manufacturers to St Thomas. Ford's facility in the city (officially referred to as Talbotville) built most of the "fleet" vehicles (taxi cabs and police cars) used on North American roads in the 1990s and early 2000s. But by the mid-2000s, the demise of the auto pact and the slowdown in the sector wrought devastation in the town's manufacturing sector. In 2004, Sterling Trucks closed its facility, with a loss of 1,400 jobs. In 2011, Ford closed its assembly facility (built in 1967 to meet auto pact requirements), resulting in another 1,000 direct jobs lost, with thousands of others along the supply and support chains also gone (Keenan 2011).

Of course, the most high-profile incident reflecting the troubles of the auto sector remains the government bailout and takeover of General Motors and Chrysler in 2009. In the context of an Obama administration that had already indicated its willingness to provide bailout funding for troubled financial services companies, the US government's decision to support the restructuring of these two iconic American companies is not surprising. Nor was the Dalton McGuinty government's decision to provide financial assistance to both companies, given the province's long-standing dependence on the auto industry: the economic consequences of a significant reduction in Big Three production would be devastating (Centre for Spatial Economics 2008). Even with towns like St Thomas facing devastation as plants closed, Ontario was determined to play a role in any support that went to the sector. More surprising, however, was the decision by Ottawa to throw its financial support behind the bailout plan. How could it be that a Conservative government in Ottawa under Stephen Harper's leadership could do this, given the ideological aversion to government support of the auto sector, and the strong representation of Mike Harris Conservatives in Harper's Cabinet?

POLICY PATHS IN AUTO MANUFACTURING

From the 1970s onwards, Ontario governments largely supported manufacturing, and explicitly supported the auto pact trade regime that underlay the auto sector. Even during the tumultuous economic and political changes from the late 1970s to the early 1990s – when the province faced dramatic political upheavals, including the transition from the Progressive Conservatives to the Liberals to the NDP between 1980 and 1995 – Queen's Park remained consistent in its support of industry, and the auto pact, no matter the government's political stripe.

Moreover, since the 1970s all provincial governments have provided financial incentives for auto firms to establish new "greenfield" plants and maintain existing operations in the province – a consequence of fear over the loss of new investment by the Big Three, and an effort to attract foreign "transplant" firms. The Progressive Conservative government of Bill Davis worked with the federal Liberal government of Pierre Trudeau to offer the Ford Motor Company a $68 million investment incentive to build a new engine plant in Windsor in 1978. Incentive packages were also provided to Volkswagen (1985), Toyota (1986), and Suzuki (under the auspices of their joint venture with General Motors) at Ingersoll through Canadian Manufacturing Industries (CAMI) in 1987. Conservative, Liberal, and NDP provincial governments willingly granted direct cash and loans to auto assemblers and parts firms, both in the form of greenfield investment incentives and ongoing financial support to maintain production in Ontario, often working with either Liberal or Progressive Conservative administrations in Ottawa.[4]

The ascendency of the Harris Conservatives in 1995 marked a sharp neoliberal turn on a host of policy issues, including manufacturing policy. The neoliberal Harris regime willingly turned away from Ontario's traditional role within Confederation as an "honest broker" (Ibbitson 2002), one which also included, in the view of Courchene (1998), an economic "unhinging" of Ontario from the federation as it sought to maximize its own economic destiny regardless of the consequences for the rest of the country. Breaking with decades of Ontario practice, Harris and his economic development ministers were ideologically predisposed against any state intervention in manufacturing, even in the high-profile auto sector. This was particularly true of investment incentives for automotive firms. After Harris resigned in 2002, incentives remained *verboten* as a policy option.[5] When he lost the party leadership to Ernie Eves, Jim Flaherty was given the Economic Development and Trade portfolio, which housed the Automotive Office and had been a key playmaker in developing incentive packages for auto companies in the 1970s and 1980s. Flaherty promptly renamed it the Ministry of Enterprise, Opportunity and Innovation, emphasizing that the government was not in the "economic development" business. No financial incentives were offered to any potential investor in the auto sector during the 1995–2003 Conservative provincial government.

During the Harris-Eves regime, a number of what political scientist Maureen Molot (2005) has called "locational tournaments" occurred across North America, with various subnational governments competing for the automotive investment that the Ontario PCs eschewed. As Harris maintained his rigid ideological refusal to engage in investment incentives, conservative and Republican-controlled jurisdictions in the US, especially in the South, binged upon incentives to attract automotive investment. Much of this new investment was by non-Big Three companies. In fact, in the period roughly corresponding to the Harris government, Japanese and German companies established eight new facilities in the American South, investing nearly US$4.5 billion in the region. US jurisdictions – governed by either political stripe – showed

Table 4.2 | Automotive investment in the US, 1993–2002 (US$ millions)

Year	Company	Investment	Incentive	% of investment
1993	BMW, South Carolina	645	130	20.2
1993	Mercedes-Benz, Alabama	380	253	66.6
1997	Chrysler, Ohio	1,200	193	17.0
2000	Mercedes-Benz, Alabama	600	119	19.8
2000	Nissan, Mississippi	930	295	28.5
2000	Ford, Michigan	2,000	222	11.1
2000	GM, Michigan	1,000	284	28.5
2002	Hyundai, Alabama	1,000	253	25.3
2002	Nissan, Mississippi	760	68	8.9

Source: Moore School of Business (2002, 24).

considerable willingness to provide significant financial subsidies to the companies to lure their investment, at a pivotal post-NAFTA moment in auto sector restructuring (as table 4.2 indicates).

The result of these investments was a veritable "Detroit South" corridor of automotive production along the I-95 highway in the southeastern United States. With every new plant established, parts facilities inevitably followed, further building up the automotive industry infrastructure in the region. Meanwhile, although Ontario remained the second-most-productive automotive region in North America behind Michigan, it failed to secure a single greenfield auto assembly investment in the 1990s and early 2000s, a period that marked one of the greatest automotive investment booms in North American history. Throughout this period, Ontario's industry, including its parts industry, largely flourished, yet the province missed a number of opportunities for new assembly investment that would have further consolidated its prominence as an auto-building jurisdiction.

The election of Dalton McGuinty and the Liberals in 2003 marked a complete reversal of the Harris-era policies. In April 2004, McGuinty established a $500 million Ontario Automotive Investment Strategy fund to provide incentives for investment. A number of high-profile investments followed from a host of auto firms, including General Motors, Ford, and Toyota. Indeed, one of McGuinty's key achievements was a $125 million incentive to Toyota for a new $1.1 billion plant in

Woodstock, Ontario, the first new auto plant in Ontario since the 1980s. The factory opened in 2008, and expanded in 2010 to build electric vehicles – the first Canadian facility to do so. In 2006, *Foreign Direct Investment* magazine labelled McGuinty the "Personality of the Year" for bringing $7 billion in new automotive investment to Ontario in 2003–06 (Yates and Lewchuck, 2017).

Federal governments also largely supported the auto industry during this period, and bipartisanship in auto industry matters prevailed even in the 1980s. Liberal policies, such as maintaining the auto pact, bailing out Chrysler (the first time), providing incentives for foreign firms, and even engaging in provocative port slowdowns and quotas aimed at Japanese producers, were keenly followed by the Brian Mulroney Progressive Conservatives, though the province and Ottawa differed on the fate of the auto pact under the FTA. The Mulroney government also offered outright incentives to Hyundai (1988) and GM (in 1990, to maintain the company's Ste Therese, Quebec plant, itself a consequence of auto pact requirements), just as they provided support to the efforts to lure Japanese and German manufacturers to Ontario (Anastakis 2013). When the Liberals returned to power in Ottawa in 1993, they continued these policies, though they were hampered in any efforts to lure new investment by the recalcitrance of the Harris Conservatives at Queen's Park.

Notwithstanding the large contingent of Harris Conservatives that migrated to Ottawa and took up government positions after the federal Conservative victory in 2006, the Harper government continued to actively support the automotive sector. Harper – a committed neoliberal whose 1993 master's thesis, "The Political Business Cycle and Fiscal Policy in Canada," was a strident attack on Keynesian economic policy – was philosophically no interventionist. In 2008, his government commissioned a report, *Compete to Win* (Canada 2008), which espoused a number of neoliberal policies around competition, trade, investment, and productivity. Yet he oversaw the largest single expenditure in Canadian government history outside of wartime by acceding to the 2009 $14.4 billion rescue package worked out between Ontario and Ottawa (and Washington) to support GM and Chrysler, essentially two bankrupt firms. The bailout of the two giant companies, shared two-thirds by the federal government and one-third by Ontario, amounted to $10.6 billion for GM and $3.8 billion for Chrysler. In the case of GM, the governments received an approximately 12 per cent stake in the company in exchange for the mixture of loans and direct support. Loans to Chrysler resulted in a 2 per cent share of the company. Both companies have subsequently paid back portions of their loans, but a fair amount of the government support has yet to be recouped by taxpayers, especially in the case of GM, since most of the support was exchanged for equity in the firm. Though GM (and Chrysler even more so) has performed very well since 2010, the company's value did not increase to the point where selling the shares derived from the government's investment could pay back the support (Shiell and Somerville 2012). Eventually, when the government sold their remaining shares by 2015, taxpayers lost approximately $3.5 billion (Keenan 2015). Ford of Canada, which also faced a difficult period in 2007–09, did not ask for government assistance, as it had launched its own recovery efforts prior to the 2009 meltdown of the other two companies.

The Harper government's willingness to engage in this kind of *dirigisme*, a sharp contrast to the Harris regime in Ontario, reflects the significance of the auto sector to the Canadian and Ontario economies. That such apparently fierce political – and ideological – competitors as McGuinty's Liberals and the Harper/Harris Conservatives could agree on the terms of the bailout gives an indication of the significance of the industry to the province and the country, and to the political calculations of parties in both Ottawa and Toronto. Since McGuinty's dramatic departure from politics in 2013, and Harper's election loss in 2015, this dynamic continued even with the leadership of Liberals Kathleen Wynne in Ontario and Justin Trudeau in Ottawa.

Indeed, if anything, despite the ongoing difficulties in the auto sector and manufacturing more generally, both Liberal governments on Parliament Hill and at Queen's Park continued to enhance market-supporting interventionist policies. In 2016, the two governments also announced research and development initiatives to support General Motors's creation of an autonomous vehicle research centre in Oshawa, employing upwards of 1,000 engineers (General Motors 2016). Investment incentives have included programs at both the federal and provincial levels to provide direct financial support to maintain existing assembly facilities, and to support parts manufacture, where there is a strong Canadian-owned sector (Keenan and Curry 2016). For example, in 2018 the federal and Ontario governments announced a $100 million grant to Linimar, a Guelph-based manufacturer, to support the development of advanced manufacturing technologies (Blatchford 2016). This, in the face of continued uncertainty in the auto sector sparked by the anti-trade policies of the Trump administration in the United States, where core trade policies, such as the 1993 NAFTA, are threatened.

NEW DIRECTIONS: THE POLITICAL IMPLICATIONS OF THE ONTARIO AUTO SECTOR

The roller-coaster story of manufacturing in Ontario, and specifically that of auto assembly and parts manufacturing, has had a significant economic impact on the province. Yet despite the dramatic circumstances surrounding the industry, certain political patterns have emerged that point to an important and telling shift in the political landscape when it comes to the auto sector: one that indicates a willingness of political actors of all stripes to continue to support the Ontario auto sector, despite partisan, ideological, or philosophical differences over the utility of state intervention in this aspect of the economy. The auto sector remains an important exception to the neoliberal story of the last twenty years, though with some important caveats.

First, it is important to recognize the long-standing political dynamic that informed auto politics in Ontario as well as federally during the postwar period. Auto towns have long played a key role in the political scene. The number and concentration of workers in several Ontario/federal ridings, from Windsor across the Golden Horseshoe to Oshawa, kept politicians sensitive to this voting bloc. Provincially, Windsor, Oshawa, and Hamilton (and other steel towns in Ontario's north) were historically NDP bastions from the 1960s to the 1990s, reflecting the concentration of auto and other manufacturing workers in those ridings and the labour movement's traditional ties to the party. In the GTA, auto towns such as Oakville, Brampton, and Oshawa, and newer auto centres such as Cambridge, Alliston, and Woodstock, have remained either Liberal or Progressive Conservative. Federally, in the 1960s and 1970s, high-profile Liberal party MPs and ministers such as Paul Martin Sr, Herb Gray, Eugene Whelan, and others were seen as stalwart representatives of auto union towns like Windsor and Essex. In Oshawa, Ed Broadbent – a political theorist whose family had worked for GM for two generations and who eventually became NDP leader – carried the party's banner for nearly two decades in the 1970s and 1980s. These were consistent political trends in this period.

Provincially, over the last two decades, the status quo has largely remained in place. Especially during the Harris years, where the government was seen as relatively unfriendly to auto workers, auto-oriented ridings have largely remained in the hands of the NDP and Liberals. McGuinty's strong support for automotive investment has not hurt the provincial Liberals in auto areas, notwithstanding the province's financial difficulties and its seeming decline, especially in manufacturing. One notable exception has been in Oshawa: Progressive Conservatives took the riding in 1995, and despite their auto policies and the efforts of labour leader Sid Ryan, who was nearly elected as an NDP candidate on four occasions (running provincially in 2003 and 2007 and federally in 2004 and 2006), they have retained it since.

Federally, there has been an even more pronounced shift. Long-time Liberal or even NDP bastions in Essex, St Catharines, and Oshawa have consistently been won by Conservative candidates since 2003. This shift reflects a number of changes. On the one hand, it reflects the general hollowing-out of the federal Liberal party in these areas, despite former CAW leader Buzz Hargrove's decision to very publicly back the Paul Martin Liberals in the 2004 and 2006 elections. At the same time, demographic and economic trends have also played a role in shaping these electoral outcomes in auto-oriented ridings in the province. The decline in the auto sector and employment has had an impact. At its height in the late 1980s, GM's Oshawa Autoplex employed nearly 20,000 workers; by the 2010s, there were fewer than 6,000 workers at the plant. As the number of active auto workers has declined, the number of retired workers has increased dramatically. Many of these former auto workers are now seniors, some a constituency for the Conservatives.

Perhaps just as significant has been the willingness of political parties of all stripes to cater to the auto sector. This is especially noticeable at the federal level. While the NDP has traditionally remained the party of blue-collar workers, and the Liberal Party has historically been seen as the party of both the auto pact and government support for auto industry, the Conservative Party now has strong support in auto ridings. For his part, during his administration Stephen Harper made an effort to retain seats taken from Liberal or NDP control by providing high-profile direct federal support for auto plants in those ridings.

A good example is Essex, a riding in Windsor. In 2008, the Ford Motor Company indicated that it would reopen its Essex engine plant if federal support was forthcoming, along with $30 million in provincial funds already offered. Initially, the Harper finance minister at the time, Jim Flaherty, was very reluctant to provide support for individual corporations, maintaining his government's approach, which contrasted dramatically with the Liberals at Queen's Park: "Once again we have Dalton McGuinty running a government with the highest taxes on business investment in Canada," he told reporters. "And taxing all businesses, as I say at the highest rate and then selecting which businesses, which corporations he wants to subsidize. That is certainly not our approach federally" (Norris 2008). Just before the 2008 election, Harper reversed course and threw financial support totalling $80 million behind the facility. The riding, won narrowly by Conservative MP Jeff Watson in the previous election, was retaken handily by the incumbent in 2008 and 2011 (though it was captured by the NDP in 2015) (CBC 2008).

Along with the 2009 bailout rescue package, such support illustrates a manufacturing policy reversal for the Conservative party. A key caveat, however, is that the Conservatives tied their willingness to support the industry through direct subsidies or bailout loans to demands for worker concessions. In keeping with his overall neoliberal economic approach, Harper supported the 2009 rescue package for Chrysler and GM on the condition that Canadian Auto Workers (now Unifor) union members agreed to substantial wage concessions, a significant "cultural shift for our organization" in the words of the CAW's economist, Jim Stanford (Montreal Gazette 2009). The resulting renegotiation resulted in a 10 per cent cut for auto workers at these plants. In the wake of the 2009 bailout, the mantra of wage concessions as the price of further government support for the auto sector has become a key point of debate. A recent, widely circulated report on the bailout and the practice of incentives came to the conclusion that the decision to support GM and Chrysler was a sound one, but that incentives in general should be avoided unless they are tied to workforce concessions, particularly around pay rates for unionized workers in the auto sector (Shiell and Sommerville 2012). Moreover, while Harper did support the 2008–09 bailout, the Conservatives continued pursuing traditional neoliberal goals overall, particularly in regard to trade agreements. This included the 2014 Canada-South Korea Free Trade Agreement, the 2016 Canada-European free trade agreement (known as the Comprehensive and Economic Trade Agreement, or CETA), and initiating discussions on the Trans-Pacific Partnership in the mid-2000s, all of which were heavily criticized by the auto workers' unions.

From a national perspective, the decision to support the auto companies has highlighted entrenched divisions within Canada, pitting Ontario against the other regions, in particular the West. Along with conflicts over equalization, representation, and policy issues such as climate change, the 2009 auto bailout exacerbated already existing regional tensions based on a historical sense of grievance against Ontario's perceived privileged status. Distaste about the auto bailout provided a rare circumstance when Westerners and Quebecers were unified: one poll indicated that while 56 per cent of Ontarians supported government aid for the industry, 62 per cent of Westerners and Quebecers were opposed (Tibbetts 2008; Strategic Council 2009).

The continued willingness of Liberal, Conservative, and presumably potential NDP governments at Queen's Park and in Ottawa to continue financial support for the auto sector – save for the exception of the Harris government – illustrates the particular place of the auto sector in the political economy of Ontario, and Canada. While Doug Ford, elected premier in 2018, promised to end all corporate subsidies (notably proposing to cancel the Jobs and Prosperity Fund), the challenges faced by the conservative protectionism of the Donald Trump administration will test the new Progressive Conservative government. It is not clear that the Conservatives have any industrial strategy beyond further business tax cuts and ending carbon pricing – both efforts to maintain Ontario as a low-cost production zone through austerity. Like banks, automotive assembly and parts companies have been deemed either economically too big or politically too important to fail. Despite the demands for worker concessions, policy towards the auto industry remains to a significant degree a statist outlier, in terms of the amount of direct state support and supporting infrastructure it receives in an otherwise increasingly market-driven economic environment.

NOTES

1. A more recent example of this phenomenon was the 1990s mantra of the Alberta-based Reform Party, "The West Wants In!" Though not specifically aimed at Ontario, the sentiment was certainly directed at central Canada. When Stephen Harper won his first minority government in 2006 he declared that "the West *is* in." Another example is the recent commentary surrounding Ontario's financial difficulties, rendering the province a "have not" under equalization (Mendelsohn 2006, 2012).
2. Despite these challenges, some have argued that manufacturing's decline is not as dramatic as the headlines suggest. See, for instance, Baldwin and Macdonald (2009).
3. In 2008, the number of cars on American roads reached 237 million for a driving age population of 238 million, resulting in an astounding ratio of 99.6 per cent. The comparable 2008 figure for Canada was 74 per cent (20 million cars for 32 million people). See DesRosiers Automotive Consultants (2009).
4. See Mordue (2007) and Anastakis (2013, chap. 7). A good example of a 1980s program was the Board of Industrial Leadership and Development (BILD), designed in part to provide $100 million in support to auto part firms in the province. Emerging firms such as Magna and Linamar benefitted significantly from BILD, as they did from an earlier Economic Development Fund (Wolfe 2002).
5. The author can attest to the unwillingness of the Harris government to consider auto incentives as a policy tool, as he was a member of the Ontario Ministry of Economic Development's Automotive Office from 2001–02. Ironically, despite his government's unwillingness to support the auto sector through incentives, Harris became the lead director for Magna following his retirement from politics.

REFERENCES

Anastakis, Dimitry. 2001. "Requiem for a Trade Agreement: The Auto Pact at the WTO, 1999–2000." *Canadian Business Law Journal* 34 (3).
– 2005. *Auto Pact: Creating a Borderless North American Auto Industry, 1960–71*. Toronto: University of Toronto Press.
– 2013. *Autonomous State: The Struggle for a Canadian Car Industry from OPEC to Free Trade*. Toronto: University of Toronto Press.

Baldwin, John R., and Ryan Macdonald. 2009. *The Canadian Manufacturing Sector: Adapting to Challenges*. Statistics Canada, Economic Analysis Division. Ottawa: Statistics Canada.

Baskerville, Peter. 2005. *Sites of Power: A Concise History of Ontario*. Toronto: University of Toronto Press.

Beine, Michel, Charles S. Bos, and Serge Coulombe. 2009. "Does the Canadian Economy Suffer from Dutch Disease?" Tinbergen Institute Discussion Paper, 09-096/4, 12 November.

Blatchford, Andy. 2018. "Federal Government, Ontario Invest $100M to Support Linamar Auto Parts Maker." *National Post*, 15 January.

Bluestone, Barry, and Bennett Harrison. 1982. *The Deindustrialization of America: Plant Closings, Community Abandonment and the Dismantling of Basic Industry*. New York: Basic Books.

Bothwell, Robert. 1999. *A Short History of Ontario*. Edmonton: McClelland and Stewart.

Canada: Competition Policy Review Panel. 2008. *Compete to Win*. Ottawa: Industry Canada.

CAW. 2002. *Getting Back in Gear: A New Policy Vision for Canada's Auto Industry*. Toronto: CAW Research Department.

CBC. 2008. "Tories Pledge $80M for Reopening of Ford Engine Plant." *CBC News*. 3 September. www.cbc.ca/news/.

Centre for Spatial Economics. 2008. "The Economic Impact of the Detroit Three Auto Manufacturers in Canada." Milton: Centre for Spatial Economics. www.cme-mec.ca/download.php?file=gp8usjo4.pdf.

Courchene, Thomas, with Colin R. Telmer. 1998. *From Heartland to North American Region State: The Social, Fiscal and Federal Evolution of Ontario*. Toronto: University of Toronto Press.

Del Balso, Michael. 1997. "Is Canada: De-Industrializing? The Industrial Restructuring of the Manufacturing Sector, 1961–1995." PhD diss., McGill University.

DesRosiers Automotive Consultants. 2010. "Employment in the Canadian Automotive Manufacturing Sector." May newsletter.

Drache, Daniel. 1989. *The Deindustrialization of Canada and its Implications for Labour*. Ottawa: Canadian Centre for Policy Alternatives.

Dudley, Kathryn Marie. 1994. *The End of the Line: Lost Jobs, New Lives in Postindustrial America*. Chicago: University of Chicago Press.

General Motors Canada. 2009. *General Motors of Canada Restructuring Plan*. Submitted to Industry Canada and Ontario Ministry of Economic Development 20 February. http://v1.theglobeandmail.com/v5/content/pdf/GMsubmission.pdf.

– 2016. *General Motors Announces Expansion of Connected and Autonomous Vehicle Engineering and Software Development Work in Canada* ... 10 June. http://media.gm.ca/media/ca/en/gm/news.html.

Gindin, Sam. 1995. *The Canadian Auto Workers: The Birth and Transformation of a Union* Toronto: James Lorimer.

Government of Ontario. 2009. *The Ontario Labour Market, 2008.* Ministry of Colleges, Training and Universities, Ontario.
- 2010. *Ontario's Long-Term Report on the Economy*, 33. http://www.fin.gov.on.ca/en/economy/ltr/.
Hart, Michael. 2003. *A Trading Nation: Canadian Trade Policy from Colonialism to Globalization.* Vancouver: University of British Columbia Press.
High, Steven. 2003. *Industrial Sunset: The Making of North America's Rust Belt, 1969–84.* Toronto: University of Toronto Press.
Holmes, John. 1990. *The Break-Up of an International Labour Union: Uneven Development in the North American Auto Industry and the Schism in the U.A.W.* Kingston: Queen's University.
Holmes, John S., S. Fitzgibbon, T. Rutherford, and P. Kumer. 2003. "Shifting Gears: Restructuring and Innovation in the Ontario Automotive Parts Industry." In *Clusters in a Cold Climate: Innovation Dynamics in a Diverse Economy*, edited by D. Wolfe and M. Lucas. Montreal: McGill-Queen's University Press.
Ibbitson, John. 2002. *Loyal No More: Ontario's Struggle for a Separate Destiny.* Toronto: Harper Collins.
Inwood, Greg. 2005. *Continentalizing Canada: The Politics and Legacy of the Macdonald Royal Commission.* Toronto: University of Toronto Press.
Keenan, Greg. 2011. "How the Economic Storm Battered St. Thomas." *Globe and Mail*, 9 July.
- 2015. "Canadian Taxpayers Lose $3.5-billion on 2009 Bailout of Auto Firms." *Globe and Mail*, 7 April.
Keenan, Greg, and Bill Curry. 2016. "Ottawa Changes Auto Fund to Issue Grants Instead of Loans." *Globe and Mail*, 14 September.
Laxer, Robert. 1973. *Canada (Ltd.): The Political Economy of Dependency.* Toronto: McClelland and Stewart.
Mellon, Steve. 2002. *After the Smoke Clears: Struggling to Get By in Rustbelt America.* Pittsburgh: University of Pittsburgh Press.
Mendelsohn, Matthew. 2006. "Ontario Staggers under Burden of Fiscal Federalism." *Toronto Star*, 6 March.
- 2012. *Back to Basics: The Future of Fiscal Arrangements.* Toronto: Mowat Centre.
Molot, Maureen. 2005. "Location Incentives and Inter-state Competition for FDI: Bidding Wars in the Automotive Industry." In *Governance, Multinationals and Growth*, edited by Lorraine Eden and Wendy Dobson. Northampton: Edward Elgar.
Montreal Gazette. 2009. "GM Agrees to Concessions Deal." 9 March.
Moore School of Business. 2002. "The Economic Impact of BMW on South Carolina." University of South Carolina. Columbia, South Carolina May.
Mordue, Greig. 2007. "Government, Foreign Direct Investment, and the Canadian Automotive Industry, 1977–1987." PhD diss., University of Strathclyde.
Norris, Gary. 2008. "Politics Plays Out at Ford Essex Plant." *Toronto Star*, 18 January.

Organisation Internationale des Constructeurs d'Automobiles (OICA). 2016. *Production Statistics*. www.oica.net.
Piva, Michael J., ed. 1988. *A History of Ontario: Selected Readings*. Toronto: University of Toronto Press.
Podgursky, Mike. 1984. "A National Industrial Policy." *Labor Studies Journal* 9 (2).
Rea, K.J. 1985. *The Prosperous Years: The Economic History of Ontario, 1939–75*. Toronto: University of Toronto Press.
Reich, Robert B., and John D. Donahue. 1986. *New Deals: The Chrysler Revival and the American System*. New York: Times Books.
Shiell, Leslie, and Robin Somerville. 2012. "Bailouts and Subsidies: The Economics of Assisting the Automotive Sector in Canada." *IRPP Study* 28. www.irpp.org.
Sobel, David, and Susan Meurer. 1994. *Working at Inglis: The Life and Death of a Canadian Factory*. Toronto: Lorimer.
Statistics Canada. 2010. "Manufacturing Establishments and Production Workers, by Province and Territory, 2006 to 2009." http://www.statcan.gc.ca/pub/11-402-x/2011000/chap/man-fab/tbl/tbl05-eng.htm.
Sweeney, B., and G. Mordue. 2017. "The Restructuring of Canada's Automotive Industry, 2005–2014." *Canadian Public Policy* s1 (January).
Tencer, Daniel. 2013. "Canada Manufacturing: Industrial Plants Disappearing at Twice the Pace of U.S., Study Finds." *Huffington Post Online*, 25 March. http://www.huffingtonpost.ca/2012/01/13/canada-manufacturing-jobs_n_1204936.html#slide=532834`.
Vieira, Paul. 2009. "Ontario in Decline: From Canada's Economic Engine to Clunker." *Financial Post*, 20 March.
Whittington, Les. 2004. "Ottawa Pledges $100M to Ford; Cash to Refit Oakville Plant, Keep Jobs Part of $1 Billion Manufacturing Boost." *Toronto Star*, 14 June.
Wolfe, David. 2002. "Harnessing the Region: Changing Perspectives on Innovation Policy in Ontario." In *The New Industrial Geography: Regions, Regulation and Institutions*, edited by Trevor J. Barnes and Meric S. Gertler. New York: Routledge.
Womack, James P., Daniel T. Jones, and Daniel Roos. 1991. *The Machine That Changed the World: The Story of Lean Production*. New York: HarperBusiness.
Yates, Charlotte. 1993. "Public Policy and Canadian and American Autoworkers: Divergent Fortunes." In *Driving Continentally: National Policies and the North American Auto Policy*, edited by Maureen Appel Molot. Ottawa: Carleton University Press.
Yates, Charlotte, and Wayne Lewchuk, 2017. "What Shapes Automotive Investment Decisions in a Contemporary Global Economy?" *Canadian Public Policy* s1 (January).

| 5 |

Northern Ontario and the Crisis of Development and Democracy

DAVID LEADBEATER

Northern Ontario has a land area of over 800,000 square kilometres – over 87 per cent of the province of Ontario. The population in 2016 was about 780,000, including over 128,000 Indigenous Peoples and 120,000 Franco-Ontarians. While it has about 6 per cent of the province's total population, Northern Ontario has about 34 per cent of the Ontario Indigenous population and about 24 per cent of the Ontario francophone population.[1]

There exists some contention over the boundary for Northern Ontario, at least its most southern portion, which divides "the North" from "the rest of Ontario" – what in Northern Ontario is usually called "Southern Ontario." In much common use, this southern boundary is taken to be from Lake Huron across the French River (la "Rivière des Français") through to Lake Nipissing and Mattawa to the Ottawa River. However, for some political purposes the boundary has been pulled south, essentially so that bordering areas, particularly Parry Sound and Muskoka, might access funds or arrangements dedicated specially to Northern Ontario. An example of this is the *Growth Plan for Northern Ontario* (Ontario 2011b) developed by the McGuinty Liberal government of Ontario. As can be seen in map 5.1, Northern Ontario includes not only the nine districts (and City of Greater Sudbury) usually identified as such, but also the bordering district of Parry Sound.[2] Some Northern political interests have challenged such enlarged boundary definitions as they could reduce the already limited provincial or federal funds available to the existing Northern districts.

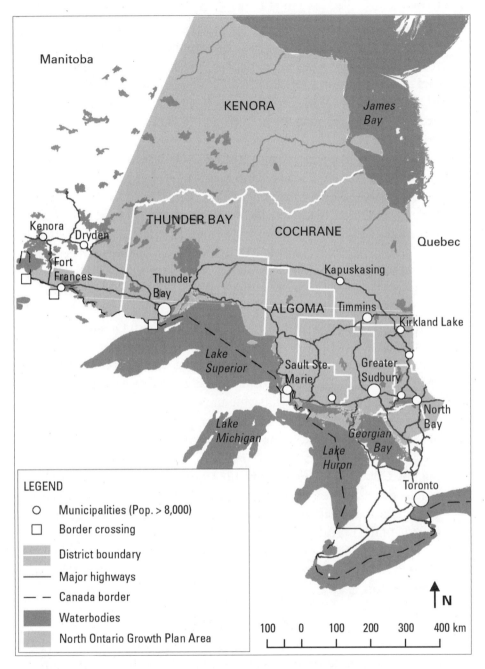

Map 5.1 | Northern Ontario as defined by the Growth Plan for Northern Ontario (Adapted from: Ontario [2011, 55], *Places to Grow: Growth Plan for Northern Ontario*)

This said, the boundary districts in question have often faced similar economic problems. One can view this conflict as reflecting the widening area of impoverishment, decline, and social division being visited on the hinterlands of Ontario and Canada. Further, it is a conflict reflecting a colonial history in which Indigenous Peoples have been excluded in determining the politico-administrative divisions of their original territories.

Despite the boundary issue, Northern Ontario is evidently vast: about 8 per cent of Canada's land area, larger than most provinces, and larger than the homelands of its early colonial masters, France and Britain, combined. Bioregionally, Northern Ontario is a creature of the Canadian Shield, the source for its fresh water, mining, forestry, hunting and trapping, and clay belt agriculture as well. The area can be seen as having two main watersheds with two main types of land cover, the Hudson Plains to the north of the Laurentian (Continental) Divide and the Boreal Shield to the south.[3]

The Ontario government recognizes that Northern Ontario has 106 First Nations, a number of Métis communities, 144 municipalities, and over 150 unincorporated communities.[4] The southern areas of Northern Ontario are relatively urbanized, and concentrated near the two transcontinental rail lines (the CPR and CN), the TransCanada highway, and Great Lakes ports (map 5.2). Some call this the "mid-North" or the "near North," preferring instead to characterize the lands above the Laurentian Divide as the "far North." Under pressures for mining, the Ontario government has moved to define the latter area and to introduce land-use planning measures in the Far North Act, 2010. Thus defined, the Far North is largely the Hudson Bay Lowlands and a portion of the Boreal Shield, which together make up over 40 per cent of the area of Ontario; most of the thirty-six communities and about 90 per cent of the 24,000 people in the Far North are First Nations (Ontario 2011a).

SETTLER COLONIZATION

As with other hinterland areas of modern Canada, the political economy of Northern Ontario has its structural foundations in the history of colonial expansion, first French and English, then Canadian internal colonization. Though colonization transformed profoundly the

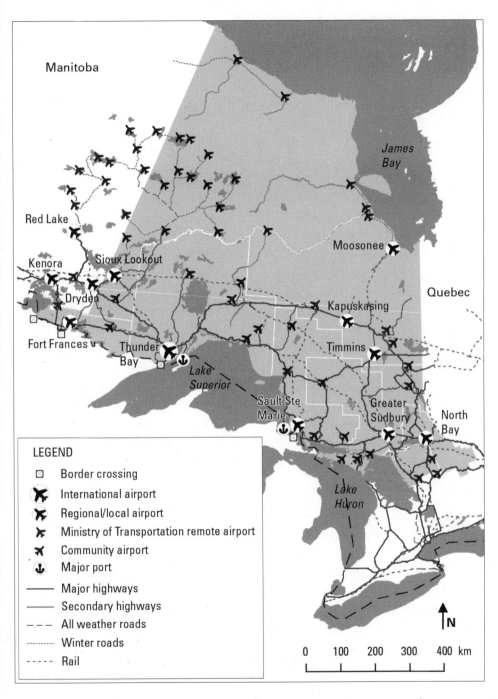

Map 5.2 | Northern Ontario transportation (Adapted from: Ontario [2011, 61], *Places to Grow: Growth Plan for Northern Ontario*)

societies and environment of Northern Ontario, the modern colonial-capitalist period has been short – perhaps 4 per cent relative to the long span of human history in the area. Archaeological evidence from the Sheguiandah site on Manitoulin Island shows an active human presence in Northern Ontario over 9,500 years ago, shortly after the last Ice Age.[5] Long before the impacts of colonization, there had evolved culturally rich, diverse, and sovereign Indigenous societies. Copper from around the Lake Superior area was used in tools and was traded; silver, too, from around the Cobalt area was traded. As Abel (2006, 16) writes of the Northeast over five centuries before European contact, "there were many small autonomous communities, but each recognized a connection to a broader regional population of similar communities, and each was also connected to the outside world through trade, intermarriage, and travel. It was a cosmopolitan society that was by no means isolated or inward-looking." The diversity one finds today includes three broad language groups in Northern Ontario, all part of the Algonquian family of languages: Anishinaabemowin (Ojibwe), Cree (Iliniimowin for the Moose Cree and Ininiimowin for the Swampy Cree), and Oji-Cree (Anishininiimowin).[6]

Colonialism in Northern Ontario first appears in the rival fur trading and religious missions of the French and English beginning in the 1600s. But the modern era of mass settler colonization and large-scale extractive industry comes two centuries later, especially following the penetration of the CPR and other railway corporations from the 1880s. This was a colonization dominated by monopoly capitalism and a ruling class based in southern Canada's metropolitan centres of Montreal and Toronto. This colonization reflected a much higher scale of capitalist accumulation and centralization than during the first phase of capitalist industrialization in Canada, which was apparent economically by the 1840s and politically in the Confederation arrangements of 1867 (Ryerson 1973). Though the participants in the colonial expansion included US and British finance capital, it was primarily a Canadian internal colonialism.

The process of settler colonization in Northern Ontario had the classic form of other hinterland areas of the old North-West Territories (Leadbeater 1984): the establishment of Canadian state power; dispossession of First Nations; railway development; natural resource exploitation; Euro-Canadian settlement; expansion of the internal market.[7] However, unlike colonization in Manitoba, Saskatchewan, or Alberta, Northern Ontario did not achieve provincehood or any state form sufficient to achieve ownership of the region's natural resources and some control of its economic and political development.[8]

The Canadian state, at both the provincial and federal level, had largely completed taking control of the territory of Northern Ontario by World War I. State power and an authoritarian administration was the sharp edge of colonization, enforcing and smoothing the dispossession and removal of Indigenous Peoples from their lands, surveying and privatizing lands, protecting the property of the mining, forestry, and railway companies, regulating settlement, and imposing a tax and customs regime to pay for its activities and help subsidize the colonization. State power was established over the vast area and depended on the balance of power against and among the Indigenous Peoples, the particular encroachments of mining and logging companies, rival federal and provincial interests, the physical advance of railways and other means of transport and communication, and the strategic direction of the state, particularly relative to US western expansion.[9]

At the time of the Confederation in 1867, the occupied land of Ontario – and of its colonial predecessors Canada West (1840) and Upper Canada (1791) – was a fraction of its current size. The new Canadian state claimed all territory north to the Laurentian Divide; the territory north of the divide was still part of Rupert's Land, ruled since 1670 as the private colonial territory of the Hudson's Bay Company. In Southern Ontario there were growing pressures centred in Toronto for northward expansion under the aegis of the Ontario government, though such expansionist pressures were evident before Confederation.[10] This gave rise to a colonial scramble for the North and a political struggle within Canada's rising ruling class. The growing capitalist power based in Toronto, particularly under the Mowat Liberals (1872–96), pressed aggressively for the expansion of the provincial boundaries against the mainly Tory federal government, with a closer British imperial interest and based in Montreal, still by far the largest city in Canada and then hub of finance.

Underlying the provincial colonial drive was the control of land and resources. The terms of the Confederation arrangements (BNA

Act, 1867, s. 92) provided for provincial control of lands and their resources ("The Management and Sale of the Public Lands belonging to the Province and of the Timber and Wood thereon"), which in the northern area would mean Ontario (Crown) ownership and resource revenues.[11] But there was more, notably the possibilities for political corruption, as Baskerville (2005, 127) expresses it: "The winner would also gain control of numerous opportunities for political patronage – in the establishment of municipal government, the granting of liquor licences, the appointment of judicial and other officials – that could be used for partisan purposes." The eventual outcome was a vast northward and westward expansion of Ontario's territory.[12]

In the mid-1800s and the early colonization period, the primary instrument of state power was the militia (the army). Professionalized public policing was then very limited, and that only starting in the largest urban centres (Greer 1992); in rural and hinterland areas there was practically none. The militia was used against Indigenous Peoples over their control of lands as early as 1849 in the so-called Mica Bay incident (Chute 1998). The Canadian government formally took charge of its own militia in the Militia Act (1868), then strengthened further the colonization process with the founding of the North-West Mounted Police (NWMP) in 1873, following the Red River (First North-West) Uprising of 1869–70. Corporations, most notably the railways and large mining companies, developed their own private police forces, which were especially active in company towns. With the growth of independent towns and local taxation, municipalities gradually increased policing under local control. In 1909, in part due to perceived lawlessness in the silver and gold boom areas of Cobalt and Timmins, the provincial government formed the Ontario Provincial Police, which marked a shift to a much expanded and direct supra-local role of the state in policing.

Canadian colonization was founded on the forced removal of Indigenous Peoples from their land and its resources, the extinguishing of legal title and reassigning of it to the colonizers, and the concentration of the Indigenous population into "Indian Reserves." Short of outright genocide, this has been a pattern typical of modern colonialism, whether seen in the US reservation, the Spanish *reducción*, or the South African bantustan. By 1860, while Canada was still under

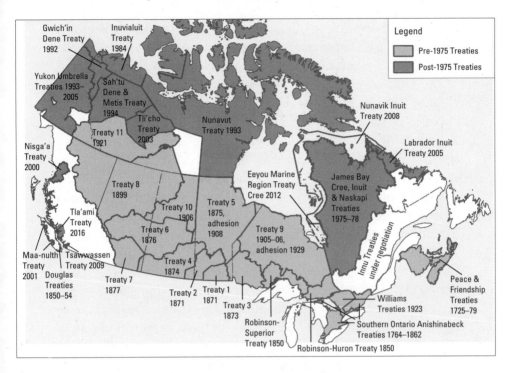

Map 5.3 | Historical and new treaties in Canada. Historical treaties are pre-1975 and modern treaties are post-1975 (*Sources*: Southern Chiefs Organization [2018]; Canada [2018])

the British colonial Province of Canada, the administration of Indigenous lands had come under Canadian settler control (Dickason 2002, 231). Although British and French colonialism have had their particular atrocities in Canada and elsewhere, what occurred in Northern Ontario was primarily a domestic Euro-Canadian colonialism led by an expanding Canadian-based capitalism seeking natural resources and transportation and communication corridors. The point deserves emphasis, given a persisting belief to the contrary among powerful parts of the Canadian population – not least Conservative prime minister Stephen Harper, who as recently as 2009 claimed that in Canada, "We also have no history of colonialism" (Ljunggren 2009).

The key means used by the Canadian state was the now well-studied process of treaty-making and administration backed by military power and economic advantage, and legitimated by racist ideology.[13] First

Nations were dispossessed in the general order in which they stood in the way of Euro-Canadian exploitation of their land and its resources. Six main treaties came to cover Northern Ontario (map 5.3).

The Ontario government was also actively initiating "province-building" measures for the development of the North – leading the era of "New Ontario." First, in 1902 the Ontario government built the Temiskaming and Northern Ontario Railway (now Ontario Northland), which reached Cochrane in 1909 and Moosenee in 1932. This stimulated a massive increase in mining, new forest-based activities, and agricultural settlement in the "Great Northern Claybelt."[14] Second, related to expanding transportation came policies and substantial expenditures for directed settlement, initially through Ontario's Bureau of Colonization then with the Northern and Northwestern Ontario Development Act (1912). Third, under popular pressure against the export to the US of raw logs and minerals with little milling or other processing, the Ontario government imposed the famous "manufacturing condition" (or value-added condition) on forest exports. Pine cut on Crown land was to be sawn in Canada (the 1898 sawlog condition) and spruce cut for wood pulp had to be manufactured in Canada (the 1900 pulpwood condition).[15] Fourth, the development of Ontario Hydro (1906), while focused initially on the Niagara and Southern Ontario, began in the 1920s to play a major role in the North, particularly in advancing electrification, providing relatively lower-cost power in the North, and transmitting power south as a large part of Ontario's hydro generation.[16]

Despite these developments, the North never achieved a balanced or self-sustained industrialization. The mining, forest, and rail towns remained essentially that, though there was some diversification in small-scale manufactures for local consumption (such as dairies and brewing) and a slowly growing secondary sector of public services. On the whole, large-scale corporate diversification did not occur. Critics have noted, for example, the failure of agriculture settlement policies, but they have also noted that adopting the heralded "manufacturing condition" was more political rhetoric than substantial in its economic effects (Kuhlberg 2014). Only Sault Ste Marie and the Lakehead appeared by World War I to be shifting towards more diversified industrialization with the capacity for export. The Sault became the centre of a heavy industry complex, from transportation and hydro power to a pulp mill, ferro-nickel plant, iron mine, and railway. At least until the 1920s, and despite a series of near-terminal financial and leadership crises, what became Algoma Steel (now the Mumbai-headquartered Essar Steel Algoma) managed to produce more iron than any operation in Ontario.[17] The Lakehead diversified even further, particularly with secondary manufacturing, from a historic base in water and then rail transportation to drydocks and shipbuilding, pulp and paper, flour milling, and rail car manufacture (now Bombardier). However, the private development was not self-sustained, and, since the 1970s, both areas have witnessed relative and even absolute employment decline, like many areas of the North.

A SUBORDINATE CAPITALISM AND THE NORTH'S NEW CRISIS OF ECONOMIC DEVELOPMENT

In the view argued here, the economy of Northern Ontario is a form of subordinate capitalism. Northern Ontario reflects the crises, impoverishment, and social disparities of capitalist development generally, but its conditions are aggravated by an additional layer of problems associated with the fact that its economic base, resource extraction, is largely owned and controlled externally and is at the sharp edge of the global environmental and imperial crisis – and that its population has lacked the political and democratic levers to reorient this. One can speak of this situation, imposed through internal colonization, as "colonial" – and, for Indigenous Peoples and a large part of the land area, it *is* indeed colonial, whether as indicated by the reserve system, the Indian Act, thwarted land rights, or unfulfilled sovereignty. For the non-Indigenous population, the situation could perhaps be characterized as semi-colonial or neo-colonial, in the sense that there is external economic control but certain forms of political representation, as limited as they are, in Parliament, the provincial legislature, and municipalities. This said, the situation does not even come close to autonomy – let alone to the formal political independence usually associated with the latter, such as occurred in the prairie provinces. In this context, I outline key elements of Northern Ontario's contemporary economic development.[18]

Table 5.1 | Class structure compared for Northern Ontario and Southern Ontario, 2017 (employed persons, in thousands)

	Northern Ontario		Southern Ontario	
	persons	%	persons	%
Total employment	348.1	100.0	6,779.9	100.0
Employees	309.3	88.9	5,710.4	84.2
Self-employed, employers	15.2	4.4	309.2	4.6
Self-employed, own account	23.2	6.7	752.9	11.1
Unpaid family workers	0.4	0.1	7.8	0.1

Employees with union coverage	Northern Ontario			Southern Ontario		
	all employees	union employees	union %	all employees	union employees	union %
All employees	309.3	119.7	38.7	5,710.4	1,491.7	26.1
Public sector	91.7	69.8	76.1	1,237.4	872.7	70.5
Private sector	217.6	49.9	22.9	4,473.0	618.9	13.8
Public sector %	29.6	58.3		21.7	58.5	
Private sector %	70.4	41.7		78.3	41.5	

Note: Northern Ontario combines the economic regions of Northeastern and Northwestern Ontario.

Southern Ontario is Ontario outside (minus) Northern Ontario.

The self-employed, employers include incorporated and unincorporated self-employed with paid help.

The self-employed, own account include incorporated and unincorporated self-employed with no paid help.

The number of unpaid family workers, reported as zero for Northern Ontario because the count was below the threshold of 1,500 for reporting, is estimated here by subtracting other self-employed from total self-employed.

Some totals do not add exactly due to rounding.

Source: Statistics Canada, Labour Force Survey, custom order.

First, the Northern Ontario economy has a largely capitalist structure as defined by the predominance of private corporate ownership of production and the capitalist labour market. In more northern areas, traditional Indigenous land-based economies continue and evolve, though much has been displaced and penetrated by capitalist relations and priorities; indeed, corporate and government policies have long aimed to push capitalist forms of development and division in the colonial hinterland. As table 5.1 indicates, capital accumulation and capitalist relations have reached a level where nearly 89 per cent of persons within the statistically measured economy are primarily wage and salary workers.[19] This level is about 5 percentage points higher than in Southern Ontario. Much of the higher level in the North can be explained by the industry structure of the Northern economy, notably the relatively small agriculture sector which historically has been a main base of small-scale independent production and self-employment.[20] As well, most of the key sectors in Northern Ontario are dominated by highly capitalized, large-scale firms, and the public sector is substantially larger. Not surprisingly, there is a relatively smaller employer class in the North. Most major corporate employers in Northern Ontario are located outside the region; for the Canadian corporations, typically in Toronto.

The wage and salary population (broadly, the working class) of Northern Ontario is not only relatively larger; it also has a higher level of unionization. The higher level of unionization in the private sector stems from the importance of large-scale resource, primary manufacturing, and transportation industries together with the history of militant unionism in the mining, forest, and transportation sectors. However, even in such a traditional bastion as hard rock mining, union coverage is below half of mining employment.

Second, as a classic colonial-hinterland region, Northern Ontario has as its economic base primary production and transportation coupled with a high level of monopoly power, external ownership, and export dependency. The main primary production is mining, forestry, and hydro-electricity. The transportation is oriented largely toward transit across the territory, principally through rail, roads, pipelines, and ports, and toward the removal of the resource commodities. Table 5.2, which compares the industry structures of Northern Ontario and Southern Ontario, reveals this division of labour. The gender division of labour follows that elsewhere in Canada. Mining, forestry, and other primary industries, as well as transportation and construction, are highly male-dominated, while public and other services are majority female.[21] Overall, though employment rates are generally lower

Table 5.2 | Industry structure of employment compared for Northern and Southern Ontario, 2017 (employed persons, in thousands)

	Northern Ontario	Southern Ontario	Northern Ontario employment as % of all Ontario
Total employment	348.1	6,431.8	4.9
Industries (% of total employment)	100	100	
Goods-producing industries	23.5	19.9	5.7
Agriculture	0.7	1.0	3.6
Forestry and logging	1.1	–	72.7
Fishing, hunting, and trapping	n/a	n/a	n/a
Metal ore mining	3.4	–	83.7
Other mining, quarrying, oil and gas extraction	1.9	0.1	43.3
Utilities	1.1	0.6	8.5
Construction	8.3	7.1	5.6
Manufacturing	6.9	11.0	3.1
Services-producing industries	76.6	80.1	4.7
Trade, wholesale, and retail	14.6	15.0	4.8
Transportation and warehousing	5.3	4.8	5.4
Information and culture	1.1	2.0	2.8
Finance, insurance, real estate (FIRE)	3.4	8.1	2.1
Professional, scientific, and technical	3.9	9.1	2.2
Business, building, and waste services	3.1	4.5	3.4
Education services	8.2	6.9	5.8
Health care and social assistance	16.9	12.0	6.8
Arts, entertainment, and recreation	2.5	2.4	5.0
Accommodation and food services	7.1	6.3	5.5
Other services (repair, religious, civic, household)	4.2	3.9	5.3
Public administration	6.2	5.2	5.8

Note: Northern Ontario combines the economic regions of Northeast and Northwest Ontario.

Southern Ontario is Ontario excluding (minus) Northern Ontario.

Employment includes both full-time and part-time employees as well as self-employed persons.

Industry categories based on the NAICS 2012. Forestry and logging includes support activities. Other mining includes support activities to mining.

Statistics Canada does not report employment numbers smaller than 1,500, which is indicated here by "n/a." "–" indicates a negligible value that would round to zero.

Due to rounding some totals may appear not to add up exactly.

Source: Statistics Canada (2018), Labour Force Survey, custom order.

in Northern Ontario, among those who are employed the percentage who are female is as high as, if not higher than, the average for Ontario. For example, contrary to some images from an earlier era, the female percentage of employed workers has been higher in both Thunder Bay and Sudbury than in Toronto.[22]

The largest part of "other primary" is the mining industry, which one can also treat as illustrative of the general situation.[23] Of Northern Ontario metals output, gold was nearly half of the value of all metals production and accounted for nearly 55 per cent of all gold production in Canada. This has been dominated in recent years by Vancouver-based Goldcorp Inc. (particularly through its ownership of the major Red Lake mine as well as four other mines in the North), and by the Toronto-based Barrick Gold Corporation, the largest gold mining corporation in the world (particularly through its ownership of Hemlo mines). The next most important metal mined is nickel, of which about 32 per cent of Canadian production comes from Northern Ontario. Since 2006, production has been controlled by Brazil-based Vale (formerly Inco), the largest nickel and iron ore mining corporation in the world, and, to a lesser degree, by Anglo-Swiss Glencore (formerly Xstrata and Falconbridge), the largest commodity trading company in the world. Though Sudbury is probably the second-largest nickel mining area in the world, the production of this industrially valuable non-renewable resource is foreign-owned and controlled. Indeed, for Canada as a whole, a majority of mining is now foreign-owned and controlled, though gold, perhaps the least socially useful of metals, remains under Canadian corporate control.

Another significant feature of the Northern economy is the larger importance of public sector employment and services. The public sector is about 29.6 per cent of all employment in Northern Ontario; it is 21.7 per cent in Southern Ontario (table 5.1). This is due in part to the vast territory over which services are provided and the limited economies of scale in key services. Some limited decentralization of government agencies to mitigate high unemployment has also played a role (for example, the headquarters of the Ontario Lottery and Gaming Corporation are located in Sault Ste Marie). However, the higher levels of public employment do not reflect higher standards, particularly in educational services and health care. The situation of public services in

Table 5.3 | Northern Ontario employment by industry, selected years, 1987–2017 (employed persons, in thousands)

	1987	1990	1992	2003	2007	2017
Total employment, Northern Ontario	342.6	367.5	335.5	371.7	368.9	348.1
Index (1990=100), Northern Ontario	93.2	100.0	91.3	101.1	100.4	94.7
Index (1990=100), all Ontario	94.3	100.0	95.0	119.6	126.0	137.2
Agriculture, fishing, hunting and trapping	4.0	4.1	5.1	3.9	3.2	2.5
Forestry and logging	6.6	5.8	7.2	4.2	4.0	4.0
Mining, quarrying, oil and gas extraction	34.9	32.1	19.8	14.9	17.6	18.3
Metal ore mining only	31.3	27.2	16.5	12.0	10.6	11.8
Utilities	4.5	4.7	4.4	3.0	4.3	4.0
Construction	18.4	23.1	19.2	22.6	21.5	28.9
Manufacturing	38.7	40.5	34.4	41.1	31.2	24.0
Wood product manufacturing only	8.8	7.5	4.8	10.7	10.1	4.6
Paper manufacturing only	11.2	14.3	10.8	13.6	5.1	3.6
Primary metal manufacturing only	9.3	9.3	6.8	4.8	5.0	3.1
Trade, wholesale and retail	52.3	55.3	51.4	57.0	58.4	50.9
Transportation and warehousing	19.9	19.3	17.3	20.7	20.6	18.4

/continued

Northern Ontario, such as the availability of medical, educational, and social services, has been worse overall.

Third, the dynamic pattern of Northern development has had a historic change – not only is there continuing cyclical vulnerability but also a long-term employment decline. As can be seen in table 5.3, for the last three decades the general level of employment in Northern Ontario has been stagnant if not declining, especially in primary industries and manufacturing. By contrast, Ontario as a whole had a general employment increase of approximately 40 per cent over this period, though this increase was insufficient to reduce unemployment

Table 5.3 | *continued*

	1987	1990	1992	2003	2007	2017
Information and culture	5.1	7.5	6.0	6.7	5.9	4.0
Finance, insurance, real estate (FIRE)	14.5	15.2	15.3	14.4	12.8	11.9
Professional, scientific, and technical	6.7	7.6	9.1	13.0	15.1	13.6
Business, building, and waste services	6.0	6.7	6.2	12.8	14.2	10.8
Education services	21.4	26.5	27.2	27.2	31.4	28.6
Health care and social assistance	38.9	42.3	41.3	55.5	53.8	58.9
Arts, entertainment, and recreation	3.8	4.6	4.0	8.3	8.1	8.6
Accommodation and food services	23.4	29.7	25.3	26.8	25.9	24.8
Other services	20.4	15.0	15.0	16.3	13.4	14.5
Public administration	23.1	27.2	27.3	23.0	27.5	21.7

Note: The year 1987 is the first for which consistent Labour Force Survey data for economic regions are available, while 2017 is the most recent year available at the time of writing.

The years 1990, 2003, and 2007 are the main employment peaks in Northern Ontario during the period; 1992 is the deepest employment trough.

Employment includes both full-time and part-time employees as well as self-employed persons.

Industry categories based on NAICS 2012. Due to rounding some totals may appear not to add up exactly.

Source: Statistics Canada (2018), Labour Force Survey, custom order.

and poverty in Ontario given current distributional policies. Further, the boom and bust pattern long associated with primary industries has not only continued, but there is evidence of an increased volatility of commodities markets associated with increased globalization and financialization (Wray 2008).

Crucial in this change has been a massive loss of employment in primary industries, especially mining and primary manufacturing. From the peak year of 1989 for the period covered in table 5.3, mining employment was 37,600; by 2017 it had fallen by half and was less than 6 per cent of Northern employment. As well, in primary manufacturing, there have been major refinery closures in Sudbury and Timmins, and, in forestry-dependent towns across the North, a swath of mill closures and downsizing. Employment in primary metal manufacturing (mainly smelting and refining) fell by around two-thirds. Wood product and paper manufacturing, which together had at least 20,000 jobs in 1987, were cut to 8,200 by 2017. The causes of this massive shift are several, the most important being corporate consolidation and technological and managerial changes, though capital export and international competition also played a role. Canadian-based transnational mining and oil corporations have become a notable domestic force pushing globalization, and are viewed by some critics as central to the rising profile of Canadian junior-partner imperialism.[24]

Mining and forestry still remain the export base of material wealth produced in the Northern economy.[25] However, for the working class and for community development in the North, lower resource employment means that a smaller proportion of the resource revenues generated goes to worker households and their communities. This situation has been aggravated by Ontario government policies to reduce levels of corporate and resource taxation, which further limits the possible benefits going to hinterland areas. Indeed, while Toronto has emerged as the leading mining finance centre in the world, the employment benefits of mining to the North have declined and mining's tax benefits are among the lowest in Canada (Deneault and Sacher 2012; Weir 2012; PricewaterhouseCoopers 2011). A parallel situation exists in the forestry sector; indeed, an even greater number of smaller Northern communities have been hit by forestry closures and losses of employment, and royalty benefits from the forestry industry may be even lower than those from the mining industry (MacDermid 2012).[26] Such grinding Northern economic conditions are barely engaged, let alone seriously challenged, by the Toronto-based corporate media, mainstream political parties, or government officials, and they are reinforced by the funding power and personal connections of resource corporations and related financial interests.[27]

Mining dependence especially is unsustainable. In the context of Northern Ontario, as a mature mining region, much of the most accessible minerals have been removed and the probability of new large finds reduced for future generations. Even more pressing, transnational mining corporations have been increasing alternative international sources of supply, particularly in countries with lower wages and weaker labour and environmental regulation. While for many decades until the 1970s Inco and Falconbridge mines in Northern Ontario almost monopolized the supply of nickel in Canada, the US, and many other countries, in 2011, Northern Ontario produced only about 5 per cent of world production, and the US had other sources of supply including Russia and Australia.[28] In gold production, Northern Ontario has been less important in world production; in 2011, the region's production was less than 2 per cent of world production, and, even for the US market, exports from Mexico surpassed those from Canada.

Fourth, environmental limits are being reached, if not already overshot. This constrains the role of primary production, especially resource extraction, as a basis for economic development, and likely some forms of growth itself. Mining in particular is known as one of the most environmentally destructive of industries, in both its effects on air, water, and habitat, and its heavily energy- and carbon-intensive production. In terms of supply, the readily accessible, lower-cost reserves are declining and so pushing exploration further into more remote and unspoiled areas, which are also areas where ownership and sovereignty are increasingly contested by Indigenous Peoples worldwide.[29] Beyond this, conventional oil and gas extraction in Canada has already reached a peak and is in decline; there is need also to consider declining ore grades and the prospect of region-specific peaking of minerals, and how the current approach to resource management is compromising the availability of non-renewable resources for future generations.

Neoliberal policies of deregulation will not alter these environmental limits, and are more likely to accelerate further environmental degradation. Ontario saw a destructive wave of environmental deregulation unleashed under the Harris Conservatives in the 1990s (Cooper 1999), and the neoliberal direction has continued since. One major event in this direction was the Conservatives' Lands for Life proposal affecting about 45 per cent of Ontario's land mass, much of it related to the boreal forest of the mid-North (about 90 per cent of Ontario's forest is publicly owned). The proposal, formalized in 1999 in Ontario's Living Legacy land use strategy and the Ontario Forest Accord, was a major shift in the direction of the privatization of the management of public lands. The proposal privileged the forest industry and initially increased mining access, while again parading over Indigenous sovereignty and land rights; a particular feature of its success was politically dividing environmental organizations, with a more conservative, parks-oriented group (formed as the Partnership for Public Lands) cooperating formally with the province to increase the role of private sectional interests in the management of such a huge land area.[30]

As a consequence of these fundamental changes since the 1970s, Northern Ontario has been facing a new crisis of economic development (Leadbeater 2008). Its economic expression is a widening and deepening of the typical capitalist tendencies to impoverishment. In terms of labour market conditions, Northern Ontario has been rendered into a labour reserve, like several other hinterland regions in Canada. The three decades of post-World War II expansion, characterized by overall growing labour demand and lower unemployment (though fluctuating) and often higher wages, are long over. Today, working people in Northern Ontario face overall lower employment rates, higher unemployment, persisting out-migration (especially of younger generations), and sharper downward pressures on wages and conditions including among unionized workers. The closures and downsizing of mines, refineries, plants, and mills across the North, such as at Elliot Lake, Smooth Rock Falls, Terrace Bay, Kirkland Lake, Porcupine, and many others, have been shown to have devastating impacts on employment conditions, loss of homes and savings, economic dependency, and bankruptcy (Leadbeater 1998, 1999). In 2016, Northeast Ontario and Northwest Ontario had employment rates of only 53.1 per cent and 54.8 per cent, respectively, compared to the Ontario average of 59.9 per cent and the two metropolitan centres of Toronto and Ottawa which were both at 61.1 per cent.[31] Predictably, there continue to be high levels of poverty, homelessness, and hunger. The mass level of poverty and the provincial government's treatment of the poor was reflected in the tragic death of Kimberly Rogers in Sudbury in 2001, which provoked province-wide outcries for change (Kuyek 2008).[32]

Along with the deteriorating employment conditions of Northern Ontario has been a persisting net outflow of population since the 1990s. For example, Statistics Canada's *Annual Demographic Estimates* showed an absolute decline between 2005 and 2010 from 817,312 to 805,247. In Northeast Ontario, the key factor in 2009–10 was out-migration to Southern Ontario, typically to places like Barrie, Toronto, and Ottawa; in Northwest Ontario, the key factor has been leaving the province, typically to a western province. This outflow includes First Nations youth, though overall the Indigenous population within the North is growing. At the same time, outside First Nations there is continuing rural and small town depopulation and re-concentration into some larger Northern centres like Sudbury and Thunder Bay, though these larger centres are facing overall decline or stagnation in population. Population stagnation or decline in itself is not necessarily a bad thing, and it may have positive features, such as reducing pressures on the environment or reversing pressures for encroachment on First Nations lands. But in the context of capitalism, such a tendency is associated with increased impoverishment and regional disparity, not social sustainability.

NORTHERN AUTONOMY, THE NATIONAL QUESTIONS, AND CLASS

Given Northern Ontario's legacy of colonialism, external corporate domination, resource-export dependence, and the new crisis in hinterland development, it is difficult to foresee fundamental change in Northern Ontario's economic and social conditions without there being a transformation in the ownership and control of the economy (especially of natural resource extraction), coupled with decolonization and a new, more democratic form of political representation and state administration. Debates about the North's socio-economic conditions have often gravitated towards calls for greater regional control, Northern autonomy, and, at times, provincehood. Greater democracy and greater regional control – the two are not necessarily the same – would have implications for class power, above all, relative to the external corporate interests commanding the Northern economy. But in Northern Ontario this class question and the issue of greater autonomy or provincehood are deeply intertwined with the question of who are to be considered the fundamental national constituents of the region, which relates particularly to Indigenous Peoples and to the

Franco-Ontarian national minority. These issues need to be dealt with *ensemble*.

Studies of Northern Ontario typically hold that its politics diverge from those of Southern Ontario. Weller (1997, 1977) has argued that the North is characterized by a "politics of disaffection," and Miller (1985) refers to "Northern alienation" within a context of four Norths ("the northeast and the northwest, and the north of the larger towns and that of the smaller communities"). Dyck (1996, 311) speaks of a northern regional political "sub-culture": "This is a culture of alienation, dependence, handouts, and frustration, based on isolated settlements, distance from Toronto, poor communications, and inadequate services."

One of the more recent expressions of opposition to the current structure has been the Northern Ontario Heritage Party (NOHP). Initiated in 1977 by Ed Deibel, a North Bay motel operator, the NOHP first emerged from leading a fight against a tax increase by the Davis Conservatives and became a small but public voice advocating provincehood for Northern Ontario.[33] There also exists a range of views short of provincehood, with some presence in local business and academe, calling for greater local and regional political control (Atkins 2006; Neiguth 2009; Whitehouse 2009; Robinson 2011). At least one strand of thinking does not foresee Northern Ontario as a single entity: Northwestern Ontario would join Manitoba, which is felt to be not only physically closer but also potentially more responsive to the Northwestern region (Di Matteo 2006). However, such proposals typically ignore Indigenous and Franco-Ontario populations as collectivities or societal constituents with histories and collective rights differing from those of the dominant Ontario population.

Elected members in the Ontario legislature, who in recent decades have been mainly NDP and Liberal, have often backed greater autonomy and improved services for Northern elements of provincial and federal programs. But there has been little action or sympathy for any major institutional shift in the form of Northern representation, let alone provincehood (Peet 2009) and decolonization. The common belief is that fewer benefits would be gained than lost, such as for health care. Overall, Northern Ontario, given its history of social struggles, its deep concerns about regional inequities, and the larger economic importance of public sector services and jobs, tends politically to the left of Southern Ontario. The 7 June 2018 Ontario general election saw a polarization that resulted in a sharp political shift to the right. While the Ford Conservatives were elected by a majority of seventy-six of 124 seats (61.3 per cent) with an electoral vote of 40.5 per cent, the NDP received forty seats (32.3 per cent) with a vote of 33.6 per cent, and the Liberals collapsed to seven seats (5.6 per cent) with a vote of 19.6 per cent. By contrast, in the thirteen Northern provincial constituencies, the NDP had a majority of eight seats (61.5 per cent) with an electoral vote of 44.2 percent, compared to the Conservatives' four seats (30.8 per cent) with a vote of 32.3 per cent, and the Liberals' single seat (7.7 per cent) with a vote of 15.6 percent.[34]

As a democratic representational system, such "first-past-the-post" voting to a single-chamber legislature is woefully inadequate for Ontario as a whole. But it is also unsustainable for the North. In the current system, Northern Ontario is actually overrepresented by population in the Ontario legislature;[35] at the same time, Northern Ontario's weight in the province, both economically and socially, continues to decline. These trends suggest that the current representational system is even less capable of defending or advancing Northern rights and needs in the long term, let alone recognizing Indigenous national rights and representation.

In terms of public administration, Ontario had a government branch (1912), then a department (1926), responsible for "northern development." Only in 1985 did the province create a ministry, and only in 1990 were the headquarters moved from Toronto to Sudbury. However, changing the Department of Mines and Northern Affairs into the new Ministry of Northern Affairs and Mines and finally into today's Ministry of Northern Development and Mines has done little to alter the long-standing, subservient position of the North. The state remains primarily as an adjunct for expanding corporate resource extraction and transportation, particularly mining and forestry.

Without fundamental change, the future form of Northern Ontario will be tied to its subordinate and colonial political economy: not only the role of external corporate control, but also the balance of class and national constituents within the North. Unlike the colonized prairie areas of the old North-West or older eastern provinces, Northern

Ontario has never seen the emergence of a strong and cohesive regionally based business class, in part because it lacked some of the province (or region)-building levers that state power would have given it. Also by comparison, the working class has had a larger socio-economic weight relative to the farmer or small-producer population, although the labour movement has yet to play a major role in leading an alternative direction in Northern development (some of the reasons for which are discussed below). Much of the North's history as a network of resource-export-based company towns and local-regional corporate monopolies still continues. The local-regional business class across most sectors and areas is highly dependent on and penetrated by the transnational corporate dominance of the regional economy, whether in mining, forestry, finance, transportation, or retail franchising; that dominance extends to the perspectives of local chambers of commerce.[36] Within the current balance of power, it is more likely that initiatives towards greater Northern autonomy would lead to strengthened external corporate domination rather than to greater democratic power.

At present, the main force compelling structural change in Northern power relations is First Nations Peoples. Among the more visible recent struggles is that of the Kitchenuhmaykoosib Inninuwug (KI) over their right to say no to mining exploration and extraction on their lands, which led to the jailing of six leaders of KI in 2008, and became a factor in revisions to the Ontario Mining Act.[37] In another historic struggle, after a decade of legal battles against the Ontario government, in 2011 the Grassy Narrows First Nation won a case before the Ontario Superior Court, which decided that the province does not have the right to authorize logging on lands protected by treaty. Starting on 11 December 2012, a hunger strike by Chief Theresa Spence of Attawapiskat First Nation (of James Bay and Treaty 9) near the federal Parliament triggered a massive wave of Indigenous-led protest in Canada and international solidarity actions against federal omnibus Bill C-45, which tramples over treaty rights and obligations to consult. The Harper Conservatives' bill, designed to promote even more aggressive corporate resource exploitation through weakening public consultation and environmental regulation, was also condemned by labour and environmental leaders, who expressed support for Chief Spence.

While the initiating focus of the "Idle No More" movement was Bill C-45, the context was ongoing government inaction and duplicity in dealing with treaties as well as with persisting poverty, health, housing, and other socio-economic crises.

As First Nations resistance has increased, the transnational corporations and their governmental allies have shifted more often to conciliatory and co-optive strategies. Hence, there has been an increased use of impact and benefits agreements between corporations and First Nations, and more talk of "consultation," "co-management," and "capacity building." However, beyond strategies that would continue corporate resource extraction in the still-colonial framework, there is a fundamental alternative that has been articulated by KI (2011):

> While others talk of co-management and even co-governance, in the wake of the KI struggle, in the wake of our jailing, our imagination of the good life returns to the law of Kanawayandan D'aaki – the sacred duty and sacred responsibility to look after our land.
> It is our land, not shared land!
> The KI are turning away from the idea of First Nations as communities with legal rights, defined under the Constitution of Canada, and in non-Aboriginal courts, towards a struggle to bring a different world for First Nations into existence.

Democratic resolution of colonial oppression and the national question[38] requires the ending of oppression of one nation by another, whether small or large, which applies to colonial situations like that of the First Nations. However, neither the dominant conception of Canada nor the Canadian constitution has recognized that Canada has not a bi-national but a *multinational* character.[39] In 2007, the Harper Conservative government, along with Australia, New Zealand, and the US, were in a tiny minority opposed to the UN General Assembly's adoption of the historic Declaration on the Rights of Indigenous Peoples. The UN declaration recognized not only that "Indigenous peoples have the right to self-determination" (Article 3), but also, among other important rights, that "Indigenous peoples have the right to the lands, territories and resources which they have traditionally owned, occupied or otherwise used or acquired" (Article 26.1). In 2010, the Harper government relented and supported the declaration as an "aspirational" and "non-legally binding" document. In 2015, the Trudeau Liberal government went somewhat further, committing the federal government to implementing the declaration, though since then there has been no fundamental change in the operative policies of the Canadian government towards recognition of First Nations territorial and self-governance rights. Nor has the Ontario provincial government transformed its approach on such fundamental democratic rights, which would seriously contradict its neoliberal policies – especially (but not only) on the ownership, control, and use of natural resources.

Indigenous political forms and expression have been many and varied (the subject is elaborated elsewhere in this volume). In terms of organizations in Northern Ontario, the largest are the Nishnawbe Aski Nation (NAN), head office in Thunder Bay, and the Union of Ontario Indians (Anishinabek Nation), head office near North Bay. There is a growing Indigenous presence and leadership in mainstream political parties and in labour unions. The North has also given rise to a small Indigenous political party, the First Peoples National Party of Canada, which among other policies expresses the need for a fundamental shift in the constitutional structure of Canada (FPNP 2011): "Abolish the Senate and [have it] replaced with an equal but second house, the First Nations House/Gimaa-gamig (First Nations elected representatives for First Nations Peoples of Canada) in the House of Commons equal to that of the present parliament."

Franco-Ontarians in Northern Ontario played a central part in the colonization process, but they themselves have also been the object of a history of English and Anglo-Canadian colonialism and prejudice in Canada. As in Quebec and Acadie, this oppression gave rise to many decades of struggle for Franco-Ontarian national minority rights, particularly on matters of language, education, and socio-economic development. Though there has been a francophone presence in Northern Ontario since the 1600s, the main wave of francophone migration and settlement, largely from Quebec, occurred in the wake of the CPR and other railways.[40] Francophone settlers worked primarily as farmers and labour in forestry and mining, though a small professional, church, and business elite came to dominate Franco-Ontarian politics over the decades. The Ontario government's efforts to expand anglophone migration and European immigration to the North were partly to limit and oppose the expansion of Quebec and the influence of the Catholic church (Bernard 1988, 33–7). In 1912, during the pre–World War I period of intense anglo-chauvinism, the Ontario Conservative government banned the use of French in Ontario schools, in the infamous Regulation 17. This unleashed a major political struggle and galvanized Franco-Ontarian political action, led by the Association canadienne-française d'Éducation d'Ontario (ACFÉO, formed in 1910). ACFÉO was able to weaken and eventually reverse the ban, though the history of the struggle remains alive in the politics of Franco-Ontario, and in the successor organizations of ACFÉO, the Association canadienne-française de l'Ontario (ACFO) and today the Assemblée de la francophonie de l'Ontario (AFO).

During the 1960s and 1970s, there emerged a more radical current of Franco-Ontarian politics that led to the Franco-Ontarian flag (1975), and gave voice to and added energy for the expansion of French-language education, culture, and services in French. Although the postwar Conservative governments gradually allowed the expansion of francophone schooling, it was not until 1984, following a ruling of the Ontario Court of Appeal, that the right of francophone students to an education in French was recognized. The Peterson Liberal government passed the French Language Services Act in 1986 and, in 1987, established public French television, La Chaîne Francaise, now TFO, as an offshoot of TVOntario. These shifts might be explained at least partly by democratic and constitutional struggles, and by the change of government from the Conservatives as the "English party" to the Liberals as the "French party." While significant, the changes were also delayed and limited in responding to class and regional pressures to Franco-Ontarian cultural and political losses.

Northern Ontario (particularly the Northeast) at one time had many majority francophone communities, but their extent was reduced in more recent decades due to rural and small town economic decline and migration, the continuing dominant anglophone pressures for assimilation, and government budgetary recalcitrance in expanding education and cultural (including media) rights. Critics of the francophone elite have also argued that the elite's often passive and accommodationist approach, ignoring working-class Franco-Ontarian realities, has been disempowering (Dennie 2008). Francophone representation in the AFO, school boards, and similar institutions is dependent largely on government funding. Religious conservatism has also been raised as an element in Franco-Ontarian politics, a division that is evident, for instance, in the existence of two publicly funded French-language school board systems (public and Catholic) which compete with each other even in small Northern communities (Boudreau 2008). The lack of broader protections and the weakness of the francophone elite are visible in a variety of educational, cultural, and social development policies. One larger example of this occurred in 2001 with the forced amalgamation of several communities surrounding Sudbury into the single-tier City of Greater Sudbury. Although this included majority francophone communities and individual concerns were voiced, the francophone leadership was notably silent in the face of this highly prominent political takeover, another neoliberal-type action that would reduce democratic representation and facilitate cuts to municipal services (Leadbeater 2008).

The diverse working-class majority population in Northern Ontario has had little effective political power in determining the direction of Northern development. Indeed, worker and community interests under globalization have been further diminished and are in a more clearly antagonistic relationship with transnational corporate power. The politics of globalization and the labour movement in Ontario are discussed elsewhere in this volume, so here I draw attention to features more particular to Northern Ontario.[41]

Overall, the corporations dominating Northern Ontario have become much larger and more diversified, and less dependent on labour or sources of supply in Northern Ontario.[42] By contrast, workers have faced relatively lower levels of employment opportunity and wages, and higher levels of unemployment and increased social insecurity, reflecting the new crisis in hinterland economic development. Hence, globalization has brought a further shift in economic and political power in favour of transnational corporations and against workers, their unions, and communities. The results are seen in declining strike activity and, when strikes do occur, they have often been protracted struggles with losses, sometimes threatening the very existence of the unions as effective bargaining forces.

Even in hard rock mining, the seven-month Mine Mill Local 598/Canadian Auto Workers (CAW)-Falconbridge (now Xstrata) strike in 2000–01, and the twelve-month United Steelworkers (USW)-Vale strike in 2009–10, were turning points where the unions suffered contract setbacks.[43] Both these Sudbury strikes were by the largest mining locals in Northern Ontario, and both unions were pressed nearly to the point of being broken as effective bargaining forces. In the end, they were able to hold together and, despite concessions, they came out of the ordeal in certain ways strengthened organizationally.[44] The two strikes were unprecedented for large-scale mining operations, in that the corporations employed professional strike-breaking firms and scab labour, which a Mine Mill lawyer likened to invasion by "private corporate armies" (Kuyek 2008). In the forest industries, too, workers suffered major setbacks, such as the 2006–07 lockout and then closure at Grant Forest Products in Timmins. Neither of the key forest unions were able to stop the epidemic of closures or consolidations, which did major economic damage to numerous Northern communities.

Second, social conditions have evolved in a contradictory fashion, though in some key ways they have weakened the labour movement. Women's much increased labour force participation has helped to transform highly male-dominated primary industry towns and to economically strengthen households. However, the main industries in Northern Ontario (mining, forestry, transportation, utilities) have remained recalcitrant when it comes to desegregating their workplaces, thus holding back the progressive social effects that greater inclusiveness and equality in these central economic activities would bring. Further, even in the midst of high levels of unemployment and underemployment, there is also a trend towards increased family and individual working time – overwork – as well as the spread of shiftwork, which weakens the free time and concerted participation of workers.

Third, the monopolization of the mass media and weakening of critical journalism has had especially negative effects in hinterland areas, which have ever fewer outlets and less competition than large metropolitan centres. Daily newspapers, already small and still the main source of local and regional news despite the enormous expansion of the internet, have seen major reductions in staffing, diminished investigative reporting, and reduced readership (St Pierre 2008), while the role of corporate public relations, media campaigns, and advertising has increased in importance.

Fourth, besides the increasingly adverse economic and social conditions, there exist unresolved political divisions. Most of the labour movement, especially in the industrial unions, has been dominated by social democracy, though a portion, more in the craft unions, has continued ties with liberalism. As the politics of capitalism itself has shifted towards neoliberalism and the right, so generally has social democracy, which has led to a greater political differentiation and conflict within and outside the labour movement. In Northern Ontario, conflicts also broke out between public sector and some private sector unions under the Rae NDP government, as well as over support for the Days of Action against the Harris Conservative government (Closs 2008). Though the North has a history of militancy and independent class action, it was also a centre of Cold War attacks and anti-communism that weakened and divided the movement. Most prominent were the USW raids against Mine Mill (now Unifor); though the division today is much reduced, it is still felt. Division is also felt over the issue of Canadian sovereignty in the labour movement. In Northern Ontario, the largest industrial union, the USW, is still headquartered in the US, as are the main craft unions in construction and transportation. Even within Canada, the internal union structures are metropolitanized to a degree, like those of capital. Despite the large number and dispersion of workers in the North, key union functions such as research, organizing, and bargaining are based in Toronto and Ottawa. Indeed, recent internal Canadian Labour Congress restructuring has reduced staff support to Northern Ontario.

Despite the many obstacles faced by the labour movement, globalization and its neoliberal policies are clashing with the interests of workers and hinterland communities and continually generating sparks of criticism, discontent, and active resistance – both organized and spontaneous. As decline continues and exasperation accumulates, it would not be surprising to see social upsurges or rapid shifts in direction. The specific forms of unity, alliance, and militancy that are needed to change the balance of power and to democratize the direction of development in the North are not yet widely discussed or clear. But for the labour movement and the interests of First Nations, Franco-Ontarians, women, the poor, and others of the excluded, they appear to converge on the issue of greater democratic control and a form of economic development that directly addresses hinterland inequalities and prioritizes social and environmental well-being rather than subordination to corporate capitalism.

NEOLIBERALISM VERSUS DEVELOPMENT AND DEMOCRACY

Provincial as well as federal government policy for Northern Ontario, driven by the regressively redistributive policies of neoliberalism, has inflicted disproportionate damage on hinterland areas. The neoliberal policy complex – coined the "the corporate agenda" in labour circles – has emerged since the 1970s into a fairly well-known form: "free trade" (more accurately, free capital movement), privatization of public assets and programs, deregulation, outsourcing, and cuts to social program standards. Conjointly, it also includes increased expenditure and power for the core repressive aspects of state power (such as policing, prisons, and the military) that are required to enforce the greater wealth concentration, social polarization, and aggressive natural resource exploitation (domestically and internationally) that neoliberalism itself generates. Further, there is a regional dimension that is less well acknowledged: the weakening of cross-regional minimum social standards and the reinforcing of metropolitan domination.

For instance, the Canada-US Free Trade Agreement (1988) and NAFTA (1993), together with the enfeebling of the Foreign Investment Review Agency, paved the way for the full foreign takeover of the nickel industry in Northern Ontario in 2006 without union, community, or public involvement – an event which was approved at the federal level with provincial support.[45] Then, for a region with higher levels of social transfer needs, the reduction of social program standards – reduced eligibility – has had disproportionate regional effects on Northern Ontario. That has occurred both with federal policy such as the Chrétien Liberals' "reform" of Unemployment Insurance (now EI), and provincial policy such as the Harris Conservatives' "reform" of Workers Compensation (now WSIB).

The overall approach of neoliberalism to regional inequality has been to devolve and withdraw from larger-scale structural and needs-oriented policies, in favour of decentralized small-scale business development initiatives, community grants and mollification, and labour market "adjustment" and training.[46] Without substantial regional employment demand, so-called "adjustment policies" have limited effectiveness and, in practice, lead to greater reliance on both large-scale resource projects and social program transfers.[47] In the context of globalization, the weakening of regional policy and the use of natural resources largely for international export is facilitating a weakening of economic links (particularly value-added links) within Canada and encouraging deeper north-south integration into the US economy (Savoie 2003, 159–60).

Though Ontario governments since the 1970s have faced legislative debate over particular neoliberal policies, to date the political division has been less about overall direction than about the pace and means of implementation – whether aggressively forcing it forward (Conservatives, 1995–2003) or trying to straddle and smooth over the social divides generated by it (Liberals, 1985–90; NDP, 1990–95; Liberals, 2003–18). Indeed, despite the experience of the financial crisis of 2008 and the mounting evidence critical of resource export-based development, current policy towards Northern Ontario continues to double down on neoliberalism and to reinforce a metropolitanist vision of the North as an area of unending natural abundance specialized in resource extraction and export in a foreordained provincial and international division of labour. Such is the corporate globalist vision of the recent *Growth Plan for Northern Ontario* (2011),[48] whose key essentials simply repeat earlier cant on resource export-based development and add little to knowledge about the North.[49]

On the core development issues of employment and distribution, the *Growth Plan* nowhere recognizes the new conditions of diminished resource employment and other reduced local benefits from resource extraction, nor the declining situation of manufacturing value-added, nor does it even discuss seriously long-standing Northern concerns about the level and sharing of resource rents and corporate taxation.[50] One is left again with the strategy of large-scale resource export-dependent development subsidized massively (in infrastructure investments and tax policy) with an emphasis on boosterist political conformity and deferential patron-client relations – as against democracy. The latest version of this is the proposed "Ring of Fire" chromite mega-project in the James Bay Lowlands, led currently by Toronto-based Noront Resources and KWG Resources. The project as proposed is – above all – not conditional on settlement of Indigenous land rights, and it would require massive government subsidies for transportation infrastructure and electricity, with little prospect for major compensating revenues during the life of the proposed mines (Kuyek 2011).

During the 2018 provincial election campaign, all parties in the legislature supported the Ring of Fire project – without a clear condition requiring the consent of the Indigenous Peoples, without limits to public subsidies, and without specified resource-revenue sharing for Indigenous Peoples and Northern Ontario – and no party proposed any substantial development alternative for the North. In August 2017, under pressures from mining interests, the Wynne Liberals made the colonial decision to start road construction for the project in 2019, but without consent from the Mattawa First Nations on whose ancestral lands the road would be located (OJAMS 2017; Powers 2018). In the campaign's Northern Ontario debate in Parry Sound, now premier Doug Ford promised an even more aggressive approach: "All we've heard is talk, talk, talk, no action ... We're going to go in there and start mining" (Meyer 2018). Once elected, Ford combined three extraction project-focused ministries under a single super-minister as the Ministry of Energy, Mines, Northern Development and Indigenous Affairs. Nishnawbe Aski Nation Grand Chief Alvin Fiddler responded that Indigenous relations had taken a "step backward" and that the move "sends a clear signal that improving relations with Indigenous Peoples is not a priority for the Ford government" (Northern Ontario Business 2018). Adding to such aggressive pressures, Noront Resources started promoting an "accidental" gold discovery in the Ring of Fire area, which could be mined and the gold flown out without road access (Friedman 2018).

The *Growth Plan* (2011, 2) feels compelled to claim that Northern Ontario "has large areas of wealth and prosperity. Its economy is diversifying and becoming less reliant on traditional resource industries." But there is no mention that Northern Ontario also has even larger areas of lower employment rates and high poverty (the word "poverty" does not appear once in the text), and the *Growth Plan* does not deign to examine why this might be so after decades of experience with the existing development model. As for the diversification notion, this is more a wishful delusion than a reckoning with the real long-term trends in market-oriented sectors, not least the massive decline in both primary and manufacturing employment. Indeed, the main source of diversifying, non-resource-based job growth has been through the public sector, insofar as it has occurred.[51]

On the Northern environment, the *Growth Plan* (39) claims to support a "culture of conservation" and sustainability practices. Yet it nowhere even asks whether minerals here, especially those that are less expensive and destructive to access, could one day be economically exhausted (and if some areas had not already seen that); nor is there a perspective on, let alone a plan for, transforming the existing non-renewable and fossil fuel-dependent energy system. And, while there is mention of the consequences of climate change – "Average temperatures are rising more quickly in the North than in the rest of Ontario" (37) – one is left with the discredited neoliberal policy of "carbon offsets markets" and nothing of substance on the climate impacts of current forms of resource extraction.[52] Further, there are no specific commitments about or even thoughtful mentions of critical recurring issues like the destruction of old growth forests, which is widely known since the Temagami struggles (Hodgins 1989; Hodgins et al. 2003), or the use of the North as an area for waste transport and disposal, which is widely known from the 1990s debates over the Adams Mine proposal for Toronto garbage (Angus 2013) and from current efforts to locate a nuclear waste disposal site in the North. Even the belated climate actions of the Wynne Liberals were deemed too much by the Ford Conservatives. Within a month of coming to power, they not only acted to revoke the cap-and-trade program but also to close the Green Ontario Fund, including support for two Indigenous-led and two municipal-led wood heating pilot projects in Northern Ontario.[53]

The brief foray of the *Growth Plan* into urban policy encourages the further weakening of smaller towns and rural areas. Communities are to be oriented to serving economic and business priorities; and larger cities, in particular, will be favoured as "economic and service hubs." This is in line with the neoliberal perspective of metropolitanization, unending scale and agglomeration economies, and, when opportune, the forced amalgamation of weakened municipalities such as occurred around Sudbury in 2001.

Unfortunately, much of what is raised today as alternative policies to challenge neoliberalism reflects thinking from the post-World War II "golden age" of the 1940s to mid-1970s: large-scale resource projects, limited Keynesian-type stimuli, and cross-regional sharing of aggregate productivity gains. Generally a period of capitalist expansion, the living standards of the mass of workers and working-class families rose, which depended on a sharing of the gains of productivity, a growing proportion of two-earner families, the expansion of social programs, and fewer immediate environmental crises. However, unemployment and inequality did increase despite it all; the "golden age" was never glittering for Indigenous Peoples, the growing numbers of poor, or the many declining towns and rural areas in the hinterland; and profound environmental issues were largely unaddressed.

Globalization and the new crisis in hinterland economic development have fundamentally altered the basis of those postwar conditions. Democratic alternatives are needed in Northern Ontario to overcome increasing corporate power and socially regressive neoliberal policies that reinforce the subordinate economy and exploitive resource export-dependent development. Alternatives deserving discussion include: public ownership, democratic control and long-term planning of resources and resource extraction to break dependence on both transnational corporations and resource export; value-added "manufacturing conditions" and research and development requirements; heightened environmental protection and restoration; an integrated, accessible, and green Northern transportation system; food, housing, and health security with renewed development of regional agriculture;

universal free public education to postsecondary levels with far greater regional content and respect for language and national rights; support for independent and local media development and measures against corporate concentration of media; and a renaissance in Northern cultural expressions. Little of this can occur without a fundamental political shift to decolonization, the ending of racial injustices, and the recognition and settlement of land rights and sovereignty issues with Indigenous Peoples. Nor will it occur without political devolution and greater regional autonomy, and, potentially, a new political structure akin to provincial status within a renewed pan-Canadian constitutional structure. Such a more radical and democratic alternative to neoliberalism is needed, actually overdue.

ACKNOWLEDGEMENTS

I would like to acknowledge the discussions and suggestions of Mary Ann Corbiere and J. Randolph Valentine on Indigenous languages, Alicia Hawkins and Patrick Julig on archaeological history, David Peerla on recent Indigenous struggles, Ugo Lapointe and Normand Mousseau on environmental issues, and John Closs and Charles Daviau on labour questions, though of course they are not responsible for the views presented here. My appreciation for their special support goes to Jane and Kate Leadbeater and to Michelle Coupal.

NOTES

1 See maps 5.1 and 5.2. For the purposes of this chapter, Northern Ontario is taken to be Statistics Canada's combined Northeast and Northwest Ontario Economic Regions. The former includes the districts of Nipissing, Parry Sound, Manitoulin, Sudbury, Timiskiming, Cochrane, and Alogoma, as well as the City of Greater Sudbury; the latter includes the districts of Thunder Bay, Rainy River, and Kenora. Geographical and population data are from Ontario (2010, 2011a) and Statistics Canada's website *Census Profile, 2016 Census*. Land area does not include freshwater area. The number for Indigenous Peoples is based on the 2016 census's Aboriginal identity counts, which are likely underestimates due to census under-coverage of First Nations areas and the currently higher growth of the Indigenous population. Southcott

(2009) calculates that between 1996 and 2006 the Aboriginal identity population of Northern Ontario grew by 52.1 per cent. A large part of the growth came from those self-identifying as Métis. By contrast, the non-Aboriginal population declined by 4.4 per cent. Hence, the Aboriginal population grew from 7.9 to 12.6 per cent of the Northern Ontario population. Southcott estimates: "If this trend continues, Aboriginals will represent the majority of the population of Northern Ontario by the year 2086." The numbers for francophones are as defined by Statistics Canada for the official language minority population based primarily on mother tongue; this likely underestimates by around 10 per cent the Franco-Ontarian national minority based on the "Inclusive Definition of Francophone" of the Ontario government, whose 2016 numbers were not published at the time of writing (see Statistics Canada 2015, s. 1).

2 Excluding the District of Parry Sound would reduce the 2016 Northern Ontario population by 42,824 (5.5 per cent); including the District Municipality of Muskoka would increase it by 60,599 (7.8 per cent). The province's Northern Ontario Heritage Fund Corporation includes the Parry Sound District in its service area, while the service area of the federal government's FedNor includes Muskoka. Statistics Canada treats Muskoka as part of the Muskoka-Kawarthas Economic Region.

3 Statistics Canada (2011b). The Laurentian Divide within Ontario marks the height of land where water to the north flows into Hudson Bay and the Arctic Ocean, and water to the south flows into the Atlantic Ocean, mainly via the Great Lakes, Ottawa River, and St Lawrence River. In Northeastern Ontario, the northern watershed is marked on Highway 11 just north of Kenogami Lake; in Northwestern Ontario, it is marked on Highway 17 near Raith, a community about an hour northwest of Thunder Bay.

4 To date in their website documentation, the Métis Nation of Ontario in collaboration with Ontario has identified at least six historic Métis communities in Northern Ontario. See also Lischke and McNab (2007).

5 For sources and further reading related to this paragraph see Julig (2002), Burnaby (1984), Abel (2006, chap. 2), and Lankton (2010, chap. 1).

6 The spelling of "Anishinaabemowin" (Northern Ontario) as distinct from Nishnaabemwin (Southwestern Ontario) reflects that "speakers of the language prefer to spell words phonetically" (Corbiere, personal communication). "Northern word[s] have vowels not found in the corresponding [Georgian Bay]/Lake Huron word[s]. The vowels are not pronounced in the latter dialect because of a prominent rule of vowel syncope, which deletes vowels that are not stressed" (Valentine 2001, 4). While among its speakers Oji-Cree is viewed as a language, linguists have tended to view it as a dialect of Ojibwe and/or Cree, though mostly of Ojibwe. An introduction to Indigenous languages in Ontario and their transmission is Burnaby (1984),

a background on the earlier European contact period in Northern Ontario is Bishop (1994), and an overview of Indigenous language populations in Canada is Norris (1998).

7   The most comprehensive historiography on Northern Ontario is Epp (1996). More recent and selective is Abel (2001), though it is limited in covering material on working-class history and political economy; as well, the large and sophisticated Franco-Ontarian literature is not addressed. The literature on Northern Ontario has recognized both rivalries and affinities with the old North-West Territories, particularly Manitoba. I would argue that understanding the specific character of colonization in Ontario requires greater emphasis on the rivalry between Ontario and Québec and their respective metropoles, Toronto and Montreal. For decades, Québec had a much larger population, industry, and territory (the latter it still has).

8   Manitoba became a province in 1870, but was not transferred ownership of natural resources until 1929; Saskatchewan and Alberta became provinces in 1905 and were not transferred resource ownership until 1930.

9   Innis (1967, 153) argued that the more active role of the state and its rapidity stemmed from the early history of colonization and the relatively later metropolitan development in Ontario:

> The advance of industrialism which followed the opening of the West and of New Ontario was accomplished by the activity of the state and of private enterprise. The rapidity of development, the long tradition of state support dating to the French régime and linked to the problem of the upper St. Lawrence waterways, and the relatively late development of metropolitan areas as contrasted with Montreal were factors responsible for the part of the government in the formation of the Ontario Hydro Electric Power Commission and of the Temiskaming and Northern Ontario Railway. The peculiarities of the economy of Ontario are deep rooted and vitally related to her position as an outpost of the lower St. Lawrence.

10 In 1858, the colonial Province of Canada established in Canada West the first two of what were northern districts, Algoma and Nipissing. They were created under pressures for mining and logging development using Lake Superior and the Ottawa River, respectively. These districts allowed for incorporated improvement districts, townships, villages, towns, and cities. However, unlike Southern Ontario with its counties, the districts were themselves not incorporated and they were without an elected council (Archives of Ontario 2009). This was followed by the districts of Parry Sound (1869), Thunder Bay (1871), Rainy River (1885), Manitoulin (1888), Muskoka (1888), Sudbury (1907), Kenora (1909), Temiskaming (now Timiskaming, 1912), and Cochrane (1921).

11 Di Matteo (1999) examines the history of resource revenues to the province. The flows and distribution of economic surplus in profits and other forms still remains to be studied.

12 Soon after the transfer of Rupert's Land to Canada, in 1874, Ontario's boundaries were expanded provisionally to the north and to the west. But the Conservative federal government clashed with Ontario over expansion into the former area of Rupert's Land, and Manitoba clashed with Ontario over control of the Kenora area. After a series of negotiations and legal battles, the federal government agreed through legislation in 1889 to the extension of Ontario's northern boundary to the Albany River and also awarded Ontario the Kenora area. The next major expansion came in 1912, when the western boundary was reduced and the northern boundary extended to its present form.

13 Ontario governments have shared responsibility for maintaining the racist structures and ideology that are fundamental to colonialism in the North. For instance, the Ontario government was central to the infamous St Catherine's Milling (1888) case. Tied to expansionist desire, Ontario premier Mowat fought the case for extending provincial jurisdiction into the North on a belief that "there is no Indian title at law or equity." In that context, the courts lined up with colonialism. As one judge expressed a prevalent racist view: "As heathens and barbarians it was not thought that they had any proprietary title to the soil." In the end, the Indigenous Peoples were allowed a right of occupancy but not title, "a personal and usufructuary right, dependent on the good will of the Sovereign" (Baskerville 2005, 127–30). See also Hall (2003, 414–17; 1991).

14 One reminiscence gives an indication of the significance of the railway (Pain 1970: 1–2):

> There is a sub-province of 100,000 people here now, and a glance at the names on a timetable of the opening up of Northern Ontario. Latchford for timber; Cobalt for silver; Haileybury as the centre of government; New Liskeard for farming; Swastika, Kirkland Lake, Larder Lake for gold; Matheson for farms, gold and asbestos. Then the fabulous Porcupine for gold again; Iroquois Falls for pulp and paper; Cochrane as the centre of an immense farming belt; and Moosenee, which is Ontario's port to the vast seas of the Arctic. They were opened up practically in that order, as the railroad started amidst misgivings and then could hardly push ahead fast enough to keep pace with developments.

15 See Nelles (2005, chap. 2), Wallace (1984), and Radforth (1987, chap. 1).

16 See Denison (1960), Manore (1999), Nelles (2005, chap. 6–7), and Luby (2016).

17 See McDowall (1984), Wallace (1984), Inwood (1987), and Beaulieu and Southcott (2010, chap. 4–7). Much has been written about entrepreneurial failure (especially of Francis Clergue in the case of the Sault), inadequate finance, adverse location, and the like in these cases, but less to discern what is systemic to the development process in colonial and hinterland conditions. Both cases can also be seen to illustrate the important if not decisive role of state policies in subsidies, tariffs, transportation, war, and procurement.

18 Limits of space prevent discussion of various single- or multiple-factor explanations that have been given for relative development failure in Northern Ontario, including adverse geography, lack of concentrated populations, transportation costs, tax and resource policies, and education. Here my focus is on the fundamental role of the political economic structure of capitalist development, particularly resource dependency in colonial and semi-colonial contexts, though such factors as those noted (as well as others) could be addressed within a larger study and are not necessarily in conflict with the present focus.

19 The overall higher level of wage and salary earnership, which is a key indicator of proletarianization in Marxist terms, must be viewed in the full context of the Northern economy. In particular, Statistics Canada's Labour Force Survey (LFS), a household survey from which the data here are collected, excludes recognized First Nations territories ("Indian reserves"), and smaller and remote areas are likely underrepresented. Discussion of inadequacies in official statistics goes beyond this chapter. However, I would emphasize that Northern Ontario, by being treated as merely another "sub-provincial" region – despite being larger than some provinces – has been denied adequate public statistical services. Neoliberal cuts to statistical services further hurt hinterland regions, such as the Harper Conservative government's elimination of the mandatory long form for the 2011 census, which was a blow to Northern Ontario as well as another attack on science.

20 It needs noting, though, for both the North and South, that a substantial portion of the self-employed are dependent contractors (frequently from corporate downsizing), so are often similar in position and interest to wage and salary earners. This would reduce further in both areas the numbers in "independent" self-employment.

21 Statistics Canada Labour Force data indicate that for primary industry occupations (which includes farming occupations), female employment in Canada in 2010 was about 21.6 per cent and had not changed or more likely declined over the previous more than 20 years. In 2011, for Ontario service-producing industries, 54.7 per cent of those employed were women.

22 According to the 2016 census, for the Toronto CMA 48.2 per cent of the employed were female, while for the Thunder Bay CMA it was 49.8 per cent and for the Sudbury CMA it was 49.3 per cent. This said, women's wages are overall lower in Northern Ontario, and the female-male wage gap has often been higher, though it has been reduced by the deteriorating conditions in wages and jobs in the higher-paid male-dominated industries in the North.

23 In 2009, Ontario mines, largely in Northern Ontario, produced about 24.4 per cent of metallic mineral output in Canada. Mineral production and a variety of related data are available from the Natural Resources Canada website under "Statistics."

24 A recent generation of such writing includes Engler (2009), Gordon (2010), and Deneault and Sacher (2012).
25 In 2006, of $8.4 billion in exports about 63 per cent were mining and primary metal products, and 24 per cent were wood and paper products, mainly to the US (Fednor 2010).
26 The "unprecedented and extended downturn" led a specially appointed "Economic Facilitator," Robert Rosehart (2008), to write in his inconsequential report: "Because the Northwest is currently facing different and more extreme challenges, standard programs and approaches of government are not sufficient to offset the significant challenges that are coming."
27 See, for example, Deneault and Sacher (2012, 64–70). MacDermid (1999) found that "the Barrick-TrizecHahn-Munk group, Munk and his spouse, TrizecHahn and subsidiaries (a development company then controlled by Peter Munk) and Barrick and its subsidiaries, made 181 contributions through 29 corporate entities totaling $312,828 to the Harris Tories between 1995 and 1997, the third largest conglomerate total after a residential developer and the companies that built highway 407." A recent study by OJAMS (2018) found that for 2014–16, metal mining companies donated $435,500 with 66 per cent going to the Liberal Party, 22 per cent to the Progressive Conservative Party, and 12 per cent to the NDP.
28 The data on nickel and gold are based on NRC (2011) and US Geological Survey (2012).
29 See, for example, Gedicks (2001) and, for Canada, the website of MiningWatch Canada (www.miningwatch.ca).
30 The three main partners in the forestry accord (and their related websites) were the Ontario Ministry of Natural Resources (http://www.mnr.gov.on.ca/en/Business/LUEPS/index.html), the Ontario Forest Industries Association (http://www.ofia.com/from_the_forest/living_legacy.html), and the Partnership for Public Lands (http://wildontario.org/). For more critical approaches from the early years, see Lindgren (1998), CELA (1999), and Weis and Krajnc (1999).
31 Data from the 2016 census. The gap of 5–10 percentage points depending on the specific area and years is a major difference and not reflected in official unemployment rate differentials of 9.3 per cent and 9.2 per cent for Northeast and Northwest Ontario, compared to 7.4 per cent for Ontario or 7.8 and 7.1 per cent for the Toronto and Ottawa regions. Nonetheless, the more on-the-ground regional rates used by the Employment Insurance Program typically show that Northern Ontario (excluding Sudbury and Thunder Bay) has the highest unemployment rate in Ontario. Taking another time, in mid-July 2011, this was 12.7 per cent compared, for example, to 8.3 per cent for Toronto and 5.3 per cent for Ottawa. Of course, all these levels are unacceptably high in terms of overall macroeconomic conditions in Canada,

but simple Keynesian-type stimulus measures will not solve the embedded structural problems confronting hinterland areas like Northern Ontario.

32 On coming to power in 1995, the Harris Conservatives imposed a series of regressive social assistance policies hardened by class prejudice that, among other things, cut social assistance levels by 21.6 per cent and imposed a zero-tolerance policy for welfare fraud. Kimberly Rogers, a forty-year-old Sudbury woman with several medical problems, committed suicide while under house arrest under the zero-tolerance policy. The jury at the inquest recommended eliminating the zero-tolerance policy, stating that it was "devastating and detrimental" to society, and the change should be made "to prevent anyone from having to go without food and/or shelter, to be deemed homeless and therefore and most importantly, to prevent the death of impoverished individuals" (Kuyek 2008).

33 The Ontario government has a chronology of "The Idea of a Separate Government" for Northern Ontario originating from the pre-1905 era, and notes that at the turn of the twentieth century "the area's resources were providing about 25 percent of Ontario's revenues" (www.mndm.gov.on.ca/en/about/history). The book associated with the NOHP and its provincehood argument is Brock (1978). Atkins (2010) considers that Deibel's campaign was crucial in establishing the Northern Ontario Heritage Fund.

34 In Northern Ontario, the Greens received 5.4 per cent of the vote, the Northern Ontario Party 1.6 per cent, and other parties and independents 0.9 per cent. The Northern voting patterns are more pronounced if the Parry Sound-Muskoka constituency is not included with the North.

35 In strict population terms, Northern Ontario has long been overrepresented. In 1996, the Harris Conservatives reduced the number of provincial electoral districts from 130 to 103, legislating that the numbers and boundaries conform to the generally larger federal electoral districts. Under this regime, Elections Canada allocated eleven ridings to Northern Ontario (including Parry Sound-Muskoka) out of the 103 or 10.7 per cent of provincial seats. In 2005, the McGuinty Liberals increased the overall number of provincial ridings to 107 but allowed the North to keep its eleven, which broke with the Harris policy, though it still meant that Northern representation fell to 10.3 per cent of seats. In 2015, the Wynne Liberals raised the total number of ridings to 122 while again keeping the Northern number at eleven. In 2017, the Liberals added two seats in the Far North for the stated reason of increasing Indigenous representation (see Ontario 2017). Hence, for the 2018 election, the North had thirteen seats out of 124 or 10.5 percent in the provincial legislature, while Northern Ontario's population is at about 6 per cent of Ontario. (If one drops the Parry Sound-Muskoka riding, the Northern representation is at twelve of 124 or 9.7 per cent.)

36 See Leadbeater (2008). One can observe this in debates on resource tax policy. Under the neoliberal impetus, Ontario has reduced corporate tax rates

substantially, including for resource corporations, to the point (as mentioned earlier) that they are lower than most other jurisdictions. Northern municipal leaders are not often heard to advocate for higher resource royalties or corporate taxation, or to campaign on the long-standing grievance against the province's exemption from municipal property taxation of the underground assets of mining corporations. More common are calls for lower corporate taxes and special low-tax zones, mimicking the orientation of corporate interests. Today, the primary orientation is to press for a bigger portion of the relatively diminishing share of corporate revenue going to the province. In a revealing moment recently, following another effort by some Northern mayors to request that the province turn over a percentage of the Ontario Mining Tax to municipalities, the corporate Ontario Mining Association actually joined in, requesting that local municipalities and First Nation communities "have a greater share in the benefits of mining through the existing levels of mining tax" (*Sudbury Star*, 6 July 2011).

37 See Peerla (2014), who considers the KI struggle to be prefigurative of a fundamentally different future. Though Ontario amended the Mining Act, the colonial "free entry" regime in mining still remains (Lapointe 2014).

38 The "national question," associated with the internationally recognized right of national self-determination, has a long, deep, and still unresolved history in Canada, and Northern Ontario is itself a microcosm of unresolved conflicts associated with it. It is now widely accepted that "nation" is not necessarily the same as, or defined by having, an independent "state," though democratic rights attach to the recognition of nations, up to and including separation and the formation of an independent state.

39 This does not imply any particular number of nations, or that language is the only marker of national status. Evidently, this is quite different in character than policies of "multiculturalism," though policies on immigration and immigrant rights are also important questions, and considered elsewhere in this volume.

40 There is a large and developing literature on Franco-Ontarians, mostly in French. Key points of access include: Choquette (1977, 1980), Vallières (1980), Arnopoulos (1982), Bernard (1988), Jaenen (1993), Gervais (1993, 2003), Ouellet (1993), D'Augerot-Arend (1995), Cotnam et al. (1995), Dennie (2001, 2008), and Bock and Gervais (2004).

41 For further discussion see Leadbeater (2008, 2014).

42 For example, Vale (formerly Inco) has about 133,000 employees worldwide relative to 4,000 in Sudbury. This contrasts to the pre-1970s decades when Inco had the vast majority of its employment and production concentrated in the region.

43 On the two strikes see Grylls (2008) and Peters (2010). The USW Local 6500, one of the largest mining locals in North America, felt compelled to accept among other things a two-tier pension system and reduced profit-sharing.

44 This was not the fate of the longest strike in recent Canadian history, against Goldcorp at Red Lake in 1996–2000, which ended with the USW local removed.
45 See Leadbeater (2008) and CAW (2006).
46 An official view of the arc of federal regional policy in Canada is Beaumier (1998). The main federally and provincially funded agencies for regional development are FedNor and the Northern Ontario Heritage Fund. Their activities, arguably more significant politically than in altering the direction of Northern economic development, deserve a more detailed and critical study than can be provided here, though an audit report such as the "Final Evaluation for the Northern Ontario Development Program" covering 2006–10 gives some perspective on how limited are the measures and the concerns about results.
47 The central problem of Northern employment conditions periodically becomes more publicly visible in large-scale layoffs, such as the mine closures at Elliot Lake in the 1990s, or the more recent wave of mill closures in the forest industry, particularly when there are actual or perceived possibilities of mass resistance, although many other thousands of smaller-scale and gradual losses are less visible. On the impacts and some lessons of such layoffs in Northern Ontario, see Leadbeater and Suschnigg (1997) and Leadbeater (1998, 1999).
48 One reads, for instance (2011, 4): "It's the year 2036 and there's a new Northern Ontario. Northern Ontario has a skilled, educated, healthy and prosperous population that is supported by world-class resources, leading edge technology and modern infrastructure. Companies scan the world for opportunities to create jobs, attract investment and serve global markets. Communities are connected to each other and the world, offering dynamic and welcoming environments that are attractive to newcomers. Municipalities, Aboriginal communities, governments and industry work together to achieve shared economic, environmental and community goals."
49 Among earlier "growth plans" were the *Design for Development* plans of the 1970s. Weller (1977, 745) wrote that the plans "indicate quite clearly that the economic development of the region will rely heavily upon raw material extraction and the other presently-established areas and that any secondary manufacturing will be related to those extractive industries and will not be of major importance; nor will the region's economy include the processing of the raw material to any high degree of manufacture."
50 Pertinent here is a comment by the right-wing *Sudbury Star* (20 October 2007), opining after the province had once again rejected a request from Northern municipalities for equitable sharing of resource revenues: "The province might still be open to dishing out more money to the North, but it will do so for projects of its choosing, and share in the political benefits, rather than simply handing over money to the municipalities."

51 Even a prominent official study on diversification found that there was little change overall and most of that was towards less diversification (Beshiri et al. 2006). Further, the typical measure used for diversification, the Herfindal Index, is formulated in such a way that, in conditions of decline, a community such as a rail town that loses its rail jobs and suffers high unemployment, loss of schools, etc., actually becomes more "diversified." Such was the case, for example, of Capreol, which is listed as the number one diversifying community in Northern Ontario. The meaning of "diversification" here as normally understood is turned on its head: most communities see it as meaning new jobs in new sectors to balance or replace existing ones, not an exercise in reducing employment to achieve more balanced relative proportions. The one area often held up as a demonstration of diversification is mining and forestry supply services, yet these are still directly tied to resource extraction and much smaller in jobs created than those lost overall in resource extraction and primary manufacturing.

52 For a critical view of Northern environmental issues, see the website of Northwatch (www.web.ca/~nwatch/).

53 The Wynne Liberals' short-lived cap and trade agreement with Quebec and California was signed 22 September 2017, came into effect 1 January 2018, and revoked effective 3 July 2018 (https://www.ontario.ca/page/cap-and-trade). On the Green Ontario program in Northern Ontario, see Church (2018) and Ross (2018).

REFERENCES

Abel, Kerry. 2006. *Changing Places: History, Community and Identity in Northeastern Ontario*. Montreal: McGill-Queen's University Press.

– 2001. "History and the Provincial Norths: An Ontario Example." In *Northern Visions*, edited by Kerry Abel and Ken Coates. Peterborough: Broadview.

Angus, Charlie. 2013. *Unlikely Radicals: The Story of the Adams Mine Dump War*. Toronto: Between the Lines.

– 2015. *Children of the Broken Treaty: Canada's Lost Promise and One Girl's Dream*. Regina: University of Regina Press.

Archives of Ontario. 2009. *The Changing Shape of Ontario: A Guide to Boundaries, Names and Regional Governments*. http://www.archives.gov.on.ca.

Arnopoulos, Sheila McLeod. 1982. *Hors du Québec point de salut?* Montréal: Libre Expression.

Arthur, Elizabeth. 1988. "Beyond Superior: Ontario's New-Found Land." In *Patterns of the Past*, edited by Roger Hall, William Westfall, and Laurel Sefton MacDowell. Toronto: Ontario Historical Society.

Atkins, Michael. 2006. "The Case for Regional Government." *Northern Life*. 2 November.

- 2010. "Is It Back to the Future for Heritage 11?" *Northern Life*, 12 May.
Beaulieu, Michel. 2011. *Labour at the Lakehead: Ethnicity, Socialism, and Politics, 1900–35*. Vancouver: University of British Columbia Press.
Beaulieu, Michel, and Chris Southcott. 2010. *North of Superior: An Illustrated History of Northwestern Ontario*. Toronto: Lorimer.
Beaumier, Guy. 1998. *Regional Development in Canada*. Ottawa: Government of Canada.
Bernard, Roger. 1988. *De Québécois à Ontarois*. Ottawa: Le Nordir.
Beshiri, Roland, Ray Bollman, and Verna Mitura. 2006. *Northern Ontario's Communities: Economic Diversification, Specialization and Growth*. Cat. no. 21-601-MIE-082. Ottawa: Statistics Canada.
Bishop, Charles A. 1994. "Northern Algonquins, 1550–1760." In *Aboriginal Ontario: Historical Perspectives on the First Nations*, edited by E. Rogers and D. Smith. Toronto: Dundurn.
Bock, Michel, and Gaétan Gervais. 2004. *L'Ontario français: Des pays-d'en-Haut à nos jours*. Ottawa: CFORP.
Bonsor, N.C. 1977. *Transportation Rates and Economic Development in Northern Ontario*. Toronto: Ontario Economic Council.
Bouchard, Daniel. 2003. "Pollution, science et pouvoir: L'histoire du désastre écologique à Sudbury (1883–1945); Derrière l'écran de fumée." PhD diss., Université d'Ottawa.
Boudreau, François. 2008. "Traditional Elites and the Democratic Deficit: Some Challenges for Education in French-Speaking Ontario." In *Mining Town Crisis: Globalization, Labour and Resistance in Sudbury*, edited by D. Leadbeater. Halifax: Fernwood.
Bray, Matt, and Ernie Epp, eds. 1984. *A Vast and Magnificent Land*. Sudbury: Laurentian University.
Brock, Gordon. 1978. *The Province of Northern Ontario*. Cobalt: Highway Book Shop.
Burnaby, Barbara J. 1984. *Aboriginal Languages in Ontario*. Toronto: Minister of Education.
Buse, Dieter, and Graeme Mount. 2011. *Come On Over! Northeastern Ontario, A to Z*. Sudbury: Your Scrivener Press.
Canada. 2018. *Pre-1975 Treaties (Historic Treaties), Post-1975 Treaties (Modern Treaties)*. Open Government Data Sets. https://open.canada.ca/data/en/dataset.
Canada. AANDC (Aboriginal Affairs and Northern Development Canada). 2018. *Treaty Guides*. Ottawa: AANDC.
CAW. 2006. *The Two Sides of the Coin: The Opportunities, and the Risks of Creating the World's Largest Nickel Producer*. Toronto: Canadian Auto Workers.
CELA (Canadian Environmental Law Association). 1999. *The 'Lands for Life Proposals': A Preliminary Analysis*. www.cela.ca.
Choquette, Robert. 1977. *Langue et religion: Histoire des conflits anglo-français en Ontario*. Ottawa: Éditions de l'Université d'Ottawa.

– 1980. *L'Ontario français, historique*. Montréal: Études vivantes.
Church, Maria. 2018. "ON Launches Wood Heat Programs for Rural, Indigenous Communities." *Canadian Biomass*, 3 May.
Chute, Janet. 1998. *The Legacy of Shingwaukonse: A Century of Native Leadership*. Toronto: University of Toronto Press.
Closs, John. 2008. "Public-Sector Unions in Sudbury." In *Mining Town Crisis: Globalization, Labour and Resistance in Sudbury*, edited by D. Leadbeater. Halifax: Fernwood.
Coates, Kenneth, and William Morrison. 1992. *The Forgotten North: A History of Canada's Provincial Norths*. Toronto: Lorimer.
Conteh, Charles, and Robert Segsworth, eds. 2013. *Governance in Northern Ontario: Economic Development and Policy Making*. Toronto: University of Toronto Press.
Cooper, Kathleen. 1999. "Guide to Environmental Deregulation in Ontario – Updated Chronology." *Intervenor* 24 (1).
Cotnam, Jacques, Yves Frenette, and Agnès Whitfield, eds. 1995. *La francophonie ontarienne: Bilan et perspectives de recherche*. Ottawa: Le Nordir.
D'Augerot-Arend, Sylvie. 1995. "La condition des femmes francophone en Ontario." *La francophonie ontarienne: Bilan et perspectives de recherche*, edited by Jacques Cotnam, Yves Frenette, and Agnès Whitfield. Ottawa: Le Nordir.
Debassige, Terry, Shelley J. Pearen, Alan Corbière, and Dominic Beaudry. n.d. "Manitoulin Treaties, Parts 1–4." *Manitoulin Expositor*. Accessed July 2018, http://www.blacksbay.com/aboriginals/treaty_series_part_1.htm.
Deneault, Alain, and William Sacher. 2012. *Imperial Canada Inc.: Legal Haven of Choice for the World's Mining Industries*. Vancouver: Talonbooks.
Denison, Merrill. 1960. *The People's Power: The History of Ontario Hydro*. Toronto: McClelland and Stewart.
Dennie, Donald. 1993. "Le mouvement ouvrier dans le Nord de l'Ontario: Les grèves de 1900 à 1945." *Labour/Le Travail* 32.
– 2001. *À l'ombre de l'Inco: Étude de la transition d'une communauté canadienne-française de la région de Sudbury, 1890–1972*. Ottawa: Presses de l'Université d'Ottawa.
– 2008. "French Ontario: Two Realities." In *Mining Town Crisis: Globalization, Labour and Resistance in Sudbury*, edited by D. Leadbeater. Halifax: Fernwood.
– 2017. *Une Histoire sociale du Grand Sudbury: Le bois, le roc et le rail*. Sudbury: Éditions Prise de parole.
Dickason, Olive. 2002. *Canada's First Nations: A History of Founding Peoples from Earliest Times*. 3rd ed. Don Mills: Oxford University Press.
Di Matteo, Livio. 1999. "Fiscal Imbalance and Economic Development in Canadian History: Evidence from the Economic History of Ontario." *American Review of Canadian Studies* 29 (2).
Di Matteo, Livio, J.C. Herbert Emery, and Ryan English. 2006. "Is It Better to Live in a Basement, an Attic or to Get Your Own Place? Analyzing the Costs and

Benefits of Institutional Change for Northwestern Ontario." *Canadian Public Policy* 32 (2).

Di Matteo, Livio, J.C. Herbert Emery, and Martin Shanahan. 2014. "Natural Resource Exports and Development in Settler Economies during the First Globalization Era: Northwestern Ontario and South Australia, 1905–15." In *Smart Globalization: The Canadian Business and Economic History Experience*, edited by Andrew Smith and Dimitry Anastakis. Toronto: University of Toronto Press.

Dubinsky, Karen. 1993. *Improper Advances: Rape and Heterosexual Conflict in Ontario, 1880–1929*. Chicago: University of Chicago Press.

Dunk, Thomas W. 2003. *It's a Working Man's Town: Male Working-Class Culture in Northwestern Ontario*. 2nd ed. Montreal: McGill-Queen's University Press.

Dyck, Rand. 1996. *Provincial Politics in Canada: Towards the Turn of the Century*. 3rd ed. Scarborough: Prentice-Hall of Canada.

– 1997. "The Socio-Economic Setting of Ontario Politics." In *The Government and Politics of Ontario*, 5th ed., edited by Graham White. Toronto: University of Toronto Press.

Engler, Yves. 2009. *The Black Book of Canadian Foreign Policy*. Halifax: Fernwood.

Epp, Ernie. 1984. "Transportation and Communication." In *A Vast and Magnificent Land*, edited by Matt Bray and Ernie Epp. Sudbury: Laurentian University.

– 1996. "Northern Ontario: History and Bibliography." In *The Historiography of the Provincial Norths*, edited by Ken Coates and William Morrison. Thunder Bay: Centre for Northern Studies, Lakehead University.

Fednor. 2010. *The State of Exporting in Northern Ontario*. Ottawa: Industry Canada.

FNCPA (First Nations Chiefs of Police Association). n.d. *Setting the Context: The Policing of First Nations Communities*. The First Nations Chiefs of Police Association with Human Resources Development Canada.

Forestell, Nancy M. 1999. "The Miner's Wife: Working-Class Femininity in a Masculine Context." In *Gendered Pasts: Historical Essays in Femininity and Masculinity in Canada*, edited by Kathryn M. McPherson and Cecilia Louise Morgan. Don Mills: Oxford University Press.

– 2001. "Women, Gender, and the Provincial North." In *Northern Visions*, edited by Kerry Abel and Ken Coates. Peterborough: Broadview.

– 2006. "'And I Feel Like I'm Dying from Mining for Gold': Disability, Gender and the Mining Community, 1920–1950." *Labour: Studies of Working Class History of the Americas* 3 (3).

FPNP. 2011. *First Peoples National Party of Canada*. http://debatecanada.ca.

Fraser Institute. 2010. *Survey of Mining Companies 2010/2011*. Vancouver: Fraser Institute.

Friedman, Gabriel. 2018. "'Accidental' Gold Discovery in Ring of Fire Prompts Noront Resources to Seek Exploration Partner." *Financial Post*, 1 July.

Gaudreau, Guy. 1999. *Les recoltes des forets publiques au Quebec et en Ontario, 1840–1900*. Montreal: McGill-Queen's University Press.

Gaudreau, Guy, with Alain Daoust, et al. 2003. *L'histoire des mineurs du nord ontarien et québécois, 1886–1945*. Sillery: Septentrion.

Gedicks, Al. 2001. *Resource Rebels: Native Challenges to Mining and Oil Corporations*. Cambridge: South End Press.

George, Peter. 1987. "Ontario's Mining Industry, 1987–1940." In *Progress Without Planning: The Economic History of Ontario*, edited by Ian M. Drummond, Peter George, Kris Inwood, Peter W. Sinclair, and Tom Traves. Toronto: University of Toronto Press.

Gervais, Gaétan. 1993. "L'Ontario français (1821–1910)." In *Les Franco-Ontariens*, edited by Cornelius Jaenen. Ottawa: Presses de l'Université d'Ottawa.

– 2003. *Des gens de résolution: Le passage du Canada français à l'Ontario français*. Sudbury: Prise de parole.

Gervais, Gaétan, Ashley Thomson, and Gwenda Hallsworth. 1985. *Bibliographie: Histoire du nord-est de l'Ontario*. Sudbury: Société historique du Nouvel-Ontario.

Gordon, Todd. 2010. *Imperialist Canada*. Winnipeg: Arbeiter Ring Publishing.

Greer, Allan. 1992. "The Birth of the Police in Canada." In *Colonial Leviathan: State Formation in Mid-Nineteenth-Century Canada*, edited by Allan Greer and Ian Radforth. Toronto: University of Toronto Press.

Grylls, Rick. 2008. "Mine Mill Local 598/CAW Reaches a Turning Point." In *Mining Town Crisis: Globalization, Labour and Resistance in Sudbury*, edited by David Leadbeater. Halifax: Fernwood.

Hall, Anthony. 1991. "*The St. Catherine's Milling and Lumber Company versus the Queen*: Indian Land Rights as a Factor in Federal-Provincial Relations in Nineteenth-Century Canada." In *Aboriginal Resource Use in Canada: Historical and Legal Aspects*, edited by Kerry Abel and Jean Friesen. Winnipeg: University of Manitoba Press.

– 2003. *The American Empire and the Fourth World*. Montreal: McGill-Queen's University Press.

– 2010. *Earth into Property: Colonization, Decolonization, and Capitalism*. Montreal: McGill-Queen's University Press.

Hodgins, Bruce. 1989. *The Temagami Experience: Recreation, Resources, and Aboriginal Rights in the Northern Ontario Wilderness*. Toronto: University of Toronto Press.

Hodgins, Bruce, Ute Lischke, and David McNab, eds. 2003. *Blockades and Resistance: Studies in Actions of Peace and the Temagami Blockades of 1988–89*. Waterloo: Wilfrid Laurier University Press.

Holland, Stuart. 1976. *Capital versus the Regions*. London: Macmillan.

Innis, Harold. 1967. "An Introduction to the Economic History of Ontario from Outpost to Empire." In *Profiles of a Province: Studies in the History of Ontario*, edited by Edith Firth. Toronto: Ontario Historical Society.

Inwood, Kris. 1984. "The Iron and Steel Industry." In *Progress Without Planning: The Economic History of Ontario*, edited by Ian M. Drummond, Peter George,

Kris Inwood, Peter W. Sinclair, and Tom Traves. Toronto: University of Toronto Press.

Jaenen, Cornelius, ed. 1993. *Les Franco-Ontariens*. Ottawa: Presses de l'Université d'Ottawa.

Jankowski, W.B., and B. Moazzami. 1996. *Northern Ontario's Economy in Transition: National and International Perspectives*. Thunder Bay: Lakehead University.

Julig, Patrick, ed. 2002. *The Sheguidandah Site: Archaeological, Geological and Paleobotanical Studies at a Paleoindian Site on Manitoulin Island, Ontario*. Ottawa: Canadian Museum of Civilization.

Kecknie, Margaret, and Marge Reitsma-Street, eds. 1996. *Changing Lives: Women in Northern Ontario*. Toronto: Dundurn.

KI. 2011. *Kitchenuhmaykoosib Inninuwug at the 37th Annual All Ontario Chiefs Conference, Toronto, Ontario*. Big Trout Lake, KI. www.http://kitchenuhmaykoosib.com.

Kuhlberg, Mark. 2014. "'Pulpwood is the Only Thing We Do Export': The Myth of Provincial Protectionism in Ontario's Forest Industry, 1890–1930." In *Smart Globalization: The Canadian Business and Economic History Experience*, edited by Andrew Smith and Dimitry Anastakis. Toronto: University of Toronto Press.

Kuyek, Don. 2008. "The State and Civility in Sudbury." In *Mining Town Crisis: Globalization, Labour and Resistance in Sudbury*, edited by David Leadbeater. Halifax: Fernwood.

Kuyek, Joan. 2011. *Economic Analysis of the Ring of Fire Chromite Mining Play*. Ottawa: MiningWatch Canada.

Laite, Julian. 1985. "Capitalist Development and Labour Organisation: Hard-Rock Miners in Ontario." In *Miners and Mining in the Americas*, edited by Thomas Greaves and William Culver. Manchester: Manchester University Press.

Langston, Nancy. 2017. *Sustaining Lake Superior: An Extraordinary Lake in a Changing World*. New Haven: Yale University Press.

Lankton, Larry D. 2010. *Hallowed Ground: Copper Mining and Community Building on Lake Superior, 1840s–1990s*. Detroit: Wayne State University Press.

Lapointe, Ugo. 2014. "The Legacy of the Free Mining System in Quebec and Canada." In *Mining Town Crisis: Globalization, Labour and Resistance in Sudbury*, edited by David Leadbeater. Halifax: Fernwood.

Leadbeater, David. 1984. "An Outline of Capitalist Development in Alberta." In *Essays on the Political Economy of Alberta*, edited by David Leadbeater. Toronto: New Hogtown Press.

– 1998. *Single-Industry Resource Communities and the New Crisis of Economic Development: Lessons of Elliot Lake*. Laurentian University, Elliot Lake Tracking and Adjustment Study. http://inord.laurentian.ca/pdf/1a15.PDF.

– 1999. "Increased Transfer Dependency in the Elliot Lake and North Shore Communities." In *Boom Town Blues: Collapse and Revival in a Single Industry Community*, edited by Anne-Marie Mawhiney and Jane Pitblado. Toronto: Dundurn.

– 2008. "Sudbury's Crisis of Development and Democracy." In *Mining Town Crisis: Globalization, Labour and Resistance in Sudbury*, edited by David Leadbeater. Halifax: Fernwood.

– 2014. "Metropolitanism and Hinterland Decline." In *Resources, Empire and Labour: Crises, Lessons and Alternatives*, edited by David Leadbeater. Halifax: Fernwood.

Leadbeater, David, and Peter Suschnigg. 1997. "Training as the Principal Focus of Adjustment Policy: A Critical View from Northern Ontario." *Canadian Public Policy* 23 (1).

Lindgren, Rick. 1998. "Lands for Life or Lands for Lumber?" *Intervenor* 23 (4).

Lischke, Ute, and David McNab, eds. 2007. *The Long Journey of a Forgotten People: Métis Identities and Family Histories*. Waterloo: Wilfrid Laurier University Press.

Ljunggren, D. 2009. "Every Nation Wants to Be Like Canada, Insists PM." *Reuters*, 25 September.

Long, John. 2010. *Treaty No. 9: Making the Agreement to Share the Land in Far Northern Ontario in 1905*. Montreal: McGill-Queen's University Press.

Luby, Brittany. 2016. "Drowned: Anishinabek Economies and Resistance to Hydroelectric Development in the Winnipeg River Drainage Basin, 1873–1975." PhD diss., York University.

MacDermid, Robert. 1999. *Funding the Common Sense Revolutionaries: Contributions to the Progressive Conservative Party of Ontario 1995–97*. Toronto: Centre for Social Justice.

– 2012. "Comment" to Weir (2012). http://www.progressive-economics.ca/2012/02/10/ontario-pitiful-mining-tax/.

MacDowell, Laurel Sefton. 2001. *Remember Kirkland Lake: The Gold Miners' Strike of 1941–42*. 2nd ed. Toronto: Canadian Scholar's Press.

Maclem, Patick. 1997. "The Impact of Treaty 9 on Natural Resource Development in Northern Ontario." In *Aboriginal and Treaty Rights in Canada: Essays on Law, Equality, and Respect for Differences*, edited by Michael Asch. Vancouver: University of British Columbia Press.

Magnuson, Bruce. 1944. *Ontario's Green Gold*. Toronto: Eveready Printers.

– 1990. *The Untold Story of Ontario's Bushworkers: A Political Memoir*. Toronto: Progress Books.

Manore, Jean. 1999. *Cross-Currents: Hydroelectricity and the Engineering of Northern Ontario*. Waterloo: Wilfrid Laurier University Press.

Martin, Chester. 1938. *"Dominion Lands" Policy*. Toronto: Macmillan.

Mawhiney, A., and J. Pitbaldo, eds. 1999. *Boom Town Blues: Collapse and Revival in a Single Industry Community*. Toronto: Dundurn Press.

McCalla, Douglas. 1992. "Railways and the Development of Canada West, 1850–1870." In *Colonial Leviathan: State Formation in Mid-Nineteenth-Century Canada*, edited by Allan Greer and Iad Radforth. Toronto: University of Toronto Press.

McDowall, Duncan. 1984. *Steel at the Sault: Francis H. Clergue, Sir James Dunn and the Algoma Steel Corporation 1901–1956*. Toronto: University of Toronto Press.

McNab, David. 1999. *Circles of Time: Aboriginal Land Rights and Resistance in Ontario*. Waterloo: Wilfrid Laurier University Press.

Mercier, Laurie. 2011. "Bordering on Equality: Women Miners in North America." In *Gendering the Field: Towards Sustainable Livelihoods for Mining Communities*, edited by Kuntala Lahiri-Dutt. Canberra: ANU Press.

Meyer, Carl. 2018. "Wynne Defends Ring of Fire Progress as Ford Touts 'Gold Mine of Minerals' in Debate on Northern Ontario Issues." *Canada's National Observer*, 11 May.

Miller, Tom. 1985. "Cabin Fever: The Province of Ontario and Its Norths." In *The Government and Politics of Ontario*, 3rd ed., edited by Donald C. MacDonald. Scarborough: Nelson Canada.

Moran, Jim. 2010. *The Sentinel: A Wildfire Story*. Bloomington, IN: Trafford Publishing.

Morrison, Jean. 1981. "The Working Class in Northern Ontario: Review Essay." *Labour/Le Travail* 7.

Neiguth, Tim. 2009. "'We Are Left with No Other Alternative': Legitimating Internal Secession in Northern Ontario." *Space and Polity* 13 (2).

Nelles, H.V. 2005. *The Politics of Development: Forests, Mines and Hydro-Electric Power in Ontario, 1849–1941*. 2nd ed. Montreal: McGill-Queen's University Press.

Norris, Mary Jane. 1998. "Canada's Aboriginal Languages." *Canadian Social Trends* Winter: 8–16. Ottawa: Statistics Canada.

Northern Ontario Business. 2018. "Provincial Cabinet Appointments Applauded, Panned by Forestry, Indigenous Leaders." *Northern Ontario Business*, 29 June.

NRC (Natural Resources Canada). 2011. *Mineral and Metals Sector Statistics*. http://mmsd.mms.nrcan.gc.ca/stat-stat/prod-prod/ann-ann-eng.aspx.

OJAMS (Ontarians for a Just Accountable Mineral Strategy). 2017. "The Ring of Fire Continues to Divide First Nations and Suck Up Monday that Should Go to Healing Communities." 13 September. http://www.ojams.ca/2017/09/.

– 2018. *Campaign Financing and the Ontario Mining Industry's Political Influence*. http://www.ojams.ca/.

Ontario. 2009. *The Far North of Ontario*. Toronto: Ministry of Natural Resources. www.web2.mnr.gov.on.ca.

– 2011a. *Aboriginal People in Ontario*. Toronto: Ministry of Aboriginal Affairs. www.aboriginalaffairs.gov.on.ca.

– 2011b. *Places to Grow: Growth Plan for Northern Ontario, 2011*. Toronto: Ministry of Infrastructure and Ministry of Northern Development, Mines and Forestry.

– 2012. *A Historical Perspective on the North*. Ministry of Northern Development, Mines and Forestry. www.mndm.gov.on.ca/en/about-ministry/history.

On the Path of the Elders. 2009–10. *Treaty No. Nine: The James Bay Treaty.* www.pathoftheelders.com/history/chapter4a-1.

Ouellet, Fernand. 1993. "L'évolution de la présence francophone en Ontario: Une perspective économique et sociale." In *Les Franco-Ontariens*, edited by Cornelius Jaenen. Ottawa: Presses de l'Université d'Ottawa.

Peerla, David. 2014. "No Means No: The Kitchenuhmaykoosib Inninuwug and the Fight for Indigenous Resource Sovereignty." In *Resources, Empire and Labour: Crises, Lessons and Alternatives*, edited by D. Leadbeater. Halifax: Fernwood.

Peet, Chelsea. 2009. "Representing the Great White North: The Northern Ontario M.P.P. Experience." Paper presented at the Canadian Political Science Association Meetings, Ottawa, 27 May.

Peters, John. 2010. "Down in the Vale: Corporate Globalization, Unions of the Defensive, and the USW Local 6500 Strike in Sudbury, 2009–2010." *Labour/Le Travail* 66.

Powers, Neil. 2018. "Ring of Fire: Homeland or Frontier?" *First Stories*, 9 January. https://1stories.wixsite.com/firststories/single-post/2018/01/09/Ring-of-Fire-Homeland-or-Frontier.

PricewaterhouseCoopers. 2011. *Digging Deeper: Canadian Mining Taxation.* www.pwc.com.

Radford, Ian. 1987. *Bushworkers and Bosses: Logging in Northern Ontario, 1900–1980.* Toronto: University of Toronto Press.

– 1998. "Finnish Radicalism and Labour Activism in the Northern Ontario Woods." In *A Nation of Immigrants; Women, Workers, and Community in Canadian History, 1840s–1960s*, edited by Franca Iacovetta, Paula Draper, and Robert Ventresca. Toronto: University of Toronto Press.

Rea, K.J. 1976. *The Political Economy of Northern Development.* Background Study No. 36. Ottawa: Science Council of Canada.

Repo, Satu. 1981/82. "Rosvall and Voutilainen: Two Union Men Who Never Died." *Labour/Le Travail* 8/9.

Robinson, David. 2011. *Why the North Doesn't Change.* Sudbury: Laurentian University, Institute for Northern Ontario Research and Development.

Rosehart, Robert. 2008. *Northwestern Ontario: Preparing for Change.* Northwestern Ontario Economic Facilitator Report. Sudbury: Ontario Ministry of Northern Development and Mines.

Ross, Ian. 2018. "Manitoulin First Nation Wants Provincial Wood Heating Program Restored." *Northern Ontario Business*, 4 July.

Ryerson, Stanley. 1973. *Unequal Union: Roots of Crisis in the Canadas, 1815–1873.* 2nd ed. Toronto: Progress Books.

Saarinen, Oiva W. 2013. *From Meteorite Impact to Constellation City: A Historical Geography of Greater Sudbury.* Waterloo: Wilfrid Laurier University Press.

Satzewich, Vic, and Terry Wotherspoon. 1993. *First Nations: Race, Class, and Gender Relations.* Scarborough: Nelson Canada.

Savoie, Donald. 2003. *Reviewing Canada's Regional Development Efforts*. St John's: Royal Commission on Renewing and Strengthening Our Place in Canada.

Sinclair, Peter. 1987. "The North and the North-West: Forestry and Agriculture." In *Progress Without Planning: The Economic History of Ontario*, edited by Ian M. Drummond, Peter George, Kris Inwood, Peter W. Sinclair, and Tom Traves. Toronto: University of Toronto Press.

Southcott, Chris, ed. 1993. *Provincial Hinterland: Social Equality in Northern Ontario*. Halifax: Fernwood.

– 2009. *Aboriginals and the Economy of Northern Ontario*. 2006 Census Research Paper No. 12. Thunder Bay: Local [Training and Adjustment] Boards of Northern Ontario.

– 2010. "Old Economy/New Economy Transitions and Shifts in Demographic and Industrial Patterns in Northern Ontario." In *Transitions in Marginal Zones in the Age of Globalization: Case Studies from the North and South*, edited by Thomas Dunk. Thunder Bay: Lakehead University Centre for Northern Studies.

Southern Chiefs Organization. 2018. *Treaty Maps*. http://scoinc.mb.ca/about/treaties.

Spencer, Loraine, and Susan Holland. 1968. *Northern Ontario: A Bibliography*. Toronto: University of Toronto.

Statistics Canada. 2010. *Canada Year Book 2010*. Cat. no. 11-402-X. Ottawa: Statistics Canada.

– 2011a. *Annual Demographic Estimates: Subprovincial Areas*. Catalogue no. 91-214-X. Ottawa: Statistics Canada.

– 2011b. *Human Activity and the Environment: Detailed Statistics*. Ottawa: Statistics Canada.

– 2015. *Portrait of Official-Language Minorities in Canada: Francophones in Ontario*. Cat. no. 89-6642-X. Ottawa: Statistics Canada.

Steedman, Mercedes. 2006. "Godless Communists and Faithful Wives, Gender Relations and the Cold War: Mine Mill and the 1958 Strike against the International Nickel Company." In *Mining Women: Gender in the Development of a Global Industry, 1670 to 2000*, edited by Laurie Mercier and Jaclyn Gier. New York: Palgrave Macmillan.

Steedman, Mercedes, Peter Suschnigg, and Dieter Buse, eds. 1995. *Hard Lessons: The Mine Mill Union in the Canadian Labour Movement*. Toronto: Dundurn Press.

St Pierre, Denis. 2008. "Strike-Breaking and the Corporate Agenda at *The Sudbury Star*." In *Mining Town Crisis: Globalization, Labour and Resistance in Sudbury*, edited by David Leadbeater. Halifax: Fernwood.

Thomson, Ashley, Glenda Hallsworth, and Lionel Bonin, with Patrick Julig. 1994. *The Bibliography of Northern Ontario / La bibliographie du nord de l'Ontario, 1966–1991*. Toronto: Dundurn Press.

Thunder Bay. 2007. *Brief History of Thunder Bay*. Thunder Bay: City of Thunder Bay Archives.

US Geological Survey. 2012. *Mineral Commodity Summaries 2012.* http://minerals.usgs.gov/minerals/pubs/mcs/.

Valentine, J. Randolf. 2001. *Nishnaabemwin Reference Grammar.* Toronto: University of Toronto Press.

Vallières, Gaétan. 1980. *L'Ontario français par les documents.* Saint-Laurent: Etudes vivantes.

Wallace, Carl M. 1984. "Industry." In *A Vast and Magnificent Land*, edited by Matt Bray and Ernie Epp. Sudbury: Laurentian University.

Wallace, Iain. 1998. "Canadian Shield: Development of a Resource Frontier." In *Heartland Hinterland: A Regional Geography of Canada*, 3rd ed., edited by Larry McCann and Angus Gunn. Scarborough: Prentice Hall Canada.

Weis, Tony, and Anita Krajnc. 1999. "Greenwashing Ontario's Lands for Life." *Canadian Dimension* 33 (6).

Weir, Erin. 2012. "Ontario's Pitiful Mining Tax." *The Progressive Economics Forum.* 10 February. www.progressive-economics.ca.

Weller, Geoffrey. 1977. "Hinterland Politics: The Case of Northwestern Ontario." *Canadian Journal of Political Science* 10 (4).

– 1997. "Politics and Policy in the North." In *The Government and Politics of Ontario*, 5th ed., edited by Graham White. Toronto: University of Toronto Press.

Whitehouse, Mike. 2009. "The Way Ahead Lies North." *Sudbury Star*, 14 November.

Wightman, W.R., and N.M. Wightman. 1997. *The Land Between: Northwestern Ontario Resource Development, 1800 to the 1990s.* Toronto: University of Toronto Press.

Woodrow, Maureen. 2002. *Challenges to Sustainability in Northern Ontario.* Ottawa: Institute of the Environment University of Ottawa.

Wray, L. Randall. 2008. "The Commodities Market Bubble: Money Manager Capitalism and the Financialization of Commodities." *Levy Institute Policy Brief*, no. 96.

Young, Peter. 2004. "The Old Hasting Colonization Road." *The Country Connection Magazine* 47, Autumn.

| PART TWO |
Transforming the Ontario State

| 6 |

New Bargains? Ontario and Federalism in the Neoliberal Period

ROBERT DRUMMOND

Federalism is a form of constitution in which legislative authority over a population is divided between at least two levels of government.[1] It normally results from an agreement among pre-existing polities who wish to join together for some purposes but to retain autonomy for others. The agreed constitutional arrangement normally gives a newly created central government authority over those matters in which the parties believe their interests will be advanced by collaboration. The same arrangement reserves to the constituent parts those matters where the parties agree that their interests are best served by maintaining difference. There is also usually some provision made to assign authority over things not explicitly bargained at the outset, and some mechanism for resolving disputes about the interpretation of the original agreement.

Once a federal constitution is in place, however, the bargain is not fixed in stone. Regions, classes, and governments will seek to promote their interests through continued bargaining and by testing the limits the constitution has placed on them through interpretation of the original arrangement. Owners of capital will generally seek to avoid regulation by asserting that the level of government least able or willing to make such laws is the only one with the authority to do so. Organized labour will seek to have employment relations managed by the level of government most sympathetic to their interests. Ethno-cultural groups that are a majority in a component part of the federation will seek to have that subnational government address cultural matters, while minorities will often look to the central government for protection from discrimination and support of their distinctiveness. Regions with the fewest resources will assert the responsibility of a central government to "level the playing field" by redistributing national income. Richer regions may prefer that all be left to their own devices. Governments with weaker tax bases will want assistance from their wealthier neighbours; those with stronger tax bases will resist efforts to spread their revenues beyond their borders. As changes occur in the economy, regions and governments may change their preferences and strategies.

In short, federalism is normally chosen as a solution to problems of competing interests (of class fractions, regional identity, ethno-nationalisms) within a collaborative project, but it really provides only a set of boundaries within which the competitions continue to be pursued. Consequently, the distribution of power among governments, regions, and classes is not immutable. Rather, it is fluid over time. In Canada we have gone, after World War II, through a period of cooperative federalism in which significant national social programmes were created with provincial agreement, to a period of neoliberal retrenchment in which governments at both levels have sought budget balance by threatening the continuation of those very programmes.

Neoliberalism prioritizes private (corporate) property rights and capital mobility for firms over equity and security for working-class households; favours private over public production of goods and services; and relies on markets to distribute such goods and services, as well as allocating the factors entering into their production and the income derived from their sale. The consequence for federalism is a downloading of social welfare policies and funding to subnational governments, usually in the name of allowing greater experimentation with market-based models of delivery. There is less support for the national government to redistribute income among provinces according to need, and there is less attention to differential taxing capacity among the subnational units now being called on to oversee the social welfare of citizens. At the same time, the national government turns its attention increasingly to international trade in what it describes as inevitable globalization, with the expectation that provincial governments will design their policies to accommodate firms engaged in that international commerce. Adam Harmes (2006, 2007) has discussed these processes of multi-level governance under neoliberalism as "market-preserving federalism." In Canada, the Stephen Harper Conservatives often used the term "open federalism" to explain their variant. But without naming it as such, the Liberals since the governments of Jean Chrétien undertook the same downloading and offered similar space for experimentation in the use of markets for service delivery.

Ontario was initially a reluctant participant in nationally funded social programmes, later an enthusiastic collaborator. Then in the late 1990s, under the Conservative government of Mike Harris, it led the neoliberal challenge to public services. In the 2000s under the Liberal regimes of Dalton McGuinty and Kathleen Wynne, the Ontario state has publicly defended social spending while simultaneously seeking cuts to that spending for "austerity" purposes, and while consistently budgeting to reduce per capita social spending and the portion of the government in the gross provincial product. Pleas to the federal government for financial assistance have been largely ineffective, with the exception of some very limited support of economic stimulus during the 2008–11 recession. Understanding the present battle requires some attention to past forms of the debate.

THE CONSTITUTIONAL BARGAIN

The federal system created by the colonies that combined to form Canada in 1867 embodied a kind of constitutional bargain. It was recognized that the willingness of Canada East (which would become Québec) to enter into the merger was dependent on their being able to maintain many local laws and traditions reflecting the history of the French-speaking, largely Roman Catholic majority in that area. At the same time, the political and economic elites of Canada West and the other colonies (New Brunswick and Nova Scotia) saw the main purpose of Confederation as the creation of an entity that could promote economic development in the British part of North America and resist the growing power of the United States. The solution adopted was a federal division of legislative authority that left local and private matters (including property and civil rights, marriage and education) in provincial hands, and reserved to the new national government control over the matters that would be essential to the development of a trade-based national economy. The national government was given authority over international and inter-provincial trade and commerce, customs and excise, money and banking, and national defence. While the provincial government could levy only direct taxes, the national government was authorized to levy taxes of any kind.[2] To better ensure that the provinces would not pass laws that interfered with national commercial development, the national government was given the right to disallow or declare invalid provincial laws. As well, they were accorded the "residual powers" of the constitution – the sole right to make laws in any area not reserved to the provinces. That at least was the apparent intent of the founders.[3]

There were some additional complications in the bargain. Agriculture and immigration – central to the nation's economic growth in the later nineteenth century, but necessarily involving much local activity – were made the joint responsibility of the two levels of government, though priority was to be given to national laws in those fields.[4] Education was to be a provincial matter, but the national government was given responsibility for preserving the educational rights of Protestant and Catholic religious minorities, particularly in Ontario and Québec. Finally, the national government had exclusive legislative authority over "Indians and lands reserved for Indians."

Over time, the original bargain was modified by decisions of the courts (including the British Judicial Committee of the Privy Council) interpreting the meaning of the Constitution. Ontario, under Premier Sir Oliver Mowat, was among the earliest challengers to the superordinate authority of the national government. Mainly (though not exclusively) as a result of his government's challenges, it came to be accepted as constitutional principle that provinces were sovereign in their own jurisdictions, and the power of disallowance fell largely into disuse.[5] More importantly, perhaps, the courts over time began to give a narrow construction to the federal government's authority over trade and commerce, and a broad construction to the provinces' authority over property and civil rights. As national governments sought to impose regulation on industry (for safety and rights of workers, product quality, etc.), owners and employers brought court cases challenging the federal government's right to make laws in those areas. The courts tended to side with the companies, ruling that only a province could make laws in those areas because it alone was allowed to make laws respecting property wholly within the province.

FINANCIAL RELATIONS WITH THE FEDERAL GOVERNMENT

Relations between Ottawa and the provinces over money have mainly to do with vertical imbalance between the federal and provincial governments in relation to their revenues and their responsibilities, and horizontal imbalance among the provinces in their capacity to provide comparable public services across the country.[6] The vertical imbalance was highlighted by the Great Depression of the 1930s, during which responsibility for poor relief fell to the provinces, while the most lucrative tax fields were available only to the federal government. Horizontal imbalance was evident then as well, though it became most important as demand grew after World War II for social programmes that fell mainly within provincial jurisdiction.

Pressure to address these imbalances came mainly from provincial governments, but also from individual political figures at the federal level. In time the federal and provincial governments settled on three main means of trying to mitigate the effect of the imbalances, apart from formal amendment to the Constitution.[7] First, the federal government (starting during the war) paid the provinces for control over fields in which both levels had the right to tax. These so-called tax rental agreements were the focus of disputes about how much control the central government should have and what amount of "rent" they should pay. They were replaced by the second programme – equalization. The federal government (starting in 1957) began to make "equalization" payments to the poorer provinces (initially all but Ontario) to address differences in tax effort.[8] In order to make it possible for provinces to provide comparable levels of public services at comparable rates of taxation, the federal government made payments out of national revenue to the "have-not" provinces to bring their revenues up to what they would have been if they had been able to levy average rates of tax on an average tax base. The third measure was born of the recognition that the national government could make a gift where it was not entitled to make a law. The "spending power of Parliament" was used initially to establish cost-sharing arrangements (a form of conditional grant) whereby the national government would agree to fund approximately half the cost of programmes within provincial jurisdiction provided that the programmes were designed to meet national objectives.[9]

The two surviving financial programmes – equalization payments and conditional grants – underwent significant change over the years since their creation, as governments argued over the amounts of money provided and the means by which they were calculated. By 1962, resource revenues had begun to enter the calculation of equalization payments, and Alberta and British Columbia joined Ontario as ineligible for federal aid. In 1967, the calculation of average rates and revenues was extended to all tax sources (rather than the three fields initially employed).[10] With the oil shock of the early 1970s, the scheme was adjusted so that equalization would not be significantly affected by the rapidly rising price of oil. That is, the revenues received by oil-producing provinces (mainly Alberta) would not be allowed to result in much higher payments to "have-not" provinces, or leave Alberta as the only province not receiving equalization. The National Energy Policy in 1980 further protected equalization from distortion by curtailing the extent to which oil and gas producing provinces would derive extraordinary revenues from high oil prices.

Despite these actions, Ontario would have been eligible for equalization payments from 1977 to 1981, but the federal government acted retroactively in 1981 to deny payments to Ontario. They further altered the calculation of entitlement to equalization by using a five-province standard (omitting the resource-rich provinces), rather than a ten-province one, to determine the "national" average tax rate and tax base. The very fact that the previous formula would have made Ontario a recipient province was seen as an indictment of the formula and a reason to change the system.

In the meantime, the federal government had become concerned with inflation in general, but especially in shared-cost programmes. Costs there were driven by provincial spending decisions without any federal control. That is, a province could increase its expenditure in a shared-cost programme and the federal government would have to match the amount. In 1977 Ottawa altered their contribution to health insurance and post-secondary education from cost-sharing to block grants – per capita transfers to the provinces known as Established Programmes Financing (EPF) in support of these "established programmes." However, funding increases were tied not to expenditure levels, but to increases in the gross domestic product. They kept social assistance as a shared-cost programme (along with some other minor federal transfer schemes that were part of the Canada Assistance Plan (CAP). The block grants were conditional on a provincial programme's meeting "national standards," and Ontario – with the largest population and programmes that helped define the national standard – had scant objection to the new transfer arrangements.

In 1984, the federal government passed the Canada Health Act to give clearer guidance about what "national standards" meant in the area of health insurance, including removing barriers to accessibility such as user fees. The new Ontario Liberal government elected in 1985 was happy to comply with the ban on "extra-billing" that the new law required, as it had been part of their election platform.[11]

A more contentious exercise of the federal spending power occurred during the recession of the early 1990s, when the federal government put an arbitrary 5 per cent ceiling on payment increases in the CAP for three provinces. It was estimated that the Ontario NDP government, faced with increased welfare costs and declining revenues, lost some $7.7 billion between 1990–91 and 1994–95 from what it would otherwise have been entitled to receive (Battle and Torjman 1995, 9).

The Constitution Act of 1982 (s. 92A) gave provinces jurisdiction over natural resources and resource revenues, limiting the ability of the national government to tax in those areas. By 2005, the exploitation of oil in the offshore fields off Newfoundland and Labrador and Nova Scotia meant that two traditionally have-not provinces would be denied equalization payments if their oil revenues were considered in the calculation. The federal government entered into bilateral agreements with those provinces to preserve their resource revenues without diminishing their equalization entitlement. In 2004, Ottawa had further changed the system to give the national government sole control over the *amount* of money available for equalization. The formula to assess the provinces' fiscal capacity would be used only to determine the *distribution* of the pool. By the middle of the 2000s, then, the system of equalization – enshrined in the Constitution twenty years earlier – had become less automatic and more subject to federal control and ad hoc agreements. Ontario was not at all pleased with these arrangements and as a result demanded that it receive some greater protection from reductions in the health and social transfers provided under the spending power. Another ad hoc agreement was made with Ontario, though not to its full satisfaction.

In 2007, the Harper Conservative government returned the equalization formula to the "ten-province standard" for determining the relative fiscal capacity of the provinces, but they included a separate treatment of resource revenues. The new system would allow provinces to receive the greater of (1) the amount to which they would be entitled if all resource revenues were excluded, or (2) the amount they would be owed if 50 per cent of such revenues were excluded. The federal government also allowed Nova Scotia and Newfoundland and Labrador to continue with the benefits of their ad hoc agreements until those agreements expired; alternatively, they could opt into the new national arrangement at any time.[12] The other reform made in the system was an agreement to tie the increase in the equalization pool to a three-year rolling average of the increase in the Gross Domestic Product.

In 1995, the federal government had changed the EPF and CAP arrangements into a new block grant system called the Canada Health and Social Transfer (CHST). The new transfer purportedly gave the provinces more autonomy in the use of the funds, but it also reduced the amount each province received. The change reflected the intention of the federal government to restrict the payments required by the distributional aspects of the federal system, as a means of imposing neoliberal austerity measures they argued were necessary to balance the federal budget. The reduction was not strongly resisted by the Ontario Conservative government of Mike Harris, as their platform favoured an even more openly neoliberal agenda of smaller government and lower social expenditures.

In 2004, the Liberal federal government again altered the "spending power" arrangements. They separated health care from other established programmes and provided a separate Canada Health Transfer, with higher payments and an agreement to 6 per cent annual increases for a period of ten years. The remaining block grants – now called the

Canada Social Transfer – were not as generously funded, but there was general recognition that the costs of health care were the main driver of increases in provincial expenditures.

The federal government claimed that their "generosity" in health care funding was intended to buy improvements in wait times for medical procedures, but it was observed by critics that public expenditures on health care had been rising at a rate of 7 per cent annually – one point above the guaranteed transfer increase.[13] In fact, the new transfer was likely to encourage provinces to seek cost savings in health care before improvements in wait times. In some provinces, that encouragement was welcomed by the proponents of "experimentation" in health care delivery – a shorthand term, some critics believed, for privatization and two-tier medicine. In Ontario, the McGuinty Liberal government had been elected on a platform that was highly critical of the Harris-Eves[14] government's "gutting" of social services, so cost savings were pursued but with at least a lip service commitment to single-payer medicare and wait-time improvements.[15] In 2004, the Ontario government did introduce a new income-related health levy as part of the provincial income tax system and removed some procedures from the list of "medically necessary" treatments. While there was a Liberal government in Ottawa, they refrained from blaming these measures on changes in federal transfers. However, more recently the Ontario government has been very vocal about the amount of tax revenue the national government raises in Ontario compared to the amount that comes back to the province in federal spending (Livingston 2006; Urquhart 2006; and Howlett 2007).

With the economic downturn of 2008, and the decline in Ontario's manufacturing sector, Ontario again became eligible for equalization. The province once known as the "milch-cow" of Confederation had become a have-not province. This time the formula was not adjusted and Ontario has received equalization payments since 2009–10. In 2015–16, the province received approximately $2.4 billion, though the provincial government is quick to point out that Ontario taxpayers still contribute much more than that to the federal treasury. A 2014 Mowat Centre study suggested that the gap between what Ontario taxpayers received and what they contributed was some $9.1 billion in the first year Ontario received equalization payments (Granofsky and Zon 2014).

Recently there has been some discussion of an expansion of the equalization system to include calculation of the different "expenditure needs" of provinces. Just as provinces have different revenue-raising potential, they also have different circumstances that affect the expenditures needed to provide comparable levels of public services. Such differences might include differences in the age, health, or income of the population to be served, or environmental factors like remoteness of communities or severity of climate (Gusen 2012). An expert panel of the federal finance department acknowledged the importance of differences in expenditure needs but then rejected a change in the system to accommodate them as too complicated (Expert Panel on Equalization and Territorial Financing 2006). Economist Peter Gusen has created a prototype form of equalization that would take account of expenditure need that he believes effectively counters objections to such a scheme. However, he admits that the addition of expenditure need would result in significantly different payments for several provinces (Gusen 2012). Ontario would be a big gainer under his prototype, while other provinces (including Québec) would not fare as well. He acknowledges that such a result would pose a political challenge.

Late in 2011, the federal government confirmed their election promise to renew the health transfer agreement to provide annual increases of 6 per cent. However, this agreement ended in 2017–18, and had the Conservatives' plan prevailed, increases would have been limited to the increase in the nominal gross domestic product (though they would not fall below 3 per cent). The Conservatives had further indicated they would not set performance goals in relation to health transfers – a move some critics saw as an invitation to "experiments" in care delivery that would increase privatization and diminish universality of access. For the most part, provinces did not object to this greater autonomy, though federal opposition parties called it an abdication of responsibility for national standards in health care. The Trudeau government elected in 2015 offered the provinces an annual increase of 3.5 per cent plus a fund for mental health and homecare in lieu of the previous plan, but provinces were initially resistant. Ultimately the national government made bilateral agreements with most provinces;

Ontario settled in 2017 for a 3 per cent annual increase plus $2.3 billion for homecare and $1.9 billion for mental health over ten years.

DIRECT FEDERAL PAYMENTS TO PERSONS

Another significant area of federal involvement in the economic life of the province is the direct payment to individuals through the Canada Pension Plan and the Employment Insurance programme.[16] Ontario has been one of the most vocal proponents of improvements in the Canada Pension Plan, which would require the agreement of a majority of provinces with a majority of the population. Changes in the plan have been resisted most recently by the Conservative government of Alberta and the conservative Saskatchewan Party government of that province. Despite the fact that it has its own contributory pension plan, Québec has also objected, probably because it would be expected to implement matching changes in its Québec Pension Plan. Ontario proposed in 2015 to create its own Ontario Pension Plan to augment the CPP for residents without an employment-based private pension. However, the newly elected Trudeau government reached an agreement with the provinces soon after its election to enhance contribution rates and payments in the CPP starting in 2019. With that agreement, Ontario put its own pension plan on hold.

In the area of Employment Insurance, the Ontario government and Ontario residents have been significantly disadvantaged. First, the changes in eligibility rules in the programme that replaced Unemployment Insurance have made it harder for unemployed workers anywhere to qualify for assistance. Despite the fact that the programme has amassed surpluses in recent years, a much lower proportion of unemployed workers – all of whom have paid premiums into the scheme – can qualify to receive benefits. The result is that provincial governments find that their welfare budgets are called upon to provide relief to the unemployed where once the federal insurance scheme would have done that job.

Unemployed workers in Ontario are doubly disadvantaged, however, since their eligibility is tied to the labour market conditions in the province. If Ontario's unemployment rate is lower than average, its workers must have worked more weeks to be entitled to benefits, and if entitled, workers are more likely to receive benefits for a shorter period. The fact that a lower proportion of the labour force is unemployed in Ontario does not make it any easier for those who *are* unemployed to make ends meet.

In short, as Ontario becomes a "have-not" province in the terms internal to the Canadian state, and as it tries to reposition its economy after the decline in manufacturing, it is disadvantaged both by the equalization programme to which its taxpayers contribute heavily and by the EI system to which its workers also contribute heavily. As it struggles to reconfigure its medical care system to limit costs and improve treatment, to maintain a first-class university and college system without burdening a generation of students with crushing debt, and to sustain social assistance in the aftermath of recession, Ontario is not all that well served by the federal transfers that supposedly aid in achieving those goals. The federal government had, prior to the advent of the Harper Conservatives and the financial downturn of 2008, managed to balance its budget and indeed create some surpluses. However, it did so to a large extent on the backs of the provinces, and Ontario was among those whose citizens most bore the burden of that set of policies.

FEDERALISM, FINANCE, AND MARKETS

Increasingly in recent years, the federal government has withdrawn from the responsibility it once accepted – to mitigate the effects of inter-provincial differences in economic wellbeing. At the same time, it has encouraged provincial autonomy in areas where it once sought to maintain national standards. The federal intervention in areas of provincial jurisdiction was always resisted in Québec, though usually in an attempt to establish that province's unique character as the locus of the French-Canadian (or more recently Québécois) nation. Québec was therefore generally willing to accept federal funds if they came without strings, and the province remains the principal recipient of equalization payments. However, the provincial position that has been served by recent federal action has its strongest expression in Western Canada. There resource-rich provinces have less need for federal funds themselves and they have been reluctant to see their wealth redistributed by federal authorities to level the national playing field.

The western provinces have also been most supportive of neoliberal policies that have privileged market "solutions" to social problems, and the demand for autonomy has sometimes been grounded in the wish to pursue private provision of public goods. Conservative governments of resource-rich provinces have been well served by a federal government that has retreated from its commitment to redistribution and its responsibility for national standards. Less conservative governments in the other provinces, including Ontario, will be less demanding of autonomy if its probable consequence is less federal support and more dependence on own-source revenues.

The federal economic policy preference – under both the Martin Liberal and Harper Conservative governments – has been to make increases in federal contributions to provincial treasuries dependent on national economic growth, rather than on local need. On occasion, it is true, they have been willing to make bilateral agreements with particular provinces to protect them from loss through the application of universal programmes. Yet it has not normally been the case that Ontario has benefitted from such favourable treatment.

In the area of transfers to persons, the preference has been to restrict eligibility in general and (in the case of Employment Insurance) to subject individual claimants to the negative consequences of provincial variations in labour market conditions. The strictures on transfers are sometimes defended as necessary cost-saving measures, but there often also seems to be an element of moral reproof. People are urged to take personal responsibility for matters that are frequently well beyond their control.

In both sorts of transfers – to governments and persons – the citizens and governments of Ontario have not been as adversely affected as those in poorer provinces, but they have felt the sting of these policies nonetheless. And as the economy of Ontario has had to adjust to global change, Ontario has come to demand the sort of federal assistance that that province once helped provide; but, with the ascendency of a resource-rich West in national politics, the federal appetite to provide such aid is no longer strong.

FIRST NATIONS AND THE ONTARIO STATE

Despite the constitutional grant of authority over "Indians and lands reserved for Indians" to the federal government, the province has had a role to play in relations with First Nations. First, not all Aboriginal persons are "Status Indians" – that is, recognized as falling under the authority of the federal Indian Act. Métis and non-status Indians are treated as ordinary citizens of the province but they may nonetheless have claims to special treatment by reason of their Aboriginal ancestry. Second, even many Status Indians reside away from the reserves in which they are entitled to live, and in those circumstances they may rely as much as any other Ontarian on the services and regulations of the Ontario government. Third, and perhaps most importantly, as First Nations have turned increasingly to issues of governance rooted in land claims, the province has been called on to take part in negotiations – separately or in conjunction with the federal government – over claims of entitlement to property that would otherwise be subject to provincial law. It may also be the case that the province is involved because it (or the colony from which it derived) had a role in events that have given rise to the claim.

In 2007, following the recommendation of Mr Justice Linden who had been appointed to investigate an incident at Ipperwash Provincial Park (see below), the Ontario government appointed former attorney general Michael Bryant as its first minister for Aboriginal affairs. The appointment came as the government was dealing with an occupation of land by Aboriginal protestors in the Grand River community of Caledonia. That occupation was one of several instances in which Aboriginal groups had taken direct action in support of land claims that they believed were not being seriously addressed by governments at any level.

Prior to Confederation, much of the land in southern Ontario had been secured for the Crown by treaties involving the surrender of Upper Canada lands and by the Robinson Huron Treaties. In 1873, the federal government signed Treaty N. 3 with First Nations in northwestern Ontario and southern Manitoba, and in 1889 they signed Treaty N. 6 involving the addition of Kenora District to Ontario, with consequent provisions for reserves in that area. In 1905–06, the federal government negotiated Treaty N. 9 (the James Bay Treaty) covering much of the north-central part of the province. For the first and only time, the provincial government of the day took an active role in those negotiations. In 1912, the boundary between Ontario and Manitoba (which had been in dispute) was finally settled, with some consequences for Indian lands and reserves on or near that border. In 1923, the federal government signed the Williams Treaties with bands in southern Ontario to resolve "uncertainties" along the northern shore of Lake Ontario (including the Toronto area). Finally in 1929, Treaty N. 9 was extended to cover the remaining areas of northern Ontario not previously addressed, thus bringing to an apparent end the cession of land from First Nations and the creation of reserves for the bands involved. In recent years, however, Ottawa has continued to receive land claims involving Ontario bands. They have signed agreements relating to four comprehensive land claims in Ontario, though all were either agreements "in principle" or frameworks for further negotiation. Specific land claims – that is, claims about non-fulfillment of treaty obligations – have been filed with the federal government in several provinces. In 2015, 7 percent of federal land claims negotiations involved Ontario bands.

In the last couple of decades, some land claims have been pursued with greater militancy on the part of First Nations groups, including some in eastern Ontario, one of which straddles the border with Québec. In 1995, protestors from the Kettle and Stony Point reserve occupied a part of the Ipperwash Provincial Park in central Ontario, claiming that the land was properly theirs. The Harris government elected to treat the issue as one of law and order, rather than Aboriginal rights, and the Ontario Provincial Police were ordered to remove the protestors from the park. In the ensuing confrontation a protestor was killed by an OPP officer, and the government was widely criticized as having been precipitous in its actions. When the McGuinty government was elected in 2003, they established a commission of inquiry directed by Justice Sidney Linden to determine responsibility for the tragic consequences of the occupation and removal, and to make recommendations for resolving the issue of the ownership of the land in question (Ipperwash Inquiry 2007).

Before Justice Linden could report, in 2006 a second occupation took place in Caledonia, in which members of the Six Nations of the Grand River took control of a building site where new homes were being created. In this case they claimed that land had been leased by Upper Canada in 1830 without proper compensation. The province in turn asserted that the land had been sold to the Crown, rather than leased, and that agreed-upon compensation had been paid. The protestors blockaded the site, with considerable inconvenience to the residents of Caledonia, but the provincial government – perhaps mindful of the Ipperwash events – chose not to try and remove the protestors. There was much criticism of the government for its decision, both because of the costs to Caledonia residents and because of the high costs borne by the provincial police in keeping order between the Aboriginal occupiers and non-Aboriginal protestors (who assembled both from Caledonia and from outside the area). The provincial government accused their federal counterparts of failing to resolve the land claim satisfactorily, and eventually both levels of government became involved in efforts to end the standoff. In the meantime, the province bought the building site from the land developer who was building the homes. In hopes of ameliorating the situation, the province agreed to transfer certain lands to Six Nations people, and the lands were placed in a federal corporation. Disputes over those lands then developed between elected band councils and a group called the Haudenosaunee Confederacy, drawn from five nations, claiming to represent a traditional government system. The province remains responsible for policing areas where protests and blockades have arisen, but it is otherwise not involved directly in the controversy.

The Caledonia and Ipperwash situations, while garnering considerable press and public attention, are by no means unique. There have been other occupations, blockades, and protests by First Nations bands in several Ontario locations, and as frustration builds over slow progress on land claims, consultation on resource exploitation, and conditions of life on reserves, one might reasonably anticipate such events to become more frequent.

At the present time, in addition to land claims filed with the federal government, the province has agreed to accept for negotiation some forty-four active land claims; it is in the process of researching and assessing seven others, and has signed nine agreements with Ontario First Nations that are currently being implemented (Canada: Aboriginal Affairs and Northern Development 2018). The provincial government committed in 2007 to transfer the land claimed in Ipperwash Park to the Kettle and Stony Point band, and in 2009 signed a framework agreement to begin negotiating the terms of that transfer.

In addition to land claims issues, the Ontario government has addressed other issues involving First Nations, including a move of one reserve (with federal agreement) from a flooded area of the James Bay region to a site nearer the city of Timmins. They also signed, in 2008, an agreement with bands across the province to share revenues from provincial gaming operations that the government estimates will provide some $3 billion over twenty-five years to First Nations communities. They further assigned some $25 million between 2008 and 2010 to assist bands in developing resources to negotiate more effectively claims for land and other treaty rights with the two levels of government. Implementation of a 2014 agreement between the province and nine First Nations has been slow, in particular with respect to road access to mineral-rich areas in northern Ontario. There have been disputes with First Nations about jurisdiction over roads. And there has been an as-yet-unrealized hope for federal financial assistance to develop the infrastructure (Government of Ontario 2016).

A significant issue that remains for negotiation is the exploitation of resources on Indian lands and the sharing of revenues from that activity. The province claims to have set aside $30 million for that purpose when an agreement has been reached.

Despite the stated aim of the provincial government to develop a cooperative climate for relations with Ontario First Nations – in conjunction with the federal government and local municipalities, and including the Métis Nation of Ontario – the process is a long one and has undoubtedly led to continuing frustration among many Aboriginal groups in the province.

OTHER ISSUES OF FEDERAL-PROVINCIAL RELATIONS

There is a range of topics falling mainly within federal jurisdiction in which the province has an interest – and often a position that they seek to have the federal government adopt (Hartmann 2017). Because they have no legislative authority in many of these areas, their influence relies on persuading the federal government that the province's position is also in their interest, or, more realistically, persuading voters to demand federal action in ways the province recommends. In either case, the process is uncertain and requires considerable time.

One such area is environmental regulation and climate change. The Ontario government has pursued expansion of renewable energy projects, though largely without federal encouragement. The federal Conservatives have been largely unwilling to support regulatory or tax initiatives to curb greenhouse gas emissions, preferring to rely on industry to respond to markets. The strength of the Conservatives in Alberta and Saskatchewan has been related (both as cause and effect) to their support for the oil and gas industry, and they have been unwilling to curb development of the oil sands to serve environmental goals. However in 2015, Alberta elected an NDP government that promised a carbon tax to reduce emissions in that province, with remarkable buy-in from the oil and gas industry. The new Liberal federal government also showed greater interest in climate change, and offered support to provinces that pursued emission reductions. Ontario introduced a cap and trade system that took effect in January 2017. In addition, Ontario's heavy reliance on nuclear generation of electricity has meant that the province is exposed to considerable uncertainty by the federal government's sale of Atomic Energy of Canada Limited (maker of the province's CANDU reactors) to SNC Lavalin in 2011.

In the area of international trade, the current federal government has been prepared to see the Canadian dollar rise in value because of demand for commodities – notably oil and gas – while the manufacturing sector centred in Ontario is priced out of international markets by the inflated currency. In 2016, the federal government concluded a comprehensive free trade agreement with the European Union. The Ontario government applauded the deal but expressed continuing concern with the impact on the province's cheese makers, wineries, and distilleries. As it has sought access to Asian markets for commodities, the federal government has discussed the possibility of abandoning agricultural supply management systems that sustain chicken, egg, and dairy production, mainly in Ontario and Québec. To date the province has not been successful in pressing its case with Ottawa. Instead it was lectured by the Conservative federal finance minister about the need to reduce corporate taxation. Canada was engaged in 2016 in negotiating with eleven other Pacific Rim countries to develop a Trans-Pacific Partnership (TPP) free trade agreement intended to counter the growing influence of China in the region. In addition to the supply management issues, there was concern in some quarters that a proposed investor-state dispute resolution mechanism in TPP might significantly curtail the ability of countries and provinces to regulate industries in the public interest. In 2016, Donald Trump was elected president of the United States, having promised to withdraw the US from the TPP and to renegotiate the North American Free Trade Agreement. Concerns with TPP are still present as the remaining countries decide whether to proceed in the absence of the US, while a whole range of issues for Ontario is opened up by any change to (or abandonment of) NAFTA.

The Conservative government in Ottawa passed a crime bill imposing mandatory sentences for a number of criminal offences. The Liberal government in Ontario opposed the change, arguing that it unreasonably constrained judicial discretion, but also that it would likely lead to higher numbers of people in jail and therefore to higher provincial costs to maintain correctional facilities. The provincial Liberals were unsuccessful in persuading the Harper Conservatives either to modify the mandatory sentencing provisions or to provide financial support for increasing prison space. The Trudeau Liberal government promised to review mandatory minimum sentencing, but to date they have been slow to proceed.

In the past couple of years, the federal government has been arguing for the need to create a national regulator for the securities industry. In this matter, the provincial government of Ontario has been supportive, assuming the regulator would be housed in Ontario, close to the country's largest stock exchange and the heart of Canada's financial industry. However, other provinces – especially in Western Canada – have argued that any national regulator should be in their area, and absent such an agreement, they prefer the fragmented regulatory system now in place. Firms seeking to avoid the stronger regulatory presence of a national body have been supportive of "provincial autonomy." So far the federal government, five provinces, and the Yukon have been developing a Capital Markets Regulatory Authority but without success in persuading the remaining provinces (especially Québec and Alberta) to join.

Finally, although Ontario has traditionally been the principal destination of immigrants coming to Canada, the province has not pressed Ottawa for much say over immigration policy (unlike Québec). As Ontario's economy weakens relative to those of Alberta and Saskatchewan and the pattern of immigrant settlement shifts west, the Ontario government may seek a bigger role in immigration policy. In the meantime, the federal government has reduced funding to Ontario for immigrant settlement programmes, citing changing patterns of immigrant destinations. With the increasing commitment to refugee settlement by the new Trudeau government, Ontario is hopeful of increasing its proportion of new arrivals and consequently its share of federal settlement support.

NEOLIBERALISM AND CANADIAN FEDERALISM

The federal government continues to have a significant impact on the province, especially in financial terms. Transfers from the federal government have constituted over 15 per cent of Ontario government revenues over most of the last decade and a half, though the share dipped as low as 8.1 per cent in the late 1990s. In 2010–11, with the province eligible for equalization and with Ottawa continuing some support for recession-fighting stimulus, the proportion rose to 21.6 per cent. In 2015–16, the proportion was 17.8 per cent (Ontario Public Accounts, various years). This fact alone gives Ottawa considerable say in what Ontario can do.

Increasing costs of health care have long been significant in driving the federal contribution, and as the new funding arrangement imposed by Ottawa takes hold, the debate over the adequacy of federal support will no doubt heat up. The fact that both levels of government have debt and deficit conditions that they treat as alarming will unquestionably lead to continuing acrimony as each blames the other for the impact of austerity measures. The era of "cooperative" federalism is becoming a distant memory, and in the new competitive environment, Ontario's ability or willingness to make sacrifices in the name of national unity or regional equity is much diminished.

For a good deal of its history, Ontario was the province on which the federal government depended for support of programmes that sought national uniformity in areas of provincial jurisdiction, or programmes to redistribute revenues to achieve greater fiscal equity among provinces. More recently, however, as commodity prices have fuelled economic growth in the West and in parts of the Atlantic region, and the manufacturing sector that is so important to Ontario has declined, Ontario has become less of a lynchpin for Confederation. Most recently, on the other hand, declining oil and natural gas prices have weakened the influence of the resource-producing provinces, while there has been some modest improvement in Ontario's manufacturing sector. Still, those changes have not significantly altered the long-term picture. Ontario's capacity to contribute to the country's economic health increasingly seems to depend either on the financial services sector (with its inherent volatility) or a rebirth of manufacturing through innovation, a weaker dollar, and/or productivity improvements.

At the same time, recent federal governments have been less interested than their predecessors in establishing national programme standards or redistributing revenue to achieve fiscal balance. There has been evidence of a neoliberal preference for reducing the federal government's role in economic management, together with an opposition to provincial rebalancing that is grounded at least as much in economic ideology as in the interests of the newly prosperous and federally powerful West. Moreover, the Liberal Ontario government – while it continued to decry the programme cuts of the Harris years – turned in tough times to a similarly neoliberal set of government budget cuts, with the same reluctance to raise taxes to sustain public programmes. Market-preserving federalism, to return to the term from Harmes, is found in the institutional logics and policy practices of the Ontario state itself under Conservative and Liberal governments alike.

In 2006, Richard Simeon reissued his classic 1971 study of Canadian federalism, *Federal-Provincial Diplomacy*, with a new preface and postscript. He claimed in the preface to that edition that many of the issues and trends of the recent past were foreshadowed in the 1963–71 period he covered in the original volume – the period of "cooperative federalism" that he describes as federal dominance and that he says effectively ended in the early 1970s. However, among the matters he cites as "foreshadowed" are challenges to the spending power of Parliament, symmetrical versus asymmetrical federalism, provincial variability instead of national standards, and a shift of influence to the provinces (Simeon 2006). While hindsight may see the roots of these conflicts in the 1960s, it is surely no coincidence that these changes – changes that favour rich provinces over poor and encourage "experiments" that increase private, for-profit corporate involvement in areas of previous public provision – come at a time when Canadian governments at both levels have adopted a neoliberal policy stance.

In Ontario at least, the debate over the efficacy of neoliberal solutions remains a lively one, and it remains possible that future governments may turn to a more progressive, actively redistributive approach. If that occurs, and absent significant change in the redistributive mechanisms of the Canadian state, Ontario is likely to change from the dependable servant of federalism into one of its most strident critics.

The election of an Ontario Progressive Conservative majority government in June 2018, however, means that a departure from neoliberalism is quite unlikely in the near future, especially given the commitment to find almost $6 billion in efficiencies (meaning cuts) in provincial spending. In addition, the campaign promises made by the new premier, Doug Ford, mean that there will be significant conflict with the federal government led by Justin Trudeau, as Ford will likely vigorously pursue a "market-preserving" federalism. Mr Ford promised to scrap the Wynne government's cap and trade programme to reduce carbon emissions, despite Mr Trudeau's insistence that provinces adopt their own carbon-reduction plan or be forced to accept a federal one. On this issue, Ontario seems likely to align with Saskatchewan (and perhaps Alberta, should Ms Notley's NDP lose its next election to the United Conservative party) in opposition to all carbon-reduction schemes. Differences with the federal government on other issues, such as Ford's opposition to safe-injection sites for drug users, or development trumping First Nations governance issues, as well as differences in communication style between the premier and the prime minister, suggest a turbulent time for Ontario in federal-provincial relations for some time to come.

NOTES

1 Not surprisingly, for a country in which national unity has long been a concern and federalism long seen as a partial solution, the academic literature on Canadian federalism is very extensive. Citing many would occupy an unjustifiable amount of space in this chapter. One of the earliest and best in the modern era is Meekison (1977). More recent works include: Anastakis and Bryden (2009); Gagnon (2009); Smith (2010); and Stevenson (2009).
2 At the time of Confederation, the bulk of taxes were levied on commercial transactions – customs and excise duties, for example. Provinces could levy taxes mainly on property, or charge fees for services within their authority. With the coming of personal income tax, of course, direct taxation became a more lucrative field.
3 An additional provision was the "declaratory power" – the right of the federal government to declare any work, though wholly within one province, to be for the general advantage of Canada, or of two or more provinces, and thus subject to federal legislative authority. The power was used over 400 times before 1961, mainly with regard to railways and to nuclear facilities. Since then it has largely fallen into disuse.
4 Another complication that had potential importance was Section 94, by means of which the federal government could legislate in areas of property and civil rights in the "common law" provinces (i.e., other than Québec) with the agreement of those provinces. The section has not in fact been used, however, and the national government has generally preferred to use the spending power to intervene in areas of provincial jurisdiction.
5 The last use of the disallowance power was in 1943. Since that time the federal government has preferred the use of the courts to determine the constitutionality of provincial legislation.
6 Even over thirty years after its publication, Smiley (1980) remains one of the best treatments of the interests and principles underlying federal-provincial financial relations.
7 One area in which the provinces and the national government did resort to constitutional amendment was unemployment insurance. Both levels agreed that the federal government should be allowed to develop such a programme, and the British government was petitioned to pass a constitutional amendment (agreed on by the national government and the provinces) to give authority over unemployment insurance to the Government of Canada.
8 Tax effort refers to the tax rates and the breadth of the province's tax bases. For example, those provinces without a manufacturing or resource base that could yield corporate tax or resource royalty revenues might have to set personal income taxes at punitively high rates to make up the difference.
9 The first such scheme was for means-tested pensions, though those were later made a federal responsibility by constitutional amendment. It was in

the areas of social assistance, hospital insurance, health insurance, and social assistance that cost sharing was most actively pursued after World War II. One of the most prolific analysts and critics of the spending power has been Thomas Courchene (2008, 2009).
10 Those fields were personal income tax, corporate income tax, and succession duties.
11 The practice of doctors charging above the rate paid for a procedure by the provincial health insurance plan.
12 Nova Scotia eventually opted into the national scheme, while Newfoundland and Labrador has not. Both are guaranteed that they will not be worse off under the national system than under the formula that was agreed in 2005.
13 In Ontario, the provincial government's expenditures on health care had increased an average of almost 9 per cent annually from 2000–03.
14 The Conservative premier Mike Harris had resigned in 2002 and been succeeded by his former finance minister, Ernie Eves.
15 Figures from 2011 suggest that Ontario has in fact been a leader among the provinces in reducing wait-times for several targeted areas of service, including bypass surgery, hip and knee replacements, and cataract surgery. See Canadian Institute for Health Information (2012). Ontario's wait times strategy was expanded by 2016 to include cancer surgery and emergency room waits. Wait times remain an issue, but Ontario figures compare favourably with other provinces.
16 In the years after World War II, the federal government also paid a "family allowance" to mothers for each child under sixteen. But that programme was cancelled in 1992 and federal government assistance to families was shifted to the income tax system.

REFERENCES

Anastakis, Dimitry, and P.E. Bryden, eds. 2010. *Framing Canadian Federalism: Historical Essays in Honour of John T. Saywell*. Toronto: University of Toronto Press.

Battle, Kenneth, and Sherri Torjman. 1995. *How Finance Re-Formed Social Policy*. Ottawa: Caledon Institute of Social Policy.

Canada: Aboriginal Affairs and Northern Development. 2018. *Reporting Centre on Specific Claims*. http://services.aadnc-aandc.gc.ca.

Canadian Institute for Health Information. 2012. *Wait Times in Canada: A Summary, 2012*. www.cihi.ca.

Courchene, Thomas. 2008. *Reflections on the Spending Power: Practices, Principles, Perspectives*. Montreal: Institute for Research on Public Policy.

– 2009. *Canada: The State of the Federation, 2008; Open Federalism and the Spending Power*. Montreal: McGill-Queen's University Press.

Expert Panel on Equalization and Territorial Financing. 2006. *Achieving A National Purpose: Putting Equalization Back on Track.* Ottawa: Department of Finance.

Gagnon, Alain, ed. 2009. *Contemporary Canadian Federalism.* Toronto: University of Toronto Press.

Granofsky, Thomas, and Noah Zon. 2014. "Cheques and Balances: The Finances of the Canadian Federation." *Mowat Research #87.* Toronto: Mowat Centre.

Gusen, Peter. 2012. *Expenditure Need: Equalization's Other Half.* Toronto: Mowat Centre.

Harmes, A. 2006. "Neoliberalism and Multilevel Governance." *Review of International Political Economy* 13 (5).

– 2007. "The Political Economy of Open Federalism." *Canadian Journal of Political Science* 40 (2).

Hartmann, Erich. 2017. *Balance of Risks: Vertical Fiscal Imbalance and Fiscal Risk in Canada.* Toronto: Mowat Centre.

Howlett, Karen. 2007. "PM Offers Ontario Cash for Transit, Environment." *Globe and Mail,* 5 March.

Ipperwash Inquiry. 2007. *Report.* www.attorneygeneral.jus.gov.on.ca/inquiries/ipperwash.

Livingston, Gillian. 2006. "Ontario Upset with Increase in Equalization, End of Child Care Deal." *Canadian Press Newswire,* 2 May.

Meekison, Peter, ed. 1977. *Canadian Federalism: Myth or Reality?* 3rd ed. Toronto: Methuen.

Ontario: Ministry of Aboriginal Affairs. 2016. *Published Plans and Annual Reports.* www.ontario.ca/page/published-plans-and-annual-reports-2015-2016-ministry-aboriginal-affairs.

Ontario: Ministry of Finance. Various years. *Public Accounts.* www.ontario.ca/page/public-accounts-ontario.

– 2011. *Budget.* www.fin.gov.on.ca/en/budget.

Simeon, Richard, ed. 2006. *Federal-Provincial Diplomacy.* Revised ed. Toronto: University of Toronto Press.

Smiley, Donald. 1980. *Canada in Question: Federalism in the 1980s.* Toronto: McGraw-Hill.

Smith, David E. 2010. *Federalism and the Constitution of Canada.* Toronto: University of Toronto Press.

Stevenson, Garth. 2009. *Unfulfilled Union.* 5th ed. Montreal: McGill-Queen's University Press.

Urquhart, Ian. 2006. "Fiscal Imbalance Battle Seems Quite Lopsided; But the Ontario Government Is Fighting Back." *Toronto Star,* 6 May.

7

Gendering the State: Women and Public Policy in Ontario

TAMMY FINDLAY

While there has been a great deal of focus on the national women's movement in Canada, there has been far less at the subnational scale (Rankin 1996).[1] This is changing with growing interest in gender and multilevel governance in the Canadian and international contexts (Haussman et al. 2010; Mahon 2005; Sawer 2007). New feminist scholarship is developing a critical political economy perspective on the relationship between neoliberalism and institutions, policy, and social forces at the provincial level.

Feminist political economy (FPE) has highlighted the negative impact of state restructuring on women, looking mainly at women as users of state programs and services, or as public sector workers. This chapter will extend this analysis to examine how neoliberal *administrative strategies*, specifically the New Public Management (NPM), have affected the politics of the women's movement in Ontario. Based on interview and archival research, the case study of the Ontario Women's Directorate (OWD), and contemporary developments, I argue that a gender regime revolving around downsizing, privatization, and managerialism has affected both the process and substance of policy for feminists working in and with the state bureaucracy in Ontario, and has undermined women's representation in the province.

I begin with an overview of gender and representation and trace the changing institutional landscape of women's policy machinery from 1990–2017, with a particular emphasis on the OWD and its successor, the Ministry of the Status of Women (MSW). I then attribute this democratic shift to the intensification of NPM after the election of the Harris government, and the subsequent restructuring of the Ontario bureaucracy. I demonstrate that neoliberalism has procedurally eroded the effectiveness of women's policy structures; and that substantively women's labour market policy has moved away from advocating for women as workers or addressing structural inequalities, and toward promoting the development of women's entrepreneurial initiative and individualism. I conclude that NPM continues to be a powerful force in the Ontario state today and that gender equality requires an alternative regime of governance.

GENDER, GENDER REGIMES, AND THE STATE

Feminist political economy is concerned with understanding the relationship, or nexus, between the state, market, family, and voluntary sector, and their intersection with gender, race, ethnicity, class, sexuality, and ability. Viewing the state as "a contested terrain" (Maroney and Luxton 1997, 87), FPE analyzes how the relations of production and social reproduction are mediated by the state within capitalist systems. Fudge and Cossman (2002) explain that in capitalism, there is a contradictory relationship between production (defined as market relation including waged work) and social reproduction (defined as the paid and unpaid work that must be done to maintain the working population). While production is valued both financially and socially over social reproduction, capitalism requires that the current and future labour force is cared for physically, emotionally, socially, and intellectually. States are, therefore, involved in negotiating this contradiction between production and social reproduction and, in the process, they regulate gender relations.

States regulate gender relations in multiple ways. They set the rules of the labour market, where women continue to be concentrated in sex-segregated, precarious work. At the same time, a sexual division of labour remains, where women are disproportionately responsible for social reproduction. States can take on some of this work, by providing public services, such as universal health care, or child care. In this way, responsibility for social reproduction shifts over time, and can be redistributed differently within the "state-market-family/household-third sector nexus," which has the effect of altering gender relations in paradoxical ways (Bezanson and Luxton 2006, 5; Porter

2003). For instance, state involvement in social reproduction can support families and women in particular, yet at the same time act as a form of social control and surveillance. FPE examines the impact of these various configurations of responsibility on social relations, and the resulting gender orders that emerge.

Feminist political economists use the notion of gender order to differentiate between the structuring, or organization, of gender relations by the state under the Keynesian and neoliberal eras. A gender order involves a particular sexual division of labour and gender discourse (Fudge and Cossman 2002). The gender order associated with the Keynesian welfare state was characterized by a positive view of state action and an expansive vision of the public sector, including recognition of the rights of social citizenship and representation of marginalized interests inside state institutions. While it relied on an implicit male-breadwinner model, in which the public-private divide and traditional gender roles were naturalized and reinforced through public policy, it did transfer some of the responsibility for social reproduction from the family (i.e., women) and the voluntary sector to the state.

With neoliberalism, state restructuring is premised on the belief that the state is the problem. The aim is to restrict the public realm, and to extend private influence over state structures or public institutions. This is a gender order marked by an erosion of social rights, the delegitimization of "special interests" participating in the policy process, and the disappearance of women from public discourse (Brodie and Bakker 2007). A universal breadwinner model, where labour market attachment is expected for men and women, is combined with the re-privatization of the costs of and responsibility for social reproduction (to the family, voluntary sector, or the market). Women, therefore, experience a double burden of paid and unpaid work.

Within a wider gender order, feminist scholars have also identified distinct gender regimes. R.W. Connell distinguishes between the concept of *gender order* to refer to the broader patterns of gender relations in society, and *gender regime* to "a regular set of arrangements about gender" within a particular institution, such as a school, or a workplace (2002, 53). The concept of gender regime stems from feminist critiques of the comparative welfare state literature. Such critiques point out that welfare state typologies, such as Esping-Andersen's Liberal, Corporatist/Conservative, and Social Democratic, ignore the different ways that gender relations are structured within regimes, and that within the varieties of welfare states, there are varieties of gender regulation based on diverse cultures, norms, ideas, policies, and institutions. Sainsbury defines a gender regime as: "the rules and norms about gender relations, allocating tasks and rights to the two sexes. A gender policy regime entails a logic based on the rules and norms about gender relations that influences the construction of policies" (1999, 5).

Gender regime theory highlights the "ways in which institutions reflect, reinforce, and structure unequal gendered power relations in wider society" (Krook and Mackay 2011, 6). The gender regime literature focuses on welfare state policy and the particular way that state negotiation of production and social reproduction is gendered in a given institutional context and how responsibility for social reproduction is distributed differently across the state/market/family/voluntary sector nexus (Connell 2002; Sainsbury 1999; O'Connor, Shaver, and Orloff 1999).

Gender regimes can be said to exist in all institutions, including those of public administration, but they differ in character across space and time. For instance, there are different ways of organizing gender relations within state administration. In a Weberian regime, the central characteristics are: hiring based on merit, standard operating procedures, hierarchy, division of labour (or compartmentalization), secrecy, neutrality, tenure, and expertise (Albo 1993, 21; Weber 1994). While designed to promote fairness and efficiency, feminists have problematized many aspects of Weberian organization due to their gendered consequences. Weberian organization often clashes with feminist principles based on challenging subordination and unequal power. It marginalizes women into bureaucratic "ghettoes." It ignores "intersectionality" and the overlapping nature of women's policy needs. And it suppresses internal advocacy for women (Findlay 2015).

State administration could be designed differently. It could be less hierarchical, and more egalitarian. It could be less segregated and more diverse. It could be less compartmentalized and more holistic. It could be less dispassionate and more just. It could be participatory. This would be a different gender regime, where gender democracy and women's substantive representation are prioritized. Gender regimes can change. The Weberian regime did. But it did not change for the better. Instead, it was displaced by NPM, which has its own gender consequences, as will be seen below.

WOMEN'S POLICY AND STRUCTURES OF REPRESENTATION IN ONTARIO

There is a variety of women's policy machinery, at both the federal and provincial levels. Although inadequate, structures were created during the Keynesian order that recognized that women have particular policy needs and that they have a democratic right to be represented within the structures of the state. In Ontario, this largely occurred through the Ontario Advisory Council on Women's Issues (OACWI) and the Ontario Women's Directorate.

As Malloy indicates, Ontario was slow to introduce women's policy structures that were similar to those implemented by the federal government after the Royal Commission on the Status of Women (RCSW) in the early 1970s. The first response was to institute the Ontario Council on the Status of Women (OCSW) in 1974, which would later become the Ontario Advisory Council on Women's Issues (OACWI) in 1985 (Malloy 2003). Like other advisory councils, members of the OACWI were appointed by the government of the day, and therefore the council was criticized by the women's movement for its partisanship and lack of autonomy. However, it did provide advice to government, engage in public education, organize formal consultations with community, and conduct independent research on a broad range of issues related to women and the environment, women and the economy, single mothers, women and mental health, women and aging, "visible minority women," women with disabilities, child care, new reproductive technologies, constitutional reform, pornography and prostitution, employment standards and pay equity. It also lobbied for the creation of the OWD (OWD 1993d). The OACWI was eliminated in 1996, based on the questionable view that it was duplicating the responsibilities of the OWD.

Bill Davis's Progressive Conservative (PC) government created the OWD in 1983 (Malloy 2003). The OWD was to take on the functions of the Women's Bureau in the Ministry of Labour and the Women

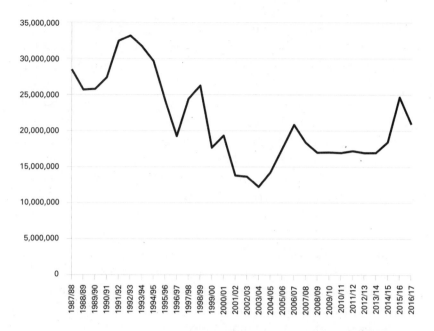

Figure 7.1 | Ontario Women's Directorate budget 1987–2016 (inflation adjusted in 2010 dollars) (*Source*: Ontario, Public Accounts, various years)

Crown Employees Office, as well as responsibility for policy and research. At that time, the position of Minister Responsible for the Status of Women was also established. Status of Women was not an independent portfolio. It was held with a minister's other portfolio, and the OWD was housed within that "home" ministry.[2] The directorate's primary role was to advise government on policy issues related to the status of women.

The directorate had forty-one staff and a budget of about $4.5 million in 1984 (Malloy 2003). It went through subsequent expansions in 1985–87 under the Liberal minority government and in 1990 under the New Democratic Party (NDP) government. Under the Liberals, the OWD had a communications branch, a program branch, and a policy and research branch. Staff numbers reached seventy-six and the budget was just over $22 million in 1991 (Public Accounts of Ontario, various years). Public servants interviewed estimated that by the mid-1990s, under the NDP, staff levels were close to one hundred.[3] The budget reached a peak in 1992 at $23 million, began a major decline in 1995 with a budget of $17.6 million, started to rise again briefly from 2004–06 under the Liberals, slipping a bit and then picking up again as Kathleen Wynne became premier, but still never returning close to the peak years of funding.

The first decade of the OWD spanned three governments: the tail end of the Bill Davis Conservative dynasty, the David Peterson Liberal minority (1985–87) and majority (1987–1990), and the NDP under Bob Rae (1990–95). Despite having different parties in power, this periodization reflects the responses in interviews, which largely stressed the similarities for the OWD across these governments.[4] Burt and Lorenzin (1997, 208–22) also submit that the NDP signalled "more of the same" in terms of a commitment to liberal democratic representation and equal opportunity, largely building on the policy framework of its predecessor. As noted above, this period represents a particular governance paradigm associated with the Keynesian welfare state and its associated gender regime.

In terms of "women's economic independence," in the directorate's words, in 1984, the directorate's *Plan of Action* outlined six main focus areas: affirmative action, child care, family violence, employment, income support, and justice. Gender analysis for Cabinet submissions and legislation was also introduced, as well as two programs, Open Doors and Jobs for the Future, that focused on encouraging women to enter non-traditional careers, and provided training for women in new technologies (OWD 1984).

These programs were expanded in 1985 and 1986 by the Liberal minority government. Child care allowances were introduced for women in training programs, more subsidized child care spaces were created, and the Ontario Skills Development Strategy included gender-based considerations such as equal access and part-time workers. Attention also turned to wages, overtime protection, worker's compensation for live-in nannies, family law (division of property in divorce), and pension reform (OWD 1985b, 1986). Progress continued on affirmative action, particularly in municipalities, school boards, universities, hospitals, and administration. Pay equity was highlighted as a priority.

There was also an early recognition of the problem of balancing work and family through a series of publications, public education materials, and conferences;[5] as well, there was an extension of parental leave (through Bill 14) and the introduction of consecutive parental leave,[6] flex time, and job sharing. The OWD also took a larger role in the administration of grants to community organizations in the late 1980s (Malloy 2003). Labour market policies demonstrated increased attention to marginalized groups (Haddow and Klassen 2004). There was a noticeable shift in directorate publications, with much more emphasis placed on diversity and contingent work.[7]

There were many gaps in the policy agenda, including child care, housing, and social assistance (Burt and Lorenzin 1997). Nonetheless, unlike later periods, there was an understanding that women's position in the labour market was determined by structural factors (Scott 1999). This stemmed from a substantive view of equality, as outlined in the directorate's 1989–90 *Year-End Report*, stating: "Although our laws now apply equally to both sexes, the significant differences in the lives of men and women must be taken into account in their application – otherwise laws can actually reinforce women's disadvantaged position" (12).

The major policies around women's labour market equality were employment and pay equity. During the Davis government, there was only cursory interest in pay and employment equity. But pay equity became a central focus of the Peterson government, and this carried through to the New Democrats. The Equal Pay Coalition, which had been organizing around pay equity in Ontario since the 1970s, had close ties to the NDP (Findlay 1997, 319). When the NDP unexpectedly won the 1990 election, they had a comprehensive women's policy program that included addressing violence against women, health care and reproductive rights, child care, family law reform, equal pay for work of equal value (pay equity), affirmative action (employment equity), and unionization (Burt and Lorenzin 1997).

Pay equity came under the mandate of the OWD, and the high priority placed on pay equity in particular raised the profile and influence of the directorate (Malloy 2003). They began working first for pay equity in the public service (OWD 1990), and it was later extended to the private sector (Burt and Lorenzin 1997). Extensive consultations occurred around pay equity and on how to put the principle of equal pay for work of equal value into practice to deal with the gendered wage gap. The work was eventually moved to the Pay Equity Commission within the Ministry of Labour for implementation.

There were certainly criticisms of pay equity. The proxy method, the most effective in reducing pay inequality, applied only to a small group of public sector workers and did not address the growing precariousness of women's work. However, pay equity challenged the idea that assigning value is best left to the market (Fudge and McDermott 1991). In fact, the early attempts at introducing equal pay for work of equal value were framed as such. In a 1985 document, the directorate's arguments for pay equity challenged several assumptions about the market. In its "Rebuttal against Market Forces," the OWD asserted that: (1) the market is not "free"; (2) the market cannot eliminate discrimination; and (3) equal value needs to be determined outside of the market (OWD 1985a). Also, the proxy method specifically recognized gendered job segregation and the need for substantial state intervention in order to combat it.

Employment equity was also introduced, starting within the Ontario Public Service (OPS), then extended to the voluntary approach in the private sector, and finally made a legislated obligation for all employers. In its early form, employment equity took a largely educational approach. For instance, the OWD, through the Change Agent project and the Urban Alliance on Race Relations, worked together to develop a handbook for employers on implementing employment equity for "visible minority" women (OWD 1989). The Office of the Employment Equity Commission was created in 1991, eventually becoming the Employment Equity Commission, which legislated employment equity in the public and private sectors (OWD 1991). The employment equity legislation took effect in 1994 and was stronger and more inclusive than its federal equivalent (Burt and Lorenzin 1997). The Act to Provide for Employment Equity for Aboriginal People, People with Disabilities, Members of Racial Minorities and Women included the provincial government and its agencies, as well as institutions in the broader public sector with more than ten employees (municipal governments, school boards, universities, hospitals, other health care), and police staffs and private sector companies with more than fifty employees. It also required employment equity plans to remove systemic barriers and an Employment Equity Tribunal to act as an enforcement body (Bakan and Kobayashi 2000).

This relatively advanced legislation had its critics. What is significant, however, is that employment equity policy constituted state acknowledgment that seemingly neutral administrative principles, like hiring based on "merit," are often tainted by systemic discrimination, and that state action is required to address it. Both employment equity and key components of pay equity were later repealed by the Tories in 1995.

NEOLIBERALISM AND STATE ADMINISTRATION IN ONTARIO

The ideas associated with the New Public Management are generally attributed to Margaret Thatcher's Conservative government during the 1980s. Thatcher emphasized three central elements of bureaucratic reform, or restructuring: increasing individual citizen, while decreasing state, control of public services; reducing the power of the public service; and advancing a market vision of "economy and efficiency" (Aucoin 2000, 1). The NPM's basic assumption is that states can, and should, be run like businesses. States around the world, including Canada, have sought to restructure public bureaucracies based on neoliberal administrative principles, or through increased "marketization" of the state (Albo 1993; Pierre 1995).

One of the central claims of neoliberalism is that out-of-control public spending had caused massive public deficits and debt. States needed, therefore, to cut spending by transferring as many programs and services as possible from the public to the private sector, through privatization, contracting-out, and public-private partnerships, and recasting citizens as "customers," "clients," or "taxpayers" (Brodie 1995). This includes the privatization of social welfare services, as well as policy advice through the growing use of private think tanks (Shields and Evans 1998). The NPM is based on public choice theory, in which "the root of any failings in the public sector ... is the self-interest of bureaucrats" (Peters 1995, 293). Privatization rescues the public, as "taxpayers," from bureaucratic extravagance.

In response to such claims, feminist political economists have emphasized that privatization includes much more than the selling of public assets. It is a gendered process that pushes services from the "public" to the "private" sphere, where the "private" includes not only the market but also the family and the voluntary sector (Brodie 1995; Fudge and Cossman 2002). This affects women who rely on the welfare state for services and good employment, and downloads the costs of social reproduction onto women, increasing their burden of unpaid labour (Brodie 1995; Bakker 1996).

This privatization is directly linked to the downsizing of public sector jobs. Blaming bureaucrats for the supposed explosion in public spending, downsizing was intended to deal with the dual evils of public expenditure and bureaucratic largesse. Influenced by firms in the private sector that "downsized" or laid off their workers to save money, advocates of the NPM suggested that states "seek to reduce the size of the public service as well as the public service payroll" (Aucoin 2000, 3). Downsizing is less about efficiency and more about political views on limiting the reach of the state. There are, moreover, negative impacts on women's work, as jobs in the public sector tend to have better wages, benefits, security, and are unionized (Bakker 1996). For those left in the public sector, jobs increasingly resemble the precarious (part-time, temporary, insecure) employment that is characteristic of the private sector (Peters 1995).

Both privatization and downsizing endeavour to take the public and place it in the private sector. However, the NPM does not stop there, since bringing the private into the public is also one of its central goals, transplanting private sector management techniques, such as business plans, quality control, target setting, customer service, merit pay, and performance measurement into government. Influenced by Osborne and Gaebler's bestselling "manual," *Reinventing Government*, NPM managerial reforms were intended to unleash "an entrepreneurial spirit, allowing organizations to innovate and excel" (Aucoin 2000, 90).

Feminist analysis has demonstrated that neoliberal state restructuring entails a variety of measures that have serious implications for equality (race, class, gender, sexual orientation, ability, age). There has been extensive feminist discussion of privatization, and downsizing, but this third element of NPM, managerialism, has received far less feminist treatment.

Borrowing from Thatcher and American neoliberals, the Progressive Conservative Party of Mike Harris argued during their 1995 Ontario election campaign that the restructuring and shrinking of government, the reduction of the deficit, and the lowering of taxes were paramount (Bradford 2003). This "reinvention" of government involved reducing the size of the state, by cutting a range of programs and services – including health care, education, welfare, child care subsidies, health and safety enforcement, environmental protections, job training, pay equity, public housing, and transfers to municipalities – and eliminating others, such as labour protection laws, and employment equity. Following the NPM recipe also meant downsizing public sector workers, privatization, commercialization, and appeals to volunteerism (Leduc Browne 1997).

Many have also pointed out that in Ontario, just as at the federal level in Canada and in other jurisdictions like Britain, Australia, and New Zealand, the NPM is really about a centralization of power in the Cabinet (ibid.). The Tories wanted to curtail the influence of both the public service and the community (Bradford 2003). The Harris government was able to radically restructure government through the 1995 Savings and Restructuring Bill, sought to introduce or amend over forty pieces of legislation, and gave the Cabinet wide-ranging powers (Weintroth 1997). The bill was followed up with the invention of the "Red Tape Secretariat" to cut onerous rules and improve efficiency and customer service (Ontario Red Tape Secretariat 2015). These functions do a good job of meeting the ends of the NPM, and advancing a very particular set of interests and power relations.

The bureaucracy was a central target for the Tories. The text of the Common Sense Revolution specifically mentions the reorganization of government as a priority. The bureaucracy was portrayed by the Conservatives as an irresponsible and inefficient monstrosity that wasted and mismanaged taxpayer money. Harris promised to "create partnerships with private business and open our administrative operations to outside competitions, where this can save taxpayers money" (quoted in Weintroth 1997, 60).

Under the Harris government, the understanding of representation clearly changed, and negatively impacted equality-oriented structures. One interview participant noted that "when the Tory government came in, they had no use for the OWD at all." This is made clear through the determined process of marginalization, the imposition of managerialism, and the undermining of community representation under the NPM gender regime.

The Conservatives' lack of interest in, and lack of support for, the OWD can be seen in many ways. Dianne Cunningham was the women's minister for most of the Tory government; the women's ministers under the PC regime generally were seen as weak in terms of decision-making, with little power or credibility in the government. In 1996, the Women's Ministry, previously stand-alone, was rolled into the new Ministry of Citizenship, Culture and Recreation (Malloy 2003). This ministry, responsible for women, immigrants, people with disabilities, seniors, volunteerism, honours and awards, was dubbed by one participant as "the Ministry of People We Don't Care About." The Conservatives also reduced the budget and the numbers of staff in the OWD (beyond the cuts made previously by the NDP). The budget in 1994–95 was $21.1 million, fell to $17.6 million in 1995–96, and then $14.2 million in 1996–97 (figure 7.1).

Budget and staffing cuts were matched with diminishing policy influence. Implicit in a lot of responses is what had been lost for state feminism over the decade. In the past, the directorate had a role in devising new policies, and in analyzing all policies with a gender lens. A former manager at the OWD said that during the Harris government, "there was no policy work going on … they were not interested in policy specifically directed at women." Although she had never heard the terminology of the NPM, she explained perfectly the impact of the new managerialism philosophy, observing: "What happened is you had a small cadre of political advisors around the premier who would basically decide on the political direction, and the civil servants' role became strictly implementation … It was as though the expertise of the civil service wasn't valued anymore."

The OWD's diminished policy presence can be seen with respect to gender-based analysis (GBA). The practice had been that the directorate's assistant deputy minister (ADM) would get all Cabinet submissions and an opportunity to comment on their impact on women, but with the Harris regime this was no longer the case. One participant spoke of the irony that she was working on GBA in an international context even though this analysis is not actively happening in Canada and especially not in Ontario since 1995. She recalled that in the Rae government, ministers were interested in the impact of policies on women, Aboriginal Peoples, racial minorities, and people with disabilities, and that the OWD had to be consulted. Under the Harris government and afterward, gender review of policies, or the incubation of new policies, was no longer seen as the mandate of the OWD.

STATE FEMINISM MEETS MANAGERIALISM

One of the main functions of the Ontario Women's Directorate was advocacy. The philosophy of managerialism, however, made advocacy illegitimate. One public servant suggested that "I bet you if you found a phone book from that period of time, that you would see advocacy, advocates on behalf of women ... that now would be entirely forbidden." In fact, this disappearance of any reference to advocacy in the Harris years can be seen by comparing the directorate's *Year-End Report, 1989–1990* to its *1998–1999 Business Plan* (OWD 1990, 1998). The expectation of "neutrality" tightened up considerably under neoliberalism, even curtailing what were established as advocacy branches of government. The Harris government, for example, wanted the OWD to acquire a much more "traditional" administrative character. As a former OWD manager put it, "the women's directorate ... in the past had some members of it who were very openly pro-active in the women's movement ... I was told very clearly that I was expected to be a corporate player and balance any personal feelings I might have with the rules we were expected to play." Despite the claims of the NPM, this certainly does not "de-politicize" the bureaucracy, but rather limits the discretion of public servants by imposing greater political control.

In order to keep the organization alive, self-censorship became a key strategy for feminist public employees working inside the Ontario state. As one official noted, "to many people's amazement, the OWD survived. It took on a much more limited mandate, a more focused mandate." A former policy analyst sensed that when she was re-hired at the directorate, her manager was concerned that she could work with the mandate because the directorate was "a pretty big target."

Besides structural changes to government administration, the new managerialism of the Harris government also brought significant discursive shifts in identifying citizen's groups. An interview participant explained that the label of "special interest groups" was applied consistently by the Harris government. This made it difficult for those working in equity-seeking areas: "under the Conservative government, we were very much made to feel as scapegoats and whipping boys ... they've done surveys, and we're down there with car salesmen and lawyers and politicians."

With the NPM "a new priority was given to the management of government ... [with] less and less attention to the development of policy alternatives" and expertise. In Ontario, knowledge of women's policy was no longer as highly valued. One interviewee insisted that from the early 1980s to the mid 1990s, all OWD staff "absolutely considered themselves feminists ... Some of the people that were hired in the mid-90s and beyond weren't even so sure they wanted to be those terms." With the loss of self-identification with feminism, the active debates within the OWD were no more. This reflects what a community worker called a "bureaucratization of the bureau" where people were no longer trained in their portfolios.

Participants also spoke of internal restructuring leading to unevenness of staff, high turnover, and lack of leadership as managerialism spread through the OWD. While high turnover was characteristic of the directorate, in the past this was because it was a place for women to get management experience and then "disseminate through the OPS ideas around looking at policy through a gender lens." But a former manager ascribed a "revolving door" scenario to the directorate. The inconsistency in staff contributed to a lack of long-term vision and planning capacity for women's policy. One former official noted that although there had always been minor shifts in governance with changes in government, the managerialism changes implemented by Harris were of a different order: "Essentially it was how to do outcomes-based planning and outcomes based measuring ... everything's a buzz word, everything's a format ... with very little thought or vision ... or planning about what the content is ... there's a whole new focus on results-based planning ... It seems like it's all rule-driven, so there can be no individual decision-making judgment." The desire for vision and long-term policy capacity by feminists working in the OWD conflicted with the neoliberal and market-driven orientation of the government.

OWD personnel noted that as the new managerialism criteria for quality management, service standards, and accountability mechanisms were introduced, all divisions and ministries had to form "business plans," with spending now more rigidly limited if it did not fit into the more narrowly defined plan. The first directorate business plan under the Harris government was created in 1996 (Malloy 2003). The former minister Dianne Cunningham hailed her government's call for business plans for all ministries as "the best thing to ever happen to the OWD." She believed it forced the latter to get focused, monitor its goals, identify "best practices," and show results. She was "fed up with reports," wanted the OWD to be more results-focused, to stop trying to do too much, and to "build on programs that work."

Cunningham's adherence to the new market-driven governance practices of the Conservatives was well illustrated in discussing her government's cuts to public service advertisements on violence against women. They were able to get the private sector to do it, she argued, because "big companies ... don't want their women coming to work every day violated. ... We in Ontario and Canada depend on the government to do things that we should be doing for ourselves."

The *1998–1999 Business Plan* consolidated the NPM discourse in the OWD, describing its role now as "a catalyst by initiating cross-sectoral partnerships in communities across the province to maximize client service and develop new solutions to issues faced by women" (OWD 1999, 3). The business plan highlighted the attention now paid to program accountability and performance measures, and away from equity advocacy or planning for women's policies. But even in terms of results-based measuring, one public servant noted that there is nothing wrong in theory with showing that what you are doing has an effect – the problem is how to measure the results in practice with respect to equity processes. She noted the difficulties in quantifying the outcomes of the directorate's intangible activities, such as consulting other ministries, and the incomplete information that is gained from these processes.

It was commented by former employees at OWD that the NPM ideas became a "very powerful model" that is "essentially [about] control mechanisms." For example, "the Harris government centralized a lot of functions and we had a much closer relationship with the Ministry of Finance ... the way they generated the numbers, they produced documents that it just looked like nothing but good news."

The desire for control is not only seen with public sector workers, but with communities outside the state as well. The NPM professes to value and support citizen engagement. Albo (1993, 25) contends that "the new right has hacked away at even modest forms of participatory administration – citizen advisory boards, funding for citizens' groups, rights of procedural justice." In Ontario, one element of the Tories' agenda in government restructuring was to eliminate a range of bodies for public consultation and local participation (Leduc Browne 1997).[8]

If one considers the relationship between feminists inside the state and activists outside in the community during the Harris period in Ontario, democratic participation was wanting. As Bradford (2003, 1018) explains: "Legislative amendments were made ... to limit the resources and policy voice of unions, social equity movements and anti-poverty activists ... structures that had institutionalized a policy role for civil society representatives, all disappeared in the government's first year." A community spokesperson said that when the Tories were elected, "real consultation plummeted," and "phony consultations" increased. When it did occur, it was much less public, and input was rarely integrated. There was a "lockdown on policy" when, for long periods of time, there were no calls for proposals or projects from the women's policy community and there was no clear funding cycle.[9]

When consultation happened, the Tory government had a very exclusive view of who was included in their "community." The Business and Professional Women's Association was one of the key organizations. It was common to hear those interviewed describing feelings of despair in the OWD, with one concluding that "it's pretty awful right now. People are pretty unhappy ... It used to be great and now it's lousy. We used to do cool stuff, now we don't." Several confirmed that it was much more difficult to keep connections to the community due to a lack of field staff, the breakdown in information from the community to the state, and the devaluing of input from so-called special interest groups. To one staffer, it seemed that the focus on efficiency and accountability is about "accountability more to the inside, than the outside." This has led Sue Findlay (1995) to maintain that shielding the public service from democratic participation is key to maintaining power relations, and that it is not surprising that restructuring has meant that the bureaucracy is even less open to "outsiders" now.

Besides the OWD, the other main agency of representation for women in the Ontario government was the Ontario Advisory Council on Women's Issues (OACWI). Unlike the cuts to the OWD, the OACWI was scrapped completely by the Harris Conservatives. The loss of the OACWI was not strongly resisted by the women's movement as it was criticized for its political appointment process and its lack of connections to the feminist community. It occurred as part of the larger implementation of the NPM which encompassed the undermining of efforts at gender democracy. The Tories believed that they didn't need policy advice, and they cut those things that were not mainstream – "women's policy issues were not at the top of agenda, they were not on the radar screen."

NEOLIBERALISM AND WOMEN'S LABOUR MARKET POLICY

Even though women's policy was certainly not a main focus of the Harris government, it did receive some attention. Under the Tories, as with previous governments, the focus of women's policy was on two main areas: violence against women and women's economic independence, with the latter being particularly revealing of the NPM practices.

Labour market policy for women during the Harris period consisted mainly of encouraging women's entrepreneurialism and their entrance into male-dominated "nontraditional" occupations.[10] For the former, other ministries provided small business loan programs for women, in combination with the OWD's own grant distribution. As Malloy (2003, 108) argues, the economic independence stream was "overwhelmingly service-oriented; it produced publications ... that emphasized women succeeding in business and as business owners." On the government website, primary emphasis was placed on "Supporting Women's Entrepreneurship." The website made grand claims: "Entrepreneurship poses an attractive career alternative, and Ontario's women entrepreneurs boast tremendous successes. Ontario women are turning good ideas and a little start-up money into thriving, growing businesses" (OWD 2003).

In addition to concentrating on women's entrepreneurialism, the OWD website paid some attention to job segregation. But this was quite different from when the central projects of the OWD were pay and employment equity. The Conservative government approach to women's job ghettoization was to exhort women to expand their occupational horizons and to individualize gender inequality. The message was that women can solve the problem of sex-segregation, and low-paid, insecure, non-unionized jobs, by making different career choices.[11]

Many OWD staff were not satisfied with such an approach to women's labour market policy. One interviewee quickly replied that "nothing" is happening, or "it's not entirely that nothing's happening, there are some targeted employment projects, specifically around women and non-traditional skills." Alan Sears (2000, 153–4) has called this approach the "new vocationalism" based on disciplining and fitting workers into the existing labour market. One example from the Harris government was the *Information Technology Training for Women* (ITTW) program. The OWD (2002b) website claimed that, as a "partnership between the Ontario government, the private and the voluntary sectors, ITTW provides low-income women in Ontario with government-funded specialized training that will help them qualify for entry level jobs in IT." The program intended to train women to be webmasters, database administrators, and software developers. While it was mentioned that the program "will let them [disadvantaged women] leave poverty behind for sustainable careers as technical office professionals," it emphasized several times that "ITTW is part of Ontario's strategy to address skill shortages in high-tech industries" (OWD 2001, 2002a, 2002b).

This was not the first time that the OWD focused on getting women into non-traditional careers. Programs like *Open Doors* and *Jobs for the Future* began under the Davis Tories, and continued under subsequent governments. The difference is that previously, such programs were but one aspect of a broader women's policy agenda to tackle job segregation in a comprehensive way.[12] During the Harris government, however, these initiatives became the primary instrument for women's labour market policy.

Women's policy advocates stressed that programs that are essential for women's economic independence, like child care and housing, "dropped out" under the Tories. The Tory agenda even resurrected the regressive "spouse-in-the-house" rule, described as "a manifestation of the deeply entrenched gender stereotyping of women as dependants of men" (Kitchen 1997, 109). For the Harris government, economic independence was not foremost about gender equality, but about reducing women's dependence on the state. One OWD staffer interviewed even charged that the Tory government "would like women to be independent because they don't want women on social assistance, and they certainly don't want women with children on social assistance for long periods of time."

Community groups clearly have a different vision of women's economic independence and labour market policy in mind. They expressed concern that the province had not clearly articulated an integrated labour market development policy that considers older workers, women, workers with disabilities, and immigrants. A former OWD staff also noticed a drastic change in the way diversity among women was treated, saying that "with the Harris government, everything was just kind of washed away. It was like women were one big lump."

The changes brought to women's policies in Ontario under the Harris government were not, as some have attempted to argue, due to a lack of a clear policy approach. Rather, the neoliberal polices that the Tories pursued, with their assumption that equality equals labour market participation, undermined the goal of women's labour market equality. Armstrong and Connelly (1999, 3) note that the Harris government "used the deficit and new discourse of eliminating red tape and global competition to justify direct attacks on pay equity legislation and wage gains in the state sector." Their assault on unions and public sector employment further undermined the limited ability of women concentrated in precarious employment to organize collectively. Furthermore, the assumption that labour market participation alone provides equality has been challenged by many immigrant women and racialized women who, despite having very high labour market participation rates, overwhelmingly lack equality with men and other women.

It is this approach to women's labour market policy that led to the Harris cuts to things like the Pay Equity Commission, Ontario Jobs Training, child care, health and safety enforcement, and the elimination of employment equity and the Ontario Training and Adjustment

Board, including the equity representation on local boards. An OWD policy analyst from this period noted:

> From '95 on, the government ... dismantled the employment equity commission, they abolished the legislation, they dismantled the programs in the broader public sector. That was a conscious decision of the ... government to do all that. So employment equity ... for all intents and purposes disappeared. Pay equity ... there was just no policy agenda to move.

Judy Wolfe, a former senior manager in OWD, recalled: "once the Conservatives were elected ... there was a moment when I was sitting in my office ... in October of 1995 ... when I was listening to the news and every single thing I had ever worked on was cancelled. That was a disheartening moment ... I still can feel that feeling." She highlighted even the loss of "gender-inclusive" language that the OWD had helped nurture before the Conservatives came into office: "Employment equity was expunged from the language after 1995. You could not use anything that sounded like that."[13] Scott (1999, 230) goes even further, assessing the Harris government policy actions as "a systematic dismantling of many of the important gains that the women's movement has made over the last 20 years."

THE NPM AND GENDER DEMOCRACY

The NPM has dominated ideas about the role of government and the form of state administration since the 1980s. The NPM in Ontario is based on privatization, downsizing, and managerialism; it has resulted in a gender regime that has posed particular problems for the women's movement and undermined gains of both procedural and substantive democracy that had been made by women's policies. Procedurally, the NPM rejects the ideas that women's policies targeted at addressing structural social inequalities are important; that feminists within the state administration should advocate for women; and that participatory forms of administration should be developed to facilitate engagement with women in the community. The traditional approach by the OWD to women's labour market policy has been eclipsed. Instead, the

NPM and neoliberal policy ideas brought into the Ontario state during the Conservative regime of Mike Harris have favoured market-based, individualized policy solutions aimed at increasing women's labour market participation as the central, and at times exclusive, objective.

But neoliberalism, and NPM strategies, have not been just about any one political party. They are about producing a particular and enduring system of power relations, which privileges private, market relations; understands inequalities in power not as collective phenomenon, but as the result of individual circumstance; and radically restricts the role of communities in the policy process. Under the subsequent Liberal governments of Dalton McGuinty and Kathleen Wynne, the Ontario Women's Directorate's presence was not significantly improved, and major advancements in women's representation and public policy have not ensued.

THE McGUINTY AND WYNNE GOVERNMENTS AND WOMEN'S POLICY: CONSOLIDATING THE NPM?

The Dalton McGuinty Liberals were elected in 2003 by distancing themselves from the harsh and punitive Common Sense Revolution, and emphasizing responsive government and social investment. However, the new discourse was not matched with a change in substance. Coulter (2009, 24) maintains that while the "Liberal government in Ontario engages in rhetoric about the value of public services, its Third Way approach ensures that neoliberal policy approaches prevail, although in camouflaged and modified forms. In this way, neoliberalism is deepened and normalized, and discussion of gender and socio-economic inequality is largely avoided by government politicians."

This is typical of versions of neoliberalism that seek a more social cast by "repackaging" the same market-oriented policies and fiscal conservatism (Coulter 2009). The result, as Fanelli and Thomas (2011, 143) show, is that "costs are socialized and profits privatized." With new emphasis on children and the social, McKeen (2007) has referred to a "neoliberal wolf in lamb's clothing." In her study of feminism in the McGuinty era, Ready also demonstrates the continuity of neoliberalism, or what she calls "new-neoliberal" initiatives, to address violence against women. She explains that "as the policies of the McGuinty government took shape, my experience was that they created new, more subtle, and in many ways, more dangerous impacts. Outwardly, the policies of this government appeared to be more supportive, yet did little to address the poverty and marginalization of women and did much to control and weaken non-profit organizations working to empower women" (2016, ix).

The basic tenets of neoliberalism remained. The McGuinty Liberals prioritized corporate and personal tax cuts; emphasized trade liberalization; continued the privatization of health care and introduced new user fees; pursued public-private partnerships for hospitals; deregulated environmental and labour standards; froze wages for thousands of public sector workers; and effectively suspended collective bargaining rights for teachers. In addition, the privatization of public assets was used as a deficit-cutting strategy (Fanelli and Thomas 2011).

While under McGuinty, the outward disdain for public services dissipated, NPM techniques such as performance measurement and public-private partnerships continued to support neoliberal governance, including in women's policy. The McGuinty government also focused on accountability, results-based planning, evaluation, logic models, outcomes, outputs, and performance measurement (Coulter 2009). This can be seen in several reports on the OWD website. In *Breaking the Cycle: Ontario's Poverty Reduction Strategy* (2008), targets, outcomes measurement, and evaluation are underscored. Public reporting on income, school readiness, education, health care, and housing is celebrated to improve accountability. "Measuring results" is also the key message in the housing strategy. Within a general climate of austerity, the generous performance pay for public sector managers is indicative of the precedence given to these measures. This shift toward "new" accountability mechanisms in Canada has not led to real improvements in public policy for women (Anderson and Findlay 2010).

Furthermore, regardless of the changing rhetoric about partnerships, collaboration, and responsiveness, community representation in the policy process remained shallow. In the Liberals' poverty reduction plan, the government committed only to provide "support to co-ordinate community revitalization projects" (Ontario Cabinet Committee on Poverty Reduction 2008, 3). Clearly, steering rather than rowing was still the order of the day. Coulter argues that the Ontario Liberals, operating through a persona of "niceness," engage in consultation that "constructs the appearance of dialogue, while postponing the need for action" (2009, 32–3), echoing the aforementioned "phony consultations" from the Tory era. The OWD's resources certainly did not reflect a desire to improve its capacity for community engagement. As seen in figure 7.1, the 2011–12 inflation-adjusted OWD budget is almost 40 per cent lower than in 1987. Collier (2016) reminds that this budget remained below the 1995 Harris level.

There is another consistent element over time. In its guidelines for OWD grants to community organizations, the priorities included projects related to micro-lending for low-income women to start small businesses, entrepreneurialism, and Women in Skilled Trades and Information Technology Training. As in the Tory era, the OWD continued to put "recognizing women" at the forefront through "the Leading Girls, Building Communities and Leading Women, Building Communities Awards [to] recognize and celebrate girls and women who demonstrate exceptional leadership in working to improve the lives of others in their communities" (2011a).

During the Progressive Conservative government, women's issues were given very low priority, and when they were taken up, it was done in a way that departed significantly from past practice. The pattern remained under the McGuinty Liberals, as is clear in women's labour market policy. There is little evidence that their agenda involved much more activity on women's labour market policy than their predecessors'. In many instances, women's economic independence is overshadowed by violence against women. Public education campaigns and resources and links are all focused on violence, with little mention of women's economic equality (OWD 2011b, 2012). Connections between poverty and violence against women are not made clear (Coulter 2009). Rhetoric on poverty reduction has not been met with action, and poverty continues to be individualized. There have not been significant changes made to welfare policy, and the clawback of the National Child Benefit Supplement was only phased out in the face of a court challenge (ibid.). The Liberal government resumed previous cuts made to the Pay Equity Commission's budget and staff (Collier 2016).

The emphasis on women in non-traditional fields was also maintained with McGuinty. In the Liberals' poverty reduction strategy,

ITTW is one of the few policies described that is directed specifically to women. The OWD lists programs on skilled trades and information technologies as its highlights (OWD 2012). In her study of the McGuinty Liberals, Coulter found that the "neoliberal ideological project ... reinforces the political culture that emphasizes and promotes individualism, individual responsibility, and choice, without any accompanying discussion about existing inequities in power and economic status or between genders, and how these influence the ability of people to make choices in their lives" (2009, 28).

Under McGuinty, gender equality continued to be absent from policy discourse. In the poverty reduction plan, even though the report figures prominently on the OWD's website, the policy agenda for women is very meagre. There is about one page of text, much of which focuses on gender-neutral "domestic violence." This is embedded in the overarching goal in the plan to reduce "child poverty" by 25 per cent in five years (Ontario Cabinet Committee on Poverty Reduction 2008). This is actually an improvement on *Ontario's Long-Term Affordable Housing Strategy* (2010) and *Open Minds, Healthy Minds: Ontario's Comprehensive Mental Health and Addictions Strategy* (2011), which also appear on the directorate's website, but fail to mention women at all, not even in reference to "domestic violence" in the housing plan (2010). The introduction of full-day kindergarten, a major investment in publicly provided, universal child care, is a central policy accomplishment of the McGuinty regime. Even so, Collier documents how "debates on child care centred on the educational needs of the child and not on the equality focus for women as it had in the past" (2016, 224). As Coulter shows, the Liberal government "promotes de-gendered, class-less neoliberal subjects, while actively avoiding consideration of the systemic causes of poverty and collective solutions that challenge the neoliberal policy paradigm" (2009, 25).

There is some unfortunate irony that this disappearance or "writing out" of gender coincides with the purported rise of GBA and GBA+ (its intersectional counterpart) over the last decade. Scala and Paterson (2017, 428) note that "replacing much of the gender equality policy architecture of the 'women's state' is an administrative machinery that seeks to integrate gender into all policies and programmes." However, this is a weak replacement since there are "no oversight mechanisms to assess the quality of analysis or to challenge those documents in which GBA is not conducted" (415–17). Ontario's approach is one of "limited consultation, favouring technocratic approaches to analysis" that "generally leave broader contexts unquestioned and rely on bureaucratic expertise to solve problems related to difference," and fail to go beyond the removal of barriers (471, 419).

There has been only minimal improvement in other internal state processes for women. Collier points out that "women have not sustained the higher levels of representation reached at the DM [Deputy Minister] or ADM levels in the 1990s." She concludes that "despite the change in regime after the McGuinty Liberals were elected in 2003, things did not improve for the OWD. It took the lead on violence against women policy and implemented the Liberals' Domestic Violence Action Plan and its more recent Action Plan to Stop Sexual Violence and Harassment, but it ceased to be an active advisor to the minister responsible on *new* gender equality policy" (2016, 220–1).

The policies that perished during the Conservative era were not revived under the McGuinty Liberals. The poverty reduction plan refers briefly to full-day learning, but makes no mention of employment and pay equity. It notes improvements to employment standards to address precarious work, but also venerates paid work (regardless of quality) through measures such as the Ontario Child Benefit, and is fully committed to a market-based approach to housing. Markets and children (future market engines) are the proper subjects of public policy. As a case in point, in the mental health and addictions strategy, the Ontario state "will focus on early intervention and support to protect our children from the many associated costs of mental illness and addictions and help steer them on the road to safe, healthy, and happy futures" (Ontario Ministry of Health 2011, 4).

In 2013, Kathleen Wynne was elected as the first female, and first lesbian, premier of Ontario (Collier 2016). Under Wynne, as of 2016, 40 per cent of the Cabinet were women, and in 2017, the OWD underwent a transformation into the Ministry of the Status of Women (MSW), and gained its first full minister. In describing its activities, the MSW says it "collaborates with women's organizations and across government to advance women's equality, support their safety and improve their economic security (Ministry of the Status of Women 2017d), signifying a more robust institutional identity than seen in the last two decades.

There are some indications that the policy ground was also changing under Wynne. Her government's sexual violence and harassment plan, *It's Never Okay: An Action Plan to Stop Sexual Violence and Harassment* (2015), which provided funding for supports for survivors, training for front-line service providers, and public education about rape and criminal justice reform, was praised by community-based advocates (Porter 2015). Important progress was made on sex-education curriculum, post-secondary tuition, pension expansion (Salutin 2016), and increasing the minimum wage. The Miss G Project secured the results of their campaign for a gender studies course for secondary school students (Ministry of the Status of Women 2017e). Plans to ensure wage parity for full- and part-time workers, to expand emergency leave, and to better enforce employment laws (Ministry of the Status of Women 2017a) were promising. After decades of advocacy by the child care movement in Ontario, and piecemeal efforts by governments, there appeared to be concrete commitments to "build a 'universally accessible' child-care system in Ontario" (Monsebraaten 2017) on the foundation of full-day kindergarten. The well-established principles set out by the child care community were finally being reflected in the government's plan to expand public and non-profit services, improve the wages and working conditions of the child care workforce, and meet the needs of families with diverse working hours and in different locations. Child care champion Martha Friendly lauded the "comprehensive system-building approach." However, the Public Policy Coordinator for the Ontario Coalition for Better Child Care, Carolyn Ferns, warned that in the past "the introduction of full-day kindergarten destabilize[d] the licensed child care sector," demonstrating the need for a system-wide, planned, and integrated approach (Monsebraaten 2017, 2).

Csanady (2016) summarizes the "many overtly feminist policies developed under Wynne: The move to force corporations to put women on their boards, or explain why they can't, has been welcomed by many feminists and academics; a sexual violence strategy recommended as a model for other jurisdictions; a move to increase wages for the lowest paid, female dominated fields of childcare and personal support work."

Perhaps the most telling signal of a turning policy tide is that investment in *social* infrastructure is increasingly taken seriously.

Yet Wynne was criticized on other policy fronts. Public sector unions have pointed out that wage freezes and cuts to public sector wages and jobs disproportionately affect women, who make up 63 per cent of the Ontario public service (Csanady 2016). Her government had ongoing pay equity struggles with LCBO employees and midwives which overshadowed the appointment of a Gender Wage Gap Steering Committee and its subsequent public consultations (Ontario Ministry of Labour 2016), and the 2014 election promise on a wage gap strategy was vague (Collier 2016). In 2017, the province held consultations (online and via written submissions) on "how to help women and girls achieve their full social and economic potential" (Ministry of the Status of Women 2017a). Nevertheless, the modest ambition to remove "barriers" for women is the persistent frame adopted in the discussion paper, often used to awkwardly describe structural inequalities related to caregiving, housing, precarity, and colonialism.

Women's entrepreneurship and the Skilled Trades and Information Technology Training Program were enduring priorities, with added emphasis on other modest initiatives such as improving financial literacy training (ibid.). The elevation of business and professional women, a longstanding preoccupation of the OWD, lingered, along with efforts to increase the numbers of women on public and corporate boards and agencies. For the Wynne government, it turned out that "empower youth" meant women in non-traditional careers and "encourage leadership" meant women in business (ibid.).

The mandate of the new Ministry of the Status of Women followed the two traditional streams of the former OWD: "to increase women's economic security and to end violence against women" (Ministry of the Status of Women 2017d). Nonetheless, the pedominance of violence against women on the Ministry of the Status of Women's website is a durable holdover from other periods. The majority of resources and references are related to violence (Ministry of the Status of Women 2017c). Consultations on the province's domestic violence action plan and gender-based violence strategy are foregrounded, along with efforts to address human trafficking (Ministry of the Status of Women 2017b, 2017e). But reviews of Wynne's Throne Speeches in 2013 and

2014 found that gender-neutral framing of child care and violence against women carried over from her predecessors (Collier 2016), and fashionable talk of GBA/GBA+ was often not translated into action. Moreover, the Ministry of the Status of Women's budget increased only marginally under Wynne and is still lower than the OWD at its height in the early 1990s.

The majority Conservative government of Doug Ford, following the June 2018 election, will have grim consequences for women's procedural and substantive equality. The vagueness of Ford's platform makes a full analysis difficult, but feminists have raised concerns about the derogatory comments he has made about women, and campaign pledges related to reproductive rights, freezing the minimum wage, replacing the sex education curriculum, and funding his promises by "finding efficiencies" in the public sector. He has already announced a public sector hiring freeze, which will likely impact women workers disproportionately. And the focus on demand-side tax credits for parents (skewed toward higher-income earners) instead of supply-side provision of child care services (favouring public provision irrespective of income) will reinforce all the problems of market and policy failure already plaguing child care in Ontario.

AFTER NEOLIBERALISM? GENDER DEMOCRACY

Gender democracy in Ontario has not fared well under neoliberalism and the New Public Management. Procedural representation, historically enabled with an active and growing architecture for women's policy in which the OWD was at the centre, has been harmed by cuts, restructuring, reorganization, mechanisms of discipline and control, delegitimization, and marginalization. More recently it is increasingly being replaced with largely superficial GBA/GBA+ processes. Substantively, traditional approaches by the OWD to women's labour market policy, which used to see gender inequality as related to a complicated set of structural factors, have been rejected in favour of marketization, individualization, and de-gendered solutions. These historic changes are not easily reversed through shifting electoral tides. Neoliberalism and NPM strategies are not about any one political party. These ideas continue to resonate in Ontario politics today.

Under the successive Liberal governments of McGuinty and Wynne, the presence of women's policy machinery remained constrained and the public policy agenda for women inadequate. At best, the Wynne government's policy approach might be captured by what Mahon (2009) has called "inclusive liberalism." The neoliberal agenda of low inflation, balanced budgets, economic liberalization, flexible labour and labour market participation, and gender erasure remain in place, but a heightened focus on investment for the future was added. With the election of Ford, Ontario is heading for a return to the aggressive neoliberalism and social conservatism of the Harris regime, which proved to be devastating for women's representation and equitable public policy. For social movements in Ontario (and agendas for research), this points to the need to focus greater attention on the political economy of governance regimes at the provincial level, and on how egalitarian struggles for gender democracy might transform them.

NOTES

1 This chapter draws on my *Femocratic Administration: Gender, Governance, and Democracy in Ontario* (University of Toronto Press, 2015), with permission of the publisher. Details of the interviews cited in this chapter can be found in this text.
2 For instance, the first minister responsible for women's issues in Ontario, Robert Welch, was also deputy premier at the time (Malloy 2003).
3 As Malloy (2003) explains, exact employment levels are not available because under the NDP's Social Contract employment levels were no longer made public.
4 These commonalities, especially due to the minority government, include a more flexible view of advocacy, stronger ministerial support, a more active policy agenda, continuity in policy, and rising staffing numbers.
5 See, for example: OWD 1993d; OWD and CAMCO 1992; OWD and Union Gas 1992; OWD and the United Food and Commercial Workers Union 1992).
6 Consecutive parental leave requires parents to take leave separately from one another. This is in contrast with concurrent leave, where parents take leave at the same time. Consecutive leave is designed so that parents (especially fathers) spend time parenting alone, encouraging a more equal distribution of caring responsibility between women and men.
7 See, for example, OWD 1993a, 1993b, 1993c; and OWD and Urban Alliance on Race Relations 1990.

8 One key exception is the Conservatives' pursuit of public-private partnerships with the business community. The directorate's *1998–1999 Business Plan* specifically refers to P3s in the context of community consultation.
9 This problem is directly related to the issue of the professionalization of groups. The OWD used to provide core funding to women's groups and centres. The funding process changed so that in order to get funds, groups now have to give project submissions, and the OWD then selects the "most worthy."
10 This was also a focus during the previous Liberal and NDP governments, but it became much more central in the Conservative agenda.
11 Jean Trickey (1997) makes a similar point about the repeal of the act. She asserts that the systemic understanding of racism that had been developed over time was replaced under the Tories with an individualized complaint approach to discrimination, largely left to the Ontario Human Rights Commission.
12 Early in the OWD, there was significant attention paid to women in non-traditional careers, technology, and small business ownership. Although of lower priority by the early 1990s, this provided a foundation for the Tories to build up their market-oriented approach to women's policy.
13 Bakan and Kobayashi (2000, 29) confirm that "in practice, even verbal use of the term 'employment equity' was considered a feature of past practice, neither relevant to, nor acceptable in, the current context."

REFERENCES

Albo, Gregory. 1993. "Democratic Citizenship and the Future of Public Management." In *A Different Kind of State? Popular Power and Democratic Administration*, edited by Gregory Albo, David Langille, and Leo Panitch. Toronto: Oxford University Press.

Anderson, Lynell, and Tammy Findlay. 2010. "Does Public Reporting Measure Up? Federalism, Accountability and Child Care Policy in Canada." *Canadian Public Administration* 53 (3).

Armstrong, Pat, and Patricia M. Connelly. 1997. "Introduction: The Many Forms of Privatization." *Studies in Political Economy* 53.

Aucoin, Peter. 2000. *The New Public Management: Canada in Comparative Perspective*. Montreal: Institute for Research on Public Policy.

Bakan, Abigail, and Audrey Kobayashi. 2000. *Employment Equity in Canada: A Provincial Comparison*. Ottawa: Status of Women Canada.

Bakker, Isabella. 1996. "Introduction: The Gendered Foundations of Restructuring in Canada." In *Rethinking Restructuring: Gender and Change in Canada*, edited by Isabella Bakker. Toronto: University of Toronto Press.

Bradford, Neil. 2003. "Public-Private Partnership? Shifting Paradigms of Economic Governance in Ontario." *Canadian Journal of Political Science* 36 (5).

Brodie, Janine. 1995. *Politics on the Margins: Restructuring and the Canadian Women's Movement*. Halifax: Fernwood Publishing.

Brodie, Janine, and Isabella Bakker. 2007. *Canada's Social Policy Regime and Women: An Assessment of the Last Decade*. Ottawa: Status of Women Canada.

Browne, Paul Leduc. "Déjà Vu: Thatcherism in Ontario." In *Open For Business, Closed to People: Mike Harris' Ontario*, edited by Diana S. Ralph, André Régimbald, and Néréee St-Amand. Halifax: Fernwood Publishing.

Burt, Sandra, and Elizabeth Lorenzin. 1997. "Taking the Women's Movement to Queen's Park: Women's Interests and the New Democratic Government of Ontario." In *In the Presence of Women: Representation in Canadian Governments*, edited by Jane Arscott and Linda Trimble. Toronto: Harcourt Brace and Company.

Cattapan, Alana, Cindy Hanson, Jane Stinson, Leah Levac, and Stephanie Paterson. 2017. "The "Budget's Baby Steps on Gender Equality." *Policy Options*, 27 March.

Collier, Cheryl N. 2016. "A Path Well Travelled or Hope on the Horizon? Women, Gender, and Politics in Ontario." In *The Politics of Ontario*, edited by Jonathan Malloy and Cheryl N. Collier. Toronto: University of Toronto Press.

Connell, R.W. 2002. *Gender*. Malden, MA: Blackwell.

Csanady, Ashley. 2016. "Does the Ontario Premier have a Gender Problem? Union Ads Question Wynne's Feminist Cred." *National Post*, 7 March.

Fanelli, Carlo, and Mark P. Thomas. 2011. "Austerity, Competitiveness and Neoliberalism Redux: Ontario Responds to the Great Recession." *Socialist Studies/Études socialistes* 7 (1–2).

Ferns, Carolyn. 2017. *Transformative Change for Early Years and Child Care in Ontario: From Market Patchwork to System*. Submission in Response to "Building a Better Future: A Discussion Paper on Transforming Early Years and Child Care in Ontario." Ontario Coalition for Better Child Care.

Findlay, Sue. 1995. "Democracy and the Politics of Representation: Feminist Struggles with the Canadian State, 1960–1990." PhD diss., University of Toronto.

– 1997. "Institutionalizing Feminist Politics: Learning from the Struggles for Equal Pay in Ontario." In *Women and the Canadian Welfare State: Challenges and Change*, edited by Patricia M. Evans and Gerda R. Wekerle. Toronto: University of Toronto Press.

Findlay, Tammy. 2015. *Femocratic Administration: Gender, Governance, and Democracy in Ontario*. Toronto: University of Toronto Press.

Fudge, Judy, and Brenda Cossman. 2002. "Introduction: Privatization, Law, and the Challenge to Feminism." In *Privatization, Law, and the Challenge to Feminism*, edited by Brenda Cossman and Judy Fudge. Toronto: University of Toronto Press.

Fudge, Judy, and Patricia McDermott. 1991. "Putting Feminism to Work." In *Just Wages: A Feminist Assessment of Pay Equity*, edited by Judy Fudge and Patricia McDermott. Toronto: University of Toronto Press.

Haddow, Rodney, and Thomas R. Klassen. 2004. "Partisanship, Institutions and Public Policy: The Case of Labour Market Policy in Ontario, 1990–2000." *Canadian Journal of Political Science* 37 (1).

Haussman, Melissa, Marian Sawer, and Jill Vickers, eds. 2010. *Federalism, Feminism and Multilevel Governance*. Farnham, UK: Ashgate Press.

Jenson, Jane. 2009. "Writing Gender Out: The Continuing Effects of the Social Investment Perspective." In *Women and Public Policy in Canada: Neo-liberalism and After?*, edited by Alexandra Dobrowolsky. Don Mills: Oxford University Press.

Kitchen, Brigitte. 1997. "'Common Sense' Assaults on Families." In *Open For Business, Closed to People: Mike Harris' Ontario*, edited by Diana S. Ralph, André Régimbald, and Néréee St-Amand. Halifax: Fernwood Publishing.

Krook, Mona Lena, and Fiona Mackay. 2011. "Introduction: Gender, Politics, and Institutions." In *Gender, Politics and Institutions: Towards a Feminist Institutionalism*, edited by M.L. Krook and F. Mackay. Basingstoke: Palgrave Macmillan.

Mahon, Rianne. 2005. "Rescaling Social Reproduction: Childcare in Toronto/Canada and Stockholm/Sweden." *International Journal of Urban and Regional Research* 29 (2).

– 2009. "Childcare and Varieties of Liberalism in Canada." In *Women and Public Policy in Canada: Neoliberalism and After?*, edited by Alexandra Dobrowolsky. Don Mills: Oxford University Press.

Malloy, Jonathan. 2003. *Between Colliding Worlds: The Ambiguous Existence of Government Agencies for Aboriginal and Women's Policy*. Toronto: University of Toronto Press.

McKeen, Wendy. 2007. "The National Children's Agenda: A Neoliberal Wolf in Lamb's Clothing." *Studies in Political Economy* 79.

Monsebraaten, Laurie. 2017. "Ontario Commits to Universally Accessible Child Care." *Toronto Star*, 6 June.

O'Connor, Julia, Ann Orloff, and Sheila Shaver. 1999. *States, Markets, Families: Gender, Liberalism and Social Policy in Australia, Canada, Great Britain and the United States*. Cambridge: Cambridge University Press.

Ontario. (various years). *Public Accounts*. https://www.ontario.ca/page/public-accounts-ontario-past-editions.

Ontario Cabinet Committee on Poverty Reduction. 2008. *Breaking the Cycle: Ontario's Poverty Reduction Strategy*. http://www.children.gov.on.ca/htdocs/English/documents/breakingthecycle/Poverty_Report_EN.pdf.

Ontario Ministry of Health. 2011. *Open Minds, Healthy Minds: Ontario's Comprehensive Mental Health and Addictions Strategy*. http://www.health.gov.on.ca/en/common/ministry/publications/reports/mental_health2011/mentalhealth_rep2011.pdf.

Ontario Ministry of Labour. 2016. "Ontario Moving Forward to Close the Gender Wage Gap: Expert Advice to Guide New Strategy." 25 August. https://news.ontario.ca/mol/en/2016/08/ontario-moving-forward-to-close-

the-gender-wage-gap.html?utm_source=ondemand&utm_medium= email&utm_campaign=p.
Ontario Ministry of Municipal Affairs and Housing. 2010. *Building Foundations: Building Futures: Ontario's Long-Term Affordable Housing Strategy*. http://www.mah.gov.on.ca/AssetFactory.aspx?did=8590.
Ontario Ministry of the Status of Women. 2017a. *Discussion Paper: Women's Economic Empowerment – A Call to Action for Ontario*. November. https://www.ontario.ca/page/discussion-paper-womens-economic-empowerment-call-action-ontario.
– 2017b. *In the Spotlight*.
– 2017c. *Publications and Resources*. http://www.women.gov.on.ca/owd/english/about/publications.shtml.
– 2017d. *About Ministry of the Status of Women*. http://www.women.gov.on.ca/owd/english/about/index.shtml.
– 2017e. *Ministry of the Status of Women Timeline*. http://www.women.gov.on.ca/owd/english/about/timeline/milestones.shtml.
Ontario Red Tape Secretariat. Ministry of Government and Consumer Services. 2015. Archives Descriptive Database.
Ontario Women's Directorate (OWD). 1984. *A Plan of Action for the Women of Ontario*. Cabinet Submission to Deputy Premier's Office. 18 April. Archives of Ontario. RG 69–1.
– 1985a. *Policy Issue: Rebuttal against Market Forces*. Archives of Ontario. RG 69-1.
– 1985b. *Questions and Answers: Women's Issues*. 2 April. Archives of Ontario. RG 69-1.
– 1986. *Minister Responsible for Women's Issues Summary of Key Announcements*. July 1985–April 1986. Archives of Ontario. RG 69-1.
– 1989. *Government Initiatives Related to Immigrant and Visible Minority Women*. May. Archives of Ontario. RG 69-1.
– 1990. *OWD Year-End Report, 1989–1990*. OWD.
– 1991. *OWD Year-End Report, 1990–1991*. OWD.
– 1993a. *Focus on Aboriginal Women*. OWD.
– 1993b. *Focus on Racial Minority Women*. OWD.
– 1993c. *Focus on Women with Disabilities*. OWD.
– 1998. *OWD 1998–1999 Business Plan*. Queen's Printer for Ontario, OWD.
– 2001. *Ontario Government Invests in Information Technology (IT) Training for Women*. OWD.
– 2002a. "Pilot Project Provides Information Technology Training for Women." OWD.
– 2002b. *Program Trains Disadvantaged Women for the IT Sector, $300,000 Presented during International Women's Week*. OWD.
– 2003. *Supporting Women's Entrepreneurship*. OWD.
– 2011a. *Recognizing Women*. OWD.
– 2011b. *Resources and Links*. OWD.
– 2012. *News Highlights*. OWD.

OWD and CAMCO. 1992. *Flexible Working Arrangements: A Change Agent Project by the OWD and CAMCO Inc.*

OWD and Union Gas. 1992. *Sharing the Balance: The Union Gas Experience: A Change Agent Project by the OWD and Union Gas.*

OWD and United Food and Commercial Workers Union. 1992. *Balancing Work and Family Responsibilities: A Change Agent Project by the OWD and the United Food and Commercial Workers Union.*

OWD and the Urban Alliance on Race Relations. 1990. *Employment Equity for Visible Minority Women, A Guide for Employers: A Change Agent Project.*

Peters, Guy. 1995. "The Public Service, the Changing State, and Governance." In *Governance in a Changing Environment*, edited by B. Guy Peters and Donald J. Savoie. Montreal and Kingston: McGill-Queen's University Press.

Porter, Catherine. 2015. "Kathleen Wynne's Bold Plan will Change the Lives of Thousands of Women in Ontario: Porter." *Toronto Star*, 6 March.

Rankin, Pauline L. 1996. "Experience, Opportunity and the Politics of Place: A Comparative Analysis of Provincial and Territorial Women's Movements in Canada." PhD diss., Carleton University.

Ready, Casey. 2016. *Shelter in a Storm: Revitalizing Feminism in a Neoliberal Ontario*. Vancouver: University of British Columbia Press.

Sainsbury, Diane. 1999. "Gender, Policy Regimes and Politics." In *Gender and Welfare State Regimes*, edited by Diane Sainsbury. Toronto: Oxford University Press.

Salutin, Rick. 2016. "Slowly but Surely, Kathleen Wynne Reveals Herself to be a Standard Issue Liberal. *Rabble.ca*, 9 December.

Sawer, Marian. 2007. "Australia: the Fall of the Femocrat." In *Changing State Feminism*, edited by Joyce Outshoorn and Johanna Kantola. New York: Palgrave.

Scala, Francesca, and Stephanie Paterson. 2017. "Gendering Public Policy or Rationalizing Gender? Strategic Interventions and GBA+ Practice in Canada." *Canadian Journal of Political Science* 50 (2).

Scott, Katherine. 1999. "The Dilemma of Liberal Citizenship: Women and Social Assistance Reform in the 1990s." In *Feminism, Political Economy and the State: Contested Terrain*, edited by Pat Armstrong and M. Patricia Connelly. Toronto: Canadian Scholars' Press.

Sears, Alan. "Education for a Lean World." In *Restructuring and Resistance: Canadian Public Policy in an Age of Global Capitalism*, edited by Mike Burke, Colin Mooers, and John Shields. Halifax: Fernwood Publishing.

Shields, John, and B. Mitchell Evans. 1998. *Shrinking the State: Globalization and Public Administration 'Reform.'* Halifax: Fernwood Publishing.

Trickey, Jean. 1997. "The Racist Face of 'Common Sense.'" In *Open For Business, Closed to People: Mike Harris' Ontario*, edited by Diana S. Ralph, André Régimbald, and Néréee St-Amand. Halifax: Fernwood Publishing.

Weber, Max. 1994. "Bureaucracy." In *Critical Studies in Organization and Bureaucracy*, 2nd ed., edited by Frank Fischer and Carmen Sirianni. Philadelphia: Temple University Press.

| 8 |

Municipal Neoliberalism and the Ontario State

CARLO FANELLI

This chapter is concerned with the municipal policy of the Ontario provincial state. A key aspect of this chapter is to consider how federal and provincial relations and public policies with respect to municipalities have been restructured over the postwar period. Neoliberal policy prescriptions rose to prominence in the 1980s, slowly displacing the politics of postwar Keynesianism. These market-reinforcing practices reconfigured public spending, social welfare initiatives, and the relationship between the state, capital, and labour. Since the onset of the 2008 recession and subsequent turn to "permanent austerity" (Albo and Fanelli 2014), the local state has come under new pressures to privatize social services and reduce the costs of public administration, often through seeking wage and benefit concessions from unionized municipal workers. The restructuring of Ontario municipalities can be understood as an extension of federal and provincial neoliberal restructuring, although in a variegated and non-linear manner (Fanelli 2016). The response of labour and social justice activists at the local level to such attacks will have important public policy implications for generations to come.

NEOLIBERALISM AND LOCAL STATES

As David Harvey has argued: "From their inception, cities have arisen through geographical and social concentrations of a surplus product. Urbanization has always been, therefore, a class phenomenon, since surpluses are extracted from somewhere and from somebody, while the control over their disbursement typically lies in a few hands" (2009, 315–16). As such, the problems of capitalist urbanization extend beyond public administration and the management of urban-suburban development as these are rooted in the concrete forms of state power and public policies through which market rule is established. In both practice and political ideology, neoliberalism is many sided, including a broad set of macroeconomic policies, a worldview, and an approach to public policy. Emerging in the economic downturn of the 1970s, neoliberal policies focused on wide-ranging transformations in economic policy, democratic structures, and the organization of work, which deepened inequalities of class, race, and gender as equity policies fell to the wayside (Brenner and Theodore 2002). At the core of neoliberalism has been an effort to reconstitute capitalist class power through re-establishing the political conditions conducive to capitalist accumulation. In this regard, the state (at various levels of public administration) has imposed austerity from above or led the charge from below, while at other times creating the conditions for capital to lead an assault against labour and social services that had been in part shielded from commodification (Albo et al. 1993; Panitch and Swartz 2003; McBride 2017).

Proponents of neoliberalism maintained that states ought to be limited to securing the institutional preconditions for a competitive market, and, once established, remolding state practices in order to ensure market rule. Understood this way, states are to be limited to the protection of private property, security, national defense, and the legal enforcement of contracts so as to embed market dependence. As a social paradigm and policy framework, neoliberalism abandons full employment and national economic development, and shifts from collective to individual responsibility (Workman 2009). This includes the limiting of wage increases to below increases in productivity, the systemic use of state power to impose market imperatives and create new spaces for accumulation, inflation-targeting by the central bank, regressive tax reforms, the erosion and dismantlement of social services, and the encouragement of foreign direct investment and trade liberalization (Burke et al. 2000; Braedley and Luxton 2010).

The restructuring of regulatory frameworks and governance arrangements between levels of government have reshaped institutional landscapes and rewoven the interconnections among them (Peck 2013). The subsequent tendency has been to limit the scope for the exercise of national discretion through socio-spatial reconfigurations along market lines. This has entailed the introduction of new state supports and mechanisms that facilitate private accumulation, as well as the retrenchment of social programs provided by the state. Thus restructuring has entailed the simultaneous devolution and upwards transference of regulatory responsibilities to other tiers of government, often without matching fiscal supports or decision-making powers. This fluid process of politico-institutional realignment prevents any one scale of government from using their regulatory authority to erect trade barriers against the goods and services from other political units, thereby entrenching capital mobility and avoiding any centralization or harmonization of market-inhibiting policies (Harmes 2005). This process can be understood as the locking-in of inter-jurisdictional competition, with the aim of commodifying all spheres of social life.

Municipalities have become critical nodal points as territorial-institutional arrangements evolve in locally specific capitalist contexts. New fiscal constraints upon municipalities from national and provincial spending cuts, for example, have intensified competitive pressures and demands for austerity. Even though the fiscal capacity of municipalities to generate revenue is weak, they are often left to provide services formerly provided by other tiers of government, such as social assistance, transit, infrastructure, and environmental protection.

In this regard, local public policy increasingly promotes conditions amenable to capital accumulation, regardless of the social costs. These policies include cost-cutting measures aimed at "administrative efficiencies," reductions to public services, state subsidies to private capital, and attacks on public sector unions (Evans and Fanelli 2018). Local states create new spaces for competition, privatization, and interlocal and regional entrepreneurialism (Leitner and Sheppard 1998). Altogether, then, municipal neoliberalism can be understood as: an uneven process of political and economic restructuring of institutional relationships across the multiple scales of governance; a policy regime promoting local processes of marketization, fiscal austerity, and flexibilization of work relations; and a process of internationalizing the local economy.

REMAKING MUNICIPAL GOVERNANCE IN ONTARIO, 1970-1994

According to Section 92(8) of the Canadian Constitution, the provinces may exclusively make laws governing municipal institutions. Understood this way, municipalities are essentially "creatures" of provincial governments that can create, modify, or eliminate a local government, as well as determine its powers and responsibilities. Ontario has one of the most decentralized municipal structures in Canada (Sancton and Young 2009). In Ontario, municipalities consist of cities, towns, villages, and townships. Above them are regional governance structures composed of regions, counties and districts, and upper-tier municipalities, on whose council sit members of lower-tier units located within its boundaries. Some cities and towns, for example Toronto and Barrie, are single-tier municipalities and exercise the full responsibilities for municipal government that are elsewhere split between tiers. Upper-tier municipalities are headed by a chair or warden, while lower-tier municipalities are headed by a mayor or reeve. As table 8.1 shows, as of 2013 Ontario has 444 municipalities of varying structures.

Despite a variety of governance arrangements, the inability of municipalities to meet their fiscal requirements has been a chronic feature of Canadian urbanism for at least the last three decades, as revenue capacities could not keep up with growing expenditure needs. Provincial and federal governments sought to "solve" their own budgetary impasses by shifting the costs of social and physical infrastructure downward to lower tiers of government (McBride and Shields 1997). Although the federal government has no constitutionally prescribed municipal powers, nearly all of its decisions affect municipalities in one way or another. However, except for some grants, bilateral agreements, and emergency relief, the federal role in municipal affairs over the last three decades has largely revolved around ad hoc agreements (Stoney and Graham 2009). Thus, there is a complete absence in Canada of a national policy for cities or for urban funding of crucial infrastructure, transportation, housing, immigration, and poverty-related issues.

From 1971–79, the federal government's Ministry of State for Urban Affairs (MSUA) attempted to institutionalize federal-municipal relations (Spicer 2011). However, as "cooperative federalism" gave way to "contested federalism" in the 1980s, the federal government scrapped

Table 8.1 | Municipal structure in Ontario as of 2013

Type of tier	Number of municipalities
SINGLE TIERS	
Southern Ontario	29
Northern Ontario	144
Total single tiers	173
LOWER TIERS	
Within a region	43
Within a county	198
Total lower tiers	241
UPPER TIERS	
Region	8
County	22
Total upper tiers	30
TOTAL NUMBER OF MUNICIPALITIES	444

Source: Slack and Bird (2013).

the ministry and abandoned any semblance of sustained urban policy. As neoliberalism gained ideological and political momentum, makeshift local agreements became entrenched as policy practice (Laycock 2002; Carroll and Ratner 2005).

Unlike the federal and provincial scales of administration, municipalities do not have the power to implement a broad range of tax measures such as income, corporate, sales, resource, and import taxes. Municipalities are also limited in their ability to incur debt.[1] As table 8.2 shows, Ontario municipalities overwhelmingly rely on property taxes to raise revenue outside of federal and provincial transfers. From this, as table 8.3 illustrates, they must provide for general government administration, social assistance and health services, social housing, fire and policing, and so forth. In reality these figures underestimate municipalities' overreliance on property-related taxes, since Toronto is also able to draw on revenue streams not available to other cities. As a result of dwindling transfers to municipalities, the 1990s saw renewed calls for greater federal involvement in municipal affairs, in particular related to revenue transfers. This resulted in the establishment of the Canada Infrastructure Works Program in 1993, which provided

Table 8.2 | City of Toronto operating revenue, 2017

Revenue sources	$millions	%
Property tax	4,046	33
Province	2,071	17
Rate programs	1,786	14
Toronto Transit Commission fares	1,246	10
Reserves, transfers from capital, investment income	826	7
User fees and fines	793	6
Land transfer tax	716	6
Other	793	6
Federal	147	1
Total	$12.33 (billion)	100%

Source: Toronto, 2017 City Budget.

Table 8.3 | City of Toronto operating expenditures, 2017

Main expenditure areas	$millions	%
Social programs	2,899	24
Other city services	2,255	18
Transit	1,955	16
Rate programs	1,786	15
Emergency services	1,781	14
Corporate and capital financing	841	7
Governance and internal services	414	3
Transportation	399	3
Total	$12.33 (billion)	100%

Source: Toronto, 2017 City Budget.

$2.5 billion over five years for local services and infrastructure. Unlike the MSUA, though, the federal government's role would be limited to providing one-time fiscal injections rather than long-term, predictable, and stable intergovernmental planning and funding arrangements.

Although Ontario has long been a province dominated by Conservative rule, by the mid-1980s Ontario had been transformed into an urbanized manufacturing and service economy in the south, and a service and extraction-based economy centered on the mineral and forest sectors in the north (MacDermid and Albo 2001). While real growth in Ontario exceeded 4 per cent per year from 1984–89 (the largest and most sustained since the 1960s), federal cuts to shared-cost arrangements made themselves felt on Ontario's fiscal position. By the late 1980s the David Peterson-led Liberals were making the case that federal downloading had resulted in over $1 billion in lost revenue (Government of Ontario Ministry of Treasury and Economics 1988). In an attempt to partially offset eroding revenues, the Liberals raised a broad range of consumption taxes on gasoline, tobacco, alcohol, and general retail sales. However, as the federal government reduced corporate and personal income taxes in the late 1980s as it began to "individualize" the welfare state, the Ontario Liberals followed suit by lowering capital taxes and reducing from ten to three the number of personal income tax brackets. This set in motion what was to become a staple of neoliberal policymaking: the erosion of public revenue through tax cuts and the downloading of service delivery to lower levels of government with even more limited fiscal capacities.

After a surprise election victory in September 1990, the Bob Rae-led NDP government continued along the course of minor increases to income security programs set by the Peterson Liberals in its first budget. This included a 7 per cent increase to basic social assistance rates and 10 per cent to shelter rates, including the uploading of single parents from municipalities and raising lone parents to the same income standard (Stapleton 2008). The NDP retreated, however, from the more ambitious increases in corporate and wealth taxes, as well as from public auto insurance, succumbing to the neoliberal orthodoxy of balanced budgets (Azoulay 2000; Walkom 1994). The evolving policy approach of the NDP, as it began to pursue governance within the constraints of neoliberalism, also meant taking distance from the report, produced under the chair of former Toronto mayor John Sewell, on the reform of the municipal planning and development system in Ontario. The Sewell Report suggested planning legislation that would place checks on urban sprawl and, at same time, densify urban development. The plan was met with a torrent of backlash from the development industry citing excessive environmental and land use regulation. The retreat from the Sewell Report ended any further attempts by the NDP at reforming provincial-municipal relations, leaving in place the ad hoc negotiations and regulations that had defined Ontario planning under the Conservatives (Desfor and Keil 2004; Walker 1994). The Fair Tax Commission suffered a similar fate. It recommended moving away from property taxes, and instead, increasing and making more progressive the provincial personal income tax.[2] All talk of municipal tax reform ended with the election of the Mike Harris Conservatives in 1995 and the hard-right pursuit of neoliberal policies began in earnest.

PUBLIC SERVICES AND MUNICIPAL TRANSFERS, 1995-2005

The 1995 federal budget terminated the Canada Assistance Plan and Established Programs Financing, replacing them with the Canada Health and Social Transfer (CHST) (McBride and Shields 1997). The CHST represented a significant reduction to provincial transfers in the realm of social assistance, post-secondary education, and health care funding. The new block funding removed the previous 50/50 cost-sharing arrangement and replaced it with a combination of cash and tax points transfers that were frozen at 1995 levels for the next five years, significantly eroding the real levels of provision due to inflation and population growth. This unilateral devolution of social welfare responsibility not only cut federal funding, it also led to an erosion of national enforcement standards and a reduction in the quality and scope of public services.

Alongside the cuts to transfers, the federal Liberals launched a series of uncoordinated programs targeted at urban issues. One was the 1998 Urban Aboriginal Strategy, which over three years provided $25 million to cities in order to build organizational capacities within urban Aboriginal communities and develop partnerships with provincial and municipal governments. The fund also sought to coordinate federal government resources with provincial and municipal departments in order to address the disparity between urban Aboriginal and non-Aboriginal groups (AANDC 2005). A year later, the federal government launched the National Homelessness Initiative as a way of channeling funds to municipalities in order to deal with poverty across the provinces and territories. In 2000, the federal Liberals put forward the Infrastructure Canada Program that, over the next decade, distributed $2 billion for local infrastructure projects, as well as the Green Municipal Fund that was to be managed by the Federation of

Canadian Municipalities and provided $125 million for local environmental initiatives. In 2001, the Green Municipal Fund was doubled and an additional $680 million was allocated to cities under the Affordable Housing Program. Another $2 billion was directed to municipalities in the form of the Canadian Strategic Infrastructure Fund, along with $600 million for the Border Infrastructure Fund.

A year later, the federal government combined various infrastructure and grant programs under Infrastructure Canada and included a notional effort to fund a New Deal for Cities and Communities (Bradford 2007). The intention was to address both municipal fiscal pressures, particularly those related to infrastructure, and public policy concerns. The 2004 and 2005 budgets included a full goods and services tax rebate worth some $7 billion over ten years, an allocation on a per capita basis of 5 cents per litre of the federal gas tax worth approximately $9 billion over five years, and $800 million for public transit distributed on the basis of transit ridership (in part to meet the needs of the large cities). In addition to new municipal revenue transfers, new intergovernmental consultative bodies were created that brought together urban development experts and community groups. Despite an influx of new federal funding and involvement, these measures were not enough to offset some three decades of combined neglect and downloading from federal and provincial governments (FCM 2012).

Parallel to the CHST cuts, the newly elected Conservative government of Mike Harris decisively turned to "slash and burn" neoliberalism with the release of its *Ontario Fiscal Overview and Spending Cuts* and *Fiscal and Economic Statement* (Reshef and Rastin 2003; Kozolanka 2007). Among the first pieces of legislation rescinded by the Harris government was the Planning Reform Act, which sought to curb urban sprawl by linking municipal requirements to provincial planning applications, zoning bylaws, and planning related documents. The catalogue of other measures undertaken by the Harris government negatively impacting the fiscal capacity and service provision of municipalities is lengthy. This includes a moratorium on the development of non-profit housing and cooperatives; suspension of $234 million worth of spending on public transportation, road, and highway maintenance; elimination of recycling funds and environmental grants to municipalities totalling $24 million; $290 million in funding cuts to the Ontario

Municipal Support Program; over $12 million in cuts to public libraries; cancellation of the conversion of private sector child care spaces into non-profit spaces; and a reduction in transfers to school boards by $400 million (Government of Ontario 1995a, 1995b). In the 1999 Speech from the Throne, the Conservatives boasted of making over ninety-nine different forms of tax cuts (Government of Ontario 1999), cuts that significantly eroded provincial revenues and increased the fiscal burden on municipalities.

The Conservatives also instituted a series of controversial municipal amalgamations. When Harris came into office there were 815 municipalities in Ontario. But the Fewer Municipal Politicians Act (1996) reduced that number to 447 by 2001, cutting the number of municipal councillors from 4,586 to 2,804 and school board trustees from 1,900 to 700 (Sancton 2000; Boudreau, Keil and Young 2009). The largest and most extensive amalgamation occurred under the provisions of the City of Toronto Act (1997), where six cities and seven governments were merged to create the single-tier City of Toronto (Boudreau 2000). This restructuring of Ontario municipalities involved a massive devolution of program spending and responsibilities onto municipalities: social services, public school services, non-profit housing, roads, public infrastructure, long-term health care, child care, shelters, children's aid societies, ambulance, fire, and police services, waste collection, and public health and transportation – all became increasingly or wholly reliant on the municipal tax base. Following the federal government strategy, the downloading of responsibilities by the Harris government onto municipalities occurred without an equivalent transfer of funding or new fiscal powers. Amalgamation was overwhelmingly rejected by urban social movements, trade unionists, and the general public across Ontario municipalities (Sancton 1996; Kushner and Siegal 2003). But this did little to deter the Conservatives from amalgamating communities. The Conservatives argued that amalgamation was in the interest of all Ontarians as it would lower costs, remove barriers to investment, enable private sector job creation, and increase the political coherence and economic efficiency of municipalities.

Invoking a report by the accounting firm KPMG (1996), the Conservatives contended that through amalgamation Toronto could realize upwards of $865 million in savings over the first three years. But this was later contradicted by a report from Deloitte and Touche (1997) that criticized KPMG's flawed report and showed that savings would be next to nothing. One year into amalgamation, the city found itself short of $164 million in tax revenues as a result of downloading, making a mockery of Harris's projected cost-savings and his freeze on commercial property taxes. In turn, Toronto Mayor Mel Lastman's promise to freeze residential property taxes for a decade was shredded.

The municipalities of Ottawa, Hamilton, Sudbury, Kingston, and Chatham-Kent, respectively, were also amalgamated as part of the Municipal Act, 2001, which consolidated dozens of municipal statutes and entrenched neoliberal administrative reforms. In what was to become a recurring saga, rather than address the structural deficit of Ontario municipalities and especially larger cities, the provincial government proceeded to provide one-time fiscal injections and short-term loans. As a result of the structural shortfall due to downloading and tax cuts, Ontario municipalities responded by seeking wage and benefit concessions from workers, contracting-out, privatization, and raising user fees. By the end of the Conservatives' second term, more than $650 million had been cut from municipal transfers.

The movement away from shared-cost provincial-municipal funding shifted the burden of revenues coming from the progressive general income and corporate taxes applied at the provincial level to the narrower base of municipal property taxes. Amalgamation of cities did little to reduce the costs of public administration; rather, it led to wide-ranging cuts to public services, diminished service levels, labour strife, and recurring budgetary shortfalls (Sancton 2000; Boudreau 2009; Albo and Fanelli 2018). The Conservative tenure at Queen's Park from 1995 to 2003 radically extended neoliberal policies. For municipalities, territorial boundaries were remade and responsibilities for delivering services increased despite the absence of an equivalent transfer of administrative powers to raise revenues.

CONSOLIDATING MUNICIPAL NEOLIBERALISM

After thirteen years of Liberal government in Ottawa, the Conservatives formed a minority government in 2006. The Harper-led Conservatives shifted the urban policy landscape away from some of the programs initiated by the Martin Liberals supporting municipalities. Instead, the Conservatives' circumscribed role for urban policy focused on piecemeal injections of funds into urban policy issues. The two most important initiatives were the Building Canada Infrastructure Plan and the Gas Tax Fund (GTF). The former provided $40 billion for municipal infrastructure over 2007–14, but covered less than 2 per cent of outstanding national needs (Warren 2013). The GTF provided Canadian municipalities with $2 billion annually, and since 2013 has been indexed to inflation.

Additionally, the 2009 federal budget provided some $12 billion in new infrastructure spending. But many municipal projects missed a federal government-mandated completion deadline in 2012, with Infrastructure Canada remaining "tight-lipped on the amount of money municipalities left on the table" (Tapper 2012). The Conservatives also provided an additional $1.25 billion in funding to support provincial, territorial, and municipal budgets, but made this funding contingent on public-private partnerships. Between 1989 and 2009, federal expenditures per capita in constant dollars fell at an average annual rate of 0.3 per cent as the retrenchment of local support continued. By 2014, general federal transfers to municipalities represented only 1.6 per cent of total municipal revenues. Over the course of nearly a decade in power, the federal Conservatives had cut some $220 billion in revenue generation in the form of corporate and income taxes as well as the reduction of the goods and services tax from 7 to 6 and later 5 per cent (Whittington 2011). The revenue foregone might have been used to repair the decimated state of municipal financing in Canada, or restoring any number of social programs.

Rather than depart from this market-led revamping of the public sector, the Dalton McGuinty Liberals further consolidated the neoliberal policy regime, with a few modest, and indeed unavoidable, amendments in the area of urban policy (Fanelli and Thomas 2011). The Liberal government, for example, extended some revenue-generating capacities to the city of Toronto with the passing of the City of Toronto Act (2006), and later, to a lesser extent, to other municipalities with the passing of the Municipal Statute Law Amendment Act (2006). The acts granted new powers to municipalities to enter into agreements with other governments, pass bylaws and levy some taxes. New powers assigned to municipalities also granted more control over the demolition of rental properties, green energy requirements, city-building standards such as height and density requirements, and faster approval of community improvement plans and brownfield remediation. While the acts expanded some powers, they stopped short of extending additional recognition of operational autonomy and capacities to municipalities in the absence of provincial oversight (for example, taxing powers related to income, wealth, or general sales). The City of Toronto's Municipal Land Transfer Tax and (now defunct) Personal Vehicle Ownership Tax served as exceptions, as a result of specific powers conferred onto the city by the province in the 2006 act allowing for more, if minor, flexible forms of revenue generation (Fanelli 2016).

In 2006, the Liberals launched the Provincial-Municipal Fiscal and Service Delivery Review (Government of Ontario Ministry of Finance 2008). Reporting in 2008, the review proposed that the province take over some (but not all) of the services and responsibilities downloaded onto municipalities during the Harris era. Beginning in 2010 and staggered over the next eight years, the province agreed to upload some of the costs associated with provincial court services, prisoner transport, public transit, and portions of the Ontario Disability Support Plan, Ontario Drug Benefit Plan, and Ontario Works. While the new arrangement provided some much-needed uploading of administrative costs and revenue transfers, it did little to address crumbling social services and housing, urban incapacities to address climate change, inadequate funding for public transit, housing, and restoring infrastructure support to pre-Harris era levels.

Between 1981 and 2017 Ontario's population grew from 8.3 million to about 14.5 million. Nearly 70 per cent live in the Greater Toronto Area, Canada's largest continuous urban area. The GTA is also the fastest growing region in Ontario, with major employment in manufacturing, financial services, agriculture, and food processing (Ali, 2008; Macdonald and Keil 2012; Donald 2005). It is worth noting that Ontario has more than one-half of the first-class agricultural land in Canada, and produces one-quarter of the country's total farm revenues. Because 90 per cent of Canadians live in a narrow band along the US border, the erosion of prime agricultural land as a result of urban sprawl, particularly in Ontario, is a significant public policy concern.[3] Lacking alternative means by which to raise revenue, many municipalities have come to rely on unchecked urban growth as a way to expand their property tax base and increase revenues.

Sara Macdonald and Roger Keil (2012) note that for decades the region has been locked into a low-density, automobile-dependent suburban growth dynamic. As a result of the uneven dispersal of population and employment between 1986 and 2001, the province saw a 53 per cent increase in the supply of new roads and a 38 per cent growth in new highways. But, at the same time, transit ridership declined over the last two decades in all regions across the GTA except for Peel (Pond 2009). Ontario residents are among the most automobile dependent in the country. In 2006, 71 per cent of workers in the Toronto census metropolitan area got to work by car, while only 22 per cent used public transit. Likewise, more than 80 per cent of all workers across other census metropolitan areas covered under the Places to Grow legislation drove to work, and less than 10 per cent took public transit. It has been estimated that congestion costs the GTA area more than $6 billion annually as automobile-dependent urban sprawl increases air pollution, congestion along trade corridors, and greenhouse gases, resulting in Ontario having the highest ground-level ozone concentrations in the country (Ali 2008; Metrolinx 2008). Expensive low-density infrastructure puts upward pressure on tax rates, raising residential and commercial costs and impeding the flow of goods and services. If left unchecked, urban sprawl over the next thirty years could absorb more than 1,000 square kilometres of land to meet projected population influxes of more than 3 million. As a result of Ontario municipalities' administrative incapacity and unwillingness to check urban sprawl – including concerns about congestion and environmental degradation – the Ontario government launched the Greenbelt Act in 2005.

The Greenbelt legislation covers 7,300 square kilometres of southern Ontario, stretching around the Toronto region from Rice Lake in Northumberland County in the east to the Niagara River in the southwest. The Greenbelt plan prohibits development outside existing municipal boundaries in designated areas close to environmentally sensitive lands, and mandates higher residential and employment densities, mixed-use communities, and infill development (Ali 2008). Under the Greenbelt plan, and its companion Places to Grow (2005) legislation, decisions about farmland and urban development have been removed from hundreds of municipal councils around the region and placed into the hands of Queen's Park (Pond 2009). The Places to Grow legislation identifies sixteen major growth areas in mid-sized cities in southern Ontario based on their capacity to accommodate population and employment growth and to provide vital linkages to transit systems in urban growth centres. The growth plan states that a minimum of 40 per cent of all annual residential development must be built within urban areas and not on greenfield sites (Government of Ontario 2012).

The Greenbelt legislation establishes planning and land-use restrictions, whereas the Places to Grow legislation sets a density target of fifty or more residents and jobs combined per hectare. The legislation requires that municipalities identify areas for density expansion in official municipal plans. The purpose of the Greenbelt legislation is to contain urban growth, preserve farmland and agrarian economies, and create compact development. The acts also aim to prevent land speculation and reduce growth pressures along sensitive ecological and hydrological lands which include the Niagara Escarpment and the Oak Ridges Moraine. Thus the Greenbelt plan is about where growth is prohibited, while Places to Grow sets out where and how this growth should happen.[4] In easing congestion, increasing the use of public transportation, and raising density requirements for residential and commercial developers, the acts also endeavour to increase the economic development of the region as a whole.

Some sectors of the development industry have predictably argued that anti-sprawl legislation is an illegitimate intervention by the provincial government into municipal affairs and that it interferes with market-based residential and commercial outcomes by placing unnecessary restraints on development (Macdonald and Keil 2012). But environmental and community groups have argued that the legislation does not go far enough and that prescribed urban densities should be even higher. They make the case that even with the Greenbelt plan, some 425 square kilometres of rural agricultural land in the Greater Toronto and Hamilton area will be lost by 2031 (SUDA 2011). Moreover, communities located outside of the Greenbelt are not subject to planning coordination and restrictions. This leaves a wide-open game for developers, with the province doing little to control competition over business incentives and inter-local erosion of tax bases from the surrounding regions. In 2017, the province announced plans to completely overhaul the Ontario Municipal Board (OMB), significantly limiting its power over land-use planning for the first time in more than a century. This is, in part, a response to a growing body of research suggesting that land speculation and development has leapfrogged the Greenbelt to the north, while prices south of the belt have risen as much of the land is owned by a small number of developers keen to take advantage of land supply constraints and rulings by the OMB that have tended to favour developers over city planners, local council decisions, and community opposition (Sanberg, Wekerele, and Gilbert 2013). In April 2017, the Local Planning Appeals Tribunal took over the responsibilities of the OMB, making good on a decade-old promise to cities to let them plan their own futures, in addition to helping citizens who have said they are "woefully unprepared" to participate on equal ground against developer interests (Pagliaro 2018).

THE GREAT RECESSION AND BEYOND

In the aftermath of the 2008 recession, the Ontario Liberal government called for a decade of austerity. The major policy planks, in the form of the Open Ontario Plan and the Open for Business Act (2010), called for tax relief, a wage freeze for public sector workers, the privatization of public assets, trade investment, capital liberalization, and regressive reforms to employment standards legislation. These initiatives placed new pressures on municipalities to extract concessions from workers and reduce social services. Between 2010 and 2017, the Liberals attempted to limit annual expenditures to nominal growth of 2 per cent per annum, which, given inflation and population increases, continues restraint through a decline in real per capita program spending by the government (the hallmark of how Liberal governments in Ontario have delivered austerity). Consecutive budgets deferred more than $2 billion in infrastructure spending while cutting corporate and personal income taxes by more than $4.6 billion as well as an additional $1.6 billion through the elimination of the Ontario Capital Tax. The measures were on top of a host of other tax cuts, corporate subsidies, and general erosion of revenue capacities (Evans and Fanelli 2018).

The ongoing tax cuts by federal and provincial governments are a core reason for the dilapidated state of much of the social and physical infrastructure of Ontario municipalities.[5] Whereas municipalities were responsible for some 36 per cent of infrastructure in 1961, this rose to nearly 60 per cent by 2017. The Association of Municipalities of Ontario (AMO) has estimated that Ontario's infrastructure deficit sits close to $60 billion: $28 billion for roads and bridges, $12.6 billion for water and wastewater, $10.7 billion for transit, $6.8 billion for stormwater, and $1 billion for solid waste (AMO 2012, 2015). In order to partly address this shortfall, in 2015 the Liberal government of Kathleen Wynne proceeded with the controversial decision to privatize a majority stake of Hydro One. As of December 2017, the province had raised an estimated $9.2 billion by selling off 53 per cent of its stake in the company, with the Liberals planning to use $5 billion to pay down leftover debt and put the remaining $4 billion toward funding transit and infrastructure projects. But this does little to address the significant infrastructure deficit currently confronting municipalities across Ontario. In fact, a 2018 report by the Financial Accountability Office of Ontario noted that financing infrastructure projects through traditional debt would have saved the government $1.8 billion had it not privatized part of Hydro One to raise the money (FAO 2018).

Rapid and uncontrolled GTA development has also increased infrastructure costs, and these expenditures are increasingly financed by municipal debt to cover the capital costs. For example, in York Region, Ontario's fastest-growing municipality, per capita debt has grown from $319 in 2000 to $1,192 by 2017 (York Region 2017, 6). Yet, much-needed maintenance and repair in urban areas is often being deferred in favour of expansion to exurban communities on the fringes (CMCC 1999; RCCAO 2010).[6] The infrastructure deficit excludes parks and recreation, cultural centres, libraries, and heritage facilities, all of which face added pressures for commercialization and privatization amidst declining municipal revenues. In addition, social housing has an estimated replacement cost of $40 billion, while an additional $50 billion is needed to expand public transit in the Greater Toronto and Hamilton Area over the next twenty-five years (AMO 2012; Metrolinx 2008).

Other levels of government have partly recognized the urban fiscal impasse but have done very little to address it in a fundamental way. Pressures for Ontario municipalities to find cost savings and new revenue sources have been growing. This has resulted in the implementation of a broad range of consumption-based taxes and user fees, as well as increases in property taxes just to keep up with existing service shortfalls. There has also been a shift away from commercial property taxes, and below-market value development charges, including shared provincial and municipal grants and financial assistance for large corporations to attract private capital (Moussaoui 2013a, 2013b; Skaburskis and Tomalty 1997; Sheppard 2008; Moore 2013). The privatization and contracting-out of municipal assets, services, and employment has been put forward as a means to restore budgets. But the evidence from outsourcing and privatization across Canadian municipalities suggests that the privatization of formerly public sector jobs – and the experiences of private sector building projects on urban transport and infrastructure projects – has correlated with more expensive and lower quality services and reduced public oversight (Whiteside 2017). There are now any number of cases – the most notable being the Walkerton water crisis – to suggest that the outsourcing and consequent deregulation of public services jeopardizes the health and safety of communities as cost-cutting and profit maximization are prioritized (Loxley 2010; Vining and Boardman 2008; Sanger 2011).

In any case, one-time fiscal injections from privatizations do not solve the underlying fiscal constraints of Ontario municipalities – receiving only 9 cents of every tax dollar collected in the province is clearly inadequate to the services and infrastructure provided. The inability of Ontario municipalities to meet revenue needs stems, in part, from governance constraints imposed from above. But the precedence in neoliberal policies given to tax cutting has also directly eroded fiscal capacities. As a consequence, all governments in Canada currently lack the fiscal capacity (and political willingness) to address the municipal infrastructure crisis.

The Doug Ford-led majority Conservative provincial government elected in June 2018 will likely continue to erode public revenue through tax cuts, with particularly damaging consequences for municipalities. Ford campaigned on a pledge to reduce provincial gas tax revenues from 14.7 cents per litre to 9.7 cents per litre (a 34 per cent cut in that revenue source), a loss of approximately $1 billion in annual provincial revenue. Since the bulk of revenues raised via the gas tax are allocated to transit and infrastructure spending, it is unclear how the province will make up for this, as the promise to find $6 billion in "efficiencies" in the public sector without cuts is difficult to envision. Moreover, the Ford platform also calls for reductions to income taxes and carbon taxes. In his 2016 book, *Ford Nation: Two Brothers, One Vision,* Ford noted: "If I ever get to the provincial level of politics, municipal affairs is the first thing I would want to change. I think mayors across the province deserve stronger powers. One person in charge, with veto power, similar to the strong mayoral systems in New York and Chicago and L.A." (quoted in Rider 2018). Such measures would concentrate decision-making in the hands of the mayor, and limit the role of municipal residents and councillors.

TOWARD A PROGRESSIVE MUNICIPAL AGENDA IN ONTARIO

Breaking the cycle of austerity and retrenchment of municipal neoliberalism in Ontario will require alternative funding arrangements. These will necessarily be premised on an alternative political vision that challenges the continued reliance on tax cuts to spur private sector-led economic growth. A first initiative might be to simply raise revenues in light of decades of federal and provincial off-loading of services and responsibilities. Orthodox policy options have focused on increasing the scope of market imperatives through a continued ideological and political assault on public services and public sector workers (CFIB 2013; University of Toronto Mowat Centre-KPMG 2009). Business and development groups continue to press these solutions on municipal councils through lobbying, local business associations, and bankrolling local campaigns for office.

The current overreliance of Ontario municipalities on property taxes is unsustainable. It has been shifting the burden of responsibility for infrastructure from capital to labour, and from one generation to the next. While municipal development charges are an important revenue source, they tend to be cyclical and rely on the unstable fluctuations of real estate markets. It is necessary, therefore, to establish dedicated funding for municipalities by other levels of government. This could come, to note the most obvious examples, from the reversal of corporate and personal income tax cuts, particularly for "one-percenters," made since the onset of the 2008 recession, and the return of the GST to 6 or 7 per cent with the increase dedicated to funding municipalities. These changes could provide consistent and secure funding that could begin to redress decades of underinvestment and neglect across Canadian municipalities. Making wealthy individuals and corporations that benefitted the most from neoliberal tax reforms pay higher taxes is important in itself. But broader anti-tax sentiments must also be challenged so that more goods and services come through public and not private consumption.

A progressive municipal agenda also needs to consider a broader range of options for mobilizing revenues, especially if user fees are to be cut and eliminated for many services. The heavy reliance on property taxes as the major source of revenue is rare. Ontario municipalities receive over 60 per cent of their own-source revenues from property-related taxation, whereas the OECD average is 36 per cent. The Nordic countries, Germany and Switzerland, for example, receive over 90 per cent of their tax revenue from income taxes, while Hungary and the Netherlands collect between 50 and 75 per cent of local revenue from various sales taxes. The same is true in France, Japan, Korea, and the US, where sales taxes compose about 20 per cent of local revenue. As the Federation of Canadian Municipalities has argued, there is no natural law dictating that local governments be exclusively dependent on the property tax; a multiplicity of revenue streams is needed to ensure diverse, predictable and long-term funding for municipalities (FCM 2012, 15).

Extensive research has demonstrated the social and economic benefits of expanding the tax base and reinvesting in public services at the local level. Such initiatives may include an employer payroll tax, high-occupancy lanes and highway tolls, land-value capture, parking space levies, municipal sales taxes, downtown congestion fees, corporate and income taxes, hotel levies, and an increase in development charges (AECOM-KPMG 2013; TRBOT 2013; Hjartarson, Hinton, and Szala 2011). The establishment of new taxation and administrative powers could be accomplished by provincial legislation and dedicated revenue streams. However, if municipalities are left to act on their own, without extra-market and extra-local planning capacities, intensified interlocal competition may result in a vicious circle of subsidies and beggar-thy-neighbour tax policies. And conferring new powers on municipal councils still requires new urban planning orientations with other levels of government.

Since federal and provincial governments possess the major powers of taxation, they have a responsibility to ensure that the needs of municipalities can be met by appropriate fiscal capacities. But municipalities cannot resolve issues related to climate change, public transportation, housing, wastewater, and so forth at the local level alone. These challenges require developing new coordinated state planning capacities with, at a minimum, dedicated funding to launch a national transit strategy, a national clean water fund, community development strategies in self-governing Northern and Indigenous communities, and long-term municipal funding for social and physical infrastructure.

New organizational capacities will be needed to make such ideas politically viable. Such initiatives would need to emphasize the social value of extending public services and shift the debate from meeting individual consumer needs to creating livable cities with decent employment, public spaces, universal services, and ecologically sustainable development (Leitner, Peck, and Sheppard 2007; Merrifield 2010; Beaumart and Dart 2010; Harvey 2012). Making the case for an expanded public sector fundamentally opposes the prevailing orthodoxy of neoliberalism – one that challenges private capital accumulation as the engine of economic growth – and raises a set of demands for non-commodified labour and services. This means not only expanding the redistributive role of the state but actually taking the lead in challenging market rule. Reducing public spending (and thus public sector employment) increases unemployment, weakens consumption, and exacerbates income inequality. One of the few silver linings of the 2008 recession has been that governments can borrow money at historically low interest rates, making large-scale public reinvestments more feasible than ever.

In the absence of organized civic political parties (they are effectively banned in Ontario by the Municipal Elections Act), trade union and community activists must fill that void. The anti-poverty movement has been the most vocal opponent of municipal service level and staff cuts. Moreover, in the face of continued gentrification (partly driven by the property tax that is tied to market value) and falling housing affordability, many working poor continue to fall deeper into debt amidst increasing social insecurity.

The political coalitions that have been thrown up across Ontario municipalities to fight the cuts over the last two decades have not been effective enough to reverse these processes. A number of notable labour-community coalitions have sprung across Ontario municipalities, including campaigns for public services, housing, living wages, fights against privatization, and demands for "good jobs for all." There are also important initiatives taking place around homelessness, poverty, anti-racist policing, Indigenous rights, and environmental movements that have opened up new spaces that challenge neoliberal diktats. These movements, campaigns, and coalitions now face new challenges in the Ford administration in Ontario, with its hard right policy platform. Activists will have to struggle with new forms of cooperation between movements, and forge shared interests and solidaristic political capacities. An alternative politics, even radical urban praxis, may yet emerge to address the social divisions of an increasingly divided province.

NOTES

1 For example, an Ontario municipality may issue long-term debt only if used for capital purposes. It cannot borrow for operations, except by issuing promissory notes that require repayment when the current tax levy is received. Other levels of government are able to refinance their debt when it matures and engage in long-term deficit management with respect to fiscal capacity. For municipalities, the principal must be amortized over the term of the debenture or bond and repaid to investors or contributions made to a sinking fund that will provide for repayment when the debt matures.

2 An exception was the NDP with Rae's "fair shares federalism" campaign, which protested the "cap on the CAP" amidst dwindling transfer funds to Ontario. However, this was far from a real critique of the *causes* of the declining revenue transfers (and the neoliberal policies that sustained them). Rather, it was a general complaint about its *consequences* – that is, declining transfers. The neoliberal paradigm remained unchallenged.

3 Only 5 per cent of the Canadian land surface is of dependable agricultural use and less than 1 per cent is Class One land. More than 52 per cent of Canada's best farmland (Class One) is in Ontario, most of it in southern Ontario where population growth is highest. Ontario's Class One through Three agricultural

land represents about 6.8 per cent of total land in the province and 16 per cent of Canada's total agricultural land. By 1996, more than 18 per cent of Ontario's Class One farmland was being used for urban purposes and effectively lost to agriculture (Government of Ontario 2009).

4   This may, on the one hand, prevent pro-growth interests from dominating local councils given the broader scrutiny and administrative protocols of the provincial government. On the other, it may simply shift the focus of business lobbying to the provincial level, and intensify the worst effects of sprawl. Some Greenbelt policies have to an extent succeeded in containing urban sprawl, preserving rural farmlands, and increasing density, while others have led to sharp increases in the value of urban lands, such as residential and commercial real estate, in addition to pushing development to areas outside of the Greenbelt where land is cheaper and building restrictions are often fewer (Ali 2008).

5   It is estimated that 82 per cent of municipal infrastructure across Canada is exhausted. For example, more than half of all municipal roads are displaying advanced deterioration, 40 per cent of pumping stations and storage tanks are in decline (with new federal water regulations expected to add some $25 billion over 20 years), and more than 30 per cent of underground pipelines are in need of replacement. Canadian municipalities now face an infrastructure deficit in the range of $125 billion, with combined provincial and federal infrastructural deficits more than double that amount (FCM 2012; AMO 2012).

6   The Residential and Civil Construction Alliance of Ontario (2010, 6–7) has argued:

> Over the next 50 years there is the risk of public infrastructure underinvestment that could cost the Canadian economy 1.1 per cent of real gross domestic product (GDP) growth ... It will cost the average Canadian worker between $9,000 and $51,000, with the younger generation disproportionately at risk, and decrease the after-tax profitability of Canadian businesses by a long term average of 20 per cent ... Results show that for every extra dollar paid in taxation revenue, the taxpayer is better off by $1.48 on average, in after-tax wage terms. That means mitigating the underinvestment risk is cost effective.

REFERENCES

Aboriginal Affairs and Northern Development Canada. 2005. *Urban Aboriginal Strategy Pilot Projects Formative Evaluation: Final Report*. Ottawa: Queen's Printer.

AECOM-KPMG. 2013. *Big Move Implementation Economics: Revenue Tool Profiles*. Markham: AECOM.

Albo, G. 1994. "Competitive Austerity and the Impasse of Capitalist Employment Policy." In *Socialist Register 1994*, edited by R. Miliband and L. Panitch. London: Merlin Press.

Albo, G., D. Langille, and L. Panitch, eds. 1993. *A Different Kind of State? Popular Power and Democratic Administration*. Toronto: Oxford University Press.

Ali, A.K. 2008. "Greenbelts to Contain Urban Growth in Ontario, Canada: Promises and Prospects." *Planning, Practice and Research* 23 (4).

Association of Municipalities of Ontario. 2012a. *Towards a New Federal Long-Term Infrastructure Plan: AMO's Submission to Infrastructure Canada*. Toronto: AMO.

– 2012b. *Annual Expenditure Report (Part I)*. Toronto: AMO.

Azoulay, D. 2000. "The CCF and Post-Second World War Politics in Ontario." In *Ontario Since Confederation: A Reader*, edited by E.A. Montigny and L. Chambers. Toronto: University of Toronto Press.

Beaumont, M. and G. Dart, eds. 2010. *Restless Cities*. London: Verso.

Boudreau, J.A. 2000. *The Megacity Saga*. Montreal: Black Rose Books.

Boudreau, J.A., R. Keil, and D. Young. 2009. *Changing Toronto: Governing Urban Neoliberalism*. Toronto: University of Toronto Press.

Bradford, N. 2007. "Placing Social Policy? Reflection's on Canada's New Deal for Cities and Communities." *Canadian Journal of Urban Research* 16 (2).

Braedley, S., and M. Luxton, eds. 2010. *Neoliberalism and Everyday Life*. Montreal: McGill-Queen's University Press.

Brenner, N., and N. Theodore, eds. 2002. *Spaces of Neoliberalism: Urban Restructuring in North America and Western Europe*. Oxford: Blackwell.

Broadbent, E. 2008. *Urban Nation: Why We Need to Give Power Back to Cities to Make Canada Strong*. Toronto: HarperCollins.

Burke, M., C. Mooers, and J. Shields, eds. 2000. *Restructuring and Resistance: Canadian Public Policy in an Age of Global Capitalism*. Halifax: Fernwood.

Canada Mortgage Housing Corporation. 1999. *Alternative Methods of Financing Municipal Infrastructure*. Ottawa: CMHC.

Carroll, W., and R.S. Ratner, eds. 2005. *Challenges and Perils: Social Democracy in Neoliberal Times*. Halifax: Fernwood.

City of Toronto. 2017. *Budget Summary*. https://www.toronto.ca/ext/digital_comm/pdfs/finance/budget-sumary-2017.pdf.

Deloitte and Touche. 1997. *Critique of KPMG Report Fresh Start: An Estimate of Potential Savings and Costs from the Creation of a Single Tier Local Government for Toronto*. Toronto: Deloitte and Touche.

Desfor, G., and R. Keil. 2004. *Nature and the City: Making Environmental Policy in Toronto and Los Angeles*. Tucson: University of Arizona Press.

Donald, B. 2005. "The Politics of Local Economic Development in Canada's City-Regions: New Dependencies, New Deals, and a New Politics of Scale." *Space and Polity* 9 (3).

Duffy, A., D. Glenday, and N. Pupo, eds. 1997. *Good Jobs, Bad Jobs, No Jobs: The Transformation of Work in the 21st Century*. Toronto: Harcourt.

Evans, B., and G. Albo. 2010. "Permanent Austerity: The Politics of the Canadian Exit Strategy from Fiscal Stimulus." *Alternate Routes: A Journal of Critical Social Research* 22.

Evans, B., and C. Fanelli. 2018. "Ontario in an Age of Austerity: Common Sense Reloaded." In *The Public Sector in an Age of Austerity: Perspectives from Canada's Provinces and Territories*, edited by B. Evans and C. Fanelli. Montreal: McGill-Queen's University Press.

Fanelli, C. 2013. "Fragile Future: The Attack against Public Services and Public Sector Unions in an Era of Austerity." PhD diss., Carleton University.

Fanelli, C., and M.P. Thomas. 2011. "Neoliberalism Redux: Ontario Responds to the Great Recession." *Socialist Studies* 7 (1/2).

Federation of Canadian Municipalities. 2003. *Alternative Funding Mechanisms: A Best Practice by the National Guide to Sustainable Municipal Infrastructure*. Toronto: FCM.

– 2012. *The State of Canada's Cities and Communities*. Ottawa: FCM.

Financial Accountability Office of Ontario. 2018. *Hydro One: Updated Financial Analysis of the Partial Sale of Hydro One*. Toronto: Queen's Printer for Ontario.

Found, A. 2012. "Scale Economies in Fire and Police Services." *IMFG Paper N.* 12. Toronto: University of Toronto Institute on Municipal Finance and Governance.

Government of Ontario, Association of Municipalities of Ontario, City of Toronto. 2008. *Provincial-Municipal Fiscal and Service Delivery Review*. Toronto: Queen's Printer.

Government of Ontario Ministry of Finance. 1995a. *Fiscal and Economic Statement*. Toronto: Queen's Printer.

– 1995b. *Fiscal Overview and Spending Cuts*. Toronto: Queen's Printer.

– 1999. *Ontario Budget*. Toronto: Queen's Printer.

– 2010. *Ontario's Tax Plan for Jobs and Growth*, http://www.fin.gov.on.ca/en/budget/ontariobudgets/2010/bk_tax.html

Government of Ontario Ministry of Infrastructure. 2012. *Places to Grow: Growth Plan for the Greater Golden Horseshoe*. Toronto: Queen's Printer.

Government of Ontario Ministry of Municipal Affairs and Housing. 2009. *Sustainability: The Intersection of Land Use Planning and Food*. Toronto: Queen's Printer.

Grewel, S. 2011. "Is It Bad for Cities to be in Debt? Not Necessarily." *Toronto Star*, 14 August.

Harmes, A. 2006. "Neoliberalism and Multilevel Governance." *Review of International Political Economy* 13 (5).

Harvey, D. 2009. *Social Justice and the City*. Athens: University of Georgia Press.

– 2012. *Rebel Cities: From the Right to the City to the Urban Revolution*. London: Verso.

Hjartarson, J., K. Hinton, and M. Szala. 2011. *Putting Canada on Track: A Blueprint for a National Framework*. Toronto: Mowat Centre.

Kozolanka, K. 2007. *The Power of Persuasion: The Politics of the New Right in Ontario*. Montreal: Black Rose Books.

KPMG. 1996. *Fresh Start: An Estimate of Potential Savings and Costs from the Creation of a Single Tier Local Government for Toronto*. Toronto: KPMG.
Krawchencko, T., and C. Stoney. 2011. "Public Private Partnership and the Public Interest: A Case Study of Ottawa's Lansdowne Park Development." *Canadian Journal of Nonprofit and Social Economy Research* 2 (2).
Kushner, J., and D. Siegal. 2003. "Effect of Municipal Amalgamations on Political Representation and Accessibility." *Canadian Journal of Political Science* 36 (5).
Laycock, D. 2002. *The New Right and Democracy in Canada: Understanding Reform and the Canadian Alliance*. Toronto: Oxford University Press.
Leitner, H., J. Peck, and E.S. Sheppard, eds. 2006. *Contesting Neoliberalism: Urban Frontiers*. New York: Guilford Press.
Leitner, H., and E. Sheppard. 1998. "Economic Uncertainty, Interurban Competition and the Efficacy of Entrepreneurialism." In *The Entrepreneurial City: Geographies of Politics, Regime and Representation*, edited by T. Hall and P. Hubbard. New York: John Wiley and Sons.
Loxley, J. 2010. *Public Service, Private Profits: The Political Economy of Public-Private Partnerships in Canada*. Halifax: Fernwood Publishing.
MacDermid, R., and G. Albo. 2001. "Divided Province, Growing Protests: Ontario Moves Right." In *The Provincial State in Canada: Politics in the Provinces and Territories*, edited by K. Brownsey and M. Howlett. Toronto: Broadview Press.
Macdonald, S., and R. Keil. 2012. "The Ontario Greenbelt: Shifting the Scales of the Sustainability Fix?" *The Professional Geographer* 64 (1).
McBride, S., and J. Shields. 1997. *Dismantling a Nation: The Transition to Corporate Rule in Canada*. 2nd ed. Halifax: Fernwood.
Merrifield, A. 2002. *Dialectical Urbanism: Social Struggles in the Capitalist City*. New York: Monthly Review Press.
Metrolinx. 2008. *Costs of Road Congestion in the Greater Toronto and Hamilton Area: Impact and Cost Benefit Analysis of the Metrolinx Draft Regional Transportation Plan*. Toronto: Greater Toronto Transportation Authority.
Moore, A.A. 2013. "Trading Density for Benefits: Section 37 Agreements in Toronto." *Institute of Municipal Finance and Governance* 2.
Moussauoi, R. 2013a. "Dealing with Developers: Municipal Bonusing Spurs Debate." CBC, 25 April. http://www.cbc.ca/news.
– 2013b. "Battle Brewing over Toronto's Development Charges." CBC, 9 May. http://www.cbc.ca/news.
Mowat Centre-KPMG. 2009. *Tough Choices Ahead: The Future of the Public Sector*. Toronto: Mowat Centre.
Panitch, L. 1977. "The Role and Nature of the Canadian State." In *The Canadian State: Political Economy and Political Power*, edited by L. Panitch. Toronto: University of Toronto Press.
Panitch, L., and D. Swartz. 2003. *From Consent to Coercion: The Assault on Trade Union Freedoms*. Toronto: Garamond Press.
Peck, J. 2010. *Constructions of Neoliberal Reason*. Oxford: Oxford University Press.

Peck, J., N. Theodore, and N. Brenner. 2013. "Neoliberal Urbanism Redux?" *International Journal of Urban and Regional Research* 37 (3).
Pond, D. 2009. "Ontario's Greenbelt: Growth Management, Farmland Protection, and Regime Change in Southern Ontario." *Canadian Public Policy* 35 (4).
Pulkingham, J., and G. Ternowetsky, eds. 1997. *Remaking Canadian Social Policy: Social Security in the Late 1990s*. Halifax: Fernwood.
Rebick, J. 2012. *Occupy This!* Toronto: Penguin.
Reshef, Y., and S. Rastin. 2003. *Unions in the Time of Revolution: Government Restructuring in Alberta and Ontario*. Toronto: University of Toronto Press.
Residential and Civil Construction Alliance of Ontario. 2010. *Public Infrastructure Underinvestment: The Risk to Canada's Economic Growth*. Toronto: RiskAnalytica.
Rider, D. 2018. "Would Doug Ford Give City Mayors More Power?" *Toronto Star*, 3 June. https://www.thestar.com/news/queenspark/2018/06/03/would-doug-ford-give-city-mayors-more-power.html.
Sanberg, L.A., G.R. Wekerle, and L. Gilbert. 2013. *The Oak Ridges Moraine Battles: Development, Sprawl and Nature Conservation*. Toronto: University of Toronto Press.
Sancton, A. 1996. "Reducing Costs by Consolidating Municipalities: New Brunswick, Nova Scotia and Ontario." *Canadian Public Administration* 39 (3).
– 2000. *Merger Mania: The Assault on Local Government*. Montreal: McGill-Queen's University Press.
Sanger, T. 2011. *Garbage In, Garbage Out: The Real Costs of Solid Waste Collection*. Ottawa: CUPE.
Shepherd, T. 2013. "Woodbine Live! Project Folds." *Etobicoke Guardian*, 6 February.
Skaburskis, A., and R. Tomalty. 1997. "Land Value Taxation and Development Activity: The Reaction of Toronto and Ottawa Developers, Planners and Municipal Finance Officials." *Canadian Journal of Regional Science* 20 (3).
Slack, E., and R.M. Bird. 2013. "Merging Municipalities: Is Bigger Better?" *IMFG Paper N. 14*. University of Toronto Institute on Municipal Finance and Governance.
Spicer, Z. 2011. "The Rise and Fall of the Ministry of State for Urban Affairs: A Reevaluation." *Canadian Political Science Review* 5 (2).
Stapleton, J. 2008. *Ontario Alternative Budget: The Last Recession Spook*. Ottawa: Canadian Centre for Policy Alternatives.
Stoney, C., and K.A.H. Graham. 2009. "Federal-Municipal Relations in Canada: The Changing Organizational Landscape." *Canadian Public Administration* 52 (3).
Streeck, W., and K. Thelen, eds. 2005. *Beyond Continuity: Institutional Change in Advanced Political Economies*. Oxford: Oxford University Press.
Sustainable Urban Development Association (SUDA). 2011. *Places to Grow: Still Unsustainable*. Mississauga: SUDA.

Tapper, J. 2012. "Billions Needed to Save Canadian Roads, Water Systems, Report Says." *Toronto Star*, 11 September.

Toronto. 2013. *2013 City Budget*. http://www.toronto.ca/budget2013/2013_budget_summary/operating_budget.htm.

Toronto.com editors. 2008. "City Hall: Council Grants Woodbine Project Massive Tax-Break." *Toronto.com*, 17 July. https://www.toronto.com/.

Toronto Region Board of Trade. 2013. *A Green Light to Moving the Toronto Region: Paying for Public Transportation Expansion*. Toronto: TRBOT.

Vining, A.R., and A.E. Boardman. 2008. "Public-Private Partnerships in Canada: Theory and Evidence." *Canadian Public Administration* 51 (1).

Walker, G. 1994. "Planning the Future of Rural Toronto: Structure Planning in the Greater Toronto Area." *Great Lakes Geographer* 1 (2).

Walkom, T. 1994. *Rae Days: The Rise and Fall of the NDP*. Toronto: Key Porter.

Warren, RM. 2013. "Politicians Ignore Creative Ways to Fund Our Infrastructure." *Toronto Star*, 19 March.

Whittington, L. 2011. "Tax Cuts Drive Harper's Right-Wing Agenda." *Toronto Star*, 19 January.

Workman, T. 2009. *If You're in My Way I'm Walking: The Assault on Working People since 1970*. Halifax: Fernwood.

York Region. 2017. *Capital: Business Plan and Budget: Financial Sustainability*. www.york.ca.

| 9 |

Class, Power, and Neoliberal Employment Policy in Ontario

CHARLES W. SMITH

More than any other Canadian jurisdiction, Ontario's postwar employment model was based on export-led growth built on natural resource extraction, and the slow buildup of specialized branch-plant manufacturing capacity. As part of this strategy, the Ontario state was influential in constructing a model of class relations that prioritized private capital accumulation and integrated the organized industrial working class into the project. An important institutional component of class integration was the Ontario Labour Relations Act (OLRA) introduced in 1943, and the Employment Standards Act (ESA) passed in 1969 (Vosko et al. 2011). The OLRA was – and remains – a rigid legal document that prioritizes collective bargaining in industries with single employers retaining large pools of workers (Smith 2009). The ESA combines several employment statutes to create a minimum "floor" for low wage (mainly non-unionized) service sector workers in the private sector (Thomas 2009). Throughout the postwar period, these two institutions contributed to relative full employment for Ontario's mostly male working class.

Between 1985 and 1999, Ontario's postwar class alliances shifted. The disappearance of state protective capacities in favour of more market-friendly policies, and the eventual transition of the domestic ruling classes to free trade with the United States and later Mexico, eroded the conditions that made Ontario's industrial base competitive under the old industrial relations system. Initially, at the end of the 1980s, successive Liberal and NDP governments attempted to craft a new deal with

Ontario's leading capitalists to promote a high value-added manufacturing strategy. When these strategies failed to get beyond partial implementation (never gaining the backing of Ontario's corporate elites), the NDP government turned to the right, choosing to tackle the province's fiscal problems through a combination of austerity and restraining the rights of workers, and losing, in turn, the support of a large part of the union movement. The Conservative government of Mike Harris accelerated the austerity agenda to further cut public services while weakening labour standards and union protection for workers. An explosion of precarious work, part-time and temporary, and a general lowering of wages, followed.

In 2003, Dalton McGuinty's Liberals promised to restore Ontario's competitiveness through new partnerships, training, and workplace fairness. McGuinty's conciliatory message led Rodney Haddow and Thomas Klassen (2006, 93–4) to argue that Ontario's labour market policies had returned to a period of "political moderation" and "the pre-1985 status quo." This conclusion, however, ignores the continuities that have remained in the spread of precarious work and neoliberal strategies in the 1990s and 2000s. For example, the Liberals embraced a form of competitiveness that prioritizes individual skills requirement on the assumption that "the more productive, innovative, entrepreneurial and global Ontario's economy becomes, the more competitive we will be" (Ontario 2012c, 1). Similarly, the Liberals bypassed unions in the formation of workplace training policy and off-loaded the cost for skills attainment onto individual students, while never seriously considering a training tax on employers. More anti-union policies followed, as the government made only minor changes to the OLRA and did little to alter the ability of workers to form unions, especially in the private sector. While Kathleen Wynne's adoption of Bill 148 in 2017 – the Fair Workplaces, Better Jobs Act – represented a significant updating of Ontario's labour laws and contains much-needed catch-up benefits for workers outside the organized working class, it continues to leave numerous workers behind. Taken as a whole, the Liberal years in Ontario should be understood as ironing out the contradictory edges of neoliberalism in the province, leaving Ontario as polarized and unequal as it was when the party first came to power in 2003. The absolute defeat of the Wynne Liberals in the 2018 provincial election by the Conservatives under the leadership of Doug Ford threatens to amplify these inequalities, in setting out a policy and political context even more pernicious for Ontario's poor and working classes.

SHIFTING EMPLOYMENT PARADIGMS IN ONTARIO

Government intervention in the labour market between 1944 and the late 1970s transformed the relationship between workers and employers throughout Canada (Panitch and Swartz 2003; Fudge and Tucker 2000). While capitalist markets continued to experience periods of crisis, active state intervention at both the federal and provincial levels assisted in levelling the extremes of capitalist downturns. In this period, Canadian governments – with Ontario at the centre – slowly institutionalized labour relations inspired by a Keynesian system of full employment and a labour relations policy known as industrial pluralism. Industrial pluralism is a systemic approach to labour relations that attempts to replace open class conflict with procedures encouraging collective bargaining in order to foster labour peace and stability between the industrial working class and employers (McInnis 2002; Russell 1995).

At its roots, industrial pluralism promotes the principles of "exclusivity" and "majoritarianism," giving unions associational rights to organize in individual job sites, bargain collectively, and strike once certain conditions have been met (Carter et al. 2002). In return, unions are required to respect the employers' right to manage the workplace free from strikes during the life of a collective agreement. For governments, industrial pluralism protects the broader "public interest" because it seeks to limit the frequency, intensity, and violence associated with workplace conflict (Peirce 2003, 339; Carrothers et al. 1986, 63–4). Within Ontario's postwar Keynesian economic model, industrial pluralism worked to stabilize labour relations so as to consolidate a broad class compromise within and between the industrial working class and employers.

That compromise began to break down in the heartland of Ontario's manufacturing centres by the 1980s. From that point forward, neoliberal employment policies became increasingly prioritized by governments of all political stripes. The foundation of neoliberal state policy is the belief that market forces excel when free from government regulation and collective pressure from workers. Neoliberals thus promote trade liberalization, lower taxation, deregulation, and the privatization of public assets in the belief that they foster free and more efficient societies (Albo 2010; Peck 2010; Harvey 2005). These freedoms flow from the strengthening of individual private property rights, defining the relationship "that people have towards each other in regard to the use and disposal of socially necessary objects" (Teeple 2004, 82). For neoliberals, the state's key function is to create an institutional framework that promotes market freedoms and protects market contracts. In order to embed these property rights, neoliberals stress the coercive elements of the state, including legal, military, police, and defense powers.

Neoliberal employment policy seeks to increase the power of owners of business property and the market freedoms of individual workers. For owners, this is power over all aspects of the workplace (wages, work time, working conditions, and the overall nature of the work). For individual workers, this is freedom from union obligations and restrictions in negotiating with employers. As neoliberals have lessened the state regulation over the workplace, the collective power of workers has also weakened, leaving them more vulnerable to market fluctuations and economic crisis. There have been a large number of changes to workplace organization in the core capitalist countries, including the introduction of flexible manufacturing processes, "lean" workplaces, new technological processes, advanced global supply chains, just-in-time management production, and a general offshoring of manufacturing work (Albo 2010; Moody 1997). These technological transformations, coupled with neoliberal employment policies, have been central to the erosion of standard, full-time employment.

A central objective of neoliberalism is to limit the collective freedoms of workers as expressed in forming a union. Amongst the numerous changes to workers' freedoms in the neoliberal era are limits on the ability to organize, bargain, and strike (Panitch and Swartz 2003). By weakening unions, neoliberal reforms have contributed to the crisis of worker solidarity and the decline of influence of unions in workplaces and over government policy (Gindin 2013; Swartz and Warskett 2012). In terms of basic employment standards, it is more difficult for workers in non-unionized, non-traditional workplaces to make a

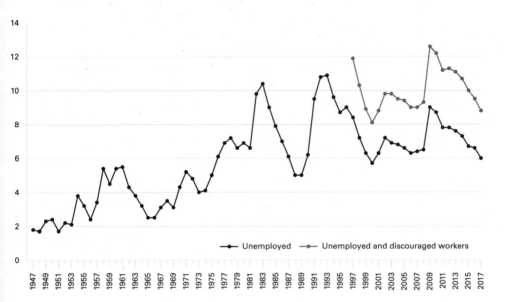

Figure 9.1 | Ontario unemployed and discouraged workers, annual average (%), 1947–2016 (*Source*: Statistics Canada (2018), CANSIM series 282-0086)

living wage or be protected from employer abuse (Fudge and Vosko 2003). These neoliberal reforms have been central to Ontario employment policy over the past thirty years.

THE LIMITS OF ONTARIO'S POSTWAR BOOM

Ontario's postwar Keynesian "golden age" was driven primarily by exports in primary and secondary manufacturing. While this growth model excluded large numbers of workers (women and most service workers), it did produce relatively stable levels of employment. As figure 9.1 illustrates, between 1947 and 1975 unemployment averaged only 3.5 per cent (Ontario 1986, 660).

The province's low unemployment levels occurred because of the staggering rate of postwar growth, with gross provincial product (GPP) increasing by an average of 5 per cent a year over the period (Foot 1974, 5–7; MacDermid and Albo 2001, 166). Aided by a growing labour force, two sectors drove the postwar boom. Throughout the North, the processing sectors in lumber, pulp, and metals provided raw materials for southern manufacturing plants. Primary and secondary manufacturing factories scattered mostly around Lake Ontario – including those in auto, steel, rubber, textiles, appliances, clothing, and food – were all closely tied to production networks in the US. By the mid-1970s, the manufacturing sector employed over 850,000 workers, many of whom belonged to large international unions (Rea 1985). The decline in well-paid jobs that emerged out of the restructuring of the 1970s and 1980s was disastrous for Ontario workers. In fact, by the end of the 1990s, Statistics Canada was tracking "unemployment fatigue," in which thousands of workers had simply stopped looking for permanent employment.

The OLRA created a standardized legal form of collective bargaining in unionized workplaces throughout the private sector. After a one-day walkout by teachers and other public sector workers in 1973, the same collective bargaining system was slowly extended to the Ontario Public Service (OPS), although these same workers were denied the ability to legally strike until 1993. Worker unrest in Ontario was compounded by the severe economic crises of the 1970s, which placed significant strain on the Conservative government of William Davis. The recession brought increasing hardship to Ontario workers, who were faced with plant closures, high levels of unemployment, double-digit inflation, and rising energy and food prices (Drummond 1983, 243). The ensuing employment restructuring led to a series of labour conflicts in the public, mining, auto, and building trades, as well as the trucking sectors. In dealing with the crisis, Davis used a series of temporary measures to limit wage increases in the public sector, including fines and criminal charges for workers engaged in public sector strikes. The most restrictive policy adopted by the Davis government was the 1982 Inflation Restraint Act, which capped public sector wage increases to 5 per cent.

WORK AND CHANGE AT QUEEN'S PARK, 1985-95

The economic challenges of the 1980s weakened the political base of the province's forty-three-year Conservative dynasty, eventually leading to a Liberal minority government that was propped up by the NDP in 1985. The agreement that sustained the Liberal government, known as the Liberal NDP Accord, promised sweeping reforms on a series of issues, including: government accountability, pay equity, environmental reform, and rent controls (Dyck 1991, 326–7; Brownsey and Howlett 1992, 163–5). The NDP was able to negotiate a much-needed update to Occupational Health and Safety (OHS) laws and an enhancement of the powers of the Workers' Compensation Board (WCB). The Liberals made several changes to the ESA that made it easier for some laid-off workers to collect severance and strengthened the ability of workers to decline Sunday work. The OLRA was also amended to compel first contract arbitration in newly unionized workplaces.

The Liberals had the good fortune of being elected in the midst of a substantial economic recovery in the province. Between 1983 and 1989, Ontario averaged annual growth rates of 5.6 per cent, hitting a high of 9.2 per cent in 1984 (Ontario 1994, table 4). This meant a substantial increase in employment, totalling 900,000 new jobs by 1989 (Ontario 1994, table 31). However, serious concerns about economic performance and long-term sustainability remained. First, the boom was sustained by higher than normal hours worked rather than significant increases in productivity: Ontario workers were simply working harder and longer. The increased output fuelled the boom, but corporations seemed to have no long-term plan to forge production in the emerging new technology sectors. Second, employment expanded but without any significant increase in the share of the unionized manufacturing sector in total employment. Rather, new jobs were predominantly in the service sector, driving up its share of all employment from 67.8 per cent in 1983 to 70.6 per cent in 1990.

The weaknesses associated with the 1980s boom were not entirely lost on the provincial government. Perhaps the most ambitious realignment of priorities was Peterson's creation of the Premier's Council in 1986.[1] The council's final report, entitled *People and Skills in the New Global Economy* (Ontario 1990), argued that Ontario was unprepared for the technological transformation of the workplace. In order to address the "training deficit," the council urged government to channel skills investment through new partnerships with private industry. This strategy included reworking labour legislation to foster harmonization across various sectors (Ontario 1990, 87–8). The report also advocated the creation of the Ontario Training and Adjustment Board (OTAB) (Ontario 1990, 90). OTAB was to be made up of management and labour representatives whose mandate would be to forge collaboration by building a cross-class consensus on the needs of both industry and labour in a more flexible, and hence more productive, workplace.

The irony of the Premier's Council's proposals for a more active state-led industrial policy was that it occurred at the same time that employers in North America were demanding workplace flexibilization on their own terms. Increased workplace flexibility meant more competition between workers over jobs, so-called lean production methods, and squeezes on compensation, all with the goal of "widening gaps between the share of value taken by capital and that taken by workers" (Crow and Albo 2005, 13). The recommendations in *People and Skills* were also out of step with the Canadian government's signing of the Free Trade Agreement (FTA) with the United States in 1989. While Ontario officially opposed the FTA, the pro-free trade opinions of the largest business groups in the province supported it. In fact, the Liberals had to contend with a dramatic repositioning of economic policy (and state protected tariffs) by the Ontario-dominated Canadian Manufacturers Association (CMA). By 1987, the CMA had dropped its historic opposition to free trade at the strong urging of the Business Council on National Issues (BCNI), and openly endorsed the free trade agreement (Langille 1987, 67–8).

The signing of the FTA coincided with a global crisis of capitalist accumulation, which had dramatic implications for workers in the province. According to Ontario's Ministry of Labour, the number of layoffs following the dual pressures of recession and a repositioning of employers after the signing of the FTA ballooned from 12,684 in 1989 to 20,554 in 1990 (Ontario 1991a; Langille 1991, 598). Moreover, the share of job losses due to permanent plant closures jumped from 35 per cent during the early 1980s recession to over 72 per cent in 1990. The restructuring from the FTA occurred at the expense of well-paid union jobs in secondary manufacturing (Wolfe and Gertler 2001). Moreover, during the recession of 1990–91 Ontario's economy contracted by 5 per cent and unemployment doubled to 10.8 per cent (figure 1). While

Ontario's unemployment rate began to ease in 1994, as of 2018 it continues to be structurally higher than the pre-FTA rate of 5 per cent (or lower). Faced with these economic challenges, the Peterson Liberals shelved the Premier's Council's "high road" manufacturing and skills strategy.

In the ensuing election, the Bob Rae-led NDP squeaked past the Liberals with the vague promise of a new *Agenda for the People* (Ontario New Democratic Party 1990). The ambiguous platform commitments left the party ill prepared to address the 1990–91 recession. Almost immediately, real provincial GDP contracted by 3.0 per cent and 2.9 per cent in 1991 (and respectively 6.3 and 8.0 per cent in manufacturing) (Ontario 1994, table 4). The 1990–91 recession was particularly devastating to Ontario's manufacturing sector, which witnessed workers in the sector dropping to 18 per cent of the total workforce by 1998, down from 21.3 per cent in 1987 (Ontario 1999, table 20). The economic dislocation of the Ontario workforce was reflected in the high unemployment of the period. By the end of 1991, unemployment was at 9.6 per cent, representing a loss of 250,000 jobs. In the following four years, unemployment averaged 10.2 per cent (figure 1). Even as the economy began to recover in the spring of 1993, workers continued to report difficulty in finding permanent employment. By 1999, the average rate of long-term unemployment (unemployed for more than twenty-seven weeks) was 29 per cent of all unemployed workers (Gertler 1995, 105).

The recession and the earlier experience of the accord with the Liberals moved the NDP to resuscitate the *People and Skills* strategy of "associative governance" (Ontario 1994, 99; Bradford 1998). These new "tripartite" structures were institutionalized in three areas: Occupational Health and Safety (OHS), OTAB, and an active industrial policy. The NDP allotted significant resources to these portfolios and appointed prominent members from business, labour, and government (OTAB also included members of equity groups) (Wolfe 1997; Haddow and Klassen 2006, 102–3). Partnerships were designed "to ensure that government support for industrial development is strategic [and] builds on the foundation of a market economy and on an appreciation of the important role that competition plays in innovation" (Ontario 1992, 3). In order to create "competitive fundamentals," the NDP prioritized public support for commercial research (often through universities) in order to encourage continuous innovation, raise skill levels, and increase businesses' technological capabilities, both in the province and abroad.

There was, however, now even less support from employers for any ambitious partnership agenda, even though it was a strategy thoroughly constructed to bolster capital accumulation. Business took the position that innovation and competitiveness could only be driven by the private sector. There was no appetite from employers to share workplace power in "partnership" with government or unions; and Ontario business was particularly antagonistic to the idea that workplace training should be centred on "worker empowerment [in] consultation with unions" (Bradford 1998, 553). Business also felt that the OHS and OTAB proposals were too intrusive, especially with regards to resource allocation, worker training, and private investment. Given this hostility, the NDP was forced to go it alone in initiating a $1.1 billion jobsOntario Training Fund that offered public money directly to private sector employers willing to train workers on provincial social assistance (Ontario 1992, 20).

Business hostility to the NDP carried over to the government's modifications to the ESA and the OLRA. The NDP increased the minimum wage from $5.40/hour to $6.85/hour and put forward the goal (never reached) of making the rate 60 per cent of the average wage by 1995 (Thomas 2009, 85). Building on past Liberal reforms, the NDP also passed an Employee Wage Protection Program (EWPP) that created a statutory mechanism for workers to collect unpaid wages when a company went bankrupt (up to $5,000). The policy also created a general public fund for employees to access when delinquent employers declared bankruptcy before paying outstanding wages (Vosko et al. 2011, 9–10). Further reforms to the ESA extended the weeks of parental leave during which worker seniority, pension, and extended health benefits continued.

The government's other main priority for employment policy was a reformed OLRA (O'Grady 1992). The new OLRA (Bill 40) sought to address several long-standing issues advanced by labour unions (Ontario 1991b, 1991c; Jain and Muthuchidambaram 1995, 1996). The eventual amendments created a "purposive clause" that promoted collective bargaining and expanded the rights of unionization to professional occupations, security guards, and domestic workers (Smith 2009; Schenk 1995; Panitch and Swartz 2003, 171). The government also gave "third parties" some access to private property for the purposes of organizing (i.e., shopping centres). The bill further reformed the grievance arbitration process; extended union abilities to apply to the OLRB for first contract arbitration; expanded successor rights; expedited the hearing process before the OLRB; eliminated the one-dollar card fee to sign a union card; and abolished employer-inspired petitions before the board. The certification procedure was also changed, allowing unions to apply for a vote when 40 per cent of employees signed union cards (down from 45 per cent). The government also passed anti-scab legislation banning the use of replacement workers during a lawful strike or lockout, but limited its application to instances where the union had obtained over 60 per cent in a strike vote.

Bill 40 only went as far as aligning Ontario's labour relations framework with both Québec and British Columbia. Yet, despite its moderation, it generated tremendous opposition from three large business coalitions (operating in unionized sectors) – Project Economic Growth, the All Business Coalition, and the More Jobs Coalition – claiming to represent 85 per cent of private sector employers in Ontario.[2] The intensity of the opposition convinced the government to eliminate provisions that would have required employers to disclose financial information to union organizers and allow organizers increased access to company property. Employers were successful in protecting their freedoms to communicate during a certification drive and in weakening the anti-scab provisions.[3] The government also balked at union demands to expand bargaining units in clerical or management positions, and at creating an institutional framework for sectoral bargaining units in the service sector (Mackie 1992).

Pressure from employers was also instrumental in moving the NDP away from its economic priorities. In early 1993, the government promised business that it would "hold the line" on the provincial deficit by introducing a three-pronged austerity strategy: a series of new tax increases; an expenditure control plan in the public service (eliminating 11,000 public sector jobs); and a new "Social Contract" with public sector workers. The Social Contract opened existing public sector collective agreements, rolled back wages and benefits, and instituted mandatory unpaid days off (dubbed "Rae Days"). The Social Contract Act shattered the NDP's relation with allies in the labour movement, yet failed to win broader support from business. In the subsequent election, a rejuvenated and stridently neoliberal Progressive Conservative Party was elected with the support of a coalition of provincial businesses, the wealthy, and middle-class voters (MacDermid 1995; Woolstencroft 1997).

NEOLIBERAL ENTRENCHMENT: THE HARRIS COMMON SENSE REVOLUTION, 1995–2003

The election of the Harris-led Conservative government was a turning point for employment relations in Ontario. The Harris agenda was a mixture of neoliberal reforms adopted in the United States and Great Britain that promised tax cuts, deregulation, and privatization. This agenda was made easier by a rebound in the world economy in the spring of 1994 that witnessed provincial economic growth of 5.9 per cent in 1994 and 3.5 per cent in 1995. The Conservatives also promised to bring "balance" back to Ontario's labour market by punishing the "have-nots" (disproportionately social assistance recipients and marginalized communities) while rewarding the hard-working "haves" (disproportionately white males in professional occupations, trades, and the self-employed).

The Harris Conservatives believed that NDP and Liberal governments had shifted Keynesian labour policy away from the realities of the competitive free market. Using the rationale of "balance" (while in fact wanting increased discipline in workplaces), Harris implemented a drastic restructuring agenda. This included: general cuts in public spending; slashing social assistance rates by 21.6 per cent; eliminating virtually all of the NDP and Liberal labour market initiatives; cancelling numerous social programs, including cutting child care spaces; privatizing key Crown assets such as Ontario Hydro; capping pay equity agreements; introducing a form of "workfare" for selected social assistance recipients; and eliminating the advisory Premier's Council (Ontario 1995). The Conservatives directly targeted the heart of the NDP's economic strategy by eliminating the jobsOntario Training Fund and trimming the provincial government's training budget by 17 per cent for 1996–97 (Haddow and Klassen 2006, 104).

The Harris government's economic priorities were overwhelmingly tied to servicing private sector competitiveness. This was, in a general sense, no different than the objectives of the Liberal and NDP governments. But if the prior Ontario government administrations attempted to do this via some notion of a "partnership" with Ontario unions and workers, the Conservatives sought to create competitiveness by targeting Ontario unions and workers. An important part of this agenda was to rewrite the OLRA (Bill 7). Bill 7 promised to restore "workplace democracy" through a new purposive clause emphasizing flexibility, productivity, and employer-employee communication. Among other things, it eliminated the NDP's anti-scab provisions and limited the ability of a union to call a strike vote before the termination of a contract. The government also eliminated card-check certification (automatic union certification based on cards signed) and opted for a mandatory secret ballot for union certification, contract ratification, and strikes (Smith 2009; Slinn 2003; Jain and Muthuchidambaram 1996).[4] The threshold to attain a vote for union certification remained at 40 per cent, while a vote for decertification was triggered at 40 per cent (from 45 per cent). The new rules further imposed a twelve-month ban on organizing if a union lost a certification vote. Not surprisingly, the Conservatives' anti-labour legislation precipitated enormous labour strife throughout Ontario (including the mass "Days of Action" political protests; see Ross, this volume).

Not deterred by worker protests, the Conservatives pushed forward with new flexibility provisions in the ESA. In 1995, the government froze the minimum wage at $6.85 per hour and eliminated the EWPP. In 1996, the government introduced the Employment Standards Improvement Act (ESIA), which limited the ability of workers to file complaints with the Ministry of Labour, capped the monetary awards for ESA violations, eliminated the ability of union members to make ESA complaints, and abolished dozens of ESA enforcement officers (Vosko et al. 2011, 10–11). In late 2000, the ESA was further amended to rewrite the long-standing provisions surrounding hours of work and overtime provisions in non-unionized workplaces. The Conservatives also eliminated the requirement that departures from the traditional forty-four-hour workweek needed Ministry of Labour consent. Under these new provisions, employers were given greater flexibility to request consent (in writing) for their employees to work a maximum of sixty hours per week (up from forty-eight). Employers and employees could also agree to average overtime over four weeks, limiting employers from paying overtime at time-and-a-half unless employees worked more than 176 hours over that period. The new ESA's emphasis on consent between employers and individual employees placed additional pressure on workers without stable employment. In essence, the changes privatized non-unionized workplace regulation: employers were given more power to control hours of work, compensation, and payment of benefits (Thomas 2009, 124).

The Harris government's restructuring of the Ontario labour market unleashed a real (and growing) wage gap in the province. Throughout the Conservative period, average GDP growth stood at 3.7 per cent while average weekly wages (less inflation) declined 0.4 per cent (Ontario 2004, tables 2 and 27). Part of these declines can be explained by changing power imbalances within the labour market. Between 1995 and 2003 there was an increase in precarious and part-time work, averaging 18.4 per cent of total employment over the period (Ontario 2004, table 24). The legislative changes introduced by the Conservatives accelerated the trend towards precarious and part-time employment. From these perspectives, the years 1995–2003 should be understood as Ontario's "class struggle from above," shifting the benefits of economic growth overwhelmingly away from the working and middle classes to the most powerful and affluent (MacDermid and Albo 2001, 190). By 2003, Ontario's labour market was tilted more in favour of employers than it had been since the consolidation of Keynesian employment policies in the 1960s.

NEOLIBERALISM AND PROGRESSIVE COMPETITIVENESS: THE MCGUINTY LIBERALS

The 2003 election of Dalton McGuinty and the Liberal party promised a new era of "balanced" and fair labour market reforms (Ontario Liberal Party 2003). McGuinty's message of change, however, had to address several structural changes in Ontario's economy that had occurred

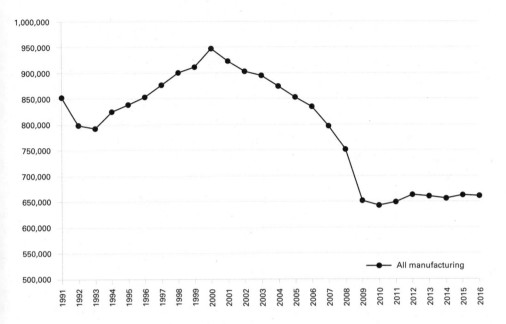

Figure 9.2 | Employment in Ontario's manufacturing industry, 1991–2016
(*Source*: Statistics Canada (2018), CANSIM series 281-0042 and 281-0051)

since the recession of the early 1990s. First, Ontario's unemployment rate remained stubbornly high. To be sure, Ontario's unemployment problems reflected broader neoliberal reforms at the federal level that trimmed unemployment benefits and prioritized the fight against inflation over employment growth. Moreover, the Harris government's radical neoliberal restructuring seemed also to contribute to the jobs crisis and relative stagnation in Ontario in the 2000s. From 2001–06, real provincial GDP growth averaged a modest 2.3 per cent, the slowest period of growth in Ontario since the 1930s (Rae 1985; Ontario 2007, table 2). When we include the dramatic economic decline during the 2008 "great recession," growth between 2003 and 2012 annually averaged a meagre 1.38 per cent (Ontario 2012c, tables 2 and 26).

Second, the Liberals also governed in a period that witnessed dramatic changes to the sectoral distribution of employment in Ontario. During the recession of the early 1990s, manufacturing employment took a devastating blow, but some rebound occurred by 1996 (figure 9.2). By the end of 2011, manufacturing represented only 11.8 per cent of total employment, an astonishing decline from an 18.1 per cent share in 1998 (Ontario 2012c, table 23).

The slide in manufacturing employment in Ontario has been part of a shift to a growing service sector. In 1981, 65.1 per cent of Ontario workers were employed in services; by 2011, it stood at 78.9 per cent (Ontario 1994; 2012c, table 23). While this workforce shift is not unique to Ontario, it has engendered an expansion in all forms of precarious employment – part-time, self-employed without employees, temporary agency placement, fixed-term contract, and casual employment (Poverty and Employment Precarity in Southern Ontario (PEPSO) 2013, 28; Law Commission of Ontario 2012, 12–15). If in 1997 about 9 per cent of Ontario workers were found in precarious employment relationships, this proportion was almost 13 per cent in 2010.[5] Put another way, the number of temporary jobs increased by 80.5 per cent over this period while permanent jobs grew by just 24 per cent. Not surprisingly, there has been a relatively flat rate of permanent employment during the 2000s in Ontario (table 1).

In 2013, PEPSO expanded the definition of precarious employment to: any worker that does not work for a single employer, who does not receive employment benefits, and who expects to be working in a different location after one year (2013, 19). Based on this definition, PEPSO found that the number of workers in precarious employment represents over 50 per cent of the working population in Ontario. These changes suggest an alarming employment reality: permanent stable employment is structurally unattainable for the majority of workers in the province. When examining the trends (table 9.1), several conclusions are noticeable. First, temporary workers have grown at a faster rate than permanent positions. Second, the volatility of the temporary workforce highlights the meaning of precariousness within Ontario's labour market. Any hint of a downturn leads first to the loss of temporary jobs, and later to permanent ones. Yet, any recovery is led first by an uptick in low-wage temporary workers and only later by increases in permanent employment. Third, since 1997, the temporary workforce has been growing, swelling the reserve army of labour that can be cast aside in a downturn or taken back temporarily as a way of suppressing permanent employee wage demands. Finally, these workers are the least likely to be protected by the OLRA, and are increasingly dependent on the ESA.

Table 9.1 | Ontario permanent and temporary employment, 1997–2012

Year	Permanent jobs	Temporary jobs	Net job increase over previous year	Net temporary increase over previous year	Temporary job increase as % of net increase	Temporary jobs as a % of all jobs
1997	4,027,300	411,500				9.3
1998	4,131,400	449,400	142,000	37,900	26.7	9.8
1999	4,274,200	468,000	161,400	18,600	11.5	9.9
2000	4,397,500	516,000	171,300	48,000	28.0	10.5
2001	4,493,700	547,800	128,000	31,800	24.8	10.9
2002	4,565,900	574,200	98,600	26,400	26.8	11.2
2003	4,714,100	580,400	154,400	6,200	4.0	11.0
2004	4,739,300	626,300	71,100	45,900	64.6	11.7
2005	4,758,400	682,300	75,100	56,000	74.6	12.5
2006	4,824,000	693,600	76,900	11,300	14.7	12.6
2007	4,865,800	717,900	66,100	24,300	36.8	12.9
2008	5,026,400	645,400	88,100	-72,500	-82.3	11.4
2009	4,824,800	665,800	-181,200	20,400	100.0	12.1
2010	4,872,000	721,400	102,800	55,600	54.1	12.9
2011	4,960,600	734,700	101,900	13,300	13.1	12.9
2012	4,997,600	742,900	45,200	8,200	18.1	12.9
2013	5,048,500	712,500	20,500	-30,400	-148.3	12.4
2014	5,086,900	735,500	61,400	23,000	37.5	12.6
2015	5,087,300	747,600	12,500	12,100	97.0	12.8
2016	5,157,500	746,100	68,700	-1,500	-2.2	12.6
2017	5,238,000	781,700	116,100	35,600	30.6	13.0

Source: Statistics Canada (2018c), Cansim series 282-0080.

The McGuinty Liberals did not try to address the causes of the growing temporary labour market. Where the McGuinty government did try to amend the province's labour market institutions, it was only to blunt the edges of the Harris years. In 2004, for instance, the Liberals amended the ESA to eliminate the Conservative allowance of an employer-imposed sixty-hour workweek. But the bill continued to allow employers and employees to agree on an extended workweek with written permission from the Ministry of Labour. The government's unwillingness to address the structural power imbalance between workers and employers meant that the ESA prioritized employers' powers to amend hours of work all the while paying below poverty wages. In another example, two amendments to the ESA in 2009 sought to address the flagrant abuse of precarious workers in temporary agencies (Bill 139) and in-home (foreign) caregivers (Bill 210). Yet neither bill addressed inadequate pay, structural precariousness, or lack of health and safety protection for workers in these industries (Vosko 2010).

There were similar problems in addressing poverty across the province, as the Liberals refused to raise the base minimum wage. By 2005, Ontario's minimum wage was a meagre $7.45 per hour. According to Statistics Canada, in 2005 a single individual with no dependents working forty hours per week in a community of half a million had to earn $10 per hour just to meet the basic poverty line (Watson 2007). Notwithstanding the fact that few Ontarians could rely on permanent full-time work, the Liberals refused to seriously address the minimum wage issue. When it became apparent that the failure to raise the minimum wage might further erode urban electoral support, the Liberals agreed to raise it, but only incrementally to $10.25 per hour by 2010. In 2014, similar forces pressured the Liberals to again raise the minimum wage, although even then it was only raised to $11.00 per hour. Demonstrating their commitment to half-measure reforms, the raises in the minimum wage continue to leave thousands labouring below the poverty line. In 2011, for instance, Statistics Canada's low-income before tax cut-off for an individual living in a community larger than half a million people was $23,298.[6] Yet, a full-time minimum wage worker in an Ontario city over half a million people would only earn $21,320 per year.

McGuinty's changes to the OLRA contained similar half-measures. When the government introduced the Labour Relations Statute Law Amendment Act in 2005, Labour Minister Chris Bentley proudly announced that the Liberals were bringing "fairness and balance" back to the province's labour relations regime. But this mainly involved restoring remedial certification powers to the OLRB. The board again had the power to temporarily reinstate workers who were fired or disciplined during a union organizing campaign. In another example, card-based certification was restored in the construction industry. For all other workers, the mandatory vote provision continued to be an obstacle for workers seeking the right to unionize. The Liberals also opposed bringing back the NDP's anti-scab provisions and maintained most of

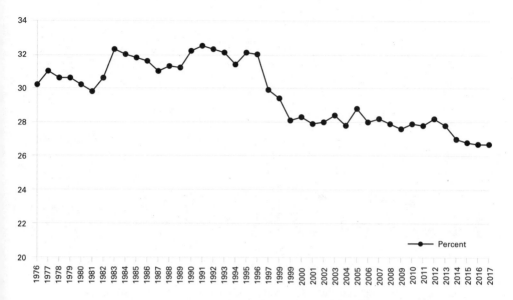

Figure 9.3 | Union density in Ontario (% of workforce unionized), 1976–2017
(*Source*: Statistics Canada, CANSIM series 279-0025 and 282-0078)

the Harris government's constraints on union organization. Since the Liberals were elected in 2003, union density has fallen, and has yet to recover from the Harris period setbacks (figure 9.3). That has been especially true in the private sector, where unionization has been declining rapidly since the Harris years while remaining relatively stable in the public sector after 2003 (figure 9.4).

The triviality of these reforms underscore the fact that the McGuinty government preserved Harris's "purposive clause" defining collective bargaining as the promotion of employer competitiveness.[7] This deference to employer power over the workplace and general opposition to the collective rights of workers was seen most prominently when the Liberals legislated striking workers back to work at the Toronto Transit Commission (TTC) (2008) and at York University (2009); in 2011, it restricted TTC workers from going on strike in the first place. Further clampdowns on union rights followed in 2012 when the self-declared "education" premier pushed through Bill 115, the Putting Students First Act, affecting the entire school sector. Bill 115 unilaterally froze teachers' wages, clawed back benefits and sick days, and eliminated the right to strike for two years.

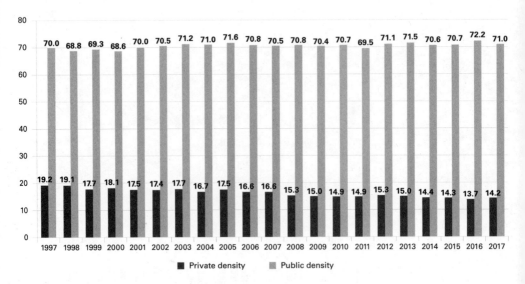

Figure 9.4 | Union density, public and private sector in Ontario (%), 1997–2017 (*Source*: Statistics Canada (2018), CANSIM series 282-0078)

While the Liberals have important allies in the labour movement (especially those in the Working Families Coalition),[8] the government has dropped most of the "partnership" consultation processes that were a staple of economic policymaking under the Peterson and Rae governments. For instance, it abandoned any pretext of including the labour movement in the creation or administration of labour market policy. Instead, employment policy has been driven almost exclusively by the demands of business. An example is the commercialization of Ontario's labour market policy with respect to skills training. Across the ministries responsible for economic development, the skills agenda has relied overwhelmingly on targeted public funding through business partnerships for commercial research, technology, and job creation. This part of the McGuinty government's skills agenda has included substantial investments in post-secondary education. In their first term (2003–07), public spending on universities grew by 45 per cent (Ontario 2008b). In 2005 alone, the Reaching Higher program committed over $6.2 billion in new funding over five years to post-secondary institutions (Ontario 2005b).

The government's priority of enhancing private sector competitiveness through skills training was highlighted in its 2008 *Skills to Jobs*

Action Plan (SJAP) (Ontario 2008a). The SJAP was designed to provide workers with skills to find new careers. Part of the SJAP was to expand access to postsecondary student loans and create programs that directly match workers with future employers. The SJAP also extended $355 million over three years for a new Second Career Strategy (giving 20,000 unemployed workers access to training), and $75 million over three years to expand apprenticeships. In 2009, the government committed an additional $700 million for skills training (on top of further corporate tax cuts to drive economic growth). The 2008 and 2009 budgets also included substantial amounts of public money for employer-specific training in the manufacturing sector, and at Toyota and Chrysler in particular (Ontario 2008a, 2009). The Liberals continued to prioritize tax cuts for businesses, including a ten-year Ontario income tax exemption "for new corporations that commercialize intellectual property developed by qualifying Canadian universities or colleges" (Ontario 2005b). Analyzed in its totality, the McGuinty Liberal policies of corporate tax cuts, workplace training, and funding postsecondary research amounted to little more than another ad hoc strategy to bolster private sector productivity in Ontario.

Three decades of neoliberal employment policies did not prepare Ontario for the great recession of 2008–09 and the continuing stagnation since. The recession was particularly devastating to the remaining vestiges of secure employment in the province's manufacturing corer. In the midst of a sharp downturn, the McGuinty Liberals proposed an initial period of fiscal stimulus via $32.5 billion for new infrastructure support (alongside targeted loans to the auto companies) over two years (Ontario 2009). But these policies were soon followed by a sharp turn to austerity that began with the Commission on the Reform of Ontario's Public Services, led by former Toronto Dominion Bank economist Don Drummond (Ontario 2012b). The Drummond Report presented a program for an even more austere Ontario state. While McGuinty (and his successor Kathleen Wynne) rejected across-the-board cuts, pressure from business to balance the budget has meant that Ontario's existing social programs are under constant pressure to cut costs and do more with less.

The one active labour market policy pursued by the Liberals after the 2008 recession was the Jobs and Prosperity Council (JPC) report released in 2012. Unlike the consultation processes of the Peterson and Rae governments, the JPC primarily consisted of corporate CEOs. The council made several recommendations that echoed the litany of problems identified by the Premier's Council in the late 1980s: Ontario employers continue to underinvest in new technologies; there remains a "skills gap" in the Ontario labour market; government needs new strategies to "drive productivity growth"; and public policies need to focus on working with private sector businesses to link entrepreneurship with new innovation services and technologies.

Reminiscent of the Premier's Council strategy under Peterson, the JPC called for greater public support for manufacturing firms competing in the export sector. The JPC maintained that government's role was to target public money to drive research and development in order to "accelerate the commercialization of new products, ideas and services in Ontario that can compete globally" (Ontario 2012a, 14). The JPC recommended: greater provincial and federal government support for venture capital initiatives to improve the quality of capital funding in Ontario; creating a stronger culture of entrepreneurship through public (and private) schools; new infrastructure spending; more public money for the skilled trades and apprentice programs; a new "Jobs and Prosperity Fund" to make business more competitive; and new incentives and tax credits to further future job creation. In contrast to the *People and Skills* report of the 1980s, the JPC ignored the OLRA and the ESA. In fact, the JPC only mentioned workers as an adjunct to private sector growth, leaving the question of wages, pensions, and workers' rights to individual workers and employers.

A CHANGE IN DIRECTION? THE LIBERAL GOVERNMENTS OF KATHLEEN WYNNE

The election of Kathleen Wynne to lead the Liberal party in 2013 was interpreted by many as extending an olive branch to disgruntled public workers, whose disputes with McGuinty had culminated in large segments of the public service losing their ability to collectively bargain. As premier, Wynne repealed controversial legislation such as the Putting Students First Act, but only after concluding a collective agreement with the province's teachers. Moreover, in their pre-election budget the Liberals clearly attempted to gain traction with left-of-centre voters by promoting a Ontario Retirement Pension Plan (later abandoned favour of Canada Pension reforms), and targeted middle-class voters with a $2.5 billion Jobs and Prosperity Fund, which directly channelled public money to private businesses in order to attract new investment. The Liberals also promised to balance the budget in 2017–18, although the details were not clear (Ontario 2014). Those promises were successful in improving Liberal party popularity and propelling Wynne back to government in the 2014 provincial election.

While Wynne's 2014 budget and the 2014 election campaign certainly suggested a change in tone from McGuinty, the government continued to walk a fine line between promoting private sector growth and appealing to a growing left-of-centre voter base that supported Wynne and her platform in 2014. That electoral division is well highlighted by the aggressive privatization agenda the party implemented in 2015. As part of its Jobs and Growth agenda, the government followed the advice of former group president and CEO of Toronto Dominion Bank Ed Clark, who was appointed head of the Premier's Advisory Council on Government Assets. Under Clark's direction, the council recommended further privatization of Hydro One in order to finance the construction of public infrastructure. The eventual sale and the resulting spike in electricity rates for Ontario consumers plagued the government after implementing one of the largest privatizations in Ontario history in 2015.

Alongside deeper privatization and public-private partnerships in skills training with private employers and universities, the Wynne Liberals' signature labour market policy was the creation of the Changing Workforce Review in 2015. In its early stages, the CWR was given the mandate to "consider the broader issues affecting the workplace and assess how the current labour and employment law framework addresses these trends and issues with a focus on the *Labour Relations Act* and the *Employment Standards Act*" (Ontario 2017, 3). Surprisingly, and notwithstanding a decade of activism by worker groups to raise the provincially mandated minimum wage, the CWR was not given the mandate to examine the provincial minimum wage.

In its final report, the CWR made several recommendations to overhaul the province's labour relations laws to reflect Ontario's changing labour market. Foremost among those recommendations to the

ESA was a fairly robust updating of employment standards, including changes to basic standards for part-time, casual, temporary, seasonal, and contract employees. In particular, the review called for limits on differential pay for various categories of employment, stating that "those who perform the work of comparable full-time employees should be paid the same accords with fairness and decency as it is grounded in equality of treatment" (Ontario 2017, 17). In addition, the CWR called for increased enforcement and access to justice for workers facing employer violations of the ESA, expanding access to personal emergency leave and paid sick days, while also clarifying and updating the definition of who is considered an employee and employer in the modern workplace. The CWR also called for eliminating many of the work exclusions from the OLRA (including those working as domestics, architectural, dental, land surveying, legal or medical workers, agricultural workers, and those employed in a professional capacity); toughening the remedies for employer misconduct during certification votes (all the while maintaining the mandatory voting process itself); opening the door for broader-based bargaining across multiple sectors; increasing remedial powers to the Ontario Labour Relations Board; and increasing legal protection for precarious workers' successor rights (Ontario 2017).

The Wynne government's response to the CWR report was Bill 148, the Fair Workplaces, Better Jobs Act, 2017. Bill 148's most prominent reform was the announcement that the government would raise the province's minimum wage from $11.60 per hour to $14 per hour in 2018 and $15.00 per hour in 2019. Although the government continued to allow for liquor servers, workers under eighteen, and those working from their homes to make less than the provincial minimum wage, Bill 148 represented a 22.7 per cent wage increase for thousands of workers. This change alone was interpreted by many as the most significant labour policy change of any government since the NDP changes in the early 1990s. While certainly a dramatic catch-up for many workers in the province, the wage change alone has to be interpreted within the context of two decades of Liberal inaction on this issue. Moreover, the impressive activism from numerous groups in Ontario – including the Fightfor$15 and Fairness campaign – certainly created the political space for the Liberals to respond.

Further changes in Bill 148 included many to the ESA that allowed for workers to access more holiday time and paid personal emergency time, mandated equal pay for equal work regardless of whether a worker is full time, part time, or temporary, and limited the ability of employers to misclassify employees as independent contractors. Additionally, Bill 148 made several changes to the OLRA, which included extending the remedial power of the OLRB to impose new units where the employer has violated the act and to consolidate units under a single employer, expanding the opportunity for first-contract arbitration, and broadening successor rights for unions. Bill 148 also extended card-check certification for the temporary agency industry, the building services sector, homecare, and community services. But these changes still did not reverse the Harris government's decision to eliminate card-check certification for all workers in the province. As such, it is unlikely to dramatically increase the possibility of workers accessing unionization outside of these sectors. Given the Liberal history on labour relations policy, it is not surprising that Bill 148 did not adopt the CWR's recommendation to adopt broader-based bargaining in the service industry; nor that it failed to go as far as the Rae NDP by introducing a ban on replacement workers during a strike.

CONCLUSION: DECLINE OF WORKERS' RIGHTS IN ONTARIO?

The neoliberalization of the Ontario state and policy regime has dramatically altered the province's labour market. The defeat of the NDP in 1995 altered the provincial state's relationship to the private sector and, in particular, repositioned Ontario's competitiveness as a low-cost, low tax zone for business. Both the Harris Conservatives and the McGuinty-Wynne Liberals have prioritized lean government and historically weaker labour laws than implemented by the Conservative governments in the Keynesian period, and have off-loaded responsibility for skills training onto individuals in order to grow the labour market. The results, however, have weakened worker protections, limited worker access to unionization, and reduced the possibility of most workers attaining full-time, permanent employment.

The changes ushered in under the OFB and JPC, or the privatization of important public assets by the Wynne Liberals, highlight the process of neoliberalization in Ontario. While the JPC mimicked many of the old themes from *People and Skills*, it included none of its formal attempts at incorporating workers and unions into the project. None of the 2012 recommendations included improving the quality of employment or worker protections in the OLRA and the ESA. While Bill 148 offers a much-needed update to the province's Employment Standards protection and raised the minimum wage, it cannot undo the transformations of Ontario employment policy implemented in the Harris years.

Notwithstanding these most recent reforms, the impact of the great recession in 2008 has been to make Ontario's labour market more flexible and precarious. Still, the province looked almost entirely to the private sector to drive the province's growth with policies that, even after Bill 148, prioritize the rights of employers over those of workers. In her time as premier Kathleen Wynne did not follow McGuinty's overt policies to erode the rights and living conditions of the province's working people, or McGuinty's use of the state to discipline public workers resisting his 2012 austerity budget. But her reforms continued to support private sector competitiveness while modestly increasing state protections of workplace standards and the capacity of unions to contest employer power in the province. Wynne's defeat in the 2018 election will test the delicate balance that the Liberals attempted to craft between private sector competitiveness and many of the half-measure reforms designed to protect workers. Because many of the workers' groups were never able to fully embrace the Liberals' competitiveness project, they are not fully committed to protecting it. The legacy of McGuinty-Wynne's reforms may indeed be similar to those of the Peterson-Rae reforms after 1995 under Harris: a full-on assault of all workers' protections by the authoritarian populism of a new Conservative premier.

After fifteen years of Liberal government, Ontario's labour market is still plagued by the same problems that existed in the 1980s: low productivity rates, weak skills training, and a decline in well-paid, value-added jobs. The goal of the neoliberal employment policies pursued by both the Conservatives and the Liberals (and partially accepted by the NDP) is to maintain low business and personal income taxes while weakening workers' protections, suppressing wages, downloading education costs to workers, and making union organization more difficult. Thus far, the strategy of market-led development – of ever-lower taxes, public sector austerity, and lean and flexible workplaces – has not reversed the long-term weaknesses of the Ontario economy. Despite this reality, the Ford Conservatives will likely be undeterred in their stubborn commitment to cut taxes while slashing government programs, all to balance the provincial budget. Unless new forms of collective power can be found in workplaces and in politics to resist the forthcoming Conservative assault, the rights and lives of workers will increasingly be precarious as government continues to prioritize corporate competitiveness.

NOTES

1 Council membership consisted of a cross-section of Ontario's businesses, including leading members of industry, manufacturing, and public utilities. There were also administrators from Ontario universities and three prominent union leaders.
2 These groups represented the largest companies in Ontario: Ford Motor Company, Chrysler, General Motors, Goodyear, Imperial Oil, IBM, McDonald's Restaurants, Brewers' Retail, Canada Trust, Coca Cola Beverages, Labatt Breweries of Canada, and hundreds of others.
3 Earlier anti-scab provisions had proposed eliminating employers' right to move personnel from other plants during a legal strike or lockout.
4 Secret ballot certification weakens the ability of unions to launch successful organizing drives because employers have time to organize anti-union campaigns.
5 Statistics Canada, *Labour Force Survey Estimates*, table 2820074. The data is for: Ontario, wages of employees by job permanence, union coverage, sex and age group, annually (current dollars unless specified). Accessed 3 February 2018.
6 Statistics Canada, *Low Income Cut-Offs before and after Tax by Community and Family Size, 2011 Constant Dollars*, table 202-0801. Accessed 3 February 2018.
7 The purposive clause of the Ontario Labour Relations Act (1995), Sched. A., s. 2. reads:
> The following are the purposes of the Act: 1) To facilitate collective bargaining between employers and trade unions that are the freely-

designated representatives of the employees. 2) To recognize the importance of workplace parties adapting to change. 3) To promote flexibility, productivity and employee involvement in the workplace. 4) To encourage communication between employers and employees in the workplace. 5) To recognize the importance of economic growth as the foundation for mutually beneficial relations amongst employers, employees and trade unions. 6) To encourage co-operative participation of employers and trade unions in resolving workplace issues. 7) To promote the expeditious resolution of workplace disputes.

8 The Working Families Coalition is a group of unions that attempt to organize to defeat the Conservatives in Ontario. The coalition consists of large public and private sector unions, including the Canadian Auto Workers, Services Employees International Union, Ontario Nurses Association, and the United Food and Commercial Workers Union. While the coalition is not aligned with any particular party, it advocated for "strategic voting," which was interpreted as a tacit endorsement of the Liberals in key ridings (Savage 2012).

REFERENCES

Albo, Gregory. 2010. "'The New Economy' and Capitalism Today." In *Interrogating the New Economy: Restructuring Work in the 21st Century*, edited by Noreen Pupo and Mark P. Thomas. Toronto: University of Toronto Press.

Bradford, Neil. 1998. "Prospects for Associative Governance: Lessons from Ontario, Canada." *Politics and Society* 26 (4).

Brownsey, Keith, and Michael Howlett. 1992. "Ontario: Class Structure and Political Alliances in an Industrialized Society." In *The Provincial State: Politics in Canada's Provinces and Territories*, edited by Keith Brownsey and Michael Howlett. Toronto: Copp Clark Pitman.

Canadian Centre for Policy Alternatives. 2007. *Ontario Alternative Budget, No Time to Lose: An Action Blueprint for Ontario*. www.policyalternatives.ca.

Canadian Federation of Students – Ontario. 2013. *Changing Priorities: Moving Towards Affordable Post-Secondary Education*. http://cfsontario.ca/downloads/CFS-ChangingPriorities-En.pdf.

Carrothers, A.W.R., E.E. Palmer, and W.B. Rayner. 1986. *Collective Bargaining Law in Canada*. 2nd ed. Toronto: Butterworths.

Carter, Donald, Geoffrey England, Brian Etherington, and Gilles Trudeau, eds. 2002. *Labour Law in Canada*, 5th ed. Markham: Butterworths.

Crow, Dan, and Greg Albo. 2005. "Neo-Liberalism, NAFTA, and the State of the North American Labour Movements." *Just Labour* 6 and 7.

Doucet, Michael J. 2004. "Ontario Universities, the Double Cohort, and the Maclean's Rankings: The Legacy of the Harris/Eves Years, 1995–2003." *Ontario*

Confederation of University Faculty Associations Research Report. http://ocufa.on.ca/.

Drummond, Robert J. 1983. "Ontario 1980." In *The Canadian Annual Review of Politics and Public Affairs*, edited by R.B. Byers. Toronto: University of Toronto Press.

Dyck, Rand. 1991. *Provincial Politics in Canada*. 2nd ed. Toronto: Prentice-Hall.

Evans, Bryan, and Charles W. Smith. 2015. "The Transformation of Ontario Politics: The Long Assent of Neoliberalism." In *Transforming Provincial Politics: The Political Economy of Canada's Provinces and Territories in the Neoliberal Era*, edited by Bryan Evans and Charles W. Smith. Toronto: University of Toronto Press.

Foot, D.K. 1974. *Provincial Public Finance in Ontario: An Empirical Analysis of the Last Twenty-Five Years*. Toronto: University of Toronto Press.

Fudge, Judy, and Eric Tucker. 2000. "Pluralism or Fragmentation?: The Twentieth Century Employment Law Regime in Canada." *Labour/Le Travail* 46.

Fudge, Judy, and Leah F. Vosko. 2003. "Gender Paradoxes and the Rise of Contingent Work: Towards a Transformative Political Economy of the Labour Market." In *Changing Canada: Political Economy as Transformation*, edited by W. Clement and L.F. Vosko. Montreal: McGill-Queen's University Press.

Gertler, Meric S. 1995. "Grouping Towards Reflexivity: Responding to Industrial Change in Ontario." In *The Rise of the Rustbelt*, edited by P. Cooke. London: University College London Press.

Gindin, Sam. 2013. "Rethinking Unions, Registering Socialism." In *The Question of Strategy: Socialist Register 2013*, edited by L. Panitch, G. Albo, and V. Chibber. London: Merlin.

Haddow, Rodney, and Thomas Klassen. 2006. *Partisanship, Globalization, and Canadian Labour Market Policy: Four Provinces in Comparative Perspective*. Toronto: University of Toronto Press.

Harvey, David. 2005. *A Brief History of Neoliberalism*. Oxford: Oxford University Press.

Jain, Harish C., and S. Muthuchidambaram. 1995. *Ontario Labour Law Reform: A History and Evaluation of Bill 40*. Kingston: Queen's University Industrial Relations Centre.

– 1996. "Ontario Labour Law Reforms: A Comparative Study of Bill 40 and Bill 7." *Canadian Labour and Employment Law Journal* 4.

Langille, Brian A. 1991. "Canadian Labour Law Reform and Free Trade." *Ottawa Law Review* 21 (3).

Langille, David. 1987. "The Business Council on National Issues and the Canadian State." *Studies in Political Economy* 24.

Law Commission of Ontario. 2012. *Vulnerable Workers and Precarious Work*. http://lco-cdo.org/en/vulnerable-workers.

MacDermid, Robert. 1995. *Funding the Common Sense Revolutionaries: Contributions to the Progressive Conservative Party of Ontario*. Toronto: Centre for Social Justice.

MacDermid, Robert, and Greg Albo. 2001. "Divided Province, Growing Protests: Ontario Moves Right." In *The Provincial State in Canada: Politics in the Provinces and Territories*, 2nd ed., edited by K. Brownsey and M. Howlett. Toronto: Broadview.

Mackenzie, Hugh. 2004. "Funding Postsecondary Education in Ontario: Beyond the Path of Least Resistance." *Study Commissioned by the Ontario Coalition for Postsecondary Education*. http://ocufa.on.ca/wordpress/assets/funding_postsecondary.pdf.

Mackie, Richard. 1992. "The Board Could Assist Such Companies by Limiting Picketing." *Globe and Mail*, 1 October.

McInnis, Peter S. 2002. *Harnessing Labour Confrontation: Shaping the Postwar Settlement in Canada, 1943–1950*. Toronto: University of Toronto Press.

Moody, Kim. 1997. *Workers in a Lean World: Unions in the International Economy*. London: Verso.

O'Grady, John. 1992. "Beyond the Wagner Act, What Then?" In *Getting on Track: Social Democratic Strategies for Ontario*, edited by Daniel Drache. Montreal: McGill-Queen's University Press.

Ontario. 1986. *Ontario Statistics*. Toronto: Ministry of Treasury and Economics.

– 1988. *Competing in the New Global Economy: Report of the Premier's Council, Volumes I and II*. Toronto: Queen's Printer for Ontario.

– 1990. *People and Skills in the New Global Economy: Report of the Premier's Council Volume III*. Toronto: Queen's Printer for Ontario.

– 1991a. *Plant Closures, Layoffs and Labour Adjustment Policy*. Toronto: Ministry of Labour.

– 1991b. *Proposed Reform of the Ontario Labour Relations Act: A Discussion Paper from the Ministry of Labour*. Toronto: Ministry of Labour.

– 1991c. *Reform of the Labour Relations Act, Cabinet Submission by Robert Mackenzie, Minister of Labour*. Toronto: Ministry of Labour

– 1992. *An Industrial Policy Framework for Ontario*. Toronto: Ministry of Industry, Trade and Technology.

– 1994. *Ontario Economic Outlook, 1994–1998*. Toronto: Ministry of Finance.

– 1995. *Ontario Fiscal Overview and Spending Cuts*. Toronto: Ministry of Finance.

– 1999. *Ontario Economic Outlook and Fiscal Review, 1999*. Toronto: Ministry of Finance.

– 2004. *Ontario Outlook and Fiscal Review 2004*. Toronto: Ministry of Finance.

– 2005a. *Ontario: A Leader in Learning (Rae Commission)*. Toronto: Queen's Printer for Ontario.

– 2005b. *Ontario Budget Speech 2005: Investing in People, Strengthening our Economy*. Toronto: Ministry of Finance.

– 2007. *Ontario Economic Outlook and Economic Review*. Toronto: Ministry of Finance.

– 2008a. *Ontario Budget: Growing a Stronger Ontario*. Toronto: Ministry of Finance.

– 2008b. *Ontario Economic Outlook and Economic Review*. Toronto: Ministry of Finance.
– 2009. *Ontario Budget: Confronting the Challenge; Building Our Economic Future*. Toronto: Ministry of Finance.
– 2012a. *Advantage Ontario: Report of Ontario Jobs and Prosperity Council*. Toronto: Ministry of Research and Innovation.
– 2012b. *Commission on the Reform of Ontario's Public Services*. Toronto: Ontario Ministry of Finance.
– 2012c. *Economic Outlook and Economic Review*. Toronto: Ministry of Finance.
– 2014. *Building Opportunity, Securing Our Future*. Toronto: Ministry of Finance.
– 2017. *The Changing Workplaces Review: An Agenda for Workplace Rights*. Toronto: Ministry of Labour.
Ontario Liberal Party. 2003. *Choose Change*. Toronto: OLP.
Ontario New Democratic Party. 1990. *An Agenda for the People*. Toronto: ONDP.
Palmer, Bryan D. 1991. *Working Class Experience: Rethinking the History of Canadian Labour, 1800–1991*. Toronto: McClelland and Stewart.
Panitch, Leo, and Donald Swartz. 2003. *From Consent to Coercion: The Assault on Trade Union Freedoms*. Toronto: Garamond.
Peck, Jamie. 2010. *Constructions of Neoliberal Reason*. Oxford: Oxford University Press.
Peirce, Jon. 2003. *Canadian Industrial Relations*. Toronto: Pearson.
Poverty and Employment Precarity in Southern Ontario (PEPSO). 2013. *It's More than Poverty: Employment Precarity and Household Well-being*. http://pepso.ca/.
Rea, K.J. 1985. *The Prosperous Years: The Economic History of Ontario, 1939–1975*. Toronto: University of Toronto Press.
Russell, Bob. 1995. "Labour's Magna Carta? Wagnerism in Canada at Fifty." In *Labour Gains, Labour Pains: 50 Years of PC 1003*, edited by Cy Gonick, Paul Phillips, and Jesse Vorst. Halifax: Fernwood.
Savage, Larry. 2012. "Organized Labour and the Politics of Strategic Voting." In *Rethinking the Politics of Labour in Canada*, edited by Stephanie Ross and Larry Savage. Halifax: Fernwood.
Schenk, Christopher. 1995. "Fifty Years After PC 1003: The Need for New Directions." In *Labour Gains, Labour Pains: 50 Years of PC 1003*, edited by Cy Gonick, Paul Phillips, and Jesse Vorst. Halifax: Fernwood.
Schwartz, Kristin. 2009. "The Successful Campaign for a $10 Minimum Wage." *Labour/Le Travail* 64.
Slinn, Sara. 2003. "The Effect of Compulsory Certification Votes on Certification Applications in Ontario: An Empirical Analysis." *Canadian Labour and Employment Law Journal* 10.
Smith, Charles W. 2009. "'Fairness and Balance?': The Politics of Ontario's Labour Relations Regime, 1949–1963." PhD diss., York University.

Statistics Canada. 2018a. *Labour Force Survey, Supplementary Unemployment Rates*. Cansim Series 282-0086. Ottawa: Statistics Canada.
– 2018b. *Labour Force Survey, Employees by Union Coverage*. Cansim Series 282-0078. Ottawa: Statistics Canada.
– 2018c. *Labour Force Survey, Employees by Job Permanency*. Cansim Series 282-0080. Ottawa: Statistics Canada.
– 2018d. *Number of Unionized Workers, Employees and Union Density*. Cansim Series 279-0025. Ottawa: Statistics Canada.
– 2018e. *Survey of Employment, Payroll and Hours*. Cansim Series 281-0042 and 281-0051. Ottawa: Statistics Canada.
Swartz, Donald, and Rosemary Warskett. 2012. "Contextualizing Labour and Working-Class Politics: Canadian Labour and the Crisis of Solidarity." In *Rethinking the Politics of Labour in Canada*, edited by S. Ross and L. Savage. Halifax: Fernwood.
Teeple, Gary. 2004. *Globalization and the Decline of Social Reform: Into the Twenty-First Century*. Toronto: Garamond.
Thomas, Mark. 2009. *Regulating Flexibility: The Political Economy of Employment Standards*. Montreal: McGill-Queen's University Press.
Vosko, Leah. 2010. "A New Approach to Regulating Temporary Agency Work in Ontario or Back to the Future." *Relations Industrielles/Industrial Relations* 65.
Vosko, Leah F., Eric Tucker, Mark P. Thomas, and Mary Gellatly. 2011. *New Approaches to Enforcement and Compliance with Labour Regulatory Standards: The Case of Ontario, Canada*. Law Commission of Ontario. http://www.lco-cdo.org.
Watson, Steve. 2007. "Struggling Against the Poverty in Ontario." *Relay* 17.
Wolfe, David A. 1997. "Institutional Limits to Labour Market Reform in Ontario: The Short Life and Rapid Demise of the Ontario Training and Adjustment Board." In *Social Partnerships for Training: Canada's Experiment with Labour Force Development Boards*, edited by A. Sharpe and R. Haddow. Kingston: Queen's University School of Policy Studies.
Wolfe, David, and Meric Gertler. 2001. "Globalization and Economic Restructuring in Ontario: From Industrial Heartland to Learning Region?" *European Planning Studies* 9 (5).
Woolstencroft, Peter. 1997. "More than a Guard Change: Politics in the New Ontario." In *Revolution at Queen's Park*, edited by Sid Noel. Toronto: Lorimer.

PART THREE

Consolidating the Neoliberal Policy Regime in Ontario

| 10 |

Poverty Policy in Ontario: You Can't Eat Good Intentions

PETER GRAEFE AND
CAROL-ANNE HUDSON

Ontario is a province with a poverty problem. For more than two decades, the province has tried to find a competitive advantage in being a high-quality, low-cost manufacturing platform in North America, and has looked to the private service sector to soak up excess labour supply. The provincial state is therefore hesitant to improve working conditions at the low end of the labour market for fear of limiting service sector growth or of putting cost pressure on a cost-sensitive manufacturing sector. The result is a labour market that fails to provide basic economic security and above-poverty living standards for many workers (MacDermid and Albo 2001). Even in the "good years" of the late 1990s and early 2000s, poverty levels crept upwards (table 10.1).[1]

The argument that those who work should do better than those who don't is then used to justify a threadbare set of social assistance programmes that keep recipients well below the poverty line and in need of additional assistance to maintain bare subsistence. Organizations like food banks, for example, originally conceived in the 1980s as solutions to temporary crises of hunger, have become institutionalized as parts of a permanent food system for dealing with the chronic cycles of hunger experienced by those on social assistance and in low wage jobs. With Ontario Works rates in 2017–18 set at $721 a month for a single person, basic survival requires food banks. Yet imagine the community time, resources, and capacity that would be freed up for other uses if social assistance rates allowed recipients to buy their own food.

There is some knowledge of the costs of poverty in terms of foregone human potential, as well as additional social costs in areas like health

Table 10.1 | Ontario labour market and poverty trends, 1985–2018

	Unemployment rate	Employment rate	% of population on social assistance	% of persons in low income (Low Income Measure, after-tax)
1985	7.9	63.0	5.1	8.8
1989	5.0	66.5	6.0	7.1
1993	10.9	59.4	12.4	9.1
1995	8.7	59.7	11.3	9.5
1996	9.0	59.6	10.3	10.9
1997	8.4	60.2	9.8	10.5
1998	7.2	61.2	8.1	10.6
1999	6.3	62.3	7.1	10.0
2000	5.7	63.2	6.0	10.1
2001	6.3	63.0	5.7	9.9
2002	7.2	62.9	5.5	10.9
2003	6.9	63.7	5.4	10.9
2004	6.8	63.7	5.3	12.3
2005	6.6	63.3	5.4	11.7
2006	6.3	63.2	5.4	13.1
2007	6.4	63.4	5.4	13.0
2008	6.5	63.5	5.6	12.9
2009	9.0	61.1	6.2	13.7
2010	8.7	61.3	6.4	13.3
2011	7.8	61.6	6.5	13.2
2012	7.8	61.3	6.5	14.5
2013	7.6	61.2	6.5	14.2
2014	7.3	61.0	6.5	13.8
2015	6.8	60.8	6.6	14.3
2016	6.5	60.7	6.6	13.7
2017	6.0		6.7	

Source: Statistics Canada (2018a, 2018b), CANSIM table 282-0002 and 206-0041.

and corrections. The Ontario Association of Food Banks has pegged the annual cost of poverty at between 5.5 and 6.6 per cent of the gross provincial product (GPP) or about $40 billion in 2011 (OAFB 2008). A more conservative analysis of the cost of poverty in Toronto in 2016 found a cost of $4.4 to $5.5 billion for the city alone (Briggs, Lee, and Stapleton 2016). Given such knowledge, the failure of existing policy to reduce poverty and the disinterest of politicians to try new approaches must reflect the ability of actors who benefit from the status quo to block change. This chapter surveys the last quarter-century of poverty policy in Ontario, paying particular attention to the return of poverty as an important policy issue in the past decade. A full account would require tracing the various policy actors involved in specific initiatives, which we have started to do elsewhere (Hudson and Graefe 2011). In this chapter, we will focus on ideas in order to capture changes in policy thinking around poverty, and to assess how successful these have been in navigating Ontario's neoliberal political context.

In the early 2000s, poverty policy moved beyond the emphasis on social assistance and workfare to take up themes of child poverty, on the one hand, and in-work poverty, on the other; these themes were taken up in varying respects in the provincial poverty reduction strategy of 2008. Nevertheless, the tangible policy content of this strategy was weak, and both the strategy and its 2013 follow-up were largely buried to make way for the post-recession austerity agenda. Overall, there have been shifts over the past decade that open opportunities for addressing the province's poverty problem. But to date, these opportunities have rarely pushed against the limits of neoliberal budgetary and labour market policies, let alone transformed them. The 2016–17 decisions to increase the minimum wage to $14 in 2018, to launch a Basic Income Pilot, and to convene a new working group for improving income security indicate some willingness to test the boundaries of neoliberal poverty policy, although much caution is needed to separate the hype from tangible changes.

POVERTY POLICY IN CONTEMPORARY ONTARIO

The politics of poverty policy in Ontario have not been subject to much academic scrutiny since the 1990s. The general story has been one of the transformation of social assistance policy towards workfare as part of the neoliberal transformation of Ontario. The "villain" here is the post-1995 Conservative government, which cut social assistance rates by 21 per cent upon taking office, changed regulations and tightened their enforcement in order to push recipients off social assistance (and keep others from applying), and introduced stronger mechanisms to push recipients (and especially the heads of lone parent families) into the labour market (Little 2001; Herd and Mitchell 2003). These accounts came as an immediate response to the Conservatives' changes in the 1995–97 period, and tended to treat the neoliberal rhetoric and ambitions of the government as reality, as opposed to appraising the net effects on an administratively complex programme. While important administrative changes were made, which in many cases channel policy thinking and delivery to this day, there is evidence of a softening of delivery in some policy areas over time, either because the irrationalities of the new system became clear, or as the result of municipal actors bending the rules to meet other, arguably progressive, ends (Marquardt 2007). That is not to ignore the short-term effects of caseload cuts and the active disentitlement of social assistance recipients through what some have termed "rituals of degradation" in the application process (Herd et al. 2005), nor the very material deprivation created by the 20 per cent cut to benefits in 1995.

The impact of further changes under the McGuinty and Wynne Liberals following their return to power in 2003 has not been greatly explored, even if partisan differences seemed to signal changes to social assistance policies in the preceding decade (Klassen and Buchanan 2006). The few analyses of that government's social policy directions that have been published often continue to characterize its policies as neoliberal (Hackworth 2008; Coulter 2009). In this reading, the Liberals are consolidating neoliberalism – while they may not be pushing for an extension of that project, they have the trust of many progressive social actors and can therefore embed neoliberal rules without great social opposition.

TAKING NEOLIBERALISM OUT OF THE CENTRE OF THE FRAME

There are a couple of dangers in making neoliberalism central to the analysis. First, there is the potential to flatten all policy under the label of neoliberalism, thereby missing the variety of policies in contention. At least at the level of problem identification and policy discourse, we have seen the emergence across the post-industrial economies of the idea of social investment to enable individuals to take and manage risks in a knowledge economy (Banting 2006), even to the extent that some speak of a *social investment state*, although the degree of its realization in Canada remains questionable (Jenson 2012; Mahon 2008). Still, the design of social policy programs remains important, both in terms of how well – or poorly – people live under neoliberalism, and in terms of potentials for challenging or transcending neoliberalism.

A second danger is to put undue causal influence on neoliberalism, as opposed to the influence of more general characteristics of capitalism, or of the long-run institutionalization of that capitalism in Ontario, in explaining policies. Poverty is an endemic feature of capitalist societies for several reasons: the tendency of capitalist labour markets to distribute income unequally; unemployment being a normal condition of capitalist labour markets; the imperative for firms to compete acting as a downward pressure on wages; and the lack of claims to income for those unable to work or who must withdraw from the labour market to care for others.[2] The actual shape of poverty in specific societies nevertheless varies based on the specific institutionalization of capitalism. Poverty is a contradictory feature in capitalism: it can be seen favourably by capitalists in that it places downward pressure on wages and produces a disciplined and compliant labour force (as the risk of job loss is felt more acutely); yet it is also problematic in suppressing the purchasing power of those in poverty, and in entailing social costs, be they in degraded skills, poor health, or policing. In Ontario, absent strong unions and left parties to push the debate on poverty within capitalism towards these more collective concerns, poverty policy thinking has revolved around questions of labour discipline: how can one sustain the poor without removing the work incentive for those in low pay? This has been compounded by the strategic positioning of Ontario as a low-cost manufacturing platform in North America, which again dampens possibilities of increasing wages and redistributing income as this would undermine the competitiveness of firms. Poverty policy in Ontario has always been highly stigmatizing and emphasized pushing people into the low end of the labour market. Neoliberalism may involve strengthening these features, or changing the categories of who is expected to take any job, but this means understanding its impact in conjunction with these more general factors. We, therefore, prefer to tease out the emergent tendencies in thinking about poverty policy over the past decade, and to consider how they are both enabled and blocked by neoliberal statecraft. The point is to relate policy to the neoliberal context – not to label it as neoliberal (or non-neoliberal), but to see how policy ideas are mobilized to extend neoliberalism, or compensate for some of its social and economic consequences, or to build towards alternative models of capitalism.

As such, in this chapter we are analytically closer to authors like Mahon and Macdonald who see an incipient "inclusive liberalism" or at least an "intrusive liberalism" in recent policy departures (Mahon and Macdonald 2010). For these authors, liberal welfare states like Ontario's reflect the influence of a variety of liberalisms. In the current context, the neoliberalism of the late 1990s has been challenged by an "inclusive liberalism" that returns to some of the developmental aspects of liberalism in order to elaborate a thicker understanding of equality of opportunity as requiring public policies around human capital formation, especially during childhood. This challenge has also opened slivers of opportunity to a more social democratic vision where poverty is combatted through intervening in labour markets and extending rights to income and services such as housing, child care, and transportation. Unlike Mahon and Macdonald, however, our goal is more descriptive than theoretical: rather than trying to establish that poverty policy is neoliberal or inclusive liberal, we work at a lower level of abstraction, sketching out some projects and noting their fit with the broader political-economic environment.

POVERTY AND POLICY IN ONTARIO UNDER HARRIS

Ontario is often classified as a "liberal welfare state," meaning that welfare is meant to flow firstly from earnings in the market and secondarily from family support. Social policies only kick in as a last-resort safety net when markets and families fail. This means that programmes like social assistance and housing are aimed at the very poor and generally are meagre so as to not improve the conditions of recipients above those of people at the bottom end of the labour market. Given the tradition of weak regulation of wages and labour standards at the low end of the labour market (Thomas 2009), it has been difficult to improve this minimum without creating horizontal hostilities between people on social assistance and people working for poverty-level wages. Through the late 1980s, however, the issue of poverty came to the fore in discussions of how to reform the social assistance programme, and led the

1985–1990 Peterson Liberal government to embrace a positive vision of enhancing the rights of social assistance recipients to adequate benefits and supports (housing, transportation, anti-violence, child care), and of providing supportive pathways to greater social participation (particularly but not exclusively through job training and placement). To the extent that the latter became centred on supporting recipients in moving into paid work, some high-profile members of the business community were willing to back this vision.

The Conservative government led by Mike Harris came to power in 1995 on a distinctly neoliberal platform and worldview. The government rejected the positive vision, but did embrace the goal of pushing social assistance recipients into work. This fit with the idea that social assistance created individual dependency on the state, and thus created disincentives to work. This view had been shared by the preceding NDP government in its thinking around social assistance, although the solution for the NDP was to provide at least some state supports (training, child care, transportation) to aid individuals in making the transition to the labour market. For the Conservatives, levels of entitlement to state benefits and the supply of public goods needed to be cut in order to provide individuals with the proper incentives and to reduce state expenditure.

To get there, existing provisions had to be rolled back or dismantled. Restructuring Ontario's social safety net began within thirty days of the installation of the Harris Conservatives. In July 1995, $2 billion was eliminated from government social spending. In October welfare rates were cut by 21.6 per cent, the construction of 17,000 non-profit housing spaces was cancelled, and many labour laws designed to protect unionized and striking workers were eliminated. The minimum wage was frozen at $6.85 and remained frozen until the Conservatives lost the 2003 election. Finally, in January 1997, the full costs for social housing, public transit, water, sewers, some highways, and responsibility for workfare were off-loaded to municipalities, placing disproportionate costs on cities with higher rates of poverty (Mocovitch 1997; Costoglu 1996). From 1996 to 1998, the existing social assistance legislation (the General Welfare Assistance and the Family Benefits Act) was rewritten to create Ontario Works and the Ontario Disability Support Program. Ontario Works included adopting new technologies to process social assistance recipients, including making it harder to apply and qualify for benefits, as well as developing greater capacity to subcontract their employability training (Herd et al. 2005; Marquardt 2007).

What is specifically "neoliberal" in this transition is not always clearly argued: below poverty-level rates, the stigmatization of recipients, and a strong push towards the labour market are all long-term features of social assistance in Ontario. The neoliberal twist was twofold. First, it ratcheted up labour market discipline through a 21 per cent cut in social assistance rates, put additional emphasis on labour force attachment (through new administrative procedures, but also by expecting mothers of young children to take paid work once their children turned two years old), and tightened eligibility. If you were without means and without work, social assistance was now harder to receive and would leave you well below basic subsistence levels. Second, while discussions of poverty in the 1980s tended to focus on social assistance, they also looked outward to the necessity of expanding a basket of social rights (transportation, child care, housing, anti-violence) on the one hand, and improved conditions at the bottom end of the labour market (minimum wages, employment standards) on the other. The reforms to social assistance in the late 1990s reduced the issue of poverty to social assistance, ignoring social rights and labour standards, as these interfered with budgetary austerity and labour market flexibility.

As the Harris government moved into a second term in office, this program became less coherent. The neoliberal zeal for labour market discipline gave way at times to a moralistic stance of policing and stigmatizing the poor, for instance through drug testing social assistance recipients. In cities like Ottawa and Toronto, responsibility for local delivery provided opportunities to blunt the full force of proposed reforms (e.g., Marquardt 2007). In addition, the government found it harder to use rhetoric to hide the fact that its policies were not containing poverty or maintaining social cohesion. For instance, food bank usage increased by 40 per cent and poverty was on the rise. Despite an improving economy, provincial poverty rates climbed steadily through the 1990s, peaking in 1998 (Finnie et al. 2004; National Council of Welfare 2000).

While much of the provincial debate on poverty had been centred on the social assistance program, the disconnect between falling social assistance caseloads and steady or rising poverty rates (see table 10.1) pushed the debate in two directions, namely in-work poverty and child poverty. By the end of the 1990s a burgeoning class of working poor was beginning to put pressure on the social state, including many welfare-leavers trapped in low-income work (HRDC 2000; Frenette and Picot 2003; Workers Action Centre 2006). The Conservative government had devised policies compelling people into the workforce. Yet many full-time workers were not able to sustain themselves or their dependents, largely because of workplace barriers like the structure of taxes and transfers, and the high cost of quality child care and transportation that exceeded the income of minimum wage workers (Maxwell 2002). The decision to keep the minimum wage frozen at $6.85 contributed to this outcome.

The issue of poverty also took on a child focus in light of the *Early Years Study* (McCain and Mustard 1999), which highlighted the importance of brain development in young children, and the high cumulative cost across the life course where programmes were not in place to support this, particularly for disadvantaged groups. This also presented a challenge to the government, as inaction on poverty threatened to have significant social *and economic* costs from foregone human capital. On child poverty, as with the working poor, there was a space for developing new interventions. As these touched on questions of human capital formation and labour market supply, they also pointed to the possibility of enlisting certain sectors of the business community in reform efforts. However, they broached the issue of poverty in a way that consciously bypassed the question of what to do with social assistance.

SETTING A NEW AGENDA FOR CHANGE?

These new possibilities, especially around child poverty, were further developed in the Panel on the Role of Government (2004) established by the Conservatives in 2002 to examine the future role of government in developing communities and promoting economic growth. The panel's report, *Investing in People: Creating a Human Capital Society for Ontario*, conceived of "human capital" in a broad sense to ensure that all members of society had the opportunity to contribute economically. Sustained growth in the new knowledge-based economy, they contended, required creating educational opportunities for all Ontarians to ensure full economic participation.

The panel's recommendations included increased spending for public services, many with an early learning focus: establishing full-day junior and senior kindergarten with free lunchtime and afterschool care; developing high quality early childhood education services; expanding licensed daycares and nurseries; increasing the stock of social housing and affordable rentals; and significantly expanding educational and skills training programs for those transitioning from welfare to work. For social assistance, the panel emphasized maintaining levels of income supports with adequate annual increases until quality transition programs were well established. This included post-employment supports such as child care, transportation, education and training, saving incentives, wage supplements, and tax credits. Underlying these recommendations was research arguing that Ontario's public policies were out of touch with "new social risks" such as in-work poverty and the care burden facing those families in which every adult was in the labour force. The panel nevertheless leaned more towards investing in education and maintaining income security than in proposing minimum wage and labour market regulation policy that might more aggressively confront working poverty.

This renewal of thinking about poverty could also be seen in parts of the business community who considered that their broader competitiveness depended on maintaining social cohesion and on ensuring the upgrading of the labour force's human capital. For instance, the Toronto City Summit Alliance (TCSA, now CivicAction), an organization of leading business people, proposed that income security reform and reducing income inequality were essential to addressing Toronto's competitiveness (TCSA 2003). In a similar vein, TD Economics (2005) argued for more decisive action on the erosion of income supplements for working age adults. Its concern arose from the poor employment outcomes of welfare-to-work programs and the need to bring all working age adults into the workforce as quickly as possible but in a manner that kept them there. It argued for a much more comprehensive approach to tackling welfare and poverty in general, including: a dramatic increase in asset limits; a working supplement and refundable tax credit for all low-income persons; the completion of the National

Child Benefit program; and finally, employment insurance reform. The sharp rollback in unemployment benefits and eligibility had left many unemployed with no recourse but to turn to social assistance.

Much of this program was repeated by the TCSA's task force, which in 2006 produced the *Modernizing Income Security for Working-Age Adults* (MISWAA) report. Established in 2004, the task force had representatives from business, unions, universities, advocacy groups, government, and income security experts. It developed recommendations for creating a more equitable income transfer system and for more effectively reducing barriers to employment, including: regular increases to the minimum wage beginning in 2007; the implementation of an integrated child benefit platform for all low-income parents; the provision of basic prescription drugs, vision care, and dental coverage to low-income workers; the strengthening of employment standards; updating employment standards to cover new forms of work; increasing asset limits for social assistance recipients; improving employment supports, training, and upgrading for recipients and low-income workers; and uploading social assistance from the municipalities to the province.

In sum, at the pivot point between the end of the Conservative government and the first years of the McGuinty Liberal government, a coherent social policy discourse that brought together social democratic and liberal social policy thinkers with reformist elements of the business community was developing around the problems of child poverty and the working poor. Our interviews also suggest that business and community actors bearing this vision had significant access to the Premier's Office, and shaped the thinking and outlook of the McGuinty government (see Hudson and Graefe 2012). However, it is one thing to observe big-picture changes in the thinking about social policy, and another to actually reform or transform policies in a manner consistent with that thinking.

POVERTY POLICY UNDER McGUINTY

The post-2003 McGuinty government was in no rush to undertake rapid changes in social assistance or poverty policy more broadly. Politically, it feared doing anything that would allow the Conservatives to mobilize the anti-welfare backlash that had helped elect Harris in 1995. Moreover, continuity in economic policy, relying on a low-wage private service sector to soak up excess labour supply, militated against moves on social assistance rates or minimum wages. This was especially the case as a rising Canadian dollar began to undercut Ontario's manufacturing cost competitiveness and cause job loss. McGuinty's initial Throne Speech and budget were virtually silent on social assistance and poverty. The provincial budgets did increase rates at roughly the rate of inflation, and passed through incremental increases in the National Child Benefit to social assistance recipients, but did nothing else to fill in the erosion from the Harris years. The government commissioned a review of employment assistance programs for social assistance and disability recipients, whose 2004 report made two broad recommendations: (1) changes within the welfare-to-work program could be made without cost to the taxpayer; and (2) eliminating poverty must be done outside welfare. Specifically, the review suggested that eligibility rules be simplified and non-punitive; that participants be allowed to supplement their incomes without penalty as they transition to full-time work; and that skills training be expanded to include the development of life skills such as budgeting and parenting (Matthews 2004). Although this review did not recommend new funding, it did signal a change in philosophy away from the assumption that people on welfare need to be carefully watched and dragged into the labour market, and towards the idea that recipients want to have meaningful lives and will choose to work if given the necessary assistance.

In response to this review, new rules were introduced in 2005, including earnings exemptions that lowered the tax-back rate on employment income to 50 per cent from 75–100 per cent. Drug and dental benefits were also extended for recipients leaving welfare. Rules that punished recipients who were living with or receiving some supports from family were eliminated. On child poverty and working poverty, progress was slow but more substantial: the freeze on the minimum wage was lifted in 2004, with rates rising from $6.85 to $8.75 in 2008; an Ontario Child Benefit for all low-income Ontarians to match the Federal National Child Benefit came online in 2008; and the province started to implement full-day learning for four- and five-year-olds. Nevertheless, it made for a first mandate (2003–07) with little substantial progress on poverty, and provided an opening for the NDP to win two by-elections (in Parkdale-High Park in 2006 and York South Weston in 2007) on "working income issues," especially the minimum wage.

Poverty policy activists saw these by-election results as an opening to push the government further. They carefully nurtured their back channels to policy advisors in the McGuinty Cabinet, which had been loosely established in the early years of the Liberals' mandate. In May 2007, a number of City of Toronto officials joined with several organizations (including the Ontario Federation of Labour, the Income Security Advocacy Centre, the Interfaith Social Assistance Reform Coalition, and the Community Social Planning Council of Toronto) in a joint call for a provincial poverty reduction strategy. The timing was fortuitous as the architect of Britain's poverty reduction strategy had held closed-door meetings with McGuinty's key policy advisors earlier that year. Through the summer of 2007, a push for poverty reduction was being developed both inside and outside government, reaching its apogee with McGuinty's election commitment to develop a set of strategies to fight poverty.

The re-elected Liberal government struck a Special Cabinet Committee on Poverty Reduction in January 2008 and tasked it with developing poverty indicators and targets and a focused strategy for reducing child poverty. The March 2008 budget also indicated commitment with another 2 per cent increase in social assistance rates, $100 million to rehabilitate existing social housing stock, an increase of the minimum wage to $10.25 by March 2010, full coverage for dental care for low-income families, a student nutritional program, and an increase to educational and parenting supports for families with children under the age of six.

The Special Cabinet Committee conducted community consultations across the province in the spring of 2008. The tone for these town hall meetings was set from the beginning: as Minister Matthews stated during the Hamilton consultation on 12 May, "tell us how we can do better with what we have." Using existing resources better had a familiar ring to it.

Despite the limitations set by the government, the broader antipoverty community mobilized to press for a more comprehensive strategy that included firm targets and which was less single-mindedly focused on child poverty. This emphasis was given by the network's name, *25in5*, which referred to its demand that the government commit to reducing poverty by 25 per cent in five years. The coalition was loosely structured, bringing together the major players in the anti-poverty community in a strategy of positive and constructive engagement with the government. More radical voices such as the Ontario Coalition Against Poverty remained outside, but the degree of joint action by a set of anti-poverty actors with different policy ideas and divergent strategies was notable.

Part of what held this group together was a common platform that avoided conflict by including multiple demands and by pushing important disputes into the future. This was laid out most clearly in *25in5*'s three-prong *Blueprint* brief, submitted to the government in August 2008. The first prong dealt with working poverty, emphasizing higher minimum wages, better labour standards, employment equity initiatives, and facilitating union certification. The second prong dealt with liveable incomes for all, including expanded child benefits, improved social assistance and disability benefits, and a housing benefit modelled on the child benefit. Finally, there was a series of proposals for developing community capacity, both in terms of supporting community groups, and in housing and early education (see Block 2009).

On 8 December 2008 the Special Cabinet Committee delivered its report. Setting out clear targets and measures for poverty reduction, as well as new funding for existing programs, the government committed to reducing the number of children in poverty by 25 per cent over five years. This proposal included additional annual investments of $1.4 billion directed to the Ontario Child Benefit, new educational opportunities such as full-day learning for four- and five-year-olds, parenting supports for low-income families, hiring twelve new employment standards officers, $5 million annually to a new Community Opportunities Fund to help coordinate neighbourhood services, and promises for a more comprehensive review of social assistance (Cabinet Committee on Poverty Reduction 2008). The government also agreed to upload all social assistance benefit costs by 2018. The impact of *25in5*'s advocacy could be seen both in the decision to set targets and in placing the question of social assistance back on the agenda. Another promising step forward was the enactment of Bill 152, "An Act Respecting a Long-Term Strategy to Reduce Poverty in Ontario," in 2009. It committed all future governments of Ontario to a set of principles to reduce poverty. These include the need to develop targets, measures, and timelines.

Overall, there were "wins" here for anti-poverty campaigners, particularly around child poverty, which became the target for reduction efforts. While the Ontario Child Benefit has between a third and a half of the value of similar benefits in Quebec, it does represent enough of an increase in the social wage to pull families working at the minimum wage over the poverty line. In terms of the working poor, the increase in the minimum wage brought individuals working full time, full year, very close to the poverty line. Those people receiving social assistance and disability benefits, by contrast, received next to nothing beyond the promise to have a commission study reforms to social assistance.

In sum, by 2009, policy around poverty had shifted since the Harris era, as the need to address issues around in-work poverty and child poverty came to the fore. As such, certain policy logics shifted in a more inclusive direction, but the neoliberal imprint is clear in continued constraints on public expenditure and a largely status quo position on labour markets. The labour market re-regulation involved correcting the worst abuses of temporary agencies and policing existing labour standards rather than raising the floor of the labour market as a whole.

AUSTERITY AND THE DISAPPEARANCE OF POVERTY REDUCTION

It is not clear what the original long-term intent of the McGuinty government was to be with the poverty reduction strategy. The government was confident that the increased child benefit coupled with improvements to federal benefits would be enough to move 25 per cent of children living in poverty over the line within five years, namely those children living in families with parents working at or near the minimum wage. What the government was thinking to do beyond 2013, when this "low hanging fruit" was gone, remains an open question, because in the face of the 2008–09 global financial crisis, poverty fell off the government's agenda.

In parallel, the anti-poverty community lost the unity of purpose that had served it in pushing for the poverty reduction strategy. Even before the government announced its strategy in 2008, there was tension between a "social liberal" faction, seeking incremental changes that largely fit within existing budgetary and labour market constraints, and a "social democratic" faction, seeking more far-reaching changes that would include putting taxes and social investment at higher settings and more aggressively regulating the labour market. In other words, the "social liberal" faction pushed for compensatory policies to deal with the dislocations of neoliberalism, but without putting into question the fundamental contours of this project. They saw a role for targeted state interventions to provide meaningful equality of opportunity for those left on the margins by neoliberalism. The social democrats, by contrast, were more willing to propose labour market and social policies that might prevent the creation of such large margins in the first place, and provide greater dignity to recipients of social assistance in the here and now. But this ultimately meant challenging neoliberal choices around taxation, spending, and flexible labour markets.

A key flashpoint between the camps was social assistance. For the social democrats, there was an immediate need to increase the adequacy of social assistance benefits, as they were too low to provide even basic physical subsistence without monthly recourse to emergency food options. This led to campaigns directly around benefit adequacy and hunger such as *Do the Math*, *Put Food in the Budget*, and *Freedom 90*. For many of the social liberals, the goal was to deconstruct social assistance from the inside, in order to create a form of guaranteed annual income. For instance, following the model of extending child benefits in social assistance to all low-income Ontarians, they sought a similar model of extending housing, dental, and vision benefits (see, e.g., Daily Bread Food Bank 2008). This group was generally cold to raising social assistance rates, both for fear of creating an anti-welfare backlash that would stymie steady progress in building a guaranteed income, and because higher rates would increase the cost of creating an annual income by increasing the likely starting level (see Stapleton 2004, 30).

The "great recession" of 2008 helped decelerate progress on poverty, not only by increasing unemployment and job insecurity, but also by strengthening the hand of Ministry of Finance officials looking to head off any new spending. The rise in social assistance caseloads as part of the 2008 recession (pushing the share of Ontarians receiving social assistance from 5.4 per cent in 2007 to 6.5 per cent in 2012) made the poverty file a cost driver in a government seeking to constrain program spending, which included delaying the full implementation of the Ontario Child Benefit. On the promised review of social assistance, the government carefully drew out the process so that no reports would be forthcoming before the 2011 election. After some delay, the government appointed a Social Assistance Review Advisory Council (SARAC) to propose terms of reference for the review, and they reported in 2010. SARAC tilted heavily in the "social liberal" direction in membership, and indeed came to argue the need to replace social assistance with a new income security architecture that would offer a basic income platform onto which training and education programs could be layered (SARAC 2010). This compared to the social democratic view, coalescing in part in a group called Poverty Free Ontario, which called for immediate increases in social assistance benefits, higher minimum wages ($12.50 by 2014), and a full housing benefit.

In the end, the government, re-elected with a minority in 2011, had no interest in either plan. Given the division in the anti-poverty community and the re-centering of business advocacy around fiscal restraint, there was little political penalty for doing the bare minimum. The government appointed a social assistance review with a mandate to improve the movement of social assistance recipients into work, but without spending new money. It was a far cry from the ambitious mandate of the SARAC, and almost entirely at odds with the social democratic emphasis on benefit adequacy.

While the social assistance review pursued its work, the poverty file remained on hold or moved backward. In the 2011 election, the Liberal platform went no further than a promise to "consider the idea" of a housing benefit, a lack of ambition mirrored by the absence of NDP commitments. This lack of interest was echoed in the 2012 Budget Speech, which had no increases in benefits (amounting to a cut due to inflation). While this was eventually changed to a 1 per cent increase (still slightly below inflation), this did not seem to be a priority for the NDP in its budgetary negotiations, as it never publicly raised social assistance (outside of the disability programme) as an issue. The budget also ended the provincial contribution to the community start-up benefit (housing) and capped special benefits (including things like dental care and burial costs), shifting a cost burden onto municipalities that led to cuts to these programmes.

It was in this sombre context that the social assistance review provided its wide-ranging report in October 2012 that included plans to collapse Ontario Works and Ontario Disability Supports into a single programme. Consistent with an employment-focused mandate, it proposed a reorientation of front-line social assistance work towards assisting recipients to develop "Pathways to Employment Plans." It also adopted the social liberal idea of extending benefits to all low-income Ontarians, including disability, drug, dental, child, and health benefits. There were a couple of nods to the social democratic view, in noting that rates were too low and should be raised by $100 while determining an evidence-based process for setting them, and in making the case for raising employment standards at the bottom end of the labour market (Commission for the Review of Social Assistance in Ontario 2012). While Kathleen Wynne, elected as Liberal party leader and premier in early 2013, spoke to the importance of implementing the report, the 2013 budget was content to pick the low-hanging fruit: allowing recipients to earn $200 a month without seeing benefits clawed back, and increasing asset limits for Ontario Works recipients. Rates were increased by 1 per cent, although single individuals on Ontario Works qualified for an additional $14 monthly top-up (bringing their benefit to $625 per month as of September 2013).

Until the election of Kathleen Wynne, there were few signs that the government had any interest in renewing its poverty reduction strategy past 2013. It did not help that the recession made the 25 per cent reduction in child poverty target unattainable (although child poverty rates did decline) and pushed overall poverty to the highest level in a generation (table 10.1). Wynne did ensure that a second five-year strategy was released, but it was developed without much public consultation, in the shadows of the more visible social assistance review. It continued to skirt social assistance, and instead placed the goal of ending homelessness at the centre of the strategy. Unlike the 2008 strategy, there were no clear timelines or intermediate targets, nor was there clarification of whether and when the government was still committed to meeting its 2008 child poverty target (Canada Without Poverty 2017).

Given the Wynne government's commitment to balancing the budget without increasing taxation, its movement on the poverty file was marked by seeking credit while minimizing expenditure. For instance, it embarked on a three-year basic income pilot, studying the impact of providing a guaranteed income of $16,989 to single individuals or $24,027 to couples, less 50 per cent of any earned income, to 4,000 social assistance recipients and low-income earners. While poverty advocates saw value in the expected evidence of how increased income adequacy improves health and social participation, given the prohibitive expense of generalizing this income, one could also portray the move as a relatively low-cost ($50 million per year) gimmick that signalled a government that was "cutting edge" on poverty even as it moved slowly on adequacy.

In terms of adequacy, when Wynne took power, social assistance rates for single individuals were lower in inflation-adjusted terms than under the Harris Conservatives. Following the social assistance review, every budget topped up rates for single individuals ($14 per month in 2013; $25 per month in 2014; $20 per month in 2015; $25 per month in 2016), such that singles received $721 per month as of 2017 (compared to $660 if the 2003 rates had increased with inflation). In the lead-up to the 2018 provincial election, the government struck three working groups (the Income Security Working Group, the First Nations Income Security Reform Working Group, and the Urban Indigenous Table on Income Security Reform) to develop a ten-year roadmap on income security reform. It engaged the social democratic demand, seen in the social assistance review's suggestion of evidence-based rates, in its first recommendation of adopting a "minimum standard income" set at the Low Income Measure, although perhaps eventually at a regionally adjusted Market-Based Measure, to be met by the end of ten years. Its second recommendation then returned to the social liberal strategy of spreading social assistance benefits to all low-income people with the idea of launching a housing benefit and of pushing all social assistance benefits for children outside of social assistance, and delivering it as a supplementary low-income child benefit. In many ways, the Working Group proposed a post-austerity version of the 2012 social assistance review, marrying a programme of more supportive and less punitive approaches to labour market placement with improved adequacy. The proposals also built on the 2012 review in paying sustained attention to social assistance for First Nations communities, and again went further in proposing greater autonomy and responsibility for designing and delivering social assistance and disability programs (Income Security Working Group 2017).

The Wynne Liberals' actions to increase minimum wages and improve labour standards in the fall of 2017 and their pre-election proposals around income security pushed at the edges of neoliberalism, in terms of pointing to the idea of a more robust right to sustenance and a willingness to "raise the floor" of the labour market. The difference between promises on social assistance and action on the minimum wage no doubt reflects in part the relative strength of campaigns on these issues, but also the Liberals' continued preference to address in-work poverty rather than stigmatized social assistance. The smaller budgetary impact of the minimum wage and labour standards measures (i.e., a compensatory lowering of the small business tax rate) compared to social assistance benefits increases probably also played a role.

With the election of a Conservative government in the 2018 provincial election, who campaigned on a platform that did not address poverty or social assistance but promised to freeze the minimum wage at $14 per hour, social assistance recipients are left to eat the good intentions of the Liberals' income security roadmap. Given the growth in incomes over the past fifteen years, the measures that the Liberals adopted over those years (such as the Ontario Child Benefit and top-ups for singles) at best allowed recipients to tread water with respect to the poverty line. The gap between social assistance benefits and the low-income measure is approximately 60 per cent of the low-income measure for singles, virtually unchanged during the McGuinty-Wynne era, and a far cry from the 40 per cent gap when the Liberals were in power in the 1980s. Child benefits have done much to help the incomes of families in poverty, but for families receiving social assistance they have at best kept the poverty gap in the 30–40 per cent range (compared to being at or above the LIM in the 1990–95 period). Compared to 2003, only couples with two children on OW have seen this gap shrink, although one can see the impact of the post-2008 emphasis on poverty in the sense that only single people receiving ODSP have a bigger poverty gap now compared to 2008 (Tiessen 2016, 10–11). Even if the Liberals had won the 2018 election, it is most realistic to assume that they would have pursued a housing benefit, to spread a social assistance benefit to all low-income Ontarians, before taking sustained efforts to fix the gap between social assistance rates and the poverty line.

Somewhat paradoxically, the victory of the Conservatives may shift the focus of poverty reduction to city-based poverty strategies. With their emphasis on improved rights to municipal services such as transportation or housing, they point to anti-poverty strategies based on an expanded basket of rights rather than improved liberal inclusion. However, as examples such as Toronto's poverty strategy indicate (Toronto 2015), even these have to navigate the Scylla of uncertain political coalitions and the Charybdis of austerity budgets.

WHAT POTENTIAL TO GO BEYOND INCLUSIVE LIBERALISM?

There has been a shift in poverty policy in Ontario over the past twenty-five years. The neoliberalism of the Harris Conservatives partially gave way to an inclusive liberalism, premised on the necessity of human capital and social cohesion for economic competitiveness and concerns about child poverty and working poverty. The mobilization of this inclusive liberal view had an impact on policy thinking and design. To simply label new initiatives as "more of the same" (i.e., neoliberalism) is to flatten some significant developments.

But how "inclusive" is this "inclusive liberalism," and how well is it rooted given the stops and starts on the poverty file? The problem of ensuring social reproduction under neoliberalism has led to new ways of thinking about social policy, but it is up to social conflict and political struggle to determine how and how far this new thinking is implemented. In Ontario, there is not a great deal of evidence of commitment to extend inclusive liberalism beyond the budgetary, redistributive, and regulatory limits of neoliberalism, although the alignment of reformist business with a wide coalition of poverty groups did provide some momentum around child poverty and the minimum wage.

This approach to the poverty file was aided by the relative silence of the Ontario New Democratic Party. While a number of MPPs from that party have consistently spoken up about poverty in the Legislature, the issue has not been at the forefront of their public demands (including the NDP's budget negotiations during the 2011–14 minority government), nor has it given rise to an encompassing policy statement. Having said that, as much as the situation for further progress in the next half-decade looks bleak, a large-scale regress under the Ford Conservative government is unlikely. It is noteworthy that the austerity agenda in Ontario, including the Drummond Report (Commission on the Reform of Ontario's Public Services, 2012), did not scapegoat social assistance recipients or directly roll back their benefits. Even the Conservative party, seemingly stuck in its 1990s mantras of attacking unions and public sector workers, had little to say about social assistance in its 2011 platform. Its 2013 policy paper on the subject was more varied, swinging between punitive approaches adopted from the US Republican Party and acceptance of the social assistance review's proposals to reduce the size of the social assistance bureaucracy and turn it towards providing employability (Ontario Conservative Party Caucus 2013). The party's 2018 platform, "Plan for the People," contained no mention of poverty or social assistance. The party did not politicize social assistance rates or the basic income pilot before or during the election campaign, although it promised to freeze the minimum wage at $14. Other than marginal interest in enhancing employment opportunities for Ontarians with disabilities (e.g., Ontario 2017), reformist business is no longer invested in immediate policy reform. Nevertheless, the importance of confronting in-work and child poverty is established firmly enough to constrain using anti-welfare backlash as a political strategy.

For those seeking to engage the state to foster more egalitarian outcomes, there are two strategic questions to confront. First, how do you mobilize groups to push inclusive liberalism beyond the neoliberal perimeter? After all, implementing a robust version of the social liberal program of health, dental, drug, and housing benefits to all low-income Ontarians would entail a significant shift in budgetary policy, to say nothing of the social democratic vision. And second, how do you move strategy beyond the needs of specific categories (social assistance recipients, single parents, the working poor, people with disabilities) to take on a low-end competitiveness strategy that necessarily creates low-wage work?

NOTES

1 While the unemployment, employment, and Low Income Measure numbers in table 10.1 are drawn from Statistics Canada, the percentage of the population on social assistance is taken from John Stapleton's (2018) calculations, using December caseloads and population figures. The Low-Income Measure is a relative measure of poverty, capturing those whose incomes are less than half the medium income. The Market-Basket Measure is more of an absolute measure, capturing those unable to buy a standard basket of goods. It has bounced around between 11.8 and 14 per cent over the past decade.
2 For a much more comprehensive discussion of poverty and labour market dynamics, see Gough, Eisenschitz, and McCulloch (2006).

REFERENCES

Banting, Keith. 2006. "Disembedding Liberalism: The Social Policy Trajectory in Canada." In *Dimensions of Inequality in Canada*, edited by David Green and Jonathan Kesselman. Vancouver: University of British Columbia Press.

Block, Sheila. 2009. *A Blueprint for Economic Stimulus and Poverty Reduction in Ontario*. Toronto: 25in5 Network for Poverty Reduction.

Briggs, Alexa, Celia Lee, and John Stapleton. 2016. *The Cost of Poverty in Ontario*. Toronto: Social Planning Toronto and Open Policy Ontario.

Cabinet Committee on Poverty Reduction 2008. *Breaking the Cycle: Ontario's Poverty Reduction Strategy*. Toronto: Ministry of Children and Youth Services.

Canada Without Poverty. 2017. *2017 Poverty Progress Profiles*. Ottawa: Canada Without Poverty.

Commission on the Reform of Ontario's Public Services. 2012. *Public Services for Ontarians: A Path to Sustainability and Excellence*. Toronto: Ministry of Finance.

Commission for the Review of Social Assistance in Ontario. 2012. *Brighter Prospects: Transforming Social Assistance in Ontario*. Toronto: Ministry of Community and Social Services.

Costolgou, P. 1996. *Summary Report of the Cutbacks in Ontario*. Toronto: Ontario Social Service Council.

Coulter, Kendra. 2009. "Women, Poverty Policy and the Production of Neoliberal Politics in Ontario, Canada." *Journal of Women, Politics and Policy* 30 (1).

Daily Bread Food Bank. 2008. *A Housing Benefit for Ontario: One Housing Solution for a Poverty Reduction Strategy*. Toronto: Daily Bread Food Bank.

Finnie, Ross, Ian Irving, and Roger Sceviour. 2004. "Social Assistance Use in Canada: National and Provincial Trends in Incidence, Entry and Exit." *Canadian Journal of Regional Science* 27 (2).

Frenette, Marc, and Garnett Picot. 2003. *Life After Welfare: The Economic Well Being of Welfare Leavers in Canada during the 1990s*. Ottawa: Statistics Canada Catalogue No. 11-010.

Gough, Jamie, Aram Eisenschitz, and Andrew McCulloch. 2006. *Spaces of Social Exclusion*. New York: Routledge.

Hackworth, Jason. 2008. "The Durability of Roll-Out Neoliberalism under Centre-Left Governance: The Case of Ontario's Social Housing Sector." *Studies in Political Economy* 81.

Herd, Dean, and Andrew Mitchell. 2003. "Cutting Caseloads by Design: The Impact of the New Service Delivery Model for Ontario Works." *Canadian Review of Social Policy* 51.

Herd, Dean, Andrew Mitchell, and Ernie Lightman. 2005. "Rituals of Degradation: Administration as Policy in the Ontario Works Program." *Journal of Social Policy and Administration* 39 (1).

Hudson, Carol-Anne, and Peter Graefe. 2011. "The Toronto Origins of Ontario's 2008 Poverty Reduction Strategy: Mobilizing Multiple Channels for Progressive Social Policy Change." *Canadian Review of Social Policy* 65–6.

Human Resources Development Canada. 2000. *Reconnecting Social Assistance Recipients to the Labour Market: Lessons Learned*. Ottawa: Human Resources Development Canada.

Income Security Reform Group. 2017. *Roadmap to Income Security*. Toronto: Income Security Reform Group.

Jenson, Jane 2012. "Redesigning Citizenship Regimes after Neoliberalism: Moving towards Social Investment." In *Towards A Social Investment Welfare State? Ideas, Policies and Challenges*, edited by Nathalie Morel, Bruno Palier, and Joakim Palme. Bristol: Policy Press.

Klassen, Thomas, and Dan Buchanan. 2006. "Ideology, Policy, and Economy: Liberal, New Democratic and Conservative Reforms of Ontario's Welfare Program." *Journal of Canadian Studies* 40 (3).

Little, Margaret. 2001. "A Litmus Test for Democracy: The Impact of Ontario Welfare Changes on Single Mothers." *Studies in Political Economy* 66.

MacDermid, Robert, and Greg Albo. 2001. "Divided Province, Growing Protests: Ontario Moves Right." In *The Provincial State*, edited by Keith Brownsey and Michael Howlett. Peterborough: Broadview.

Mahon, Rianne. 2008. "Varieties of Liberalism: Canadian Social Policy from the 'Golden Age' to the Present." *Social Policy and Administration* 42 (4).

Mahon, Rianne, and Laura Macdonald. 2010. "Anti-Poverty Politics in Toronto and Mexico City." *Geoforum* 41 (2).

Marquardt, Richard. 2007. "The Progressive Potential of Municipal Social Policy: A Case Study of the Struggle over Welfare Reform in Ottawa during the Common Sense Revolution." PhD diss., Carleton University.

Matthews, Deb. 2004. *Review of Employment Assistance Programs in Ontario Works and Ontario Disability Support Program*. Toronto: Ministry of Community and Social Services.

Maxwell, Judith. 2002. *Smart Social Policy – Making Work Pay*. Ottawa: Canadian Policy Research Networks.

McCain, Margaret Norrie, and J. Fraser Mustard. 1999. *Reversing the Real Brain Drain: Early Years Study Final Report*. Toronto: Ontario Children's Secretariat.

Moscovitch, Allan. 1997. "Social Assistance in the New Ontario." In *Open for Business, Closed to People*, edited by Diana Ralph, André Régimbald, and Nérée St-Amand. Halifax: Fernwood.

National Council of Welfare, 2000. *Welfare Incomes 1999*. Ottawa: National Council of Welfare.

Ontario. 2017. *Access Talent: Ontario's Employment Strategy for People With Disabilities*. Toronto: Queen's Printer for Ontario.

Ontario Association of Food Banks. 2008. *The Cost of Poverty: An Analysis of the Economic Cost of Poverty in Ontario*. Toronto: Ontario Association of Food Banks.

Ontario Conservative Party Caucus. 2013. *Pathways to Prosperity: Welfare to Work*. Toronto: Conservative Party.

Panel on the Role of Government. 2004. *Investing in People: Creating a Human Capital Society for Ontario*. Toronto: Queen's Printer.

Social Assistance Review Advisory Council. 2010. *Recommendations for an Ontario Income Security Review*. Toronto: Ministry of Community and Social Services.

Stapleton, John. 2004. *Transitions Revisited: Implementing the Vision*. Ottawa: Caledon Institute of Social Policy.

– 2018. *The East Steeles Nexus of Poverty*. http://openpolicyontario.com/presentations.

Statistics Canada. 2018a. *Labour Force Survey*. CANSIM table 282-0002. Ottawa: Statistics Canada.

– 2018b. *Low Income Statistics by Age, Sex and Economic Family Type*. CANSIM table 206-0041. Ottawa: Statistics Canada.

TD Economics 2005. *From Welfare to Work in Ontario: Still The Road Less Travelled*. Toronto: TD Economics.

Thomas, Mark. 2009. *Regulating Flexibility: The Political Economy of Employment Standards*. Montreal: McGill-Queen's University Press.

Tiessen, Kaylie. 2016. *Ontario's Social Assistance Poverty Gap*. Toronto: Canadian Centre for Policy Alternatives.

Toronto. 2015. *TO Prosperity: Toronto Poverty Reduction Strategy*. Toronto: City of Toronto.

Toronto City Summit Alliance. 2003. *Enough Talk: An Action Plan for the Toronto Region*. Toronto: Toronto City Summit Alliance.

– 2006. *Time for a Fair Deal: Report of the Task Force on Modernizing Income Security for Working-Age Adults*. Toronto: Toronto City Summit Alliance.

Worker's Action Centre. 2006. *Working, Yet Poor in Ontario*. www.workersactioncentre.org.

| 11 |

Reforming Health Services in Ontario: Contradictions

PAT ARMSTRONG AND HUGH ARMSTRONG

Health care remains Canada's most popular social program[1] and ranks high on the list of priorities for most Canadians,[2] for good reason. It has delivered quite consistently good quality services on a relatively equitable basis. Despite widespread attacks in the media, those who use public health care services rate them highly. And despite multiple efforts to turn many services or aspects of them into profit-making enterprises, most of the system remains in non-profit hands. It is a rare politician who would launch a direct assault on such a popular program, and former Ontario Liberal premier Dalton McGuinty was not one of them. Indeed, McGuinty initially campaigned on a platform that promised a strengthening of the public system. But there were multiple contradictions in the McGuinty government's policies and practices in health care, making it no simple task to evaluate what these mean in terms of equity in access, in quality of care and of care work, or in terms of his promises. Health care is a huge, complex, and multi-faceted system and we are able to touch on only some aspects here. The assessment of the 2003–13 McGuinty government record is organized around the broad headings of funding and restructuring; and we indicate how these trends were extended into the Liberal governments of Kathleen Wynne.

FUNDING ONTARIO HEALTH CARE

As required by the federal Canada Health Act, in return for the transfer of federal funds to each province, Ontario pays for all medically necessary hospital and doctor care. The province also pays for selected other services, such as some homecare and parts of long-term residential care. Contrary to much of the media coverage, public health care costs are not out of control.[3] During the McGuinty years, per capita public spending on health care rose in real terms (after inflation is factored out) by less than 1 per cent a year, while the comparable increase in private spending was over 1.5 per cent a year; and per capita health spending fell on average each year since 2013–14 under the Wynne period (CIHI 2012, 2018). Health spending actually declined quite substantially as a share of total program spending by the province, from 45.0 per cent in 2004–05 to an estimated 40.3 per cent in 2011–12, remaining in this lower expenditure range since, with the Wynne government steadily trying to further reduce health expenditures (CIHI 2012, series F.1.1.4; CIHI 2018, series B.4.4.). Even with a slowly aging population, then, health spending has not been "crowding out" public spending on schools, roads, parks, subsidies to industry, and so on.

Indeed, there is ample evidence that Ontario could and should spend more on health. Despite growing wait times for homecare and admission to long-term residential care facilities, and despite still being a relatively prosperous province, Ontario spends less per capita on health (an estimated $6,367 in 2017) than any other province except British Columbia ($6,321). The estimates for the other provinces range from New Brunswick ($6,643) to Alberta ($7,329). For Canada as a whole, the estimated figure, including Ontario, is $6,604 (CIHI 2018, 21). Ontario continued to remain below national per capita expenditures on health across the entire period of the Wynne government (CIHI 2018, table F1.1.2). It is therefore appropriate to begin this assessment of the Liberal record with a look at funding.

TAXES FOR HEALTH

During the 2003 election campaign, McGuinty promised not to raise taxes. He broke that promise in 2004 by introducing an individual health premium collected through the income tax system, with the $3 billion in revenue to be dedicated to health care (Ontario Ministry of Finance 2013). This levy did not replace the employer health levy introduced in 1989 by a previous Liberal government. Although the move contradicted his promises, the tax was somewhat progressive. Those with taxable incomes less than $20,000 in 2010 paid no premium and the amounts rose with income, with the top payment of $900 for those with taxable incomes over $200,600 (Ontario Ministry of Finance 2011). As the former US Supreme Court justice Oliver Wendell Holmes put it, "Taxes are the price we pay for civilization," and health care qualifies as a critical component of civilization. So breaking this promise could be seen as a move forward to equity rather than as a move backwards, especially given that it was supposed to protect some funds for health care. However, the cap on taxes limited the extent to which the tax was progressive, and there is no clear mechanism for ensuring that the money goes to public care. Both the Ontario Health Premium and the Employer Health Tax remained in place under the Wynne government, as did these contradictions in the funding of health care.

PUBLIC-PRIVATE PARTNERSHIPS

Another broken McGuinty promise had much clearer inequitable consequences. In April 2003 before the election that would bring him to power, McGuinty vowed to "end the Harris-Eves agenda of creeping privatization" (Urquart 2003a); he also promised to scrap the public-private partnerships (P3s) "as soon as we can" (Urquart 2003b). And, as a new premier, he announced after the October 2003 election that: "We are turning those private hospitals [the Brampton hospital and the Royal Ottawa] into publicly-owned hospitals" (Greenberg 2003).

There was, however, no real turn. The Liberals in fact pressed ahead with P3s, albeit under the new label of "alternative financing" arrangements. As of 2008, twenty-six hospitals were built or planned under these schemes (Silversides 2008a), but later tallies put the number at forty-three by the end of 2012 (CCPPP 2013). They retained the key features of what had been termed P3s, with the private partner(s) bearing all or most of the responsibility for designing, financing, constructing, and operating the facility in question. At the end of the lengthy partnership agreement, often thirty years in length, ownership of the facility will be in public hands. Under Premier Wynne, the Liberals continued their reliance on P3s in health care provisioning. According to the P3 tracking report put out by the Canadian Council of Public-Private Partnerships, the Ontario government was using P3s for sixty-two health care projects (almost all related to hospitals) with a "total market value" of $18.469 billion in 2018 (CCPPP 2018).

The first argument advanced for P3s, including alternative financing arrangements, is that the private sector has the expertise to make the schemes more efficient. The claim is that the private sector will build on time and within budget, introducing innovative design, construction, and operational features to the project. Another argument is that P3s are said to transfer the risks associated with construction and operation from the public sector to the private sector. A third, if unspoken, advantage to government is that the design and construction costs are neither allocated from current tax revenues nor added to the public debt.

The actual experience with P3s in Ontario and elsewhere, in the health sector and many other sectors,[4] refutes the claims of increased efficiency and transferred risk with P3s. The actual construction of hospitals (and other public buildings) has always been in private hands, at least since the transition in the late 1940s from a wartime economy (Armstrong 1977). So there is no particular advantage there. As for design, P3 projects routinely entail reduced capacity. One of the early Ontario examples, the William Osler hospital in Brampton, ended up with only 479 beds instead of the 608 initially promised (Ontario Health Coalition 2005). According to the auditor general of Ontario (2008, 104), "the all-in cost could well have been lower had the [Brampton] hospital and the related non-clinical services been procured under the traditional approach, rather than the P3 approach in this case." Note that the language of "alternative financing" was not used in this report.

An obvious reason for the lack of cost-effectiveness in P3s, and thus their reduced capacity, is that the public sector can borrow more cheaply than any private consortium. Another reason is that the private consortium is involved in order to make a profit at all stages of the project. Indeed, if it sees itself failing to make what it regards as a sufficient return on its investment, it either negotiates higher charges or it pulls out. In the Brampton case, the construction costs alone rose from a projected $350 million to $550 million.

Part of the cost increase is attributable to design changes made after the initial agreement had been reached. This cannot be entirely surprising, for it is very difficult to specify every detail in advance, and even more difficult to anticipate changing needs and appropriate ways of meeting these needs. The facility's owner has more freedom to specify and anticipate whether it employs or hires its own architects and engineers at the design stage, than if it has to rely on the design plans brought to it by the private consortium.

Design and construction costs are multiplied at the operational stage. In addition to the ongoing need to monitor whether the private consortium is living up to all its obligations, responding to an unforeseen crisis such as the SARS outbreak requires a new set of negotiations and additional payments to the consortium. These institutional "transaction costs" are considerable. The presumption of dishonesty involved in purchaser-provider splits is particularly intense when the provider's prime objective is to turn a profit, not to offer a public service.

At another level, the operational stage is likely to include contracting out, to one or more of the consortium's partners, some or all support services (food preparation, building cleaning and maintenance, laundry, record keeping, purchasing, security, etc.), and perhaps even some "clinical" services (such as diagnostic, lab, and rehab services). At the Royal Ottawa Hospital, also an early P3 project, extra funds have to be identified and paid in order to reconfigure the chairs and tables in a meeting room. In another example, the nurse employed by the hospital may no longer be able to ask the housekeeper to clean up vomit without going through a manager from the private firm (Kahnamoui 2005). The for-profit management and operation of support services is based on the assumption that they are not health services, whatever the rhetoric about "teamwork" on the ward and whatever the health care skills the workers involved have and require.

The claim that greater efficiency results from for-profit management is particularly problematic in terms of quality, finances, and equity. According to a World Health Organization study (McKee, Edwards, and Atun 2006, 895), any savings on time or building costs "seem often to be at the expense of quality" and there is a "reluctance to undertake evaluations" that would test the claims for benefits. Unions and health coalitions have tried to fill the gap. In the case of the Brampton hospital, for example, they had to go to the courts to pry information out of the government on its "Value for Money Benchmark" (VFMB) for the project (Ontario Health Coalition 2007). Another case is particularly telling: that of the 2008 comparison of a P3 hospital in North Bay with a public hospital in Peterborough. "Peterborough had 127% of the bed capacity of the North Bay P3 but was only 35.8% of the cost" (Ontario Health Coalition 2008). The drive to cut costs contributes to major health risks, such as hospital-acquired infections for patients and rising illness and injury rates for workers. All the hand-washing in the world cannot make up for beds and bathrooms that are insufficiently cleaned. The public purse ends up paying. Meanwhile the private partners save money on supplies, training, and staffing levels, and may reduce worker pay, benefits, and employment security (CUPE 2009a).

The contracting-out of these support services to private firms that are more familiar with managing hotels and food outlets than health care facilities is disproportionately felt by the women and, in many parts of the province, by the immigrant and racialized individuals who do the work. They are disparagingly labelled "ancillary workers" performing "hotel services," with negative implications not only for their pay and working conditions, but also for safe care (Armstrong, Armstrong, and Scott-Dixon 2008).

Turning briefly to the argument about transferring risk, it is simply a mirage. No government can allow a hospital to be left partially built or to close if the consortium fails or decides to walk away. As a former director in the Audit Operations Branch of the Office of the Auditor General for Canada put it, "when there are essential services and institutions, if a major material risk actually takes place, the public sector must step in, even if it has already paid a large premium for risk transfer costs" (Auerbach 2008). In addition, there are significant problems with democratic control because consortiums claim that they must have privacy in order to ensure competition. The justification for such confidentiality is extended well beyond the bidding for the contract, even though the competition is over and all the money comes from the public purse.

That risk cannot be transferred to the private "partner" is underscored by the 2017 collapse of Carillion, the huge UK firm that is currently heavily involved in P3 projects at several Ontario hospitals (Loxley 2018). Should its Canadian operations be liquidated, the government will have to protect, at least in large part, the jobs, incomes, and pensions of potentially[5] thousands of workers. It is inconceivable that these public hospitals would be closed.

These problems are well documented and known to many of those in charge. In her two-part series for the *Canadian Medical Association Journal*, Ann Silversides (2008b, 991) quotes a former chair of a hospital that adopted the partnership approach as saying: "It is a tough dilemma for [hospital] boards. We know the downside [of public–private partnerships] ... We know there is money involved and there are risks and transparency issues, but in the end ... we have something [built] in 5 to 7 years as opposed to possibly never." In other words, the move to P3s has happened in spite of the evidence demonstrating the negative consequences, and in spite of promises to avoid them. Indeed, from recent reports of the Ontario auditor general, the evidence continues to mount on the costs from P3s to the health care sector (OHC 2015; Hemingway 2016).

A NEW FUNDING MODEL

While the P3s follow in the Conservatives' footsteps and represent a marked departure from Liberal promises, the current funding mechanisms have no such legacy. The Health Based Allocation Model (HBAM) for hospitals is presented as

> a sophisticated tool that draws on years of clinical and demographic information collected across the province in order to model the expected demand and expenditures for health services. HBAM accounts for differences across communities in age, socioeconomic status and existing health conditions. The model develops a cost profile for every patient based on their clinical diagnosis, type of treatment received and the characteristics of the hospital they received their care from. (Ontario Ministry of Health and Long-term Care 2010)

Perhaps surprisingly given its title, HBAM is funding mainly based on past utilization. As Michael Rachlis (2008) explains, it thus involves a perverse incentive given that past high levels of usage are rewarded. At the same time, the formula ignores past inequities and unmet needs. In the case of homecare, the auditor general (2010, 9) concluded that a "reliance on historically-based funding rather than on an assessment of current client needs ... creates the risk that people with similar levels of need may not receive similar levels of care, depending on where they live in Ontario." For Rachlis, this means that the system is likely to perpetuate rather than address inequities among individuals and regions.

Meanwhile, if HBAM were to become a more explicit activity-based funding (ABF) scheme, hospital revenues would be more clearly linked to volumes of activity, as distinct from historical patterns. The concern here is that ABF could promote price competition from private, for-profit clinics that "cherry-pick" those discrete services from which profit is to be had (eye surgery, joint replacement surgery, etc.), leaving the public system to care for those with chronic conditions and complex or multiple health problems. The effect would likely be to reduce quality and to fragment services, to the detriment of vulnerable patients and providers alike (Canadian Doctors for Medicare 2010).

In addition, the McGuinty government's incentive payments to physicians were intended to encourage the delivery of specific services to specific patient populations. However, the evidence concerning their effectiveness in ensuring the delivery of quality care is quite mixed (Hutchison 2008), and there is some indication that such pay-for-performance approaches can even increase disparities among different cultural groups (Millet et al. 2009). Pay-for-performance is yet another example of how the Liberals followed the Tory lead in promoting for-profit practices within the public system.

At the same time, since 2010 the government has required hospitals to balance their budgets. This undermines another promise, one about nurses. In keeping with their commitment to nurses, 10,000 more nurses were hired in the years following the initial Liberal victory. And as promised, there was also a significant increase in full-time employment for nurses. However, as a consequence of the need to balance budgets, many hospitals began laying off nurses and moving others to part-time work. The government distanced itself from these cuts by maintaining that the decisions to cut back on nurses were made locally, with the hospital boards and Local Health Integration Networks (LHINs) blamed for the reductions. Given that well over nine out of ten nurses are female, this was an indirect attack on women's work.

Equally important, the McGuinty government passed legislation that restricted compensation increases for non-union employees. Except for certain restrictions, Bill 16, or the Creating the Foundation for Jobs and Growth Act (2010), for example, froze compensation in the broader public sector between 24 March 2010 and 31 March 2012.[6] Although most managers were also affected by this freeze, it had the greatest impact on those in services such as child care and homecare where wages are already low, where mainly women work, and where many are from racialized and/or immigrant groups. The freeze did not affect a couple of scandal-prone areas that caused much grief to the Liberal government: the implementation of e-health records by private consultants earning thousands of dollars a day, and the arms-length agency set up to operate ORNGE, the province's air ambulance service, whose former CEO acquired millions in various ways and which itself spun off some for-profit subsidiaries with huge revenue from the public purse.

The Ontario government's Action Plan for Health Care brought in Health System Funding Reform, and further entrenched HBAM (with its attempt to link volume of activities – medical procedures – to prices established as incentives for the transfer of money) at the centre of funding. Starting in 2012–13, the new funding model was phased in over four years, and now provides 70 per cent of the funding for hospitals with 30 per cent coming from other sources (Ontario Ministry of Health and Long-Term Care 2018).

DRUG PRICES

It came as a surprise to many that the government decided to tackle drug prices. Although Ontario does not have a public drug plan, it does cover the cost of most medications in hospital and many that are prescribed to children, seniors, the disabled, and those on welfare. Drugs eat up a substantial portion of health care budgets, making them a likely target for controls, rising from 7.7 per cent under Harris in 1995–96 to 9.5 per cent in 2004–05 (CIHI 2012, series F.3.6.1). But previous governments in Ontario had not been willing to take on the drug companies.

As background, it is important to know that brand-name drugs are those initially patented by a pharmaceutical company under a trade name, and a generic drug is one that is basically a copy introduced when the brand drug patent has run out. Generics are usually significantly cheaper than brand-name ones. The province regulates the prices pharmacies can charge the public sector for generic drugs. Generics compete with each other and with brand-name ones for shelf space and sales. As Steven Lewis (2010) explains, generic firms had offered rebates to pharmacies in order to ensure that their drugs were strategically placed and previous governments had basically supported this by naming them "professional allowances" and capping them at 20 per cent of the wholesale price. This money went to pharmacies rather than to those buying the drugs, and the result was high drug prices compared to European countries.

The McGuinty government developed a plan to change the price structure for generic drugs and to negotiate better prices for the brand-name ones at the same time as it allowed greater interchangeability between generic and brand-name drugs. Despite strong opposition from the pharmacies and drug companies, the new rules removed the hidden rebates paid to pharmacies by generic drug companies as a means of promoting their sales. The government instead pays a professional fee to pharmacists, with special additional fees to support pharmacies in rural areas. Lewis, in response to this initiative, concluded that "patients will get cheaper drugs. Pharmacists in rural and remote areas will get higher dispensing fees. It's not a revolution, but it is an improvement. And if Ontarians are lucky, it will be just the beginning" (2010). Ontario has extended its universal pharmacare program to those aged 18–24, and has urged the federal government to lead in the development of a national program covering all ages. The Wynne health minister, Eric Hoskins, resigned in early 2018 to head a federal advisory council to further study this proposal.

STAGNANT FUNDING

In sum, the McGuinty government had a mixed record when it came to its funding promises, with varied results for equity at best. It promised not to raise taxes, then imposed an individual health premium, but one that was and remains modestly progressive except for the wealthy. This was accompanied by tax cuts for corporations in particular, reducing the fiscal room available to the province. The Liberals promised to eliminate P3s for hospital design, financing, construction, and operation. But they then introduced many more P3s, with all their disadvantages (costs, capacity, rigidity), only partly hidden by the misleading label of alternative financing.

As well, the Liberals introduced a Health Based Allocation Model for hospitals, shifting some funding away from historically based global budgets to more evidence-informed allocations based on demographic factors (population growth and aging) and clinical activity levels. In the process, however, this effectively cut hospital resources in an unstable, unpredictable fashion without adding sufficient capacity to long-term residential care or to homecare. As a result, both experienced substantial and predictable wait time increases, leading to a critical bed shortage that was addressed in an equally piecemeal fashion by the Wynne government. Finally, it cut what it paid for generic drugs, prompting futile opposition from the large pharmacy chains in particular.

Continuing trends established during the previous Conservative governments under Premiers Mike Harris and Ernie Eves, the McGuinty government cut the shares of its health spending on hospitals from 41.2 per cent in 2004–05 to 36.1 per cent in 2014–15, while increasing slightly the shares going to other institutions (notably long-term residential care and homecare) from 9.6 per cent to 10.9 per cent, and to public health from 7.4 per cent to 9.1 per cent. Meanwhile, the share going to physicians rose appreciably (21.2 per cent to 24.8 per cent), and the share spent on drugs rose slightly from 9.6 per cent to 10.9 per cent (CIHI 2018, series F.3.6.1). The reallocation of resources from hospitals to long-term residential care, to homecare, to public health, and especially to physicians masked the reality that overall public spending on health care was under McGuinty quite stagnant in real per capita terms, while it used a shrinking share of program spending and kept Ontario near the bottom of the provincial ladder in per capita support for health care. From 2005 to 2015, the health share of total program spending dropped from 43.9 per cent to 38.8 (CIHI 2018, series B.4.4). The Wynne period reinforced all these trends in further reducing real per capita health care spending as a whole, cutting the share of spending for hospitals, increasing the share to physicians, and maintaining other funding shares (CIHI 2018, series F.3.6.2). Together, these trends help set the stage for an analysis of the province's restructuring of health services.

RESTRUCTURING HEALTH SERVICES

Although not very evident in initial election promises, the McGuinty government moved to restructure the system. Many health services have been reorganized into Local Health Integration Networks (LHINs), building on regionalization efforts timidly initiated by previous governments. Tighter new rules have been introduced in homecare. A new medical school has opened in Northern Ontario, and the number of both doctors and nurse practitioners has increased significantly. New family health teams have been established to meet primary care access issues at the same time as hospitals have been closed. Here, too, the consequences for care and equity are mixed.

LOCAL HEALTH INTEGRATION NETWORKS

Several decades ago, other Canadian jurisdictions began regionalizing their health services. McGuinty started the process in Ontario in a serious way just as others were rethinking or even reversing their regionalization strategies. According to the government, the province's fourteen LHINs, which assumed authority in 2008, are "responsible for funding a wide range of health service providers and for managing the majority of service agreements with these providers. The government's role is to provide stewardship of Ontario's health system, setting direction, strategic policy and system standards and delivering provincial programs and services" (Ontario Ministry of Health and Long-Term Care 2011a). The services under the LHINs include hospitals but not doctors. Including hospitals in regional planning could be a way to balance resources, given that hospitals take up such a large share of budgets. But it could also be a way for hospitals to exert a powerful influence over others, especially in the case of large teaching hospitals. The board for each LHIN is appointed by the government, making it more likely that large players will have influence and less likely that there will be more democratic community control. As an indication of relative power, its CEO is paid much less than the CEOs of the large hospitals in the region. The LHIN mandate also excludes public health, which is controlled by municipal governments, prescription drug distribution, and important other aspects of the system, such as cancer diagnosis and treatment, which is the responsibility of Cancer Care Ontario.

The ministry website promised that this structure would bring decisions closer to the people in ways that respond to their needs (Ontario Ministry of Health and Long-Term Care 2011a), and more recently in ways that improve access and patient experience by integrating health services (Ontario LHINS 2018). However, the very structure of LHINs makes it virtually impossible for the LHINS to fulfil this promise. First, with populations usually over a million, and often spread across vast areas, the regions are very large and do not reflect communities or localities. Instead, their boundaries were set in a mathematical calculation based on hospital usage and in an attempt to make the regions roughly equal in terms of population. The result was a split in some communities (notably the Greater Toronto Area) and some huge regions (especially in Northern Ontario) that could not possibly be seen as communities.

Second, the funding limits placed on the LHINs mean that they, rather than the provincial government, are saddled with some tough, unpopular decisions. As the Ontario ombudsman put it in his scathing assessment, the ministry has "been able to distance itself from difficult decisions surrounding the integration and funding of regional health services" (Marin 2010, 1).

A third problem relates to democracy and the composition and practices of the provincially appointed LHIN boards. According to the ombudsman, "the reality of community decision-making has fallen far short of the political spin" (ibid.). Decision-makers may be from the community but are not of the community in the sense of representing them. The ombudsman found that, contrary to policy, some LHINs far too frequently met behind closed doors in what were called "education" meetings, making transparency and local control impossible.

The government was reluctant to require that all but the most limited number of meetings be open, as the ombudsman recommended. New standards for openness were introduced by the government, but they fall short of what the ombudsman recommended and fail to address the undemocratic nature of appointed boards.

The Ontario Health Coalition, an organization that brings together unions, community groups, and individuals, held public hearings to investigate the impact on small and rural hospitals. In those public forums, LHINs were blamed for closures and cutbacks that significantly reduced access to care. Large regions meant that small communities had no voice and little defence against priorities set far away in the sense of geography, class, and the priorities of local residents. This is particularly the case in terms of having hospitals close to home, even if they cannot provide the full range of services offered in larger centres. The coalition's report (2010; cf. 2011) on the hearings calls for new provincial standards that would contribute to equity, and for new, accountable, smaller regional bodies. So far, the government has not responded positively to its demands. Indeed, the Wynne government's December 2015 White Paper on Health Care, *Patients First: A Proposal to Strengthen Patient-Centred Health Care in Ontario*, proposed to further expand the power of the LHINs, including public health units and other local health providers. The LHINs have taken over the functions of the Community Care Access Centres (CCACs), reducing administrative costs slightly, as some senior CCAC managers with controversial high salaries were let go.

HOMECARE

Homecare is one area that falls under the direction of the LHINs. Access to homecare is through the Community Care Access Centres (CCACs). The thirty-odd agencies introduced by the previous Conservative government were reduced in number by the McGuinty government to match the boundaries of the fourteen LHINs. In June 2017, under the Wynne government the LHINs took over from the CCACs the provision of government-funded home services and long-term care homes. Like the fourteen CCACs before them, the LHINs negotiate contracts with homecare provider organizations, and their case managers assess the homecare needs of individual patients on the basis of regulations set down by the government and by their LHIN.

Although homecare received a big financial boost under Liberal governments and no fees were charged for services provided through the CCACs,[7] the increase happened in the context of bed shortages in hospitals, a dramatic rise in day surgeries, and long waiting lists for residential care. Partly as a result, the focus for public homecare services was on patients recently discharged from hospitals and on palliative care, too often leaving many of the vulnerable, poor, and frail older people living in private homes – most of whom were and are women – without support.

The McGuinty government did introduce new regulations in July 2009 that indicated a commitment to extend homecare services and to protect care workers (OHA 2009), and the government under Wynne raised the wages for the personal support workers in homecare to a minimum of $15 an hour. The amendments expanded the role of the case managers who are in charge of services for individual clients, allowing them to handle entry to a broader range of services. The amendments to the regulations also added a wide range of community support services such as emergency response services and foot care to those that could be provided by the LHINs. In addition, the regulations say that the environment in which the services are to be provided must be safe for the worker. The new labour legislation of the Wynne government, which requires equal pay for part-time workers and some sick leave, may also help workers in this sector.

But at the same time, the McGuinty regulations established a maximum number of hours of nursing service that any one person could receive. For example, for those receiving the most intensive care at home there is a limit of 120 visits in a thirty-day period from a nurse or registered practical nurse. Equally important, the LHINs have only a restricted budget and rising demands so that even this number of visits may not be forthcoming. As the *Toronto Star* series, "Begging for Care" (Boyle and Welsh 2011), made clear, many people go without necessary care or even promised care.

The problem may be compounded by Liberal governments' continuation of the legacy of the Tory competitive bidding strategy for homecare. Under this strategy, Ontario had become the only Canadian jurisdiction to rely on competitive bidding in this field. In response to research and public protest, much of it centred in the Hamilton area and organized by the Ontario Health Coalition, the government agreed to a moratorium on bidding but left existing contracts in place. A 2008 study commissioned by the Ontario Health Coalition and the Service Employees International Union concluded that the "input and research shows that assessing bids and monitoring performance is very costly and involves significant challenges. Competition has generated a climate of fear and reluctance to share best practices" (Kushner, Baranek, and Dewar 2008, 2).

The hearings for this report also indicated that the quality of care declined as a result of disruptions caused by both contracts and the employment practices of the competing companies. Non-profit organizations were forced to compete with for-profit ones, and often lost because they did not have the resources to put in the bids and because they could not as readily do loss-leader bids to obtain initial contracts, as was the case for large, for-profit agencies.

The moratorium on competitive bidding remains in place, but could be lifted at any time. In response to research and protests demanding a return to the days when homecare was provided by non-profit agencies such as the Victorian Order of Nurses and the Red Cross, the government merely agreed to extend the length of the contracts in the hope that this would increase stability in the sector. While this means lower turnover in employers, it also means that bad employers can remain in place longer. And it ensures that public money for care goes to profit rather than to care, too often leaving the most vulnerable without options or care, and workers with low wages and little security.

The additional financial resources for homecare are part of the Aging at Home strategy (from 2007, reworked under the Wynne government in 2017 as Aging with Confidence: Ontario's Action Plan for Seniors). However, the emphasis on staying out of hospitals and long-term care facilities has not been accompanied by enough resources to provide adequate care at home. Indeed, the real emphasis seems to be on "responsibilization," that is, individuals and families taking responsibility for their own care. This responsibility usually falls on women, given traditional divisions of labour and the lack of structural supports. Yet the expectation that women have the time and skills to take on unpaid care ignores the fact that the majority of women have paid jobs and few have the skills required for the high tech demands of homecare today. For those who can afford to pay for care at home, there are options, but for those who cannot, the result too often is no care.

LONG-TERM CARE

The LHINs now also handle admissions to long-term residential care facilities that receive government funding. Ontario has long provided financial support for residential care. Entry is not means tested, so there is little obvious class discrimination in terms of entry. Residents pay an "accommodation fee" meant to cover the room and board that is distinguished from care. This fee is carefully controlled, set for basic rooms at an amount low enough to be mainly covered by public pensions and with rate reductions that make it possible for virtually everyone to afford. "Preferred accommodation" is available for those able to pay higher fees, creating a class bias. However, these fees, too, have a maximum rate that is relatively low. In 2010, the Liberals extended the list of income sources that could be excluded from calculations for rate reductions, most notably allowing deductions for a dependent family member in the community.

Money is not a major barrier to entry, but supply is. According to recent calculations, over 24,000 people were waiting to get into long-term residential care in 2010, and this had become over 32,000 in 2017 (Munro 2011, 4; OLTCA 2017). It is important to recognize that only those with complex needs are now deemed eligible for such care. For those with financial resources, the alternative is private retirement homes where residents pay the full cost. Reliance on these private care homes has an obvious class bias. Less obvious is the gender bias which reflects the fact that women are more likely than men to need admission to such a facility but are less likely to have the financial resources required for admission.

The lack of spaces in publicly funded facilities is not the only problem in long-term care. The quality of care is also important. Under the Tories, the regulations requiring minimum staffing standards had been removed just as the care needs of residents increased. With staffing a critical – and even the most critical – component in quality, the removal of staffing standards was a major issue (CUPE 2009b). Responding to deputations from the nurses' organizations, the Liberal government restored the requirement to have a registered nurse on every shift. In 2008–09, the government provided some additional funding intended to allow a minimum of three-and-a-half direct care hours per resident per day, with the aim of reaching four hours by 2012 (Munro 2011, 5). There is still no regulation to this effect. As Munro's report for the Conference Board of Canada explains, "generally, facilities provide levels of care that are below these [intended] levels."

A private member's bill to establish a mandatory minimum of four direct care hours did receive unanimous support in the Legislature at second reading in late 2017. When it called the general election for June 2018, the Wynne government had not yet initiated the committee hearings required before it could come back to the Legislature for third and final reading, and so the bill died on the order paper.

The Liberals not only failed to require minimum staffing levels; they also failed to challenge the ownership structure. Under the Tories, most of the licences for new facilities went to for-profit facilities. As a result, a majority of Ontario facilities and beds are now for-profit ones (ibid., table 1). Based on their review of the literature, McGregor and Roland (2011, 35) conclude that "there is sufficient empirical evidence in the peer-reviewed literature to conclude that providing public funding for residential long-term care to for-profit facilities is likely to produce inferior outcomes." Unions and community groups have used such evidence to demand a shift to non-profit care, but to no avail. The Wynne government's 2015 strategy for homecare, *Patients First: A Roadmap to Strengthen Home and Community Care*, promised increased funding, but mainly on the for-profit, benchmarking assessment, and flexible caregiver model put in place under the McGuinty years.

These groups have also pushed for the effective regulation of retirement homes. Until now, retirement homes were basically unregulated and the problems with them have become more evident as they have moved to provide for those with higher care needs. In 2011, the McGuinty government passed legislation to regulate the care and conditions in residential care facilities. While the principle of regulation was welcomed, licensing, inspection, and enforcement have been assigned to a body independent from government and entirely funded by the owners of facilities. In effect, they are self-regulating and dominated by for-profit homes.

Groups representing seniors have had some success in gaining input into the daily operation of homes. When the government brought charitable homes, nursing homes and homes for the aged under a single piece of legislation in 2007, it also provided for resident and family councils as well as for unannounced inspections.

FAMILY HEALTH TEAMS

The McGuinty government promoted the growth of family health teams, creating 200 of them since 2005 (Ontario Ministry of Health and Long-Term Care 2012). The teams are intended to provide integrated services by bringing together a range of practitioners, usually centred on doctors, although a few new ones are led by nurse practitioners. The teams include not only nurses, but also other health professionals such as social workers, dieticians, and pharmacists. In addition, the services are promoted as offering extended hours and weekend services, with an emphasis on keeping people healthy. In theory, this health promotion work is encouraged by rostering. Patients sign up for the team's service, and teams are paid a capitation fee for each patient rather than for each service, thus encouraging them to keep the people who are signed up healthy.

In theory, the approach could both widen access to care and provide more integrated services at one location in ways that improve care for those most in need. It could also be more responsive to diverse needs, because teams are located in communities and are under the direction of their LHIN. There is not a large body of Canadian literature evaluating this theory in practice (Glazier et al. 2012), but there are reasons to be cautious about the claims. The data on individual team websites do not all suggest extended hours. A Hamilton team, for example, indicates hours from 8:30 a.m. to 5:00 p.m., Monday to Friday, making it difficult for those employed during similar hours, and without the flexibility in their workplace hours to access the services (Ontario Ministry of Health and Long-Term Care 2011). The rostering system may have the perverse incentive of encouraging teams to avoid those with chronic diseases, who could potentially make significant claims on their time without any additional financial benefit (Lanktree 2008).

The Ontario Health Quality Council's 2010 *Yearly Report* suggests that many moves toward health promotion have stalled, that there has been only slight progress on care for those with chronic diseases, and that a majority say they wait too long to see a doctor. These are all areas that the health care teams were intended to address. Cardiovascular care has improved, and wait times in some areas have declined, but it is difficult to tell what role teams, as distinct from more funding, may have played in these improvements. Meanwhile, teams in rural areas are unlikely to include anyone other than a doctor and nurse. The government did, however, prohibit the development of for-profit clinics providing day surgery.

The shortcomings persist. Reporting under the Wynne government in 2017, the Quality Council records only modest improvements in screening and wait times to see a surgeon, but also records continued problems – sometimes even alarming ones – in access of patients to the health system, caregiver distress levels, transitions from emergency to hospital beds, and equity of health care services by income group and region. Next to other comparable jurisdictions, the Ontario health system could at most be ranked "average to good" in terms of longevity of the population and nursing home quality, the worst at "ability to get a primary care appointment the same or next day when sick," and among the worst in terms of the cost of drugs (2017, 4).

CONCLUSION: MORE CARE FOR PROFIT

In conclusion, the impact of the Liberal governments are mixed. Unions and community groups, as well as the media, researchers, and the ombudsman, had some impact on the Liberals' policies. As a result of their efforts, a moratorium on competitive bidding in homecare was established, an additional 2,000 hospital beds were temporarily opened to address serious overcrowding, family practice teams were promoted and a prohibition on new for-profit hospitals was reinstated and indeed strengthened, and new standards for openness in LHINs and new regulations on retirement homes were established. The government may also legislate minimum staffing levels in long-term care, reduce the six-month wait before patients moving to Ontario to be close to family can receive palliative care, and require patient groups to reveal funding that they receive from pharmaceutical and medical devices companies – but these reforms likely depended on its winning the June 2018 election. All these measures had the potential to improve access and quality, thus contributing to equity among Ontarians.

At the same time, however, the McGuinty and Wynne governments failed to reverse the Tory neoliberal measures of public-private partnerships and more for-profit delivery (notably for-profit addiction clinics, given the opioid drug crisis), and they expanded the P3 ownership pattern (except in the case of day surgery clinics). The very structure of the LHINs that the government introduced has blocked democratic control and prevented any reflection of local needs. The LHINs have served to transfer responsibility for cutbacks without being very responsive to their communities. Those most clearly harmed by the reliance on for-profit methods are the most vulnerable patients in Ontario and the workers in the Ontario health care system, especially those workers at the bottom of the hierarchy, whose work is too often defined as outside of the purview of health care. But we all suffer from more of our money going to profit rather than to care.

Under the leadership of Doug Ford, the Conservatives won a parliamentary majority in the June 2018 election, despite the absence of a full or costed platform. The Conservatives did promise, however, to "end hallway medicine" and not to lay off nurses or public employees. But they also promised billions in tax cuts and to balance the provincial budget in four years while reducing provincial spending by 4 per cent through unspecified "efficiencies." There is good reason to believe that the provincial health spending can be insulated from more austerity cuts (Mehra 2018). What the next four years will bring is, to say the least, in doubt. The prospects for increased spending on health care and on the social determinants of health are not promising.

NOTES

1 In a recent poll, universal health care ranked first as a source of personal or collective pride in Canada, with 74 per cent regarding it as very important and another 20 per cent as somewhat important (Leger 2012, A7). An Ekos poll in January 2018 found that 93 per cent of Canadians consider a strong public health care system to be very important, (Ekos 2018).
2 A poll from 2011 (Health Edition 2011, 1) indicated that 91 per cent of Canadians support increased spending on health care, behind only increased support for low-income seniors (92 per cent). According to the Environics polling firm in 2012, 66 per cent strongly agreed that Canada should have a public health system that covers everyone and is fully supported through taxes, and another 26 per cent somewhat agreed, while 8 per cent somewhat disagreed and 2 per cent strongly disagreed (Morrow 2012, A6).
3 See Robert G. Evans, "Don't Panic: The Fiscal Sustainability of Medicare, Past and Future" (Vancouver: UBC Centre for Health Services and Policy Research, 2010). The presentation (accessed from www.medicare.ca on 23 March 2011) shows that provincial/territorial spending on Medicare only increased from over 4 per cent of GDP in 1975 to under 5 per cent in 2009. Medicare is the component of health spending covered under the Canada Health Act, which was applied across Canada by 1975. All provincial/territorial health spending, including long-term and homecare, as well as prescription drugs, increased from about 5 per cent to close to 8 per cent of GDP during this period, with a sharp jump estimated in 2009 because of the decline in GDP.
4 On P3 experiences across Canada, see Loxley (2010) and Whiteside (2016). On the Private Finance Initiative (PFI) program, the pioneering approach to P3s in the United Kingdom, see Pollock, Price, and Player (2005).
5 Carillion employs 6,000 workers in Canada, including at ten P3 projects (seven of which are Ontario hospitals). It also operates road maintenance projects in Ontario and Alberta, and owns a BC power lines construction and maintenance firm with a large electricity transmission project in Manitoba (Loxley 2018).
6 Government of Ontario, Creating the Foundation for Jobs and Growth Act (2010). The bill had thirty schedules. Schedule 25 of Bill 16 creates The Public Sector Compensation Restraint to Protect Public Services Act (2010).
7 The provincial lead for the Ontario Seniors Strategy did recommend, as the McGuinty era came to a close, that the government should "explore the implications of developing an incomes-based system towards the provision of homecare and community support services" (Sinha 2013, 11). The Liberal minister of health and long-term care Deb Matthews seemed to agree to this challenge to universality, and a vigorous debate on it may now be anticipated under the Ford government.

REFERENCES

Armstrong, Hugh. 1977. "The Labour Force and State Workers in Canada." In *The Canadian State: Political Economy and Political Power*, edited by Leo Panitch. Toronto: University of Toronto Press.

Armstrong, Pat, Hugh Armstrong, and Krista Scott-Dixon. 2008. *Critical to Care: The Invisible Women in Health Services*. Toronto: University of Toronto Press.

Auditor General of Ontario. 2010. *Annual Report*. Toronto: Queen's Printer.

Auerbach, Lewis. 2008. "P3 Risk Transfer – An Expensive Insurance Policy?" *Canadian Medical Association Journal*, 6 November.

Boyle, Theresa, and Moira Welsh. 2011. "Begging for Care." *Toronto Star*, 25 February.

Canadian Doctors for Medicare. 2010. *Activity-Based Funding (ABF)*. http://www.canadiandoctorsformedicare.ca.

CCPPP (Canadian Council for Public Private Partnerships). 2013. *Canadian PPP Project Data Base*. http://projects.pppcouncil.ca/ccppp/src/public/.

– 2018. *P3 Spectrum Data Base*. http://www.p3spectrum.ca/project/.

CIHI (Canadian Institute for Health Information). 2012. *National Expenditure Trends, 1975–2012*. Ottawa: Canadian Institute for Health Information. http://www.cihi.ca.

– 2018. *National Expenditure Trends, 1975–2017*. Ottawa: Canadian Institute for Health Information. http://www.cihi.ca.

CUPE (Canadian Union of Public Employees). 2009a. *Health Care Associated Infections: A Backgrounder*. 2 March. http://cupe.ca.

– 2009b. *Residential Long-term Care in Canada: Our Vision for Better Seniors' Care*. Ottawa: CUPE.

Denton, M., M.H. Wilcox, F. Parnell, D. Green, V. Keer, P.M. Hawkey, J. Evans, and P. Murphy. 2005. "Role of Environmental Cleaning in Controlling an Outbreak of Acinetobackter Baumannii on a Neurosurgical Intensive Care Unit." *Intensive Critical Care Nursing* 21 (2).

Ekos. 2018. *Canadian Views on Health Care Privatization: Summary Report*. Toronto: Ekos Research Associates.

Glazier, Richard H., Alexander Kopp, Susan E. Schultz, Tara Kiran, and David A. Henry. 2012. "All the Right Intentions but Few of the Desired Results: Lessons on Access to Primary Care from Ontario's Patient Enrolment Models." *Healthcare Quarterly* 15 (3).

Greenberg, R. 2003. "McGuinty Confirms Death of P3 Hospital." *Ottawa Citizen*, 21 November.

Hemingway, Alex. 2016. "The Biggest Waste of Money in Canadian Healthcare? The Private, For-Profit Sector." *Policy Note*. BC-CCPA. www.policynote.ca.

Hutchison, Brian. 2008. "Pay for Performance in Primary Care: Proceed with Caution, Pitfalls Ahead." *Healthcare Policy* 4 (1).

Kahnamoui, Niknaz. 2005. "After Outsourcing: Working Collaboratively to Deliver Patient Care." MA thesis, Simon Fraser University.

Kushner, Carol, Patricia Baranek, and Marian Dewar. 2008. *Home Care Change: Report on the Ontario Health Coalition's Home Care Hearings We Need.* www.web.ner-ohc/summary and notesnov1708.pdf.

Lanktree, Graham. 2008. "Ontario Family Health Teams Inspire Envy." *National Review of Medicine* 5 (3).

Leger Marketing. 2012. "Public Opinion: National Symbols." *Globe and Mail*, 26 November.

Lewis, Steven. 2010. "Ontario Generic Drug Wars, Part 4: Lessons for Medicare." http://www.longwoods.com.

Loxley, John. 2010. *Public Service, Private Profits: The Political Economy of Public/Private Partnerships in Canada.* Halifax: Fernwood.

– 2018. *The Collapse of P3 Giant Carillion and Its Implications.* Winnipeg: CCPA-Manitoba.

Marin, Andre. 2010. *The LHIN Spin.* http://www.ombudsman.on.ca.

McGregor, Margaret, and Lisa A. Ronald. 2011. *Residential Long-Term Care for Canada's Seniors: Nonprofit, For-Profit or Does It Matter?* Montreal: Institute for Research on Public Policy.

McKee, Martin, Nigel Edwards, and Rifat Atun. 2006. "Public-Private Partnerships for Hospitals." *Bulletin of the World Health Organization* 84 (11).

Mehra, Natalie. 2018. "Punitive Austerity: Ford, the Tories and the Coming Cuts." *The Bullet*, 5 June.

Millett, C., G. Netiveli, S. Saxena, and A. Majeeed. 2009. "Impact of Pay for Performance on Ethnic Disparities in Intermediate Outcomes for Diabetes: A Longitudinal Study." *Diabetes Care* 32 (3).

Munro, Daniel. 2011. *Elements of an Effective Innovation Strategy for Long Term Care in Ontario.* Ottawa: Conference Board of Canada.

Morrow, Adrian. 2012. "Grassroots Causes Gain Support." *Globe and Mail*, 21 November.

OHA (Ontario Hospital Association). 2009. *Backgrounder: Strengthening Home Care Services in Ontario, July.* http://www.oha.com.

Ontario Health Coalition (OHC). 2007. *What's Happening to the Brampton Hospital.* www.ontariohealthcoalition.ca.

– 2008. *Cost Comparison Analysis of P3 Projects Versus Public Hospitals.* www.ontariohealthcoalition.ca.

– 2010. *Toward Access and Equality: Realigning Ontario's Approach to Small and Rural Hospitals to Serve Public Values.* 17 May. www.ontariohealthcoalition.ca.

– 2011. *Submission Regarding the Rural and Northern Framework/Plan.* www.ontariohealthcoalition.ca.

– 2015. *Privatized Hospitals and Projects Cost $8 Billion More.* http://www.ontariohealthcoalition.ca.

– 2016. *Summary and Analysis of Minister of Health's White Paper on Health Care Reform.* http://www.ontariohealthcoalition.ca.

Ontario Health Quality Council. 2010. *Yearly Report.* http://www.ohqc.ca/en/yearlyreport.php.

- 2017. *Measuring Up 2017*. http://www.hqontario.ca/portals/0/Documents/pr/measuring-up-2017-en.pdf.
Ontario Long Term Care Association. 2018. *Facts and Figures*. https://www.oltca.com/OLTCA/Documents/SectorDashboards/ON.pdf.
Ontario Ministry of Finance. 2011. *Health Premium*. https://www.ontario.ca/page/h-premium.
- 2013. *2013 Ontario Budget*. http://www.fin.gov.on.ca/en/budget/ontariobudgets/2013/.
Ontario Ministry of Health and Long-Term Care. 2010. *Excellent Care for All*. http://www.health.gov.on.ca/en/ms/ecfa/pro/ecfa_pbp.aspx.
- 2011a. *Local Health Integration Networks*. www.health.gov.on.ca/transformation/lhin/lhin_history.html.
- 2011b. *Family Health Teams, Hamilton Health Teams*. 26 January. http://www.inform.hamilton.ca/record/HAM4728.
- 2012. *Ontario's Action Plan For Health Care*, http://www.ontario.ca/health.
- 2015. *Patients First: A Proposal to Strengthen Patient-Centred Health Care in Ontario*. http://www.ontario.ca/health.
- 2018. *Health System Funding Reform*. http://www.health.gov.on.
Pollock, A.M., D. Price, and S. Player. 2005. *The Private Finance Initiative: A Policy Built on Sand*. London: UNISON.
Rachlis, Michael R. 2008. *Health Equity and Ontario's Health Based Allocation Model*. Toronto: Wellesley Institute.
Silversides, Ann. 2008a. "Public-Private Partnerships, Part 1: The Next Hospital Wave." *Canadian Medical Association Journal* 179 (9).
- 2008b. "Public-Private Partnerships, Part 2: Calculations of Risk." *Canadian Medical Association Journal* 179 (10).
Sinha, Samir K. 2013. *Living Longer, Living Well: Highlights and Key Recommendations from the Report Submitted to the Minister of Health and Long-Term Care on Recommendations to Inform the Seniors Strategy for Ontario*. http://www.health.gov.on.ca/en/common/ministry/publications/reports/seniors_strategy/docs/seniors_strategy.pdf.
Urquart, Ian. 2003a. "Muzzles Firmly in Place Over Hospital Plans." *Toronto Star*, 21 April.
- 2003b. "Hospital Deal Could Get Messy." *Toronto Star*, 22 September.
Waterloo Wellington Local Health Integration Network. 2010. *Health-Based Allocation Model Frequently Asked Questions*. May. http://www.waterloowellingtonlhin.on.ca/uploadedFiles/HBAMFAQ.pdf
Whiteside, Heather. 2016. *About Canada: Public-Private Partnerships*. Winnipeg: Fernwood.

| 12 |

Competing Policy Paradigms and the Search for Sustainability in Ontario Electricity Policy

MARK WINFIELD AND BECKY MACWHIRTER

The design and role of Ontario's electricity system have been central elements of debates about the province's economy and environment since the system's origins at the beginning of the twentieth century. Although electricity accounts for only one-fifth of the province's total energy consumption, questions around the generation, distribution, and conservation of electrical energy dominate Ontario's energy policy discourse (Joshi 2012). The scale of Ontario's electricity system is substantial. The province has planned expenditures in the range of $87 billion over the next twenty-five years on its maintenance and expansion (Ministry of Energy 2010), a level of investment comparable to what has been anticipated in the development of Alberta's oil sands.[1] The consequences of the decisions made about the direction of Ontario's system are of no less economic, social, and environmental importance to Canada's future.

For the first seventy years of their existence, the institutions and policies that defined the province's electricity system operated in an environment of relative stability. In contrast, the past three decades have been characterized by growing policy instability. Since the late 1970s, Ontario has moved through a succession of apparently contradictory policy models: supply planning; "soft" energy paths and integrated resource planning; a "market" model; a "hybrid" model combining market and planning elements; a renewable energy paradigm centred around the 2009 Green Energy and Green Economy Act (GEGEA); and most recently an ad hoc approach driven by political management considerations. The consequences of the latter model played no small role in Premier Dalton McGuinty's October 2012 resignation announcement (Howlett, Morrow, and Waldie 2012). Despite this outcome, the ad hoc political management paradigm was continued and eventually formalized through legislation by the government of McGuinty's successor, Kathleen Wynne. The long-term implications of this approach are uncertain, but seem unlikely to serve the goals of advancing either policy stability or sustainability, particularly in light of the outcome of the 2018 election.[2] The new premier, Doug Ford, was elected, in part, on the basis of platform commitments to undertake major changes in the electricity sector to reduce electricity rates (Ontario Progressive Conservative Party 2018).

In a political economy context, the primary focus of energy policy discussions has been on the tensions between the liberal and particularly neoliberal emphasis on markets as the most efficient mechanism for making decisions about developing energy resources and, alternatively, state-centred approaches, which stress the importance of democratic control over energy policy. In contrast, progressive students of energy policy – generally following the pioneering work of Amory Lovins (1980) – have emphasized the importance of the technical and planning paradigms around which energy systems have been designed as being more central to understanding energy policy decisions. These approaches are grounded in the observation that both publicly and privately owned and controlled energy utilities have suffered from the same "hard" path pathologies of massively overbuilding large, capital-intensive, inflexible, high environmental impact, high catastrophic-event-risk energy supply technologies (e.g., nuclear and coal), and underemphasizing the "soft" path options of energy efficiency and smaller, more flexible low-impact renewable energy sources. Authors working on energy-related questions within political economy frameworks have tended to highlight the centrality of the specific material character of energy resources (e.g., their particular physical properties and the nature of the technologies and infrastructure required for their use) to the understanding of governance and public policy issues around them (Mitchell 2011).

The underlying normative framework for this chapter considers how the Ontario electricity system can be configured to advance sustainability and system stability. Sustainability is defined here as incorporating the core Brundtland (WCED 1987) elements of both *inter*generational and *intra*generational justice. The chapter also draws on more recent reflections on sustainability (Gibson 2006) and works specific to energy issues (Jaccard 2005; Winfield, Gibson, Markvart, Gaudreau, and Taylor 2010; Winfield 2016). These contributions incorporate considerations regarding the importance of system resilience, adaptive capacity, and the avoidance of path dependency; precaution, particularly with respect to the potential for catastrophic events; the need for economic and resource efficiency; the centrality of socio-ecological civility and democratic governance; and the avoidance of geopolitical risks in energy system design. Such a framework leans towards the soft path technological options, but also highlights the importance of the role of the state in system planning to ensure democratic governance.

Within these theoretical contexts, the chapter argues that the present electricity policy situation in Ontario reflects the extent to which the long-standing historical consensus around the objectives of the province's electricity system of providing cheap and abundant electricity, and the planning models used to support those objectives, has broken down. New actors, including organized environmental interests and, more recently, an emergent renewable energy industry, have challenged the system's traditional assumptions and directions in terms of their environmental and social consequences, their ability to deliver electricity reliably and at least cost, and their capacity to adapt and respond appropriately to the rapid changes occurring in the province's economy and society. The result has been a highly unstable policy environment in which different constituencies, or "policy entrepreneurs," have been able to take advantage of the "policy windows" (Kingdon 1995) created by convergences of problems and crises, political circumstances and the availability of new policy ideas, taking control of the electricity policy agenda – until the arrival of the next window.

In this environment, decision-making around electricity became explicitly politicized to an extraordinary degree during the latter stages of the McGuinty government, a practice continued and formalized under his successor, Kathleen Wynne. The resulting policy environment has come to be defined by a combination of low legitimacy and high instability. Premier Ford and the province's future premiers face decisions about the overall design and course of the province's electricity system in the face of uncertainty about the future direction of electricity demand. A series of emerging socio-technological revolutions in the energy sector, including the rapid deployments of "smart" grids, as well as dramatic improvements in the technological performance of renewable energy and energy storage technologies, further complicate the landscape (Winfield 2017). These are questions that will require far more than day-to-day political management to resolve.

In attempting to understand the origins of the province's current situation, this chapter pays particular attention to the competing policy and governance paradigms (Skogstad 2008) for the electricity system being advanced by different actors. The importance of the role of underlying normative concepts and factors in understanding public policy, particularly energy policy, has been highlighted by a number of authors (Doern and Toner 1985; Doern and Gattinger 2003; Dryzek 2005; Winfield and Dolter 2014). There has been a tendency in the mainstream Canadian public policy literature to address these questions through proxies of state and non-state actors rather than to treat them as important variables in their own right. As such, the chapter explores the six policy paradigms that have defined the system, from its origins in 1906 under the auspices of Sir Adam Beck's Ontario Hydro-Electric Power Commission (HEPC), in terms of their normative assumptions, the institutional and societal actors that supported them, and the circumstances that led to their demise and the emergence of new paradigms.

PARADIGM 1: SUPPLY PLANNING

A supply planning paradigm guided Ontario's electricity system over the first seventy years following the creation of the Ontario Hydro-Electric Power Commission (HEPC) by the Conservative government of James Whitney in 1906. The supply planning model sought to expand electricity capacity to meet projected demand growth by way of centralized, large-scale generation facilities whose economies of scale yielded lower electricity rates (Swisher, Jannuzzi, and Redlinger 1997). Supply planning typically led to monopoly system structures, rapid capacity expansions in the form of capital-intensive energy mega-projects, hierarchical transmission and distribution systems, the active encouragement of electricity consumption as it was believed to be essential to economic growth, and political interventions to keep rates low. In Ontario, the HEPC and its successor, Ontario Hydro, are widely regarded to have been archetypical supply planning entities – monopolies responsible for planning, building, and operating the electricity generation and transmission system. The model defined the role and approach of most publicly and privately owned utilities in North America until the 1980s.

Anticipating an ever-increasing demand for electric power, the HEPC set out in the 1920s to develop or purchase all of the viable hydroelectric sites available in Ontario. The exhaustion of accessible and economic hydraulic sites, coupled with increasing post-World War II electricity demand, led to the addition of coal-fired generation from the early 1950s onwards (Macdonald et al. 1996). The availability of uranium deposits in Northern Ontario prompted recommendations that in the longer term, large-scale nuclear power plants provide the foundation of both new supply and the development of an export-oriented nuclear industry in the province. By the late 1960s the province's first nuclear generating station (Douglas Point) was online, another (Pickering) was under construction, and plans for further stations were announced (Freeman 1996, 126).

Private industry played a major role in sustaining the supply planning model in Ontario. Major industrial energy consumers supported the supply planning model, believing that its "economies of scale" approach provided cheap, abundant, and reliable supplies of energy. The interests of three primary actors were supported by this governing paradigm, namely the HEPC and its successor (Ontario Hydro), industrial energy consumers, and the Conservative/Progressive Conservative "dynasty" that dominated the province's politics for most of the twentieth century (Swift and Stewart 2004, 14).

PARADIGM 2: SUPPLY PLANNING MEETS SOFT ENERGY PATHS – INTEGRATED RESOURCE PLANNING

Debates began to emerge throughout North America over the prudence of the supply planning policy paradigm from the mid-1970s onwards. These arguments were driven by a combination of concerns over the widespread and massive cost overruns on the utility-sponsored nuclear projects that the model had spawned, the environmental impacts of coal-fired electricity, energy security concerns resulting from the "oil shocks" of the mid-1970s, and the safety implications of the 1978 Three Mile Island nuclear accident (ibid., 3). The central figure in the emerging critique was Amory Lovins, an energy researcher trained in physics. Lovins (1980, 176, 191) challenged the supply planning-based "hard" energy path and its emphasis on large-scale centralized technologies on the basis that:

- it is inflexible and results in path dependency, limiting the ability of future decision-makers to adopt new and superior technologies;
- it is inefficient and costly due to its capital-intensive nature and its tendency to overbuild supply; and
- the scale and complexity of hard path infrastructure subjects the system to greater risk of malfunction and disruption.

Lovins argued instead for an approach based on "soft" technologies such as energy efficiency and renewable energy. The principles of the soft path paradigm were as follows:

- Perpetual growth in electricity demand is not necessary for economic prosperity;
- The environment is a finite system – the environment has limits;
- Distributed generation is preferable to centralized control;
- The electricity system should be flexible, diverse, sustainable, and benign;
- Conservation and efficiency should be pursued first, renewables second;
- Energy supply should be matched to end-use needs in terms of scale and quality;
- There must be opportunities for broad participation in the energy system; and
- Low impact fossil-fuel technologies (e.g., natural gas) should be used to enable the phase-out of nuclear and other "hard" path technologies.

Lovins's critics, particularly established actors in the energy sector, viewed his ideas as unnecessary, infeasible, and even dangerous (Robinson 1982, 27). To others, however, they represented an alternative policy paradigm – one that, to this day, continues to provide much of the intellectual foundation of critiques of conventional approaches to energy system planning and technological choices. In Ontario, criticism of the supply planning model and Ontario Hydro's expansionary aspirations had begun to emerge even before Lovins's articulation of the soft path concept. A diverse and fragmented group of anti-nuclear advocates, environmental organizations, opposition party politicians, and energy experts had already started to argue that Ontario Hydro was grossly overestimating future electricity demand, hiding the true costs of nuclear projects, and ignoring the potential for improvements in energy efficiency and the emergence of new renewable energy technologies (Swift and Stewart 2004).

In response to the emerging public concerns over Ontario Hydro's approach and activities, a Royal Commission on Electric Power Planning, chaired by Arthur Porter, was established by the Davis government in 1975. The Porter Commission was mandated to investigate Hydro's demand forecasts and nuclear program. The commission's 1980 final report challenged the soundness of Ontario Hydro's planning assumptions and recommended that "the rigidity of supply planning, with its fixation on large-scale nuclear plants, be abandoned for the flexibility of demand management and smaller-scale additions to generation capacity" (ibid., 28). The government nominally accepted the bulk of the commission's recommendations, and Ontario Hydro initiated some energy conservation programs, but the focus on the development of major nuclear energy projects, particularly the Darlington facility east of Toronto, continued (Winfield 2012, 34).

The fall of the Progressive Conservative "dynasty" after the 1985 provincial election and its replacement by a minority Liberal government, led by David Peterson, seemed to reinforce the shift in direction toward a softer path. Neither partner in the Liberal-NDP accord that brought Peterson to power was politically committed to nuclear energy; indeed both parties had been regular critics of Ontario Hydro's approach to electricity matters during the Davis period. The 1986 final report from the Legislature's Select Committee on Energy, established under the auspices of the accord and delivered in the aftermath of the Chernobyl nuclear accident, echoed many of the Porter Commission's conclusions, further legitimizing the soft path option. The committee found that Ontario Hydro's nuclear expansion plans impeded conservation efforts and recommended a focus on small-scale generation and investments in energy efficiency (Swift and Stewart 2004, 54–6).

Despite concerns over the extent of the cost overruns on the Darlington project, the Peterson government ultimately authorized its completion, but also pressed Ontario Hydro to move in the direction of more integrated resource planning (IRP) that considered the supply *and* demand sides of the province's electricity needs while adding conservation and renewable energy sources to its list of more traditional options. The resulting 1989 Ontario Hydro Demand Supply Plan (DSP) seemed to reflect some of these directions, incorporating extensive conservation programs and environmental analyses of the options it proposed. But the plan also still strongly reflected Ontario Hydro's supply planning heritage – it was based on assumptions that economic growth required increasing amounts of electric power, and it called for the construction of new nuclear and natural gas-fired generating facilities (Winfield 2012, 59).

Bob Rae's NDP government, which succeeded the Peterson Liberals in 1990, seemed poised to move even more substantially in a soft path direction, with strong policy commitments to energy efficiency in its platform, and the announcement of a moratorium on future nuclear construction in its initial Speech from the Throne. These directions would, however, be overtaken by a series of new crises involving the electricity file. The recession of the early 1990s resulted in declining, rather than growing, electricity demand, first leading to the deferral of any new generating projects and then to the withdrawal of the 1989 DSP. Dramatic increases in electricity rates, excessive generating capacity in the context of declining demand as the Darlington facility came into service, and a $26 billion debt largely arising from Darlington and the earlier Pickering and Bruce nuclear projects, led Ontario Hydro's incoming chairman, Maurice Strong (1992–95), to declare the utility a "corporation in crisis" (Ontario Power Generation Review Committee 2004). Plans for both nuclear construction and energy efficiency programs were abandoned as the corporation's staff was reduced by 30 per cent (Winfield 2012, 75).

The effort to create an Integrated Resource Planning model by injecting the supply planning model with softer path elements effectively had collapsed. The province found itself in a vacuum with respect to the direction of electricity policy and with a provincial utility whose credibility as the planner, builder, and manager of Ontario's electricity system was seriously damaged (Daniels and Trebilcock 1996, 63).

PARADIGM 3: DEREGULATION AND COMPETITIVE MARKETS

The "Common Sense Revolution" platform that helped carry Mike Harris's Progressive Conservatives to victory in the 1995 provincial election said little about electricity policy beyond the promise of a five-year rate freeze. In practice, however, the Harris government embarked upon the most significant restructuring of the province's electricity system ever undertaken to that point, propelled by the combination of the ongoing collapse in confidence in Ontario Hydro, its own strong neoliberal ideological orientation, and the influence of market-based policy models being adopted in the United Kingdom and the United States in response to failures of supply planning models in those jurisdictions.

The Advisory Committee on Competition in Ontario's Electricity System was quickly established to outline future directions for the electricity system. The committee's recommendations sought to transition the electricity system from a publicly owned monopoly to a competitive system controlled and administered by a mix of private and public enterprise (Macdonald et al. 1996, 27). The system planning functions of Ontario Hydro would be eliminated. Instead, private investors would make decisions about investment in new generating capacity, acting in response to the potential returns on investment that would flow from meeting anticipated future demand. In theory this would avoid the problem of the massive over-construction of generating assets that had led Ontario Hydro and many US utilities into financial crisis.

Rather than having prices set by Ontario Hydro or a utility regulator, the consumer price of electricity would be determined by the wholesale market, into which any qualified generator could sell power. As a result, electricity consumers would face a rate system characterized by far greater price fluctuations and potential for price increases in response to high demand than the previous model. Ontario Hydro itself would be broken up, and the portion of the electricity market controlled by its successor companies reduced (ibid., 26, 33–4).

The market-based model was to be implemented through the 1998 Energy Competition Act. The Ontario Energy Board (OEB) was given an expanded mandate to regulate the wholesale and retail electricity markets and an Independent Market Operator (IMO) (later renamed the Independent Electricity System Operator (IESO)) was created to manage the day-to-day operation of the electricity market. Ontario Hydro itself was split into a series of provincially owned entities: Ontario Power Generation (OPG) assumed control of Ontario Hydro's generating assets; Hydro One took responsibility for the management and operation of the transmission and rural distribution network; and the Ontario Electricity Financial Corporation (OEFC) absorbed $22 billion of Ontario Hydro's "stranded" debt, effectively transferring it from the successor corporations to the provincial government.[3] An Electrical Safety Authority took over Ontario Hydro's electrical safety regulation functions.

The drive towards markets was not based on widespread public support. In fact, the constituency for the market model was relatively narrow: academic economists; large industrial power users represented by the Association of Major Power Consumers of Ontario (AMPCO); the market-oriented non-governmental organization (NGO) Energy Probe; potential builders of new generating facilities; and investment dealers hoping to profit from the anticipated privatization of OPG's fossil fuel and hydro-electric assets and Hydro One (Swift and Stewart 2004, 120, 147, 154).

The government's initial plan was for competitive electricity markets to open within two years of the adoption of the Energy Competition Act. In practice, the process of introducing markets proved much more complex than suggested by the elegant neo-classical economic theories that had underlain the Macdonald and subsequent market design committee reports. The implementation of competitive markets required the development of major new capacities and regulatory frameworks on the part of the OEB, IESO, and local electricity distribution companies.

In the meantime, seven of the province's twenty nuclear power reactors had to be taken out of service in 1997 as a result of serious concerns over maintenance and operating practices under the auspices of a Nuclear Asset Optimization Plan (NAOP). The missing power was made up through dramatic increases in generation from OPG's coal-fired plants. The resulting growth in air pollution and greenhouse gas (GHG) emissions made the plants the target of high-profile campaigns. Environmental and public health organizations, led by the newly established Ontario Clean Air Alliance and including the Ontario Medical Association, advocated closing the plants, rather than selling them to private operators. The repair and refurbishment of the out-of-service reactors at the Pickering and Bruce facilities was itself subject to major delays and cost overruns (Winfield 2012, 140). The government's attempt to privatize Hydro One was blocked by a court challenge led by the Canadian Union of Public Employees and the Communications, Energy, and Paperworkers Union (Gans 2002).

Competitive wholesale and retail electricity markets did eventually open in Ontario on 1 May 2002, nearly two years behind the government's original schedule. Complications began to arise almost immediately. The summer of 2002 was exceptionally hot, with the result that electricity demand, driven by air conditioning loads, reached record highs. The retail and wholesale markets reacted to this situation precisely as they had been designed, pushing consumer electricity costs upwards. The public, which had been repeatedly assured by Premier Harris and Minister of Energy, Science and Technology Jim Wilson that markets would "help keep [electricity] prices low," reacted angrily (Benzie 2001). The government responded with a major retreat from the market model, terminating the competitive retail electricity market in November 2002 and fixing the consumer electricity price at 4.3 cents per kWh for the next six years, retroactive to 1 May 2002. Picking up on themes raised in the June 2002 report of the Legislature's Select Committee on Alternative Fuels (Galt 2002), a number of modest initiatives related to energy conservation and renewable energy, options that had been almost completely ignored in the design of competitive markets, were announced at the same time.

Adding to the government's problems were growing concerns, particularly among major industrial electricity consumers, about the security of the province's long-term electricity supply. Industrial consumers, who had originally been strong supporters of the move to competitive markets, now began to question the model's ability to ensure that future demand would be met through private investments in new generating capacity, particularly as the bulk of the province's coal-fired and nuclear power plants would reach the end of their normal operational lives over the coming twenty years. In response, an Electricity Conservation and Supply Task force was established by the government in June 2003 with a mandate to develop a plan for attracting new generation, promoting conservation, and enhancing system reliability. The task force's creation signalled a further potential retreat from the market paradigm.

The concerns about security of supply and the government's management of the system were dramatically reinforced by the August 2003 blackout that affected eastern North America. The episode highlighted questions about the ability of the electricity transmission system to cope with the stresses being placed on it by the introduction of competitive electricity markets throughout North America.

The Harris government's response to the apparent failure of the supply and integrated resource planning paradigms and resulting financial and operational crises at Ontario Hydro was a dramatic move in the direction of a competitive electricity market. When that model began to collapse in the face of a host of practical and political challenges the government of Harris's successor, Ernie Eves, responded with a series of ad hoc measures: the termination of the retail electricity market; the implementation of a consumer rate freeze; a very modest reengagement with the soft path options of conservation and renewables; a retreat from the privatization of Ontario Hydro's successor companies and assets; and perhaps most importantly, the establishment of the Electricity Conservation and Supply Task Force. But by the time of the October 2003 election, no coherent vision for the way forward with the electricity system had emerged.

PARADIGM 4: THE PLANNING/MARKET HYBRID

The Conservatives' misadventures with the electricity file perhaps did as much as the Walkerton water disaster (O'Connor 2002) to undermine their reputation for administrative competence, and played no small role in their defeat in the 2003 provincial election. The province's new Liberal government, led by Dalton McGuinty, arrived with a commitment, driven by concerns over the air quality impacts of the post-1997 NAOP expansion of coal-fired generation, to phase out coal-fired electricity by 2007. But they had little else in terms of a sense of the way forward on the electricity file. The new government was ideologically neutral with respect to the electricity system, but had built strong alliances while in opposition with the environmental and public health critics of the market model adopted by the previous government. In practice the McGuinty government would find itself compelled to invent a new policy paradigm combining planning and market elements as it responded to a new succession of crises, both perceived and real.

The origins of this new "hybrid" paradigm lay in the work of the Electricity Conservation and Supply Task Force – the body established by the previous government to review the electricity system in the face of the effective collapse of the market experiment. The task force delivered its report in January 2004, warning that electricity demand in the province would continue to grow and that an "electricity supply shortfall" was looming in Ontario as a result of the premier's commitment to a coal phase-out and the anticipated end of the nuclear facilities. The task force, whose members were primarily large industrial power consumers, effectively recommended a return to long-term planning, to be led by the IMO. But they also concluded by recommending that "private investment and risk taking ... be the mainstay of the future power system, following competitive principles" (Electricity Conservation and Supply Task Force 2004).

In response to the task force's recommendations, an Electricity Restructuring Act was adopted at the end of 2004. The act's central feature was to create the Ontario Power Authority (OPA) to conduct long-term planning for electricity generation, demand management, conservation, and transmission, and to develop an integrated power system plan (IPSP) for Ontario. At the same time the OPA was also mandated to facilitate a long-term transition towards a market-based model. As an interim measure until the IPSP was developed by the OPA and approved by the OEB, the act permitted the minister of energy to issue "directives" to the OPA and other agencies regarding the development of new generation and conservation resources.

The OPA's planning mandate was first put into practice in May 2005, when the minister of energy sent a request to the OPA for advice on options for an appropriate supply mix for Ontario's future electricity system. This would then provide the basis for the minister's Supply Mix Directive to the Ontario Power Authority. The directive, issued to the OPA on 13 June 2006, took the unusual approach of specifying targets for individual technologies within the plan, as opposed to setting high-level policy objectives under which the OPA could formulate a plan and the OEB review it. While identifying minimum targets for conservation and demand management (CDM) activities and new renewable energy supplies, the directive made it clear that nuclear power would remain the foundation of the province's electricity system, calling for 14,000 MW of nuclear generating capacity – a target that would require refurbishing existing nuclear plants and building new reactors. The directive also required that the OPA plan for the phase-out of coal-fired generating facilities "as early as possible" – a retreat from the original 2007 phase-out target (Duncan, 2006). Breaking with the precedent established during the handling of the 1989 Ontario Hydro DSP, the IPSP was exempted from review under Ontario's Environmental Assessment Act. Rather, the OPA was required to demonstrate that it had "considered" environmental sustainability in developing the plan (Winfield 2016).

The McGuinty government would never issue a white paper or any other document explaining how the new model was to actually function. In practice, the model evolved in a direction where the OPA undertook planning activities in response to the minister's directives, determined the need for new resources, and then contracted the construction of new supply from the private sector. Such contracts were sometimes established on a competitive bid/request for proposal (RFP) basis, although sole-source contracts were employed with respect to the nuclear refurbishment projects at the Bruce and Pickering facilities with Bruce Power and OPG respectively.[4] In an atmosphere of near panic about the future of the province's electricity supply, the contracts for new supply typically guaranteed both minimum prices and minimum revenues for project developers, regardless of whether the facilities were actually required to generate power, or whether the power could be used by the electricity system. The potential for new generation to be developed on a market basis by private developers without contracts with the OPA, as envisioned in the original market model, virtually disappeared as the OPA contracted new nuclear, natural gas, and renewable energy projects. The latter types of projects were acquired through both RFPs and a small Feed-in-Tariff (FIT) program for projects under 10MW, initiated in 2006. Although with the entry of new private and community-based sources of generation and the eventual phase-out of OPG's coal-fire plants, OPG's portion of total generation fell relative to that of Ontario Hydro (85 per cent as of 1997), the provincially owned company's assets still dominated the system, providing approximately 62 per cent of total output in 2016 (OPG 2016; IESO 2017a).

With the OPA's submission of the first IPSP to the Ontario Energy Board (OEB) in August 2007 (OPA 2007), the re-election of the McGuinty government a few months later, and the initiation of OEB hearings on the plan in September 2008, it looked as if some form of closure was at hand with respect to the future direction of the province's electricity system. In practice it would prove to be anything but. A host of unresolved issues around the province's direction, in combination with radically changed economic circumstances, would provide the opportunity for the emergence of another new policy paradigm.

PARADIGM 5: THE RENEWABLE ENERGY ECONOMY

The OPA's Supply Mix Advice and the government's Supply Mix Directive regarding the IPSP had been the target of extensive criticism from NGOs following the electricity file. Greenpeace Canada, the Pembina Institute, the Ontario Clean Air Alliance, and WWF-Canada found that the product of the hybrid model looked suspiciously like the outputs of the old supply planning model. These organizations felt that the OPA's plan emphasized hard path supply options, particularly nuclear power, and was based on over-ambitious projections of growing electricity demand and hostility to larger roles for conservation and renewables (Gibbons 2008).

These criticisms, which had been pointedly ignored by the OPA, would find an apparently more receptive ear in the new energy minister, George Smitherman, who was appointed after the 2007 election.

A few weeks into the OEB's hearings on the IPSP, Smitherman directed the OPA to revise the plan to incorporate more ambitious targets for renewable energy sources and conservation, compelling the authority to withdraw the plan while it was redrafted. While the new directive seemed to signal a greater emphasis on the role of "softer" energy sources and technologies in the displacement of coal power, the minister also reiterated the province's commitment to a nuclear capacity goal of 14,000MW and the continuation of its new build nuclear procurement process (Smitherman 2008).

At the same time, Smitherman began to be exposed to new policy ideas regarding the potential for the rapid expansion of renewable energy sources, particularly wind and solar photovoltaic energy, in Ontario. The adoption of feed-in-tariff programs in Germany, Spain, and Denmark for these technologies had produced dramatic growth in their deployment in Europe (Hamilton 2008b). These programs paid renewable energy developers a guaranteed price for any energy they produced, and assured them access to the electricity grid. The strong commitments of the incoming Obama administration in the United States on renewable energy and energy conservation (Weiss 2010), and growing state-level activity around these options (Rabe 2010), further reinforced the province's interest in the potential expansion of their roles in Ontario (Winfield 2015). A coalition of environmental, agricultural, Aboriginal, and renewable energy interests had already come together over the summer of 2008 under the banner of the Green Energy Act Alliance to begin lobbying for a "Green Energy Act," establishing a large/utility scale European-style FIT program in Ontario (Hamilton 2008a).

The final element in the downfall of the original IPSP and the emergence of a new policy paradigm defined by green energy was the fall 2008 global economic downturn. Contrary to the OPA's projections, as shown in figure 12.1, electricity demand in Ontario had already begun to decline rather than grow from 2005 onwards, a trend that was accelerated by the 2008 crisis. The impact of this downward trend affected the province's manufacturing sector particularly strongly (Ministry of Finance 2010). The downturn had the twin effects of further undermining the assumptions behind the IPSP regarding the growth in electricity demand, and creating demand for a provincial economic recovery plan.

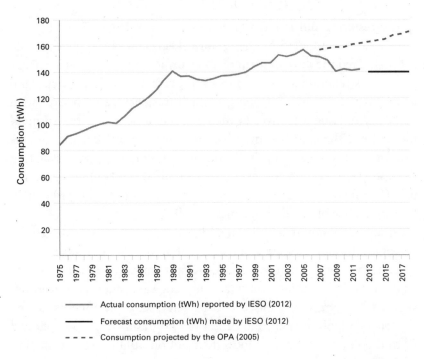

Figure 12.1 | Ontario electricity consumption in terawatt hours/year (tWh/yr) (*Sources*: Actual 1975-2012 [OPA 2007]; Forecast 2013-2018 [IESO, 2012a])

In this context, the Green Energy Act Alliance demonstrated some extremely deft policy entrepreneurship and positioned its proposed green energy legislation as an economic development strategy. A rapidly expanding renewable energy industry would offer support for renewable energy development in Aboriginal and rural communities, and also provide the basis for the emergence of a new green energy technology manufacturing and services sector similar to that which had developed in Germany and Denmark in response to their FIT programs. Within this ecological modernist (Dryzek 2005) vision, green industry would become a driving force of Ontario's future economy (Green Energy Act Alliance 2008). The government itself repeatedly highlighted the potential for a green energy strategy to produce 50,000 jobs in Ontario (Ministry of Energy 2011b). Domestic content requirements regarding the sourcing of renewable energy equipment would be built into the resulting program to promote the development of a renewable energy industry in the province (OPA 2010).

The resulting Bill 150, the Green Energy and Green Economy Act (GEGEA), was adopted by the Ontario Legislature in May 2009. The act mandated the development of a FIT program for renewable energy projects, streamlined the approvals process for such projects, and provided the minister of energy and infrastructure with expanded authority to issue directives to the OPA and OEB to ensure its implementation.[5] The following month Smitherman announced the suspension of the province's new build nuclear procurement process, citing the unexpectedly high cost estimates contained in all of the competing bids (Winfield et al. 2010). In doing so he apparently further cemented the emergence of a new green energy policy paradigm.

As an expression of a policy paradigm, the GEGEA emphasized the ecological modernist theme of the potential for positive links between green technologies and economic development, and seemed to embed an open-ended commitment to adding renewable energy sources, developed by community-based and private sector proponents, to the electricity supply mix through the FIT program. OPG was excluded from the FIT program, and local distribution utilities were limited to projects under 10MW. The program implied a significant disruption of the OPA's IPSP planning process, further delaying the revision of the plan.

At the same time, there were concerns, even among members of the Green Energy Act Alliance itself and particularly on the part of those with long-standing involvement on energy issues, about the extent to which the legislation provided a complete and coherent model for the path forward. The legislation departed from the conventional soft path model in a number of important ways, emphasizing the development of renewable energy over other resources, including conservation. More broadly, there were concerns about the extent to which the leadership of the alliance distanced itself from earlier critiques of the planning assumptions that guided the IPSP (Ontario Sustainable Energy Association 2012), avoiding criticizing the government's overall policy direction in order to pursue a FIT program (confidential interview, May 2010). The alliance's approach was seen to ignore the risk that if electricity demand turned out to be less than the OPA's predictions, the centrality of nuclear energy in the IPSP process could ultimately restrict the potential for the expansion of renewable energy sources.

The initial public and investor response to the FIT and accompanying MicroFIT[6] programs, launched in October 2009, was extremely strong. The MicroFIT program generated 47,000 applications, while the overall program produced applications for nearly 21,000 MW of new renewable energy capacity (Weis et al. 2011). As of April 2011, contracts were in place under the program for 3,759 MW of new renewable energy generating capacity (IESO 2017c). With respect to economic development, the government claimed that $26 billion in investment had been committed as a result of the legislation and 20,000 jobs created through the program by the end of 2011 (Ministry of Energy 2011c). Notwithstanding the government's rosy assessments, the FIT program faced a host of complications. The GEGEA and FIT program were never popular with the major institutional actors within the province's electricity system – the OPA, IESO, and OEB. These entities saw the GEGEA as a political override and effective rejection of the supply and/or integrated resource planning models that had re-emerged through the hybrid system planning paradigm.

The institutional landscape was further complicated by Smitherman's departure to run (unsuccessfully) for the position of mayor of Toronto in the October 2010 municipal election, robbing the GEGEA of its most important internal champion beyond the premier himself. Declining electricity demand, driven by the province's weak economic situation and longer-term restructuring of the Ontario economy away from energy intense manufacturing and resource processing industries, added to the challenges. With demand declining rather than growing as the OPA had assumed, the province began to face surpluses of electricity supply, principally as the new natural gas-fired and nuclear refurbishment projects that had been committed to during the perceived 2003–08 supply "crisis" (Spears 2011) produced an expansion of the province's installed generating capacity from 30,006MW in 2003 to 38,600MW in 2017 (Ministry of Energy 2010, figure 5; IESO 2017b).

In this context the FIT program was seen to be encouraging new supply that was no longer needed. This was particularly the case if the government attempted to proceed with its plans for new nuclear reactors at Darlington and the refurbishment of the existing Darlington and Bruce B nuclear facilities. However, the economic viability of these projects, in comparison to conservation, renewable energy, and natural gas-based alternatives, was seriously questioned (Ontario Clean Air Alliance 2010; Haines, Weiss, and Anderson 2011). The operational inflexibility of the existing nuclear facilities was already the primary driver of the IESO's need to offer negative electricity prices to in- and out-of-province consumers during periods of low demand to use surplus supply from sources of generation whose output could not readily be reduced (IESO 2012b).

The rates paid for electricity under the FIT program became a major target of criticism. The FIT prices were well above the typical hourly electricity price in the Ontario wholesale market, prompting arguments that the province was paying more than it needed to for new supply (Auditor General of Ontario 2011; Dachis and Carr 2011).

It was pointed out by FIT supporters that the market price largely reflected the costs of supply from historic nuclear and hydro-electric assets whose capital costs had since been retired or "stranded," as opposed to the actual contracted or projected costs of conventional (i.e., gas or nuclear) new supply. These costs were, at best, much closer to the FIT rates, particularly for wind, especially if consideration was given to the avoided environmental costs and fuel price risks provided by renewables. As a result, the impact of the program on consumer rates relative to the costs of developing non-renewable alternatives was marginal (Weis and Partington 2011). These arguments found limited political traction (Winfield and Dolter 2014). The criticisms over costs were sufficient to prompt the province to introduce an Ontario Clean Energy Benefit, effectively reducing residential electricity bills by 10 per cent, and an additional Northern Energy Benefit for Northern residents (Ministry of Energy 2011). The costs of the "benefit" programs were estimated as exceeding $1 billion per year, and criticized for encouraging energy consumption rather than conservation (Environmental Commissioner of Ontario 2011).

Renewable energy proponents also found themselves facing the emergence of some surprisingly well-organized local resistance to wind energy projects in rural southern Ontario. While the arguments of wind opponents regarding negative health impacts of wind energy were increasingly discredited (Ontario Chief Medical Officer of Health 2010; Ellenbogen et al. 2012; Saxe 2013), significant conflicts have emerged in rural communities between wind proponents, including farmers and landowners hosting facilities, and their critics (Stokes 2013). The situation has become serious enough to prompt the Ontario Federation of Agriculture, a key member of the original Green Energy Act Alliance, to adopt, at the beginning of 2012, a new position of opposition to further wind development in rural areas until the current conflicts are resolved.

Even the GEGEA's proponents were disappointed by the relatively low levels of community-based participation in the FIT program. In Germany and Denmark, individuals, cooperatives, and other community-based actors constitute a high proportion of FIT project proponents (Gipe 2007; Szarka 2007). By contrast, such proponents in Ontario constituted less than 4 per cent of the total number of FIT contracts and less than 9 per cent of the total power contracted (Martin 2011, table 7). With Ontario community proponents being far less organized than their German and Danish counterparts, participation in the program was dominated by large corporate developers. These proponents generally did not require the rates offered under the FIT program for their projects to be viable (Winfield 2015).

The overall result was increasing uncertainty over the government's actual direction. A new Supply Mix Directive was issued in February 2011 (Dugiud 2011). The directive limited the total contribution of new, non-hydro, renewable energy sources to 10,700 MW. In practice, this left little room for growth beyond what has already been contracted through the FIT program and previous initiatives. The plan also maintained a commitment to a system that was approximately 50 per cent nuclear, justifying both the pursuit of the refurbishment of the existing Darlington facility and the construction of two new reactors at the same location. Finally, the directive affirmed the OPA's assumptions that growth in demand would continue and in fact accelerate beyond 2018.

The political focus on electricity intensified in the run-up to the October 2011 election. Local conflicts over proposed off-shore wind projects, and their potential impact on the government's electoral fortunes, particularly in Southern Ontario, led to an abrupt ban on such projects in February 2011. The decision reversed the government's 2008 position in favour of such projects and abandoned provisions in the FIT program specifically designed to encourage them, further shaking confidence in the government's commitment to green energy. The GEGEA itself became a significant issue in the 2011 election campaign. The Progressive Conservatives proposed an outright repeal of the legislation, while the NDP committed to limiting the FIT program to community-based projects and, to the dismay of soft path energy advocates, turning large-scale renewable energy development over to OPG. Even the Green Party's platform made reference to restoring "local decision-making for energy projects" (Green Party of Ontario 2011), in an attempt to assuage wind energy opponents in rural Ontario. In the midst of the campaign, the government abruptly stated that it would relocate proposed gas-fired electricity plants that were the targets of strong local opposition away from Liberal-held ridings in Oakville (Jenkins and Artuso 2012) and Mississauga (CBC News 2011).

Given the positions of the opposition parties, the GEGEA's proponents breathed a sigh of relief over the McGuinty government's re-election, albeit as a "major minority" (Canadian Press 2011) with its implication of the continuation of the FIT program.[7] Indeed, the government's November 2011 Throne Speech noted: "Your government remains fully committed to clean energy and the 50,000 new, good jobs in one of the world's fastest-growing economic sectors." In practice the commitment would prove less categorical, particularly as some of the government's losses of rural seats were blamed on conflicts over GEGEA-inspired wind energy projects (Howlett and Ladurantaye 2011). A scheduled two-year review of the FIT program was initiated immediately after the election, but was accompanied by a moratorium on new FIT applications for the duration of the review.

The review report, prepared by the deputy minister of energy and delivered in March 2012, recommended a continuation of the FIT program, and even the possible expansion of the province's renewable energy targets, subject to reductions in the FIT rates and an increased focus on projects that were community initiated or supported (Amin 2012). The report also belatedly recommended the development of a sectoral industrial development strategy for the renewable energy sector. The strategy was initiated in the aftermath of the report (Ministry of Energy 2012). However, it was not until December 2012 that a short window for new small (<500Kw) FIT applications was opened.

Among other things, the more than year-long moratorium on new projects had a devastating effect on the emerging renewable energy sector (Hamilton 2012), whose development was one of the main purposes of the legislation. The sector's fortunes were further darkened by a World Trade Organization ruling, in response to complaints from Japan and the European Union, against the local content requirements of the FIT program, resulting in the withdrawal of the requirements (Canadian Press 2013).

PARADIGM 6: POLITICAL MANAGEMENT

In practice the 2012 FIT review marked the beginning of the end for the program. With an endorsement of the government's overall direction on electricity in the report of the Commission on the Reform of Ontario's Public Services (Drummond 2012, chap. 12) the OPA's hybrid planning paradigm found itself in little better shape. The plan's forecasts of resumed demand growth continued to collapse in the face of the province's weak economic performance and changing economic structure. In fact, the Drummond Commission's only forecast about the future was to describe it as a "cone of uncertainty that broadens the further out into the future we look" (ibid., chap. 1).

The federal government's June 2011 sale of Atomic Energy of Canada (AECL) to SNC Lavalin removed any possibility of realizing the province's long-held hope of a federal underwriting of the risks of new nuclear project cost overruns or delays in Ontario. Along with SNC Lavalin's stated lack of interest in new build projects (McCarthy 2011), and the March 2011 Fukushima nuclear disaster, this raised questions about the viability of any future new build nuclear project, a core element of the plan.

The McGuinty government's final response to this situation was to move to formalize the drift towards a model of short-term decision-making driven by political management considerations, exemplified by the Clean Energy Benefit, the off-shore wind moratorium, mid-election natural gas plant relocations, and hesitation on the continuation of even a modified FIT program. Bill 75, the Electricity System Operator Act, introduced in April 2012, was on the surface another response to opposition criticism of the government's handling of the electricity file, particularly the proliferation of an "alphabet soup" of gencies, merging the OPA and the IESO. However, the bill also incorporated an abandonment of any form of formal long-term planning, removing the OPA's mandate to produce an IPSP and instead making it clear that the system was to be guided solely by ministerial directives. The bill died on the order paper with McGuinty's October 2012 resignation over the controversies regarding the gas-fired power plant cancellations prior to the 2011 election, and prorogation of the Legislature.

McGuinty was succeeded as premier by Kathleen Wynne in February 2013. Wynne's leadership platform was silent on electricity issues, beyond a commitment to continue the coal phase-out (Wynne 2013). The phase-out would ultimately be completed at the end of 2014. In practice the other core themes in evidence at the end of the McGuinty government on the electricity file would continue under Wynne. The FIT program for larger projects was formally terminated in May 2014, and for smaller projects in 2017. The 2013 and 2017 Long-Term Energy Plans confirmed no commitments to the development of new renewable energy sources beyond 2018. Although the intention to build two new nuclear reactors at Darlington was abandoned in 2015 in the face of continuing weak demand, a surplus of inflexible supply, and cost concerns, the refurbishments of the Bruce B and existing Darlington reactors were to continue, as was a "life-extension" for the Pickering B station, at a total cost of at least $26 billion. In light of the massive cost overruns on the previous Pickering and Bruce refurbishments, many observers expect the actual costs to be much higher (Gibbons 2017).

Despite the disastrous political consequences for McGuinty of the political management approach to the electricity file, the model continued under Wynne, following her unexpected majority government victory in the June 2014 provincial election.[8] The government's April 2015 budget announced the intention to sell a majority of the Hydro One provincial electricity transmission grid and its rural distribution services. The stated intention was to use the proceeds to capitalize transit investments. There was no apparent electricity policy rationale for the decision. Concerns were raised around the sale given the natural monopoly inherent in the transmission and rural distribution infrastructure, the central role of that infrastructure in the evolution of the electricity system toward a "smart" grid, its importance in the integration of renewable energy sources into the electricity grid, ... Hydro One's role in the delivery of residential, commercial, and industrial energy efficiency programming in areas not served by municipal local distribution companies (Cohn 2015).

The Wynne government then, in October 2015, introduced Bill 135, the Energy Statute Law Amendment Act, 2016. The legislation was effectively the same as that first proposed as Bill 75 by the McGuinty government. The bill, which was ultimately adopted in June 2016, merged the IESO and OPA, and eliminated the requirement for the development and publication of IPSPs by the merged entity or for their review by the OEB before implementation. Instead, system plans would be developed by the minister of energy and approved by the cabinet. The OEB and IESO would then be required to implement those plans. In effect, the legislation dropped the pretense of rational planning, subject to meaningful independent public review, for the province's electricity system, and formalized the paradigm of political management.

A major expression of that political management paradigm came at the beginning of March 2017. With high hydro costs being consistently identified as the leading public concern facing the province (Nanos 2016), the government announced a "Fair Hydro Plan," intended to reduce electricity rates by 25 per cent for the following five years, beginning 1 July 2017 (Office of the Premier 2017). The intention was to remove the issue of hydro rates from the political agenda before the provincial election in 2018. The plan relied principally on extending the financing period for debt associated with new electricity infrastructure, typically from twenty to thirty years. The potential additional financing costs of this approach, along with the elimination of the HST on hydro bills, have been estimated at $45 billion, with the costs largely falling on future consumers (Auditor General of Ontario 2017). The approach of extending the amortization period for assets also effectively extends the expected life of those assets, reducing the technological flexibility of the system at a time of very rapid technological change in the electricity sector. Rising electricity pricing have particularly affected low-income consumers. However, their situation could have been addressed much more cost-effectively through targeted measures, rather than across-the-board rate cuts, which benefit the largest (and typically higher income) consumers the most.

ADVANCING SUSTAINABILITY AND STABILITY?

A supply planning model governed electricity policy from the beginning of the twentieth century. By the 1970s, the weaknesses of this model were becoming evident. The "bigger is better" mentality was contested by emerging social movements responding to the negative environmental, social, and economic costs of such a model. Its planning assumptions were challenged by emerging economic realities. Attempts to incorporate emerging soft energy path elements related to conservation and renewable energy sources into an integrated resource management model collapsed as the financial legacy of the supply planning model drove Ontario Hydro towards virtual bankruptcy.

The adoption of the market model attempted to improve the efficiency of the province's electricity system by moving away from central planning and instead relying on private investment to plan the system. The failure of that paradigm led to an ad hoc hybrid model, which attempted to incorporate elements of both the integrated resource planning and market models.

A combination of criticism of the resulting IPSP, overly optimistic demand forecasts and underestimated nuclear costs, the emergence of new ideas regarding the potential roles of green energy options, and the 2008 economic crisis opened a window for yet another potential paradigm, embodied in the 2009 GEGEA. However, that paradigm failed in the face of resistance from key institutional actors in the electricity system, criticism over costs and technical viability, and the emergence of well-organized local opposition to wind energy projects. In its final stages the McGuinty government moved in the direction of formalizing a framework of explicit political management through the proposed Bill 75. The government of McGuinty's successor, Kathleen Wynne, continued the political management paradigm, ultimately adopting the core contents of Bill 75 as Bill 135, and moving forward with the sale of Hydro One Networks, costly and risky nuclear refurbishments, and the enormously expensive Fair Hydro Plan. The costs and risks associated with these paths, in the absence of any widely accepted underpinning economic, environmental, technical, or social rationales for them beyond political expediency, suggest that further major shifts in direction are following the June 2018 election. Indeed, the new Progressive Conservative premier, Doug Ford, has committed to further electricity rate reductions, a review of new and existing supply contracts, changes to the funding of conservation programs, and the restructuring of the province's relationship with Hydro One (Progressive Conservative Party of Ontario 2018). Table 12.1 summarizes the elements that have come together to create policy windows through which each new system paradigm has advanced over the past century, as well as the key policy entrepreneurs responsible for pushing the paradigm forward.

The overall picture over the past three decades is one of remarkable policy instability, where different constituencies have taken the opportunity provided by each policy window to move the system in radically different directions. The primary contributor to this instability has been the increasing complexity of the political, social, and economic environment in which electricity policy must be formulated and implemented.

The historical consensus around the system's goal of cheap and abundant electricity has collapsed in the face of the need to address wider societal concerns around environmental sustainability and develop more sophisticated economic strategies. Core assumptions about demand growth and its relationship to economic prosperity and the cost, safety, and reliability of nuclear energy have broken down, while new ideas, technologies, and constituencies have emerged and gained strength. However, none of the policy paradigms of the past thirty years has carried sufficient legitimacy to survive the next policy window, a problem enhanced by the increasing politicization of decision-making. The election of the new Conservative government has only compounded these problems.

At the same time, despite the instability in terms of the various governments' policy directions, the inertia of Ontario Hydro's hard path, supply orientation has continued to define much of the system's actual path. Nuclear now constitutes a substantially higher portion of supply than it did at the beginning of the millennium (61 per cent of generation in 2016, versus 42 per cent in 2003) (Ministry of Energy 2010; IESO 2017a). This hard path momentum has continued to carry the system in the opposite direction of the principles of sustainability outlined at the beginning of the chapter. The pattern of radical changes

Table 12.1 | Policy paradigms in Ontario electricity policy, 1906–2017

Paradigm	Policy	Problem	Politics	Policy Entrepreneur
Supply planning (1906–80)	"Power at cost"	Private development of Niagara hydroelectric resources	"The politics of development"	Sir Adam Beck
Integrated resource management (1980–95)	Lovins; "soft" energy paths; Porter Commission	Darlington delays and cost overruns; supply overconstruction	Fall of the PC "dynasty"; Liberal/NDP "quiet revolution"	Liberal and NDP ministers and staff; ENGOs
Markets (1995–2002)	Competitive market models from US and UK	Collapse of DSP and Ontario Hydro in "crisis"	The "Common Sense Revolution"	Academic economists; Energy probe; AMPCO
Planning/market hybrid (2002–09)	Electricity Conservation and Supply Task Force report; Select Committee on Alternative Fuels	Failure of market experiment	2003 election; arrival of McGuinty government	Minister, political staff, and Premier's Office
The green energy economy (2009–11)	Germany and Denmark FIT programs; US states and Obama administration	2008 economic downturn; coal-phase-out	ENGO criticism of IPSP; 2007 election and Smitherman appointment; need to respond to 2008 economic crisis	Green Energy Act Alliance
Political management (2011–)	Premier's Office and ministers' offices	Collapse of IPSP demand assumptions; wind opposition; gas plant crisis; FIT cost debates	2011 election; opposition pressure on energy file	Premier's Office, party and ministerial staff

in policy direction and hard path inertia seems destined to continue unless steps are taken to build consensus around the system's goals and structure.

Although there have been a number of semi-formal and ad hoc reviews, there has been no comprehensive and open review of the system's goals, structure, and options since the report of the Porter Commission, now more than thirty years ago. Such a review, undertaken by an entity outside of the existing institutional structure and without interests within it, may be the only way that assumptions about the system's role in the province's society and economy – and the social, economic, environmental, and technological context within which the system must operate – can be examined and debated openly. Such a process offers the best hope for overcoming conflicting visions and the emergence of some form of enduring consensus – which has not been made any easier with the 2018 election – around the system's purposes and direction.

Whatever emerges, the system will need a planning framework to guide its long-term direction. That framework, however, must be far more resilient, flexible, and adaptive than anything that has gone before it. It must also integrate the wider range of objectives now being sought through the province's electricity system in a manner that captures an appropriate democratic and ecological balance while advancing sustainability.

ACKNOWLEDGMENTS

The authors wish to thank Sarah Goldstein for her research and editorial assistance in preparing this chapter.

NOTES

1 The government of Alberta (2012) most recently estimated domestic and international investment commitments to the oil sands in the range of $100 billion.
2 The election outcome was Progressive Conservatives seventy-six; NDP forty; Liberals seven; Green one.
3 This was debt that the corporation had no reasonable prospect of being able to repay and which would have rendered the successor corporations, particu-

larly OPG and Hydro One, unable to function effectively. The debt was paid down through a "debt retirement charge" on consumers' electricity bills.
4 Bruce Power is a private consortium that took over operation of the Bruce Nuclear Facility in 2001 as a result of the Harris government's directive that OPG reduce its share of the province's electricity generation capacity from over 85 per cent to 35 per cent by 2010.
5 Legislation established a process for setting CDM targets for electricity distribution utilities, but also eliminated the position of chief energy conservation officer and the Conservation Bureau within the OPA. The energy conservation officer's reporting responsibilities were transferred to the environmental commissioner of Ontario.
6 For projects 10 kilowatts or less in capacity.
7 The election outcome was: Liberals fifty-three seats, Progressive Conservatives thirty-seven, and NDP seventeen.
8 The Liberals emerged with fifty-eight seats (a gain of ten seats), the PCs twenty-eight (a loss of nine seats), and the NDP twenty-one.

REFERENCES

Amin, F. 2012. *Ontario's Feed-in Tariff Program: Two-Year Review Report.* http://www.energy.gov.on.ca/docs/en/FIT-Review-Report.pdf.
Auditor General of Ontario. 2011. *Reports by Year: 2011.* http://www.auditor.on.ca.
– 2017. *Special Report: The Fair Hydro Plan: Concerns about Fiscal Transparency, Accountability and Value for Money.* Toronto: Queen's Printer.
Benzie, R. 2001. "Harris to Impose Speedy Deregulation of Hydro in Ontario." *The National Post*, 1 March.
Canadian Press. 2011. "Horwath says McGuinty Would Be Wise to Work with Opposition." *iPolitics*, October 7. http://www.ipolitics.ca.
– 2013. "Ontario to Change Green Energy Law after WTO Ruling." *The Globe and Mail*, 29 May.
Canwest News Service. 2010. "Ontario Signs Green Energy Deal with Samsung Team." *The Financial Post*, 21 January.
CBC News. 2011. "Liberals Halt Mississauga Power Plant: Gas-Powered Plant Will Be Relocated." *CBC News.* http://www.cbc.ca/news/canada/toronto/story/2011/09/24/tor-election-power-plant.html.
Cohn, M.R., 2015. "Why Kathleen Wynne's Hydro One Sell-off Is a Sellout: Cohn." *Toronto Star*, 18 May.
Dachis, B., and Carr, J. 2011. *Zapped: The High Cost of Ontario's Renewable Electricity Subsidies.* Toronto: C.D. Howe.
Daniels, R.J., and Trebilcock, M. 1996. "A Future for Ontario Hydro: A Review of Structural and Regulatory Options." In *Ontario Hydro at the Millennium: Has Monopoly's Moment Passed?*, edited by R. Daniels. Toronto: University of Toronto Press.

Doern, B., and Gattinger, M. 2003. *Power Switch: Energy Regulatory Governance in the Twenty-First Century.* Toronto: University of Toronto Press.

Doern, G.B., and Toner, G.B. 1985. *The Politics of Energy: The Development and Implementation of the National Energy Program.* Toronto: Methuen.

Drummond, D. 2012. "The Need for Strong Fiscal Action." In *Commission on the Reform of Ontario's Public Services.* Ministry of Finance. http://www.fin.gov.on.ca/en/reformcommission/.

Dryzek, J. 2005. *The Politics of the Earth: Environmental Discourses.* New York: Oxford University Press.

Duguid, B. 2011. *Ministry of Energy Supply Mix Directive.* http://www.powerauthority.on.ca/sites/default/files/new_files/IPSPdirective20201110217.pdf.

Duncan, D. 2006. *Directive to OPA re: Integrated Power System Plan.* Toronto: Ministry of Energy.

Electricity Conservation and Supply Task Force. 2004. *Tough Choices: Addressing Ontario's Power Needs.* http://www.ospe.on.ca.

Ellenbogen, J., S. Grace, J.W. Heiger-Bernays, J.F. Manwell, D.A. Mills, K.A. Sullivan, and M.G. Weisskopf. 2012. *Wind Turbine Health Impact Study: Report of Independent Expert Panel.* Boston: Massachusetts Department of Health Protection, Massachusetts Department of Public Health.

Environmental Commissioner of Ontario. 2011. *Managing a Complex Energy System.* http://www.eco.on.ca/index.php/en_US/pubs/energy-conservation-reports/cdm10v1-managing-a-complex-energy-system.

Freeman, N. 1996. *The Politics of Power: Ontario Hydro and Its Government 1906–1995.* Toronto: University of Toronto Press.

Galt, D. 2002. *Select Committee on Alternative Fuel Sources: Final Report.* Legislative Assembly of Ontario.

Gans, Hon. A. 2002. *Transcript of Oral Judgement, Ontario Superior Court of Justice Bryan Payne on his own behalf and on behalf of all members of the Communications, Energy and Paperworkers Union of Canada, and Judy Darcy on her own behalf and on behalf of all members of the Canadian Union of Public Employees, and James Wilson and Her Majesty the Queen in Right of Ontario.* 19 April (File No. 01-CV-227522 CM3).

Gibbons, J. 2008. "Ontario's Energy System Ripe for Shakeup." *Toronto Star*, 29 June.

– 2017. "Ontario's Electricity Options: A Cost Comparison." *Fact Sheet*, 3 October. http://www.cleanairalliance.org/wp-content/uploads/2017/10/options-2017.pdf.

Gibson, R.B. 2006. "Sustainability Assessment: Basic Components of a Practical Approach." *Impact Assessment and Project Appraisal* 24 (3).

Gipe, P. 2007. *Wind Energy Cooperative Development in Anglophone Canada: For the Canadian Cooperative Association.* http://www.cpfund.ca/pdf/windenergy.pdf.

Government of Alberta. 2012. *Alberta Energy – Oil Sands Facts and Statistics.* http://www.energy.alberta.ca/oilsands/791.asp.

Green Energy Act Alliance. 2008. *A Vision of a Greener Energy System for Ontario.* http://www.greenenergyact.ca/Storage/22/1366_A_Vision_of_a_Greener_Energy_System_for_Ontario_23-09-08.pdf.

Green Energy Act Alliance, Shine Ontario, and others. 2011. *Ontario Feed-in-Tariff: 2011 Review.* The Pembina Institute. https://www.pembina.org/reports/on-feed-in-tarif-2011-review.pdf.

Green Party of Ontario. 2011. *It's Time: A Five Point Plan for Ontario's Future.* Toronto: GPO.

Haines, G., T. Weiss, and K. Anderson. 2011. *Analysis New Nuclear: Darlington Environmental Impact Statement.* Drayton Valley: Pembina Institute.

Hamilton, T. 2008a. "Time for Green Act in Ontario." *Toronto Star*, 2 June.

– 2008b. "The Wind at His Back." *Toronto Star*, 27 September.

– 2012. "Ontario Teaches World How Not to Run a FIT Program." *Toronto Star*, 5 October.

Howlett, K., and Ladurantaye, S. 2011. "How McGuinty's Green-Energy Policy Cost Him a Majority in Ontario." *The Globe and Mail*, 7 October.

Howlett, K., Morrow, A., and Waldie, P. 2012. "Ontario Premier Dalton McGuinty Resigns." *The Globe and Mail*, 15 October.

Independent Electricity System Operator (IESO). 2012a. *18-Month Outlook: From December 2012 to May 2014.* http://www.ieso.ca/imoweb/pubs/marketReports/18Month_ODF_2012nov.pdf.

– 2012b. *Supply Overview.* http://www.ieso.ca/imoweb/media/md_supply.asp.

– 2012c. *Surplus Baseload Generation.* http://www.ieso.ca/imoweb/pubs/consult/se91/se91-20120808-SBG_Explanation_FPFG.pdf.

– 2017a. *2016 Year End Data.* http://www.ieso.ca/corporate-ieso/media/year-end-data.

– 2017b. *Ontario's Supply Mix: Installed Capacity – Transmission System.* Toronto: IESO. http://www.ieso.ca/learn/ontario-supply-mix/ontario-energy-capacity.

– 2017c. *A Progress Report on Contracted Electricity Supply: Fourth Quarter 2016.* IESO.

Jaccard, M. 2005. "What is Energy Sustainability?" In *Sustainable Fossil Fuels: The Unusual Suspect in the Quest for Clean and Enduring Energy*, edited by M. Jaccard. New York: Cambridge University Press.

Jenkins, J., and Artuso, A. 2012. "Cancelled Oakville Gas Plant to Be Moved to Napanee." *St Catharines Standard*, 25 September.

Joshi, R. 2012. *Energy Security for Ontario.* Toronto: Mowat Centre for Policy Innovation.

Kingdon, J.W. 1995. *Agendas, Alternatives and Public Policies.* New York: Harper Collins.

Legislative Assembly of Ontario. 2009. *Green Energy and Green Economy Act.* S.O. 2009, c. 12, Bill 150.

Lovins, A. 1980. "Hard versus Soft Energy Paths. *Alternatives* 8 (3/4).

Macdonald, D.S., Carr, J., Grant, J., Gillespie, R., Mckeough, W. Darcy., Sutherland, S., and L. Waverman. 1996. *A Framework for Competition: The Report of the Advisory Committee on Competition in Ontario's Electricity System to the Ontario Minister of Environment and Energy.* Ontario Ministry of Environment and Energy. https://ozone.scholarsportal.info/bitstream/1873/6669/1/10258213.pdf.

Martin, S. 2011. *The Sustainability Case for Community Power: Empowering Communities Through Renewable Energy.* MA research paper, York University.

McCarthy, S. 2011. "Ottawa to Sell AECL to SNC-Lavalin." *The Globe and Mail,* 27 June.

Mitchell, T. 2011. *Carbon Democracy: Political Power in the Age of Oil.* London: Verso.

Ministry of Energy. 2010. *Ontario's Long-Term Energy Plan.* Toronto: Queen's Printer.

– 2011a. *Ten Per Cent Relief on Electricity Bills Starts Today: McGuinty Government Helping Families with Energy Costs, Increasing Consumer Protections* [News release]. http://news.ontario.ca/ mei/en/2011/01/ten-per-cent-relief-on-electricity-bills-starts-today.html.

– 2011b. *Green Energy Act Creates 20,000 Jobs: McGuinty Government Supporting Clean, Renewable Energy* [news release]. http://news.ontario.ca/mei/en/2011/07/green-energy-act-creates-20000-jobs.html.

– 2011c. *Ontario's Solar Energy Industry Creating Jobs: McGuinty Government Building a Clean, Modern, Reliable Electricity System* [news release]. http://news.ontario.ca/mei/en/2011/12/ontarios-solar-energy-industry-creating-jobs.html.

– 2012. *Expanding Ontario's Clean Energy Economy: McGuinty Government Launches Clean Energy Economic Development Strategy* [news release]. http://news.ontario.ca/mei/en/2012/04/expanding-ontarios-clean-energy-economy.html.

– 2013. *Ontario's Long-Term Energy Plan.* Toronto: Queen's Printer.

– 2017. *Ontario's Long-Term Energy Plan.* Toronto: Queen's Printer.

Ministry of Finance. 2010. *2010 Ontario Budget: Chapter II; Ontario's Economic Outlook and Fiscal Plan.* http://www.fin.gov.on.ca/en/budget/ontariobudgets/2010.

Nanos Research. 2016. "Hydro Rates are the Top Issue For Ontarians; PCs Lead and Wynne Takes an Image Hit." November. http://www.nanosresearch.com/sites/default/files/POLNAT-S15-T711.pdf.

O'Connor, D. 2002. *Walkerton Commission of Inquiry Reports.* Ontario Ministry of the Attorney General.

Office of the Premier. 2017. *Ontario Cutting Electricity Bills by 25 Per Cent: System Restructuring Delivers Lasting Relief to Households across Province* [news release]. March 2.

Ontario Chief Medical Officer of Health. 2010. *Potential Health Impact of Wind Turbines.* Toronto: Ministry of Health and Long-Term Care.

Ontario Clean Air Alliance. 2010. *Darlington Rebuild Consumer Protection Plan* Toronto: Ontario Clean Air Alliance.

Ontario Power Authority. 2007. *Re: Ontario Power Authority, Integrated Power System Plan and Procurement Process, Ontario Energy Board File No.: EB-2007-0707.* http://www.rds.oeb.gov.on.ca/webdrawer/webdrawer.dll/webdrawer/rec/12969/view.

– 2010. *FIT Program, microFIT Program.* http://fit.powerauthority.on.ca/home.html?q=domestic-content-1.

Ontario Power Generation. 2016. *Annual Information Form for the Year Ended December 31, 2015.* Toronto: OPG. https://www.opg.com/about/finance/Documents/OPG_2015_AIF.pdf.

Ontario Power Generation Review Committee. 2004. *Transforming Ontario's Power Generation Company.* Toronto: Ministry of Energy.

Ontario Sustainable Energy Association. 2012. *Advocacy: Feed-In Tariffs.* https://ontario-sea.org/advocacy.

Progressive Conservative Party of Ontario. 2018. *For the People: A Plan for Ontario.* Toronto: Progressive Conservative Party of Ontario. https://www.ontariopc.ca/plan_for_the_people.

Rabe, B., ed. 2010. *Greenhouse Governance: Addressing Climate Change in America.* Washington: Brookings Institution Press.

Robinson, J.B. 1982. "Apples and Horned Toads: On the Framework-Determined Nature of the Energy Debate." *Policy Sciences* 15 (1).

Saxe, D. 2013. "Anti-Wind Litigation: Is There an End in Sight?" *Environmental Law and Litigation*, 12 February. http://envirolaw.com/.

Skogstad, G. 2008. *Internationalization and Canadian Agricultural Policy: Policy and Governing Paradigms.* Toronto: University of Toronto Press.

Smitherman, G. 2008. *Notes for Remarks.* Toronto: Ministry of Energy and Infrastructure.

Spears, J. 2011. "Ontario's New Dilemma: Too Much Power." *Toronto Star*, 20 January.

Stokes, L.C. 2013. *Energy Policy* 56.

Swift, J., and K. Stewart. 2004. *Hydro: The Decline and Fall of Ontario's Electric Empire.* Toronto: Between the Lines.

Swisher, J.N., G.M. Jannuzzi, and R.Y. Redlinger. 1997. *Tools and Methods for Integrated Resource Planning: Improving Efficiency and Protecting the Environment.* United Nations Environment Programme Working Paper No. 7.

Szarka, J. 2007. *Wind Power in Europe: Politics, Business and Society.* Hampshire: Palgrave Macmillan.

Weis, T. 2010. *Canada Falling Even Further Behind the U.S. in Sustainable Energy Investments Per Capita.* The Pembina Institute. http://www.pembina.org/pub/1979.

Weis, T., and P.J. Partington. 2011. *Behind the Switch: Pricing Ontario Electricity Options.* The Pembina Institute. http://www.pembina.org/pub/2238.

Winfield, M. 2012. *Blue-Green Province: The Environment and the Political Economy of Ontario*. Vancouver: University of British Columbia Press.
– 2015."Ontario's Green Energy and Green Economy Act as an Industrial Development Strategy." In *Work and the Challenge of Climate Change: Canadian and International Perspectives*, edited by S. McBride and C. Lipsig-Mummé. Montreal: McGill-Queen's University Press.
– 2016. "Electricity Planning and Sustainability Assessment: The Ontario Experience." In *Sustainability Assessment: Applications*, edited by R.B. Gibson. London: Earthscan.
– 2017. "Energy Policy Is Falling Behind the Energy Revolution." *The Globe and Mail*, 15 May.
Winfield, M., and B. Dolter. 2014. "Energy, Economic and Environmental Discourses and Their Policy Impact: The Case of Ontario's Green Energy and Green Economy Act." *Energy Policy* 68.
Winfield, M., Gibson, R., Markvart, T., Gaudreau, K. and Taylor, J.. 2010. "Implications of Sustainability Assessment for Electricity System Design: The Case of the Ontario Power Authority's Integrated Power System Plan." *Energy Policy* 38.
World Commission on Environment and Development. 1987. *Our Common Future*. Oxford University Press.
Wynne, K. 2013. "Enable Communities to Prosper." KathleenWynne.ca.

| 13 |

Schooling Goes to Market: The Consolidation of Lean Education in Ontario

ALAN SEARS AND JAMES CAIRNS

Education policy was central to the agenda of Ontario's Liberal government for the fifteen years after it was elected in 2003. Dalton McGuinty, premier from 2003 to 2013, sought to be known as the "Education Premier" (Urquhart 2002; *Toronto Star* editors 2009). His successor, Kathleen Wynne (premier from 2013 to 2018), also framed improving education policy as her top priority. Wynne, who was a Toronto School Board trustee before being elected to the Ontario Legislature, told a CBC reporter in 2015: "I got involved in politics because I believe education is a cornerstone of our democracy" (Council of Ontario Universities 2015). Portraying itself as substantively different from the prior Conservative administrations of Mike Harris and Ernie Eves, the Liberal government's first Speech from the Throne promised "to bring stability and peace to a system that has been racked by turmoil for too long" (Bartleman 2003). Wynne's second Throne Speech praised the Liberal government for "strengthening what is already one of the best education systems in the world, working collaboratively with our partners across the education sector" (Dowdeswell 2016).

Despite the Liberal government's claim of providing substantive change in the field of education, its record was not marked by a sharp departure from the fundamental framework of "lean education" introduced by the previous Conservative government of Mike Harris (Pinto 2016, 2012). On the contrary, the main argument of this chapter, which aligns with the overall theme of this book, is that the Ontario government led by Dalton McGuinty and Kathleen Wynne consolidated the lean education framework through initiatives and partnerships that normalized the new state of affairs. We are using the term "lean education" here to describe the specific education regime that has developed in the context of a neoliberal policy framework to prepare students for conditions of lean production in workplaces and a narrower conception of citizenship without a social safety net. On the 2018 election campaign trail, and during Doug Ford's first days in office, the new premier threatened to overhaul education policy implemented by the McGuinty/Wynne Liberals. It is not yet clear whether Ford's Conservative government will significantly change schooling in Ontario; however, there is no doubt that whatever alterations the Conservatives make, and however aggressive they are in making them, Ford's policy agenda is fully consistent with the lean education model prevailing in Ontario since the 1990s.

The Harris Conservative government moved dramatically on the education front in the early years of its mandate, particularly from 1995 to 1998. The three key elements of the Conservative government's education agenda were universal standardized testing, the reorientation of curriculum, and the restructuring of education system governance. Universal testing – measuring the performance of all students in key areas at specific moments through the Education Quality and Accountability Office (EQAO) – was central to the Conservative government's reorganization (although it grew out of legislation introduced by the previous NDP government) (Gidney 1999, 237; Spencer 2006). Curriculum reorientation included sharper focus on specific subject content, as well as steps back towards streaming in high schools (Gidney 1999, 240–1). The restructuring of education system governance included implementing new forms of teacher professional regulation through the Ontario College of Teachers (again, envisioned by the previous NDP government), crucial changes to the funding formula (Mackenzie 2002), and a dramatic reduction in the power of elected school boards (Gidney 1999). Not one of these key Conservative policies was changed during the term of the Liberal government.

Indeed, at the end of the Liberal era, the overall framework established by the Harris government remained substantially in place. Education scholar Laura Pinto wrote that the McGuinty/Wynne government that replaced that Harris/Eves Conservatives "continued the same political course with little change to educational policy" (Pinto 2016, 98). Standardized test scores were the key success measures used to evaluate the education system, and areas that were not directly aligned with these goals, such as music/arts learning and staffed school libraries, continued to be squeezed. By the end of the Wynne years, teacher-librarians were present in fewer schools (down to 52 per cent of elementary schools and 68 per cent of secondary schools in 2016–17, from 80 per cent and 76 per cent respectively in 1997–98), and there was a notable lack of counselling services, with 61 per cent of elementary schools and 50 per cent of secondary schools reporting inadequate access to psychological services (People for Education 2017). The fundamental core of the highly contentious funding formula introduced during the Harris years, which focused resources narrowly on classroom teaching and dramatically reduced support for ancillary services, remained in place. It was, however, tweaked by adjustments that reduced the proportion of school board funding based exclusively on a per student basis from 75 per cent in 2002–03 to 66 per cent in 2007–08. This was largely due to new school-based grants rooted in particular policy considerations (Ontario Ministry of Education 2009b, 16). This slightly tweaked funding formula remained in place through the years of Liberal government, so that a 2017 assessment reported that "the Ministry has not addressed at all the issues raised by the narrow definition of education embedded in the funding formula" (Elementary Teachers' Federation of Ontario 2017, 16).

The Harris government focused largely on breaking the hold of the existing policy framework of public education established in the postwar decades. If it was to introduce a new educational regime that repudiated the prevailing order, first it had to undercut the legitimacy and the institutional foundations of the existing framework. To this end, the Conservative government's education policy deliberately whipped up antagonism towards teachers, explicitly politicized the realm of education policy, and fostered an exceptional situation in schools, colleges, and universities (see Kozolanka 2007, chap. 6). Mike Harris's first education minister, John Snobelen, described this overall approach as inventing a crisis: "If we really want to fundamentally change the issue ... we'll have to first make sure we've communicated brilliantly the breakdown in the process we currently experience. That's not easy. We need to invent a crisis" (Kuehn 1995, 12).

The Harris government went to battle with the defenders of the old regime of welfare state education and basically won. But the victory was costly to the government, because it provoked resistance among educators and school boards, and increasingly disgruntled parents. By contrast, the McGuinty/Wynne government attempted to stabilize the new lean order: to present it as rational and inevitable, and make allies out of former opponents. As the McGuinty government steered education out of the crisis created by the Conservatives, it embarked upon a new consolidation phase of lean education. The McGuinty government started with an emphasis on replacing antagonism with partnership, politicization with ostensibly neutral policy science, and the exceptionalism of crisis with the normalization of new ways of conceiving of public education. The aftermath of the 2008 economic crisis, however, pushed the McGuinty government towards a more adversarial relationship with education workers, while maintaining the broad consolidation frame. Bill 115, the Putting Students First Act introduced in 2012, forced contracts on education workers and undermined their legal right to strike. The replacement of McGuinty by Wynne in 2013 provided the context for a shift back towards a partnership strategy that included the repeal of Bill 115. In the face of a court challenge to the attack on collective bargaining rights in Bill 115, Wynne-era education minister Liz Sandals explained that legislation in terms of specific conditions, stating, "Those were the circumstances at the time" (Rushowy, Ferguson, and Benzie 2016).

There are important parallels between the Liberal government's consolidation of lean education in Ontario and the work of Tony Blair's "New Labour" government in Britain (Burden, Cooper, and Petrie 2000; Clarke 2001; Wrigley 2003, 2004). It is no coincidence, for example, that one of Dalton McGuinty's top advisors on education was Michael Fullan: chosen by McGuinty on account of his being instrumental in overhauling education in the UK under New Labour (Boyle 2004, H04). Research on the restructuring of British education helps frame our analysis of developments in Ontario.

TRANSFORMING POLICY FRAMEWORKS

Our characterization of education policy as moving through phases of crisis and consolidation draws on the Italian Marxist Antonio Gramsci's understanding of state formation. The foundation of Gramsci's approach was the concept of "hegemony," in which rulers not only dominate by force but also seek a degree of consent from the population being governed. Gramsci argued that "the fact of hegemony presupposes that account be taken of the interests and tendencies of the groups over which hegemony is to be exercised, and that a certain compromise equilibrium is formed." He noted, however, that these compromises are constrained because they must preserve the core features of the capitalist system: such compromises "cannot touch the essential" (1971, 161).

Compromises of this sort develop through processes of state formation that seldom resemble structured negotiations between representatives of contending parties. Rather, hegemonic settlements involve formal and informal processes through which policymakers seek to solve problems (Taylor 2001). There is rarely a straightforward granting of demands on the part of government, but rather "a process of transformation, reformulation and displacement" between demands from below and state policies (Topalov 1985, 259).

A successful hegemonic settlement frames popular expectations and guides the actions of major parties, including unions, management, and policymakers (Eagleton 2007, 112–21). The settlement contains and regulates conflict as long as it holds. A settlement can be broken from below, as popular mobilization challenges the limitations of the existing framework, such as in periods of activist upsurge like the 1960s. But a settlement can also be broken from above, as employers and state policymakers view the existing framework as an obstacle to meeting their goals because it serves as a fetter on innovation, encourages a sense of entitlement, or is seen as being financially unsustainable (Cairns and Sears 2012, chap. 8).

In the 1980s and 1990s, members of the Centre for Contemporary Cultural Studies at the University of Birmingham developed a specific application of Gramscian conceptions of social policy to the realm of education policy. They developed the term "education settlement" to describe "the balance of forces in and over schooling" (Education Group 1981, 32; Education Group II 1991). They noted that in light of the fact that education settlements emerge out of contending forces, settlements are never permanent but rather "are highly unstable and deeply contradictory arrangements which easily pass into crises" (Education Group 1981, 32). It is difficult, therefore, to mark off clear boundaries between one settlement and another. Despite this conceptual difficulty, the notion of education settlements is a useful tool in identifying crucial differences between the aims and organization of educational policy in different periods (cf. Taylor 2001). In this chapter, we trace key moments in the transition from the education policy framework associated with the broad welfare state at its most expansive moments (roughly, the late 1960s to early 1970s) to the framework associated with neoliberalism and the social policy of the lean state (which grew gradually from the mid-1970s until advancing rapidly in the mid-1990s).

The broad "welfare state education" settlement focused on social inclusion. It sought to bring students into the nation by means of a relatively flexible schooling system that could retain a varied population and meet wide-ranging social needs. This framework was focused on student-centred learning that was designed to accommodate individuals rather than hold all students to universal standards. For example, it was under the welfare state education settlement that standardized high school graduation tests were abolished.[1] In this period, curriculum was opened up, vocational streams in high schools were upgraded, community colleges were introduced, and the university system was dramatically expanded. These changes were driven in part by mobilizations from below, which included an activist student movement (Gidney 1999, 85), the unionization of teachers, and various struggles for the educational inclusion of women, people of colour, and people with limited incomes.

Our goal is not to portray welfare state education as a lost golden age. Even at the height of this period the education system was bureaucratic, centered on eurocentric conceptions of knowledge, and deeply implicated in the reproduction of heterosexuality, as well as class, gender, and racial/ethnic inequalities. Indeed, it was partially problems in welfare state education that made it possible to erode that settlement (Education Group 1981). Nevertheless, the core project of this education settlement was to foster a relatively expansive form of citizenship – in which the lives of citizens were increasingly bound up in relations with the nation-state.

By contrast, the emerging lean state education framework (which we call "lean education") introduced a harsher regime (Spring 2015). Its central aim has been to hold students to universal standards and narrow the curriculum. The emphasis of lean education is less on incorporating students into the state as full citizens and more on exposing them to the market, to a life of selling their capacity to work in order to be able to purchase goods and services.[2] Lean education is about "teaching cognitive skills and knowledge needed in the workplace, and shaping behavior in schools and by government to meet the needs of corporations and to sustain free market economics" (ibid., 3). The core of this project of marketization is to restructure the education system so that state power (for example, the compulsion to attend school) is used to promote market relations as inevitable and desirable. It does this through shifts in the content of education (for example, more emphasis on career outcomes), the outsourcing of some educational activities to the private sector, and the use of market model mechanisms in institutional governance. These changes were driven in large part from above, as policymakers and employers sought to reconfigure the educational system to align with the emerging system of lean production and the social policy of the lean state associated with neoliberalism (Sears 2003; Regan 2009).

One important moment in this shift of policy frame was the Harris government's construction of a crisis to break the hold of the welfare education settlement. Before a new framework for education could be established, the old one had to be undermined. This was no small challenge. The welfare state education settlement was deeply embedded and had powerful constituencies, including not only teachers and the educational administrative apparatus, but also large numbers of parents. Despite resistance to its willful destruction of the previous settlement (Kozolanka 2007, chap. 6), the Harris government did not draw back from making enemies in the education field, waging a war on teachers, reorganizing school governance to reduce democratic control at the local level by dramatically reducing the power of elected school boards, and shifting the funding formula towards a narrow enrollment-driven metric in a way that sent a financial shock through the system (Gidney 1999, chap. 14).

The destructiveness that allowed the Harris government to accomplish its goals of extinguishing familiar practices, relations, and expectations created sharp polarization that hampered the development of a new settlement. A clear and concerted strategic shift was required to develop a reconfigured education system with genuine hold – for, as the Education Group at Birmingham argues, in order for a new policy framework to become normalized, educators, parents, unions, and community groups need to find reasons to willingly participate in a new way of doing things. A settlement cannot be reached if these major players view themselves as opponents of the emergent regime.

Although establishing a new settlement does not require electoral transition, a change in government has the potential to be a useful mechanism for achieving a shift in policy frame. A change of government creates opportunities to consolidate a new settlement within the framework that shaped the destructive phase. In this regard, Blair's New Labour government in Britain consolidated the education reforms associated with the previous Thatcher Conservatives (Burden, Cooper, and Petrie 2000, chap. 5; Foot 2005, 420–2). In Ontario, the McGuinty/Wynne Liberals consolidated the lean reforms begun under Harris, though this has been an uneven process. Consolidation requires an agile response to shifting political conditions, which was evident in the retreat from, and subsequent return to, partnership with education workers in 2012–13. Indeed, the shift from McGuinty to Wynne was associated with a renewed commitment to deepen consolidation by returning to partnership and adding new elements (such as sex education and equity commitments) that radicalized the break with the Harris government's strategies while maintaining the core policy frame of lean education.

CONSOLIDATING LEAN EDUCATION

Consolidating lean education requires new governance strategies aimed at ending polarization, establishing partnerships, and normalizing reforms through routinization. McGuinty made this shift central to the Liberal election campaign of 2003 and, as premier, signalled its centrality from day one: "The path to a better society, and a more prosperous economy, runs through our public schools. Your new government believes that, for too long, that path has been strewn with conflict, cuts, and chaos. It's time to begin to build a new path, with cooperation, creativity, and a genuine commitment to what's best for our children" (Bartleman 2003). As early as 2006, McGuinty declared that his administration had moved beyond "conflict, cuts, and chaos." Assessing the contribution of resigning education minister Gerard Kennedy, the premier announced: "There is peace and stability and a positive environment in our schools" (McGuinty 2006). The government interrupted this focus on social peace in 2012 with Bill 115 in response to the economic and political aftermath of the 2008 economic crisis, but returned to it in 2013 with the accession of Premier Wynne. Peace was highly valued in this case because it was a precondition for establishing a new education settlement rooted in the lean framework of standardization and marketization. The return of "peace and stability" normalized lean education; taking it out of the realm of heated contention and making it the taken-for-granted premise of education policy.

The consolidation of lean education under the Liberals had three main elements. First, it emphasized partnership, stressing the importance of teachers and other former resisters, and finding new ways of bringing them into the lean educational order. Second, it drew heavily upon so-called "neutral policy science" to frame educational decision-making as technical rather than political. And third, it developed curricular programs that encouraged students to conceptualize their role as citizens in terms of civility and work-readiness, as opposed to liberal democratic conceptions of citizenship, which involved both responsibilities to the nation-state and the benefits of state-provided entitlements. The Liberal government pulled back from the exceptional crisis environment created by the Conservative government and sought ways of normalizing lean education, of altering fundamentally the DNA of Ontario's education system.

As stated above, the consolidation of a settlement requires agility to navigate shifting political and economic conditions. The fact that dissent against the dominant order is never fully extinguished further complicates matters.³ In the aftermath of the 2008 economic crisis, there was a period of turbulence in social and economic policy both in Ontario and globally (McNally 2011). Many predicted that a break with neoliberalism would be required: "the catastrophic stuttering of the neoliberal strategy of consolidating the state as enabler of financialised accumulation prompted widespread predictions of recomposition" (Salvage editors, 2015). In the end, however, "the recomposed social settlement at the end of neoliberalism was more neoliberalism" (ibid.). The Liberal government shifted course within the broad frame of a consolidation strategy that deepened the neoliberal commitment to lean education in Ontario.

There have been contradictory trends developing within the new education settlement. On the one hand, the expansion of the reach of education, particularly at the post-secondary level, has been presented as the crucial basis for developing a national labour force sufficiently skilled to be competitive in "an era of globalization and a knowledge-based economy" (McGuinty quoted in Radwanski 2009). Yet, on the other hand, entitlement to accessible education has been being portrayed as something that needs to be ended, both because it is unaffordable in present conditions and because it develops a population dependent on the state (Cairns 2017, chap. 4). The outcome of these and other contradictory aspects of the current education settlement will depend upon struggles in the coming years – the balance of forces between those who seek to further entrench lean education, and those who push from below for more expansive educational policies.

CONSOLIDATION THROUGH PARTNERSHIP

Ending the war on teachers was a crucial component of the early period of the McGuinty government, for a new education settlement organized around standardization and marketization could not be established without the active participation of key players within the education field. The *Reaching Every Student* (2008) report issued to mark the McGuinty government's second term in office announced success on this front:

> Four years ago, the new government faced the fact that a staggering 26 million learning days had been lost in our schools in the previous eight years due to strikes, lockouts, and work stoppages. We committed, instead, to respect all education staff and to work in partnership with them. The government's first-term "peace and stability" priority was highly successful in

establishing four years of a positive climate where not a single learning day was lost to strikes by full-time teachers. (Ontario Ministry of Education [hereafter OME] 2008b, 13)

This new partnership with teachers was necessary to transform classroom practice and the broader framework of educational relations. The nature of the teaching labour process is that it is performed with considerable autonomy (Wrigley 2003). Teacher professionalism is crucial to the regulation of this substantially autonomous practice, establishing standards for self-discipline and external assessment. Early in the establishment of neoliberal education policies, teacher professionalism was an impediment to the new regime as it was firmly integrated with welfare state education and provided considerable opportunity for resistance. The nature of substantially autonomous work is that it is difficult to sharply reorganize from above. Both the Thatcher government in Britain and the Harris government in Ontario attacked teacher professionalism, at times intentionally belittling teachers (Walkom 1997).

Despite the brief policy shift towards confrontation in 2012–13, the Ontario Liberal government generally shared the focus of the Blair Labour government in Britain on seeking partnership with teachers to remake teacher professionalism. John Furlong argued that the Blair government's agenda was "to change the ground rules of what teacher professionalism actually meant in order to harness that professionalism closely to the government's own educational reform agenda" (2008, 727). The Blair government focused on a number of areas in promoting the remaking of teaching around a preconceived idea of professionalism, including increased teacher retention, increased regulation, greater differentiation among teachers and school leadership, and a renewed emphasis on professional development (729–33).

An early working paper for the McGuinty government stressed its shift in approach to teacher professional development: "As a result, we reject outright the overly formalized and controlled PLP or Professional Learning Program unilaterally imposed by the past government. The program was not respectful of teachers and exceedingly prescriptive. It created a unique professional jeopardy by tying a particular set of courses to the revoking of the license to teach" (OME 2004, 1). The McGuinty government stated: "School-improvement needs, as well as board and ministry strategies at work in a particular school, should be drivers for teacher development, but in ways that respect teacher autonomy" (ibid., 4).

Part of this shift was simply to ease the pressure on teachers. Data from the OME (ibid., 2–3) confirmed that the Conservative government's war on teachers created serious retention issues within the profession, which led to concerns about continuing high rates of teacher turnover. Certainly the goal of easing the drain on human capital and increasing retention was part of the shift in policy. More importantly, however, the Liberal policy was rooted in a commitment to cultivating new forms of non-punitive accountability measures among teachers (Mehta and Schwartz 2011). No longer battered by a government committed to smashing the traditional model of education, teachers were invited by the Liberal government to play a larger role in assessing their own performance. For instance, the new School Effectiveness Framework (introduced in 2007–08, updated in 2013) was founded on the assumption that "Ontario educators wish to monitor their own effectiveness" (OME 2007–08, 5). The framework rejected accountability measures that were "imposed from external sources," and, by contrast, conceived of accountability as "transparent processes that lead to individual and collective responsibility for strong evidence-based practice and continuous improvement in student learning and achievement" (OME 2013, 45).

The development was contradictory, however. Although the Liberal government deliberately and publicly took a more respectful approach to teachers, it did not move to enhance any genuine form of teacher autonomy. The aim of the SEF and policies like it was for teachers to realign their self-conception of effective education so that it is consistent with the lean model (Spring 2015, 18). For example, in an era when teacher effectiveness is largely measured by how students score on standardized tests, teachers are less likely to explore more creative pedagogical approaches and more likely to "teach to the test" (Casas and Meaghan 2001, 149). So while it is true that the SEF did not define exactly how teachers are supposed to behave in the classroom, by attaching the notion of effectiveness to the results of standardized testing, this "self-assessment" tool strongly encouraged certain traditional teaching models and discouraged others. Thus, the SEF should be viewed as a manifestation of concerns among "the professionally oriented new middle class who are committed to the ideology and techniques of accountability, measurement and 'management'" (Apple 2000, 104). Using Clarke's (2001, 23) language of the "performance culture" that has grown out of neoliberal restructuring, the SEF is part of the neoliberal trend "to generate a greater level of individual worker efficiency and accountability which it is argued will have a subsequent effect on the overall organisational capacity ... to respond appropriately to the needs of the 'client' (i.e. student) whilst at the same time enhancing the overall quality of 'service delivery' (i.e. teaching)."

Despite the government's friendlier disposition, teachers in Ontario in fact saw their level of autonomy in schools narrowed under the consolidation phase of lean education. Cowans (2004, 5), writing in the OSSTF publication *Update*, clearly doubted that there was much for teachers in the change from Conservative to Liberal rule: "The repeal of the Professional Learning Programme (or PLP) has removed the initiative which most epitomized the Tory regime's callous disregard for teachers. But what will the Liberals now do with its equally odious companion: the Teacher Performance Appraisal[?]" Indeed, the Liberal government maintained the Teacher Performance Appraisal (OME 2018). From the government's perspective, the key to forming new partnerships with teachers was ensuring that the standards by which teachers assessed themselves were consistent with the logic of lean education. In the consolidation phase of the lean education system, disciplinary mechanisms were less overtly coercive than they were under the first phase; specifically, they were designed to draw on the unique practical knowledge and self-monitoring capacity of workers in schools and school boards.

CONSOLIDATION THROUGH POSITIVIST POLICY SCIENCE

The Ontario Liberal government's project of consolidation recognized the inevitability of some debate over the most effective techniques for transmitting content in the classroom, but it operated as though the ends of public schooling were given. The substance of province-wide, compulsory standardized tests made it clear that basic literacy and numeracy skills were privileged above all other types of learning

(Pinto 2016). The framework of positivist policy science reduces political questions to technical ones, making issues "tangible, measureable and testable" (Fay 1975, 22). The government's embrace of this policy science frame normalized the administration of lean education.

The hallmark of the standardized testing regime introduced to Ontario by the Harris Conservatives was the compulsory standardized literacy and numeracy tests administered to all grade three, six, nine, and ten students. The introduction of this testing regime was contested during the Harris years, but since then has largely become a taken-for-granted feature of the educational environment in Ontario. McGuinty-Wynne Liberals retained the EQAO and made standardized testing central to their education policymaking. In fact, during the Wynne government there was "support by all three [main political] parties to standardisation and centralised assessment for accountability" (Pinto 2016, 98). Despite claiming "a different point on the political spectrum," each main party aligned itself with the new normal of standardized testing when it came to the "policy ideology" of education (ibid., 98).

The Ontario government used the EQAO and its testing regime as the foundation upon which to erect professional accountability programs like the School Effectiveness Framework. As noted earlier, the SEF was designed to facilitate the government's commitment to "continuous improvement" in Ontario schools (OME 2013, 3). The term "continuous improvement" emerges from the lean production literature and is associated with the ongoing intensification of work (Robertson et al. 1992; Garrahan and Stewart 1992; Sears 1999). Of course, no one could be opposed to improvement in schools, but the term "continuous improvement" raises questions about the criteria used to evaluate change. Standardized testing establishes a specific set of measures for school effectiveness, sidelining many aspects of the educational endeavour to focus exclusively on quantitative measures of reading, writing, and mathematical abilities (Casas and Meaghan 2001; Pinto 2012; Wrigley 2004).

The template for teacher self-assessment that organized the SEF was a chart that defined the "indicators" of teaching outcomes in one column, and included an adjacent blank column in which assessors were to provide "evidence" that the outcomes are being achieved

(OME 2007–08, 29–55). The program was designed to help a school develop its own unique "school improvement plan," and yet the key components of such a plan were prescribed in the first instance. They included: "a clear focus on literacy and numeracy"; "a small number of priorities that are determined through analysis of school data"; "ambitious achievement targets"; "specific strategies to meet the targets"; "clear timelines"; and "identification of measurable indicators of success" (25).

In short, the SEF used test results as the lever to transform schools, creating a rigid, narrow set of criteria. From the start, then, the SEF was not the autonomous sphere of self-reflection that it was billed to be. Rather, it was a way of ensuring that the work practices and workplaces of education professionals were aligned with the growing "'economic rationalism' in education – the replacement of a values discussion by one about 'performance' and 'efficiency'" (Wrigley 2004, 240).

The measurement framework was used to shift the mission of schools. Political ideas of democratic accountability, through school boards for example, were supplanted by supposedly technical measures. The Liberal government did nothing to restore the powers of locally elected school boards that were dramatically curtailed by the Harris government. Rather than discussion and debate in democratic processes, education policy was seen in technical terms as doing what was necessary to improve standardized test scores. Joel Spring, a sociologist of education, described policy tools like the SEF as part of an emerging "'audit state,' which continually monitored performance … [in order] to measure the contribution of national school systems to economic growth" (2015, 14). The new assessment regime, which "configures the word 'value' as 'exchange value' rather than 'worth' … places important curricular questions beyond discussion; what children learn is a 'given', and the teacher's role is merely to deliver it so that the transmission can be measured" (Wrigley 2004, 234). There is nothing inherently wrong with quantifiable indicators of the education system, but there are limitations to what this sort of research can assess. "Though characteristics of effective schools are rarely capable of precise delineation, the appearance that they can be conveys the aura of scientific objectivity while simultaneously leaving them open to political reinterpretation and manipulation" (Wrigley 2003, 17).

Clarke (2001) notes the ways that the shift to target-setting in schools has led to increased stress among teachers (cf. Sears 1999), as well as an overall "experience of fragmentation where the conception of what will be learnt is detached from the immediate execution and experience of teaching" (Clarke 2001, 29). When the end of education is reduced to a numerical score on a standardized test, the spontaneity, creativity, autonomy of teachers, and rich learning experience of students is severely restricted. The standardized testing regime in Ontario has led "to the prioritisation of certain policies while eclipsing other laudable educational aims," and many teachers and their unions "express dissatisfaction with standardised testing" (Pinto 2016, 104). These trends would be worrisome if the aim of the education system were to develop students' intellectual curiosity and capacity for critical inquiry; however, this is not the aim of the education system. The lean education system in Ontario is primarily about reorganizing the capacity for learning on the principles of the market and simultaneously diminishing the expectations of students.

Under the welfare state education settlement, the state ideologically positioned itself as responsible for the education of all citizens and therefore tried to increase participation and graduation rates, in part by reducing possibilities for failure. Learning was characterized as entailing more than the ability to produce correct answers on standardized tests. In the words of the Ontario Government's Hall-Dennis Report of 1968: "A child who is learning cannot fail" (PCAOESO, 62). By contrast, the regime of standardized testing brought in by the Harris government and embraced by the Liberals provides students with increased opportunities to fail, as students who could not achieve certain test scores were not allowed to graduate. This approach prepares students for the precariousness of the neoliberal world, in which the safety net is eroded and life opportunities derive only from selling one's capacity to work in order to purchase goods and services (Sears 2003, 20–2).

The logic behind the quantified, standardized measurement regime was seen in the Liberal Throne Speech of 2007. The speech explained that Ontario must "ensure that still more of our children meet the provincial standard in reading, writing and math, so that we are assuming our shared responsibility to equip them to succeed in the hyper-competitive global economy of the 21st century, and to measure their progress" (Onley 2007). In contrast to the previous Harris government, the Liberals included specific targets for increasing the high school graduation rate in their metrics for system evaluation along with improved test scores. Indeed, the proportion of Ontario high school students completing to graduation increased from 68 per cent in 2003–4 to 82 per cent in 2011 (Levin 2012). The consolidation phase of the standardized testing regime included some measures to staunch the outflow of students from school before graduating, which was created by the failure and attrition rates associated with this testing regime.

CONSOLIDATION THROUGH DE-POLITICIZED CITIZENSHIP

New forms of citizenship education have also helped to consolidate a model of public education in which responsibility is increasingly understood in terms of market relations, as opposed to the state (Pashby, Ingram, and Joshee 2014). The fundamental principle of neoliberal government is that citizens should look to the market to satisfy their wants and needs (McNally 2006). This ethos of self-reliance – that is, dependence on the market – was a core of the Harris and Eves governments' education framework. The creation of a sink-or-swim atmosphere configured around test scores contributed to forming a student body prepared and expected to "make it" on its own. Those students who failed to live up to the increasingly narrow and rigid standards of success laid down by the new standardized testing regime and a range of other punitive policy frameworks (for example, the zero-tolerance policy on student conduct) were a model to everyone of the cost of not keeping up (cf. Gough, Eisenschitz, and McCulloch 2006).

Yet, this approach created problems for the Conservative government. For one thing, the steadily increasing failure and dropout rate at the secondary school level produced a growing body of under-credentialized (and therefore underemployed and potentially disruptive) young people, as well as growing numbers of angry – and voting – parents (see Honey 2001; Rushowy 2001). More broadly, an education system founded upon individual achievement or failure undercuts its own effectiveness in preparing students for society.

The Liberal government addressed these problems at a number of levels, including new measures to increase graduation rates and raise school participation rates through full-day kindergarten. Central planks in Ontario's curriculum for the twenty-first century have included cultivating an entrepreneurial ethos among all students, and specific courses teaching entrepreneurship at multiple levels (Cairns 2007; Gordon 2017; Newstadt 2015). Related to these efforts at preparing students for life without a social safety net, the Liberal government also launched a new character education initiative.

Character development in schools became a means through which the *extra-individual* was recognized and nurtured. However, crucially, in the context of character education, this was framed in terms of assuming individual responsibility for helping others, and a commitment to civility and work-readiness, as opposed to the more political aspects of liberal citizenship.

In the words of the Ministry of Education's founding document on character education, character development was

> the deliberate effort to nurture the universal attributes upon which schools and communities find consensus. These attributes provide a standard for behaviour against which we hold ourselves accountable. They permeate all that happens in schools. They bind us together across the lines that often divide us in society. They form the basis of our relationships and of responsible citizenship. They are a foundation for excellence and equity in education, and for our vision of learning cultures and school communities that are respectful, safe, caring and inclusive.
> (OME 2008a, 3)

Viewed in light of the lean education system's market focus, character development involved an interesting tension between the state's need for both socialization and atomism among its citizens. In one sense, then, character development was preparing students to be moral social beings, to ensure that they accepted the increased personal responsibility required of citizens in a neoliberal state. In contrast to the standardization of other elements of Ontario education policy, character education stresses the need for students to participate in a variety of experiences, from "involvement in leadership in the classroom" (22), to "volunteer activities" and "civic engagement" outside the school (12), to "work-experience programs that reflect the call from the business community for schools to develop well-rounded individuals capable of thriving in a global economy" (24). The program helped to embed a lean conception of citizenship in Ontario schools by developing within each individual student the values that were once vested in the collective, namely the welfare state. In their analysis of character education documents in Ontario, Pashby, Ingram, and Joshee (2014, 13) wrote that "interconnection and independence become part of a neoliberal frame of social cohesion through a notion of individual respect for difference and 'finding common ground,' despite those differences." But "in the Ontario documents, the main locus for social cohesion is the individual student-citizen … The documents lack in-depth attention to systemic inequality based on race, culture, gender, sexual-orientation, religion, or other group-based exclusions."

Sennett argues that the emphasis on rapid change and flexibility in the era of lean production "corrodes trust, loyalty, and mutual commitment." The stability of welfare state social relations, though problematic in many ways, offered at least the discursive grounds upon which people could imagine a narrative for their lives, a "shape to the forward movement of time, suggesting reasons why things happen" (1998, 24, 30). By contrast, argues Sennett, within neoliberal social relations it is increasingly difficult for people to cultivate a long-term view of themselves and their families. The market is prone to rapid change, and the state offers less and less protection from the unpredictability of the market (McNally 2006, chap. 3). We should not be surprised, says Sennett, when a society increasingly governed by the amoral movements of the market propagates amorality.

Character education, therefore, was on one level part of the state's response to its self-inflicted weakened capacity to protect and nurture its own citizens. The character development initiative sought to instill an ethic of personal responsibility in young people who could no longer look to the state for traditional forms of regulation and assistance (on the increasing "conditionality" of entitlements in the UK, see Dwyer 2004). It aimed to provide students ways of conceptualizing social differences as aspects of individual personalities that could be transcended through hard work and the acceptance of individual agency for success and failure. The Wynne government shifted this character education in a way that suggested a break with its social conservative implications by introducing a controversial sex education program that included explicit discussions of same-sex preferences, gender equality, and consent in 2015 (Brown, 2015).

Even with more inclusive and explicit sex education, and the promotion of values such as civic engagement, respect for differences, and hard work, the character development initiative was preparing students to be *amoral*, atomistic rational agents by normalizing the centrality of market relations. The same initiatives that sought to fortify students' sense of self, "to develop self-discipline and the personal management skills that will make their communities and workplaces the best that they can be" (OME 2008a, 9), promoted personal responsibility on the assumption that individuals must look within if they were to survive and thrive in the competitive global market society. The new capitalism described by Sennett (1998, 84) requires a permanent state of risk, but "being continually exposed to risk can ... eat away at your sense of character."

In order to reproduce itself, "capitalism by and large ... requires that traditional values are subverted" (Apple 2000, 3); which is why, in the words of Ontario's character development initiative, it is so important that individual students understand and act upon the "ethical principles ... needed to guide decision making for the common good" (OME 2008a, 18). In the neoliberal era, we cannot rely upon the state to act as a moral force in society. If morality is to be salvaged, the responsibility for moral action falls to the individual. By shifting the location where the citizen understands responsibility to reside – from the state to the self – character education realigns citizenship toward market relations and therefore drives neoliberalism deeper into Ontario's political DNA. Curricula like the character development initiative are ideological allies of the establishment of a new educational settlement based on the primacy of market relations.

CONCLUSION: EDUCATION MOVEMENTS IN ONTARIO

The durability of an education settlement depends not only upon the force with which it is imposed from above, but also upon the extent to which groups and individuals throughout society view it as legitimate, and willingly work within its frame. The Mike Harris Conservative government drastically reconfigured education policy in Ontario in the mid-1990s by openly attacking the welfare state education settlement of earlier decades. However, in doing so, it also provoked widespread, coordinated militant resistance to a system of lean education from teachers, unions, parents, school boards, and students. The previous settlement had been broken, but the task of building broad, stable support for lean state education policy required both a more conciliatory approach and the development of new initiatives designed to normalize the emergent hegemonic settlement. The education policy of the McGuinty/Wynne Liberal government was certainly less antagonistic than that of the preceding Conservative government. But its aim was to consolidate the gains of lean state education, not to reverse them or to push for a fundamentally different education settlement in Ontario. The newly elected Conservative government of Ford may well adopt a much more antagonistic approach to governing – particularly toward teachers' unions – than the Liberal approach of 2003–18. Ford certainly has promised to restructure provincial government and policy even more thoroughly in the lean mould.

In spite of this dominant trend, resistance to elements of lean education did not disappear over the period of the Liberal government. For example, in 2010–11, groups such as Jane-Finch On the Move and the Save Our Schools campaign launched inspiring fight-backs against school closures in their area, using the government's own Accommodation Review Committee process (designed to force local participants into identifying for themselves which schools to close) as a forum to publicize their grassroots protests and at least temporarily grind the school closure movement to a halt (Brown 2010; Gopaul 2008). Teacher activists mobilized against Bill 115 in 2012, even if their unions favoured a strategy of appealing to the courts to overrule the legislation (Hewitt-White 2015). The lobby group People for Education released reports describing and condemning "privatization by stealth" in Ontario schools (Walkom 2010). A chorus of teachers, parents, and school boards unsuccessfully called for EQAO testing to be suspended as it underwent a provincial review (Alphonso 2017). In its call for increases to education funding, the Campaign for Public Education (2011) – a coalition of unions, community groups, and parents – decried the fact that "we are still living under the Mike Harris framework for education funding." Faculty held the longest strike in Ontario college history in 2017, fighting against the precarious labour conditions and top-down managerialism associated with lean education (Gillmore 2017).

However, without downplaying the significance of these and other examples, there was no broad-based mobilization against the shift to a system of lean state education during the Liberal era. Community organizing tended to occur below the surface of mainstream public debate, and, as opposed to the massive coalitions mobilized during the Harris years, there was no overarching, pan-provincial network of resistance that brought together teachers, unions, parents, and activists under an "anti-lean education" banner. Whether this sort of mobilization will re-emerge over the period of the Ford Conservative government depends upon numerous complex factors. Most importantly, future struggles will be shaped by (1) the Conservative government's focus on continued consolidation or a new round of disruptive policies; and (2) the mass politicization and democratic forms of organizing that are necessary to transform what are now relatively small and isolated nodes of resistance into a much larger, unified, explicitly anti-lean education movement.

NOTES

1 A fuller description of welfare state education is developed in Sears (2003, 44–56).
2 These ideas are further developed in: Apple 2000; Cairns 2007; Clarke 2001; and Wrigley 2003, 2004.
3 This idea follows the thinking of Gramsci (1971). This legacy for Ontario schools is described in Hammer (2010, 2011), and can be found in the campaigning work and YouTube videos of the "Save Our Schools" Campaign.

REFERENCES

Alphonso, Caroline. 2017. "Ontario School Boards Want EQAO Testing Halted Amid Review." *Globe and Mail*, 1 November.

Apple, Michael W. 2000. *Democratic Education in a Conservative Age*. 2nd ed. New York: Routledge.

Bartleman, Hon. James K. (Lieutenant Governor of Ontario). 2003. *Speech from the Throne: Strengthening the Foundation for Change.* 20 November. http://www.ontla.on.ca/web/house-proceedings/.

Boyle, Theresa. 2004. "Making a Difference in Students' Lives." *Toronto Star*, 31 July.

Brown, Louise. 2015. "Busting the Myths around Ontario's New Sex-Ed Curriculum." *Toronto Star*, 5 May.

Burden, Tom, Charlie Cooper, and Steph Petrie. 2000. *"Modernising" Social Policy: Unravelling New Labour's Welfare Reforms.* Aldershot: Ashgate.

Cairns, James. 2017. *The Myth of the Age of Entitlement: Millennials, Austerity, and Hope.* Toronto: University of Toronto Press.

Cairns, James, and Alan Sears. 2012. *The Democratic Imagination: Envisioning Popular Power in the Twenty First Century.* Toronto: University of Toronto Press.

Cairns, Kate. 2007. *Partnership, Community and the Young Entrepreneur: Exploring Educational Partnerships in Canada.* MA thesis, Ontario Institute for Studies in Education, University of Toronto.

Campaign for Public Education. 2011. *About Us.* http://campaignforpubliceducation.ca/?page_id=2.

Casas, Francois R., and Diane E. Meaghan. 2001. "Renewing the Debate Over the Use of Standardized Testing in the Evaluation of Learning and Teaching." *Interchange* 32 (2).

Clarke, John, and Janet Newman. 1997. *The Managerial State: Power, Politics and Ideology in the Remaking of Social Welfare.* London: Sage.

Clarke, Paul. 2001. "Feeling Compromised: The Impact on Teachers of the Performance Culture." *Improving Schools* 4 (3): 23–32.

Council on Ontario Universities. 2015. "Leveraging Skills and Talent of Ontarians Key to Economic Growth, says Premier Wynne." 9 January. http://cou.on.ca/blog/leveraging-skills-and-talent-of-ontarians-key-to-economic-growth-says-premier-wynne/.

Cowans, Jon. 2004. "The End of PLP: Now What about Teacher Performance Appraisal?" *Update: Ontario Secondary School Teachers' Federation* 31 (8).

Dowdeswell, Hon. Elizabeth (Lieutenant Governor of Ontario). 2016. *Speech from the Throne: A Balanced Plan to Build Ontario Up for Everyone.* 12 September. https://news.ontario.ca/opo/en/2016/09/speech-from-the-throne.html.

Dwyer, Peter. 2004. "Creeping Conditionality in the UK: From Welfare Rights to Conditional Entitlements." *Canadian Journal of Sociology* 29 (2).

Eagleton, Terry. 2007. *Ideology: An Introduction.* Revised ed. London: Verso.

Education Group, Centre for Contemporary Cultural Studies. 1981. *Unpopular Education: Schooling and Social Democracy in England since 1944.* London: Hutchinson.

Education Group II, Department of Cultural Studies, University of Birmingham. 1991. *Education Limited: Schooling, Training, and the New Right in England since 1979.* London: Unwin Hyman.

Elementary Teachers' Federation of Ontario. 2017. *Shortchanging Ontario Students: An Overview and Assessment of Education Funding in Ontario*. Toronto: Elementary Teachers' Federation of Ontario.

Fay, Brian. 1975. *Social Theory and Political Practice*. London: George Allen and Unwin.

Foot, Paul. 2005. *The Vote: How It Was Won and How It Was Undermined*. London: Viking.

Furlong, John. 2008. "Making Teaching a 21st Century Profession: Tony Blair's Big Prize." *Oxford Review of Education* 34 (6).

Garrahan, Phillip, and Paul Stewart. 1992. *The Nissan Enigma: Flexibility and Work in a Local Economy*. London: Mansell.

Gidney, R.D. 1999. *From Hope to Harris: The Reshaping of Ontario's Schools*. Toronto: University of Toronto Press.

Gillmore, Meagan. 2017. "Ontario College Teachers: It's Not Over Yet." *Rabble.ca*, 22 November.

Gough, Jamie, and Aram Eisenschitz, with Andrew McCulloch. 2006. *Spaces of Social Exclusion*. London: Routledge.

Gopaul, Sabrina. 2008. *Jane-Finch On The Move*. http://jane-finch.com/videos/janefinchonthemove.htm.

Gordon, Andrea. 2017. "Ontario Launches Plan to Teach High School Kids Financial Skills." *Toronto Star*, 23 March.

Gramsci, Antonio. 1971. *Selections from the Prison Notebooks*. Edited and translated by Q. Hoare and G.N. Smith. New York: International Publishers.

Hammer, Kate. 2010. "Ontario Teachers Call for Timeout on Standardized Tests." *Globe and Mail*, 17 August.

– 2011. "Toronto Board Backs Off Controversial School Reviews." *Globe and Mail*, 10 February.

Hewitt-White, Caitlin. 2015. "The OSSTF Anti-Bill 115 Campaign: An Assessment from a Social Movement Unionism Perspective." *Alternate Routes* 26.

Honey, Kim. 2001. "What's Wrong at Our Schools? Tougher New Curriculum Poses Bigger Challenge for High-School Students." *Globe and Mail*, 29 November.

Kozolanka, Kirsten. 2007. *The Power of Persuasion: The Politics of the New Right in Ontario*. Montreal: Black Rose Books.

Kuehn, Larry. 1995. "Education Roundup." *Our Schools/Our Selves* 72 (44).

Mackenzie, Hugh. 2002. *Cutting Classes: Elementary and Secondary Education Funding in Ontario 2002–03*. Ottawa: Canadian Centre for Policy Alternatives.

McGuinty, Dalton. 2006. *Public Education: Progress Made, Progress To Continue*. http://www.premier.gov.on.ca/news/event.php?ItemID=4846&Lang=en.

Mehta, J.D., and R.B. Schwartz. 2011. "Canada: Looks a Lot Like Us but Gets Much Better Results." In *Surpassing Shanghai: An Agenda for American Education Built on the World's Leading Systems*, edited by M. Tucker. Cambridge: Harvard Education Press.

McNally, David. 2006. *Another World Is Possible: Globalization and Anti-Capitalism*. 2nd ed. Winnipeg: Arbeiter Ring.
– 2011. *Global Slump: The Economics and Politics of Crisis and Resistance*. Oakland: PM Press.
Newstadt, Eric. 2015. "From Being an Entrepreneur to Being Entrepreneurial: The Consolidation of Neoliberalism in Ontario's Universities." *Alternate Routes* 26.
Onley, Hon. David C. (Lieutenant Governor of Ontario). 2007. *Speech from the Throne: Moving Forward the Ontario Way*. 29 November. http://www.ontla.on.ca/web/house-proceedings/house.
Ontario Ministry of Education (OME). 2004. *Teacher Excellence: Unlocking Student Potential Through Continuing Professional Development*. http://www.edu.gov.on.ca/eng/general/elemsec/partnership/potential.html.
– 2007–08. *The School Effectiveness Framework: A Collegial Process for Continued Growth in the Effectiveness of Ontario Elementary Schools*. http://www.edu.gov.on.ca/eng/literacynumeracy/framework.html.
– 2008a. *Finding Common Ground: Character Development in Ontario Schools, K–12*. http://www.edu.gov.on.ca/eng/literacynumeracy/character.html.
– 2008b. *Reach Every Student: Energizing Ontario Education*. www.michaelfullan.ca/Articles_08/EnergizingFull.pdf.
– 2009a. *News Release March 9, 2009*. http://www.edu.gov.on.ca/eng/document/nr/09.03/nr0309.html.
– 2009b. *Planning And Possibilities: The Report of the Declining Enrolment Working Group*. http://www.edu.gov.on.ca/eng/policyfunding/DEWG.pdf.
– 2013. *School Effectiveness Framework: A Support for School Improvement and Student Success*. http://www.edu.gov.on.ca/eng/literacynumeracy/SEF2013.pdf.
– 2018. *Teacher Performance Appraisal System*. http://www.edu.gov.on.ca/eng/teacher/appraise.html.
Pashby, Karen, Leigh-Anne Ingram, and Reva Joshee. 2014. "Discovering, Recovering, and Covering-Up Canada: Tracing Historical Citizenship Discourses in K–12 and Adult Immigrant Citizenship Education." *Canadian Journal of Education* 37 (2).
People for Education. 2017. *Annual Report on Schools: Competing Priorities*. http://peopleforeducation.ca/report/annual-report-2017/.
Pinto, Laura Elizabeth. 2012. *Curriculum Reform in Ontario: Common Sense Processes and Democratic Possibilities*. Toronto: University of Toronto Press.
– 2016. "Tensions and Fissures: The Politics of Standardised Testing and Accountability in Ontario, 1995–2015." *Curriculum Journal* 27 (1).
Provincial Committee on Aims and Objectives of Education in the Schools of Ontario (PCAOESO). 1968. *Report* [Hall-Dennis]. Toronto: MOE.
Radwanski, Adam. 2009. "McGuinty's Education Talk Put to the Test." *Globe and Mail*, 6 October.
Regan, Bernard. 2009. "Campaigning against Neoliberal Education in Britain." In *Contesting Neoliberal Education: Public Resistance and Collective Advance*, edited by Dave Hill. New York: Routledge.

Robertson, David, James Rinehart, Christopher Huxley, and the CAW Research Group on CAMI. 1992. "Team Concept and Kaizen: Japanese Production in a Unionized Canadian Plant." *Studies in Political Economy* 39.
Rushowy, Kristin. 2001. "Grade 9 Failure Rate Soars." *Toronto Star*, 28 November.
Rushowy, Kristin, Rob Ferguson, and Robert Benzie. 2016. "'Remedy' for Ruling on Bill 115 Could Be Costly." *Toronto Star*, 21 April.
Salvage editors. 2015. "Salvage Perspectives #1: Amid This Stony Rubbish 2015." *Salvage* 1. http://salvage.zone/in-print/salvage-perspectives-1-amid-this-stony-rubbish/.
Sears, Alan. 1999. "The 'Lean' State and Capitalist Restructuring: Towards a Theoretical Account." *Studies in Political Economy* 59.
– 2003. *Retooling the Mind Factory: Education in a Lean State*. Aurora: Garamond Press.
Sennett, Richard. 1998. *The Corrosion of Character: The Personal Consequences of Work in the New Capitalism*. New York: W.W. Norton.
Spencer, B. 2006. "The Will to Accountability: Reforming Education through Standardized Literacy Testing." PhD diss., Ontario Institute for Studies in Education, University of Toronto.
Spring, Joel. 2015. *Globalization of Education: An Introduction*. 2nd ed. New York: Routledge.
Taylor, Alison. 2001. *The Politics of Educational Reform in Alberta*. Toronto: University of Toronto Press.
Topalov, Christian. 1985. "Social Policy from Below: A Call for Comparative Historical Studies." *International Journal of Urban and Regional Research* 9 (2).
Toronto Star Editors. 2009. "Editorial: Words Bite Education Premier." *Toronto Star*, 23 January.
Urquhart, Ian. 2002. "Revitalized McGuinty Makes his Move." *Toronto Star*, 9 November.
Walkom, Thomas. 1997. "The Truth behind Mike Harris' Handling of Teachers." *Toronto Star*, 30 September.
– 2010. "School Fees are Slowly Eroding 'Public Education.'" *Toronto Star*, 4 September.
Wrigley, Terry. 2003. *Schools of Hope: A New Agenda for School Improvement*. Stoke on Trent: Trentham Books.
– 2004. "'School Effectiveness': The Problem of Reductionism." *British Education Research Journal* 30 (2).
Yuen, Jenny. 2009. "Bad-Faith Bargaining Charged by Teachers." *Toronto Sun*, 12 March.

PART FOUR
Democratic Politics and Social Movements

| 14 |

Colonialism, Indigenous Struggles, and the Ontario State

JAMES LAWSON

A comprehensive account of settler-Indigenous relations in Ontario is impossible at any length. Ontario is too complicated, First Nations and Métis people too diverse; history's lessons are unavoidable in the account. The overview here can therefore touch on only a few key themes; a fuller account belongs to the Indigenous Peoples.[1]

Like the other chapters, this one emphasizes developments in its subject matter under Liberal premiers Dalton McGuinty (2003–13) and Kathleen Wynne (2013–18), a "Liberal era" that now has closed. It compares these governments with the previous government of Progressive Conservative (PC) premier Michael Harris (1995–2002), and it makes some tentative remarks on what the future may hold under the Doug Ford PC government elected in June 2018. Its central concern is the settler state's impact on Indigenous Peoples' economic, social, and political conditions, their resistance and resurgence.

The chapter stresses the land question. But it also considers the drone of routinized violence on Indigenous bodies. It emphasizes capitalism's role.[2] But colonialism, dispossession, assimilation, racism, environmental destruction, and patriarchy also poison Indigenous lives, settler-Indigenous relationships, and the moral claims of settler society. Capital entwines them all. Against them all, Indigenous people, leaders, and allies resist and build anew.

These Liberal governments were part of a specifically neoliberal age, in which particular pro-capitalist ideas prevail. Neoliberalism generally insists upon the efficiency and equity of deregulated markets, of private-property rights, and of competitive and possessive individualism. It seeks rollbacks in state redistribution, in pay for reproductive labour, and in rates of pay and working conditions more generally.

These are familiar enough themes in capitalism's history; neoliberalism reaffirms their centrality and universality, even outside the economic realm.

Of course, the varied tendencies and interests in a society receive neoliberalism differently. When linked to the right wing of the North American political spectrum, neoliberalism upholds unequal social outcomes alongside formal equality of opportunity; promotes family-based privatism over public and collective activism; and variously combines libertarian proposals with punitive state responses to crime and dissent (Brown 2006). Increasingly, cracks in its carapace and deviations from its faith claims have surfaced, including from elements in right-populist tendencies worldwide. The latter tendencies, alongside neoliberalism proper, gave rise to the incoming premier Doug Ford. That said, since the late 1980s, core neoliberal policy prescriptions became nearly axiomatic, even for liberal or social democratic governments. They promise to be central to the Ford government as well.

Some Indigenous Nations and individuals have concluded in this neoliberal era that confident, autonomous participation in capitalism can lessen Indigenous poverty and social suffering. Through social programs and limited state activism, Liberal governments underwrote this idea. Others see such participation as a recipe for further Indigenous dispossession, assimilation, and exploitation. In the present, still-colonial context, this chapter does not presume to adjudicate this debate. The chapter does affirm that capitalism expands as it exploits, exploits as it expands. In good times and in bad, in good faith or in bad, capital's rhythms and modes of operation renew settler society's pact with colonial expansion, inequality, and other forces that mar Indigenous lives.

In accounts of Ontario Aboriginal policy, the Liberal era rarely appears as a low point. Its leaders appeared generally to have wanted better relations. Aboriginal policy also allowed Liberals to signal moderation to the wider electorate in an otherwise inauspicious time: in addition to the neoliberal restructuring that had intensified across North America, security fears had risen after September 11, 2001, and the province's industrial base was in general decline. Liberal measures targeted violence in Indigenous households and communities, injustice in the judicial system, and unilateral practices in negotiations. Liberal governments pointedly avoided some confrontations over Aboriginal policy that earlier governments would have joined; in some truth-telling, they broke new ground. Yet the destructive backdrop conditions remain.

One central puzzle in assessing the legacy of the Liberal era is the Liberals' self-conscious self-presentation as moderate progressives through – of all things – settler-Indigenous relations. This policy area addressed (and addresses) crying needs, but it touched (and touches) few Ontario voters directly. A second puzzle: if the tensions and distress were (and are) ongoing, what would it have taken to go further, and why did the Liberals not do so?

Three factors are offered here by way of explanation. First, makers of Aboriginal policy normally present Indigenous conditions as exceptions to settler society. Second, the prevailing neoliberal consensus sharply restricts policy alternatives that could otherwise signal moderate progressivism. Third, all capitalist governments must facilitate capitalist growth.

This last factor means territorial expansion and periodic relocation of capitalist activities; in the context of settler states, that means ongoing Indigenous dispossession. Doing less than what is needed for a small, deeply marginalized population, but doing so visibly, allows government to postpone two reckonings in such a context: first, with the roots of that population's problems in colonial expansion; and second, with mounting inequality in settler society (see other chapters in this volume).

The following section considers the Ipperwash crisis, a symbol of both PC "toughness" and McGuinty moderation, and a symbolic spectre of the past for some of the major programming under Wynne. Next, the chapter sketches the severity of Indigenous social conditions in the Liberal era, and then points to their historical roots. It suggests neoliberal and welfare-therapeutic alternatives have influenced successive Ontario government policy styles, but that important regional variations mark settler-Indigenous conflicts. The chapter points to the visibility of Indigenous social conditions to settler populations and the perceived threats of Aboriginal policy to their interests to explain these variations.

In the end, the chapter returns to the two puzzles with which it began. Ethical consistency and policy effectiveness require a decisive break with Liberal moderation, but not the kind that PC campaign rhetoric prescribed in the 2018 election. The Conservatives appear to be determined to stimulate the economy through tax cuts and shrink the government, particularly with reference to targeted social programming and environmental programs. By implication, that project will proceed with a much more limited commitment to Indigenous difference as a positive feature of Ontario politics. That combination should mean a revived basis for colonial expansion and ecological imperialism at Indigenous expense, fewer official channels for handling Indigenous concerns, and therefore intensified settler-Indigenous conflict.

IPPERWASH AND MCGUINTY MODERATION

On 6 September 1995, well before the Liberal era, a violent confrontation broke out at Ipperwash Provincial Park between Indigenous activists and the Ontario Provincial Police (OPP). Anishinabaek activist Dudley George died from gunshots; two others were injured (Windspeaker Staff 1995). For years after, critics alleged that the Premier's Office – or even Premier Harris – had directly shaped these events.

The Ipperwash conflict crystallized the Harris government's approach to Aboriginal policy, just as it was consolidating power. The conflict opened up tensions between the provincial police, the premier, and Cabinet. The later investigation marked the preferred policy style of the incoming Liberal government. But it also exposed the wider role of state violence in settler-Indigenous relations, and the fragility of settler claims to land ownership.

By 1995, Ipperwash was already a charged symbol. Its original 1928 sale to private owners had angered the Stoney Point Ojibway (Anishinabaek). Ontario had then bought the land in 1936, and it founded the park without consulting them (Barnsley 2006a, Harries 2008). Subsequent governments simply assumed that Ontario's ownership was legitimate. Against Stoney Point objections, the Canadian military expropriated more reserve land in the Second World War: Camp Ipperwash endured into the 1990s.

In 1993, Indigenous activists reclaimed the camp's site. At about the time the Harris government took power in 1995, activists moved to reclaim the park as well. The new government wanted the "occupiers" removed. The activists countered that the land was unceded and that its original sale was improper: effectively, they considered the province itself the "occupier."

Harris's position reflected the wider PC stance toward protest. Facing premiers David Peterson (1985–90) and Bob Rae (1990–95), some Indigenous leaders, environmentalists, and others had made gains through protest and high-pressure bargaining outside normal channels. By 1995, many Ontarians supported the PCs' "tougher" stand against these tactics: they regarded protesters as lawless "special interests" and dangers to the economy. Harris's Common Sense Revolution catapulted these perceptions into power.

When Ipperwash went tragically wrong, the Harris government disavowed responsibility, but remained "tough" in handling other protests. Long criminal proceedings against front-line police at Ipperwash delayed a broader debate. In 1997, a court convicted former OPP sergeant Kenneth Deane of criminal negligence, for which appeals ended only in 2001 (Barnsley 1997, 2001). George's family then launched a wrongful death suit. This broadened the debate somewhat – Harris himself had to testify – but it delayed a wider inquiry.

By 2002, even many conservatives had tired of Harris's "toughness": his successor Ernie Eves changed few policies, but he did seek a kindlier image. A serious change in this direction could have meant addressing Ipperwash, but that had its own risks for the government: George's death, unresolved but not forgotten, reminded voters of the PCs' controversial style. The Georges' suit provided grounds for Eves to wait (Birchbark Staff 2002).

Meanwhile, McGuinty's Liberals were crafting a moderate image. They tied Eves to Harris's "excesses," and convinced many that a return to the New Democratic Party (NDP) would be divisive. When the Liberals won the October 2003 elections, they announced Justice Sidney Linden's inquiry into George's death the very next day (Barnsley 2003). Ipperwash therefore introduced the McGuinty brand to Ontarians, just as it had introduced Harris's.

The Linden inquiry lasted nearly a full electoral cycle. The public heard testimony that PC officials had pressured police at Ipperwash, often through angry, even abusive interventions. Some witnesses implicated Harris himself in this, though he denied remembering the incident (Barnsley 2006b). For many undecided voters and some disillusioned conservatives, the reports and speculations poisoned the PC brand for a second election.

In May 2007, Linden's lengthy report faulted the provincial and federal governments of 1995, and the police (Linden 2007). Crucially, it also considered wider issues, documenting a long history of racism and marginalization. But while exculpating Harris personally, Linden believed that the minister, high officials, and police had talked about accelerating police action just before George's death (Lawson 2007).

In 2008, McGuinty's government promised to return the park. They pointedly launched a $25 million New Relationship Fund to assist First Nations in future negotiations (Harries 2008, Windspeaker 2008), and subsequently avoided or defused some overt confrontations. They engaged more with official Indigenous leaders and generally fostered a more "welfare-therapeutic" approach to Aboriginal policy (on this approach and its meaning, see below). Many expected better days in Ontario-Indigenous relations.

WYNNE: BROADENING REFORM

After ten years of McGuinty government, Wynne stressed a renewed progressivism, including enhancement of the "new relationship" with First Nations and Métis people. This file's prominence undoubtedly reflected personal convictions of the core leadership. But it also helped to fend off an NDP recovery at the Liberals' expense. In part, it also responded to Canada-wide developments: the federal Truth and Reconciliation Commission (TRC) on residential schools (2010–15), the Idle No More protest movement since 2012, the persistent campaigning on behalf of missing and murdered Indigenous women and girls, and a breakthrough court case securing land rights and obligations for Métis people across Canada.

In 2014, Aboriginal Affairs announced a $70 million, seven-year Economic Development Fund to build business development, economic diversification, and regional partnerships. New Relationship Fund grants at $90 and $50 thousand annually were to build negotiating and administrative capacities in First Nations communities. On 24 August 2015, Wynne signed a political accord with Ontario First Nations (Ontario: Aboriginal Affairs 2015). Negotiated over a year, it stressed procedural reforms and capacity-building in Ontario-First Nations relations, and inaugurated a new Treaty Recognition Week.

Two other documents staked out ground less associated with the facilitation of economic deal-making. In 2016, *Walking Together* announced a three-year, $100 million collaboration against sexual violence and harassment of Indigenous women. It was responding to the campaigns for missing and murdered Indigenous women, as well as to the legacies of the province's residential schools, foster care, and adoption programs. Over $95 million of this program supported family healing from intergenerational trauma, and counselling and crisis support (Ontario: Office of the Premier 2016b).

Queen's Park pointedly accepted all the TRC's Calls to Action. *The Journey Together* (2016a) responded in detail. It pledged $250 million over three years, mainly for recovery programs in mental health and addictions. It also put $45 million towards justice system reforms and $30 million to cultural revitalization. Twenty million dollars supported study and education about the schools' legacy, and $5 million went to reconciliation initiatives. The Ministry of Aboriginal Affairs was renamed Indigenous Relations and Reconciliation.

Beyond these two documents, Wynne convened a special assembly of legislators and Indigenous leaders on 30 May 2016. The premier apologized formally for Ontario's past Aboriginal practices, including its support for residential schools, and committed it to a path of reconciliation (ibid.). Both opposition leaders supported the apology. However, NDP leader Andrea Horwath's speech tellingly raised a confidential report that had been released the same day. The report revealed that in the 1990s, industry and government had known that severe mercury contamination from the 1960s had continued on the Wabigoon River. Almost certainly, this implied contamination of the Grassy Narrows First Nation had continued into 2016; previous governments had claimed that the mercury would gradually disperse (Benzie 2016; see below). Indigenous experience, therefore, still pointed to the limits of the new relationship.

INDIGENOUS PEOPLES IN ONTARIO: DEMOGRAPHIC AND PUBLIC HEALTH DATA

The Indigenous population in Ontario is both Canada's largest by raw numbers (374,395 in 2016, or 22.4 per cent of the Indigenous total), and one of the smallest, proportionate to the population as a whole (2.8 per cent [Statistics Canada 2017]). Primarily First Nations or Métis, the Indigenous people in Ontario are ethnically, culturally, and institutionally diverse. All have roots in hunting, fishing, and gathering, but many in the south also have deep agricultural traditions. Wider shifting trade, diplomatic, and cultural networks linked nations up within and beyond Ontario's borders, hundreds if not thousands of years before Europeans arrived.

In 2006, approximately 139 state-recognized "bands" inhabited some 208 communities, including 189 reserves. By then, only 37 per cent of Ontario's Indigenous people lived on reserve (Canada Aboriginal Affairs and Northern Development 2011, 2017; compare Ontario Trillium Foundation 2008, 8, 10, 15). A small remnant of their lands remains – in 2011, only about 0.7 per cent of Ontario. Often beset with problems, reserves remain touchstones for many Indigenous people off-reserve (Canada Aboriginal Affairs and Northern Development 2011).

Indigenous social problems were daunting during McGuinty's first term. From 2001–06, Indigenous unemployment was at least double the provincial rate. In 2005, average Indigenous incomes ran some $12,000 below provincial ones. One-third of Indigenous children lived below the low income cut-off. Exceptionally few on-reserve First Nations members completed high school. While post-secondary achievements were now approaching settler rates, overall post-secondary credential rates were low (Spotton 2006, 21, 16–17, 20, Ontario Trillium Foundation 2008, 22).

As of 2006, Indigenous people in Ontario lived shorter lives, and experienced more serious health conditions and contagious diseases. Proportionately more died young; died more often from injury, vehicle accidents, and suicide; and experienced violent crime, especially women and children (Chartrand and McKay 2006). Indigenous women also faced higher health risks of other kinds (Grace 2003). Indigenous children were far more likely to be abused or placed in foster care (Statistics Canada 2012), and Indigenous people were far more likely to be jailed, addicted, or mentally or emotionally impaired.

THE ROOTS OF SETTLER-INDIGENOUS RELATIONS

Repeating these hard truths could reinforce anti-Indigenous racism. The point here is instead to understand the impacts of a deeper and ongoing colonial history. This section shows that the broad patterns of that history are clear, but that important details vary by region.

Several Iroquoian-language confederacies, the Anishinabaek (Ojibwa), and the Omàmìwinini (Algonquin) all had pre-contact ties to Southern Ontario. Alliance-building and missionizing established France's fragile claims in the area: virtually no French lived there. But many of these Nations collapsed, weakened, or relocated long before the British conquered New France in 1759–63. After initial Indigenous uprisings against the British throughout the Great Lakes basin, the Royal Proclamation (1763) and the Treaty of Niagara (1764) secured the British as the region's new European alliance-builders.

Successively reorganized as "Indian territory" (1763–74), part of Québec (1774–91), Upper Canada (1791–1840), and then as Canada West within the Province of Canada (1841–67), these lands changed most substantially with the multiracial wave of English-speaking Protestant refugees from the American Revolution. Unquestionably serving these Loyalist settlers' needs, the British Crown and military still arranged treaties and reserves, both for their incoming Haudenosaunee (Iroquois/Six Nations) allies and for the Nations already present. While settlers pressed for treaties to speed land transfers, the resulting reserves became as controversial for their size and location as Crown and clergy reserves did. For decades more, the British military steered settler-Indigenous relations through colonial rebellion and war.

Starting in the 1820s, capitalist growth came to Ontario, first to the Ottawa Valley timber trade and then to the towns of the southwest, sped by canal and rail investments (McCalla 1993; Page and Walker 1991; Wood 2000). Colonial authorities increasingly moved First Nations beyond the lines of settlement and shrank existing reserves. After responsible government in 1848–49, the Province of Canada was deeply involved in negotiating the Robinson treaties of 1850; this tapped resources north and east of the upper Great Lakes. In 1860, the elected colonial government gained control over Indian Affairs.

When Indian Affairs shifted to Ottawa with Confederation (Constitution Act [1867], s. 91.24), the new province of Ontario retained control over most Crown land and resources (s. 92.5). Over several decades, it pushed its borders north and west onto Anishinabaek, Nehiyaw (Cree), and Anishininiwag (Oji-Cree) territories (Armstrong 1981, 14–22); new transportation corridors then drove through new lines of resource investment and labour. By the early decades of the twentieth century, two sides of one capitalist coin, expansion and dispossession, thus minted Northern Ontario as a pulp and paper giant, a hydroelectrical powerhouse, and a mining hub (Nelles 1974).

Meanwhile, Ottawa's Indian Act (1876) consolidated wide-ranging control over First Nations. Harshest from 1885 to 1945, it imposed over the years an inferior, assimilationist, and abusive school system; a demeaning system of elected but long-powerless chiefs and councils; exclusionary and patriarchal definitions of an "Indian"; a ban on legal and political organizing; and an off-reserve pass system.

For its part, Queen's Park built infrastructure and social services for swelling settler populations. Off-reserve, it enforced the Dominion's laws and its own. Its provincial police and forest and wildlife officials increasingly disrupted more First Nations' lives and livelihoods, though their actual enforcement capacities grew more slowly. Ontario's land disputes with Ottawa periodically brought Indigenous rights and treaties into court, though seldom to resolve Indigenous grievances. To protect the fiscal autonomy for Ontario that came with resource revenues in those years (Smiley [1937] 1963, 100, 106),[3] Ontario broadly opposed Indigenous land rights (Armstrong 1981).

All the while, capitalist expansion and extraction prevailed, led by government surveys and land registries. Over time, gaps in treaty coverage emerged that put investments themselves at risk. Small wonder: treaty-making procedures had been deeply flawed, and typically ignored Indigenous understandings. Furthermore, some First Nations had not signed the treaties purportedly covering their lands. The federal Indian Act overrode or neglected treaty provisions and included some Nations retroactively and without their consent. The Williams Treaties (1923) closed some of these gaps before Ottawa banned Indigenous land litigation altogether, but many other cases went dormant for generations.

Only in the 1950s did Ottawa revoke some of the Indian Act's most openly racist restrictions and legalize land-rights litigation again. At the same time, postwar capital intensification and concentration were driving many Indigenous farms, fishing operations, and firms out of business and onto government aid: Indian Act property and wardship rules deprived them of access to loans. The act's new Section 88 in 1951 opened up a new era of delegated provincial social service provision for Indigenous people, with decidedly mixed effects. Provincial schools began replacing federal ones, though some activists also began to struggle for schools of their own. Only in the 1990s and 2000s did settler society open discussions about the legacy of the residential and day schools (Milloy 1999, 1996). Provincial child welfare programs took Indigenous children *en masse* from their families and communities (Johnson 1983).

Initially, Section 88 programs had to treat settler and Indigenous alike. However, in the late 1970s, courts allowed targeted Indigenous programs (*Kruger et al. v the Queen* 1978; *Dick v the Queen* 1985). This opened up some tensions in contemporary provincial social policy between the principle of legal equality, the structural racism of inferior treatment, and the practical need for exceptional resources to serve Indigenous needs.

INDIGENOUS PEOPLES AND THE LAND IN THE LIBERAL ERA

Ontario now considers most of its lands to be under treaty. But Indigenous people have contested historic violations of their land rights and their meaning with growing effect, whether under treaty or not. Overall, as of 2018, the Ontario government had accepted some fifty land claims for negotiation, three were at the research and assessment stage, and eleven settlement agreements were at the implementation stage. At the end point of the Liberal era, the government could claim to have participated in some eighteen settlements since McGuinty's first victory in 2003 (Ontario: Ministry of Indigenous Relations and Reconciliation 2018). Starting in the 1970s, Ottawa and Queen's Park began to negotiate the few cases in which no treaties had previously been agreed. Despite federal jurisdiction over treaties, Ontario joins such talks as presumptive Crown landowner and resource regulator. In May 2013, well into the Liberal era, four such "comprehensive claims" talks were underway. In 2018, with the addition of the Métis Nation of Ontario, there were five.

Such cases are always marathons. Some ultimately settled their claims under an existing neighbouring treaty. One in Ontario, with the Algonquins of Ontario, has now reached a final agreement and was in the still-thorny implementation stage at the time of writing. If fully implemented, the Algonquin claim over much of the Ottawa River watershed will be Ontario's first modern treaty, and the province's largest. In Indigenous circles, such cases rest on rights of prior occupation, ongoing sovereignty, and recently the UN Declaration of the Rights of Indigenous Peoples. Federal and provincial governments stress domestic and common-law rights (Kulchyski 1994). Recent rulings have considerably extended protections under the latter, which do not cede Canada's sovereignty claims (e.g., *Sparrow* (1990), *Van der Peet* (1996), *Delgamuukw* (1997), and *Tsilhqot'in* (2014)).

Given this history, frequent litigation is understandable. The courts' remedies are limited: they generally lead to treaties that still extinguish Aboriginal title, but *before* private land sales and territorial expansion, rather than after. Indigenous lands still become alienable Crown property – and then commodities – but by *legal* means and at a higher price than might otherwise have been the case. Treaties typically leave First Nations as lesser private landowners with new funds (usually after deducting litigation costs). Self-government and remaining jurisdiction over the land are either left out or are made firmly subject to Canadian sovereignty. Non-extinguishment of rights and shared sovereignty, though common Indigenous demands (e.g., Ontario, Canada, and Algonquins of Ontario 2017, 3–4), are usually deal-breakers.

In the Algonquins of Ontario case, a court ruling in the early 1980s denied that the Omàmìwininì (Algonquins) had the Royal Proclamation itself as their treaty for 36,000 km² of the Ottawa Valley: this meant they had inadvertently retained their Aboriginal title since the conquest of New France. The comprehensive talks, begun in the 1990s, quickly faced problems. First, most Algonquin territory was private land, except near the treasured Algonquin Park. Second, Pikwakanagan (Golden Lake Reserve) had been at first the sole Algonquin negotiator, but other communities lacking Indian Act status demanded separate representation (Lawrence 2012a). Third, Québec Algonquins claimed to share land interests in Ontario with the Algonquins of Ontario. Internal and inter-governmental negotiations finally reached an agreement-in-principle on 18 October 2016, involving Indigenous retention of 47,550 hectares of provincial Crown land and potentially federal lands as well.

"Specific claims" cover the grievances of First Nations already under treaty, and are far more numerous. They form the basis of some of the key regional land conflicts outlined here, including the Camp Ipperwash case. The federal Conservatives under Stephen Harper accelerated their settlement. A high proportion of those negotiated or

Table 14.1 | Specific claims cases, Ontario and Canada, 2013 and 2018

	Ontario 2013	Canada 2013	Ontario cases as % of Canadian 2013	Ontario 2018	Canada 2018	Ontario cases as % of Canadian 2018
IN PROGRESS						
Under assessment	10	101	9.9	7	158	4.4
Research	4	50	8.0	3	56	5.4
Justice preparing opinion	2	24	8.3	–	48	0.0
Legal opinion signed	4	27	14.8	4	54	7.4
In negotiations	50	230	21.7	54	242	22.3
Active	44	173	25.4	53	241	22.0
Inactive	6	57	10.5	1	1	100.0
Total in progress	60	331	18.1	61	400	15.2
CONCLUDED						
Settled by negotiation	47	377	12.5	61	461	13.2
No lawful obligation found	60	402	14.9	60	432	13.9
Resolved by admin remedy	7	33	21.2	7	32	21.9
File closed	59	320	18.4	65	342	19.0
Total concluded	173	1,132	15.3	193	1,267	15.2
OTHER						
Active litigation	57	82	69.5	49	61	80.3
Specific claims tribunal	2	37	5.4	4	72	5.5
Total other	59	119	49.6	53	133	39.8

Source: Canada: Aboriginal Affairs and Northern Development (2018).

Table 14.2 | Current claims and land-related negotiations involving Ontario

	2013	2018
Settlement agreements in implementation	10	11
Claims accepted by Ontario for negotiations	42	50
At research and assessment stage	8	3
Total	60	64

Source: Ontario Aboriginal Affairs (2018).

litigated in the Liberal era, as well as of those closed or dismissed, were in Ontario (table 14.1). Ontario's own involvement in these cases is not automatic, and is calculated separately (table 14.2).

ONTARIO SOCIAL POLICY STYLES AND IMPACTS ON INDIGENOUS PEOPLES

In recent years, two broad policy styles have dominated Ontario's Aboriginal social policy. The pure "neoliberal" style places core responsibility on Indigenous individuals and families. The state contains protest, weans individuals from "welfare dependence," and limits program costs. Apart from private and spiritual expressions, Indigenous identity appears primarily as a negative deviation from settler norms – as an "exception." Its alignment to settler norms should ideally be quick, final, and simple, using transitional agencies or ones designed for settlers. Less committed to universal outcomes, this approach can countenance relatively selective consultation to legitimize state action, for instance with "model" groups or individuals.

The federal Liberals' 1969 White Paper had once proposed to end Indian status and the Indian Act in this way (Canada: Indian Affairs and Northern Development 1969), but sharp Indigenous retorts (e.g., Cardinal 1969, 1999) and court cases intervened. After a hiatus, this style re-emerged, mostly in neoliberal garb on the right of the political spectrum (e.g., Alcantara, Flanagan, and Dressay 2010; Flanagan 2000).

A second, "welfare-therapeutic" policy orientation has dominated the Liberal era. Here, the onus for change rests more on special, permanent agencies, civil-societal groups, and quasi-governmental organizations. Policy responses are more often targeted, quasi-therapeutic interventions. Indigenous chiefs, councils, and agencies may demand, legitimate, administer, deliver, and (increasingly) set limited priorities. Core Indigenous social problems are still generally deemed to be exceptions in settler society, but the framing of Indigenous difference often includes a more genuine and apparently positive form: a collective identity that constitutes a unique tile in the Canadian ethnic mosaic and a rightful and distinctive public-policy partner. In keeping, by 2003, with trends in most Canadian court rulings, this generally favours consultations that are more comprehensive, official, and hence expensive.

This distinction is imperfect. Targeted Aboriginal policy can be neoliberal, for instance, like workfare or means-testing. "Equal treatment" can mean reinserting individuals into "normal" jobs and social behaviours like ordinary settlers or affirming the equality of Indigenous and settler collectivities. In any case, wider neoliberal efforts to balance the books can render either approach moot (Roslin 2004; Kulchyski 2007). Either policy style may also mark emergency measures the state may take when shocking examples of the "Indigenous exception" suddenly become visible to settler society. Sometimes these emergency policy moves yield breakthroughs, but the limited room for consultation and preparation cause many to miss their mark.

Each approach is also vulnerable to settler backlash, increasing the effort and expense behind policies that may still fail Indigenous people. Backlash can be expressed against "special treatment," supposedly in favour of formal equality, because the distinctively Indigenous problems addressed by targeting may be too distant, invisible, or unbelievable to settlers. Invisibility and distance can also block support for still deeper change in the relationship, because they hide policy failures – and the human costs of half-measures.

Equal (and even inferior) treatment can also provoke settler backlash, based on disbelief that such a small population could generate such high service demands. A related reason can be simple resentment at costs, amidst growing inequality in settler society (Fiscal Realities 2010, 7). Of course, costs for *adequate* or *effective* change can be far higher. A final reason for backlash is more obvious: simple racism can support the conclusion that desperate social conditions are "just how things are," or raise the question of "what is wrong with Indigenous people."

A subtler problem is "white supremacy." This is not necessarily an ideology of extreme racism, but is rather the ideological assumption, found across the political spectrum, that Euro-Canadian values and institutions are the universal ones. This can be another source of policy failure, even in well-funded and well-meaning programs. Funding and accountability conditions, administrative convenience, and settler program control can all favour ill-fitting settler-inspired policy instruments and procedures. Program targeting then becomes the alignment of Indigenous difference to settler norms.

Nuance here is crucial. For instance, where internalized violence is exceptionally high in Indigenous communities, it must not – and cannot – be naturalized on liberal-democratic grounds. However, settler definitions of "normal" (in parenting styles, schooling, justice systems, and so on) have notoriously added to Indigenous social problems through policy and program design intended to address such violence.

An alternative to supposed Indigenous "deviance" for explaining "what is wrong" better fits the facts: The primary causes of often-shocking Indigenous social statistics lie in the wider society of Ontario. The latter cannot operate without repeatedly confronting Indigenous Nations and their territories as a barrier: capitalism, and thus growth driven by atomized self-interest and exploitation, are central to it. "The problem [therefore] isn't poverty. It's theft" (Kulchyski 2011). Though responsibility for that problem, like benefit from it, is differentiated by class, ethnicity, and gender, settler society depends overall on Indigenous dispossession. Characterizing this as unquestionable or unalterable makes effective responses to Indigenous suffering and demands appear unreasonable; only the more "realistic" (but inadequate) measures remain.

The *political economy* of capitalism and colonialism therefore turns our explanatory attention from social policy questions to the centrality in settler society of separating Indigenous people from the land: capitalism itself drives Indigenous land loss, and therefore Indigenous social problems. *Political ecology* draws additional explanatory attention to the land's material transformation, as asset and as ecosystem (e.g., Wood 2000; compare Storper and Walker 1989 and Harvey 1982). We now turn to this material side of capitalism's growth imperative.

ECOLOGICAL TRANSFORMATION AS COLONIALISM

With or without treaties and sales, settler expansion felled, burned, and plowed over forests; built dams and roads; drained and cultivated bogs and wetlands; and erected buildings. This has served industrial, consumer, and reproductive needs (Harris 2009). In the process, game has fled; berry bushes have been uprooted, meadows fenced, and topsoil and water degraded, all this deeply destabilizing the original land-based peoples. Such "changes in the land" (Cronon 1983) support capitalist accumulation, because they deprived First Nations of burial grounds and sacred sites, but also health and livelihoods. They concretized and intensified legal losses. Notwithstanding many creative adaptations, many Indigenous land relationships became harder, impractical: at the limit impossible.

As one kind of qualitative change in the land, many "improvements" that contribute to monetary gain depend on destroying non-monetized assets. For instance, land reshaped to store toxic waste may generate profit and therefore count as "improved," even as it destroys assets and homelands. The terms environmental racism (Bullard 1993) and ecological imperialism (Crosby 1986) name "investment" of this kind.

The exposure of such patterns was common in the Liberal era. The Haudenosaunee of Akwesasne near Cornwall developed and publicized proof of industrial contamination of their "country food" over decades, including the contamination of their mothers' milk (Tarachansky 2008, 36). Aamjiwnaang residents near Sarnia publicized petro-chemical impacts on male/female birth ratios (Scott and Smith 2011). New uranium exploration began on Algonquin lands (Lawrence 2012b, chap. 8) and on lands of the Kitchenuhmaykoosib Inninuwug (KI) (Cuthand 2008). Both communities' leaders went to jail to stop the mining and assert their rights. Embarrassed by the uranium conflicts, which also affected settlers, Ontario moved to amend corporate access under the Mining Act (Ontario: Northern Development and Mines 2012a). That in turn affected the Ring of Fire development negotiations (see below).

To oppose Abitibi-Consolidated clear-cuts, the Asubpeeschoseewagong (Grassy Narrows) people conducted repeated blockades near Slant Lake (e.g., Willow 2010). Meanwhile, 86 per cent of them had suffered from mercury poisoning, because Reed Paper (now defunct) had dumped waste in the Wabigoon River system decades earlier (Shkilnyk 1985, 177–230); (Braun 2003). But as mentioned above, old reports released in 2016 showed that government officials had known in the 1990s that very high contamination had continued, and had wrongly reassured the First Nation for years that it would abate. Ontario asserted that this report came to it only in 2016 (Bruser and Poisson 2017; Leslie 2016) and launched studies for an $85 million decontamination program.

As this case shows, changes in the land and their impacts did not always follow a treaty or sale immediately. Indigenous people often continued to use such land. Indigenous secrecy and settler ignorance played a role in this: clandestine trapping, for instance, showing up intermittently as "poaching." Often ongoing use reflected Indigenous understandings of their rights, and even features of the written treaties themselves. Consequently, new waves of investment in already-transferred lands often determined when Indigenous Peoples felt the right, need, and capacity to resist.

Where Indigenous practices had continued on the land, new visions of Indigenous social renewal can also more readily include future land uses in renewal efforts. Some simply imagine adapting settler land practices on recovered land. This may challenge particular owners, users, and investments, but not capitalist land use. A different and more radical kind of renewal rebuilds historical ties to land, including non-capitalist uses (Corntassel 2012). Susan Hill writes, "It does nothing for us to regain territory if we do not treat it as we were instructed at the time of Creation" (2009, 495). The scale of this challenge to capitalism depends on the lands sought, on the scale and profitability of any capitalist investments it interrupts, and on whether the land's role in capital accumulation is altered.

Some Indigenous activists have experimented with such renewal without prior negotiations (see Caledonia and Tyendinaga, below). Despite the risk of state coercion and settler antipathy, advocates argue that this approach has its own therapeutic effects internally (Alfred 2005; Gindin 2008). This can also create uncertainties for capital, particularly if prior investments in the land are still contributing to capitalist profitability.

DEVELOPMENTS UNDER THE LIBERALS: CONFLICT IN SOUTHERN ONTARIO

We have seen that much of Ontario's agro-industrial heartland came under treaty as early as the 1780s, yet dispossession and resistance continued there into the Liberal era. Many Indigenous people live in the South; their communities are among the largest and best endowed. But rebuilding an Indigenous land base in the South, often hotly demanded, is difficult and expensive.

Settler repression and Indigenous resistance have long histories there. After the Haudenosaunee sought international recognition in the early 1920s, for example, the RCMP took their wampum belt records, suppressed longhouse governance, and imposed a band council. That council system, modified, still affects Haudenosaunee politics (DeVries 2011, 3; Hill 2009, 482).

Agro-industrial expansion also shaped Southern settler-Indigenous relations. Early treaties had enabled Loyalist refugee settlement, but ordinary settlers blamed Crown, clergy, *and Indian* reserves for blocking market access and settler capitalist development. Freehold tenure prevailed in the 1830s, stimulating rapid growth; municipal governments founded at mid-century accelerated infrastructure financing, and thus real estate values. Today the predominance of privately held, transformed lands exacerbates outstanding land grievances: they are commonly excluded from compensation packages in settler-Indigenous land talks, or are expensive to buy back. In the Liberal era, several controversies, triggered by late waves of industrial and residential construction, highlighted the flawed treaty-making and improper sales at the root of private property rights in Southern Ontario.

One such conflict concerned the Ohsweken (Six Nations) action near Caledonia. It also showed to what lengths the Liberal government would go to avoid "another Ipperwash." With about 22,000 residents, the Six Nations' Grand River reserve is Canada's most populous. Activists there contested the loss of the much larger 1784 Haldimand Tract. This tract rewarded Thayendanega's (Joseph Brant's) Six Nations followers as British allies during the American Revolution. The proclamation set aside some 385,000 hectares running six miles inland from both banks of the Grand River. Colonists gradually took or bought much of that tract. In 1841, one questionable deal transferred land along the Plank Road, later Highway 6. In 1987, the federal and provincial governments finally agreed to discuss this transfer (Hill 2009, 481). In 1995, Six Nations leadership had filed for court relief on about half of the related claims. In 2004, they withdrew their case and three-way talks began.

Meanwhile, however, a firm slated forty hectares for housing construction on this tract, between the reserve and Caledonia. In late February 2006, activists reclaimed the site. Their action, long and complex (e.g., DeVries 2011), began small (Lawson 2006). But an OPP raid on 20 April drew hundreds (CBC News 2006e). A seven-week blockade affected nearby highways, roads, and electrical power, and some non-Indigenous residents clashed with protestors (Hill 2009, 481–2). Police intervened and positions hardened.

After further protester conflicts with the OPP and the courts, the Liberal government withdrew the police and bought out the construction firm (CBC News 2006a). But Justice David Marshall then ordered the site cleared in May, and in August sought to block negotiations until Indigenous "occupation" ended. Police and the government ignored Marshall, favouring direct talks to end the conflict (CBC News 2006c, 2006d). Police costs ultimately reached tens of millions of dollars. Several commentators and the PC opposition demanded decisive law-and-order action to enforce the injunctions (Blatchford 2010; compare DeVries 2011). On 7 June, a rally drew 100 chiefs from across Ontario, while the elected council challenged the original deal in court. In October, federal-provincial meetings ended acrimoniously (CBC News 2006b). Controversy simmered on for years. Crucially, though damaged politically for not being "tougher," the government withheld harsher measures. Resolution did not come quickly. The Six Nations renewed their court case in 2009 (Ontario: Indigenous Relations and Reconciliation 2013, 2017).

On 29 June 2007, a Kanienkehake (Mohawk) protest addressed similar issues at Tyendinaga near Deseronto on the shore of Lake Ontario (Tyendinaga Support Committee 2007; Pawlick 2009). Four years before, Ottawa had acknowledged historical problems regarding an historical tract that now included a nearby quarry. Sidelining both the Assembly of First Nations and their own elected council, Indigenous activists targeted the quarry and a neighbouring subdivision. Frustrated that quarrying had continued during negotiations, and citing its profits amidst substandard reserve conditions (Gude 2009), protestors reclaimed the quarry in November 2006.

The following April, they briefly blocked the major arteries between Toronto and Montreal (Hamilton Spectator 2007). The OPP laid charges, but avoided direct confrontations with drivers by closing Highway 401; CN Rail and VIA suspended rail traffic (Lawson 2007). Some settler interests then took a harder line than the government: CN filed injunctions and sought multi-million-dollar damages. The new PC leader John Tory supported CN, hoping suits would reduce costly future protests. Meanwhile, the protestors challenged the more moderate band leadership, stuck in frustrating land talks (Pawlick 2009, 225).

On 5 July, protest spokesperson Shawn Brant turned himself in to police over the April blockade (Hamilton Spectator 2007). The Crown initially sought a twelve-year sentence. In September 2008, Brant was sentenced to probation on reserve, pleading guilty to reduced charges. In the process, Brant's defence obtained and publicized wiretaps of OPP commissioner Julian Fantino threatening Brant verbally in June. They suggested that this had undermined OPP protocols established after Ipperwash (Fantino had been controversial there, too). The defence contested the wiretaps' constitutionality, and protesters alleged that the OPP broke a promise of immunity for protesters over the April blockade (CBC News 2008b, 2008a). In this case, the government's cultivated image only partly mirrored its own behaviour and the OPP's.

DEVELOPMENTS UNDER THE LIBERALS: NORTHERN AND CENTRAL RESOURCE FRONTIERS

Resource extraction is now a relatively small part of the Ontario economy. It remains important to the North, and also helped to stabilize conditions for growth in Southern population centres for much of the twentieth century. Northern and Central Ontario forestry, mining, and hydro-electric activity have been troubled in recent decades, but sustained many towns and cities for years: "places to stand" for the residents. As capitalist undertakings, however, resource industries also needed "places to grow": a succession of new lands open to extraction.

While late twentieth-century land-use and environment planning have complicated the picture, resource capital and government have had a freer hand in the North. Harold Innis's metaphor of "cyclonics" (Barnes, Hayter, and Hay 2001) vividly captures the social and environmental consequences. The region's economy is highly cyclical, as a consequence of both larger investment cycles from the swings in commodity prices and the longer gestation period of individual projects (Prefasi 1992). Putting down and pulling up roots, these temporary extractive operations collide with established communities, including Indigenous ones. Twentieth-century management principles of "scientific" conservation or "wise use" reshaped the cyclonic patterns, though frequently to the further detriment of First Nations' rights and authority over the land (Gillis and Roach 1986).

Unlike Southern land-based projects, most Northern ones occur on Crown lands (e.g., Nelles 1974). Investment on this basis initially creates important provincial revenues, but generally spares firms the costs of ownership and clean-up. Through the twentieth century, provincial permitting required local secondary processing (Armstrong 1981, 33–48). The recent decline of this practice has hollowed out local economic benefits.

Northern First Nations, the tourism industry, and environmentalists have gradually become important "stakeholders" alongside government and industry. Crown land dominance has simplified modern land talks with First Nations: if pressed enough, Ontario can cede larger environmental preserves and Indigenous settlement lands without buying back private holdings. But resource capital's growth imperatives impede enduring compromises. In the 1980s and 1990s, Indigenous opponents of resource capital defended their subsistence and land-based practices. Sometimes they joined wilderness and recreationist activists. However, by the Liberal era, the resource sector also offered First Nations some compelling direct "win-win" arrangements for cooperating with them. In part, courts required such deals (Morellato 2008); in part, they were simpler for the parties than government mediation.

Many Northern First Nations welcome regulated resource projects, despite their concerns about damaging subsistence activities on the land. For instance, the Nishnawbe-Aski Nation (NAN) central office was not happy when the Liberals' Far North Act (2010) set aside some 225,000 km² of Ontario's remotest forest and muskeg, partly in the name of carbon sequestration. The act did not block resource extraction elsewhere, and it offered Indigenous Peoples some planning influence. NAN called the consultations inadequate and the plan economically destructive. It argued that carbon, if priced as planned, properly fit under Indigenous land rights and had to be negotiated. More generally, NAN wanted a freer economic hand in its territories (Nisnawbe Aski Nation 2012). The bill did pass, but at the Liberals' cost in the North.

From 2007–09, Northern mining claims had doubled to 8,200. Much government energy centred in this period on claims in the so-called Ring of Fire. Initial diamond exploration about 550 unserviced kilometres north of Thunder Bay exposed massive metal and mineral finds there. Discoveries only grew from 2002–07; by 2011, nearly 100 firms had staked claims and some thirty-five juniors were exploring chromite, nickel, copper, and other ores (Gismondi 2017; MiningWatch Canada 2011). The region's minerals, by then commonly estimated at some $60 billion, rivalled the Sudbury basin's (Scales 2017); widely cited figures at the time predicted 3,600 start-up and 3,000 ongoing jobs (MiningWatch Canada 2011).

Cliffs Natural Resources fielded the first major project, intended to be Canada's first chromite mine. Noront Resources, initially a junior, blossomed rapidly, and announced another leading project (2010). Each firm backed a separate transport route into the region. Initially, preparations proceeded rapidly. After investing over half a billion dollars, Cliffs withdrew angrily in 2013–14, blaming regulatory burden and government delays (Koven 2014; Scales 2017). One barrier was major Mining Act reform, including changes to miners' access rights. This process continues (Mines 2018). The rails necessary for chromite extraction are also expensive to put in. Ultimately, other projects came to the fore (2010), and Noront remained (Scales 2017).

Indigenous rights, environmental integrity, and public health had fed rapidly growing dissent about the Ring of Fire. In 2009, three environmental organizations deplored limited provisions for government oversight, Indigenous participation, and environmental assessment. Doubtful waste management, weak water protection, and dangers to wildlife also concerned them. Their allegation that firms were making fraudulent mining claims to control prospective railway routes (MiningWatch Canada, Wildlands League, and Ecojustice 2009) led to a lengthy court case (Koven 2016).

On 16 September 2010, two First Nations agreed to negotiate impacts and benefits with Ontario and the industry. But at different times in 2010–11, Matawa Tribal Council members prepared to blockade corporate facilities to increase their participation in the bonanza (2010). With Idle No More leadership centring on nearby Attiwapiskat, and aware of the community disruptions of bitumen mining in Northern Alberta, First Nations representatives also struggled to sort out their overlapping interests (Scoffield 2012). When not hostile to mining itself, some Indigenous protesters criticized staking that had happened without prior Indigenous permission and participation. They demanded consultations and for their consent to be built into corporate planning, both to increase Indigenous benefits (such as corporate use of First Nation airstrips and community road service) and to minimize environmental and social costs (2011a). They sought funding to build their negotiating capacities. At the same time, local First Nations and several environmental organizations demanded a thorough regional strategic environmental assessment for the whole Ring of Fire, shared between Ottawa and Queen's Park (Hart and MiningWatch Canada 2011). But in October 2011, the Canadian Environmental Assessment Agency angered its critics by approving a "comprehensive" assessment of just the Cliffs project alone (2011b).

By summer 2012, key chiefs were preparing eviction notices against project officials (Friends of MiningWatch 2012), even as the Anishinabek Nation called for more attention to existing treaties relationships in resource projects (2013). The Liberals rushed to respond to the First Nations in a way that also saved industrial expansion. In 2011, McGuinty had appointed a special secretariat (Gismondi 2017). By 2013, former premier Bob Rae resigned as Liberal MP to negotiate for the Matawa Tribal Council (Gismondi 2017). Ontario hired as its representative retired Supreme Court justice Frank Iacobucci, who was just ending his inquiry into Indigenous people in the justice system (Rennie 2013).

In 2013, Wynne announced a $1 billion Ring of Fire infrastructure package (Gismondi 2017). The federal Conservative government, anxious to appear supportive of the development, was at the same time reluctant to underwrite costly programs. In February 2014, Ontario openly decried Ottawa for anaemic budget support (Leslie 2014; Rennie 2014), as did the Ontario Chamber of Commerce (Babbage 2014; Wright 2014).

Meanwhile, First Nations talks moved forward, buttressed in 2014 by new Supreme Court rulings (Hasselback 2014). Ontario signed a framework agreement that year (2014), and in 2015 announced plans for an all-season road serving both communities and new mines (Scales 2017). In 2016, a $785,000 study closed a key phase in follow-up talks. Details to resolve (Gismondi 2017) included environmental protections for local hunting, gathering, and fishing. Talks with the First Nations had not been cheap: $30 million by 2017. Noront developed special underground tailings storage to signal its own good faith. On 29 August 2017, two key First Nations agreed to a multi-purpose transport corridor, with environmental assessments leading to the start of construction in 2019.

In 2018, on the eve of a provincial election, Northern business and opposition critics intensified their criticism of the pace of First Nations talks on the Ring of Fire, while the Matawa Council continued to insist on the principle of Indigenous consent for development agreements. In June, the premier finalized agreements across the North with the Grand Council Treaty No. 3, Wabun Tribal Council, and Mushkegowuk Council to pass 45 per cent of forestry stumpage, 40 per cent of royalties and taxes from existing mines, and 45 per cent of royalties and taxes from future mines. For his part, Conservative Party leader Doug Ford pointedly promised some $30 million in resource revenues to all Northern communities, not just Indigenous ones, while the NDP's Andrea Horwath promised Indigenous communities the revenues from Ontario's mining taxes. Reports on the agreements suggested that the Matawa Council, absent from the agreement Wynne announced, was working on a separate process at a different pace for revenue-sharing for the Ring of Fire, and was apparently held up by the road access talks (Ross 2018).

SETTLER-INDIGENOUS RELATIONS: REGIONAL VARIATIONS

Regional differences in Indigenous people's visibility and impacts on settler society affect wider public support in Ontario. For instance, well-publicized Indigenous activism against Northern and central resource projects can gain more sympathy in the South than similar actions in the South do. (The deep connections between Toronto finance and Northern resources [e.g., Ontario: Northern Development and Mines 2012b] are often not especially visible to Southerners.) Acknowledging Northern Indigenous land rights with apparently impressive figures can seem relatively low-cost to Southern Ontario, preferably if the resource projects still go forward. But Southern knowledge of and attention to Northern conditions are often weak and the extreme distances can stretch state capacities to deliver support (e.g., Shah, Gunraj, and Hux 2003; Skinner, Hanning, and Tsuji 2006).

In Central Ontario, support for Indigenous activism can be more intense because Southerners' direct experience of the land is more often involved. To many, especially among established elites and middle class professionals, this is cottage and summer camp country, evoking nostalgic, often nationalist bonds. If First Nations and settler environmentalists often campaign together against resource capital there, they may disagree over parks and nature preserves. Indigenous-industrial pacts also occur: pro-wilderness campaigns may backfire if they antagonize resource workers, many of whom are Indigenous people.

Indigenous land interests and protests in the South pose the greatest challenge for gaining the support of the Southern majority. They can visibly threaten major industrial, recreational, and residential projects, and are likelier to inconvenience more settlers. The treaties are older, and extensive land privatization makes "win-win" settlements expensive. Thus, alliances and simple toleration can be difficult, except for the settlers with the fewest landed interests. These regional differences return us to the opening puzzles of Liberal moderation and the peculiar salience of this policy area for Ontario politics.

CONCLUSION: SETTLER-INDIGENOUS RELATIONS AS SETTLER IDEOLOGY

Drawing on a phrase from Ontario's pop anthem of the 1960s (Claman, Morris, and Toth 1967), capitalist Ontario needs "a place to grow," but its moral and sometimes legal rights to the land rarely have a "place to stand." *All* its growth must take place on lands taken or dubiously bought from First Nations, but not yet fully occupied or depleted by settlers. Direct resource revenues may have become less important for Ontario, but they still limit taxes on settlers. Financial and manufacturing jobs, activities seemingly insulated from the resource economy and centred in the South, still benefit from this need for a "place to stand." Ontario therefore needs projects like the Ring of Fire. Urbanization and population growth also impel projects in the South, like the subdivision at Caledonia or the quarry near Deseronto.

Round after round of expansion has layered the costs onto Indigenous Peoples. But members of any advanced settler society are encouraged to think of it as a place of justice, prosperity, and democracy (e.g., Adam 2003, esp. 59, 111–12), notwithstanding the wider cynicism about government in this neoliberal era. It is easy for settlers to seek contrary evidence or excuses when confronted about their society's unjust, immiserating, and undemocratic impacts on Indigenous people. For sixteen years, they could turn to evidence of Liberal-era initiatives to benefit Indigenous people. Or they could stress the importance of community isolation in explaining Indigenous hardships, instead of the layered impacts of colonialism (Urban Aboriginal Task Force 2007; Menzies 2005).

This positive settler self-image is singularly at odds with Indigenous social conditions: such a stark rebuke, in fact, that a self-consistent liberal democracy must respond. And recent Ontario governments have responded – up to a point. After some sixteen years of Liberal moderation, the price now evidently strikes many citizens of Ontario as large, exceptional, and burdensome. Yet the problems remain. One way out of this predicament is to write off Indigenous conditions as a narrow, insoluble "exception" to a society that otherwise functions well. One version of this is overtly racist; another simply reflects disillusionment with pro-Indigenous reform. A second way seems to be the Ford government's initial approach: solve Indigenous problems by treating them as much as possible like those of other Ontarians, and drawing First Nations where necessary into resource capitalist growth strategies.

But an alternative account to Indigenous exceptionalism would run something like this: settler Ontario arose entirely on Indigenous territories, massively disrupting their ecosystems and ways of life. As part of Canada, Ontario participated in wide-ranging experiments to police, segregate, marginalize, and assimilate First Nations. These were strikingly ineffective, if their point was benevolent assimilation. If their point was dispossession, however, they have worked remarkably well. The negative effects have been profound: they will be difficult and expensive to undo.

As *exceptions* to settler society, Indigenous problems may appear expensive, but they still imply, reassuringly, that "normal" society can come to the rescue. As *foundations* to settler society, Indigenous problems are politically explosive, and the solutions become virtually unthinkable. As responses to an "exception," the most significant reforms to date appear as the outer limits of settler generosity, yet they necessarily fall short of what is needed. Elites may even make a virtue of the apparent generosity – a risky political gambit, for as the early days of the Ford government have already shown, the scale of the costs repels some settlers.

Painting Indigenous people as exceptional problems is no elite conspiracy: it is a predictable axiom of a whole society that would otherwise have to face the structural forces at its core. That elites engage in over-selling the reforms they achieve explains little by itself, until the underlying structures are understood. Pointing to increasingly undemocratic economic inequality more generally (the justification of which is central to neoliberalism) also fails to explain why *Indigenous* outcomes are particularly unequal. In combination, however, colonial racism and the landed dimensions of capitalist growth do provide such an explanation.

Even people of untouchable personal integrity shy away from the implications of dealing seriously with the impacts of colonial capitalism: "massive restitution, including land, financial transfers and other forms of assistance to compensate for past harms and continuing injustices committed against our peoples" (Alfred 2005, 152). In the end, those implications appear, not so much as wrong or unwarranted, but as staggeringly unrealistic. And so they are – for settler society as it is.

The problem is that the status quo is also unrealistic – for Indigenous people. Indigenous people name this unreality – this madness – in their resurgent activism and community service to push back and seek a different way. But the staggering rates of suicide, mind-numbing addictions, internalized violence, and neglect in their communities also bear witness to that unreality.

Many settlers – decent people – increasingly know about the symptoms of colonial capitalism, though they may not name them as such. Other settlers also question what they themselves gain from the status quo. But the people experiencing those symptoms typically lie far outside everyday settler experience. Ordinary Indigenous people are routinely mistaken on the street for Filipinos or Mexicans, or if recognized, are approached as walking "problems" that settlers can commonly avoid in their daily lives (compare DuBois [1903] 1994, 1–7). That everyday mutual isolation is the product of centuries (Satzewich and Wotherspoon 1993, 15–41).

As real restitution has become harder to contemplate, limited action, talk about action, or purely cultural accommodation can become safe, even imperative in policy terms, especially if Indigenous conditions become visible to settler society. For Ontarians have retained self-conceptions of equality, prosperity, and democracy in the face of neoliberal policies that increasingly undermine them. Partial answers to Indigenous inequality may be expensive per capita and they may be unequivocally necessary in themselves. But they are also cheap and uncontroversial nods to justice, measured against the costs of full and effective restitution – and of a more egalitarian and democratic settler society. Limited Aboriginal policy reform can thus nurture Ontarians' self-conceptions ideologically, *even if* the problems are not solved, and *even as* democratic equality and social provision decline in settler society (Mehra 2012). "Something" must be done – but always only "within reason."

Settler society rests on Indigenous territory. Its capitalist foundations repeatedly compel it to expand and thus to appropriate and to transform the land. Presenting this as natural and inevitable makes Indigenous rights and well-being secondary. What remain are not understandable compromises, but ethically compromising ones. They will not turn Indigenous collective life decisively towards health and self-determination. Ontario Liberals tried, within moderation, to do better by reforming the colonialism of the capitalist growth they facilitated.

Their successors in the new Ford government have not been elected to be moderate. Despite the vagueness of the PC electoral platform on Indigenous issues, it is hard to see how retrenchment by tax cuts and deregulation will serve decolonization or reconciliation better, let alone move towards radical and restorative restitution. Early indications, such as the elimination of a separate ministry for Indigenous relations and reconciliation or the "colonial-blind" campaign promises related to revenue sharing in the North, are that Ford's government intends to return to an openly neoliberal conception of Indigenous relations and away from welfare-therapeutic or government-to-government conceptions. That apparent intention will operate to the extent that Indigenous militancy, the courts, and the momentum of existing negotiation processes permit.

Rekindling the Ontario economy through cutting social and environmental programs and disciplining labour may or may not work on their own terms, at the cost of deepened inequality in settler society. Under pressure to generate dignity for their people through work, Indigenous leaders may well be sympathetic to strategies to renew capitalist growth by drawing First Nations into resource extraction and other branches of capitalist enterprise. But among the negative consequences of such developments would be the rekindling of the very forces of colonial capitalism that have driven Indigenous social problems and Indigenous resistance. Cutting future commitments to Métis people and First Nations in final agreements and similar talks may help to balance budgets for one or two electoral cycles, in a similar spirit of neoliberal austerity. But it would be purchased with deepening resentments and worsening relations for future generations. For their part, those who will one day succeed Doug Ford's government must decide in the coming years whether the imperatives of decolonization and a more decisive turn towards just relations in settler-Indigenous affairs can bear a return to simple moderation.

ACKNOWLEDGMENTS

The author thanks Heidi Stark, as well as anonymous peer reviewers, for sparing readers many errors of omission and commission in reading earlier drafts of this chapter. The remaining errors are mine.

NOTES

1 "Settler" is an imperfect term (Abele and Stasiulus 1989). It deceptively conjures up both frontier agriculture and permanency, though most settlers today live urban, relatively mobile lives. "Settler" also conceals the white privilege and white supremacy that marginalizes non-white settlers, appearing to indict all those with immigrant roots equally: "whites" appear merely to *predominate*, together with their norms, practices, and institutions. "Indigenous" is increasingly preferred to "Indian," "Native American," or "Aboriginal." Many now consider "Aboriginal" derivative of Canadian state

recognition in the Constitution Act (1982) of "Indians" (those placed under the federal Indian Act), Métis, or Inuit. The specific term "Aboriginal policy" (versus "Indigenous policy") therefore implies settler initiatives, constitutional frameworks, and points of view. However, "Aboriginal" is still used by many Indigenous people and their allies. Recent Canadian practice refers to "First Nations" rather than "Indian bands" or "tribes," whether historically for larger polities, or more recently for individual "bands" under the Indian Act.

2 Capitalism is the dominant logic of how things are made and exchanged in Western societies. It rests on production under private ownership using waged labour, for the purpose of selling the products for the private benefit of the owners. From the difference between workers' wages and what their work contributes to the products' value, and from the competitive pressures on owners to reinvest their profits, flows the system's need to grow and to profit through exploitation (Harvey 1982). This understanding differs from more common definitions, in which private property rights, free markets, or entrepreneurial spirit are central.

3 By comparison, Ontario's 2012 resource royalties were just $200 million, about 0.2 per cent of its revenues (Public Accounts of Ontario 2011–12).

REFERENCES

Abele, Frances, and Daiva Stasiulus. 1989. "Canada as a 'White Settler Colony': What about Natives and Immigrants?" In *The New Canadian Political Economy*, edited by Wallace Clement and Glen Williams. Montreal: McGill-Queen's University Press.

Adam, Michael. 2003. *Fire and Ice: The United States, Canada and the Myth of Converging Values*. Toronto: Penguin.

Alcantara, Christopher, Tom Flanagan, and André Le Dressay. 2010. "Beyond the Indian Act: Restoring Aboriginal Property Rights." In *Beyond the Indian Act: Restoring Aboriginal Property Rights*, edited by Tom Flanagan, Christopher Alcantara and André Le Dressay. Montreal: McGill-Queen's University Press.

Alfred, Taiaiake. 2005. *Wasáse: Indigenous Pathways of Action and Freedom*. Peterborough: Broadview Press.

Armstrong, Christopher. 1981. *The Politics of Federalism: Ontario's Relations with the Federal Government, 1867–1942*. Toronto: University of Toronto Press.

Babbage, Maria. 2014. "Ottawa and Ontario Must Fund Plan to Build Transportation to Ring of Fire: Study." *The Canadian Press*, 20 February.

Barnes, Trevor J., Roger Hayter, and Elizabeth Hay. 2001. "Stormy Weather: Cyclones, Harold Innis, and Port Alberni, BC." *Environment and Planning A* 33 (2).

Barnsley, Paul. 1997. "Minimal Sentence for Deane." *Windspeaker* 15 (4).

– 2001. "George Family Member Demands Federal Inquiry." *Windspeaker* 18 (11).

– 2003. "Ipperwash Inquiry Called." *Windspeaker* 21 (8).
– 2006a. "Ipperwash Park Surrender Illegal – Lawyer." *Windspeaker* 23 (12).
– 2006b. "Mike Harris Star Witness at Inquiry." *Windspeaker* 23 (12).
Benidickson, Jamie. 1996. "Temagami Old Growth: Pine, Politics and Public Policy." *Environments* 23 (2).
Benzie, Robert. 2016. "Kathleen Wynne Offers Indigenous People 'A Formal Apology for the Abuses of the Past.'" *Toronto Star*, 30 May. https://www.thestar.com/news/canada/2016/05/30/kathleen-wynne-to-reveal-ontarios-response-to-truth-and-reconciliation-commission.html
Birchbark Staff. 2002. "Still No Action on Ipperwash Inquiry." *Ontario Birchbark* 2.
Blatchford, Christie. 2010. *Helpless: Caledonia's Nightmare of Fear and Anarchy, and How the Law Failed All of Us*. Toronto: Anchor Canada.
Braun, Wil. 2003. "Treaties, Trees and Sharing: Report from the Grassy Narrows Blockade." *Canadian Dimension* 37 (3).
Brown, Wendy. 2006. "American Nightmare: Neoliberalism, Neoconservatism, and De-Democratization." *Political Theory* 34 (6).
Bruser, David, and Jayme Poisson. 2017. "Ontario Knew about Grassy Narrows Mercury Site for Decades, but Kept It Secret." *Toronto Star*, 11 November. https://www.thestar.com/news/canada/2017/11/11/ontario-knew-about-mercury-site-near-grassy-narrows-for-decades-but-kept-it-secret.html.
Bullard, Robert D., ed. 1993. *Confronting Environmental Racism: Voices from the Grassroots*. Boston: South End Press.
Canada. Aboriginal Affairs and Northern Development. 2010. *Fiscal Realities: The True Cost of First Nation Government*. Ottawa: Aboriginal Affairs and Northern Development Canada.
– 2011. *Reports: Ontario Region*. Environment and Natural Resources. Mining and Minerals.
– 2017. *Ontario First Nations Map*. http://www.aadnc-aandc.gc.ca.
– 2018. *Reporting Centre on Specific Claims*. http://services.aadnc-aandc.gc.ca.
Canada. Indian Affairs and Northern Development. 1969. *Statement of the Government of Canada on Indian Policy*. Ottawa: Queen's Printer.
Canada Newswire. 2010. "Historic First Nations Signing for Ring of Fire Discoveries." 16 September. https://www.newswire.ca/news-releases/historic-first-nations-signing-for-ring-of-fire-discoveries-545549862.html.
– "'Treaties Must Be Part of Resource Discussions': Lake Huron Chief." 6 December.
Canada. Truth and Reconciliation Commission. 2015. *Calls to Action*. Winnipeg: TRC.
Canadian Press. 2010. "NW Ont. First Nation Plans Blockade of Exploration Activity in Ring of Fire Area." 18 January.
– 2011a. "First Nations Chiefs Unite against Unauthorized Ring of Fire Mining Projects." 14 July.

- 2011b. "First Nation Planning Blockade Near Ring of Fire in Northern Ontario." 28 February.
- 2014. "Ontario Inks Framework Agreement with First Nations in Ring of Fire Region." 26 March. http://www.cbc.ca/news/canada/thunder-bay/ontario-first-nations-ink-framework-deal-on-ring-of-fire-region-1.2588317.

Cardinal, Harold. (1969) 1999. *The Unjust Society: The Tragedy of Canada's Indians*. Toronto: Douglas and McIntyre.

CBC News. 2006a. "Buying Caledonia Land Will Cost Ontario Government $12.3M." 23 June. http://www.cbc.ca/news/canada/buying-caledonia-land-will-cost-ontario-government-12-3m-1.629086.
- 2006b. "Feds Scrap Planned Caledonia Meeting." 31 October. http://www.cbc.ca/news/canada/toronto/feds-scrap-planned-caledonia-meeting-1.611766.
- 2006c. "Judge Orders End to Talks until Caledonia Occupation Stops." 8 August. https://web.archive.org/web/20071106030824/http://www.cbc.ca/story/canada/national/2006/08/08/caledonia-decision.html.
- 2006d. "Judge Wants to Know Why Caledonia Order Not Enforced." 29 May. http://www.cbc.ca/news/canada/judge-wants-to-know-why-caledonia-order-not-enforced-1.598828.
- 2006e. "Tensions Grow as Native Protesters Return to Ontario Site." 20 April. http://www.cbc.ca/news/canada/tensions-grow-as-native-protesters-return-to-ontario-site-1.583738.
- 2008a. "Mohawk Protester Brant Gets Light Penalty for Blockades." 29 September. http://www.cbc.ca/news/canada/mohawk-protester-brant-gets-light-penalty-for-blockades-1.761843.
- 2008b. "NDP Calls for Fantino 'To Resign Or Be Fired' over Brant Wiretaps." 21 July. http://www.cbc.ca/news/canada/ndp-calls-for-fantino-to-resign-or-be-fired-over-brant-wiretaps-1.708472.

Chartrand, Larry, and Celeste McKay. 2006. *A Review of Research on Criminal Victimization and First Nations, Métis and Inuit Peoples 1990 to 2001*. Ottawa: Department of Justice Canada.

Corntassel, Jeff. 2012. "Re-envisioning Resurgence: Indigenous Pathways to Decolonization and Sustainable Self-Determination." *Decolonization: Indigeneity, Education and Society* 1 (1).

Cronon, William. 1983. *Changes In the Land: Indians, Colonists, and the Ecology of New England*. New York: Hill and Wang.

Crosby, Alfred W. 1986. *Ecological Imperialism: The Biological Expansion of Europe, 900–1900*. Cambridge: Cambridge University Press.

Cuthand, Doug. 2008. "'KI Six' Jailed in Fight for Land Rights." *Leader Post*, 31 March. https://www.pressreader.com/canada/regina-leader-post/20080331/281599531213316.

DeVries, Laura. 2011. *Conflict in Caledonia: Aboriginal Rights and Rule of Law*. Vancouver: University of British Columbia Press.

DuBois, W.E.B. (1903) 1994. *The Souls of Black Folk*. Mineola, NY: Dover Publishing.

Eccles, W.J. 1969. *The Canadian Frontier, 1534–1760*. Albuquerque: University of New Mexico Press.

Friends of MiningWatch. 2012. *Chiefs Prepare Eviction Notice to Mining Companies Working in the Ring of Fire*. https://miningwatch.ca/news/2012/6/25/chiefs-prepare-eviction-notice-mining-companies-working-ring-fire.

Gillis, R., and Thomas R. Roach. 1986. *Lost Initiatives: Canada's Forest Industries, Forest Policy and Forest Conservation*. Westport: Greenwood Press.

Gindin, Jonah. 2008. "Stone by Stone: What Does the Mohawk Cultural Resurgence at Tyendinaga Have to Teach Us about Aboriginal Youth Suicide Prevention?" *Briarpatch*, June/July. https://briarpatchmagazine.com/articles/view/stone-by-stone-rail-by-rail.

Gismondi, Angela. 2017. "Ring of Fire Road 'A Huge Win for Northern Ontario.'" *Daily Commercial News* 90 (166). https://web.archive.org/web/20170829110111/http://dailycommercialnews.com/en-US/Projects/News/2017/8/Ring-of-Fire-road-a-huge-win-for-northern-Ontario-1026744W/.

Grace, Sherry L. 2003. "A Review of Aboriginal Women's Physical and Mental Health Status in Ontario." *Canadian Journal of Public Health* 94 (3).

Gude, Stephanie. 2009. "The Great O.P.P. Cover-Up at Tyendinaga." *Canadian Dimension* 43 (1).

Hamilton Spectator. 2007. "Protester Surrenders." *Hamilton Spectator*, 6 July.

Harries, Kate. 2008. "Ipperwash Park Returned to Local First Nations." *Windspeaker* 25 (11).

Harris, Cole. 2009. *The Reluctant Land: Society, Space, and Environment in Canada before Confederation*. Vancouver, BC: University of British Columbia Press.

Hart, Ramsey, and MiningWatch Canada. 2011. *What Kind of Environmental Assessment for Ontario's "Ring of Fire"?* Toronto: MiningWatch Canada. https://miningwatch.ca/blog/2011/10/12/what-kind-environmental-assessment-ontarios-ring-fire.

Harvey, David. 1982. *The Limits to Capital*. Chicago: University of Chicago Press.

Hasselback, Drew. 2014. "'Sky Not Falling' over Aboriginal Court Decisions." *National Post*, 30 July.

Hill, Susan M. 2009. "Conducting Haudenosaunee Historical Research from Home: In the Shadow of the Six Nations-Caledonia Reclamation." *American Indian Quarterly* 33 (4).

Johnson, Patrick. 1983. *Native Children and the Child Welfare System*. Ottawa: Canadian Council on Social Development.

Knight, Rolf. 1978. *Indians at Work*. Vancouver: New Star Books.

Koven, Peter. 2014. "Ring of Fire Futile: Cliffs; New CEO Sees 'Zero Hope.'" *National Post*, 29 October.

– 2016. "Ontario Court Ruling Opens Up Potential Access to Ring of Fire." *Financial Post*, 26 February. http://business.financialpost.com/commodities/mining/

ontario-court-ruling-opens-up-potential-road-access-to-ring-of-fire-mineral-belt.

Kulchyski, Peter, ed. 1994. *Unjust Relations: Aboriginal Rights in Canadian Courts.* Toronto: Oxford University Press.

– 2007. "The Violence of the Letter." *Canadian Dimension* 41 (1).

Lawrence, Bonita. 2012. *Fractured Homeland: Federal Recognition and Algonquin Identity in Ontario.* Vancouver: University of British Columbia.

Lawson, James. 2006. "The Caledonia Occupation." *Relay* 12.

– 2007. "The AFN Day of Action." *Relay* 32.

Leslie, Keith. 2014. "Sousa Says Ontario Ripped Off by Federal Budget, Calls It Kick in the Teeth." *The Canadian Press*, 11 February.

– 2016. "It's Possible to Safely Remove Mercury from Wabigoon River, Report Says." *Toronto Star*, 30 May. https://www.thestar.com/news/canada/2016/05/30/possible-for-mercury-to-be-safely-removed-from-wabigoon-river-report-says.html.

Linden, Sidney B. 2007. *Report of the Ipperwash Inquiry.* Toronto: Ontario, Attorney-General.

Marketwire. 2011. "MiningWatch Canada/Federal Decision Ignores First Nations and Public Input: Likely to Hinder Development in Ontario's 'Ring of Fire.'" 13 October.

McCalla, Douglas. 1993. *Planting the Province: The Economic History of Upper Canada.* Toronto: University of Toronto Press.

Mehra, Natalie. 2012. *Falling Behind: Ontario's Backslide in Widening Inequality, Growing Poverty and Cuts to Social Programs.* Toronto: Ontario Common Front.

Menzies, Peter M. 2005. "Orphans within Our Family: Intergenerational Trauma and Homeless Aboriginal Men." PhD diss., Ontario Institute for Studies in Education, University of Toronto.

Milloy, John S. 1999. *A National Crime: The Canadian Government and the Residential School System, 1879–1986.* Winnipeg: University of Manitoba Press.

MiningWatch Canada. 2011. *Government and Industry Steam Ahead on Ring of Fire Developments, First Nations Left Waiting on the Platform.* https://miningwatch.ca/news/2011/1/13/government-industry-steam-ahead-ring-fire-developments-first-nations-left-waiting.

MiningWatch Canada, Wildlands League, and Ecojustice. 2009. *A "Free for All" as Mining Claims More Than Double in Carbon-Rich Ecosystem.* https://miningwatch.ca/news/2009/12/14/free-all-mining-claims-more-double-carbon-rich-ecosystem-public-interest-groups-call.

Morellato, Maria. 2008. "The Crown's Constitutional Duty to Consult and Accommodate Aboriginal and Treaty Rights." In *Research Paper for the National Centre for First Nations Governance.* Ottawa: National Centre for First Nations Governance.

Nelles, H.V. 1974. *The Politics of Development.* Toronto: Archon Books.

Nishnawbe Aski Nation. 2012. *Ontario's Far North Act.* http://www.nan.on.ca/article/ontarios-far-north-act-463.asp.

Ontario, Canada, and Algonquins of Ontario. 2017. *Draft Environmental Evaluation Report: Proposed Settlement Lands.* https://files.ontario.ca/draft_environmental_evaluation_report.pdf.

Ontario. Aboriginal Affairs. 2018. *Current Claims and Land-Related Negotiations.* http://www.aboriginalaffairs.gov.on.ca/english/negotiate/claims.asp.

Ontario. Aboriginal Affairs and Chiefs of Ontario. 2015. *Political Accord.* Toronto: Queen's Printer for Ontario.

– 2016b. *Walking Together: Ontario's Long-Term Strategy to End Violence against Indigenous Women.* Toronto: Queen's Printer for Ontario.

Ontario. Indigenous Relations and Reconciliation. 2017. *Six Nations of the Grand River.* https://www.ontario.ca/page/six-nations-grand-river.

– 2018. *Current Land Claims.* https://www.ontario.ca/page/current-land-claims.

Ontario. Northern Development and Mines. 2012a. *Mining Act Modernization.* Northern Development and Mines. http://www.mndm.gov.on.ca/en/mines-and-minerals/mining-act/mining-act-modernization.

– 2012b. *Mining in Ontario – Facts and Figures.* http://news.ontario.ca/mndmf/en/2012/05/mining-in-ontario---facts-and-figures.html.

– 2018. *Modernizing the Mining Act.* https://www.mndm.gov.on.ca/en/mines-and-minerals/mining-act/modernizing-mining-act.

Ontario. Office of the Premier. 2016a. *The Journey Together: Ontario's Commitment to Reconciliation with Indigenous People.* Toronto: Queen's Printer for Ontario.

Ontario Trillium Foundation. 2008. *Aboriginal Communities in Profile: Ontario – Building Healthy and Vibrant Communities.* Toronto: Ontario Trillium Foundation.

Page, Brian, and Richard Walker. 1991. "From Settlement to Fordism: The Agro-Industrial Revolution in the American Midwest." *Economic Geography* 67 (4).

Pawlick, Thomas. 2009. *The War in the Country: How the Fight to Save Rural Life Will Shape Our Future.* Vancouver: Greystone Books.

Prefasi, Ron. 1992. "Temagami." In *At the End of the Shift: Mines and Single-Industry Towns in Northern Ontario*, edited by Matt Bray and Ashley Thomson. Toronto: Dundurn.

Rennie, Steve. 2013. "Retired Supreme Court Justice Named Ontario's Lead Ring of Fire Negotiator." *Canadian Press*, 2 July. https://ipolitics.ca/2013/07/02/former-scc-justice-frank-iacobucci-named-ontarios-lead-ring-of-fire-negotiator/.

– 2014. "Social Services in Ring of Fire May Strain Ottawa." *Globe and Mail*, 4 January.

Roslin, Alex. 2004. "Bill C-6: Land Claims Gutted." *Canadian Dimension* 38 (1).

Ross, Ian. 2018. "Playing Politics with Resource Revenue Sharing: Municipal Leader Wants Mining, Forestry Benefits Deal for All Northern Communities." *Northern Ontario Business* 38 (8).

Satzewich, Vic, and Terry Wotherspoon. 1993. *First Nations: Race, Class, and Gender Relations*. Scarborough: Nelson Canada.

Scales, Marilyn. 2017. "Road to the Ring of Fire." *Canadian Mining Journal* 138 (2).

Schmalz, Peter S. 1991. *The Ojibwa of Southern Ontario*. Toronto: University of Toronto Press.

Scoffield, Heather. 2012. "Natural Resources Key to Aboriginal Peace, Northern Ontario Leaders Say." *Canadian Press*, 21 December.

Scott, Dayna Nadine, and Adrian A. Smith. 2011. "The Green Teens of Aamjiwnaang Make the Connection." *Canadian Dimension* 45 (6).

Shah, Baiju R., Nadia Gunraj, and Janet E. Hux. 2003. "Markers of Access to and Quality of Primary Care for Aboriginal People in Ontario, Canada." *American Journal of Public Health* 93 (5).

Shkilnyk, Anastasia M. 1985. *A Poison Stronger than Love: The Destruction of an Ojibwa Community*. New Haven: Yale University Press.

Skinner, Kelly, Rhona M. Hanning, and Leonard J.S. Tsuji. 2006. "Barriers and Supports for Healthy Eating and Physical Activity for First Nation Youths in Northern Canada." *International Journal of Circumpolar Health* 65 (2).

Smiley, Donald V., ed. (1937) 1963. *The Rowell-Sirois Report: An Abridgment of Book One of the Royal Commission on Dominion-Provincial Relations*. Toronto: McClelland and Stewart.

Smith, Donald B. 1989. "The Dispossession of the Mississauga Indians: A Missing Chapter in the Early History of Upper Canada." In *Historical Essays on Upper Canada: New Perspectives*, edited by J.K. Johnston and Bruce G. Wilson. Ottawa: Carleton University Press.

Spotton, Noelle. 2006. *A Profile of Aboriginal Peoples in Ontario*. Toronto: Ipperwash Inquiry.

Statistics Canada. 2013. *National Household Survey: Aboriginal People, 2011*. http://www12.statcan.gc.ca.

Storper, M., and R. Walker. 1989. *The Capitalist Imperative: Territory, Technology and Industrial Growth*. Oxford: Basil Blackwell.

Tarachansky, Lia. 2008. "In Their Backyard: Turning Indigenous Lands into Toxic Dumps for Industry." *Canadian Dimension* 32 (6).

Tyendinaga Support Committee. 2007. *In Support of the Mohawks of Tyendinaga*. Toronto: Tyendinaga Support Committee.

Urban Aboriginal Task Force. 2007. *Final Report*. Toronto: Ontario Federation of Indian Friendship Centres.

Watson, Denis McLean. 1971. *Frontier Movement and Economic Development in Northeastern Ontario, 1850–1914*. MA thesis, Department of Geography, University of British Columbia.

Wiebe, Sarah Marie. 2016. *Everyday Exposure: Indigenous Mobilization and Envrionmental Justice in Canada's Chemical Valley*. Vancouver: University of British Columbia Press.

Willow, Anna. 2010. "Cultivating Common Ground: Cultural Revitalization in Anishinaabe and Anthropological Discourse." *American Indian Quarterly* 34 (1).
Windspeaker. 1995. "Blood Spilled at Ontario Provincial Park." *Windspeaker* 13 (6).
– 2008. "New Funds to Enhance Land and Resources." *Windspeaker* 26 (3).
Wright, Lisa. 2014. "Action Plan Tries to Light Ring of Fire under Ottawa." *Toronto Star*, 20 February.

| 15 |

Unequal Futures: Race and Class under Neoliberalism in Ontario

GRACE-EDWARD GALABUZI

This chapter explores race and the changing composition and nature of the working class in the early twenty-first century in Ontario. It focuses on the ways in which the intersection of race and class is integral to the contemporary working-class experience, shaped by the neoliberal restructuring of provincial, Canadian, and global economies. It argues that racialization is a key organizing process of capitalist relations of production. The racial and gender identity of workers is essential to the process of class formation under neoliberalism. The intersection of class with varied social distinctions and identities (such as race, gender, and disability) is integral to the structuring of differential exploitation. By differential exploitation we mean here the unequal occupational status and pay between white and non-white workers, but also other aspects of social equality such as unequal treatment in the policing and judicial systems, or in educational access, and so forth. Data is provided to demonstrate these effects in the Ontario context and to describe the resistance they provoke in communities. The ways in which communities are subjected to modes of differential exploitation, and respond to the processes of racialization that structure access to workplaces, are of particular interest.

Anti-racism struggles are documented as they shift towards addressing questions of workplace access and related institutional arrangements under a neoliberal economy in which class formation has a distinctly racialized character and work is increasingly precarious. The chapter concludes by looking at the emergence of the Colour of Poverty Coalition, as an example of a coalition of community-based organizations that attempts to mobilize racialized communities in Southern Ontario in response to the racialization of poverty. Such anti-racist coalitions may become even more important in a province that is likely to become further divided along lines of class and race under the hard-right neoliberal policies of the Conservative government of Doug Ford.

THE CHANGING DEMOGRAPHY OF ONTARIO

Aboriginal people and racialized groups are becoming a significant proportion of the Ontario population through higher birth rates and increased immigration. A snapshot can be found in the 2011 National Household Survey of trends that will continue over the next few decades in Ontario (Statistics Canada 2011).[1] Between 2006 and 2011, the Aboriginal population grew by 20.1 per cent compared to the rest of the Canadian population at 5.2 per cent. Ontario is home to the largest number of Aboriginal people (301,425 or 21.5 per cent of the Aboriginal population in Canada in 2011). Only 37 per cent of those registered under the Indian Act were living on reserve. In 2011, the median age of Aboriginal people in Canada was 28 years as compared to 41 years for the rest of the Canadian population.

Ontario was also home to 53.3 per cent of all Canadian residents born outside the country (3,611,400 people). Most of these were members of racialized populations.[2] The racialized population in Ontario in 2011 accounted for 3,279,600 people, or 52.3 per cent of all racialized people in Canada and 26 per cent of the population of the province, and had a median age of 33.4 years compared to 40.1 years for the rest of Canadians (ibid.). Concentrated in Southern Ontario, racialized group members constituted 47 per cent of the Greater Toronto Area and 50 per cent of the Region of Peel, one of Ontario's fastest growing areas. While Ontario welcomed 501,000 immigrants between 2005 and 2011, differential experiences with the labour market have emerged between racialized immigrants to Ontario and non-racialized immigrants, with Asian-, Caribbean-, and African-born immigrants experiencing lower employment rates and higher unemployment than immigrants born in Europe in 2006 (Gilmore 2008).

These developments bring the material conditions and the differential exploitation that defines the work lives of Aboriginal and racialized peoples into sharp political focus. The growth in racial diversity in the province means that racial inequality has become a significant policy issue in Ontario. The province's future social, economic, and political well-being will be determined by how the differential life chances for Aboriginal and racialized peoples who will constitute over a third of the province's population by 2030 are addressed (Malenfant, Lebel, and Martel 2010).

Numerous studies and reports speak to a growing awareness of the racial disparities in labour market access and compensation, income, health outcomes, housing and residential patterns, and political participation (Block 2010; Hou and Coulombe 2010; Wilson and Macdonald 2010; Burleton and Gulati 2012; Siemiatycki 2011). These disparities threaten sharper social polarization and the potential for negative intergenerational impacts as they emerge from the deepening of the neoliberal form of capitalist social relations. It is through an exploration of the dominant relations of production under neoliberal capitalism that one can best appreciate the implications of the interplay between race and class (and gender) in the structuring of the racialized and Aboriginal realities in the "Great White North" of Ontario. The role racial discrimination plays is critical to understanding how the "Canadian experience" shapes the incorporation of racialized groups into the labour market in a manner that reproduces differential exploitation (Block and Galabuzi 2011; Baldwin, Cameron, and Kobayashi 2011). It also offers a window into the agency of working people and the significance of the social movements they produce.

A major shift in the form of immigrant labour coming to Canada under a variety of temporary worker programs, driven by employers demanding greater workforce flexibility, is also occurring in Ontario. These include the Temporary Foreign Worker Program for Skilled Workers, the Low Skilled Worker Pilot Project, the "Foreign Labour Agreement" annex to the Canada-Ontario Immigration Agreement, the bilateral reciprocal agreements between sending and receiving countries, and the Provincial Nominee Program, among others (Faraday 2014; House of Commons 2009; UFCW 2011; Valiani 2009). Ac-

Table 15.1 | Racialized population in Ontario, 2011

Group	Population	Group %	%
Total visible minority	3,279,565		25.9
South Asian	965,985	7.6	
Chinese	629,140	5.0	
Black	539,210	4.3	
Filipino	275,385	2.2	
Latin American	172,560	1.4	
Arab	151,640	1.2	
Southeast Asian	137,875	1.1	
West Asian	122,530	1.0	
Korean	78,290	0.6	
Japanese	29,090	0.2	
Visible minority, other	81,125	0.6	
Multiple visible minority	96,735	0.8	
Not a visible minority	9,372,225		74.1
Total population	12,651,795		100.0

Source: Statistics Canada (2011), *National Household Survey*.

Table 15.2 | Aboriginal Peoples in Canada and Ontario

Group	2006	2011
Total Aboriginal	1,172,790	1,400,685
Ontario	242,490	301,425
North American Indian	698,025	851,560
Métis	389,785	451,795
Inuit	50,485	59,445

Source: Statistics Canada (2011), *National Household Survey*.

cording to Faraday (2014), 252,124 permanent immigrants and 280,000 temporary foreign workers entered the country in 2009, signalling the shift from "nation-building" through permanent migration to reliance on vulnerable commodified migrant labour.[3]

While the Aboriginal population is also growing at a rate that outpaces other groups, its labour market performance is lagging behind that of non-Aboriginal Canadians. The Ontario Aboriginal population grew by 20 per cent between 2006 and 2011, from 242,490 to 301,425, and is much younger than the non-Aboriginal population. According to the 2011 National Household Survey, 28 per cent of the Aboriginal population in Canada was 14 years of age or younger compared to 16.5 per cent among the rest of Canadians; and 18.2 per cent of the Aboriginal population was between 15 and 24 compared to 5.9 per cent among other Canadians in 2011.

Racialized group populations make up a majority or near majority in Toronto (49 per cent racialized), Mississauga (53.7 per cent), Brampton (66.4 per cent), and Markham (72.3 per cent). The cumulative impact of racially segmented labour markets and other dimensions of racial inequality have heightened social exclusion for whole segments of racialized groups (Mississauga News 2013). Increased immigration, persistent devaluation of racialized human capital, social marginalization, and racial polarization in the labour market all implicate racialized groups as a form of "reserve army of labour" that produces a dividend for capital in a labour market where workers are ushered into competition along racial lines. Yet, beyond intensifying competitiveness between workers, the struggles of racialized groups increasingly display a surprising level of class consciousness, as segmentation transforms racial affinity into class interests in the sectors where they are disproportionately represented (Teelucksingh and Galabuzi 2004; Satzewich and Liodakis 2017, chap. 5).

The global and local articulations of capitalist relations today impose material burdens on people in the Global North and South through market disciplines; they also provoke transnational migrations and concentrations of displaced, migrating racialized workers in particular sectors of the economy. This capitalist logic of seeking to lower the cost of labour globally and locally creates conditions in central economies like Canada that Saskia Sassen (1998) has referred to as the "South in the North," that is, racialized populations from the Global South living on the social margins in the North. The question as to whether these are class phenomena, or ethnic or racialized ones, may be misplaced since they appear to be mutually constitutive, through the course of capitalist development. As Stuart Hall has remarked: "Race is thus, also, the modality in which class is 'lived,' the medium through which class relations are experienced, the form in which it is appropriated and fought through" (1980, 341).

RACE AND PRECARITY IN THE ONTARIO ECONOMY

A key consideration here is how the neoliberal restructuring of the Canadian economy has intensified racial hierarchies in Ontario's economy. One manifestation of that is the stratification of the labour market along racial lines during a time of retreat for the Canadian state from its regulatory role (Block and Galabuzi 2011; Pendakur and Pendakur 2010). The process of racialization in the labour market is accentuated by the emergence of precarious or non-standard forms of work in sectors with disproportionately high levels of racialized groups' employment (Block 2010; Precarious Employment and Poverty in Southern Ontario 2013; Law Commission of Ontario 2012; Vosko 2006). Canada's reliance on immigrants from the Global South has increased the numbers of racialized members in the labour market and contributed both to a reconsideration of the process of class formation and to a phenomenon we refer to as the racialization of poverty.[4] The impact is reflected in sectoral participation patterns and related differential social and economic indicators such as income, the incidence of low income, and unemployment (Block 2010). The sectoral segregation exemplified by the disproportionate concentration of racialized populations in retail and other service sector employment, light manufacturing, and the textile and hospitality industries – in other words, sectors with precarious work as the dominant mode of labour organization (part-time, temporary, contract, and low-paid work) – converges with other exclusions to create conditions of overrepresentation in low income neighbourhoods with substandard and increasingly segregated housing, higher health risks, and growing tensions between racialized communities and the criminal justice system.[5] Increasingly, racialized poverty is concentrated among racialized and Aboriginal groups in Ontario's urban centres, as table 15.3 suggests for the early 2000s (a trend that has continued).

This raises the question of racialized and Aboriginal peoples and the process of class formation. How do gendered and racialized processes of entry into the labour market, and the corresponding struggles mounted against the barriers they face, redefine the process of class formation in the early twenty-first century?

Table 15.3 | Racialized groups in low-income areas in Ontario urban centres, 2001–06

	% of population		% in low-income areas	
	2001	2006	2001	2006
Racialized groups	22.8	26.9	39.4	45.8
All other	77.2	73.1	60.6	54.2
	100.0	100.0	100.0	100.0

Source: Statistics Canada (2006).

This chapter offers the observation that in specific periods of history, the racial character of labour plays a more determinative role in the processes of class formation. This was the case during the periods of colonization when an ideology of white supremacy, during and immediately after the Atlantic slave trade triangle, played a key legitimating role in the political and economic ordering, establishing a structural racial regime that determined which group membership entitled one to access various labour market opportunities (Loomba 1998; Roediger 1991; Du Bois 1935; Mackey 2002; Creese 1991; Shadd 1987; Satzewich 1991). In the last decades in Canada, racialized immigration has become a key source of labour market regeneration, and flexibility in the deployment of labour determines differential rewards. It is difficult to understand the process of class formation without considering the process of racialization that structures the integration of migrants in Canadian society, as well as the imperatives of migration from societies and economies, in Asia and Africa for example, that are being integrated into global capitalist relations (Galabuzi 2006; Li 2003).

There are a number of approaches used to explain the processes of labour market sorting that produce differential outcomes for immigrant and racialized workers. In the Canadian context, Porter (1965) initially identified what he called a "vertical mosaic" based on ethnicity arising out of "occupational inequality" among ethnic groups. Subsequent research suggested three possible explanations for these inequalities: a slow acquisition of soft skills (language or Canadian cultural norms); a high degree of employment discrimination; and a changing structure of employment in Canada in favour of experiences of precariousness and incorporation into lower-paid sectors. There is some evidence that all three apply, to various degrees, to the condition of racialized workers in Canada now (Porter 1965; Pendakur and Pendakur 1998; Wanner 1998; Galabuzi 2006).

Canadian scholarship today largely deploys four theoretical approaches that reflect these earlier explanations. First, the "assimilation thesis" is rooted in the idea that these conditions are temporary phenomena, possibly due to immigration status, and will ease over time. This approach also subsumes what is called the "entrance status thesis" – immigrants and marginalized populations enter the labour market from the lowest status jobs but migrate up the labour market over time. Second, the "human capital" thesis places emphasis on the quality of the individuals' human capital due to educational attainment, low job skills, age, low geographical mobility, and health. Immigrants from countries of the Global South are often assumed to have a low quality of human capital. Third, the "discrimination thesis" contends that lower economic performance and blocked access to the labour market arises from systemic discrimination in employment such that even high human capital leads to diminishing returns and explains why highly educated racialized group members have occupational status and incomes that are inferior to those of non-racialized people and non-immigrants. Finally, the "period effect" thesis suggests that the nature of the economic conditions in a particular moment – say during periods of economic restructuring – structures vulnerabilities for particular groups that have historical disadvantages in accessing the labour market, such as women, youth, racialized people, immigrants, and Aboriginal Peoples (Portes 1995; Gordon 1995; Borjas 1994; Basran and Zong 1998; Li 1998; Grant and Oertel 1998; Reitz 1998).

South-north migration has always arisen out of the various forms of displacement and dislocation generated by global capitalist accumulation. These processes have engaged various modes of racialization at local and global levels to facilitate the production of "unfree" migrant and local labour. This was historically through slavery, indentured and contract labour, and others, and now through the intensification of conditions of precarious and "flexible" employment. Precarious employment is often the basis for intensifying exploitation.[6]

There is a growing body of evidence that, under neoliberalism, Aboriginal and racialized workers are operating under conditions of high exploitation, in unsafe work environments, and with unstable work arrangements and tenure, low wages, limited or no control over their work, income insecurity, and deteriorating health status (Office of the Fairness Commissioner 2013; Wilson et al. 2011). These reports also suggest that precarious employment is connected to growing neighbourhood instability and insecurity of livelihoods. Further, that precarious employment imposes differential impacts on historically vulnerable communities – women, immigrants, racialized people, and off-reserve Indigenous people and youth.

Precarious employment is characterized by increased economic insecurity, reduced entitlement to ongoing employment, limited control over work schedules, low pay, limited benefits, and fewer opportunities for career advancement (Vosko 2006). It is a shift from the once-standard employment relationship based on full-time, continuous work with good wages and benefits towards intensified exploitation through heightened economic insecurity. In a recent study, precariousness is described as changes in types of work from permanent to contract, temporary work, irregular schedules, and low pay (Precarious Employment and Poverty in Southern Ontario 2013). In seeking to structure maximum flexibility, precarious employment undermines labour power, the ability of workers to have decent incomes, decent lives, and a stable community life.

It's More than Poverty (2013), an important study of the Greater Toronto Area by the Precarious Employment and Poverty in Southern Ontario (PEPSO) Project, reported that 40 per cent of workers experienced precariousness and that such employment rose by 50 per cent among workers in Southern Ontario. These developments are consistent with other neoliberal policies that seek to diminish labour market regulation, including privatization, contracting out, and other forms of austerity recently imposed on the province. While the epicenter of precarious employment has been the private sector, it has been extended to the public sector. A recent federal government Public Service Commission report called for the need to investigate the increasing use of temporary employment agencies for filling federal public service vacancies (Public Service Commission of Canada 2010).

The temporary agency has emerged as an institutional form that acts to normalize precarious employment by matching temporarily employed workers to employers who seek maximum flexibility and minimum encumbrances. By 2012, there were 1,000 temp agencies in Ontario that processed most of the 740,000 temporary and part-time workers. Temp agency workers typically earn 40 per cent less than their coworkers who were hired directly by the company. Agency workers receive less pay, fewer or no benefits, little protection against employment rights violations, and no protection against termination (Law Commission of Ontario 2012). Despite their temporary status, agency workers often work for months and years beside workers doing exactly the same work. Racialized workers, women, and young workers are disproportionately represented among precariously employed workers and so among temp agency employees. Standing (2011) refers to the emergence of a "precariat" – a class of temporarily employed people who have distinctive relations of production. In Ontario, temporary foreign work is another form of labour market flexibility that deploys a form of unfree, and often coerced, labour given the limited rights of these workers (Faraday 2014).

These various schemes of precarious work represent a form of differential exploitation dependent on the conditions for labouring being constructed around the identity of workers – immigrant, Aboriginal, racialized, female, youth, or disabled. Some indicators of the differential conditions of exploitation that reflect the vulnerability to precarious conditions of work that Aboriginal and racialized workers endure include: unequal access to the labour market, unequal employment income, higher levels of unemployment, and sectoral segmentation in the labour market.

RACE IN THE PROCESS OF CLASS FORMATION

Racialization is a crucial subtext to the processes of class formation in that it helps form class consciousness and thus the particular interests and characters of working-class institutions. As E.P. Thompson (1963, 9) commented, "class happens when some men, as a result of common experiences (inherited or shared), feel and articulate the identity of their interests as between themselves, and as against other men whose interests are different from (and usually opposed to) theirs. The class experience is largely determined by the productive relations into which men are born – or enter involuntarily."

It is exactly this consolidation of interests along racial lines that Thompson speaks of – racialization constructing racial identities as "real" modes of distinction. Hall's earlier quoted observation that "race is the modality in which class is lived" is particularly relevant to understanding racialization as part of the process of creating class consciousness, a process that is always dynamic and transforming (Hall 1980; Omi and Winant 1995). It is particular in that the dominant group against which the working class is defined is not just the capitalist class, but also incorporates the dynamic of "whiteness" within the ranks of workers themselves. It includes those defined "into whiteness" by dominant racial hierarchies because they acquire varying degrees of integration, mediated by class position, that always define the racial particularity of class relations (Dunk 1998; McCarthy 2016). In essence, the relations of domination that structure gender and racial oppression also legitimize an exploitative socio-political economic order and differential exploitation. Class, gender, and other forms of oppression intersect with race to intensify the relations of domination experienced by Indigenous and racialized group members in capitalist societies.

In twenty-first-century Ontario, class formation involves the incorporation of immigrant racialized labour from the Global South into Ontario as part of the capitalist transnationalization of racially hierarchical relations of production (Bond 2003). This reality is built on historical colonial regimes that marginalized Aboriginal peoples within the Canadian economy founded on European agriculture settlement and the extractive industries. The building of capitalism involved territorial dispossession that often still transgresses Indigenous claims (Mackey 2002).

The process of neoliberal restructuring and deregulation combines with the legacies of colonization and racialization to intensify racial inequalities. In the process of capital accumulation, racialization reproduces labour market segmentation, generating particular racialized working-class experiences, structures, and subjects. In so doing, working class formation is racialized, as is a wage gap, occupational segmentation, and poverty. In a capitalist society, where most survive by selling their labour, the racial character of that labour continues to matter. The process of class formation, in the broad sociological sense adopted by Thompson, is contingent on the agency of its subjects. Along with the structures and processes that determine the modes of incorporation of particular groups into the labour market, the hierarchical patterns of racialization determine the points of entry and mobility in the labour market (Thompson 1963). Racialization is, therefore, mutually constitutive with the processes of exploitation in class formation; the minority construction of groups on the basis of race, gender, and other key distinctions is socially produced (Hall 1980; Satzewich 1990).

RACIALIZED GROUPS IN ONTARIO'S LABOUR MARKET

Aboriginal and racialized workers and their communities are mobilizing under conditions not of their choosing. They have to do so within conditions of differential access to employment, employment income, and sectoral distribution for Aboriginal and racialized group members in Ontario. Aboriginal peoples in Ontario were the subject of colonial relations, complete with colonial institutions and systems imposed on them in place of their sovereign institutions, leading to the dismantling of traditional territorial claims and political and economic means of governance. The impact of a European colonial process is still manifest in the social marginalization of Aboriginal peoples (Trigger 1985; Maaka and Anderson 2006).

According to the 2011 census, just over 2 per cent of the Ontario population identified as Aboriginal. In table 15.4 below, key labour force characteristics for the Aboriginal population are compared with the total Ontario population. According to the census, 61.9 per cent of the Aboriginal population over the age of 15 was in the labour force as compared to 65.6 per cent of the non-Aboriginal population in 2011. Aboriginal people had a significantly higher unemployment rate of 13.9 per cent, as compared to 8.2 percent for the non-Aboriginal population (Wilson and Macdonald 2010; Block 2010).

The average incomes of Aboriginal people in Ontario are significantly lower than those of non-Aboriginal people. According to table 15.5, in Canada, Aboriginal men make 72.5 cents for every dol-

Table 15.4 | Labour market profile, Aboriginal Peoples in Ontario, 2011 (%)

	Aboriginal			Non-Aboriginal		
	Men	Women	Total	Men	Women	Total
Participation rate	65.1	59.1	61.9	70.0	61.5	65.6
Employment rate	55.1	51.7	53.3	64.3	56.5	60.3
Unemployment rate	15.3	12.5	13.9	8.1	8.2	8.2

Source: Statistics Canada (2011), National Household Survey, catalogue no. 99-012-X2011039.

Table 15.5 | Average employment income for Aboriginal groups in Ontario, 2011 ($)

	Average employment income for those with employment income		Aboriginal as % of non-Aboriginal income
	Aboriginal	Non-Aboriginal	
Men	37,209	51,329	72.5
Women	29,698	36,303	81.8
Both	33,400	44,045	75.8

Source: Statistics Canada (2011), *National Household Survey*, catalogue no. 99-014-X2011041.

lar that non-Aboriginal men earn, while Aboriginal women make 81.8 cents for every dollar that non-Aboriginal women make; and Aboriginal women make 57.8 cents for every dollar that non-Aboriginal men make.

Labour force data also show that a smaller share of Aboriginal workers are in management, business, science, and health occupations, and are more concentrated in sales and service, trades, and primary and other manufacturing industries than the rest of the labour force. There is also a gender effect, with fewer non-Aboriginal men in sales and service occupations compared to a significantly disproportionate number of Aboriginal women in those occupations. Aboriginal people in Ontario are also far more likely to live in poverty (roughly two times more likely) than the rest of the population (Block 2010).

Racialized Ontarians have always been – and continue to be – subject to economic exclusion. As disproportionate victims of precarious forms of employment, racialized workers have lower incomes than

Table 15.6 | Labour market profile of racialized groups in Ontario, 2011 (%)

	Racialized			Non-racialized		
	Men	Women	Total	Men	Women	Total
Participation rate	70.8	61.4	65.9	69.6	61.5	65.4
Employment rate	63.9	54.4	58.9	64.2	57.0	60.5
Unemployment rate	9.7	11.4	10.5	7.8	7.3	7.5

Source: Statistics Canada (2011), *National Household Survey*, catalogue no. 99-012-X2011038.

non-racialized workers. They also have higher rates of unemployment and are more likely to live in poverty. While on average, racialized workers have more years of education than other Canadians, this does not translate into higher incomes and occupational status. Internationally educated professionals and tradespeople particularly continue to confront barriers to employment in their chosen profession or trade (Office of the Fairness Commissioner 2013). Racialized women's labour market experience reflects the impact of both racism and sexism in employment.

Table 15.6 shows key labour market characteristics for racialized (following the Statistics Canada definition of visible minorities excluding Aboriginals) and non-racialized Ontarians in 2011. While racialized Ontarians, both male and female, had a slightly higher participation rate (65.9 per cent compared to 65.4), they also had higher rates of unemployment at 10.5 per cent compared to 7.5 per cent for the rest of the population. In other words, while more likely to be working or available to work, Ontarians from racial minorities were more likely to be out of work.

There is some value to disaggregating the data to show the differentiated labour market experience of particular groups. Table 15.7 shows a breakdown of aggregate labour market data by racialized group. Among them, people of Arab, West Asian, Chinese, Korean, and Japanese background had lower participation rates than other non-racialized Ontarians, while all other racialized groups had higher participation rates. All racialized groups, except for those who identify as Filipino or Japanese, had higher unemployment rates than non-racialized Ontarians. Those of Arab, West Asian, and Black backgrounds had significantly higher unemployment rates.

Table 15.7 | Labour market profile by racialized groups in Ontario, 2011 (%)

	Participation rate	Employment rate	Unemployment rate
Total racialized population	65.9	58.9	10.5
South Asian	66.0	58.8	11.0
Chinese	62.3	56.7	9.0
Black	67.0	58.3	13.0
Filipino	75.0	70.2	6.5
Latin American	71.3	63.9	10.4
Arab	59.4	51.6	13.1
South East Asian	67.9	60.3	11.1
West Asian	61.3	53.4	12.8
Korean	57.8	52.0	10.0
Japanese	59.9	56.0	6.4
Visible minority, other	67.3	59.7	11.3
Multiple visible minorities	66.7	59.5	10.8
Non-racialized population	65.4	60.5	7.5

Source: Statistics Canada (2011), *National Household Survey*, catalogue no. 99-012-X2011038.

Table 15.8 | Gender, race, and employment income in Ontario, 2011 ($)

	Average employment income for those with employment income		Racialized % of non-racialized
	Racialized	Non-racialized	
Men	43,604	53,322	81.8
Women	32,936	37,189	88.6
Both	38,340	45,536	84.2

Source: Statistics Canada (2011), *National Household Survey*, catalogue no. 99-014-X2011041.

These patterns of incorporation into the labour market extend to differential average employment income between racialized and non-racialized Ontarians, as shown in table 15.8. These differences in earnings between the groups also illustrate the interactions between race and gender with the employment earnings gap between racialized women and non-racialized men perhaps the most glaring. While racialized men in Ontario made 81.8 cents for every dollar that non-racialized men made, racialized women made 61.8 cents for every

Table 15.9 | Average employment income by racialized group in Ontario, 2010 ($)

	Men	Women	Total
Total racialized population	43,604	32,936	38,340
South Asian	44,662	31,632	38,790
Chinese	47,519	36,821	42,144
Black	38,367	33,105	35,588
Filipino	39,629	33,304	35,844
Latin American	39,859	29,063	34,613
Arab	47,409	31,612	40,967
South East Asian	42,823	29,554	36,392
West Asian	42,133	29,415	36,622
Korean	42,751	30,198	36,535
Japanese	63,513	40,521	51,695
Visible minority, other	41,144	32,602	36,740
Multiple visible minorities	44,253	33,271	38,630
Non-racialized population	53,322	37,189	45,536

Source: Statistics Canada (2011), *National Household Survey*, catalogue no. 99-014-X2011041.

dollar that non-racialized men made in 2011. The gap was significantly smaller between racialized women and non-racialized women, partly because of the much lower wages that non-racialized women made, which were also lower than those of racialized men. Racialized women made 88.6 cents for every dollar that non-racialized women made. However, the difference between racialized men and women was smaller than the difference between non-racialized men and women. While racialized women made 75.5 cents for every dollar that racialized men made, non-racialized women made 69.7 cents for every dollar that non-racialized men made.

These patterns of differential income are present for almost all racialized groups. Table 15.9 below is a breakdown of average employment income by group. It shows that the pattern of lower employment earnings for racialized workers is consistent across all groups except for Japanese-Ontarians. There are, as well, significant income gaps within the racialized category itself, with particularly the Latin American, Black, and Filipino groups having significant income gaps with non-racialized Ontarians.

Table 15.10 | Racialized labour market distribution by occupation in Ontario, 2011 (%)

	Racialized		Non-racialized	
	Men	Women	Men	Women
All occupations	12.5	11.8	39.2	36.5
Management	12.2	7.5	49.4	31.0
Business, finance, and administration	9.1	16.4	21.9	52.7
Natural and applied sciences and related occupations	25.6	7.8	52.1	14.5
Health	6.6	20.1	13.4	59.9
Education, law and social, community and government services	6.2	14.6	26.8	52.3
Art, culture, recreation, and sport	8.9	9.2	37.6	44.2
Sales and service occupations	12.3	14.3	31.2	42.2
Trades, transport, and equipment operators and related occupations	16.9	1.4	76.6	5.1
Natural resources, agriculture, and related production occupations	6.8	2.4	70.5	20.3
Occupations in manufacturing and utilities	20.4	15.5	46.2	17.9

Source: Statistics Canada (2011), National Household Survey, catalogue no. 99-010-X2011038.

The labour force participation of racialized groups can also be defined by a significant degree of segmentation, as demonstrated by the occupational distribution within industrial sectors. As presented in table 15.10, the racialized share of the total labour force was 12.5 per cent for men and 11.8 per cent for women. In that case, any industry that has a racialized labour force share lower than those amounts can be said to represent an underrepresentation of racialized workers, while any industry that has a higher share shows an overrepresentation of the groups. Racialized men are overrepresented in: manufacturing and utilities; trades, transportation, and related occupations; and natural and applied science occupations. In contrast, racialized women are overrepresented in: business, finance, and administration; health; education, law and social, community and other government services; sales and service; and manufacturing and utilities.[7]

The racialization of poverty represents the disproportionate experience of poverty among racialized people. As we saw with the Abori-

Table 15.11 | Low income by racialized group after tax in Ontario, 2010 (%)

	Men	Women	Total
Total racialized population	19.7	20.5	20.1
South Asian	17.6	17.5	17.5
Chinese	18.7	19.2	18.9
Black	23.5	26.5	25.1
Filipino	9.5	10.2	9.9
Latin American	19.6	22.1	20.9
Arab	31.4	33.4	32.3
South East Asian	17.0	18.9	18.0
West Asian	32.3	33.9	33.1
Korean	32.0	32.0	32.0
Japanese	9.0	12.4	10.8
Visible minority, n.i.e.	16.6	19.5	18.1
Multiple visible minorities	16.0	17.0	16.5
Non-racialized population	10.9	12.4	11.6

Source: Statistics Canada (2011), National Household Survey, catalogue no. 99-010-X2011038.

ginal population, the differential access to employment and employment incomes gaps are responsible for structuring higher levels of poverty among racialized Ontarians. Table 15.11 below shows the significantly higher levels of poverty among racialized groups compared to non-racialized Ontarians, except for the Japanese and Filipino groups. Poverty rates were three times those of non-racialized families for West Asian, Arab, Korean, and Black groups, for the 2011 census data. Women tend to systematically suffer a higher degree of poverty than men, for both racialized and non-racialized groups.

ORGANIZATIONAL RESPONSES TO THE RACIALIZATION OF THE DIVISION OF LABOUR

The persistent racial inequalities of Aboriginal and racialized groups in the Ontario labour market have led to organizational mobilizations that reflect both a class and racial conscious. Racialized groups have long experienced precarious employment in the Canadian labour market. By the 1980s, the inequities of employment were on the policy agenda. The differential employment participation and outcomes for racialized populations were identified by various studies, including the Royal Commission on Equality in Employment (Abella 1984), as forms of discrimination in employment, and they emerged as social and political problems that demanded state remedies.

The most assertive responses to these labour market inequalities have employed the racialization framework and organized around demands for legislated anti-discriminatory policies and programs (inspired by Section 15 of the Canadian Charter of Rights and Freedoms). The most prominent of these initiatives have included pay and employment equity policies. Employment equity addresses differential treatment in common workplaces and, to some degree, issues of income, access, and mobility within sectors. According to the Abella Report, it is a policy "designed to obliterate the present residual effects of discrimination and to open equitably the competition for employment opportunities to those arbitrarily excluded" (Abella 1984, 214). The mobilizational approaches responsible for securing employment equity as a regulatory regime for addressing employment discrimination were largely community based, although the labour movement, after a long period of ambiguity, sought to influence the nature of regulation that became increasingly inevitable in the 1980s. Legislated employment equity programs emerged in the 1980s and 1990s at the federal level and in some provinces, notably Ontario, through the Act to Provide for Employment Equity for Aboriginal People, People with Disabilities, Members of Racial Minorities and Women 1993 (Bakan and Kobayashi 2000). The designated groups in the legislation included women, persons with disabilities, visible minorities (racialized people), and Aboriginal peoples.

Eventually passed in 1994, the employment equity legislation and its institutions, the Employment Equity Commissioner and Tribunal, were however quickly expunged by the newly elected Conservative government of Mike Harris in 1995. A key part of the Conservatives' election campaign was their view of unfair "preferential treatment" in employment for designated groups. Although the government regulation was meant to combat discrimination in employment, the discourse around the legislation became highly racialized and precipitated a backlash. Subsequently, legislated employment equity programs at the federal and provincial level have lacked the full support of the state and the enforcement powers necessary to succeed, as well as a relapse in their legislative action (Abu-Laban and Gabriel 2002).

In any respect, these programs represent a limited approach to dealing with the unequal power relations structuring the labour market. Bakan and Kobayashi's (2000) review of provincial programs, for example, suggests that they have been ineffective in eliminating discriminatory structures in the labour market because of the persistence, and often re-emergence, of public discourses inspired by racist and sexist practices and views. In this sense, legislated employment equity programs are not well equipped to address the intersecting multiple oppressions that are fundamental to the racialized experience of social exclusion in Canada and Ontario. Neoliberal market reforms have, moreover, imposed new competitive tensions among workers, as opposed to expanding employment opportunities for all segments of society.

Subsequent attempts to address issues of employment inequality through systemic approaches have been largely abandoned, including by the Liberal governments of Dalton McGuinty in the 2000s. Liberal government action focused on more generic approaches such as the introduction of the Poverty Reduction Strategy (which set a notional target of lowering child poverty by 25 per cent in five years), or reforms to the Employment Standards Act, or a modest increase in the minimum wage (Government of Ontario 2008). These efforts shift the focus away from the processes of racialization, and hope to indirectly impact discriminatory patterns in the labour market (Government of Ontario 2013; Workers' Action Centre 2012). In its last year in office, the government of Kathleen Wynne moved to more aggressively raise the minimum wage to $15 and improve employment standards through Bill 148, the Fair Workplaces, Better Jobs Act (2017). As well, an Anti-Racism Directorate was established in 2016 and shortly proposed an anti-racism strategic plan, *A Better Way Forward* (Ontario: Anti-Racism Directorate 2017), focused on community collaborations and education and awareness about systematic racism, in particular anti-Black and Indigenous racism and Islamophobia.[8]

But the lack of a systemic organizational response at the level of the Ontario state has meant that dealing with labour market discrimination has been left to community organizing. This requires building on an analysis of colonial and racial dimensions that construct precarious conditions in the labour market and differential exploitation. It also requires society to recognize the extent to which these conditions create precarity in the community and neighbourhoods in which we live.

Countering neoliberalism means addressing issues of race and class. This means empowering Aboriginal and racialized workers to utilize collective action in the workplace. Unionization is a well-established workplace-based approach that has proven effective in improving employment and income opportunities and protections. However, this has to include community concerns and interests, or what has been called social/community unionism (Crawford, Gellatly, Ladd, and Vosko 2006; Sawchuk 2006; Schenk 2006). Coalition-building across class, race, and gender lines is needed to strengthen collective bargaining rights. But such a political movement would also strengthen the ability of racialized workers to resist demands for more flexibility and casualization of labour, and address issues of privilege and unequal power relations.

The documented overrepresentation of racialized groups in certain sectors, industries, and occupations where unions are weak suggests that unionization of these sectors would improve wage levels. Numerous studies now show the impact of the union advantage for racialized workers, particularly in precarious work environments, while also raising prospects for new forms of class consciousness (Jackson 2002; Reitz and Verma 1999; Galabuzi 2006). However, traditional union models of organizing are not always able or willing, due to the legislative regime/priorities, to address the needs of precariously employed or unemployed workers.

The formation of new types of workers' associations and action centres represents an important organizational response to the precarious nature of the neoliberal labour market. The emergence of the Ontario Coalition of Black Trade Unionists, the Asian Canadian Labour Alliance, INTERCEDE (a domestic workers' association), Black Lives Matter, Idle No More, Justice for Migrant Workers, Ontario Coalition Against Poverty (OCAP), Colour of Poverty, and other related workers associations, all represent innovative approaches to employing an integrated approach to racial oppression and class exploitation. Such organizing campaigns have been complemented by new workers' action centres in a number of communities across the country, such as the Toronto Workers' Action Centre, the Migrant Farm Workers' Support Centre (supported by UFCW), and the Windsor Workers' Action Centre. Community unionism represents an effective local response to neoliberalism that is both more democratic and ensures greater participation for racialized and Aboriginal peoples in unions. The province-wide campaign to raise the minimum wage and employment standards over the last few years, the Fight for $15, has been led by a coalition of these centres, local labour councils, and campus groups. There is a potential with these campaigns to build union power by connecting workers' activism to political empowerment of the membership in a community-union alliance framework. Kim Moody has suggested that such strategies "assert the centrality of union democracy as a source of power and broad social vision ... (and uses outreach) as a means of enhancing that power" (1997, 4).

Social unionism coupled with community organizing represents a "new" or "renewed" form of working class organizing and organization. In assuming a broad notion of community and attention to democratic participation, particularly for historically marginalized groups, it represents a critique of the traditional forms of economic unionism. Social or community unionism should be understood both as a process and an organizational form. As a process, it refers to cooperation between a union and community to achieve a common objective. As a form of organization, it represents an autonomous community-based labour organization

The idea is to extend the focus of organizing to community issues beyond workplace concerns. This can be done by linking workplace issues like the minimum wage, unpaid work, job security, and working conditions that arise from racialization to non-workplace concerns about inadequate community health care, child care, housing, immigration settlement, anti-racism, policing, welfare, a living wage, and so on. If it is a challenge to take labour out of competition under neoliberalism, it is possible to make gains if community standards for compensation can be imposed through political action and community bargaining. Similarly, in a period of precarious workplaces, community unionism can help develop a sense of solidarity when a union member is laid off and would normally lose contact with the union. While some unions maintain contact for a time with those who lose jobs, and some may offer some training and support, it is not unlimited. Community unions can help cultivate political participation and community engagement and encourage workers to act collectively to challenge powerful interests and governments.

THE COLOUR OF POVERTY CAMPAIGN

The Colour of Poverty Campaign is an initiative that builds on some of these ideas of community unionism. The campaign was launched in 2007 to call attention to the growing racialization of poverty in Ontario and to organize and mobilize racialized communities for policy action. The fact that a disproportionate number of racialized Ontarians were living in poverty, and that conditions related to access to the labour market exacerbated these conditions of economic exclusion, motivated many racialized community activists to develop a campaign around a set of fact sheets that made clear the connection between race, income insecurity, and poverty, as well as employment inequality and related adverse outcomes in housing, health, and criminal justice. These issues of differential access to the labour market created a condition of marginality that increasingly defined the lived experience of many racialized peoples in Ontario's urban centres (Ornstein 2000; Galabuzi 2001).

Led by the executive director of the Metro Chinese and South Asian Legal Clinic, along with the Ontario Council of Agencies Serving Immigrants (OCASI), the Canadian Arab Federation (CAF), the Council of Agencies Serving South Asians (CASSA), the African Canadian Legal Clinic, the South Asian Legal Clinic, and the Hispanic Development Council (among others), the Colour of Poverty began organizing community dialogues to educate and discuss strategies for political action aimed at reversing the racialized poverty of those in low income neighbourhoods.

In its initial media statements, the campaign addressed both workplace and neighbourhood concerns through building a grassroots movement and undertaking community-based action to end poverty. The anti-racism and anti-poverty analysis acknowledged that poverty is about power and its uneven distribution; it called on allies to commit to building an inclusive anti-poverty and social justice movement to achieve fairer distribution of power and wealth in society. The campaign demanded a comprehensive, multi-sector response to racialized poverty with adequate targeted policies and programs from the various levels of government, aimed at mitigating the growing experience of poverty among racialized groups, as well as addressing overall poverty in Canada (Colour of Poverty Campaign 2012).

The Colour of Poverty Campaign undertook a series of community-based "dialogues" built around the various dimensions of vulnerability to poverty – income, health, education, employment, housing, neighbourhoods, and contact with the criminal justice system – as experienced by racialized people. By the end of the initial dialogues, a "Shared Framework for Action" emerged. It focused on key determinants and institutional arrangements, but also integrated anti-racism and equity into the analysis, along with targets and timelines. It articulated a vision of anti-poverty action that acknowledged that poverty is not a generic, colour-blind experience, but rather is differentially experienced related to the distribution of power in the society, and to the historical racial and gendered hierarchies that determined the vulnerabilities of communities and individuals to poverty.

A central point of the campaign was the recognition that although income measures are vital, they cannot be the exclusive focus for poverty reduction. Attention also needs to be paid to housing and child care in racialized neighbourhoods, and to education, health care, and overall public investment in public services and community development. A range of policies addressing labour market inequalities was also put forward: income security initiatives; employment equity legislation; living wage ordinances as well as raising the minimum wage; fair access to employment insurance for precarious workers; strengthening employment standards legislation and enforcement; extending access to collective bargaining; a series of anti-racism policies and initiatives; and accreditation of international qualifications.

The plan of action also specifically addressed the racialization and feminization of poverty (Colour of Poverty et al. 2016). It called for people living in poverty to be included in defining and planning responses to poverty, as well as targeted outreach to reflect the demographics of those disproportionately affected by poverty. It sought measures or indicators for success to be disaggregated to include clear statements on progress on racialized poverty, and for data collected on poverty to be disaggregated to make transparent the experiences of racialized groups, Aboriginal peoples, persons with disabilities, seniors, women, children, and youth, among others.

CHALLENGING RACIAL INEQUALITIES IN NEOLIBERAL ONTARIO

To understand the process of class formation in Ontario in the period of neoliberal globalization, it is important to factor in the experience of Aboriginal and racialized workers. Racialization always needs to be set in relationship to processes of capital accumulation, and the way this reproduces racial segmentation in labour markets. Particular racialized working-class experiences, structures, and subjects are generated within these processes, racializing, in turn, a wage gap, poverty, and working class formation. In capitalist societies like Ontario, the racial character of labour continues to matter.

Aboriginal and racialized workers and their communities are not passive victims of these processes. Their mobilizations reflect a form of working-class consciousness expressed through racially based organizing using community-based institutions and the existing legal apparatus. An organized response to neoliberal labour market conditions must build on an analysis of colonial and racial dimensions of the dominant relations of production. It requires a direct response to the conditions that construct precarious conditions in the labour market, exposing all workers to intensified exploitation and Aboriginal and racialized workers to differential exploitation. The emergence of workplace-based, community-supported and racially conscious organizing, like the Colour of Poverty Coalition and the Fight for $15, reflect the potential of community-union alliances to address racial inequalities in neoliberal Ontario.

These anti-racist and social movements will now confront new challenges from the new Conservative government. It has been commonly observed that Ford's political base differs from that of Donald Trump in the US in its bridging of racial divides, at least to some degree, by attracting Conservative support in some of the most diverse suburban and exurban areas. And neither the Conservative Party nor Ford offered policy positions directly on matters of race and racism (other than "coded" planks, e.g., respect for the police and the curtailing guns and gangs). It is difficult, however, to imagine any scenario in which the Conservatives' policies of austerity do not hit redistributional policies such as welfare, education, training, employment, and several others, thus magnifying the social divisions produced by racialization.

Indeed, the initial actions and statements of the Ford government presage the sharper racial divides likely to emerge (*Globe and Mail* editorial 2018). As soon as they took office, the new policing oversight laws proposed by the Wynne government in the Ontario Special Investigations Unit Act, partly in response to the Black Lives Matter protests, were blocked. Similarly, the Conservative election manifesto hinted at a re-launch of the Toronto Anti-Violence Intervention Strategy (TAVIS), disbanded in 2017 for its aggressive practice of "carding" individuals in racialized neighbourhoods. As premier, Ford immediately started a major spat with the federal government over costs for re-settling refugees, (falsely) declaring many of the claimants "illegals" whom Ontario should not be paying for. It is also quite unclear whether the modest effort of the Anti-Racist Directorate formed by Wynne will survive Ford's pursuit of administrative "efficiencies." The new phase of neoliberalism that Ontario is entering will require community-union alliances to further step up their anti-racist commitments and politics.

NOTES

1 The National Household Survey is a new voluntary source for the census data set that replaced the mandatory long form census survey, ended by the federal Conservative government in 2010. The national survey's reliability is unlikely to match the former survey's mandatory compliance (Woolley 2013). The latest census was becoming available only after this chapter and overall project were completed. It will confirm the trends presented here.
2 The term "racialized group" is used to denote the social construction of racial categories imposed on certain groups on the basis of superficial attributes such as skin colour. These categories form the basis of inequalities experienced by the identified groups. For the purpose of data collection, the term "visible minority" approximates the category here termed "racialized group"

and continues to be used both by Statistics Canada and in the federal employment equity program.
3   Since 2000, the population of temporary migrant workers in Canada has more than tripled to 338,213 by 2012. The number of temporary migrant workers in Toronto alone grew by 237 per cent between 2006 and 2012 (Faraday 2014).
4   The racialization of poverty refers to the disproportionate level of racialized group members living in poverty in Canada and the disproportionate levels of poverty among those groups. A particular concern has been anti-black racism in urban areas (City of Toronto 2017).
5   This is a large and specialized literature, but see: Halli and Kazemipur (2001); Wilson et al. (2011); McGibbon (2012); Tanovich (2006); and Comack and Balfour (2004).
6   A series of recent reports all speak to the growing prevalence of forms of precarious work in Ontario's labour market: Law Commission of Ontario (2012); Precarious Employment and Poverty in Southern Ontario (2013); and Workers' Action Centre (2007).
7   These data are drawn at a very broad industrial level and do not provide the clearest picture of the racial concentrations and segregation occurring in the Ontario economy (Teelucksingh and Galabuzi 2004).
8   A similar anti-racist strategy formed at the City of Toronto (2017) to address anti-black racism, partly in response to carding and other policing issues that spurred Black Lives Matter protests.

REFERENCES

Abella, Rosalie. 1984. *Report of the Commission on Equality in Employment, Volume 1.* Ottawa: Supply and Services Canada.
Abu-Laban, Yasmeen, and Christina Gabriel. 2002. *Selling Diversity: Immigration, Multiculturalism, Employment Equity and Globalization.* Peterborough: Broadview Press.
Agócs, Carol. 2002. "Canada's Employment Equity Legislation and Policy, 1987–2000: The Gap between Policy and Practice." *International Journal of Manpower* 23 (3).
Bakan, Abigail B., and Audrey Kobayashi. 2000. *Employment Equity Policy in Canada: An Interprovincial Comparison.* Ottawa: Status of Women Canada.
Baldwin, Andrew, Laura Cameron, and Audrey Kobayashi, eds. 2011. *Rethinking the Great White North: Race, Nature and the Historical Geographies of Whiteness in Canada.* Vancouver: UBC Press.
Basran, Gurcharn S., and Zong Li. 1998. "Devaluation of Foreign Credentials as Perceived by Non-White Professional Immigrants." *Canadian Ethnic Studies* 30 (3).

Belgrave, Roger. 2012. "Government Inspectors Focus on Temp Agencies." *Brampton Guardian*, 9 June.

Block, Sheila. 2010. *Ontario's Growing Gap: The Role of Race and Gender*. Ottawa: Canadian Centre for Policy Alternatives.

Block, Sheila, and Grace-Edward Galabuzi. 2011. *Canada's Colour Coded Labour Market: The Gap for Racialized Workers*. Ottawa: Canadian Centre for Policy Alternative.

Bond, Patrick. 2003. *Against Global Apartheid: South Africa Meets the World Bank, IMF and International Finance*. New York: Palgrave Macmillan.

Borjas, George J. 1994. "The Economics of Immigration." *Journal of Economic Literature* 32 (4).

Burleton, Derek, and Sonya Gulati. 2012. *Debunking Myths Surrounding Canada's Aboriginal Population*. Toronto: TD Economics.

City of Toronto. 2017. *The Interim Toronto Action Plan to Confront Anti-Black Racism*. www.toronto.ca/legdocs/mmis/2017/ex/bgrd/backgroundfile-104623.pdf.

Colour of Poverty Campaign. 2012. *Submission to the Commission for the Review of Social Assistance in Ontario in Response to the Options Paper*. www.mcss.gov.on.ca/documents.

Colour of Poverty Campaign, Ontario Council of Agencies Serving Immigrants, Metro Toronto Chinese and South East Asian Legal Clinic, and South Asian Legal Clinic of Ontario. 2016. *Joint Submission to the Committee on the Elimination of Discrimination Against Women*. www.ocasi.org/joint-submission-cedaw.

Comack, Elizabeth, and Gillian Balfour. 2004. *The Power to Criminalize: Violence, Inequality and the Law*. Halifax: Fernwood.

Crawford, Cynthia J., Mary Gellatly, Deena Ladd, and Leah Vosko. 2006. "Community Unionism and Labour Union Renewal: Organizing for Fair Employment." In *Paths to Union Renewal: Canadian Experiences*, edited by P. Kumar and C. Schenk. Toronto: Broadview Press.

Creese, Gillian. 1991. "Organizing against Racism in the Workplace: Chinese Workers in Vancouver before the Second World War." In *Racism in Canada*, edited by O. McKague. Saskatoon: Fifth House Press.

Du Bois, W.E.B. 1935. *Black Reconstruction in America: An Essay towards a History of the Part which Black Folk Played in the Attempt to Reconstruct Democracy in America, 1860–1880*. New York: Harcourt Brace.

Dunk, Thomas. 1998. "Racism, Ethnic Prejudice, Whiteness and the Working Class." In *Racism and Social Inequality in Canada*, edited by V. Satzewich. Toronto: Thomson.

Faraday, Fay. 2014. *Profiting from the Precarious: How Recruitment Practices Exploit Migrant Workers*. Toronto: Metcalf Foundation.

Galabuzi, Grace-Edward. 2001. *Canada's Creeping Economic Apartheid: The Economic Segregation and Social Marginalization of Racialized Groups*. Toronto: Centre for Social Justice.

- 2006. *Canada's Economic Apartheid: The Social Exclusion of Racialized Groups in the New Century.* Toronto: CSPI.
Gilmore, Jason. 2008. *The Canadian Immigrant Labour Market in 2006: Analysis by Region or Country of Origin.* Catalogue no. 71-606-X2008002. Ottawa: Statistics Canada.
Globe and Mail editorial. 2018. "Doug Ford's Troubling First Week." *Globe and Mail*, 10 July.
Gordon, Ian. 1995. "The Impact of Economic Change on Minorities and Migrants in Western Europe." In *Poverty, Inequality and the Future of Social Policy*, edited by K. McFate, R. Lawson and W. Wilson. New York: Russell Sage.
Government of Ontario. 2008. *Breaking the Cycle: Ontario's Poverty Reduction Strategy.* Toronto: Cabinet Committee on Poverty Reduction.
- 2013. *Protecting Ontario's Vulnerable Workers: Province Introducing Stronger Rules and Enforcement Measures for Increased Fairness.* Toronto: Ministry of Labour.
Grant, Hugh M., and Ronald R. Oertel. 1998. "Diminishing Returns to Immigration? Interpreting the Economic Experience of Canadian Immigrants." *Canadian Ethnic Studies* 30 (3).
Hall, Stuart. 1980. "Race, Articulation and Societies Structured in Dominance." In *Sociological Theories: Race and Colonization.* Paris: UNESCO.
Halli, Shiva, and Abdolmohammad Kazemipur. 2001. "The Changing Colour of Poverty in Canada." *Canadian Review of Sociology and Anthropology* 38 (2).
Hou, Feng, and Simon Coulombe. 2010. "Earnings Gap for Canadian-Born Visible Minorities in the Public and Private Sectors." *Canadian Public Policy* 36 (1).
House of Commons. 2009. *Temporary Foreign Workers and Non-Status Workers.* Ottawa: Standing Committee on Citizenship and Immigration.
Jackson, Andrew. 2002. *Is Work Working for Workers of Colour?* Toronto: Canadian Labour Congress.
Law Commission of Ontario. 2012. *Vulnerable Workers and Precarious Employment.* Toronto: Law Commission of Ontario.
Li, Peter. 1998. "The Market Value and the Social Value of Race." In *Racism and Social Inequality in Canada*, edited by V. Satzewich. Toronto: Thompson.
- 2003. *Destination Canada: Immigration Debates and Issue.* Toronto: Oxford University Press.
Loomba, Ania. 1998. *Colonialism/Postcolonialism.* London: Routledge Books.
Maaka, Roger C.A., and Chris Anderson, eds. 2006. *The Indigenous Experience: Global Perspectives.* Toronto: CPSI.
Mackey, Eva. 2002. *The House of Difference: Cultural Politics and National Identity in Canada.* Toronto: University of Toronto Press.
Malenfant, Éric C., André Lebel, and Laurent Martel. 2010. *Projections of the Diversity of the Canadian Population: 2006–2031.* Catalogue no. 91-551-X. Ottawa, ON: Statistics Canada.

McCarthy, Michael. 2016. "Silent Compulsions: Capitalist Markets and Race." *Studies in Political Economy* 97 (2).

McGibbon, Elizabeth. 2012. *Oppression: A Social Determinant of Health*. Halifax: Fernwood.

Mississauga News. 2013. "Racism Thriving in Peel." 19 November.

Moody, Kim. 1997. *Workers in a Lean World: Unions in the International Economy*. New York: Verso.

Office of the Fairness Commissioner. 2013. *A Fair Way to Go: Access to Ontario's Regulated Professions and the Need to Embrace Newcomers in the Global Economy*. Toronto: Queen's Printer.

Omi, Michael, and Howard Winant. 1995. *Racial Formation in the United States: From the 1960s to the 1990s*. New York: Routledge.

Ontario. Anti-Racism Directorate. 2017. *A Better Way Forward: Ontario's 3 Year Anti-Racism Strategic Plan*. www.ontario.ca/page/anti-racism-directorate.

Ornstein, Michael. 2000. *Ethno-Racial Inequality in Toronto: Analysis of the 1996 Census*. Toronto: Access and Equity Centre of Metro Toronto.

Pendakur, Krishna, and Riva Pendakur. 1998. "The Colour of Money: Earnings Differentials Among Ethnic Groups in Canada." *Canadian Journal of Economics* 31 (3).

– 2010. *Colour by Numbers: Minority Earnings in Canada 1996–2006*. Vancouver: Metropolis British Columbia.

Porter, John. 1965. *The Vertical Mosaic*. Toronto: University of Toronto Press.

Portes, Alejandro. 1995. "Children of Immigrants: Segmented Assimilation and its Determinants." In *The Economic Sociology of Immigration*, edited by A. Portes. New York: Russell Sage.

Precarious Employment and Poverty in Southern Ontario. 2013. *It's More than Poverty: Employment Precarity and Household Well-Being*. Toronto: United Way of Toronto.

Public Service Commission of Canada. 2010. *Use of Temporary Help Services in Public Service Organizations*. Ottawa: Public Service Commission of Canada.

Reitz, Jeffrey G. 1998. *Warmth of the Welcome: The Social Causes of Economic Success or Immigrants in Different Nations and Cities*. Boulder: Westview Press.

Reitz, Jeffrey G., and Anil Verma. 1999. "Immigration, Ethnicity and Unionization: Recent Evidence for Canada." Presented at *Forging a Labour Community Agenda: Race, Class and Gender and the Fight for Economic Justice*, 8–11 April. Atlanta: AFL-CIO Education Centre.

Roediger, David R. 1991. *The Wages of Whiteness: Race and the Making of the American Working Class*. New York: Verso.

Sassen, Saskia. 1999. *Globalization and Its Discontents: Essays on the Mobility of People and Money*. New York: New Press.

Satzewich, Victor. 1991. *Racism and the Incorporation of Foreign Labour: Farm Labour Migration to Canada since 1945*. New York: Routledge.

– 1990. "The Political Economy of Race and Ethnicity." In *Race and Ethnic Relations in Canada*, edited by P. Li. Toronto: Oxford University Press.

Satzewich, Victor, and Nikolaos Liodakis. 2017. *"Race" and Ethnicity in Canada*. 4th ed. Toronto: Oxford University Press.

Sawchuk, Peter H. 2006. "Anti-Colonialism, Labour and the Pedagogies of Community Unionism: The Case for Hotel Workers in Canada." In *Breaching the Colonial Contract: Anti-Colonialism in the US and Canada*, edited by A. Kempf. New York: Peter Lange.

Schenk, Chris. 2006. "Union Renewal and Precarious Employment: A Case of Hotel Workers." In *Precarious Employment: Understanding Labour Market Insecurity in Canada*, edited by L. Vosko. Montreal: McGill-Queen's University Press.

Shadd, Adrienne L. 1987. "Dual Labour Markets in 'Core' and 'Periphery' Regions of Canada: The Position of Blacks Males in Ontario and Nova Scotia." *Canadian Ethnic Studies* 19 (2).

Siemiatycki, Myer. 2011. *The Diversity Gap: The Electoral Under-Representation of Visible Minorities*. Toronto: The Greater Toronto Leadership Project.

Standing, Guy. 2011. *The Precariat: The New Dangerous Class*. London: Verso.

Statistics Canada. 2006. *Census Data: Ethnocultural Portrait of Canada Tables*. Ottawa: Statistics Canada.

– 2011. *National Household Survey*. Ottawa: Statistics Canada.

Tanovich, David M. 2006. *The Colour of Justice: Policing Race in Canada*. Toronto: Irwin Law.

Teelucksingh, Cheryl, and Grace-Edward Galabuzi. 2004. *Working Precariously: The Impact of Race and Immigrant Status on Employment Opportunities and Outcomes in Canada*. Toronto: Centre for Social Justice.

Thompson, Edward P. 1963. *The Making of the Working Class*. New York: Vintage Books.

Trigger, Bruce. 1985. *Natives and Newcomers: Canada's "Heroic Age" Reconsidered*. Montreal: McGill-Queen's University Press.

UFCW. 2011. *Report on the Status of Migrant Workers in Canada*. Toronto: UFCW Canada.

Valiani, Salimah. 2009. *The Shift in Canadian Immigration Policy and Unheeded Lessons of the Live-in Caregiver Program*. Ottawa: Mimeo.

Vosko, Leah F. 2006. "Precarious Employment: Towards an Improved Understanding of Labour Market Insecurity." In *Precarious Employment: Understanding Labour Market Insecurity in Canada*, edited by L. Vosko. Montreal: McGill-Queen's University Press.

Wanner, Richard A. 1998. "Prejudice, Profit or Productivity: Explaining Returns to Human Capital Among Male Immigrants to Canada." *Canadian Ethnic Studies* 30 (3).

Wilson, Daniel, and David Macdonald. 2010. *The Income Gap Between Aboriginal Peoples and the Rest of Canada*. Ottawa: Canadian Centre for Policy Alternatives.

Wilson, Ruth Marie, Patricia Landolt, Yogendra B. Shakya, Grace-Edward Galabuzi, Z. Zahoorunissa, Darren Pham, Felix Cabrera, Sherine Mohamed, Abdel

AzizDahy, and Marie-Pier Joly. 2011. *Working Rough, Living Poor: Employment and Income Insecurities Faced by Racialized Groups in the Black Creek Area and Their Impacts on Health.* Toronto: Access Alliance Multicultural Health and Community Services.

Woolley, F. 2013. "How Employment Equity Will Take a Hit from Dodgy National Data." *Globe and Mail*, 8 May.

Workers' Action Centre. 2007. *Working on the Edge.* Toronto: Workers' Action Centre.

– 2012. *Temp Agency Workers Entitled to Public Holidays. It's the Law!* Toronto: Workers' Action Centre.

– n.d. *Inclusion and Protection: Vulnerable Workers in Canada.* Toronto: Workers' Action Centre.

| 16 |

The Democratic Imagination in Ontario and Participatory Budgeting

TERRY MALEY

In this chapter I want to assess a fairly recent set of democratic interventions in Ontario politics that lie on the border between community/social movement activism and the formal government/state budget-making process at the municipal level. In the Ontario context, these experiments in *participatory budgeting* (PB) are not one of the more radically anti-capitalist protest strategies we have seen in Greece and the European Union (EU) after the economic crash of 2008–09. *Participatory budgets* (PBs) have tried to make government budget processes and public finances more accessible to citizens. The slowly growing number of PB experiments in Ontario – in Guelph, Peterborough, Hamilton, Ottawa, Toronto, North Grenville in 2019 – may, in the future, have the potential to point in broadly transformative directions beyond budgeting, toward what Baiocchi and Ganuza (2014) call the "empowerment dimension." When PBs first appeared in the province some commentators saw in them the potential to spark broader democratic renewal in an era of austerity that began to dominate Ontario politics in the mid-1990s. But in their migration to Ontario (and Canada) their scope is still limited.[1]

The fledgling Ontario PBs share some common themes. One is that there are more "horizontal" or equal ways for citizens to participate in budget processes that allocate public resources. Other shared themes are the ideas that "ordinary" people are perfectly capable of participating in complex processes like budgeting; that this involves power-sharing with state/government officials; and that this, in turn, requires a "dual" strategy, as UK commentator Hilary Wainwright (2013) has argued, of both working with (sympathetic) civil servants and politicians inside government, *and* building democratic capacities outside of it. Such a strategy involves very different assumptions about representation and how democracy works than those currently embedded in the parliamentary framework that defines the budget process in Ontario. PB experiments in (mostly local) participatory democracy clearly show that there are alternative ways to organize budgets that do not completely accept the neoliberal or market-based view that (a) governments should run like businesses and be concerned primarily with deficits and tax cuts, and (b) that budgets can only be created and understood by technocratic experts and administrators.

PBs represent a response to, and protest against, two related things. The first is what commentators have called the "democratic deficit" in Canada. This "deficit" has grown out of the historical intersection of the institutional structures of representation in our Westminster system of government with neoliberal austerity over the last forty years. The parliamentary system is defined by the centralization of power in the hands of prime ministers and premiers and a few senior ministers. Elected MPs and MPPs have little control over Cabinet or budget decision-making. There is also little direct input into, and no control over, the machinery of government by the majority of citizens between elections in any case. In the last twenty years, this model, which used to be called the plural-elite or brokerage model of politics, has come under heavy criticism.[2] It has been seen as exclusionary, working in favour of the established white, male business elites who dominate the mainstream political parties. It has also been criticized for not supporting more extensive democratic participation from below.

Since the mid-1970s these elites have aggressively pursued what has been called a "neoliberal" agenda in Ontario and Canada. Even after pumping billions into the Ontario economy after the 2008 global financial meltdown, neoliberal business leaders, politicians, and commentators in the mainstream media continue to focus on themes such as the need to make government smaller, cut social spending, and lower taxes.[3] At the same time, wages for working people – especially for young, racialized, and immigrant workers and women – have, in real dollar terms, declined; social assistance has only increased marginally in twenty years; but profits for corporations and the income of the "1%" have risen dramatically.

Since the late 1990s social movements have protested against the "democratic deficit," and for more egalitarian, participatory political alternatives. And since the 2008 financial crash the gross inequalities of global capitalism have received renewed attention, though they are certainly not new. The protest movements of the 2000s, which came together after Seattle and at the World Social Forum in Porto Alegre, Brazil in 2001 under the slogan "Another World is Possible," have focused on the crises of economic and social inequality produced by a highly undemocratic global economic system. This system of free trade, created by governments in the Global North and international institutions such as the IMF, World Bank, and WTO, has been aggressively promoted over the last thirty years by a global plutocracy that has benefitted hugely from the neoliberal "counter-revolution" against the redistributive policies of the Keynesian welfare state. The established institutions of the global political-economic system have excluded marginal, mostly racialized people from any real decision-making power – the aged, women, minorities, new immigrants, migrant workers, the "precariat" (young people in precarious, low-wage, part-time jobs), as well as older, laid-off workers in Ontario's shrunken manufacturing sector. The result has been that the democratic deficit, and the gap between the "99%" and the "1%," continues to grow.

Other, more radical kinds of democratic protests outside of the parliamentary arena have sporadically erupted in Ontario. The G20 protests, Occupy, and now Idle No More have reached the steps of Queen's Park and Bay Street. These forms of extra-parliamentary protest have gone beyond demands for reforming the electoral system, and have challenged the deep cuts to social programs and citizen entitlements that neoliberal governments of all political stripes have made in Ontario and in Canada since the 1990s. They have also challenged budget "deficit" politics in Ontario that governments from the federal Harper Conservatives to the Ontario McGuinty Liberals and Toronto's former populist mayor Rob Ford took to be normal.

Budgets have traditionally been seen as the most important annual political events through which governments engage the public. The annual Budget Speech, usually presented in March or April after the federal finance minister's budget, allows the Ontario finance minister to showcase his/her government's economic agenda, good governance, and achievements.

Yet it is only recently that discussions of the democratic "deficit" have taken into account the fact that ordinary citizens, and especially marginal ones, have been largely excluded from the formal institutional budget process at Queen's Park. In addition to the growing economic inequality created by neoliberalism, activists and citizens are calling attention to something that has been part of the machinery of "democratic" government for a long time. That is the gap in "fiscal democracy," or the lack of citizen control over where government revenues and "tax payers' money" is spent. This exclusion from *democratic control* over government budgets at all levels (municipal, provincial and federal) was taken for granted in Ontario for decades by business leaders, elected representatives, and the public. It has now come under scrutiny not only from right-wing supporters of tax cuts and smaller government (Dachis and Robson 2014), but from progressive civil society groups and citizens as well. A key government process – the allocation of public finances – is being contested from below in Ontario, to some extent at least, by movements and communities outside of the halls of government power. This is because, as UK commentator Hilary Wainwright says, "existing parliamentary democracy effectively tends to … reinforce inequalities of wealth and power unless directly challenged" (2013, 154).

Before discussing the emergence of PBs in Ontario and how their strategies relate to some of these movements, I first want to look at how the established provincial government *budget consultation* process works. What I want to note in this description of the Ontario budget cycle of the Ministry of Finance is how little space is devoted to citizen participation.

Although modern budget-making is a continuous year-round process, the annual budget cycle involves the following steps which begin as soon as the annual Budget Speech is presented by the Ontario minister of finance each spring, usually in April–May. The process begins with the development of the fiscal plan by Ministry of Finance officials. The plan identifies both an "expenditure strategy" and "the province's revenue outlook and resulting deficit or surplus." The cycle begins each year when the "Cabinet and Policy and Priorities Board, or P&P, the Cabinet committee made up of key Ministers confirm the Government's strategic priorities ... for the upcoming fiscal year." In early summer, officials from the Ministry of Finance "draft proposals on fiscal strategies that reflect the economic environment." The fiscal plan is then finalized in early fall and the "business planning process" begins. This involves the preparation, by the Finance Ministry, of a revenue strategy, as well as the preparation of a strategy for expenditure allocations by the Management Board Secretariat (MBS, the bureaucratic policy branch of Management Board; MB is the Cabinet committee in charge of government spending by the ministries).

In late fall or early winter Cabinet approves the "recommended preliminary allocations," and "MBS then issues business plan and allocation instructions for ministries." Cabinet Office (the central policy agency, or policy "department" for Cabinet) consults with the Premier's Office (the premier's political central agency). In early February MB and Cabinet approve business plans and allocations for each ministry. In the next phase, "the Ministry of Finance begins the budget preparation process, including pre-budget consultations, drafting budget papers, speeches, legislation." Pre-budget consultations involve an all-party legislative committee, the Standing Committee on Finance and Economic Affairs (SCFEA). The SCFEA tours the province to hear brief presentations by a wide variety of interest groups. Public pre-budget consultations are one phase in a complex political and administrative process. I want now to look at the way that the commentary on budget consultation is framed by an expert commentator on the legislative part of the process, specifically at how the "public" is portrayed. This allows me to point to its limited nature when compared to PB processes.

Yet as Ian Burns, a former Queen's Park Legislative staffer, notes, the budget consultation process had traditionally been quite secretive, involving unpublicized meetings with leading members of the business community. Burns writes: "Historically, the Treasurer/Minister of Finance would hold *in camera* meetings with interested stakeholders in the budgetary process. These consultations were not advertised and it was not widely known that they took place" (2007, 3). Burns and Evert

Lindquist have observed that in the 1980s, an attempt was made to "open up" the budget consultation process to the public federally and in Ontario (ibid., 2, 4; Lindquist 2010). In 1985, the Ontario budget included a discussion paper called "Reforming the Budget Process." It contained proposals for greater involvement of *elected members* of the Legislature in the budget consultation process. In 1987 the Standing Committee on Finance and Economic Affairs (SCFEA) began to hold open public consultations. As Burns puts it, this "opened up what was widely considered a closed process" (2007, 5). In its document "Pre-Budget Consultation 1990," the SCFEA said that the annual committee hearings provide a "framework through which members of the public can express their views on Ontario's economy and the upcoming budget" (cited in ibid., 3). By the end of the 1980s, "The roster of individuals and organizations the Minister consulted with had expanded to include labour and social organizations" (ibid.). In the standard Ontario politics text of the 1990s, Mark McElwain (1990, 372) notes that "the opening up of the budget process to ... greater ... input with the public and the Legislature can assist in developing budgets that are increasingly reflective of citizens' views." As late as 2000, around the same time that PBs emerged in the EU and the first Ontario PB appeared in Guelph, a former legislative staffer argued that "Ontario has been the pioneer in formal pre-budget consultations" (cited by Burns 2007, 2). Another argued that Ontario's pre-budget consultation hearings "make an original contribution to the process leading up to the budget by providing the general public with an opportunity to take part, which no doubt has an influence on the government's decisions" (ibid., 13). These are very optimistic views of the budget process by experts with an intimate knowledge of its internal workings.

One thing that is striking in these positive assessments and in official committee and legislative documents is that the term "public" is used in a very specific way. Reading the documents carefully, it becomes clear that the "general public" consists of a limited number of officially recognized business and other interest groups that have participated in the process for some time. It is true that the groups that now appear at pre-budget consultations represent a wider segment of the "public" than before the 1980s. Not only business associations but unions, environmental groups, social service agencies, NGOs, and other organizations have their ten minutes in front of the SCFEA committee. For example, Burns notes that in the 2004 round of pre-budget consultations, "business, labour and social welfare groups were united in calling for the elimination of the Ontario Health premium" that was going to be proposed in the budget by Finance Minister Greg Sorbara (Burns 2007, 9). The participation of different groups was emphasized by the McGuinty government. Liberal budgets since 2004 have focused on a different theme each year. Yet the list of core participants remains largely the same.

Beyond the groups that already participate, the term "public" is not differentiated. There is no sense of the need to acknowledge that the "groups" that make up the "public" have been historically unequal and are, under neoliberalism in Ontario, becoming more so. As Wainwright (2013, 155) has argued, the "entrenched institutions ... take [existing economic and social inequalities] as given and beyond their responsibility." Institutions such as the SCFEA committee and the Ministry of Finance do this because the official language of both "public" consultation and parliamentary representation still assumes the formal political equality of individual citizens and civil society groups.

But this assumption leaves the inequality of differently situated members of the "public" unrecognized. More profound forms of inequality – systemic differences of class, gender, race, disability, age – do not appear in the official record of "individuals and groups" from the "public" which present briefs to the committee. The unequal ability of groups to participate in the hearings and their lack of control over budgetary decisions remains unacknowledged in the official government record of the pre-budget consultations. At one point, Burns defends the accessibility of the current process in these terms: "The traditional arguments against the Ministerial consultations on the budget were that they were too closed and the public was not able to hear what recommendations were being made; this is alleviated *somewhat* by the public consultations of the committee, *the Hansard of which is readily available to the public*, thus enhancing the accountability of the Legislature" (2007, 13, my emphases).

Members of the "public" from the most marginal communities in the province *do not* easily have access to *Hansard*, or even know what it is. In a diverse city such as Toronto, language barriers compound this. A relatively obscure yet public document such as *Hansard* might be seen as a subtle example of an institutional barrier. The Liberal government in Ontario had been hard-pressed to demonstrate greater transparency in times of austerity. The transcripts of the groups that present their briefs to the committee in pre-budget consultations are now available on the Ministry of Finance website. Thus, a bit more openness has been built into the routine of pre-budget consultations.

But the *processes* of budget consultation and particularly decision-making have not changed much since "opening up" in the 1980s. Pre-budget consultations still consist of ten-to-fifteen minute deputations, mostly by well-resourced "stakeholders" in front of the all-party SCFEA, which is typically chaired and dominated by the governing party. What Burns's and the other insiders' comments do not capture is that the actual budget-making process, beyond public consultations, has changed relatively little. It is still expert-driven, top-down, and controlled by the minister of finance and a small group of senior officials.

Burns (2007, 13) writes that "much of the criticism surrounding SCFEA's pre-budget consultations is that the hearings have little discernable effect on the budget process." He has noted, for example, that in the 2007 budget round, the SCFEA's committee's report was tabled in the Legislature just three days before Finance Minister Sorbara delivered the Budget Speech. The committee's report and its recommendations were far too late to be included in the budget itself.

The budget consultation process has historically assumed different, hierarchical roles for participants. Citizens are consulted, they have limited opportunity to be heard, and they occupy the bottom tier of the legislative hierarchy. Above them are the elected politicians on budget or finance committees and those further up the ladder, the few actually involved in key budget decisions (ministers, mayors). In between are bureaucratic officials with highly specialized public finance expertise. The assumption behind the current consultation process is that it is sufficient for the state, through the system of representative democracy, to consult citizens annually, while technocratic experts and politicians engage in the decision-making processes that actually determine outcomes.

John Loxley addresses this issue, noting that the "nature of Canada's parliamentary system makes decision making highly centralized, particularly at the federal and provincial levels" (2003, 158). This makes it difficult for ordinary citizens, and especially more marginal groups outside of the parliamentary system, to influence the minister of finance who, along with a small number of officials, controls the top-down budget-making process. Even elected MPPs from the government party have no influence over the budget process and no control over the outcome.[4] Except for the limited annual process of "budget consultations," which are dominated by professional lobby/industry groups with substantial resources, ordinary citizens have little input into, and no say in, actually creating the budget. The Italian councillor Ann Pizzo (2008, 7) contends that *"established political institutions"* (emphasis added) are the most "powerful brake" on more far-reaching democratic change.

PBs have sought to open up democratic space. They seek a different balance between these roles so that citizens without specialized technical expertise or institutionally entrenched power can: (a) be heard more equally; (b) be more active participants in the design of the process; and (c) actively participate in deliberations and decisions over how to spend public funds. Advocates of PBs argue that what now passes for democratic participation in this process needs to change radically so that budget decisions are not shaped mostly by powerful business interests. The current budget consultation process acts as a *barrier* to more direct citizen-based PBs.

PORTO ALEGRE: THE ORIGINAL PARTICIPATORY BUDGET

PBs first emerged in the 1980s in Latin America as a response to not only dictatorships but, as Loxley (2003, 157) puts it, to "the daily fiscal violence visited on people by neo-conservative structural adjustment programs imposed by the IMF and World Bank." PBs were a reaction to extensive cutbacks to, and the privatization of, public services imposed by these international institutions on cash-strapped governments in the Global South. They caught the popular democratic imagination in Latin America, which had long been known, under authoritarian regimes, for the "clientelistic" politics whose legacy was huge gaps between the rich and poor, widespread poverty, and the exploitation and suppression of rural peasants, the urban working class, Indigenous and racialized peoples, and women. PBs challenged the neoliberal order as well as the long-standing custom of elite budget-making.

The experiment in citizen participation in Porto Alegre, Brazil has become a symbol of protest against top-down neoliberal economic austerity "reforms" by political and economic elites. Sergio Baierle, one of the leading Latin American commentators on PBs, sees the Porto experience as a moment that signalled the creation of a "plebian public sphere." The Porto Alegre PB began after the 1988 municipal election of the Worker's Party (Partido dos Trabalhadores, or PT) and continued in its original spirit until 2004, when the PT lost power to a new coalition of parties that were pro-business and not as committed to the PB process.[5] Porto Alegre became well known for the way in which it democratically engaged local citizens from the poorest areas of the city in more democratic, "horizontal," decision-making processes. The PB co-determined a comparatively high proportion (about 20 per cent) of the city's annual budget. Under the PT, issues of social justice and equitable allocation of resources were central to PB deliberations. The process was constructed around the social needs of the city's poorest residents. Deliberations, facilitated by local government officials and elected PT councilors, were constructed collaboratively by local citizens, and included the previously excluded – women, the city's black minority, the illiterate, and the poor. All of this was made possible by the historical experience of a long-standing social justice tradition in the city and the province before 1988.

Wainwright has discussed the unique role of the PT party in the transition from dictatorship to democracy in Brazil. As a left-wing party committed to social justice, the PT reacted to both the memory of past injustice *and* to the emergence of neoliberalism in the region by seeing the role of the state differently. Instead of an institution of the elites, the PT saw the state as a "resource for transformation by campaigning for electoral office in order then to decentralize and redistribute power." This was part of a *dual strategy* that "combined initiatives for change from within government structures with support for developing wider, more radical sources of power outside" (2013, 139–40).

Porto Alegre signalled a paradigm shift in how marginal citizens in a large urban centre (1.4 million) could make democratic decisions about public finances. Porto embodied the idea that an alternative to the neoliberal fiscal downsizing of the state could be successfully implemented and, to a degree, institutionalized (Sintomer, Herzberg, and Röcke 2008; Gret and Sintomer 2005; Loxley 2003, Baiocchi and Ganuza 2014). It is also an important example of how the imagination of a more democratic politics could go *beyond resistance* to neoliberalism, and produce a new, quasi-institutionalized process whose outcomes gave citizens real democratic control over a portion of public finances. This was so even though commentators realize that the Porto experience grew organically out of a specific political and historical setting, and that it has not been without its complexity and flaws (Baierle 2003).

PBS IN THE EU

There are now over 200 PB experiments in over twenty European countries. They have been seen as local responses to the lack of democratic control over state-driven budget processes (Sintomer, Herzberg, and Röcke 2008, 173; Lerner and Van Wagner 2006, 25). They can also be seen as precursors to the massive protests against state-led austerity in Greece, Spain, Italy, and Portugal (Mayer 2007; Wainwright 2013).

For Sintomer (2008), PBs have to have: (a) discussion of the financial aspects of governance; (b) a municipal government that can implement decisions; (c) a repeatable process; (d) forums for public deliberations, not just public committee meetings; and (e) some accountability. Sintomer et al. (2005) have also developed a range of models, and four, to some degree, are comparable to those in Ontario.

- Porto adapted for Europe: This model most resembles Porto Alegre. It includes the working class, women, the poor, and the illiterate; social justice issues are central; and citizen's decisions are implemented by supportive local governments. In Cordoba, Spain (pop. 320,000), Grottamare, Italy (pop. 150,000), and recently Barcelona, new kinds of participation influenced by anti-globalization movements and social justice concerns have been established. The Albacete Participation Forum successfully allocated part of the Albacete city budget for an Office of Roma Affairs to address issues in the Roma community (Wainwright 2008, 12; Sintomer, Herzberg and Röcke 2008, 174; Sintomer 2005).

- Participation of organized interests: Here "participation is not directed towards individual citizens." Instead, organizations "such as NGOs, unions and organized groups are the main actors."
- Proximity participation: Popular in France and Germany. This PB deals mostly with neigbourhood goals and investments – community centres, language training, or cultural events/centers – or symbolic ideas such as "beautiful cities."
- Consultation on public finances: This is the least participatory PB, involving only "selective listening" by local governments. Popular in Germany, randomly chosen citizens are invited to a citizen's forum on the budget that is only consultative. There is no citizen deliberation or decision-making. Citizens are "included" as clients or customers. Modernization of public administration is a goal but accountability is low (Sintomer, Herzberg and Röcke 2008, 172; Allegretti and Herzberg 2005, 10).

Sintomer found that only models like "Porto adapted for Europe," where social mobilization and institutional change are *combined*, really engaged citizens democratically (Wright and Fung 2003). Only where working-class and marginal citizens were central to the process did a "plebian public space in local politics" emerge (Baierle 2003, 300). Subirats sees these PBs as one answer to the question, "How can democracy be restructured to recover ... transformative, egalitarian and participatory aspects ...? How can we move beyond a democracy that is ... formalist and minimalist, and that conceals the deep inequalities that still exist?" (2008, 9). Allegretti and Herzberg argue that the EU PBs emerged "against the context of neoliberal economic policies, the financial crisis of cities, intensifying urban conflict, struggles against privatization and the deepening crisis of the legitimacy of representative democracy" (2005, 10).

As reported by Victoria Boelman in LabCities, there has recently been a resurgence of PBs in the EU in response to both the austerity measures the EU imposed in the post-2008 crisis period, the inaccessibility of EU institutions, and the rise of far-right nationalism/xenophobia. Cities like Paris, Barcelona, and Reykjavik are adopting a combination of more traditional PB local meetings with a range of online (and in Barcelona's case, democratically created) web tools for democratic participation and decision-making beyond budgeting. The progressive mayor of Barcelona, Ada Colau, for example, who is part of the DiEM25 movement (Democracy in Europe Movement 2025), has embraced PBs as part of a larger process of democratic renewal in the EU.

FOUR ONTARIO CASES

PB experiments are relatively new in Ontario. They have not yet caught the popular imagination the way they have in Latin American and the EU, and have a mixed history in the province. The Ontario PBs arose in different local political/economic contexts. Of the four Ontario examples I want to look at, two have been in cities of different economic significance – Toronto and Guelph – and one in a city agency in Toronto, the Toronto Community Housing Corporation (TCHC) (Lerner and Van Wagner 2006, 6). The other is the Ontario version of a national PB, the Alternative Budget (AB) of the Canadian Centre for Policy Alternatives.

Toronto and the Miller Consultations: In 2004, newly elected mayor David Miller initiated the *Listening to Toronto* budget consultation exercise. Miller was a member of the (informal) New Democratic Party (NDP) caucus at City Hall, and was seen as a moderate, progressive social democratic councillor before he successfully ran for mayor. Miller was aware of the anger of Toronto residents with both the previous (radically) Conservative Harris provincial government and the previous pro-business mayor, Mel Lastman. He was anxious to appear more democratically connected to Toronto's citizens (Boudreau 2005). Porto Alegre participants were even brought in as advisors. But *Listening* turned out to be consultative only; it resembled two of the weakest of

Sintomer's models, "consultation on public finances" and "proximity participation."

Toronto community groups such as the Metro Network for Social Justice and social service agencies such as the Community Social Planning Council initially applauded *Listening*, which held seven open community meetings around the city. The meetings involved about 1,100 residents in discussions of budget priorities for Toronto in 2004. But after its first year, the exercise was scaled back by Miller. In 2005 only one large meeting was held, and it focused on symbolic issues such as "How can we make Toronto clean and beautiful?" and "How can the city strengthen neighbourhoods?"

Listening only minimally engaged citizens; there was little active deliberation by participants, and no decision-making power. Social justice concerns disappeared from the consultations and many of those who attended were not the poor or marginal, but "professional citizens." Participants tended to be middle-class or upper-income professionals, well-educated, and white, and from a social stratum whose members "seem to attend public consultations as a hobby" (Lerner and Van Wagner 2006, 16). These "professional citizens" were much more likely to have the education or "social capital" to understand the complexity of Toronto's budget. This was a kind of informal form of representation that was based on class and race.

Toronto is Canada's biggest city (in 2004, the first year of the *Listening* exercise, Toronto's budget was around $7 billion; in 2013, the city's combined capital and operating budgets were $14 billion), and it is a bigger fiscal entity than the three smallest provinces in Canada. Understanding its budget is not simple. Those "professional citizens" were likely to have a better understanding of the impact of the deep cutbacks visited on Toronto by the Harris government.

If the Miller *Listening* exercise was inadequate from a participatory point of view, the version of municipal pre-budget consultation in Toronto under Mayor Rob Ford was even more limited. In the 2012 city budget round, Ford was grilled in the local media for offering to hold *one night* of round-the-clock budget "consultations" with the public, in which citizens could present their ten-minute proposals in front of the mayor, his budget chief, and the Executive Committee within one twenty-four-hour period – an all-nighter in which citizens lined up to give their deputations at 3 and 4 a.m. in front of an exhausted mayor. After the all-nighter, the budget was hammered out in the usual manner by the budget chief, his committee, the city manager, and management staff. Neither Mayor Miller's *Listening* process nor Mayor Ford's version of budget consultations came close to meeting the challenges of addressing the democratic deficit or the needs of Toronto's most marginal citizens. Toronto has a very diverse urban population in which language, cultural differences, and deepening socio-economic inequalities need to be built into a PB process. *Listening*, which did not emerge from a bottom-up, grass-roots process, failed to produce a new political space in which ordinary citizens could participate in a more democratic budget-making process.

While a small community group remained active in Toronto around PBs after the *Listening* exercise (and after the financial crash of 2008–09), the idea was revived in 2015 by community groups and city councillor Shelley Carroll in her Don Valley East Ward 33 as a pilot project (PB33). Its principles are similar to other PBs in Canada – local consultations and decision-making by area residents around spending $250,000 on community projects such as wellness playgrounds, accessibility, park benches, and hiking trails. The top item/amount last year was $75,000 for a playground in a park, but most projects were between $25,000 and $50,000. And hers is the only ward/area of the city that has such a PB project. The city budget process remains largely as it was before the chaotic Rob Ford all-nighter budget consultations of a few years ago.

Toronto Community Housing and Tenants: There has been, however, a different PB in Toronto that outlasted *Listening*. It began in one of the city's biggest autonomous agencies, the Toronto Community Housing Corporation, or TCHC. The TCHC is the largest public housing agency in Ontario (and Canada), and provides subsidized housing to 165,000 low-income, senior, and disabled residents. As Lerner and Van Wagner (2006, 8) note: "Since 2001 the TCHC has used a PB process to involve tenants in budget decision-making, as part of their Tenant Participation System." Staff at the mid-management level initiated the process in 2000 in the face of deep budget cuts by the City of Toronto. After their re-election in 1999 the Harris Conservatives made more funding cuts to Ontario municipalities for social housing, public transit, and other areas for which cities had shared responsibility with the province. Harris's mantras were the now-familiar ones that government needed to be "leaner," and had to "do more with less."[6]

Yet it was against this backdrop that mid-level managers at the TCHC *encouraged* tenants to demand greater participation in decision-making regarding living conditions and maintenance issues in their apartment buildings. After the development of a deliberative, participatory process that involved extensive tenant participation from the building level up to area-wide tenant councils, tenants "decided on budget priorities through 'dotmocracy.'" Dotmocracy was an adult education technique used to overcome language and literacy barriers in a culturally diverse, mostly immigrant tenant population. It consisted of placing dots beside pictorial representations of issues. By doing so, the tenants "ranked projects by marking dots next to those they support" (Lerner and Van Wagner 2006, 9).

This process resembles Sintomer's "Porto adapted for Europe" to the extent that it involved marginal citizens, TCHC residents, directly in a deliberative decision-making process. Tenants decided on how to allocate about $9 million a year in spending, or 13 per cent of the TCHC annual capital budget of $70 million (Lerner 2006). While the TCHC is a huge organization with an overall operating budget of over $600 million a year, its PB did not fundamentally shift political priorities in the city of Toronto or affect citizens from other social classes or areas of the city. It was limited in this respect. Yet, Lerner and Wagner (2006) note that it was able to grow *because* the TCHC is not directly controlled by senior staff at City Hall or by the mayor or Toronto city council. The politics of the institutionalized budget process at City Hall, which involves pressure on locally elected councillors (the majority of whom were champions of fiscal austerity and supported Mayor Lastman) from developers and other entrenched business interests, could easily have derailed the PB initiative at the TCHC. The TCHC tenants who have participated in the experience found it very positive, in much the same way that Porto residents did. While the experience has changed the lives of tenants for the better, it has not altered the larger economic or social circumstances that led them to become TCHC tenants in the first place – poverty, disability and other socio-economic and cultural barriers, all exaggerated by the Harris government's neoliberal austerity policies (including cuts to public housing).

While the TCHC may be autonomous from the city, it is not monolithic. In other ways it continues, like other parts of the state, to operate under neoliberal principles of administrative "efficiency" that are oriented towards top-down control of tenants. Al Gosling, an eighty-two-year-old tenant, was evicted for missing a rent payment in 2009. He ended up homeless on the street for a week and died. This tragedy reflects the "belt-tightening" and budget-cutting principles of "efficient" public administration brought in by the Harris Conservatives and subsequently expected of even arm's-length agencies like the TCHC in Ontario. Fiscal tightening of the rules has made tenants more vulnerable and easier to evict. This example stands in stark contrast to the effort of mid-level managers within the same agency to "democratize" participation and decision-making in the TCHC through the budgetary process.

The TCHC PB process was discontinued in 2016 after the agency faced public criticism and scrutiny for mismanagement, misspending, and a leadership scandal – all painfully detailed in an ombudsmen's report that resulted in the resignation of two CEOs (in 2014 and 2017). None of the issues afflicting the TCHC were directly related to or caused by the PB process, which had been a unique experiment in limited but still significant self-governance by the poor. But part of the organizational re-think at the TCHC involved re-thinking the PB experiment in light of both neoliberal pressures for greater internal administrative efficiency and accountability, and government funding shortfalls and the resulting deferred maintenance issues that have plagued the organization for many years. The TCHC PB has now been redefined as the broader-sounding "tenant-led decision-making process." But the scope of this participation process, held in four city-wide meetings over three days in August 2017, has been reduced and now includes much less ambitious "projects" such as "benches, bike racks, fitness equipment, gardening materials" (TCHC Information Sheet 2017).

Guelph and Community Planning: The Ontario example from the city of Guelph comes close to some of Sintomer's PB models. Guelph is a medium-sized city of 120,000 in central Ontario. It is an affluent university town with income and education levels above the national average. It has also had progressive city councils. As Pinnington, Lerner, and Shugarensky note, "Since 1999, Guelph residents have used participatory budgeting to allocate part of the city budget and other funds" (2009, 463). While the mayor and city councillors still allocate the municipal operating and capital budgets (a $349 million gross operating expenditure budget and a $76 million gross capital expenditure budget for a total expenditure budget of $425 million in 2013), the coalition has worked with mid-level city bureaucrats and social service partners such as the United Way on a participatory community-based process to allocate discretionary funds ($225,000 in 2012) for neighbourhood projects. It is the only city in the province (in fact, in Canada) "implementing participatory budgeting through its municipal budget" (ibid., 456).

The Guelph example initially seemed hopeful (ibid., 466). Community groups began forming in the 1990s to address the diverse needs of marginal and minority residents in Guelph in the face of the provincial government cutbacks to cities. The PB only got underway, however, when it was initiated by the city's manager of community development, Janet Loveys-Smith, in 1999. A participatory process was facilitated by Loveys-Smith's staff in which local residents received training, created priorities within their own neighbourhood groups, discussed them with social service agency partners, and brought them to the NSC. Priorities were decided by consensus when members from the different groups met in larger sessions, with members outnumbering agency partners by a two-to-one ratio.

By the mid-2000s, some social service agencies had come to rely on the PB for part of their own funding, producing tensions when the funding to the Neighbourhood Support Coalition (NSC) was cut back by the city. In addition, some more affluent neighbourhood associations chose not to participate, focusing instead on more middle-class and business issues such as economic development and zoning. Most participants were not used to being public decision-makers. Some who were hired by the PB for two-year terms to help their communities implement projects struggled to let go of their positions at the end of their terms. Others struggled with detailed, complex transparency requirements in the applications for project funding.

The Guelph PB survived for a little more than ten years. When it had the support of Community Development staff (though staff from other city departments argued that scarce funds should be spent on other programs) and a progressive city council from 2003–06, it grew to cover the whole city. PB decisions were made city-wide on social and community development spending, and were linked to the city's formal budget. By 2005, the NSC's PB "had funded 460 community events and programs, including peer support groups ... summer camps and language classes. Roughly 10,000 people have participated in these activities" (Lerner 2006, 5), most of them from marginal and minority neighbourhoods. Yet in 2010 a steering committee recommended to Guelph City Council that the NSC be incorporated as a non-profit agency with an executive director.

With regard to the Guelph and TCHC cases, Pinnington, Lerner, and Shugurnensky (2009) make a key observation. They point out that these participatory processes occurred only *because* politicians were *not* involved until the PBs had already been established by mid-level bureaucrats working with community groups. By contrast, Allegretti and Herzberg (2005) have noted that many of the successful PBs in the EU have, paradoxically, been *initiated* top-down by leftist mayors and their officials from social democratic or socialist parties. Allegretti (2006) found this in sixteen of nineteen EU cases he studied. The Guelph and TCHC PBs relied on mid-level bureaucratic leadership *instead of* political leadership from city council. Instead of either a top-down, or truly bottom-up process, we might say that the early Ontario PBs were "mid-down" processes.

The municipal budget process is also somewhat different from the provincial process described earlier. The budget chief and committee (as well as the mayor and city council) set budget priorities. They work with the city manager (in Toronto, or CAO in Guelph) and department managers to construct a budget consisting of capital and operating expenditures. The public also makes deputations to the budget committee. Many of the "stakeholders" are the same groups and associations (or their local versions – i.e., Chambers of Commerce) that participate in pre-budget consultations at the provincial level.

The main difference from the provincial level, and the main constraint, as Pinnington, Lerner, and Schugurensky (2009, 461) note, is "the limited autonomy of municipal government" fiscally. As "creatures of the province" constitutionally, municipalities rely for revenue on grants from the provincial government, local property taxes, and user fees. They write that "since cities do not have much financial or legal autonomy to ... change their budgets, there is less incentive for residents to participate in municipal budget processes." Yet "neoliberal restructuring has resulted in changing roles, greater demands, and fewer resources for ... municipal governments." One of the "changing roles" that municipalities have taken on is "increasing the economic value of the city as a business location, facilitating private sector growth and business development [...] As cities increasingly focus on creating better environments for business, it becomes more difficult to justify programs geared towards social inclusion, equity or popular participation." This is perhaps another reason why progressive administrators interested in facilitating PBs avoided austerity-minded elected politicians who were engaged in the legislative budget process and instead went "under the radar" in initiating local PBs. Yet economic and political constraints impinged on the Guelph PB to the point where it could no longer escape the attention of Guelph City Council and was abandoned in 2012. It moved to a grant application model, adjudicated by a small board, and a new name, the Guelph Neighbourhood Support Coalition, in 2013.[7]

Ontario and Alternative Budgeting: Alternative Budgets (ABs) first emerged in Manitoba in the 1980s, where activists and community groups took on the city of Winnipeg and the (early) neoliberal government of Conservative premier Gary Filmon over issues such as cuts to social housing, women's shelters, and social services for the urban poor, including Winnipeg's large Indigenous population. A coalition of activists, community groups, labour council representatives, and unions formed a grassroots collective, *Cho!ces*, that formulated an alternative budget for the city of Winnipeg.

With the help of trade union economists – Jim Stanford from the Canadian Auto Workers (CAW) and Hugh MacKenzie from the United Steel Workers (USWA) – the Canadian Centre for Policy Alternatives organized a similar exercise on the national level. The CCPA formulated its first Alternative Federal Budget (AFB) in 1995 to counter the neoliberal austerity budget of Liberal finance minister Paul Martin. Martin's budget cut more than $6 billion in transfer payments to the provinces for health care, post-secondary education, and social assistance. In Ontario beginning in the same year, Premier Harris's attempt to "revolutionize" the province's finances through the neoliberal shock therapy of deep cuts to social services, education, and health care led the Ontario Federation of Labour (OFL), along with community and civil society groups, to produce a similar alternative budget for the province in 1997.

The ABs of the CCPA have offered an alternative to neoliberal federal and provincial budgets for more than a decade now. Instead of budgets that offer tax cuts and smaller government, the ABs have had, as Loxley puts it, "a pronounced emphasis on reducing poverty, a plausible position on the environment, in terms of both expenditure and revenue initiatives, and a clear gender component with respect to the spending side" (Loxley 2003, 163–4). The alternative budgets offer another version of a PB.

Alternative budgets seek to achieve two objectives. First, they show that there *can be* alternative approaches to neoliberal economic, fiscal, and social policies. Second, they can foster political education. Their material is now accessible on the CCPA website and is disseminated through social media. The CCPA's strategy has been to influence public opinion more broadly by also gaining a mainstream media presence. Canada's biggest national daily newspaper, the *Toronto Star*, often reports favourably on the CCPA AB's policy alternatives. The ABs have often, though not always, been supported by the federal and Ontario New Democratic Party.

Daniel Shugurensky is critical of them, however, arguing that the "PB goes beyond alternative budgets, which are mainly academic exercises that do not deal with real budgets" (2004, 5). He thus differentiates ABs from the more participatory PBs. This criticism is not quite fair. The CCPA ABs do deal with, and are quite critical of, real neoliberal government budgets. But Shugurensky is right when he says that ABs do not produce a more extensive *participatory budget* involving larger numbers of citizens who deliberate and make decisions collectively. The "Westminster" parliamentary and institutional system in Ontario (with its tight control of public budgeting by a small group of elected politicians and officials at the top of the system of representative government) has blocked the participatory potentiality of ABs. In this context, whether as a matter of strategy or necessity, ABs have not involved poor, marginal, or working-class citizens in an extensive process like Porto Alegre or even Guelph. This strategy is based on the pragmatic acceptance of the existing institutional arrangements of representative democracy in Ontario within which the state-led budget process occurs. The CCPA ABs are an example of Sintomer's "participation by organized interests" model. They are produced by highly trained trade union and social agency staff, whose organizations are committed to a more equal redistribution of public resources based on principles of social justice rather than only market "efficiency."

Strategically, ABs are important for offering concrete policy alternatives to the neoliberal policies that have been the staple of both Conservative and Liberal government budgets in Ontario since 1995. The ABs focus on Keynesian fiscal and policy alternatives, but *not on democratizing the budget process itself*. Neoliberal parties in Ontario have been hostile to the ABs' policy, taxation, and spending proposals. In the absence of left-leaning parties at the municipal and provincial levels, the CCPA ABs have come to fill a void in democratic participation on budget issues.

NEW FORMS OF DEMOCRACY IN ONTARIO?

PBs show the need to rethink the meaning of democratic participation in the public allocation of financial resources in times when the ideology of austerity is still predominant among political and economic elites. Wainwright (2013, 154) sees this rethinking, as we have noted, as part of a *dual strategy* that needs to move along two tracks at the same time. On the one hand, PBs are an example of the creation of "non-state democratic power." They have often opposed the market-led policies of neoliberal governments. On the other hand, PBs and ABs have also tried to influence the distribution of public resources allocated *by* local governments. They recognize the importance of the state in redistributing public resources. They have also tried to open up state institutions in which "services and resources are still managed through hierarchical and secretive systems that stifle the creativity of public service staff in their relationship with the public" (Wainwright 2008, 12). Wainwright stresses the need to work in the "borderline spaces" between movements and state processes. For Subirats (2008, 8–9), this begins with the idea that PBs work "at the limits of what is conventional to create new spaces of autonomy." How successful PBs are in carving out those new spaces for democratic participation depends on how deeply – and unevenly – neoliberalism is entrenched compared to other historical ways of seeing the relationship between government, the economy, and politics. Some have noted that Anglo-American jurisdictions (such as Ontario) do not have a historical legacy or memory of radical politics to the left of social democracy (Dobrowolski and Jenson 2004, 154–80; White 2001, 385–405).

In Latin America, the social movements that created PBs emerged from historical experiences of colonial domination, dictatorship, and huge socio-economic inequalities. Neoliberal austerity and cuts to social services for the poor added to an already deep sense of social injustice. In the EU many cities have socialist, communist, or regional/separatist histories. Even though social democratic, labour, and socialist parties there have adopted neoliberal policies when in government (Albo and Evans 2011, 290), there has been a broader radical tradition to the left of social democracy in the EU that has allowed local pockets of resistance to emerge. Mayors from leftist parties supported PBs, helping to create spaces for marginal citizens to participate more democratically. By contrast, Royson James (2009, 5), the municipal affairs columnist for the *Toronto Star*, has noted that in the context of Ontario politics the moderately social democratic mayor David Miller may have been "as left as a Toronto mayor can be and still hold power."

In addition to these differences in political culture, there is another institutional difference as well. As Margit Mayer (2007, 105) reminds us, in the EU the party system (including left parties) is much more active at the municipal level. Loxley (2003, 158) points out that in Canada (and Ontario) "the lack of a clearly defined party system at the civic level has been a long-term obstacle" to producing alternative budget processes.

This means that the pressure from below, from outside the state and/or from left parties within the established electoral system, has been weak and localized in Ontario. Resistance to neoliberalism in Ontario has been less organized, less broadly based, and less militant than many spaces in the EU. And it does not have a voice in the system of party/parliamentary representation in the province. This partly explains why few PBs have emerged in the province. Instead of relying on either social movements or leftist political parties, the two PBs in Ontario that lasted the longest, the TCHC and the Guelph NSC, came about when progressive mid-level bureaucratic officials in government, and then local politicians, supported them. Under neoliberal fiscal pressures, when that support from local politicians stopped, these local PBs were shut down. Yet what these mid-level managers did in the mid-2000s was to innovatively link the users of social and community services to a process of democratic deliberation that did not previously exist *within the governmental budget process*. I want to make a few final points in relation to this.

There is an *affinity* between the Ontario PBs and the social justice campaigns of public sector unions, anti-poverty activists, and community groups who argue that the state can be used for a more progressive redistribution of public resources. What they share is the common goal, as Albo and Evans (2010, 290–2) have noted, of preserving public sector social services that neoliberal governments want to cut back. The most progressive PBs have all shared this basic orientation.

This has not been easy, however, and not all of the Ontario PBs have survived neoliberal pressures. The Ontario examples from Guelph and the TCHC illustrate Mayer's more general point that, "when ... new coalitions for social justice are picked up by supportive local politicians, they still confront the problem of the very real limits of municipal policy in an age of capital mobility and neoliberal hegemony" (2007, 105). PBs in Ontario still run up against the established institutions and ideologies of government and budget-making, even as PBs slowly proliferate in the province. The CCPA ABs that have been produced for more than twenty years now have not been adopted by any level of government. Nor have the local Ontario PBs been able to create democratic structures that have replaced the existing institutions of budget decision-making. But both have influenced public debates about budgets.

Baiocchi and Ganuza (2014, 36–7) have noted that the global proliferation of PBs has raised the issue of the degree to which entrenched, institutional state processes can be changed or reformed based on extensive citizen participation and decision-making. In the best cases PBs have provided a new institutional connection between collective deliberative practices that local citizens create themselves, social justice issues, and administrative structures within the state. In the PBs that have been closer to the Porto Alegre experience, the technical expertise of administrators has been partially subordinated to, and has worked cooperatively with, local citizens who do not have political or administrative experience, or social or actual capital. The important question they raise is the degree to which existing state structures, never static to begin with, can be reformed, or new institutional patterns created that empower actual citizen (not top-down, bureaucratic) decision-making *within* government. They refer to this as the *empowerment dimension*, which thus far has often been limited to localized citizen decision-making and discretionary spending on smaller community projects.

By contrast, there is another aspect of the PB process that features the "open structure of transparent meetings to decide on projects and priorities." Baiocchi and Ganuza (2014, 32) refer to this as "the *communicative dimension* because the meetings are based on procedures that regulate the conditions of communication, democratizing the nature of demand making in civil society." PBs can provide both platforms for citizen learning, and can create new institutional forms within public administration, even though they have at times faced both political and bureaucratic resistance. As they note, it is the communicative dimension – the local, popular assemblies and public priority-setting meetings – that has migrated globally to a far greater extent than the empowerment dimension, in which local citizens have been co-equals with technocrats in actual budget decision-making.

We can summarize the discussion this way. Local government *can* be flexible in engaging citizens in "bottom-up" forms of direct, participatory decision-making. But the party system, electoral representation, existing legislative budget processes, and the entrenched neoliberal ideology of austerity are often barriers to the fuller realization of the far-reaching democratic change implied in the idea of the "empowerment dimension." My discussion suggests that ordinary citizens and working-class people need to rely on multiple kinds of political organizations and institutions, not just the established ones, to pursue social justice agendas. This means that diverse groups of citizens can have common goals but approach them through a variety of tactics, organizations, and levels. Thus, as Wainwright (2013, 152–5) argues, there is "no necessity for different activities and organizations that share common values to be part of a single political framework." The range of PBs in Ontario and globally shows, as Wainwright continues, that "there is a wide variety of ways in which common values can be communicated and shared" (ibid.). But whether we will witness more robust forms of PB that include a significant empowerment dimension, changing the institutional structures of budget participation in Ontario's cities or in the province, remains to be seen. If the Conservative government led by Doug Ford introduces further austerity and cuts funding to municipalities (cloaked as part of the electoral pledge to find almost $6 billion in "efficiencies"), then coalitions of citizens, supportive politicians, and administrators may find it even more challenging to expand the scope of the formal PB initiatives in the province. But popular budgeting efforts, from social agencies to unions to social movements, will still form one part of the repertoire of resistance movements searching for alternatives to the inequalities and declining social services that are the inevitable outcome of neoliberal policy regimes.

NOTES

1 Other Canadian cities in which limited PB projects have been initiated are Calgary, Vancouver, and Victoria, BC, and the Montreal borough of Plateau-Mont Royal.
2 See, for example, C.B. Macpherson's classic, *The Life and Times of Liberal-Democracy* (1977).
3 Even though the federal Trudeau Liberals have deviated from the neoliberal orthodoxy of deep tax cuts and no deficits, newly elected Premier Doug Ford of Ontario has reaffirmed his commitment to these neoliberal mantras. I draw on the vast literature on neoliberalism but do not outline it in detail in the chapter. A formulation in the early 1990s, by Albo, Langille, and Panitch (1993), noted the twin dynamic of neoliberalism: that cutting social services/entitlements shifted the costs of social reproduction to low-income citizens, while deregulation implemented by neoliberal states creates economic

growth that benefits the wealthy. Neoliberal policies thus have very different political impacts on citizens. Neoliberalism is underpinned by "the discourse of the market – privatization, entrepreneurialism, competition," along with ideas of limited government and tax cuts, "worshipped as a populist remedy to the inefficiencies of ... an anachronistic welfare state," as Coté, Day, and de Peuter (2007, 318) note. As Harvey (2005) argues, the neoliberal view of the state is contradictory. Debts and deficits still plague neoliberal governments, caused in part by deep tax cuts for the business classes. In order to manage these contradictions politically, neoliberal states use technocratic top-down forms of administrative rule, as with budgets. These forms of control do not exclude limited forms of "public" inclusion – potentially PBs.

4 This is becoming a chronic dysfunction of the representative system and a key example of the stubbornness of the democratic deficit. Under Harper's Conservatives, for example, the top-down budget process became incomprehensible to the public. The Conservative government began using huge, complex "omnibus" legislation (many unrelated bills folded into the one huge budget implementation bill) to pass the federal budget.

5 The new mayor, elected in 2004, instituted a framework called Local Solidarity Governance, which emphasizes "partnerships" with third sector groups, civil society groups, and business groups. This reduced the social justice orientation of the PB while still paying lip service to it.

6 The neoliberal view that governments are more "efficient" and work better when they do "more with less" has been cogently challenged by one of Canada's leading commentators on public administration, Donald Savoie (2013).

7 In one of the latest studies of the now-famous Guelph PB, Pin (2014) sees it as an example of neoliberal rationality. For an earlier view of the Guelph PB before it was shut down see Maley (2010).

REFERENCES

Albo, Greg. 2007. "The Limits of Eco-Localism: Scale, Strategy, Socialism." In *Coming to Terms with Nature: Socialist Register 2007*, edited by Leo Panitch and Colin Leys. London: Merlin Press.

Albo, Greg, and Bryan Evans. 2010. "From Rescue Strategies to Exit Strategies: The Struggle over Public Sector Austerity." In *The Crisis This Time: Socialist Register 2011*, edited by Leo Panitch, Greg Albo, and Vivek Chibber. London: Merlin Press.

Albo, Greg, David Langille, and Leo Panitch, eds. 1993. *A Different Kind of State? Popular Power and Democratic Administration*. Toronto: Oxford University Press.

Allegretti, Giovanni. 2006. "The Challenge of Participatory Budgeting in Europe." *Council of Europe Forum for the Future of Democracy*. Stockholm, June.

Allegretti, Giovanni, and Carsten Herzberg. 2005. "Participatory Budgets in Europe: Between Efficiency and Growing Local Democracy." *TNI Briefing Series*. Amsterdam: Transnational Institute and the Centre for Democratic Policy Making.

Baierle, Sergio. 2003. "The Porto Alegre Thermidor? Brazil's Participatory Budget at the Crossroads." In *Fighting Identities: Socialist Register 2003*, edited by Leo Panitch and Colin Leys. London: Merlin Press.

Baiocchi, Gianpaolo, and Ernesto Ganuza. 2014. "Participatory Budgeting as if Emancipation Mattered." *Politics and Society* 42 (1).

Boudreau, Julie-Anne. 2005. "Toronto's Reformist Regime, Municipal Amalgamation and Participatory Democracy." In *Metropolitan Democracies: Transformations of the State and Urban Policy in Canada, France and Great Britain*, edited by Phillip Booth and Bernard Jouve. Burlington: Ashgate.

Burns, Ian. 2007. "Pre-Budget Consultations in the Ontario Legislature: A Case Study of the Standing Committee on Finance and Economic Affairs." Paper delivered at the CPSA Congress, Saskatoon, June.

Coté, Mark, Richard Day, and Greig de Peuter. 2007. "Utopian Pedagogy: Creating Radical Alternatives in the Neoliberal Age." *The Review of Education, Pedagogy, and Cultural Studies* 29.

Dachis, Benjamin, and William B.P. Robson. 2014. *Baffling Budgets: The Need for Clearer and More Comprehensible Financial Reporting by Canada's Municipalities*. Toronto: C.D. Howe Institute.

Dobrowolski, Alexandra, and Jane Jenson. 2004. "Shifting Representations of Citizenship: Canadian Politics of 'Women' and 'Children.'" *Social Politics* 11.

Fung, Archon, and Eric Olin Wright, eds. 2003. *Deepening Democracy: Institutional Innovations in Empowered Participatory Governance*. London: Verso.

Good, David, and Evert Lindquist. 2010. "Discerning the Consequences and Integrity of Canada's Budget Reforms: A Story of Remnants and Resilience." In *The Reality of Budget Reform: Counting the Consequences in Eleven Advanced Democracies*, edited by J. Wanna, L. Jensen, and J. de Vries. Northampton: Edward Elgar.

Gret, Marion, and Yves Sintomer. 2005. *The Porto Alegre Experiment: Learning Lessons for Better Democracy*. London: Zed Books.

Harvey, David. 2005. *A Brief History of Neoliberalism*. New York: Oxford University Press.

James, Royson. 2009. "Wooing Moderates Key to Beating Miller." *Toronto Star*, 8 August.

Lerner, Josh. 2006. "Let the People Decide: Transformative Community Development through Participatory Budgeting in Canada." *Shelterforce Online* 146.

Lerner, Josh, and Estair Van Wagner. 2006. *Participatory Budgeting in Canada: Democratic Innovation in Strategic Spaces*. http://www.tni.org/newpolitics.

Loxley, John. 2003. *Alternative Budgets: Budgeting as if People Mattered*. Halifax: Fernwood.

Maley, Terry. 2010. "Participatory Budgeting and the Radical Imagination: In Europe but Not in Canada?" *Affinities: A Journal of Radical Theory, Culture and Action* 4 (2).
Mayer, Margit. 2007. "Contesting the Neoliberalization of Urban Governance." In *Contesting NeoLiberalism*, edited by Helga Leitner, Jamie Peck, and Eric Sheppard. New York: Guilford Press.
McElwain, Mark. 1990. "Ontario's Budgetary Process." In *The Government and Politics of Ontario*, 3rd ed., edited by Graham White. Scarborough: Nelson.
Pin, Laura. 2016. "On Global Austerity and Local Democracy: The Case of Participatory Budgeting in Guelph, ON." *Canadian Political Science Review* 10 (1).
Pinnington, Elizabeth, Josh Lerner, and Daniel Schugurenksy. 2009. "Participatory Budgeting in North America: The Case of Guelph, Canada." *Journal of Budgeting, Accounting and Financial Management* 21 (3).
Pizzo, Anna. 2008. "Participation in Italy." *Eurotopia: Participatory Democracy at the Crossroads* 5.
Savoie, Donald. 2013. *Whatever Happened to the Music Teacher?: How Government Decides and Why*. Montreal: McGill-Queen's University Press.
Shugurensky, Daniel. 2004. *Participatory Budgeting: A Tool for Democratizing Democracy*. www.ed.acrewoods.net/ideas.
Sintomer, Yves, Carsten Herzberg, and Anja Röcke, eds. 2005. *Participatory Budgeting in a European Comparative Approach*. Berlin: Centre Marc Bloch.
– 2008. "Participatory Budgeting in Europe: Potentials and Challenges." *International Journal of Urban and Regional Studies* 32 (1).
Subirats, Joan. 2008. "If Participatory Democracy is the Answer, What is the Question." *Eurotopia: Participatory Democracy at the Crossroads* 5.
Wainwright, Hilary. 2008. "Facing the Problems, Learning the Lessons." *Eurotopia: Participatory Democracy at the Crossroads* 5.
– 2013. "Transformative Power: Political Organization in Transition." In *The Question of Strategy: Socialist Register 2013*, edited by Leo Panitch, Greg Albo, and Vivek Chibber. London: Merlin Press.
White, Linda. 2001. "Child Care, Women's Labour Market Participation and Labour Market Policy Effectiveness in Canada." *Canadian Public Policy* 27 (4).

| 17 |

The Challenges of Union Political Action in the Era of Neoliberalism

STEPHANIE ROSS

Since the early 1990s, the Ontario labour movement's approach to political action has been deeply divided. Indeed, Larry Savage (2010, 14) has characterized it as "the most divided labour movement in Canada." Since the infighting and fragmentation in political strategy that characterized labour's response to the Social Contract Act, introduced by the New Democratic Party (NDP) government of Bob Rae in 1993, Ontario labour has had little influence over governments. Nor has it been able to block the ongoing spread of neoliberalism as the basic terrain on which public policy choices are made. Labour's declining political influence has several sources: stagnating union density (and hence economic and political weight); declining economic leverage in key sectors (such as manufacturing); a growing material gap between the unionized and non-union working class; an inability to stop the spread of precarious employment throughout the labour market; and the ideological marginalization of organized labour in Canadian society. In this context, labour continues to search for viable political strategies. Various Ontario unions, reflecting their deep divisions, committed to very different strategic directions between 2003 and 2018, the period that the Liberal Party governed Ontario. Although some glimmers of hope emerged with the successful mobilizations to improve Ontario's labour and employment standards, organized labour's political fragmentation has only accelerated.

For a brief period, however, the potential seemed to exist for a reinvigorated political strategy for fighting neoliberalism. The Ontario Days of Action, a series of eleven spirited and creative community-based mass walkouts between 1995 and 1998 that protested the neoliberal policies of Premier Mike Harris's Conservative government, were widely considered evidence of a political turning point (Moody 1997). This extra-parliamentary movement, which emerged in the wake of a severe discrediting of social democratic electoralism and in the face of an unprecedented anti-union neoliberal agenda, held out the promise of a more politically unified labour movement. This movement generated the largest demonstrations in the history of the Ontario communities that organized them, and, in Toronto on 26 October 1996, the largest single demonstration in Canadian history up to that time.[1]

Beyond such numerical successes, the Days seemed to have important impacts on individual activists' and leaders' ideological orientations, the labour movement's repertoire of struggle, the resulting political-strategic orientation of the movement, and working-class organizational structures and capacities. The Days of Action addressed the impact of neoliberalism on both labour and non-labour constituencies, engaged union members and the public in a discussion of the terms of social citizenship, and tied together the interests of many segments of Ontario society. They expanded the Ontario labour movement's repertoire of struggle, using the withdrawal of labour for an explicitly political rather than economic purpose and challenging the legal (and ideological) restrictions placed on the strike weapon by the postwar industrial relations framework. This had the effect of displacing, for a time, social democratic electoralism from the centre of labour's political strategy. The Days also brought unions and community groups together in a formal coordinating structure that promised greater unity within the working class. Observers and participants argued that the Days would build union members' political and organizational capacities in a lasting way, thus potentially democratizing internal labour movement relationships. For many activists, these struggles were crucial episodes in their political development and resulted in the mobilization, training, and politicization of a layer of previously uninvolved union members.

The political dynamics that played out during and after the Days of Action, however, resulted in an even more fragmented labour movement. Despite the movement's capacity to bring nearly 250,000 people onto Toronto's streets in October 1996, the Harris government's neoliberal policies were at best slowed down, not turned back. Much post-mortem commentary on the Days of Action has focused on the reasons for their ultimate demise and failure.² However, while these assessments importantly inform how this period is remembered and understood, they need to be examined in relation to the longer-term *implications* of the Days of Action on the Ontario labour movement's political strategies and capacities to the present. From this vantage point, many of the early positive predictions of the Days' effects have not been borne out.

Since 1998, the Ontario labour movement has not sustained effective, coordinated, mass mobilization and participatory strategies on any front, whether to counter manufacturing job loss, organize new workers into unions, undo Harris-era policies, or mount a concerted electoral challenge to the McGuinty or Wynne governments. While some unions' repertoire of struggle expanded in a more permanent way, elsewhere in the labour movement the effectiveness of mass extra-parliamentary mobilization was marginalized as a social change strategy. Instead, many unions returned to electoral strategies with enthusiasm. For some this has meant a re-engagement with social democracy, while others have settled for Gomperist strategic voting for the least bad alternative to the Conservative variant of neoliberalism. Finally, the failure to create new forms of working-class organization that could unite union and non-union workers has left labour and other social movements floundering in the context of both the economic crisis and government's (re)turn to austerity. Thus, the divisions over labour movement political strategy under the Rae and Harris governments not only remain, but in some ways have deepened in the McGuinty and Wynne era, hampering both effective coordination and the possibilities for renewal at the provincial level.

THE RAE GOVERNMENT AND THE CRISIS OF SOCIAL DEMOCRACY

In the 1980s, the Canadian labour movement's political strategies underwent important transformations related to the declining effectiveness of both "pure and simple" collective bargaining and electoral strategies pursued on their own. The Ontario Days of Action can thus be seen as part of a longer wave of politicization, growing militancy, and expanding strategic repertoire for many unions. Beginning in the mid-1970s, many segments of the Canadian labour movement increasingly engaged in coalition work around legislated wage controls, interest rates, pay and employment equity, reproductive rights, and the fight against free trade (Rapaport 1999, 58; Panitch and Swartz 2003, 157–8; Bleyer 1992). The rise of neoliberalism in this period further reinforced these tendencies, particularly amongst public sector unions. Cuts to public services and jobs twinned with restrictions on their collective bargaining rights through practices of "permanent exceptionalism" politicized these workers further, highlighted the growing inadequacy of narrow forms of unionism focused only on workplace-oriented collective bargaining, and drove them to seek allies amongst the voting public (Panitch and Swartz 2003). These pressures led many unions to adopt a mass-mobilization rather than merely electoral variant of social unionism (although by no means were these two approaches mutually exclusive).[3]

The movement towards extra-parliamentary strategies and tactics by Ontario unions was also shaped in important ways by the policy choices of the Rae government, which represented a more general crisis in social democracy as a political expression of working-class politics. As with many NDP provincial governments before it (Evans 2012; McBride 1996), the contradictions of the Ontario NDP's rule from 1990–95 challenged the notion that electing a "labour-friendly" government would necessarily produce "labour-friendly" results. In 1993, in response to a major recession which had produced unprecedented strain on state finances, the Rae government introduced the controversial Social Contract Act, which sought to extract over $2 billion from public sector workers' contracts through legislation rather than negotiation (McBride 1996, 80).[4] Stephen McBride (1996, 69) argues that the Social Contract Act was not merely a product of "electoral opportunism and moderation"; it was rooted in the NDP's failure to produce "a theoretically coherent account of contemporary capitalism." This resulted in the party's inability to do anything but "replicate the policy objectives of its political rivals" and alienate its key supporters. Panitch (1986) suggests that the tendency of social democratic governments to use their special relationship with organized labour to elicit working-class consent for – or demobilize resistance to – wage restraint is a long-standing feature of parliamentary socialism. This dynamic was clearly in play in the case of Ontario.

The Ontario labour movement was deeply divided by the Social Contract. The Canadian Union of Public Employees (CUPE), the Ontario Public Service Employees Union (OPSEU), and the Ontario Secondary School Teachers Federation (OSSTF) had all mobilized support for the NDP in the 1990 election, and felt deeply betrayed by the suspension of their collective bargaining rights (Kerr 2006, 21).[5] Liz Barkley of the OSSTF appealed to the government "not to abandon its social democratic principles in favour of a destructive neo-conservative agenda" (Martell 1995, 79). Concerted attempts by the Rae government to divide the Public Services Coalition – formed in April 1993 by the public sector unions in an attempt to present a common front at a central negotiating table – were initially unsuccessful. Eventually, however, most unions broke ranks and sought to "negotiate" the terms of the Social Contract at separate sectoral tables (ibid., 74). Nonetheless, the Canadian Auto Workers (CAW) sided with the public sector unions, with then-president Buzz Hargrove pledging to "stand side by side with the Public Sector Unions against any attacks on their rights by the Government of Ontario" (quoted in ibid., 83).

The NDP government's "betrayal" fostered a cynicism in the labour movement about the utility of permanent alignment with a particular political party in an era of neoliberal hegemony, when all governments, left and right, adopted broadly similar policies.[6] At minimum, their base had to send a political message to the NDP. Geoff Bickerton (1993, 11) put it this way: "A withdrawal of support by labour may result in more Liberals, Tories or Reformers being elected [federally]. This may be a short term price to pay to ensure that the parliamentary caucus that remains is prepared to promote party policies. It might be similarly argued that the only way to preserve the NDP as a progressive force in Ontario is to defeat all of the caucus members who supported the social contract." This criticism of the NDP, and of the particular way the parliamentary party and the party's major constituency would relate to each other, opened many public sector unions up to other forms of social unionism, and to union-community coalitions and extra-parliamentary mass mobilization in particular.

Although Panitch and Swartz (2003, 178) suggest that the Social Contract "shattered the confidence of trade unions in their central political strategy," this was not true of all sections of the labour movement. Many private sector unions with long-standing ties to the NDP argued that the labour movement had to remain loyal to "their" social democratic government, particularly in a time of deep recession and attacks from the business class. After all, the Rae government was in the process of developing pro-labour reforms to the Employment Standards Act and Ontario Labour Relations Act, including banning the use of replacement workers in the event of a labour dispute, and extending the right to organize to agricultural workers[7] and the right to strike to Ontario civil servants.[8] They were also to make major improvements to pay equity legislation and introduce employment equity in both the public and private sectors.[9] Importantly, the Rae government would save Algoma Steel from closure, setting up a form of worker ownership and mitigating through this and other means the crisis in manufacturing. These public policy initiatives complicated the political calculation for unions outside the public sector. A prevalent view amongst them was that, since the members of private sector unions "had born[e] the brunt of the economic recession [which began in 1990], it was now up to public sector workers to make some sacrifices," even if this came at the expense of their collective bargaining rights (Neimeijer 2000, 3). This response was contradictory in that it appealed to broader working-class unity (in the form of continued support for the NDP) while also positing a sectionalist claim about the relative importance of the interests of the "wealth generating sector" over those of public sector workers, who were merely a "drain" on the public purse (Ryan 2008, interview; Zeidenberg 1996, 20).

These tensions came to a head at the November 1993 Ontario Federation of Labour (OFL) Convention, which solidified the two political factions that were to endure through the Days of Action. On the one hand, members of the Public Services Coalition, supported by the CAW, put forward a resolution "stipulating that no money, volunteers or other resources would be made available to the party in the next provincial elections unless the social contract legislation was repealed" (Reshef and Rastin 2003, 136). While the majority of voting delegates supported this resolution,[10] those from twelve private sector unions, sensing impending defeat, walked out before the conclusion of the debate.[11] Soon afterwards, these pro-NDP unions formed the "Pink Paper" Group, so-named for having printed their dissent from the OFL resolution on pink paper, and issued a strategic plan to re-elect New Democrats. This conflict over political strategy and over the boundaries, interests, and internal relations within the union movement was to frame the dynamics of protest over the next five years.

THE 1995 PROVINCIAL ELECTION AND THE TURN TO EXTRA-PARLIAMENTARY MOBILIZATION

The union movement's strategic disarray was on full view in the 1995 provincial election. The Public Services Coalition, although very troubled by the deep job and service cuts being promised by the rising Conservative Party and its leader, Mike Harris, remained committed to its refusal to endorse the NDP. Instead, these unions opted for a third-party media campaign focusing on the value of public services, and its prominent leaders – Sid Ryan of CUPE Ontario and Buzz Hargrove of the CAW – were reported as "probably not vot[ing] in the election" (Van Alphen 1995, A9). For their part, the Pink Paper unions mobilized for NDP candidates as usual. However, the unions' divided efforts, combined with the Liberals' failure to court disaffected NDP and working-class voters and the Tories' potent message of right-wing populism, contributed to the Rae government's defeat.

The election of the Harris government in June 1995, the rapidity with which it began implementing its anti-union "Common Sense Revolution" (CSR),[12] and the fact that nearly every non-elite constituency was targeted by the government's policies provided a much-needed unifying element in the labour movement. Within five months, the Days of Action strategy emerged and began to consolidate the fragmented, single-issue, and sectoral protests against the Harris government into a broad, multi-sectoral mobilization that went far beyond the union movement. This strategy was formally and unanimously adopted by the 2,000 delegates to the OFL Convention in November 1995 in the form of a city-by-city fightback. As Rapaport (1999, 53) points out, this decision was part of a rising tide of protest that began immediately after the election of the Conservative government: "What started as a relatively small opposition of social protest groups in the summer of 1995 had evolved into a full-blown social movement by the winter. On a warm sunny day in July about a thousand demonstrators showed up at Queen's Park to protest cuts to day care. Just seven months later, on a cold and wet wintry day, 100,000 Ontarians showed up in Hamilton to protest the CSR outside a Tory policy conference." The Days soon came to take on a common form, with one part of the day involving shutting down of workplaces with cross-picketing – that is, pickets by people from other workplaces who could not be held responsible under the Ontario Labour Relations Act for engaging in an illegal strike – followed by a march and speeches.[13] These tactics had the important effect of breaking down divisions between workers and movements, and broadening the sense of shared struggle.

The emergence of the Days of Action strategy raises the question of how previously isolated struggles and protests were consolidated and woven into something greater. Organizations and activists could have turned to fighting each other, as they had under Rae and as the "poor-bashing" discourse of the Harris electoral campaign had encouraged. Instead, a broad-based alliance emerged, expressed through a popular and universalist framing of problems as well as new forms of organizing and political action, raising the *possibility* of sustained shifts in class consciousness and political strategy.

A central part of the coalition's ideological framing targeted Harris and his government ministers, giving a face to the abstraction of neoliberalism and mobilizing visceral emotions. T-shirts proclaimed, "*We Want Harris Out the Door*," and buttons with a red line through the premier's face were widespread and popular. The personification of the enemy in the person of Harris (and his various ministers) resonated deeply and widely, given the particular arrogance with which the government addressed dissenters, and was something everyone could easily agree on. A related discourse concerned the "authoritarian" nature of "the Tory style of governance," evident in its notable disinterest in building broad consensus around policy changes or negotiating with opposition groups and including their concerns. This governance style raised the spectre of the end of democracy, and hence legitimated taking steps outside the established political process. Finally, the labour movement's own discourse emphasized the government's "anti-labour" or "corporate agenda," and drew links between Harris and the Ontario business class.

The movement also framed the collective bargaining struggles of both public servants and teachers so as to become lightning rods for broader opposition to the government. OPSEU was the first group of workers to face the collective bargaining implications of the CSR. Their first-ever strike in February 1996 to defend job security language lasted three weeks and rapidly politicized the membership – not least because of the significant level of Ontario Provincial Police (OPP) violence involved in policing the strike. Then-OFL president Gord Wilson characterized the OPSEU strike as "one of the first jets that lifted the rocket off" (Rapaport 1999, 56). The OPSEU strike became a symbol of the government's authoritarianism and thus the importance of supporting any form of resistance against it. Ontario teachers were also prominent participants in the Days of Action as part of their struggle against Bill 160, the Education Quality Improvement Act,[14] which would radically restrict the scope of teacher collective bargaining (Sears 2003; Kerr 2006, 19). As particular targets of the Harris reforms, teachers came to engage in an unprecedented political mobilization, not only turning out thousands of their members for the Days – the February 1996 rally in Hamilton was a sea of OSSTF toques – but also, in the fall of 1997, undertaking an illegal two-week political strike against the legislation. Ontario teachers had engaged in prior waves of militancy, most notably in the 1973–75 mass resignations campaign to oppose the imposition of compulsory arbitration by the Davis government (Laxer 1977, 217–24), and they were gradually moving closer to the labour movement, but they had remained officially outside the labour federations until 1996. The Harris government and the Days of Action thus brought teachers into the labour movement proper (at least in some ways), and, in their engagement in coalitions with parents and students to defend public education, opened them up to both goals and strategies beyond the workplace and collective bargaining.

The Days also mobilized people around a very diffuse set of demands, which in part was a reflection of the fragile nature of the coalition and the need to maintain all sectors' support. Rapaport (1999, 62) gives a sense of both the broader base of the opposition movement and the wide range of issues motivating people's participation:

Unions opposed changes to labour law; teachers opposed cutbacks to the education system; students opposed cutbacks to postsecondary education and projected tuition increases; day-care workers opposed cutbacks in their centres; women's groups opposed cutbacks to pay equity programmes; minorities opposed the dismantling of employment equity; poor people opposed the cutbacks to social assistance; injured workers opposed the cutbacks to workers compensation; judges opposed the cutbacks to the justice system; police opposed the hard line in bargaining that the government was taking with civil servants; and OPSEU members opposed cuts to the public service.

The establishment and structure of local organizing committees reflected the desire for co-leadership between the union movement and the social justice movement, and for a kind of "common front" strategy. After the London Day of Action, each local organizing committee designated "co-chairs," usually the president of the local labour council and the head of the local social justice coalition (if it existed). This commitment to fully representing the diversity of groups harmed by the CSR was also reflected in the choices for speakers at the demonstrations themselves, which reflected a balance of labour and community voices.

The Days also introduced the general political strike into the Ontario labour movement's repertoire and discourse, challenging the boundaries between the economic and the political. This required the development of new capacities amongst workers. In order to convince people to participate, unions serious about mobilizing for the Days had to engage their own members and social movement activists in political discussions over the nature of the economy, its relation to the state, and the question of which "side" one was on. This was particularly important as local chambers of commerce and media stoked a moral panic about "anarchy," "chaos," or the breakdown of social order, and as employers attempted to get injunctions against picketing or use disciplinary procedures against their own employees. Because the Days of Action strategy of shutting down workplaces meant potential risk – a day's pay, the employer's discipline, the wrath of one's neighbours – a deeper form of political education was required. Participants had to know what was at stake: why they were using economic power as a political strategy in order to be able to mobilize co-workers, talk to their neighbours, and justify their participation when challenged. A significant internal education campaign within the public sector unions and the CAW was undertaken to equip people to deal with these challenges. This organizing work, in CUPE for example, involved booking off hundreds of member-activists to do political education about the government's policies and get locals set up to picket their workplaces. It activated a layer of people who had never been involved in union or political activism and brought the level of debate in workplaces to a fever pitch.

CONTRADICTIONS IN THE DAYS OF ACTION

Even as they worked to mobilize thousands of people, and may have provided the "necessary basis" for unifying a deeply divided union movement, these discursive and organizational choices nonetheless contained important limitations and contradictions that have had lasting effects. First, although personalization is a very common part of social movement framing, this emphasis often worked to mask the way in which Harris represented both a larger ideological and political movement and reflected the interests of a real social base in the suburbs and exurban and rural areas, as well as amongst some segments of the unionized working class (Ross 1996). Ultimately, the Days of Action discourse about the causes of the problem did not lead to a deep analysis of neoliberalism in the short run, or equip movement leaders and activists to see the penetration of neoliberal ideas and policies in the other electoral alternatives.[15]

Second, the inability to focus the struggle on a core set of demands for fear of alienating some coalition partners meant that there were no real conditions for "success" except the complete reversal of the CSR. The extent to which movement participants genuinely integrated their related but distinct struggles into a common political analysis and set of commitments was variable, and depended on the particular way that unions mobilized their members. Overall, the Days represented a "reactive opposition," a militant defense of the *status quo ante* whose "primary aim was damage control" (Rapaport 1999, 54) and the preservation of the basic terms of Fordist industrial relations and Keynesian social policy. This aim of returning to an era of relative labour peace and cooperative relations was expressed this way by CAW staffer Ron Pellerin, initially tasked with being the CAW's fightback coordinator: "They're going to have to learn to work with labour to resolve the issues we're all facing" (CAW 1995).

A third limitation was the inability of the labour movement to work through the relative importance of, and relationship between, parliamentary and extra-parliamentary strategy. From the outset, the Pink Paper unions remained both deeply resentful of the role played by public sector unions in defeating the NDP in 1995 and very skeptical of mass mobilization.[16] It was common to see people at the Days sporting Steelworker-made t-shirts reading "Don't Blame Me, I voted NDP." Indeed, these unions feared the impact that militancy would have on the NDP's chances in the 1999 election, and emphasized the need to marshal resources to re-elect the NDP. As Neimeijer (2000, 5) recounts, the Pink Paper group would only clear the way for the OFL's financial support of Days of Action strategy in exchange for revisiting disaffiliation from the NDP and on the condition that they themselves would not be expected to support the mobilizations financially or organizationally, and that "this lack of commitment ... [would not] be politicized in any way." As a result, the official leadership of these unions, for instance, "did not actively support" the London Day of Action, though many of their locals participated in the work stoppages and some later negotiated days off for members to participate (Bickerton 1996, 38; Neimeijer 2000, 6). As such, they failed to confront the very real problems of late twentieth-century social democracy by simply reasserting the necessity of loyalty to the party regardless of its ideological or policy orientation.

The city-by-city strategy was itself a product of the limitations placed on the CAW-public sector alliance. A province-wide action would be impossible to pull off without the full support of the entire labour movement, and hence a regional concentration of efforts was necessary. While this regional focus allowed for stronger place-based coalitions to form, they were ephemeral in many places: only a minority of activists were involved in all the Days of Action, and most were involved only briefly before returning to their normal lives (Neimeijer

2000, 5). In that sense, the Days of Action did not necessarily create the conditions for a sustained expansion of class consciousness or solidarity beyond the community level.

Despite the Pink Paper unions' "tolerance" of the Days of Action strategy, there was an ever-present sense that these unions were biding their time, confident that the extra-parliamentary strategy would fail. Indeed, two weeks after the October 1996 Toronto Days of Action, a significant debate emerged amongst union leaders at the OFL, not only over where to hold future Days of Action rallies but also over whether to continue with them at all. The Toronto demonstration brought upwards of 250,000 people into the streets. Yet the government remained unmoved, providing the Pink Paper unions with the evidence they needed to conclude that the strategy had run its course. On November 7, 1996, the Pink Paper group held their own press conference to announce that they were finished with the protests, with spokespeople indicating that the thirteen unions would return to focusing on "workplace issues" and building support for the NDP (Rusk 1996).

However, it was not merely the Pink Paper unions' failure to support the Days that limited the extra-parliamentary strategy. Given the ideologically diffuse nature of the alliance behind the Days, few seriously considered what it would mean to follow the extra-parliamentary path to its logical conclusion: a provincial and open-ended strike creating conditions of "un-governability" in order to produce political change from outside the electoral system. Short of that, the extra-parliamentary strategy necessarily remained one of "voice" rather than an attempt to extract concrete concessions from the government. There was vocal support amongst certain quarters of now-activated union memberships for at least a provincial day of action, even if little consideration was given to its character or ultimate aims. A compromise emerged that attempted to appease both sides: while the OFL executive voted to end further city-based protests against the Harris government, the delegates at the 1997 OFL convention unanimously voted in favour of calling a one-day province-wide day of action before the end of 1998 and to work in the upcoming election to defeat Harris and elect an NDP government (CUPE Ontario 1997). Despite the convention's call for a one-day general strike, the hotly contested election for the presidency of the OFL, in which Steelworker and Pink Paper unionist Wayne Samuelson narrowly defeated the CAW's Paul Forder,[17] foreshadowed the fate of the Days of Action. Soon after the 1997 OFL convention, the federation's executive cancelled the province-wide action, leading to a long period of demobilization and demoralization.

DAYS OF CONFUSION: UNION POLITICAL STRATEGY AND REALIGNMENT SINCE 1999

In the wake of the Harris government's re-election in 1999, the divisions in the labour movement were deepened by a political fracturing between the unions at the core of the Days of Action coalition. As the Days of Action strategy (and the financial resources behind it) dissipated, Ontario unions were faced with a choice about how best to engage in the upcoming 1999 election. The CAW, OPSEU, and the teachers' unions adopted strategic voting to defeat Harris, which ironically, in most ridings, meant voting for the Liberal Party, a political formation to the right of the NDP (Savage 2010, 2012). The CAW (2002, 16) struck an internal task force to explore the union's approach to political action, concluding that although members were politicized, wedded to the union's vision of social unionism, and wanted the union to issue "report cards" on the parties' approaches to important issues, most "wanted to make up their own mind and not be told how to vote." This anti-partisan politics laid the logical foundation for the CAW's turn to strategic voting. For its part, CUPE Ontario opted to re-engage social democratic electoralism as its main political strategy in concert with many of the Pink Paper unions. CUPE Ontario President Sid Ryan, one of the Social Contract's harshest critics, even ran (unsuccessfully) for the party in the 1999 provincial election.

The results of both strategic voting and social democratic electoralism in 1999 were limited. The Harris government was re-elected with an even greater share of the popular vote in 1999 and the Ontario NDP fared poorly in the two elections following the Days of Action, losing official party status after both the 1999 and 2003 provincial elections. Since that time, with a few prominent exceptions, Ontario's unions have been in a constant state of flux, changing their partisan alignments in each election and making it difficult for observers to keep track.

Since 2003, union-sponsored negative attack ads by the Working Families Coalition have underpinned union-sponsored strategic voting efforts that have largely benefitted the Liberal Party, notably in helping elect them to government in 2003 (Walchuk 2010). The CAW's turn to strategic voting has only solidified in successive provincial and federal elections and remains a strong commitment for Unifor, the product of the merger of the CAW with the Communications, Energy, and Paperworkers Union in 2013. Interestingly, SEIU, which had been amongst the Pink Paper group's participants in 1993, has also moved into the strategic voting camp.

Other Ontario unions, however, give their efforts exclusively to the NDP, some unwaveringly (like the United Steelworkers, and CUPE Ontario since 1999), and some in more recent realignments. OPSEU, for example, was solidly within the strategic voting camp in 1999, but has gradually drifted to the NDP in successive elections, albeit without establishing official affiliation with the party. No doubt these decisions are coloured by the fact that the provincial government – and hence the governing party – is the employer of most of OPSEU's members, and the Liberal Party was their employer throughout this period.

However, Savage and Ruhloff-Queiruga (2017) show that even unions with public partisan alignments with the NDP have been hedging their bets and donating money either to strategic voting initiatives like the Working Families Coalition or directly to Liberal Party candidates. Indeed, although union donations to the NDP have increased over the past two decades, "the Ontario Liberal Party [has] eclipsed the provincial NDP as the primary recipient of union campaign contributions" (ibid., 247).

Any strategic political unity achieved in the Ontario labour movement since 1999 has in fact been centred on strategic voting initiatives and has been fleeting. The OFL's #StopHudak campaign in the 2014 election is the key case in point. Developed under the leadership of then-OFL president Sid Ryan, #StopHudak aimed to block the election of a Tim Hudak-led Conservative government whose policy documents clearly showed they would pursue draconian austerity measures and a renewed attack on unions' organizational strength. The campaign drew widespread participation from unions of all political alignments, who could fit their particular electoral strategy under the #StopHudak banner (ibid., 270). However, divisions flared up almost immediately after the election, with OPSEU criticizing the effort for having re-elected a Liberal government still bent on austerity and culminating in Ryan's ouster from the helm of the OFL at its 2015 convention.

Attempts to move the OFL back to a formal partisan endorsement of the NDP exposed the enduring divisions over union political strategy. The 2017 convention debate over the OFL's political action strategy was especially fractious. With support for the NDP initially omitted from the plan, upon its insertion by the delegates, a lengthy debate ensued, with leaders from Unifor, OSSTF, SEIU, and the Ontario English Catholic Teachers visibly opposed. The effects of the continuing divisions over partisan alignment showed again in the 2018 provincial election. The OFL followed through on the convention's endorsement of the NDP. Even if efforts did not live up to the intentions of the controversial convention resolution, the OFL organized telephone and in-person town halls and a dozen labour canvasses for NDP candidates in strategically chosen ridings. Their endorsement of the NDP was also made clear in official statements and social media posts. Other realignments followed, with ETFO joining CUPE and the Steelworkers in endorsing the NDP and leaving the Liberal fold early in the election (Iwanek 2018). For other affiliates, however, strategic disarray was more evident. Despite the Wynne Liberals' abysmal polling numbers throughout the campaign, some unions committed to "activating [members'] electoral participation" (Unifor 2018) or strategic voting (OSSTF) were very slow to shift their support clearly to the NDP. While the NDP was in a statistical dead heat for first place for much of the campaign, and despite repeated pleas from CUPE Ontario and the Steelworkers that the NDP was the "strategic vote," OSSTF's Toronto local only rescinded their endorsement of several Toronto-area Liberals on 30 May, a mere week before election day (Ferguson 2018). Similarly, Unifor only made it clear that the best chance to defeat a Doug Ford-led Conservative government was a vote for the NDP in the final week of the campaign (Rizvi 2018). Although the NDP became the official opposition and achieved its best result since 1990, Ford was still elected with a majority government. It remains an open question whether a more unified electoral strategy by unions could have made the crucial difference.

While most unions in Ontario remain committed to some type of electoral activism, extra-parliamentary mobilization has not been completely extinguished. Since 1999, there have been several impressive waves of extra-parliamentary activity, in the form of the global justice, anti-war, and Occupy movements. However, none of these movements (in North America, at any rate) has presented a significant obstacle to neoliberalism in the province (or elsewhere). Labour-based extra-parliamentary mobilization against the McGuinty government, even in the wake of the financial and economic crisis of 2008–09, the loss of manufacturing jobs, and the return to public sector austerity, has also been relatively muted and ineffective (Ross 2011). There has also been little effort to go beyond the dichotomy of social democratic electoralism and extra-parliamentary activism, or to think through how to articulate them together for greater effect. Rather, what demonstrations have been organized have remained one-off events to address a specific policy or event, rather than been part of an escalating strategy to exert political pressure, whether electorally or through ongoing disruption and public debate.

One major exception to this overall situation is the Fight for $15 and Fairness, a provincial campaign coordinated by the Toronto Workers' Action Centre to force an increase to the provincial minimum wage and a host of employment standards reforms that would address rising levels of poverty and precarity in the labour market. Initiated in 2015 but building on previous iterations, the campaign developed an impressive network of activists across the province carrying out coordinated monthly public interventions, awareness-raising, petition drives, and activist capacity-building. When the Liberal government announced its Changing Workplaces Review in 2015, the campaign was uniquely positioned to take advantage of the space opened, with a clear and coordinated set of demands and cadre of well-trained local activists ready to intervene in hearings (Bush and Abdelbaki 2016). The resulting 2017 legislation – Bill 148, the Fair Workplaces, Better Jobs Act – made the first significant improvements to Ontario's labour and employment standards legislation in a generation. The campaign worked vigorously through the 2018 provincial election to mobilize voters to defend these wins, highlight the threat that Ford posed to them, and convince candidates to sign a Decent Work pledge, but opted not to declare partisan support for either the Liberals or the NDP (Fight for $15 and Fairness 2018). Whether or not this was the right or only strategy for such a movement to adopt, the election of the Ford-led Conservatives in 2018 places the legislative achievements of the Fight for $15 and Fairness in serious jeopardy. In sum, this campaign points to the real and continuing possibilities of extra-parliamentary action, yet its strategies and tactics have not had wider impact on the unions themselves. Moreover, given the campaign's dependence on a sympathetic provincial government, thinking through the relationship between parliamentary and extra-parliamentary strategy remains crucial.

Another of the major claims made about the Days of Action was that participation in the local joint coordinating committees had created lasting relationships and partnerships in the various communities and made evident the utility of engaging in union-community coalitions (John Cartwright in Mirrlees 2004, 1). Undoubtedly, many lasting relationships between individual activists and organizations were forged in this period, creating new forms of social capital and solidarity, reducing isolation in some quarters, and opening access to new resources for mobilization and support in the struggles to come. In CUPE Ontario, for instance, the already-existing tendency towards coalition work was solidified and expanded, such that the community has come to feature centrally in the union's political strategy documents.

However, not all unions internalized these lessons to the same extent, and at the municipal level, few enduring structures remain that could bring together the labour movement and the social justice community in regular collaboration at a common table. Instead, as Crow and Albo (2005, 15) rightly point out, "these [coalition] strategies remain ad hoc and generally do not last beyond individual battles." Windsor is an interesting example, particularly since its CAW-dominated labour movement has had a reputation for social unionism and community engagement. While one legacy of the Days was the creation of a permanent "Social Justice Representative" on the Windsor and District Labour Council executive, the scope of groups involved in WDLC activity are actually quite narrow, limited to the United Way's labour representatives and other union activists formally representing their locals but also involved in other groups like the Windsor Peace Coalition and the Citizens' Environmental Alliance. Moreover, Windsor's local social justice coalition collapsed in the late 1990s, diffusing whatever capacity existed for coordination amongst the community-based organizations. Therefore, in March 2007, when the CAW initiated the organization of a community-wide rally to defend manufacturing jobs, it was necessary to reinvent those organizational ties between the labour and social justice communities. Though the May 2007 rally was immensely successful in resource mobilization terms, bringing out 38,000 people and making a universalist appeal to defend "our jobs, our community, our future," the sectionalism of the Pink Paper unions had also crept into the CAW's discourse. It now came with a twist: public sector unions (and the broader community) were told that they should support manufacturing because CAW workers are the "tax base" (or the "wealth-generating sector") for public services (Ross 2008). As with the Days of Action, attempts to consolidate that community coalition were ineffectual. Instead, the mobilization had the character of a last hurrah: Windsor experienced a serious backlash against organized labour after the 2007 financial crisis as the then-CAW negotiated successive rounds of concessions to secure government loans for their near-bankrupt employers and solidarity for municipal workers on strike in 2009 was minimal. In that sense, the repeated references to the Days of Action during strategic discussions at the community jobs coalition were nostalgic rather than aimed at learning lessons from past successes and failures.

Although the Toronto labour scene is different, and seems to have sustained a greater ongoing capacity for union-community collaboration and mobilization (as is evident in the Toronto District Labour Council's "Million Reasons" $10 minimum wage campaign, their related mobilization around the election of Cheri DiNovo as an NDP MPP in a 2006 by-election, and their Good Jobs for All Coalition), there is still a widespread sense that the labour movement must continuously rebuild relationships in every new round of struggle. In particular, the opportunity presented by the Days to create a new form of working-class organization, one that transcended the boundaries of unions and organized workers, would articulate sectional struggles together, and would permanently maintain and deepen relationships, solidarities, and collective identities, was missed in most places. This new type of organizational form could have provided a space for non-union workers to participate in the labour movement. It might build the potential for union expansion and narrow the social, economic, and political gap between unionized and non-union workers. The implications of this lost opportunity continue to be evident. In many communities, a concerted multi-sectoral resistance against employer and government strategies for dealing with economic recession or austerity is either absent, or struggling to be re-founded. In this sense, the Ontario labour movement clearly remains divided on both extra-parliamentary and electoral strategies, with little learned from the Days of Action process about either approach.

THE POLITICS OF LEARNING FROM STRUGGLE

The last two decades of union political action in Ontario raise an important set of questions about how to understand the impact of movement dynamics, outcomes, successes, *and* failures on the strategic thinking, capacities, and repertoires of movements. As argued above, the Days did have a number of positive outcomes in some quarters, and the commitment to union-community coalition and the combination of electoral and extra-parliamentary strategies was deepened in some unions and activists' orientations. However, it is difficult to avoid concluding that they were, in important ways, a failure. They did not block the passage of any piece of legislation introduced by the Harris government, nor did they translate popular anger at the government into an electoral defeat in 1999. While they slowed down and moderated the Common Sense Revolution, and undermined the legitimacy of the *government* (John Cartwright in Mirrlees 2004, 1; Ryan 2008, interview), the Days did not block the consolidation of *neoliberalism's* more general ideological dominance (John Clarke in Mirrlees 2004, 2). Moreover, the victory of the Ontario Liberals in 2003 ushered in a more moderate neoliberalism, and though the Liberals' style of governance was (until 2012) much less polarizing, the shift in approach was not accompanied by a major shift in substance. Finally, the NDP did not benefit from this popular mobilization until the 2018 election, and even then it was not enough to put them in government. All of this raises questions about the lessons drawn from this round of struggle and the impact on the formation of class capacities and repertoires of struggle.

As Adams (2003) argues, even when movements succeed, their impacts on participants can be negative and emotionally difficult, ushering in a period of isolation and disillusionment. We would expect these dynamics to be at play even more clearly in movements that fail, particularly if the process of learning from them is ad hoc and uneven.

Kim Voss's work on the collapse of the Knights of Labor in the 1880s provides some interesting insights into how we might understand the strategic lessons derived from the outcome of the Days of Action. Voss (1996, 227–8) argues that one of the longer term implications of the Knights' failure was the delegitimization of their collective action frame of "new inclusive labor ideologies and organizational forms through which less-skilled wage earners were incorporated into the labor movement." Despite their successes in the early 1880s, the eventual collapse of the Knights meant that "the labor activists who had once championed radical reform and class-wide organizations were demoralized, the organizational forms which had been used for the purpose of incorporating less skilled workers into the labor movement were discredited, and the strategic frame that had been constructed by the Knights lost its power to mobilize workers."

The Days have held a similarly complex and contradictory place in the minds of many Ontario labour activists, serving as a source of nostalgia for the feeling of exhilaration and unity but also as an "example" of the futility of mass political action. This, I would argue, is related to the way that the Days of Action raised very high expectations amongst large segments of the population, while failing to provide a set of structures and strategies that would have much hope of fulfilling them. It promised the possibility of moving beyond bureaucratic to direct forms of action, based on mass mobilization, through which the populace might actually intervene to block harmful policy decisions rather than relying on elected representatives or other intermediaries. As Neimeijer (2000, 1) put it, soon after they were wound down, "the initial disappointment at the lack of effectiveness of the Days of Action turned into pessimism and defeatism." The delegitimation of mass extra-parliamentary action as an effective strategic option in future cycles of struggle has occurred not least because, as Camfield (2000, 312) argues, "the experience of engaging in struggle with a strategy that is not working ultimately corrodes hope."

However, a return to examining this period of labour movement upsurge also reveals clues to the kinds of organizational structures that effectively brought together a broader section of the working class and had the potential to consolidate, extend, and deepen class unity and consciousness. Although these city-wide organizations were generally not preserved, their capacity to challenge the boundaries between organizations, and force a conversation about what unites them and what differences must be worked through, was an important contribution to the Ontario labour movement's repertoire. From the vantage point of 2018, with organized labour more isolated than ever in a climate of economic inequality, employment precarity, and union density stagnation, and the election of a provincial government that promises a return to the policies of the Harris years, a retrieval of the class-wide organizational forms generated by the Days of Action is now an urgent task.

ACKNOWLEDGMENTS

I wish to thank Larry Savage, Peter Graefe, and Suzanne Mills for their invaluable feedback on this chapter.

NOTES

1 The 1976 National Day of Protest against wage controls drew a million people across the country, but nowhere did upwards of 250,000 people gather in one place as in Toronto in October 1996.
2 Various commentators have located this failure in the timidity of the labour bureaucracy (John Clarke and Carolyn Egan in Mirrlees 2004); the divisions between public and private sector unions and the latter's narrowness and failure to embrace coalition work and a social justice agenda (Palmer 1998); the dominance of electoralism as a political strategy (ibid.); or the entrenched attachments to bureaucratic relationships and ways of organizing in the movement as a whole (Camfield 2000).
3 Generally speaking, social unionism is an approach to union activity that defines workers' interests as extending beyond the boundaries of the workplace to include other forms of class and other inequalities, takes the community of interest as larger than the existing union membership, and uses a range of strategies and tactics beyond collective bargaining that reflect these expanded understandings. However, there is enormous variation in how such commitments are acted upon, ranging across electoral action, lobbying, coalition work, and mass demonstrations. For a more extensive discussion of these terms and their contested usage see Ross (2012, 2008, 2007).
4 The Social Contract Act's approximately $7 billion in cost savings were primarily achieved with $4 billion in program cuts, and $2 billion from workers'

wages and benefits via a three-year freeze and twelve mandatory unpaid days' leave per year (popularly known as "Rae Days"). After initial attempts to get the unions to "voluntarily" negotiate the implementation (but not the extent) of these cuts failed, the government used legislation to force the unions to various sectoral bargaining tables to avoid agreements being imposed upon them. The details and political struggles leading up to the Social Contract Act's passage in July 1993 are well documented elsewhere, namely in Walkom (1994), Martell (1995), McBride (1996), and Panitch and Swartz (2003).

5 Interestingly, beyond a few small local demonstrations and one at the NDP provincial council meeting in June 1993, there was no serious attempt at mass mobilization or direct resistance to the Social Contract. Even though CUPE Ontario held out the longest by refusing to participate in the sectoral tables, the possibility of a province-wide action was not even raised at the CUPE all-presidents meeting in the summer of 1993 (M. Roy [president, CUPE Local 2323] 1993, pers. comm.). Instead, public sector unions focused on negotiating agreements with employers that would contain the damage, indicating that the break with social democracy was incomplete at best (Neimeijer 2000, 3). McBride (1996, 88) calls this evidence of labour's "division and weakness."

6 This view was echoed internationally, as European new left activists were increasingly concluding that strong, independent social movements and union-community coalitions were central to effective social justice struggles and to ensuring the accountability of left parties (Wainwright 1994).

7 Agricultural Labour Relations Act (1994).

8 Ontario civil servants gained the right to strike in 1994 with the passage of the Crown Employees Collective Bargaining Act (Rapaport 1999, 28).

9 With the Pay Equity Amendment Act (1993), the NDP introduced the proxy method of comparison, which allows for a female-dominated job class without a relevant male comparator in their own workplace to use one from a sufficiently similar workplace in order to establish whether a gender-based pay inequity exists. This closed one of the major gaps in the pay equity legislation that blocked women in female-dominated workplaces from having their work revalued.

10 Neimeijer (2000, 3) reports that this margin was quite narrow, even though many who would have voted against had left.

11 Those walking out of the OFL Convention included the United Steel Workers, the Communication Energy and Paperworkers Union, the Service Employees International Union, the United Food and Commercial Workers, the International Association of Machinists, and the Amalgamated Clothing and Textile Workers Union (later UNITE-HERE); they were later joined by CUPE Local 1000, also known as the Power Workers Union (representing workers at Ontario Hydro).

12 The elements of the Common Sense Revolution are detailed quite extensively by other sources. See Panitch and Swartz (2003); Reshef and Rastin (2003); OFL (1999); and Ralph et al. (1997).
13 Days of Action took place in the following communities: London (December 1995, 10,000); Hamilton (February 1996, 100,000); Kitchener-Waterloo (April 1996, 20,000); Peterborough (June 1996, 10,000); Toronto (October 1996, 250,000); Sudbury (March 1997, 7,000); Thunder Bay (April 1997, 5,000); North Bay (September 1997, 30,000); Windsor (October 1997, 40,000); St Catharines (May 1998, 4,000); and Kingston (June 1998, 5,000).
14 In addition to the major restructuring of educational governance promulgated by the Fewer School Boards Act (1997), which reduced the number of boards from 129 to seventy-two and the number of trustees from 1,900 to 700 (Glasbeek 1999, 807n5), Bill 160 made significant changes to the scope of teacher collective bargaining, including: removing principals and vice-principals from bargaining units and placing them in management; centralizing in the Ministry of Education and Training control over class sizes and preparation time; and removing from trustees the local power to tax (thus placing fiscal limits on local collective bargaining) (MacLellan 2009, 63).
15 This is a similar dynamic observed by Panitch and Swartz (2003, 158) in their discussion of the 1988 fight against the US-Canada Free Trade Agreement: that coalition's "discourse ... reduced the state to the government of the day and failed to treat the state as a constituent element of capitalist domination."
16 The Pink Paper Group continued to operate as a working group in the wake of the 1993 OFL convention throughout the Days of Action. Senior staff strategized over how to retake control of the OFL and labour councils from those sympathetic to the Public Services Coalition, and invest significant resources in a "joint political-action-&-education program, in partnership with the New Democratic Party," to mobilize electoral support for the party during the Harris years (Mackenzie 1996, 9). In the former goal, they were successful, pushing CUPE's Julie Davis and Sid Ryan off the OFL Executive in November 1995 (Zeidenberg 1996, 20).
17 Forder was the OFL's Days of Action coordinator.

REFERENCES

Adams, J. 2003. "The Bitter End: Emotions at a Movement's Conclusion." *Sociological Inquiry* 73 (1).

Bickerton, G. 1993. "Labour Re-evaluates the NDP." *Canadian Dimension* 27 (5), September–October.

– 1996. "Ontario Labour on the Move." *Canadian Dimension* 30 (1), February–March.

Bleyer, P. 1992. "Coalitions of Social Movements as Agencies for Social Change: The Action Canada Network." In *Organizing Dissent*, edited by W. Carroll. Toronto: Garamond.

Bush, D., and R. Abdelbaki. 2016. "Fight for $15 and Fairness." *Global Labour Research Centre Working Paper N. 1*. Toronto: GLRC.

Camfield, D. 2000. "Assessing Resistance in Harris's Ontario, 1995–1999." In *Restructuring and Resistance: Canadian Public Policy in an Age of Global Capitalism*, edited by M. Burke, C. Mooers, and J. Shields. Halifax: Fernwood.

Canadian Dimension. 1996. "The Pink Group Woos." *Canadian Dimension* 30 (2), April.

CAW. 1995a. "There Will Be Another City and Another and Another ..." *Contact* 25 (44), 19 December. http://www.caw.ca/en/4500.htm.

— 1995b. "Ontario Federation of Labour Picks London as Target for Day of Protest." *Contact* 25 (40), 19 November. http://www.caw.ca/en/4496.htm.

— 2002. *Task Force on Working Class Politics in the 21st Century: Recommendations to the Collective Bargaining and Political Action Convention*. Toronto: CAW.

Crow, D., and G. Albo. 2005. "Neo-Liberalism, NAFTA, and the State of the North American Labour Movements." *Just Labour* 6/7.

CUPE Ontario. 1997. "OFL Elects Irene Harris, Votes for One-Day Strike." *One Strong Voice* [newsletter], December. http://archive.ontario.cupe.ca/newsletters/osv-97-12-30.html.

Davis, M. 1986. *Prisoners of the American Dream*. London: Verso.

Evans, B. 2012. "The New Democratic Party in the Era of Neoliberalism." In *Rethinking the Politics of Labour in Canada*, edited by S. Ross and L. Savage. Halifax: Fernwood.

Ferguson, R. 2018. "Teachers Union Pulls Support from Wynne's Campaign After Liberal Accusation." *Toronto Star*, 30 May.

Fight for $15 and Fairness. 2018. "The Clock Is Ticking. Every. Vote. Counts." 25 May. https://www.15andfairness.org/every_vote_counts.

Gindin, S. 1995. "London, December 11, 1995: What Does It Mean, What Does It Change?" *Contact* 25 (44), 19 December. http://www.caw.ca/en/4500.htm.

Iwanek, M. 2018. "Ontario's Largest Education Union Opts to Endorse NDP over Liberals." *The Globe and Mail*, 10 May.

Kerr, L. 2006. *Between Caring and Counting: Teachers Take on Education Reform*. Toronto: University of Toronto Press.

Laxer, R. 1977. *Canada's Unions*. Toronto: James Lorimer.

Mackenzie, D. 1996. "Recommendations from Pink Staff Working Group" [memorandum]. Reprinted in *Canadian Dimension* 30 (2), April.

McBride, S. 1996. "The Continuing Crisis of Social Democracy: Ontario's Social Contract on Perspective." *Studies in Political Economy* 50.

Mirrlees, T. 2004. *Remembering the Days of Action, Re-Orienting Socialist Strategy* [unpublished workshop report]. Toronto: Socialist Project.

Moody, K. 1997. *Workers in a Lean World: Unions in the International Economy.* New York: Verso.

Munro, M. 1997. "Ontario's 'Days of Action' and Strategic Choices for the Left in Canada." *Studies in Political Economy* 53.

Neimeijer, M. 2000. "The Ontario Days of Action: The Beginning of a Redefinition of the Labour Movement's Political Strategy?" Unpublished manuscript.

Ontario Federation of Labour. 1999. *The Common Sense Revolution: 1,460 Days of Destruction, 1999 Election Edition.* Don Mills: OFL.

Palmer, B. 1998. "Teachers, Bureaucrats and Betrayal: Halloween in Harrisland." *Canadian Dimension* 32 (1), January–February.

Panitch, L. 1986. *Working-Class Politics in Crisis: Essays on Labour and the State.* London: Verso.

Panitch, L., and D. Swartz. 2003. *From Consent to Coercion: The Assault on Trade Union Freedoms.* Toronto: Garamond.

Ralph, D.S., A. Régimbald, and N. St-Amand, eds. 1997. *Open for Business, Closed to People: Mike Harris's Ontario.* Toronto: Fernwood.

Rapaport, D. 1999. *No Justice, No Peace: The 1996 OPSEU Strike against the Harris Government in Ontario.* Montreal: McGill-Queen's University Press.

Reshef, Y., and S. Rastin. 2003. *Unions in the Time of Revolution: Government Restructuring in Alberta and Ontario.* Toronto: University of Toronto Press.

Rizvi, N. 2018. "This is How We Stop Doug Ford." Uniforvotes. May. https://www.uniforvotes.ca/this_is_how_we_stop_doug_ford.

Ross, S. 2007. "Varieties of Social Unionism: Towards a Framework for Comparison." *Just Labour* 11, Fall.

– 2008. "Social Unionism and Membership Participation: What Role for Union Democracy?" *Studies in Political Economy* 81.

– 2011. "Social Unionism in Hard Times: Union-Community Coalition Politics in the CAW Windsor's Manufacturing Matters Campaign." *Labour/Le Travail* 68.

– 2012. "Business Unionism and Social Unionism in Theory and Practice." In *Rethinking the Politics of Labour in Canada*, edited by S. Ross and L. Savage. Halifax: Fernwood.

Rusk, J. 1996. "Major Unions Withdraw from Protests." *Globe and Mail,* 8 November.

Savage, L. 2010. "Changing Party-Union Relations in Canada." *Labor Studies Journal* 35 (1).

– 2012. "Organized Labour and the Politics of Strategic Voting." In *Rethinking the Politics of Labour in Canada*, edited by S. Ross and L. Savage. Halifax: Fernwood.

Savage, L., and S. Ross. 2014. "Divisions in Labour Movement Undermine Effort to Stop Harper." *RankandFile.ca,* 11 December.

Savage, L., and N. Ruhloff-Queiruga. 2017. "Organized Labour, Campaign Finance, and the Politics of Strategic Voting in Ontario." *Labour/Le Travail* 80.

Sears, A. 2003. *Retooling the Mind Factory: Education in a Lean State.* Toronto: Garamond.

Unifor. 2018. "Unifor Commits to Make Ontario Election Count for Workers." 9 May. https://www.unifor.org/en/whats-new/press-room/unifor-commits-make-ontario-election-count-workers.
Van Alphen, T. 1995. "Protest Cuts, Unions Tell Voters." *Toronto Star*, 25 May.
Voss, K. 1996. "The Collapse of a Social Movement: The Interplay of Mobilizing Structures, Framing, and Political Opportunities in the Knights of Labor." In *Comparative Perspectives on Social Movements: Political Opportunities, Mobilizing Structures, and Cultural Framings*, edited by D. McAdam, J. McCarthy, and M. Zald. Cambridge: Cambridge University Press.
Wainwright, H. 1994. *Arguments for a New Left: Answering the Free Market Right*. Oxford: Blackwell.
Walchuk, B. 2010. "Changing Union-Party Relations in Canada: The Rise of the Working Families Coalition." *Labor Studies Journal* 35 (1).
Walkom, T. 1994. *Rae Days: The Rise and Fall of the NDP*. Toronto: Key Porter.
Zeidenberg, J. 1996. "Labour's Dirty Secret." *This Magazine*, November–December.

Contributors

GREG ALBO teaches political economy in the Department of Politics at York University. He is co-editor (with Leo Panitch) of the *Socialist Register* and recent books include *Rethinking Democracy* and (with Jerome Klassen) *Empire's Ally: Canada and the War in Afghanistan*.

DIMITRY ANASTAKIS is professor of history at Trent University. His most recent book is *Re-Creation, Fragmentation and Resilience: A Brief History of Canada Since 1945*.

HUGH ARMSTRONG is professor emeritus of social work and political economy at Carleton University. He has published widely on the political economy of the long-term care sector, and his most recent book (co-authored with Pat Armstrong) is *About Canada: Health Care*.

PAT ARMSTRONG is distinguished research professor of sociology at York University. Her recent books include (co-edited with Ruth Lowndes) *Creative Team Work: Developing Rapid, Site-Switching Ethnography* and (co-authored with Suzanne Day) *Wash Wear and Care: Clothing and Laundry in Long-Term Residential Care*.

JAMES CAIRNS is associate professor of social and environmental justice at Wilfrid Laurier University. His most recent book is *The Myth of the Age of Entitlement: Millennials, Austerity, and Hope*.

ROBERT J. DRUMMOND is university professor emeritus in politics and public policy and administration at York University. His research interests include Ontario politics, health policy, and the politics of aging.

BRYAN EVANS is a professor in the Department of Politics and Public Administration, Ryerson University. Recent publications include the co-edited volumes (with Steve McBride) *Austerity: The Lived Experience* and *The Austerity State*.

CARLO FANELLI is assistant professor of work and labour studies in the Department of Social Science at York University. He is editor of *Alternate Routes: A Journal of Critical Social Research*, author of *Megacity Malaise: Neoliberalism, Public Services and Labour in Toronto*, and co-editor (with Bryan Evans) of *The Public Sector in an Age of Austerity: Perspectives from Canada's Provinces and Territories*.

TAMMY FINDLAY is an associate professor and chair in the Department of Political and Canadian Studies at Mount Saint Vincent University. She researches feminist intersectionality and social policy, child care policy, and women's representation and democratic governance. She is the author of *Femocratic Administration: Gender, Governance and Democracy in Ontario*.

GRACE-EDWARD GALABUZI is an associate professor in the Department of Politics and Public Administration at Ryerson University. His recent books include (co-edited with Tanis Das Gupta and others) *Race and Racialization: Essential Readings (2nd ed.)*, and *Canada's Economic Apartheid: The Social Exclusion of Racialized Groups in the New Century*.

PETER GRAEFE is associate professor of political science at McMaster University. He has published widely on social policy, federalism, and Ontario and Québec politics.

CAROL-ANNE HUDSON is a senior policy analyst with the Ministry of Municipal Affairs and Housing for the government of British Columbia. She has written extensively on income supports, living wages, and poverty reduction policy.

JAMES LAWSON is an associate professor in the Department of Political Science at the University of Victoria. He researches Canadian natural resource politics and political economy.

Contributors

DAVID LEADBEATER is associate professor of economics at Laurentian University in Sudbury. He is the editor of *Resources, Empire and Labour: Crises, Lessons and Alternatives* and *Mining Town Crisis: Globalization, Labour and Resistance in Sudbury*.

BECKY MACWHIRTER is a graduate of York University's Master of Environmental Studies program. She is currently working as the Green Programs coordinator for the City of Belleville focusing on the development of environmental programs and community engagement.

TERRY MALEY teaches critical and radical democratic theory in the Department of Politics and in Social and Political Thought at York University. He has worked with the trade union movement on alternative budgets. His recently edited book is *One-Dimensional Man 50 Years On: The Struggle Continues*.

JOHN PETERS is associate professor of labour studies at Laurentian University. His research focuses on the politics of inequality and labour market deregulation. His most recent book is *Jobs with Inequality: Financialization, Post-Democracy and Labour Market Deregulation in Canada* (forthcoming).

STEPHANIE ROSS is an associate professor in the School of Labour Studies at McMaster University. Her latest book (co-edited with Larry Savage) is *Labour under Attack: Anti-Unionism in Canada*.

ALAN SEARS is a professor in the Department of Sociology at Ryerson University. His recent publications include *The Next New Left: A History of the Future* and (with James Cairns) *The Democratic Imagination: Envisioning Popular Power in the 21st Century*.

CHARLES W. SMITH is an associate professor in the Department of Political Science at St Thomas More College, University of Saskatchewan. His research interests include Canadian and international political economy, public law, and labour unions. As well as co-editor of *Labour/Le Travail*, he is the author (with Larry Savage) of *Unions in Court: Organized Labour and the Charter of Rights and Freedoms*, and co-editor of *Transforming Provincial Politics*.

STEVEN TUFTS is an associate professor in the Department of Geography at York University. His current areas of research include union strategy, labour market adjustment, unions and urban austerity, and populism and labour in North America.

MARK WINFIELD is professor of environmental studies at York University. He has published on a wide range of environmental and energy law topics, particularly climate change and electricity issues in Ontario. He is the author of *Blue-Green Province: The Environment and the Political Economy of Ontario*.

Index

ability, 213, 222. *See also* disability
advocacy, 215, 225, 227, 238, 241n4, 319, 321–2, 325
agriculture, 43–4, 64, 78, 89, 138–44, 163, 167n14, 190, 259–61, 266n3, 268n3, 269n3, 374, 430–2, 452n1, 471, 477, 544n7; agricultural workers, 49, 64, 298, 482, 527; clay belt, 132, 138, farmers, 152, 154, 168n21, 379; Ontario Federation of Agriculture, 379; supply management of, 204
agro-industry. *See* agriculture
Alberta, 126n1, 135, 166n8, 192, 197, 204–6, 208, 335, 355n5, 359, 387n1, 446
Alberta New Democratic Party, 204, 208. *See also* New Democratic Party (federal party); Ontario New Democratic Party; social democracy
alienation, xviii, 32, 150
alternative budgets (AB), 493–519
American Revolution, 431, 441
anti-globalization movement, 33, 503. *See also* globalization
anti-privatization, 34, 268, 336, 370, 501, 504
army. *See* military
austerity, xviii, 36n3, 236, 248, 500–5, 508, 512–17, 541; in Brazil, 502–3; by the NDP, 19, 36n3, 276, 285; effect on poverty reduction, 311, 316, 323–9; federal government austerity, 10, 31, 194, 206, 513; in European countries, 503, 505; and health spending, 354; ideology of, 512, 517; municipal, 249, 265; Ontario provincial government austerity, 15, 19–22, 26–36, 79, 125, 189, 194, 262, 276, 295, 300–1, 452, 469, 486, 493–5, 500, 536, 538; opposition to, 28, 34–5, 300, 524, 541; "permanent austerity," 27, 247

authoritarianism, 135, 300; authoritarian tendencies within neoliberalism, xviii; in Harris government, 20, 529–30; in Latin America, 501–2
automotive industry, 13, 43, 49, 56; "Big Three" automakers, 51, 54–55, 103, 105, 112–18. *See also* manufacturing

Bank of Canada, 31, 61
banking, 25, 47–50, 57–60, 68, 79, 83, 87, 103, 126, 190, 248; World Bank, 495, 501. *See also* Bank of Canada
bankruptcies, 148; in automotive industry, 103, 116, 120, 540; during 2008–09 financial crisis, 54, 540; in mining industry, 148; of Nortel Networks, 61; of small businesses, 55; wage protections for workers during, 49, 248; of US Steel, 55; virtual bankruptcy of Ontario Hydro, 384
basic income. *See* guaranteed annual income
Basic Income Pilot Project. *See* guaranteed annual income
Bay Street, 20, 28, 495
Black Lives Matter, 35, 481, 486, 487n8
bonds, 24, 47, 57, 448
Brampton, 122, 336–7
Britain, 15, 46, 56, 132–7, 189, 209n7, 223, 286, 321, 340, 386, 397, 401, 404, 412, 431, 441
British Columbia, 63, 192, 285, 335

Caledonia conflict, 200–2, 440–1, 448
Canada Pension Plan (CPP), 13, 197, 297
Canadian Auto Workers (CAW), 32–3, 51, 54, 107, 109, 114, 123–4, 157, 172n45,

302n8, 512, 526–8, 532–6, 539–40. *See also* Unifor
Canadian Centre for Policy Alternatives (CCPA), 505, 512–16
Canadian Dollar, 13, 19, 53
Canadian Union of Public Employees (CUPE), 24, 32, 34, 95, 369, 526–39, 544n5, 544n11
cap and trade, xvi, 29–30, 125, 162–3, 173n53, 204, 208, 444
capital mobility, 46, 188, 249, 516
casinos. *See* gaming
Catholicism, 155–6, 189–90; Catholic school boards, 156
childcare, xvi, 26, 29, 79, 82–3, 213–16, 218–19, 223, 230–1, 236–40, 258, 286
China, 54, 81, 105, 111, 205
Chrétien, Jean, 56, 108, 160, 189. *See also* Liberal Party
Chrysler, 54, 103, 112–16, 119, 120–1, 124–5, 295, 301n2
class: creative class, 80, 82, 93, 95–7; Franco-Ontarian working class, 156, 166n7; gap between union and non-union working class, 522; industrial working class, 275; middle class, 12, 15, 286, 288, 297, 406, 448, 506, 510; ruling class, 13, 31, 134–5, 248, 275–6, 313; urban working class, 502; working class, 5–6, 12, 94, 163, 166n7, 188, 288, 461–86; working class experience, 461, 471, 485; working class in Northern Ontario, 141, 146, 152, 156–8, 166n7; working class participation in participatory budgeting, 503–4, 514, 517; working class political mobilization, 522–4. *See also* unions
class struggle, 6, 82, 94, 156–7, 268, 403, 415, 465–6, 504, 541; from above, 7, 20, 24, 30, 288; war on teachers, 400, 403–5, 414. *See also* Common Sense Revolution; Days of Action; unions
climate change, xvi, 24, 35, 125, 162, 196, 204, 259, 267. *See also* environment
coalitions, 7, 32–3, 481, 502, 516, 531; *25in5* coalition, 322; alternative budgeting, 512, 518; anti-poverty coalition, 322–4, 329; business coalitions, 285–6; *Cho!ces* coalition (Winnipeg), 512; East Toronto Community Coalition, 95; Equal Pay Coalition, 219; Fairbnb, 97; Guelph Neighbourhood Support Coalition, 512; "One Ontario" coalition, xiii, xv; Ontario Coalition for Better Child Care, 238; social movement and labour coalitions, xvii, 95–7, 268, 339, 374, 414–15, 461–2, 481, 512, 525–6, 530–3, 535, 539–40, 541, 543n2, 543n3, 544n6, 545n15; Public Services Coalition, 526–9, 545n16; Working Families Coalition, 294, 302n8, 535–6. *See also* Colour of Poverty campaign; Days of Action; Fight for $15 and Fairness; Ontario Coalition Against Poverty; Ontario Health Coalition
colonialism, xiii, xvii, xix, 4, 132–9, 141, 149, 151–4, 161, 166n10, 167n13, 167n17, 168, 171n37, 239, 423–52, 471–2, 481, 485, 515; reconciliation, 429, 451
Colour of Poverty campaign, 461, 481, 483–5
commercialization, 21–7, 223, 263, 294–6. *See also* privatization
commodities, 7–8, 18, 24, 47–8, 52–3, 55–6, 80, 84, 141–7, 168n23, 169n25, 204, 207, 434
Common Sense Revolution, xiii–xv, 20–2, 31–2, 35, 90, 233, 286–8, 367, 386, 427, 528, 541, 545n12; *Common Sense Revolution Manifesto*, 20, 223
communism, 515; anti-communism, 158. *See also* socialism
Confederation, 4, 103, 106, 109, 134–5, 189, 195, 200, 431; Ontario's traditional role within, 118, 207, 209n2
conservatism, xiii; neo-conservatism, 501, 526; religious, 156; social, xvi, 233, 241. *See also* Conservative Party (UK); Conservative Party of Canada
Conservative Party (UK), 221–3, 401
Conservative Party of Canada, 3, 31, 63, 106–8, 117–21, 124–5, 152–4, 168n19, 189, 194, 196–9, 204–5, 257–8, 434, 446, 486n1, 519n4
contracting-out, xv, 15, 21, 28, 30, 221, 257, 264, 339, 469. *See also* privatization
cooperatives, 255, 379
courts, 153, 167n13, 190, 209n5, 235, 259, 339, 369, 397, 414, 427–8, 432–6, 442, 446, 452; Ontario Court of Appeal, 155;

Ontario Superior Court, 36n8, 152; US Supreme Court, 336
criminal justice, 205, 238, 280, 424, 427, 430, 438, 466, 483–4, 531. *See also* courts; policing; prison

Davis, Bill, 13, 17, 117, 216–19, 230, 280, 365, 530. *See also* Progressive Conservative Party of Ontario
daycare. *See* childcare
Days of Action, 22, 32, 158, 287, 522–543, 545n13
deindustrialization, 50–6, 104–9. *See also* manufacturing
demonstrations. *See* protest
Department of Mines and Northern Affairs. *See* Ministry of Northern Development and Mines
deregulation, xiv, 17, 27, 45–9, 56–7, 105, 147, 159, 278, 286, 367–70, 423, 451, 471, 518n3
disability, 461, 499, 508; benefits, 320–3, 325–8; Ontario Disability Support Plan (ODSP), 259, 315, 326. *See also* ability
diversity, xv, 93, 134, 219, 231, 463, 531
domestic violence. *See* women: violence against
domestic workers, 49, 64, 285, 481
Drummond Report, 28, 91, 295, 330, 381

ecological imperialism, 426, 439
economic recession, 15, 18–19, 50, 59, 166, 193, 277, 280, 282–3, 289, 366, 525–7, 540; Great Recession (2008–09), 7, 25, 53, 55, 103, 112–13, 189, 198, 206, 247, 262–7, 295, 300, 311, 324–6; Great Depression, 12, 191
education: commercialization of, 11, 295; elementary, 396; expansion of college and university system, 14, 399; secondary schools, 396, 399, 410, 430; school boards, 21, 27, 156, 218, 220, 256, 294, 395–7, 400, 405–8, 414, 545n14; post-secondary, xv, 36n6, 88, 192, 238, 254, 294, 403, 430, 513; university and college workers, 24, 415; vocational training, 18, 230, 399. *See also* unions: teachers' unions
elites, 448, 450, 494, 502, 514; economic, 3, 14, 155, 189, 276; francophone, 156; "liberal," 30; media, 31; political, xiii–xiv, xviii, 31, 35; "Toronto," 95. *See also* class

Employment Insurance (EI), 63, 160, 169n31, 197, 199, 209n7, 319, 484
energy policy, 11, 24, 33, 103, 192, 359–71, 373–88; green energy, 24–5, 33, 204, 259, 359–62, 364–70, 373–86
environment, 134, 139, 149, 159, 162–3, 172n48, 173n52, 216, 255, 259–61, 267–8, 364–9, 371–2, 378, 384–5, 387, 388n5, 426, 443–7, 513; air pollution, 260, 369, 371; carbon emissions, 29, 70, 147, 204, 208, 260, 265, 369, 444; effect of mining on, 147, 445; environmentally friendly industry, xv, 29, 109, 375–6; environmental organizations, 33, 35, 148, 261, 361, 365, 373–4, 427, 444, 498, 539; environmental regulation, 17, 26–7, 147, 152, 204, 223–34, 249, 253, 260; political ecology, 438; toxic waste, 162, 439; environmental racism, 439. *See also* ecological imperialism
equalization payments, 191–6, 198, 206
European Union (EU), 204, 381, 493
Eves, Ernie, 118, 195, 210n14, 336, 344, 370, 394–5, 410, 427. *See also* Progressive Conservative Party of Ontario
evictions, 446, 509
exports, 10, 13, 22, 43, 53–6, 79–81, 92–3, 109–10, 113, 138–64, 196n25, 275, 296, 363. *See also* extractive sector; manufacturing
extractive sector, 12–16, 43, 78, 109, 134, 139, 147–9, 153, 161–3, 172n49, 173n1, 252, 275, 443–5, 452, 471; oil and gas, 13, 58, 109, 113, 142, 144, 146–7, 192–3, 204, 207, 359, 373, 376–8, 387n1; resistance to, 35, 152. *See also* environment; exports; mining

farming. *See* agriculture
federalism, xvii, 31, 187–208, 250, 209n1, 268n2
feminism, 212–13, 225–6, 228–9, 232, 233, 238, 240. *See also* feminist political economy; women
feminist political economy (FPE), 212–35
Fight for $15 and Fairness, 34, 298, 482, 485, 538. *See also* precarity; wages
First Nations, 4, 35, 130–40, 147–54, 159, 161, 163–4, 164n1, 165n6, 166n6, 167n13, 168n19, 171n36, 200–3, 208, 267–8, 327–8, 423–53, 469, 471, 480, 502, 512. *See also* Caledonia conflict; colonialism; ecological imperialism; environment:

environmental racism; Idle No More;
Ipperwash conflict; land; Métis people;
race; reserve system
Ford, Doug, xiv–xvi, 4, 30–5, 70, 94–8,
125, 151, 161–2, 208, 240–1, 264–5, 268,
277, 301, 330, 354, 355n7, 360–1, 385, 395,
414–15, 418, 423–4, 447–52, 462, 485–6,
537–8, 545n17. *See also* Progressive
Conservative Party of Ontario
Ford, Rob, 495, 506–7
Ford Motor Company, 103, 112, 114–17, 119,
121, 124, 301n2
Fordism, 12–13, 533
France, 48, 109, 132, 166n9, 226, 431; French
settlers, 132, 134, 137, 431; New France,
434
free trade, 5–7, 20–2, 32, 49, 52, 103–26, 159,
204–5, 275, 282, 495, 525, 545n15
French language, 171n40, 189; French
school boards, 155–6
French-Canadian nation, 198

gaming, 23, 27, 95–8, 143, 208. *See
also* Ontario Lottery and Gaming
Corporation
gender democracy, 215, 229, 232–3, 240–1
General Motors (GM), 54, 103, 112–16, 119–
21, 123–5, 301n2
gig-economy. *See* sharing economy
globalization, 3, 16, 32–3, 44–8, 145–6,
156, 160, 163, 188, 403, 485, 503. *See also*
anti-globalization movement
gold, 136, 143, 147, 162, 167n14, 169n28
Golden Horseshoe (region), 105, 108–9, 122
Great War. *See* war: World War I
Green Party of Ontario (GPO), 380, 387n2
Greenbelt (protected area), 260–2, 269n4;
Greenbelt Act (2005), 260
gross domestic product (GDP), 58–9, 61, 77,
269n6, 283, 288–9, 355n3
guaranteed annual income, 29, 311, 324–30
Guelph, 86, 122, 493, 498, 505, 510–2, 514,
516, 519n7

Hamilton, 51, 55, 86–7, 122, 257, 261, 321,
349, 352, 493, 529, 530
Harper, Stephen, 125, 126n1, 137. *See also*
Conservative Party of Canada

Harris, Mike, xiii–xv, 4, 19–26, 30–2, 36n4,
36n5, 49, 56, 63, 90, 106–8, 116–25, 126n5,
147, 158–60, 169n27, 170n32, 170n35, 189,
194–5, 201, 201n14, 207, 212, 223–35, 241,
254–9, 276, 286–300, 314–23, 327–9, 336,
342, 344, 367–70, 388n4, 394–415, 423–8,
479, 495, 505–13, 523–4, 528–35, 541–3,
545n16
Haudenosaunee Confederacy, 202, 431,
439–41
healthcare, xv, 9, 23–9, 74, 84–9, 116,
142–5, 150, 153, 192–7, 206, 210n13, 213,
219–23, 231, 239, 251, 254–6, 309, 334–54,
355n1–3, 355n7, 482–4, 513; benefits, 326,
330; devolution to municipalities, 256;
Indigenous health, 429–30; preventative,
79; privatization of, 27, 34, 90, 95, 234,
239; mental health, 196–7, 216, 236–7, 429
Honda, 110, 115
housing, 11, 17–18, 26–9, 47, 53–7, 87, 94–7,
153, 163, 219, 223, 230, 234–51, 255–9, 263,
267–8, 314–30, 463, 466, 482–4, 505–12.
See also Toronto Community Housing
Corporation
Hudak, Tim, xv, 34, 536. *See also* Progressive Conservative Party of Ontario
human capital, 24, 87, 92, 94, 314, 317–18,
329, 405, 465, 468
human trafficking, 239
hydro, xv, 13, 35, 139, 141, 166n9, 362–87,
432, 443; hydro rates, 30, 383–4; Hydro
One, 23, 29, 263, 297, 369, 382–5, 387–
8n3; Ontario Hydro, 13, 21, 24, 35, 138,
286, 362–8, 370–3, 384–6, 544n11. *See
also* energy policy

Idle No More, 32, 35, 153, 428, 445, 481, 495
immigrants, 44, 62–4, 77, 87–9, 96, 224, 231,
339, 342, 452n1, 462, 466–71, 481–3, 487,
494–5, 508. *See also* migration
indentured labour. *See* slavery
Indigenous people. *See* First Nations
inequality, 213, 248, 277, 399, 412, 424–5,
437, 495, 499, 504, 543n3; economic,
78, 84, 94, 233, 496, 543; gender, 230–3,
239–40; income inequality, 45–8, 62–70,
89–90, 220, 267, 318, 450; Indigenous
inequality, 450–2; in Latin America, 515;

racial inequality, 463–7, 471, 478–80, 483–6; regional, 159–63
information technology, 43–44, 47–56, 230, 235, 239
infrastructure, xvi, 8, 10–17, 23–7, 69, 90, 126, 161, 172n48, 203, 249–52, 254–67, 269n5, 295–7, 360, 376, 382, 432, 441, 446
insurance, 47, 58–9, 61, 63, 69, 85–9, 142, 145, 192–3, 210n9, 210n10; public auto insurance, 19, 253. *See also* Employment Insurance
intellectual property. *See* property: intellectual property
interest rates, 15, 22, 26, 31, 47, 56, 110, 267
Ipperwash conflict, 200–3, 425–8, 441, 443
Islamophobia, 480

jail. *See* prison

Keynesianism 4–6, 13, 120, 163, 214–18, 247, 277–9, 286–8, 299, 495, 514, 533; "emergency Keynesianism," 25. *See also* welfare state
Kingston, 86, 545n13; forced amalgamation of, 257
Knights of Labour, 542

labour movement. *See* unions
Lake Ontario, 109, 201, 280, 442
land: Canadian and Ontario control of, 135–7, 190, 200, 202–3, 426, 430–4; capitalist accumulation and, 440, 443, 448, 450, 451; colonial drive for control of resources and land, 135–8, 161, 203, 438, 443, 451; Crown land, 138, 431, 434, 444; dispossession of Indigenous peoples from, 135–6, 426, 430, 438, 441, 448; environmentally sensitive lands, 260; European land enclosures, 5; farmland, 261, 268n3, 269n4; Indigenous land claims, 4, 164, 200–3, 426, 432–5, 441–4; Indigenous land-based economies, 140, 438–40, 444; Indigenous land rights, 148–9, 161, 164, 428, 434, 444, 447; industrial land, 92, 96; land area of Northern Ontario, 130, 132, 164n1; land transfer tax, 252, 259; land surveying, 298; land-use planning and regulation, 91, 132, 147–8, 254, 261–2; Living Legacy land use strategy, 147; privatizing of, 135, 448; resistance to resource extraction on Indigenous lands, 139, 152–3, 349; settler nationalist bonds to, 448; treaty settlements, 200–1, 431, 439–40; urban sprawl, 260; wetlands, 438. *See also* Caledonia conflict; environment: environmental racism; Ipperwash conflict; property; reserve system
land-value capture, 266
lean education, 394–415
lean production, 28, 105, 278, 282, 299–301, 508. *See also* lean education; manufacturing
liberal democracy, xiv, 9, 31–2, 218, 402, 437, 449. *See also* liberalism; social democracy
Liberal Party of Canada, 3, 5, 63, 258, 518n3; Canadian Auto Workers union support for, 107–8, 123; climate change policy, 204; crime policy, 205; and Declaration on the Rights of Indigenous Peoples, 154; and federal transfers to provinces, 199, 254–5; role in downloading social welfare policies, 189; support for auto industry, 107–8, 118, 124; support for private sector growth, 15; Unemployment Insurance reform, 160
liberalism: conceptions of citizenship, 402, 411; "inclusive liberalism," 329–30, 449; liberal democratic institutions, xviii, 218; liberal democratic states, 9; social policy thinkers, 319; "liberal" markets, 6, 46; liberal welfare states, 314; political system of, 32; "social liberal" faction of, 324–7; tensions with neoliberalism on issues of energy policy, 360; ties of labour movement to, 158. *See also* Liberal Party
liberalization: of employment protections, 50, 241; financial, 57; of economy and state, 6, 110, 262; of trade, 234, 248, 278; under NAFTA, 52. *See also* deregulation; free trade
libertarianism, 424
lobbying, 32, 95, 265, 269n4, 374, 414, 501, 543n3

Local Health Integration Networks (LHINs), 342, 345–8, 350, 352–4. *See also* healthcare
lockouts, 157, 285, 301, 403
London, 86, 104, 107, 531, 533, 545n13
low income assistance. *See* social assistance

Manitoba, 135, 150, 166n7–8, 167n12, 200, 335n5
manufacturing, 12–13, 89–92, 103–26, 252, 522, 540; branch-plant production, 13–16, 104, 275; capital mobility in, 81; continental integration of, 107, 280; decline of in Canada, 5, 12, 104, 126n2; decline in North America, 47, 51, 105, 278; decline of in Ontario, 52, 56, 69, 108, 112, 123, 195, 198, 290, 349, 374, 377, 527; employment conditions in, 282–3, 295; employment in GTA, 259; green technology, 375, increased debt-to-equity leverage ratios in, 58; "intensive," 44; job loss in, 15, 43, 51–3, 55, 84, 104, 112–14, 162, 283, 289–90, 320, 524, 538–9; lack of development strategy for, 98; low-end, 44; "manufacturing condition" on forest exports, 138–9; manufacturing workers support for NDP, 122; Ontario as low-cost manufacturing platform, 309, 313; Ontario as Canada's "manufacturing heartland," 43, 103, 106; primary manufacturing, 145, 172n51, 279; protectionism for, 105; provincial and federal policy, 109, 117–26, 161, 296, 301n1; racialization of manufacturing work, 473, 477; rebirth of, 207; restaurants and hotels classification as, 78–9; secondary manufacturing, 172n49, 279, 282; wood and paper, 146, 279. *See also* automotive industry; free trade; lean production
Martin, Paul, 108, 123, 199, 258, 513. *See also* Liberal Party of Canada
McGuinty, Dalton, xiii–xvi, 4, 23–34, 36n6, 49, 90, 107–24, 130, 170n35, 189, 195, 201, 233–41, 258, 276, 288–312, 319–28, 334–6, 341–54, 355n7, 360–1, 371–3, 380–6, 394–407, 414, 423–33, 446, 480, 495, 499, 524, 538. *See also* Ontario Liberal Party
media, 18, 31, 103, 146, 156–8, 164, 334–5, 353, 483, 494, 506, 513, 528, 531, 537

medicare. *See* healthcare
Métis people, 132, 137, 165n1, 200, 203, 423, 428–9, 433, 452, 453n1, 464
Mexico, 52–3
migration, 5, 13–14, 63–4, 87, 148–9, 155, 171n39, 190, 206, 250, 462–8, 493, 517. *See also* immigrants
military, 136–7, 159, 278, 426, 431
militia. *See* military
mining, 27, 49, 52, 54, 80, 89, 132–6, 138–9, 141–8, 151–4, 157, 161–2, 171n47, 280, 432, 439, 443–7. *See also* Ring of Fire
Ministry of Aboriginal Affairs. *See* Ministry of Indigenous Relations and Reconciliation
Ministry of Citizenship, Culture and Recreation, 224
Ministry of Economic Development and Trade, 24, 118, 126n5
Ministry of Education, 396, 405, 411, 545n14
Ministry of Enterprise, Opportunity and Innovation. *See* Ministry of Economic Development and Trade
Ministry of Finance, 228, 324, 496–7, 499–500
Ministry of Health and Long-Term Care, 346–7
Ministry of Indigenous Relations and Reconciliation, 429, 451
Ministry of Industry, Trade, and Technology, 17
Ministry of Labour, 216–17, 282, 287–8, 291
Ministry of Natural Resources, 95, 169n30
Ministry of Northern Affairs and Mines. *See* Ministry of Northern Development and Mines
Ministry of Northern Development and Mines, 151
Ministry of Public Infrastructure Renewal, 23
Ministry of Research, Innovation and Science, 24
Ministry of State for Urban Affairs (federal ministry), 250–1
Ministry of the Status of Women, 212, 217, 224, 237, 239–40. *See also* Ministry of Citizenship, Culture and Recreation
Ministry of Training, Colleges and Universities, 24

Mulroney, Brian, 109, 120. *See also* Conservative Party of Canada
multinational corporations, 45–51, 104
municipalities, 21, 92, 132, 136, 139, 163, 171n36, 172n48, 172n50, 203, 218, 220, 223, 247–68, 269n5
mutual funds, 57, 60

nationalism, 188, 505
New Brunswick, 189, 335
New Democratic Party (federal party), 3, 107–8. *See also* Alberta New Democratic Party; Ontario New Democratic Party; social democracy
New Public Management (NPM), xv, 20–2, 36n2, 212–16, 221–40
Newfoundland and Labrador, 193–4, 210n12
Nishnawbe Aski Nation (NAN), 154, 161, 444
North American Free Trade Agreement (NAFTA). *See* free trade
North-West Territories, 134
Nova Scotia, 189, 193–4, 210n12
nuclear power, 209n3, 360, 366, 370–4, 377–8, 382–5; accidents, 55, 364, 366, 381; anti-nuclear advocates, 365; Atomic Energy of Canada, 204, 381; Bruce Nuclear Facility, 366, 369, 372, 377, 382, 388n4; CANDU reactors, 204; cost overruns, 363–5, 376, 381, 384; as export-oriented industry, 363; Liberal-NDP criticism of, 365; Nuclear Asset Optimization Plan (NAOP), 369; Pickering Nuclear Generating Station, 366, 369, 372, 382; phasing out in favour of "soft" path technology, 360, 364; Ontario's reliance on, 204, 372, 379, 385; waste disposal, 162. *See also* energy policy; environment
Nunavut, 137

Oakville, 107, 114, 122, 380
Occupy movement, 32, 495, 537
omnibus bills, 20, 519n4
"one province" ideology, xiii, vx, xviii, 7, 12–13, 16, 18–19, 23, 27–35
Ontario Coalition Against Poverty (OCAP), 322, 481

Ontario Disability Support Plan (ODSP). *See* disability
Ontario Federation of Labour (OFL), 32–4, 321, 513, 527–30, 533–7, 544n11, 545n16, 545n17. *See also* unions
Ontario Health Coalition, 34, 95, 347–9. *See also* healthcare
Ontario Liberal Party, 22–35, 36n4, 334–6, 387n2, 388n7–8; Aboriginal policy, 424–30, 433, 442–52; budgets, 495, 499–500; changes to electoral districts, 170n35; education policy, 394–7, 401–11, 414–15; energy policy, 359–61, 365–6, 371–84, 386; environmental policy, 173n53; as "French party," 155; healthcare policy, 193, 195, 334–7, 340–8, 350–4, 355n7; labour market flexibilization, 49–50; Liberal-NDP Accord, 16, 280–3, 365; loss of support in Northern Ontario in 2018 election, 150–1; mining corporation donations to, 169n27; neoliberal policy, xiii–xvi, 4–7, 106–9, 189, 207, 233, 239, 258, 262, 276–7, 423, 541; Northern Ontario policy, 130, 135–6, 161; poverty reduction policy, 319–28, 480; "progressive competitiveness" program, 16–19, 288–300, 315; "strategic voting" for, 302n8; support for auto industry, 117–25; women's policy, 217–19, 233, 235–9, 241, 242n10
Ontario Lottery and Gaming Corporation, 23, 95–6, 143. *See also* gaming
Ontario New Democratic Party (ONDP), xvii, 18–19, 94, 275, 283–6, 315, 538; adoption of "third way" position, xv–xvi, 5; anti-poverty policy, 325, 329; anti-scab provisions, 287, 292, 299; austerity under, 19–20, 285–6; auto towns' traditional support for, 122–5; business hostility to, 285; education policy, 395; energy policy, 366, 380, 386; increasing in social spending by, 17–18, 253; inept campaigns, 27–8; labour policy changes in 1990s, 298, 525–6; labour support for, 528, 534–7, 545n16; Liberal-NDP Accord, 16, 280–3, 365; mining corporation donations to, 169n27; neoliberal policy implementation, 160, 275–6, 300; Northern Ontario support for, 150–1; Social Contract,

19, 286, 522, 527, 544n5; support for alternative budgets, 513, 535; support for auto industry, 117; support for minimum wage increases, 320-1; women's policy, 217-19, 224. *See also* Alberta New Democratic Party; New Democratic Party (federal party); social democracy
Ontario Provincial Police (OPP), 136, 201-2, 426-8, 432, 441-3, 530. *See also* policing
Ontario Public Sector Employees Union (OPSEU), 95, 526, 530-1, 535-6; support for NDP, 536
Ontario Public Service (OPS), 20-1, 220, 226, 239, 280
Ontario Secondary School Teachers' Federation (OSSTF), 406, 526, 530, 537; strategic voting by, 537. *See also* unions: teachers' unions
Ontario Works (OW), 259, 309, 315, 326. *See also* social assistance
opioid drug crisis, 354; Ford Government opposition to safe-injection sites, 208
organized labour. *See* unions
ORNGE air ambulance service, 342
Oshawa, 86, 107, 114, 116, 121-2; capture by Conservatives from NDP, 108, 122-3
Ottawa/Ottawa-Gatineau: employment and, 86, 148; equalization payments, 193, 206; health and education spending, 192; interventionist approach to auto industry, 106, 117, 120, 125; land claims, 201, 442; Liberal governments in, 195; migration from Northern Ontario to, 149; monetary and banking policy centered in, 25; municipal social assistance, 316; Ottawa-Gatineau region, 78, 169, 257; as part of Canada's research "triangle," 58; participatory budgeting in, 493; preferential treatment for Ontario manufacturing, 103, 120; relationship with Ontario provincial government, 117-18, 120-1, 125, 206, 433, 446; responsibility for Indian Affairs, 431-2; Royal Ottawa Hospital, 336, 338; seat of federal government, 108, 118; supply management systems, 204
Ottawa River, 130, 165n3, 166n10

Ottawa Valley, 431, 434
outsourcing, 49, 68, 113, 159, 264, 400. *See also* manufacturing

part-time work, 44, 52-4, 60-7, 91, 142, 145, 218, 222, 238, 276, 288, 290, 298-9, 341, 348, 466, 470, 495. *See also* precarity
patriarchy, 423. *See also* women
pay equity, 17, 216, 218-21, 223, 230-7, 239, 281, 286, 298-9, 348, 350, 461, 470, 479, 525, 527, 531, 544n9. *See also* women
pension funds, 44, 47, 57-8, 60, 87; sale of bonds to, 57; public sector, 58. *See also* pensions
pensions, 34, 47, 49, 197, 209n9, 238, 284, 296, 340; Ontario Pension Plan, 197, 238, 297; for precarious workers, 62; private pension plans, 197; two-tier pension systems, 171n43; workers' loss of, 61. *See also* Canada Pension Plan; pension funds
Peterborough, 86, 104; as regional service centre, 87, 95; public hospital, 339; Day of Action Protest in, 545n13
Peterson, David, 4, 16-18, 109, 155, 218-19, 253, 281-3, 294, 296, 300, 315, 365-6, 427. *See also* Ontario Liberal Party
pharmacare, xvi, 29, 259, 319-20, 326, 330, 342-3
pharmaceutical industry, 25, 56, 59, 342-4, 354
policing, 21, 92, 116, 220, 256, 278, 448-9, 531; "carding," 486, 487n8; North-West Mounted Police (NWMP), 136; opposition to racial biases in, 35; private police, 136; Royal Canadian Mounted Police (RCMP), 441; Toronto Anti-Violence Intervention Strategy (TAVIS), 486. *See also* Ontario Provincial Police (OPP)
populism, xv-xvi, 300, 528
Porto Alegre, 495, 501-8, 514, 517
poverty, 61, 67, 144, 153, 250, 268, 292, 309-30, 331n1-2, 324, 462, 469, 502, 508, 538; anti-poverty organizations, 33, 228, 267, 325, 481, 516; food banks, 309-10, 316; in Northern Ontario, 148, 162; racialization of, 424, 438, 462, 466, 471-4, 477-8, 483-

486, 487n4; reduction of, 18, 25–9, 230, 234–7, 254, 291, 314, 321–6, 329, 480, 513. *See also* Colour of Poverty Campaign; inequality; Ontario Coalition Against Poverty; precarity; wages

precarity, 5, 44–5, 61, 64–5, 84, 213, 222, 231, 237–9, 276, 288–92, 298–301, 409, 415, 461, 466–478, 481–5, 487n6, 495, 522, 538, 543. *See also* part-time work; poverty

prison, 152–3, 159, 205, 259, 430, 439. *See also* criminal justice

privatization, xiv, 14–15, 21–30, 34–5, 49, 77, 90–1, 95–7, 148, 159, 195–6, 212, 221–3, 232–4, 249, 257, 263–8, 278, 286–8, 297–9, 336, 370, 414, 424, 448, 469, 501, 504, 519n3; of Indigenous lands, 135; "re-privatization," 15, 214. *See also* commercialization; public-private partnerships (P3s)

Progressive Conservative Party of Alberta/ United Conservative Party (Alberta), 197, 204, 208

Progressive Conservative Party of Ontario, 4, 16, 34, 207, 210n14, 242n10, 387n2, 394–410, 447, 495; capture of traditional NDP strongholds by PCs, 108, 123–4, 151; changes to electoral districts, 170n35; education policy, 394–410, 414–15; employment equity programs, 479–80; energy policy, 362–5, 367–70, 380, 385; as "English party," 155; environmental policy, 147–8, 162; healthcare policy, 340, 354; inept campaigns, 27; intervention to support private sector growth, 15; labour and employment policy; 287–8, 293–9, 301, 536–8; lack of industrial strategy, 125; lack of intervention into auto industry under Harris, 106–7, 118, 121; mining corporation donations to, 169n27; neoliberal policy, 7, 14–15, 22, 30–1, 63, 70, 189, 194, 208, 264–5, 276, 286, 462, 508–9, 514, 518, 523–4; Northern resource development, 161; political domination of Ontario by, 252, 280; poverty reduction policy, 311–19, 328–30; pursuit of public-private partnerships, 242n8; reform of Workers Compensation, 160; relationship with First Nations, 423–8; right populism, xiv, xvi, 94–5; support for auto industry, 117; tax reform, 150, 254; view that social assistance created individual dependency on the state, 315; women's policy, 216–40. *See also* Common Sense Revolution; conservatism; Days of Action; Saskatchewan Party

property: corporate property rights, 33, 135, 188, 248, 278; division of property in divorce, 218; First Nations claims over entitlement to, 200; Indian Act property rules, 432; intellectual property, 25, 295; property taxes, 171, 209n2, 251–2, 254, 257, 260, 264–7, 512; union access to company property, 285. *See also* land; rights: property

protest, 7, 22, 32–5, 49, 95, 152, 200–2, 287, 349, 414, 427–8, 436, 442–8, 486, 487n8, 493–5, 503, 522, 528–9, 534, 543n1. *See also* Days of Action

public consultation, 25, 153, 202, 216, 219, 228, 235, 239, 242n8, 249, 296, 321, 326, 446; budget consultation, 496–501, 505–7, 511; lack of, 20, 237, 436–7, 444

public-private partnerships (P3s), xv, 11, 23–4, 90–1, 95, 221, 234, 242n8, 258, 276, 297, 336–40, 344, 354, 355n4–5

Quebec, 63, 120, 125, 154–5, 166n7, 173n53, 189–90, 196–8, 201, 204–6, 209n4, 285, 323, 431, 434

race: affirmative action, 479–80; anti-Indigenous racism, 430–3, 437, 450; Anti-Racism Directorate, 29, 480, 486; African slavery, 5; and labour market participation, 474–5, 480–3; multiracial refugees from American Revolution, 431; racial biases, 35; racial consciousness, 478; racial injustice, 164, 399, 450, 471, 481; racial minorities, 225, 339, 462–8, 473–9, 483–5, 486n2, 495, 502; racial stratification, 4, 342, 399, 463–5, 466–71, 474–8, 480–6, 487n7; racialization of poverty, 466, 477–8, 483–5, 487n4; racialized immigrants, 462; racialized

women, 231, 474; racialized work, 5, 463–8, 470–2, 477–81, 485; racialized workers, 77, 83, 98, 342, 461, 466–81, 485, 494; union participation and, 481–2; role in class formation, 470–2, 481. *See also* Colour of Poverty campaign; First Nations; immigrants; inequality; migration; policing
racism. *See* race
Rae, Bob, 4, 16–19, 31, 158, 218, 225, 253, 268n2, 283–6, 294–300, 366, 427, 446, 522–9, 544n4. *See also* Ontario New Democratic Party
religion, 412
renewable energy. *See* energy policy: green energy
rent controls, 18, 281
replacement workers, 18, 49, 157, 285, 287, 292, 299, 301n3, 527
reproductive labour. *See* social reproduction
reproductive rights, 219, 240, 525
Republican Party (US), 118, 330
reserve army of labour, 81, 290, 465. *See also* unemployment
reserve system, 136–9, 148, 168n19, 190, 200–3, 426, 430–4, 441–3, 462, 469
rights, 18, 27, 151–6, 164, 180, 189–90, 209n4, 214–15, 242n11, 314–16, 329, 444–8; Charter of Rights and Freedoms, 36n8, 479; Indigenous, 151–4, 161, 201, 268, 432–4, 439–40, 444–7, 451; property, 13, 33, 188–9, 209n4, 278, 298–301, 397, 423, 441, 453n2; tenant, 97; workers', 49 190, 234, 276–7, 285, 293, 296, 470, 481, 525–7. *See also* land: Indigenous land rights
Ring of Fire, 27, 161–2, 439, 445–8. *See also* extractive sector; mining

Saskatchewan Party, 197, 204
Saskatchewan, 135, 166n8, 206, 208
scabs. *See* replacement workers
Second World War. *See* war: World War II
self-employment, 44, 61–8, 140–5, 168n20, 286, 290
Service Employees International Union (SEIU), 308n8, 349, 536–7, 544n11
sharing economy, 77, 81, 83, 94, 97

slavery, 5, 467–8
social assistance, 21–33, 63, 85–9, 142–5, 170n32, 193, 198, 210, 219, 231, 249, 251–4, 284–6, 296, 309–30, 331n1; child benefits, xvi, 26–7, 210n16, 213, 218, 223, 235–7, 318–28. *See also* Ontario Works (OW); poverty
social democracy: crisis of, 524–8, 533; domination of labour movement by, 158; European, 19, 515; social democratic critique of welfare state, 213–14; social democratic politicians, 505, 515; "third way," 19–20, 158; and the NDP, xv, 3, 525–8; union reengagement with, 524, 544n5. *See also* New Democratic Party
social justice, 17, 28, 32, 218, 247, 484, 502–6, 514–18, 519n5, 531, 539, 543n2, 544n6
social liberalism, 324–7, 330
social movements, xvii, 15, 32–6, 82–3, 90, 97, 153, 212, 216, 225–32, 238–41, 256–7, 267–8, 384, 399, 415, 428, 463, 483–5, 493–6, 503–5, 515–18, 529–32, 537–8, 541, 544n6
social reproduction, xiv, 82–3, 213–15, 222, 329, 482, 518n3
socialism, 18, 515; parliamentary socialism, 526; socialist movement, 5; socialist parties, 511. *See also* communism; social democracy
sovereignty: Canadian, 158, 434; of Indigenous peoples, 134–9, 147–8, 164, 167n13, 433–4, 472; Ontarian, 190. *See also* land
St Catharines, 86, 107, 114, 123, 167n13
steel industry, 34, 43, 49–55, 104, 107–12, 122, 139, 280, 527. *See also* Hamilton; United Steel Workers (USW)
strikes, 22, 32, 43–54, 67, 91, 157, 171n43, 172n44, 277–8, 280, 285–7, 293, 299, 301n3, 403–4, 415, 523, 529–34, 540
subsidies, xv, 8–16, 21–4, 119, 124–5, 161, 167n17, 223, 249, 262, 266, 335
suburbs, 20, 87, 98
Sudbury, 86, 130, 143, 146–51, 157, 164n1, 166n10, 168n22, 169n31, 171n42, 172n50; forced amalgamation of, 156, 163, 257, 445, 545n13
support for NDP, 536–7, 545n16

taxes, 10–30, 36n9, 44–6, 55–60, 124, 135–6, 161, 171n36, 188, 190–5, 209n2, 209n8, 210n10, 210n16, 248, 251–67, 269n6, 276–8, 299–300, 310, 317, 324, 335–7, 355n2, 447–8, 512–14, 540, 545n14; anti-tax populism, xv; cuts and incentives, xvi, 11, 15–16, 20–30, 49, 53, 69–70, 106, 125, 146, 204–5, 234, 240, 286, 292–6, 301, 318, 328, 344, 354, 426, 451, 494–6, 518n3, 519n3; General Sales Tax (GST), 19; increases, xvi, 17–19, 150, 207, 285, 327. *See also* subsidies; taxpayers

taxpayers, 90, 121, 195, 198, 221, 223, 269n6, 320, 496

temporary employment agencies, 69, 292, 299, 323, 469–70. *See also* temporary workers

Temporary Foreign Worker (TFW) program, 64, 463–4, 470, 487n3

temporary workers, 52–3, 61–8, 91, 222, 276, 290–1, 298–9, 463, 466, 469–70. *See also* temporary employment agencies; Temporary Foreign Worker (TFW) program

Thunder Bay, 86–7, 143, 149, 154, 164n1, 165n3, 166n10, 168n22, 169n31, 445, 545n13

Timmins, 136, 146, 157, 203

Tories. *See* Conservative Party of Canada

Toronto Community Housing Corporation, 505–11, 516

Toronto District Labour Council, 96, 540

Trudeau, Justin, 109, 121, 154, 196–7, 205–8, 518n. *See also* Liberal Party

Trump, Donald, 122, 125, 205, 485

Tyendinaga, 440, 442

unemployment, 15, 44, 48–51, 61–3, 68, 143–4, 148, 156–7, 163, 169n31, 173n51, 197–8, 209n7, 267, 279–83, 289, 310, 313, 319, 324, 331n1, 430, 462, 466, 470–5; youth unemployment, 17. *See also* Employment Insurance (EI)

unemployment insurance. *See* Employment Insurance (EI)

uneven development, 8, 10, 77, 84, 94, 97–8

Unifor, 33, 51, 124, 158, 536–7. *See also* Canadian Auto Workers (CAW)

Union of Ontario Indians (Anishinabek Nation), 154

unions, 14, 18, 24, 33, 123, 125, 158, 219, 301n1, 319, 499, 542n3, 543n2; activism in healthcare, 251, 253; Canadian Labour Congress (CLC), 158; casualization of unionized workforce, 91, 95; collective bargaining, 234, 301n7, 530, 545n14; Conservative government opposition to, 20, 22, 231, 330, 536; decline of, 44, 51–5, 67, 81, 124, 140, 157, 222, 228, 293–4, 313, 322, 481, 522, 543; divisions within labour movement, 34, 158, 522, 527, 532; electoral strategy, 524–43; extra-parliamentary strategies, 35–6, 525, 537–8; and Fordism, 13–15, 43, 66–7; industrial pluralism, 277; labour law reform, 47–9, 97, 219, 276, 280–1, 284–5, 287–8, 292, 299–301, 302n7, 315, 513; low unionization rate in private service sector, 79–80, 92; and nationalism, 105; non-union workers, 26–7, 43, 52–5, 67, 79, 91–2, 230, 275, 278, 288, 342, 540; in Northern Ontario, 141, 148, 154, 157, 159; Ontario's non-union growth model, 44–6, 50, 67, 98, 106, 284; opposition to municipal amalgamation by, 256; opposition to privatization, 338–9, 369; organizing, 18, 67, 91–2, 97, 277–8, 285, 292, 299, 301n4, 322, 399, 481; participation in Ontario Health Coalition, 347–9; participation in Working Families Coalition, 302n8, 536; participation in participatory budgeting, 504, 512, 514, 516, 518; "Pink Paper Group," 528, 533–6, 540; public sector unions, 26–7, 32, 88, 90, 247–8, 516, 525–6, 532; role in municipal politics, 267; social/community unionism, 481–3, 485–6, 525–6, 531, 535, 539–41, 544n6; teachers' unions, xvi, 28, 33, 296, 399, 401, 409, 414–15, 526, 530–1, 537; strategic voting by, 535–7; stratification of union and non-union workers, 62, 67, 108; unionized manufacturing workforce, 5, 107, 280–2. *See also* coalitions; Days of Action; Ontario Federation of Labour (OFL); Ontario Secondary School Teachers' Federation (OSSTF); Unifor; United Food and

Commercial Workers (UFCW); United Steel Workers (USW)
United Food and Commercial Workers (UFCW), 241n5, 302n8, 482, 544n11
United Kingdom. *See* Britain
United States of America, 3, 13–15, 22, 45–8, 51–6, 62–6, 93, 103–13, 116–22, 134–8, 147, 153, 158–60, 169n25, 189, 205, 259, 266, 275, 280–2, 286, 330, 336, 367, 374, 386, 486, 545n15
United Steel Workers (USW), 54, 157–8, 171n43, 172n44, 512, 544n1; raiding, 158; support for NDP, 536
uranium, 439. *See also* nuclear power
urban development and planning, 93–6, 163, 248, 253, 255, 260–1, 263–4, 267, 269n3, 269n4
user fees, 27–8, 193, 234, 252, 257, 264, 266, 512

violence: anti-violence as social right, 315–16; against Indigenous people, 423, 426; fiscal violence of structural adjustment programs, 501; in Indigenous communities, 424, 437–8, 450; workplace conflict and, 277, 530. *See also* criminal justice; policing
Volcker shock, 15

wages, 5, 13–20, 36n7, 43–70, 78–98, 112–14, 124–5, 141, 147–8, 156, 168n18, 168n20, 213, 218, 223, 247–8, 268, 275–80, 284–6, 288–93, 296–8, 301, 309–30, 339–42, 348–9, 423, 453n2, 469–71, 476–85, 494–5, 525–6, 452, 543n1, 544n4; minimum wage, xvi, 18, 21, 25, 33–4, 63–70, 90, 95, 238–40, 275, 284, 287, 292–300, 311–30, 348, 480–2, 484, 538–40; public sector wages, 15, 19, 26–31, 222, 231–4, 239, 246, 257, 262; women's wages, 168n22, 220–2. *See also* Fight for $15 and Fairness
Walkerton water crisis, 264, 270
war: anti-war movement, 537; Cold War, 158; colonial war against Indigenous people, 431; "permanent war," 22; "war on terror," 33; World War I, 4, 135, 138, 155; World War II, 2, 148, 163, 188, 191, 210n9, 210n16, 363, 426
waste management, 21, 91, 142–5, 162, 256, 263, 445. *See also* environment; nuclear energy
welfare programs, 17, 20, 47, 170n32, 188, 193, 197–223, 235, 247, 254, 315–20, 425–8, 433, 436, 451, 482, 486; anti-welfare backlash, 320, 324, 330; welfare-to-work programs, 318, 320. *See also* Ontario Disability Support Plan (ODSP); Ontario Works; social assistance
welfare state, xiii, 5–20, 214–18, 253–4, 314–15, 396, 399–404, 409, 412–14, 415n1, 495, 519n3. *See also* welfare programs
Windsor, 86, 114, 117, 123–4, 539–40, 545n12; as historical NDP bastion, 122. *See also* Workers' Action Centre (Windsor)
women, 35, 44, 62, 77, 84, 87–8, 96, 98, 141, 143, 157, 159, 168n21–2, 212–41, 237–8, 241n2, 241n6, 242n8, 242n12, 279, 339, 342, 348–50, 399, 428–30, 449, 468–79, 485, 494–5, 502–3, 512, 531, 544n9; feminization of poverty, 484; violence against, 218–19, 227, 229, 233–40. *See also* feminism; feminist political economy; patriarchy; pay equity; reproductive rights
Woodstock, 104, 114–15, 120–2
Workers' Action Centre (Toronto) (WAC), 482, 538. *See also* Fight for $15 and Fairness
Workers' Action Centre (Windsor), 482
Workers' Party (Brazil) (Partido dos Trabalhadores, PT), 502
workfare, 21, 286, 311, 315, 436. *See also* welfare programs: welfare-to-work programs
Wynne, Kathleen, xiv–xv, 4, 28–34, 69, 107–9, 121, 161–2, 170n35, 173n53, 189, 208, 218, 233, 237–41, 263, 276, 295–312, 326–8, 334–6, 343–54, 360–1, 382–4, 394–402, 407, 413–14, 423–9, 446–80, 486, 524, 537. *See also* Ontario Liberal Party

youth, 17, 149, 239, 468–70, 485
Yukon, 137, 205